STOCKPORT FROM ABOVE
Yesterday & Today

JD Smith & Webbaviation.co.uk

SBP
Publishing

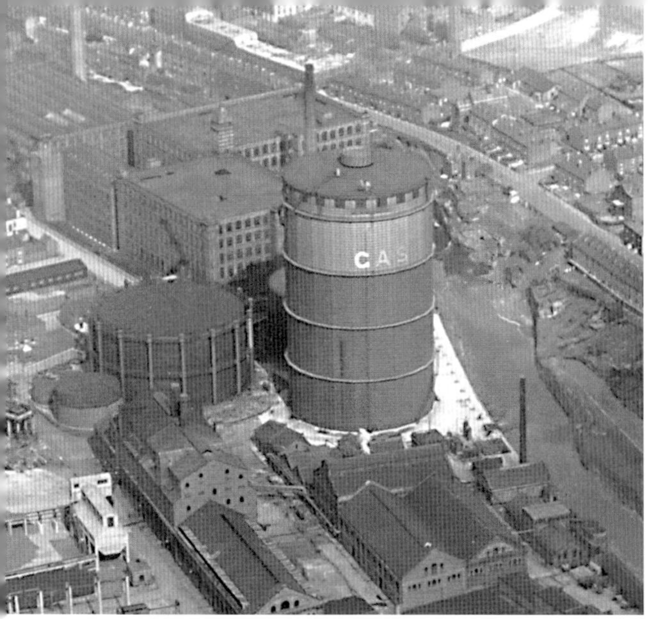
GAS
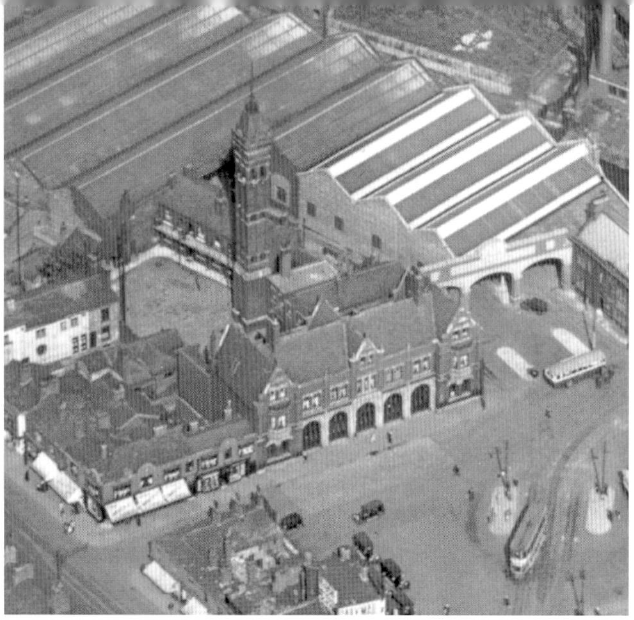
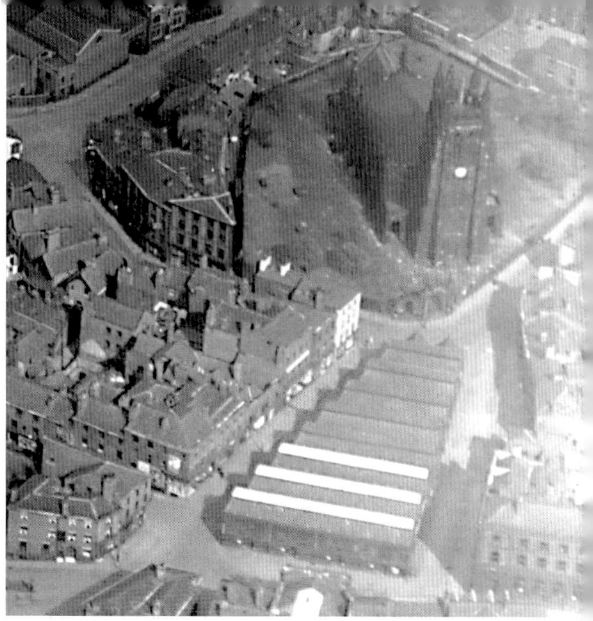
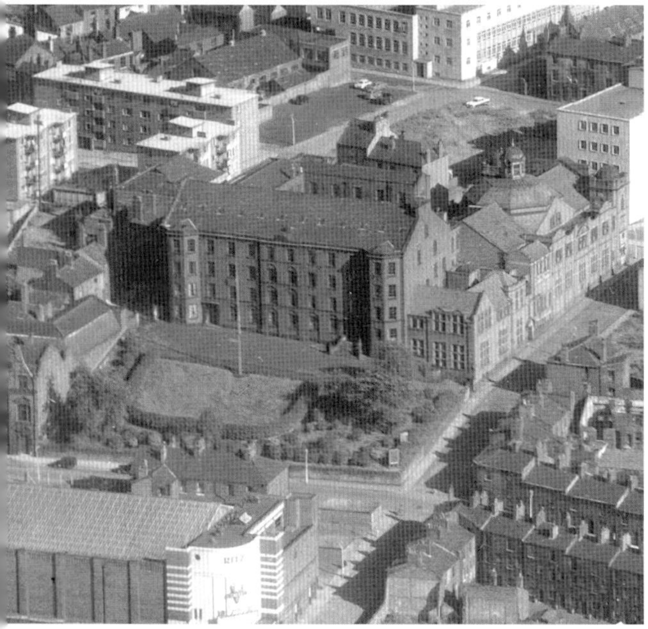
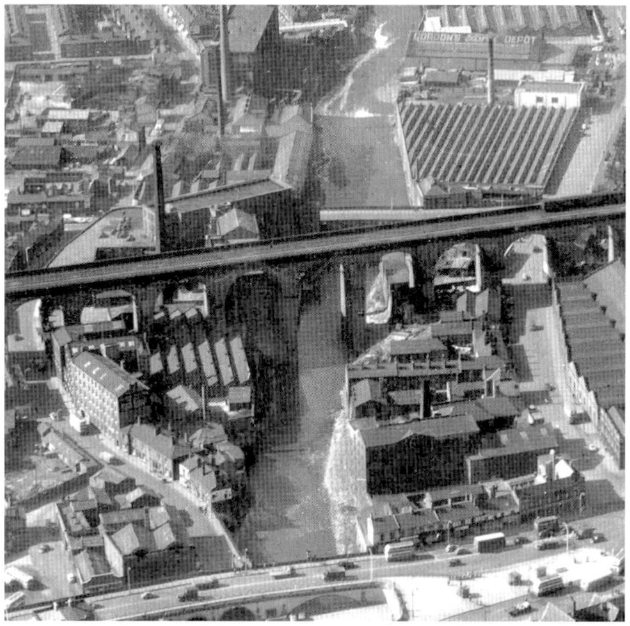
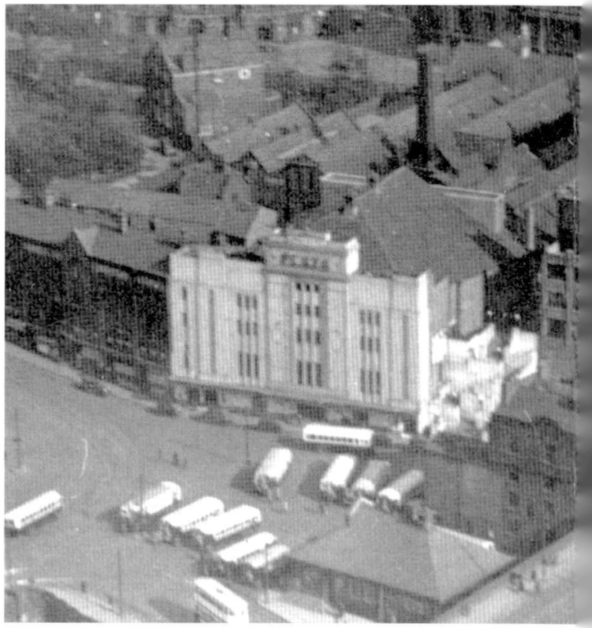
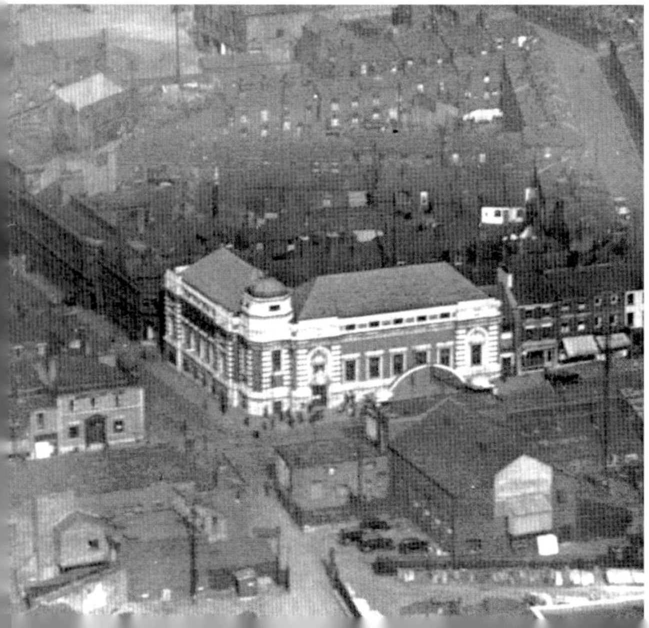
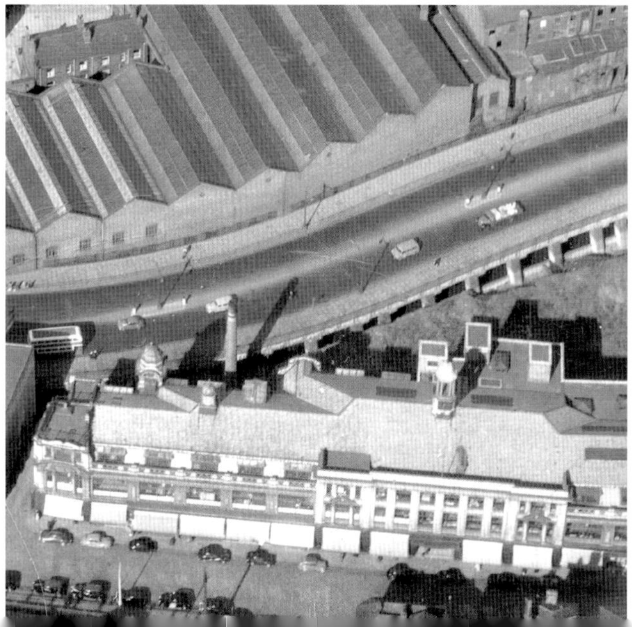
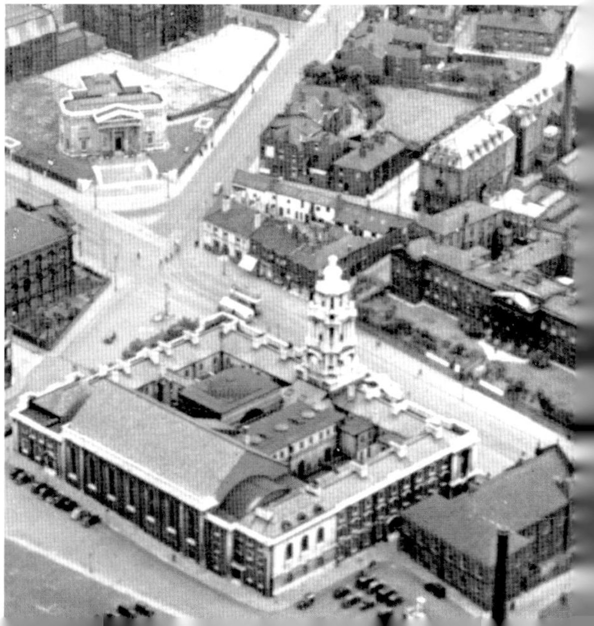

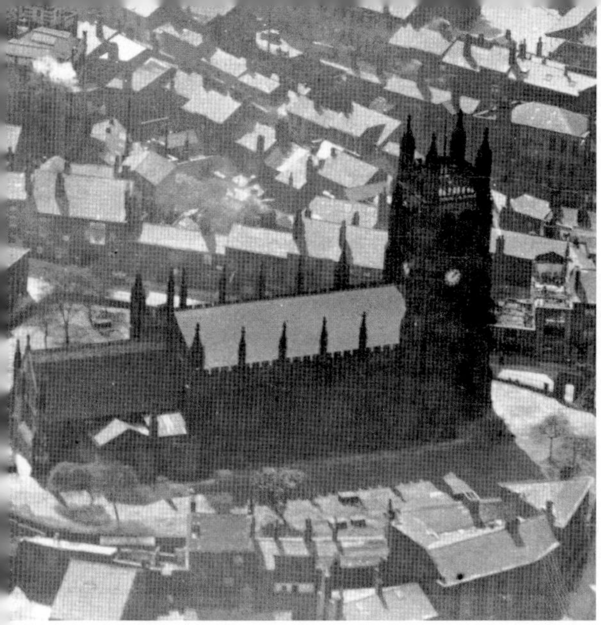

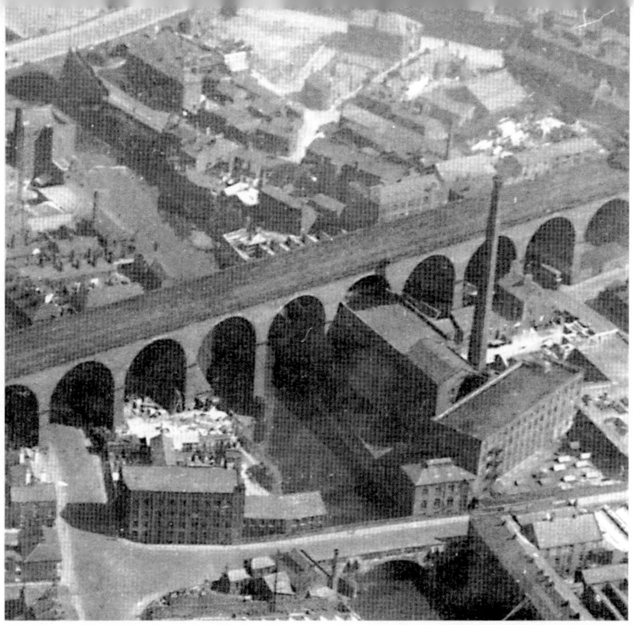

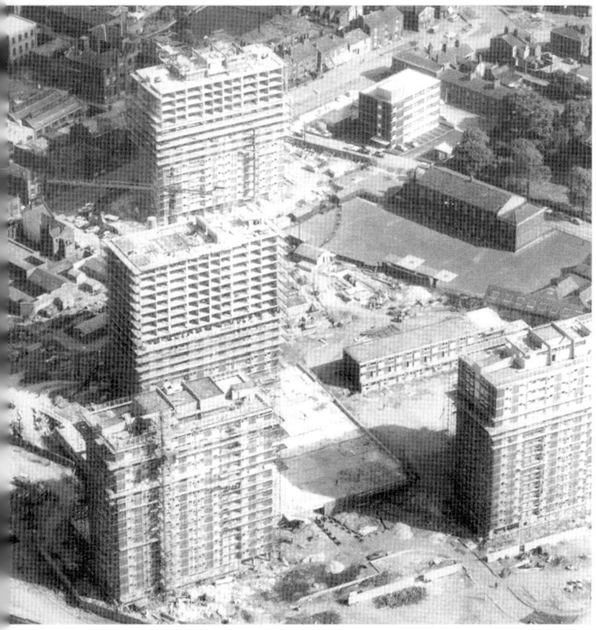

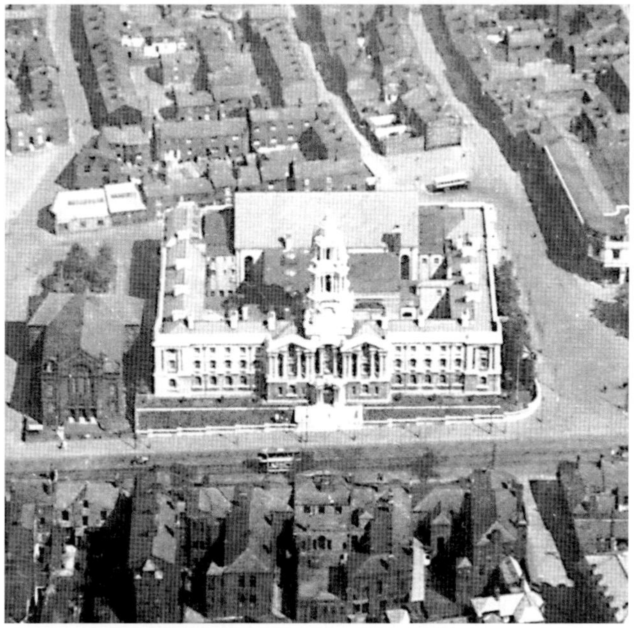

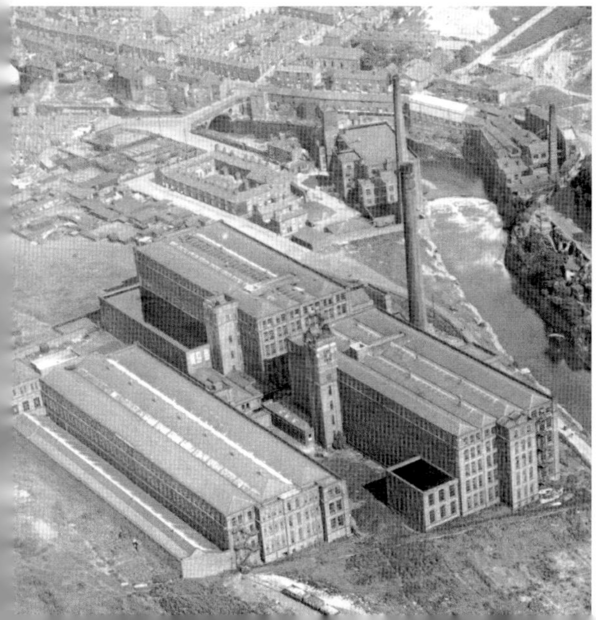

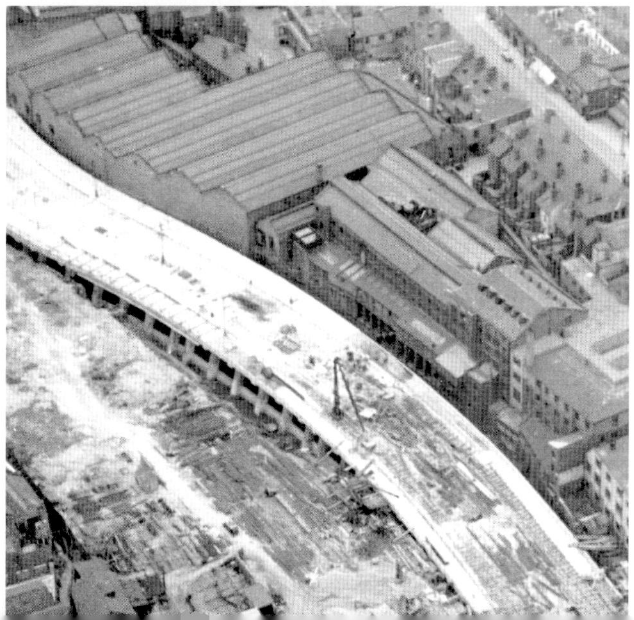

Contents

Introduction

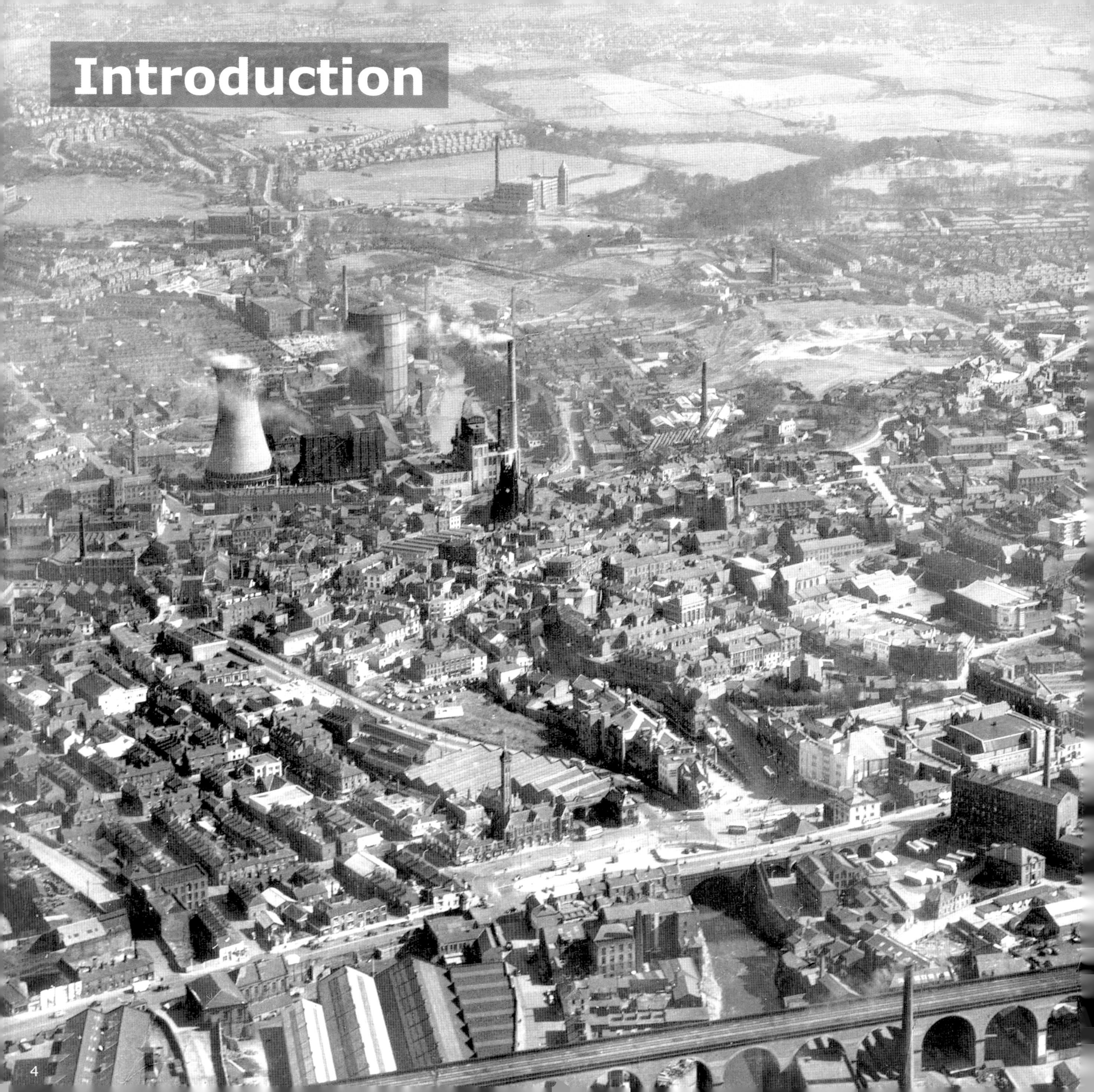

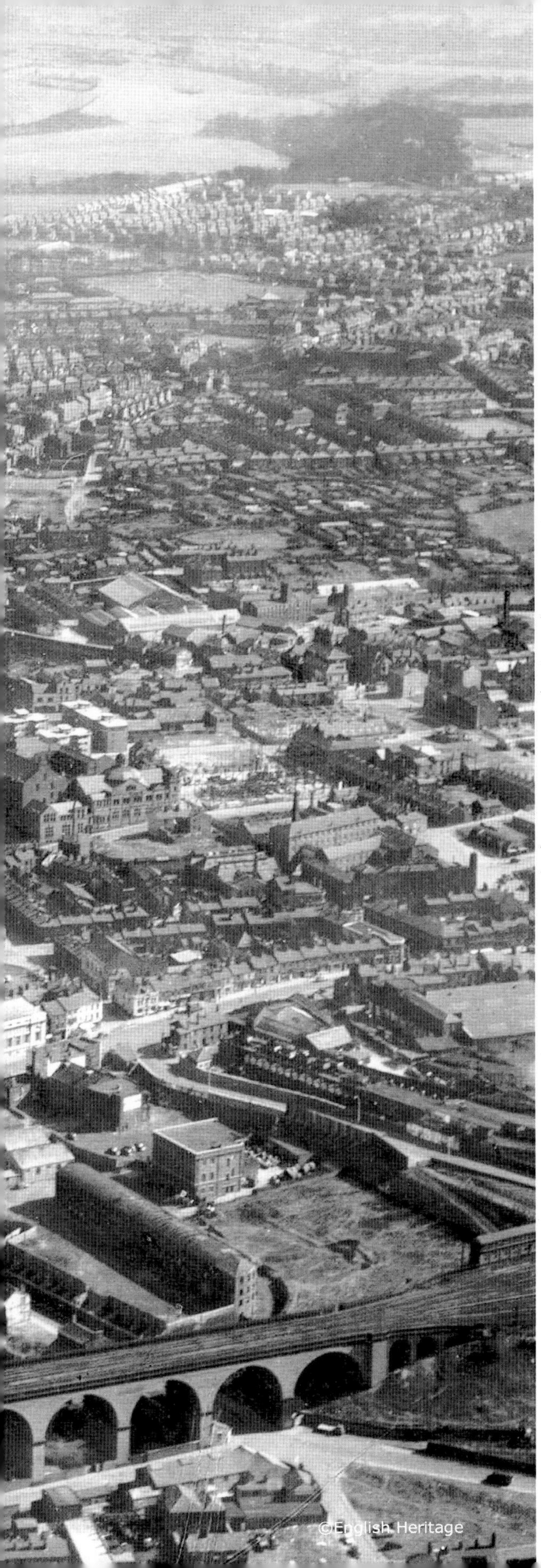

About the book

Stockport From Above: Yesterday & Today gives a new perspective on the historic market town of Stockport. The images in this book show a varied and unique landscape, both urban and rural, industrial and agricultural, that has all but vanished over the course of the 20th century. This book will give people the chance to view the area from a vantage point that they may never have seen before, and the combination of historic and modern images will show the huge changes that have taken place since the first aerial photograph of the town was taken in April 1926. It will also allow us to see which areas have remained relatively unchanged through the course of time, and to ponder what might have been if only a little more foresight had been utilised before buildings of the previous age were swept away in the name of progress. Before this book, modern aerial views of Stockport were hard to come by due to the presence of the flight path to Manchester Airport directly above the town. The airport continues to grow in size, and it has been predicted that within a few years aerial photography within the area may be banned due to the increase in the number of commercial aircraft using the airspace. For this reason alone, we believe that this book will be of great importance to the town's history and heritage for many years to come.

The old images

The old images have come from the archives of Stockport Heritage Library, with a few additional pictures provided by the Manchester Heritage Library and the Stockport Express. Almost all of these images are previously unpublished, meaning that this book will allow people the chance to view them for the very first time. The aerial image archive is quite small, numbering around 300 pictures ranging from 1926 to the present day. Of these images, there are only around 100 or so pre-World War Two aerial photographs. The majority of the early images were taken for the Stockport Borough Surveyors Department in the 1920s and 1930s. From the 1950s onwards, most of the images were taken by a company called Airviews Manchester that operated out of Manchester Airport. Airviews continued flying until 1991 when they were bought by Aerofilms, one of the largest aerial photography companies in the UK. The Aerofilms archive, which includes over 800,000 aerial photographs of the UK dating back to 1919, was recently bought by English Heritage in order to preserve it for the nation. There are still some historic aerial photographs of Stockport from the Aerofilms collection that remain unpublished. English Heritage only acquired the archive in Summer 2007, so these images are not yet available for public use.

The new images

The new images have been taken by Webb Aviation of Bramhall. Run by Jonathan Webb, Webb Aviation fly out of Barton Aerodrome and have one of the largest online aerial images galleries in the world, which can be seen at www.webbaviation.co.uk. For this book we have undertaken the largest ever aerial survey of Stockport, with over 1200 new pictures taken. Where possible we have attempted to take new images that match the old ones as closely as possible to enable us to see the major changes that have taken place since 1926. Due to the small number of historic images we only have new images for some areas, whereas in other areas we only have old images. This is because of the great difficulty and cost of taking aerial images within Stockport's Airspace. We have tried to make sure that all of the main areas are covered, whether it is just with old pictures, just with new pictures, or with both.

Left: Stockport Town Centre in April 1956, looking towards Bredbury

About Stockport

Stockport is a historic Cheshire market town situated at the edge of the Peak District and the Pennine Mountains in the north west of England. The town grew up by a ford at the River Mersey which was the meeting point of several Roman roads. This included the road running from Mamucium (Manchester) to Aquae Arnemetiae (Buxton), and another heading to the east towards Melandra (a fort near Glossop). It is believed that the Romans also established a fort at the site in order to guard the ford, which would have been a strategically important location.

The name of Stockport has elicited several meanings, two of which are often quoted. The Anglo-Saxon word "Stoc" is said to refer to a stockaded place or a castle, whilst the word "port" was said to mean a wood, giving us the definition of "a castle in a wood". Another theory, which is currently more widely used, is that the Anglo-Saxon word "Stoc" meant a market place, and "port" meant hamlet or a minor settlement, giving us the name of the "market at the hamlet". The first recording of the modern name is in 1170, when it was written as "Stokeport". Other written names have included "Stopford", "Stokport" "Stockporte" and "Stoppart". Of these, those most commonly cited is Stopford, which survives to this day in the name given to the town's residents – Stopfordians.

Following the Norman conquest of England, a castle was built at the site of the ford on the sandstone bluff overlooking the river. It is recorded as having existed in the 12th century, and was rebuilt several times over the years. The castle would survive until 1775 when it was demolished. Where previously Stockport had been a settlement within a manor, by this time it had grown to become a manor in its own right, At the turn of the 12th century the Lord of the Manor was Robert de Stokeport II. He also had control over many neighbouring manors, and this led to the creation of the Stockport Barony. By 1248, the barony contained Brinnington, Bredbury, Offerton, Bosden (now part of Hazel Grove), Marple & Wybersley, Torkington (Hazel Grove), Norbury (Hazel grove), Poynton, Woodford and Stockport Etchells (Heald Green & Gatley). It also included parts of Sharston & Ragel (later to be known as Northern Etchells, and now Sharston and Northenden in Manchester) and Hattersley (now in Hyde). The manors of Werneth and Romiley were added to the barony later on in the century. The manors of Cheadle and Bramhall were not included within this barony, and it is likely that they had their own Barons at that time. In 1326, Cheadle was divided into two separate manors: Cheadle Bulkely (Cheadle) and Cheadle Moseley (Cheadle Hulme).

These manors would go on to form the major districts and townships that make up Stockport today. The baronial system would last until the 19th century, with the manors and townships passed down through the generations between many important families, all of whom played their part in shaping the area. The most populous of these manors was the manor of Stockport, but it did not begin to develop fully until it was granted a market charter in 1260. This helped establish Stockport as a town, and saw it's importance rise. During the medieval period, the town had grown sufficiently to become the fifth largest in Cheshire, behind Chester, Nantwich, Macclesfield and Congleton. In 1664 the population was estimated at 1,500. The population of Chester was around 7,500, and neighbouring Manchester in Lancashire was estimated at 4,000.

The first seeds of the industrial revolution took hold in the late 17th and early 18th centuries. The first major industry was silk manufacturing, but this would go on to be superceded by the cotton trade. Later, hat manufacturing would become the dominant industry in the town. The arrival of Cotton resulted in massive growth around the medieval centre, and Stockport soon started to spread out and engulf the old areas of the barony. By 1835 the medieval town had spread over the River Mersey int Heaton Norris, where a township had now been established. Th population by this time had reached over 25,000 within the confines of th old town, with a further 11,000 in the Heaton Norris Township.

The rule of the old baronial system was finally ended in that year when th Municipal Corporation Act came into being, establishing a series of loca self governing authorities in England and Wales. Amongst other things the act allowed the new boroughs to appoint a mayor, something that th smaller districts could not do. The manors still existed, but the Lords c the time now had to work side-by-side with the people, which wasn without conflict. The Heaton Norris township, parts of Brinnington, an parts of Cheadle Bulkeley and Cheadle Moseley (Edgeley and Brinksway were added to the Stockport township to create the new Municipa Borough of Stockport. As the town continued to grow the boundaries wer regularly extended to include the newly developed urban areas.

In 1837 a Poor Law Union was established in Stockport comprising of 1 local townships. The Unions were a system of local government designe to assist the administration and funding of the Poor Laws for the poor c those areas by pooling resources of local parishes. The Stockport Unio consisted of the townships of Stockport, Bramhall, Bredbury, Brinnington Cheadle Bulkeley, Cheadle Moseley, Heaton Norris, Marple, Norbury Offerton, Reddish, Romiley, Stockport Etchells, Torkington, and Werneth It also included Handforth cum Bosden and Hyde, which had been part c the original barony. This brought together all of the ancient townships tha now make up Stockport for the first time under one banner. In 1841 th combined population of these townships had reached 78,882, whic included 50,154 in the Stockport Municipal Borough area.

In 1889 Stockport was upgraded to become a County Borough. I recognition, the town's football club changed its name to Stockport Count FC. The new status heralded further periods of expansion into th neighbouring districts as the population continued to swell. The late 19 century saw the creation of many Urban Districts by The Loca Government act of 1894. These Urban Districts were based upon previou Sanitary Districts and the Poor Law Unions and were generally area smaller than towns. Six new urban districts were created in the Stockpor area. These were: Bredbury & Romiley Urban District, Cheadle & Gatle UD (Including Cheadle Moseley, Cheadle Bulkeley and Stockport Etchells) Hazel Grove & Bramhall UD, Heaton Norris UD, Marple UD and Reddis UD. A seventh, Compstall Urban District, was created in 1902, and with a population of just 875 was said to be the smallest in the land.

In 1901 the suburb of Reddish, which had previously been in Lancashire was joined with Stockport and moved into Cheshire. Other parts of Haze Grove & Bramhall, Cheadle & Gatley, Bredbury & Romiley and part o Heaton Norris were also added. In 1913 the whole of the remainder o Heaton Norris Urban District (the area comprising of Heaton Chapel Heaton Mersey and Heaton Moor, all in Lancashire) was amalgamated int the town, rejoining it with the township of Heaton Norris. A small area o the Urban District adjoining Burnage became part of Manchester. Th urban districts were abolished in 1974 when the Local Government Act o 1972 reunited all of the old townships under the one name.

Stockport has come a long way since that first settlement by the rive crossing, and it is now one of the largest areas in the UK without city status. It has managed to evolve into a major urban centre whilst stil retaining its historic character and attractive suburban districts. With several major redevelopments on the cards within the town centre, it may not be too long before it is confirmed as a city for the 21st Century.

Right: Stockport Town Centre, October 195

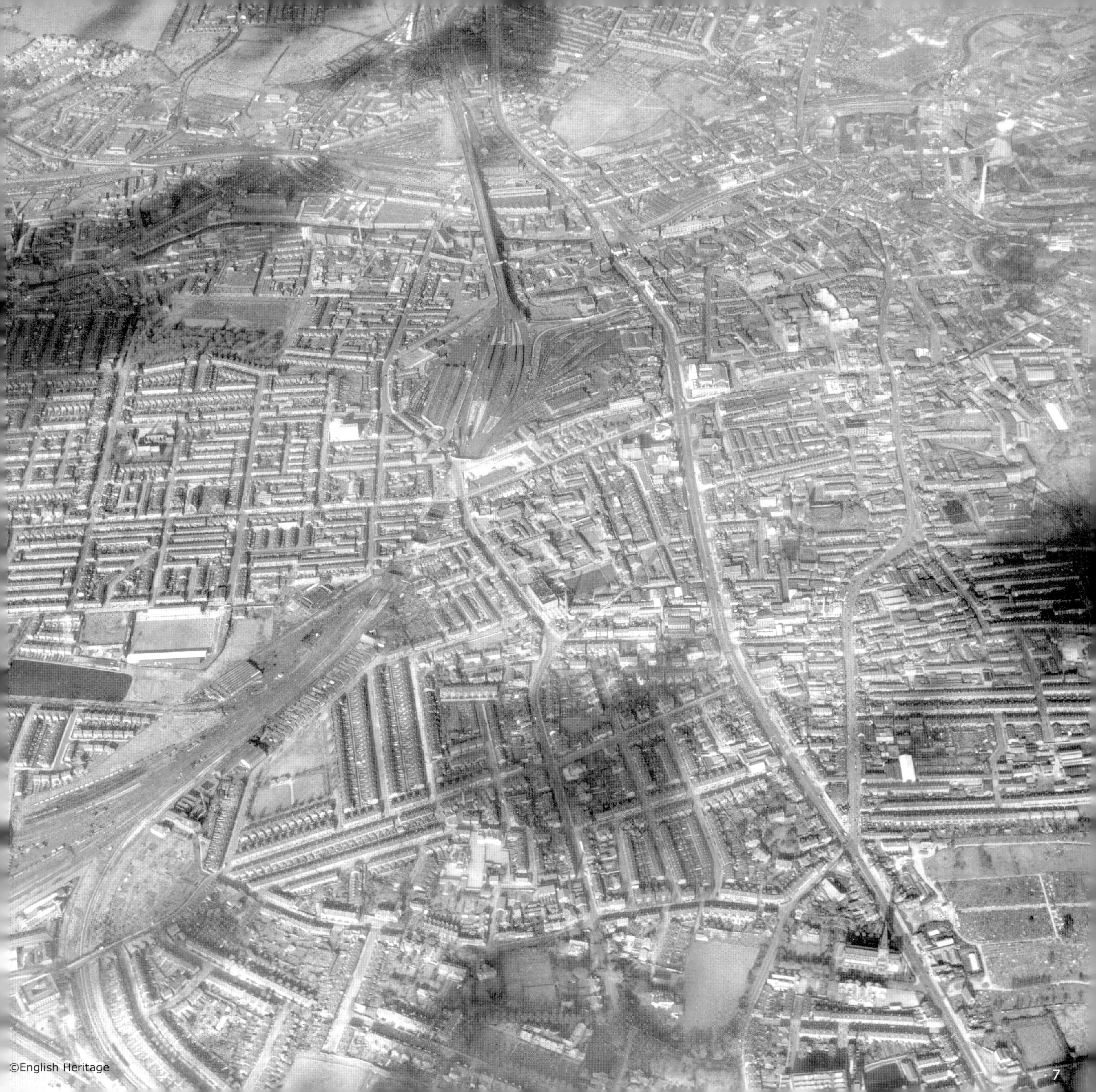

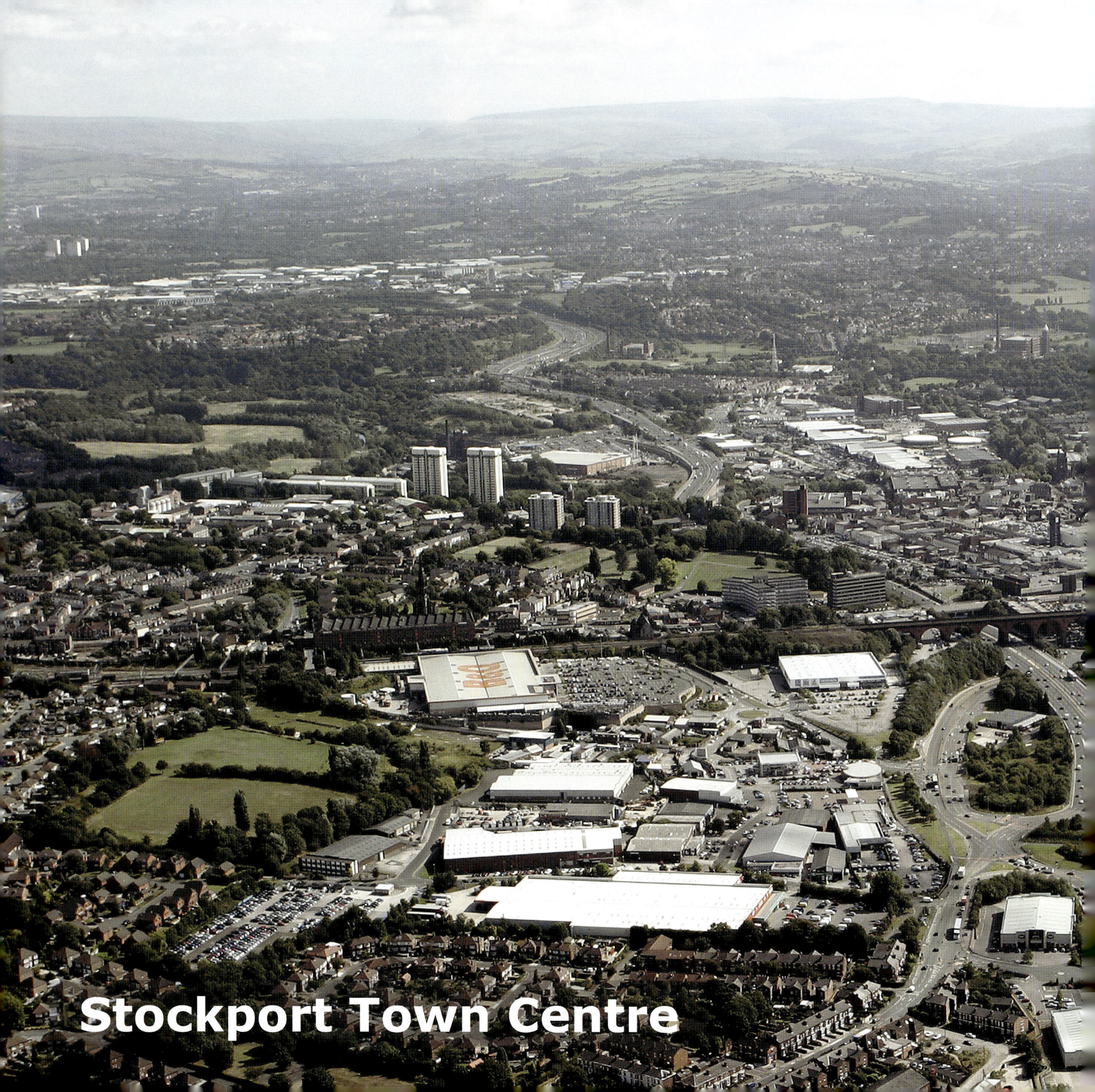
Stockport Town Centre

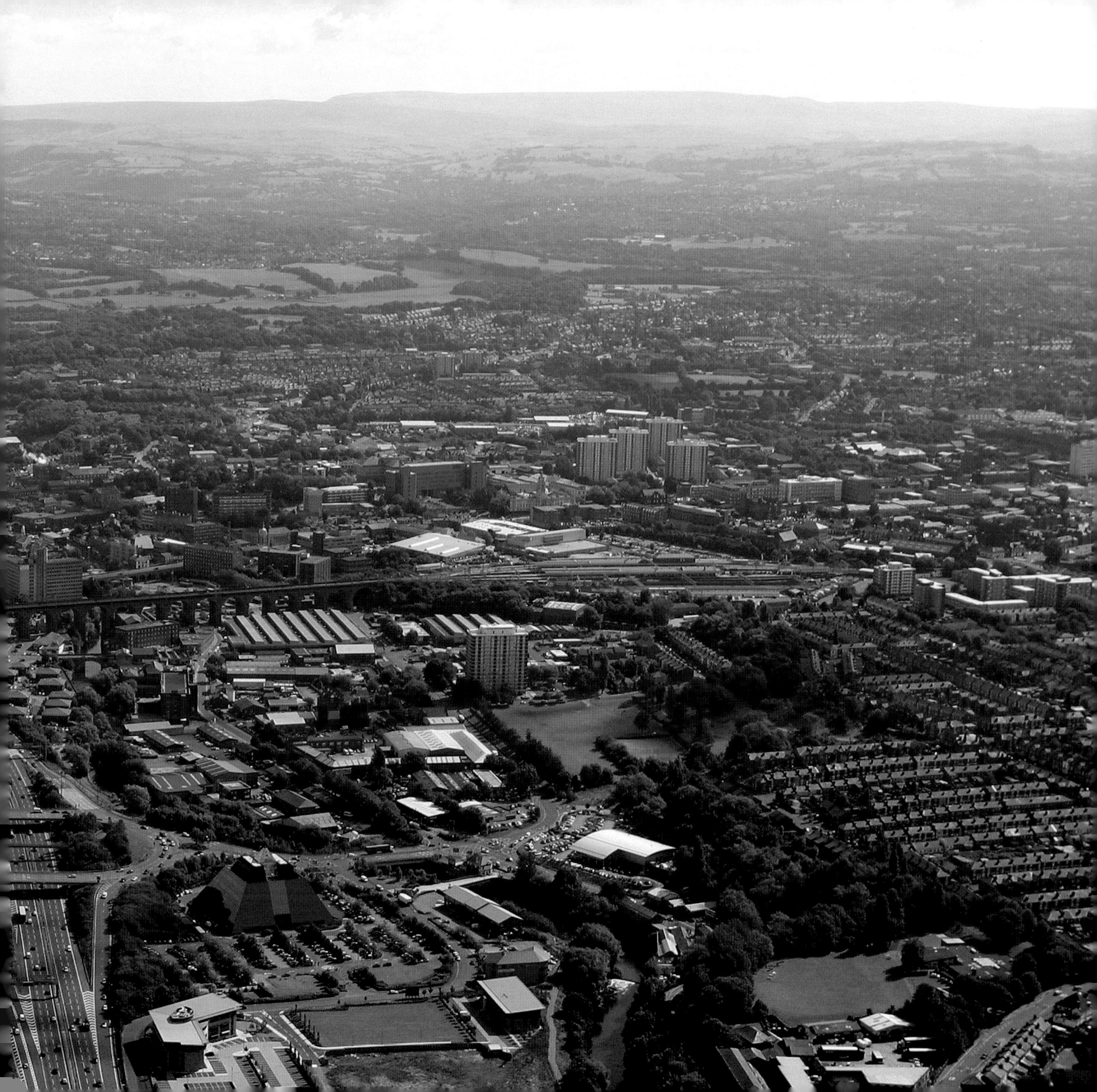

The Old Town

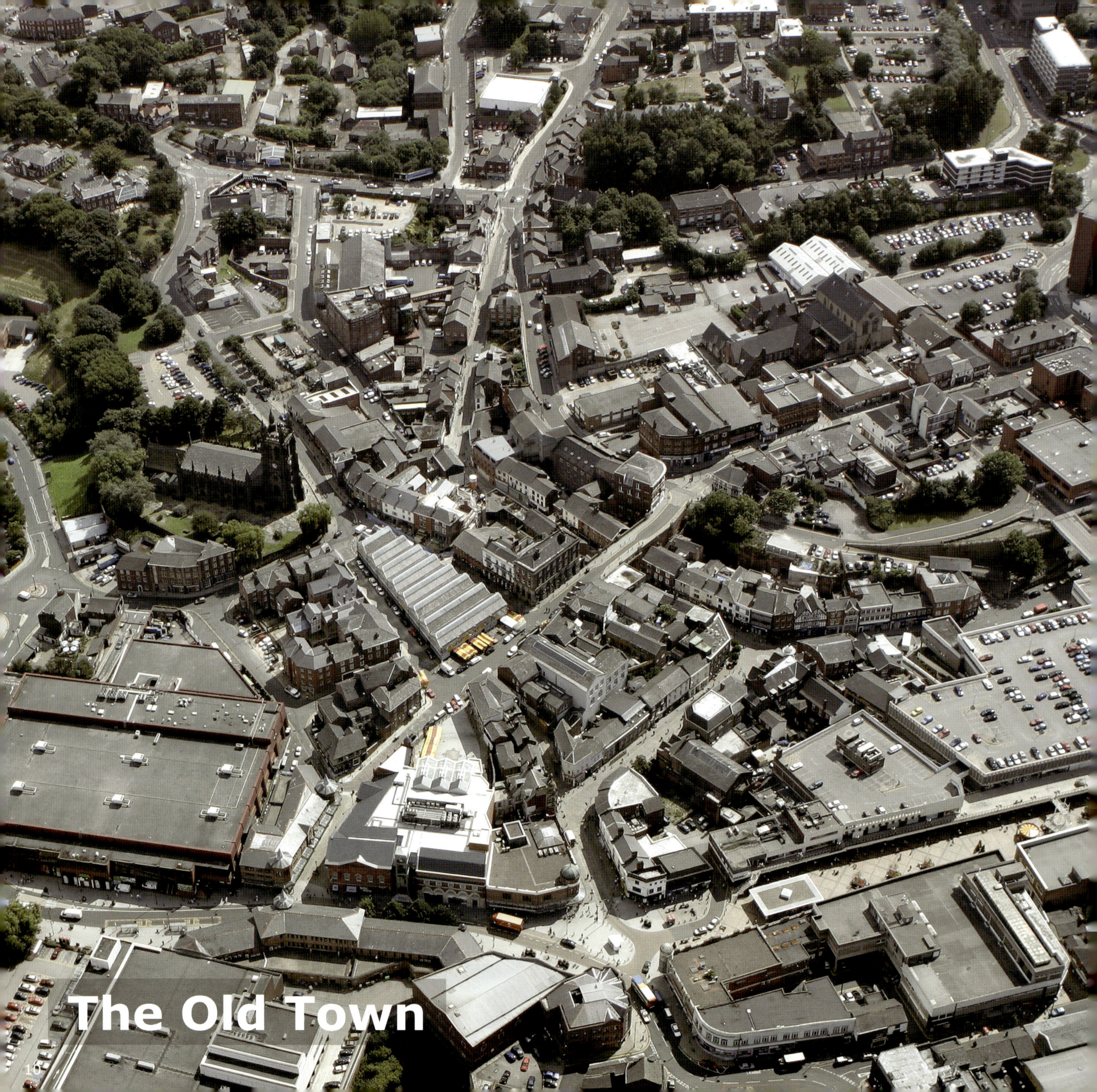

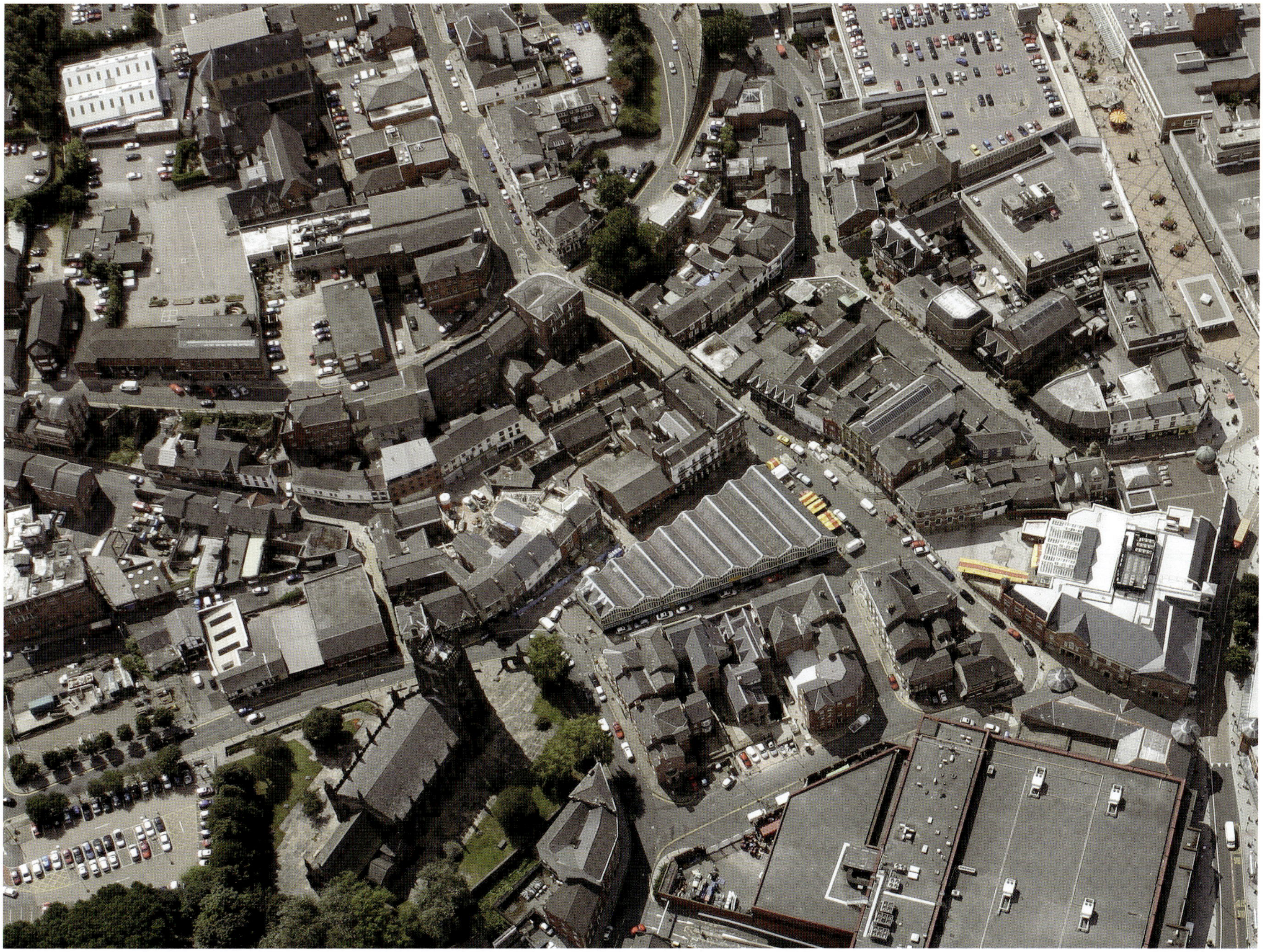

The Old Town encompasses the area that grew out of the original settlement based around the old Norman Castle. With a narrow, winding medieval street-pattern, the Old Town is the most historic part of Stockport Town Centre and contains some of its finest and most important buildings, with some dating back over 500 years. The layout of these streets has remained almost unchanged since first put down, and today they resemble something more likely to be seen in a popular seaside resort instead of a large industrial town. The main road through the medieval town traversed these small streets and was for centuries the only route through the town centre until major new developments occurred in the 19th century. From the river crossing at Lancashire Bridge (middle bottom, left picture), the route took in Bridge Street (straight ahead), Great Underbank (first right), Little Underbank (first left) and finally Hillgate (top centre of image). Because of developments over the course of the 20th century, the Old Town is now tucked away from the main focal points of the town centre and is almost hidden from view. This does have the advantage of keeping the area peaceful, but visitors may not be aware of its presence and the startling differences these streets present to the rest of the central business district. There were plans in the 1970s to demolish much of the historic area around the market place, but thankfully these were rebuffed, and the Old Town is now the jewel in the crown of Stockport Town Centre.

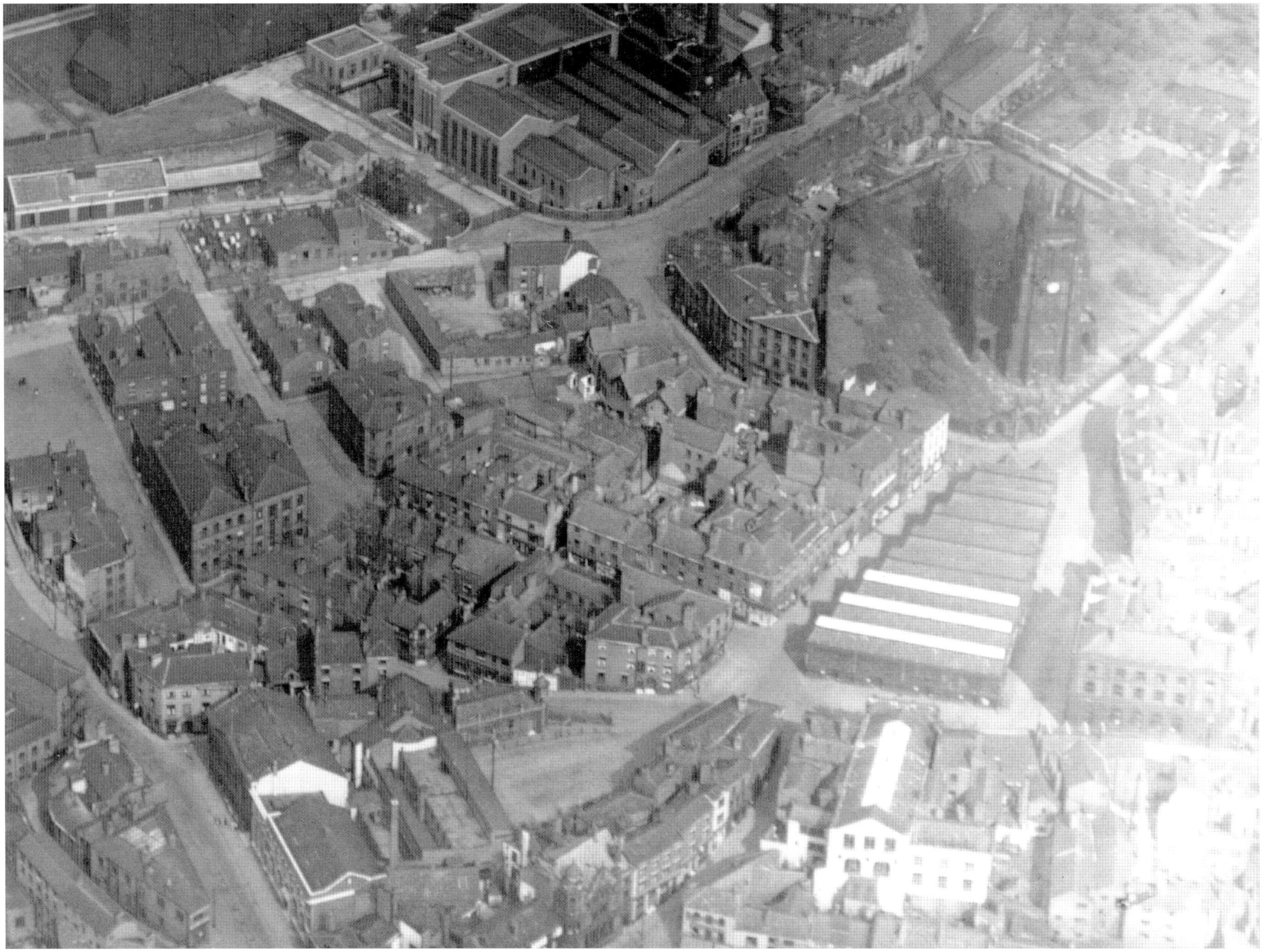

The Market Place 1933

At the heart of the Old Town is the Market Place. A Market Charter was granted on September 6th 1260 to the Lord of the Manor of the Stockport Barony, the third Robert de Stokeport, son of Robert de Stokeport II. It was given by Prince Edward, Earl of Chester, who was the son of Henry III and would later become King Edward I (also known as Edward Longshanks). The charter allowed a market to be held every Thursday and also an annual fair, which would take place from St Wilfred's day (October 12th) and last for eight days. The fair was an extension of the regular market, and would attract traders from further afield. The market was almost certainly in existence before this charter, but it's granting acted like an official seal of approval. The market has played a central role in the history of the town for nearly 750 years since. The old market square was the place for local traders to sell their produce, but many unconventional items were available as well, and the last wife sale in England is said to have taken place here. The Market was first held in the yard of the Norman Castle that stood on the bluff overlooking the River Mersey, and took place within the outer defensive walls. Although the castle was demolished in 1775, the yard remained.

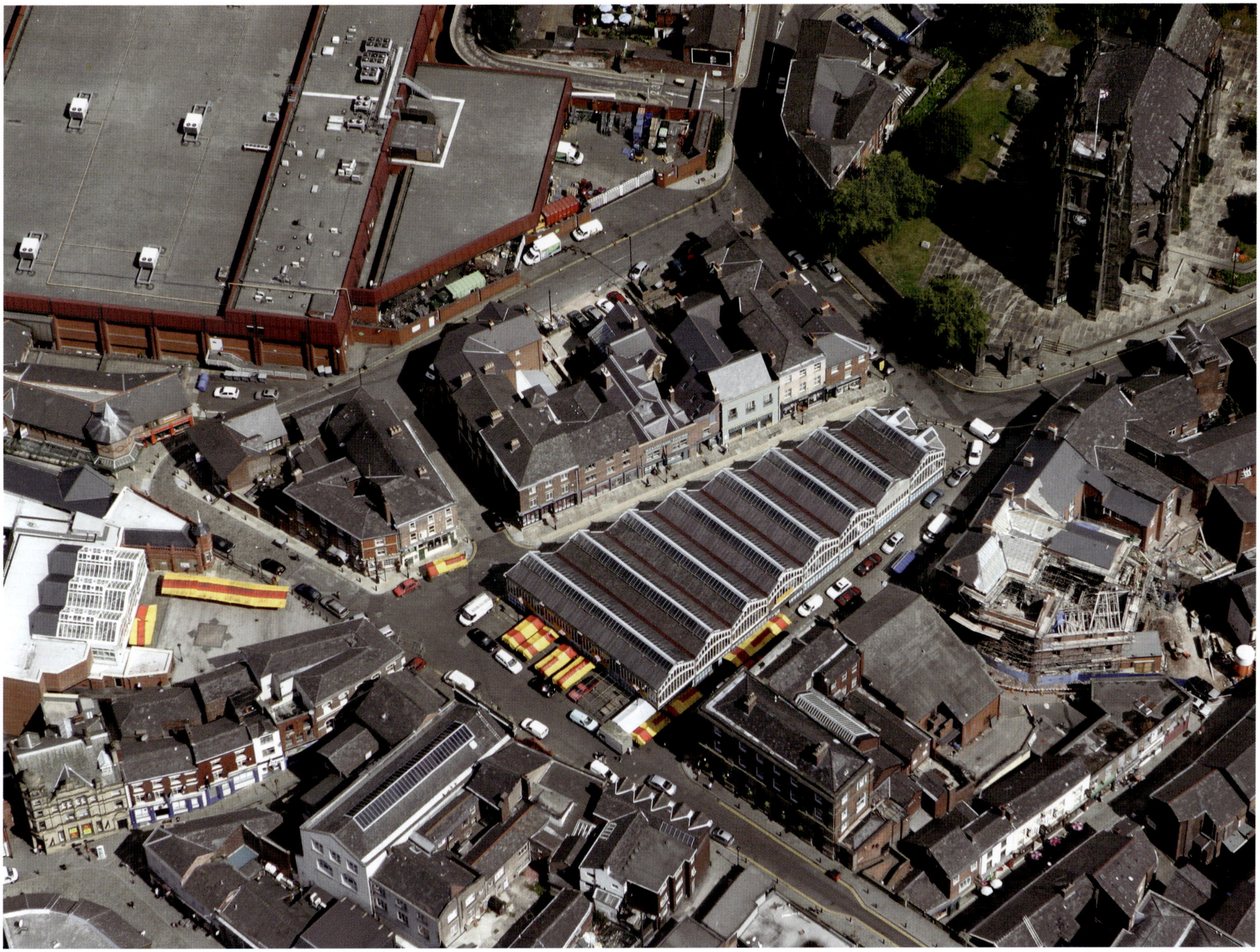

The yard was later the site of Castle Mill: a cloth weaving mill that was demolished in 1841. Castle Yard is visible on the middle left of the picture above. The building next to it with the glazed triple span roof built to ape the design of the market hall, is the old Magistrates Court. This was opened in 1824 and has recently been converted into a shopping complex, known as The Courts. The yard was lowered in 1853 to make it the same level as the rest of the market place, and it became home to a cattle market. This was subsequently moved to Portwood. Since then the yard has been an extension of the main market place, and is still a popular place to pitch a stall on market days, which are now held every Tuesday, Friday and Saturday. Little has changed around the market hall in the years between these photographs. The greatest changes have been in the surrounding buildings, with the giant Asda supermarket now dominating the area where houses once stood. One such house to survive is Staircase House, facing the Market Hall. This 15th century Town House (the fourth building from the right, left of the turquoise building) was built in around 1460 and was occupied for over 600 years. The building, which takes its name from its carved cage newel staircase – one of only 3 remaining in England - was nearly destroyed in a fire in 1995, but it has now been restored and converted into a museum, allowing people to experience what life was like in Stockport through the ages.

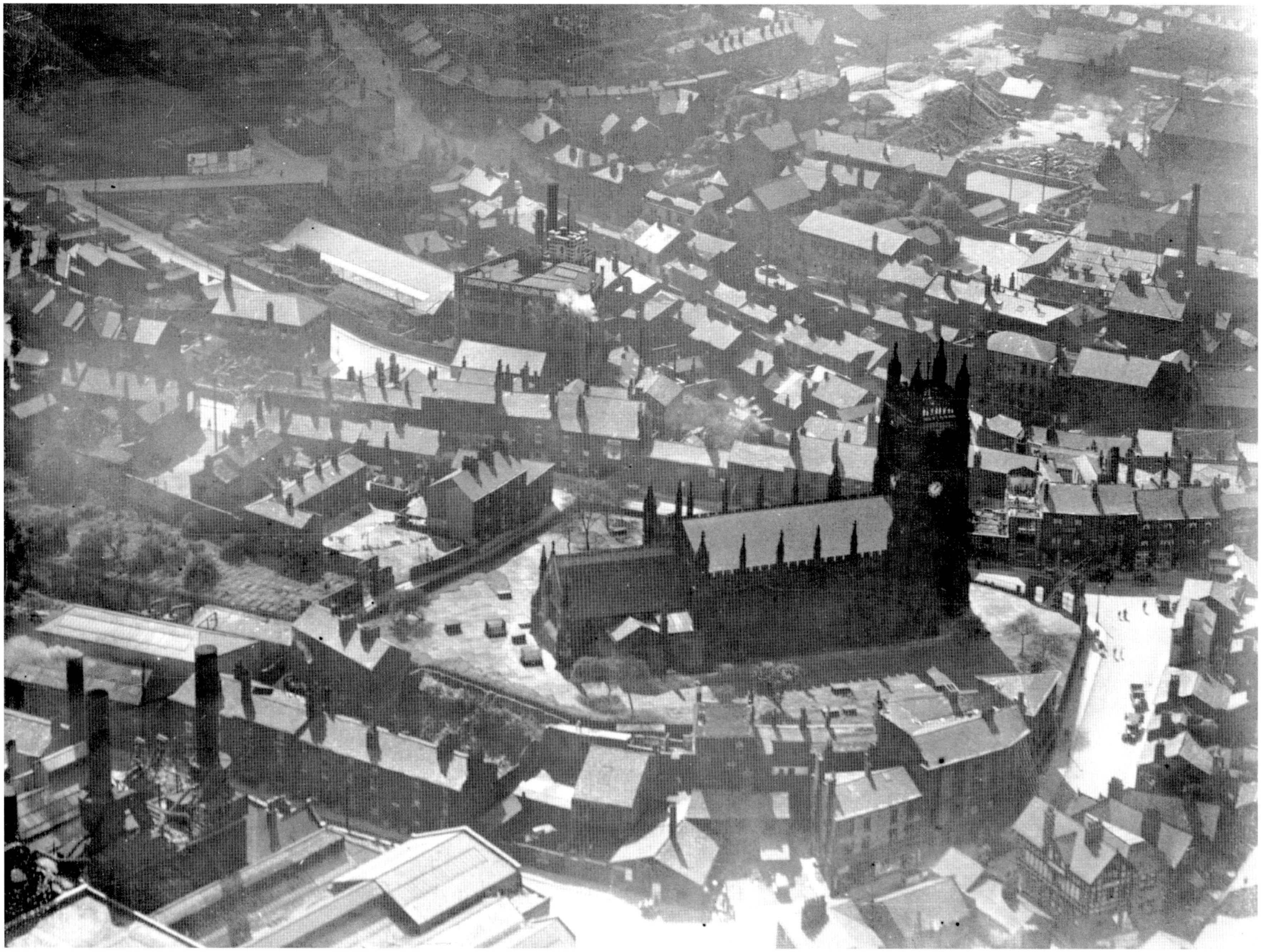

St Mary's Church 1933

Standing proud and tall over the market is St Mary's Parish Church, also known as "St Mary's in the Market Place". Originally built in the 14th Century, the church was rebuilt from 1813-1817 to today's design after the building began to literally fall apart. The Nave and the 125 foot Tower were the first sections to be rebuilt after part of the tower collapsed, apparently after a vigorous bell-ringing session to celebrate Admiral Nelson's victory over Napoleon at Trafalgar in 1805. Only the red stone Chancel (the low section at the rear on the left) remains from the original building. The Chancel is now home to the Stockport Heritage Centre, which is run by the Stockport Heritage Society.

In the background is the Unicorn Brewery, home to Frederic Robinson's Brewers since 1838. The present building dates from 1929. Famed for producing high-quality real ales with a distinctive flavour, the water for Robinson's beers is taken from their very own well, situated deep below the brewery buildings. The company now owns over 400 pubs throughout the North West.

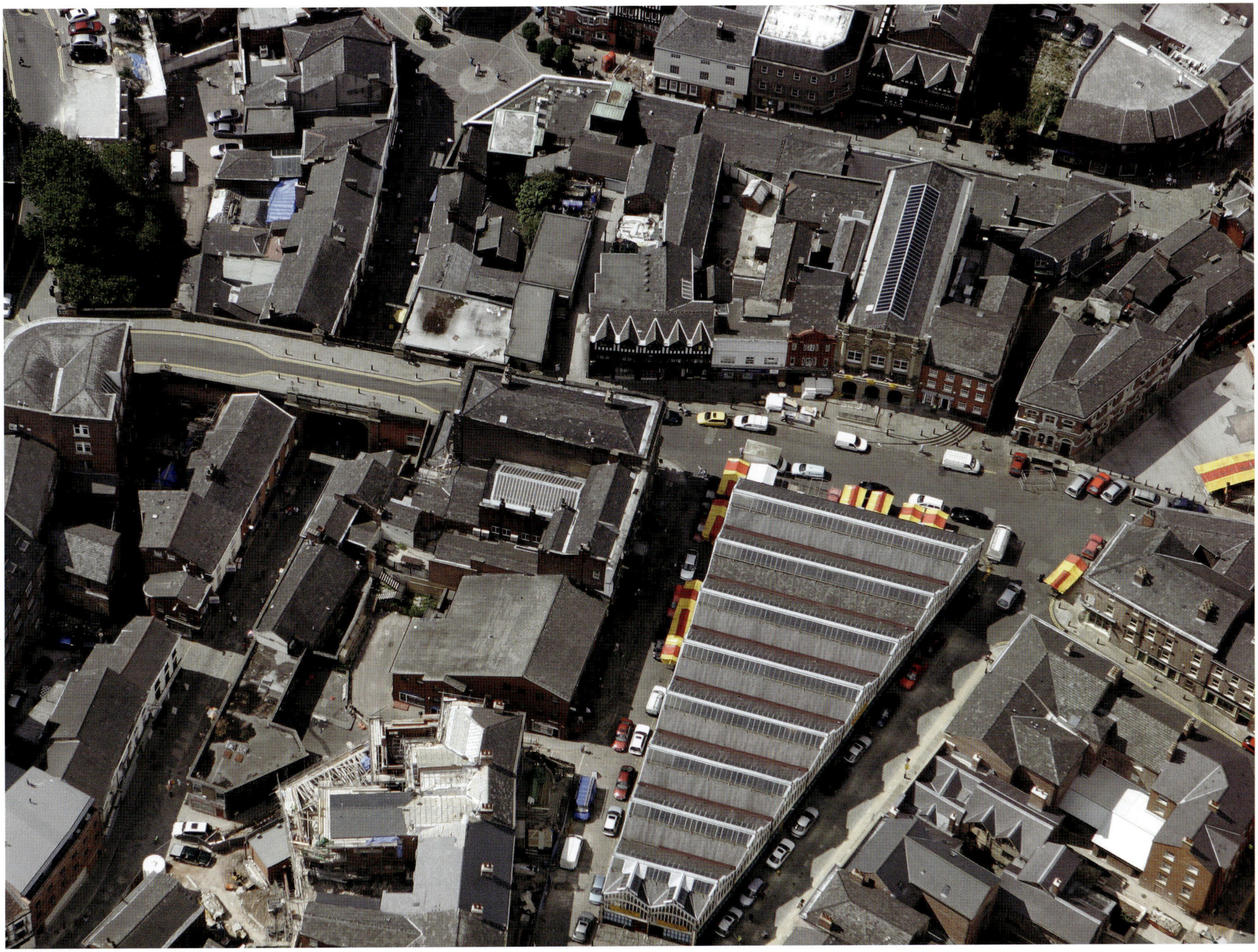

Market Hall & Produce Hall

The grand Victorian Market Hall was erected in 1862 and quickly gained the nickname "the Umbrella on Stilts". The intricate steelwork-and-glass frame was originally open to the elements along the sides, leading to the nickname being chosen. The hall was eventually boxed-in between 1898-1900 to help shield the traders inside from the weather. The Produce Hall was built in 1851, and was known locally as the Hen or Cheese Market. It offered a variety of local items such as eggs and butter, but particularly specialised in Cheshire Cheeses. Built of yellow Yorkshire stone, the hall has four Corinthian columns on its facade, as well as a balcony for public orating. The balcony was added when the building was extended upwards. It was originally only a single storey building but the upper floors were added in 1875. The upstairs became home to Stockport's free Library, which had been based at Vernon Park Museum. The Library eventually moved as the smells emanating from below are alleged to have put-off those reading upstairs. Amongst other things, the building also housed a dungeon in the lower levels. Beyond the Produce Hall can be seen Great Underbank, and to the left is Little Underbank running underneath St Petersgate Bridge.

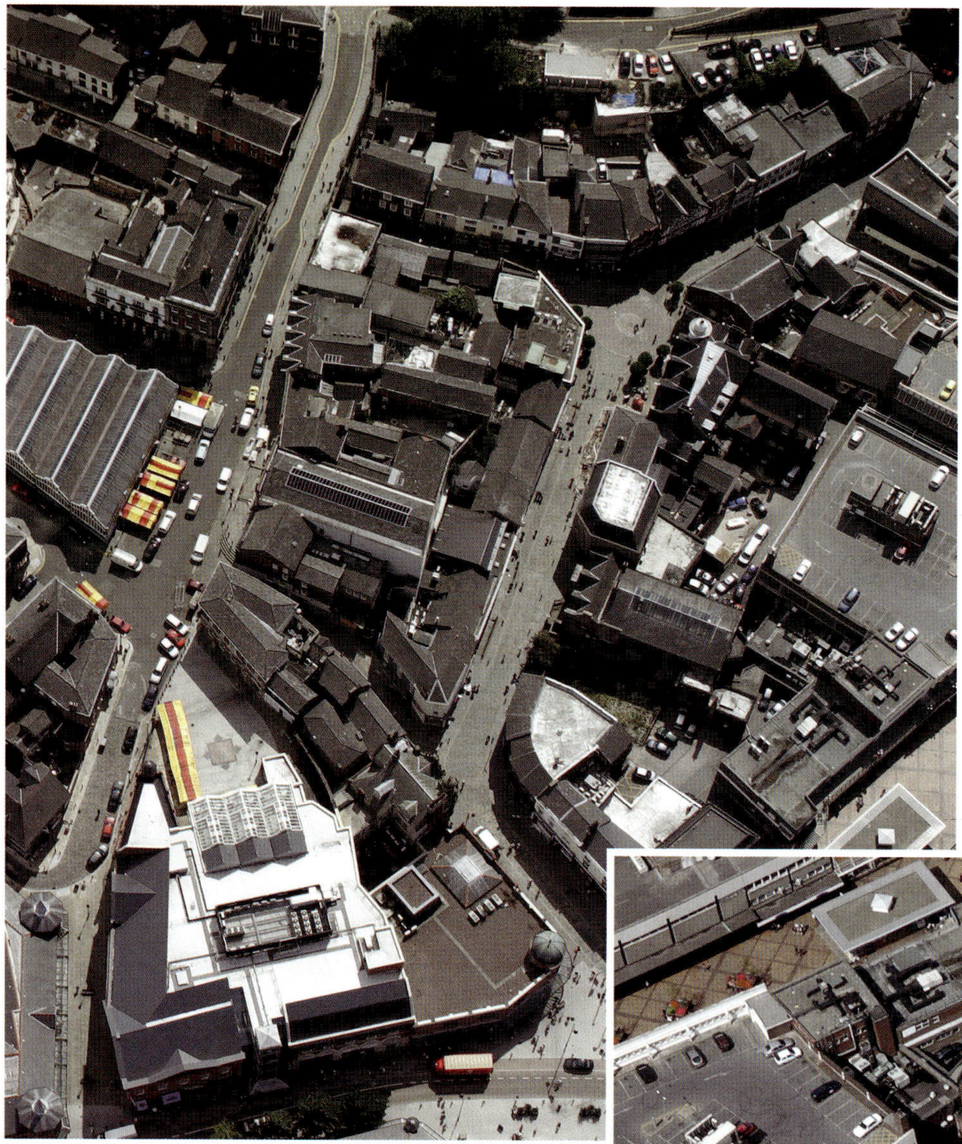

The Underbanks

The Underbanks formed the central part of the original route through Stockport. The narrow medieval streets, which would once have been frequented by horse-and-cart or those driving cattle to market, led to or from the only crossing of the River Mersey in the developing town at Lancashire Bridge. As such, many prominent buildings were constructed along the route, including the Grade-1* Listed Underbank Hall along Great Underbank. Built c1580, this black and white timber framed townhouse was the home of the Arderne family of Arden Hall, Bredbury. Since 1824 it has been used as a bank.

Other buildings include the Three Shires Inn, built c1637, and the prominent White Lion Public House, which was rebuilt in 1904. The original White Lion was a two-storey inn dating back to the 15th Century. It sat in the space at the front of the present building. The new structure has four floors, topped by the white domed corner tower. The Three Shires was originally the Town House of The Legh Family of Adlington and is now a wine bar. Like Underbank Hall, it is a fine example of a black and white Tudor building, and its double gabled roof can be seen on the left in the picture below.

Leading off Great Underbank, Little Underbank follows the course of the old Tin Brook, a tributary of the Mersey which now flows out of site underground. Along Little Underbank are the chiming clocks of Winters Public House, formerly a Jewellers' shop. St Petersgate Bridge was built from 1864-1868 to provide an easier route to the market from the west. The historic bridge actually consists of 5 brick arches, but due to the proximity of the neighbouring buildings, only the cast iron section over Little Underbank is visible. This area has often been referred to as "Little Chester", due to its resemblance to the Eastgate Clock and bridge along Chester's main high street.

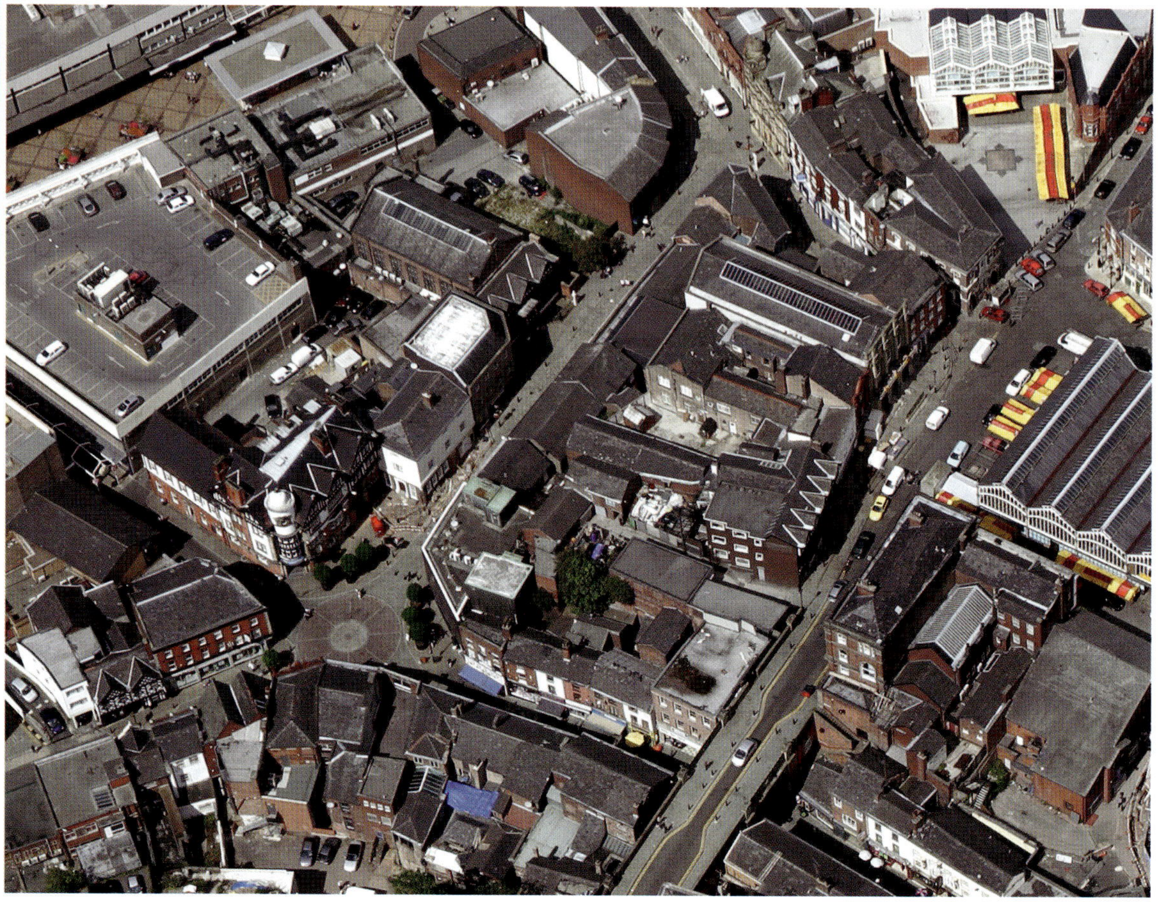

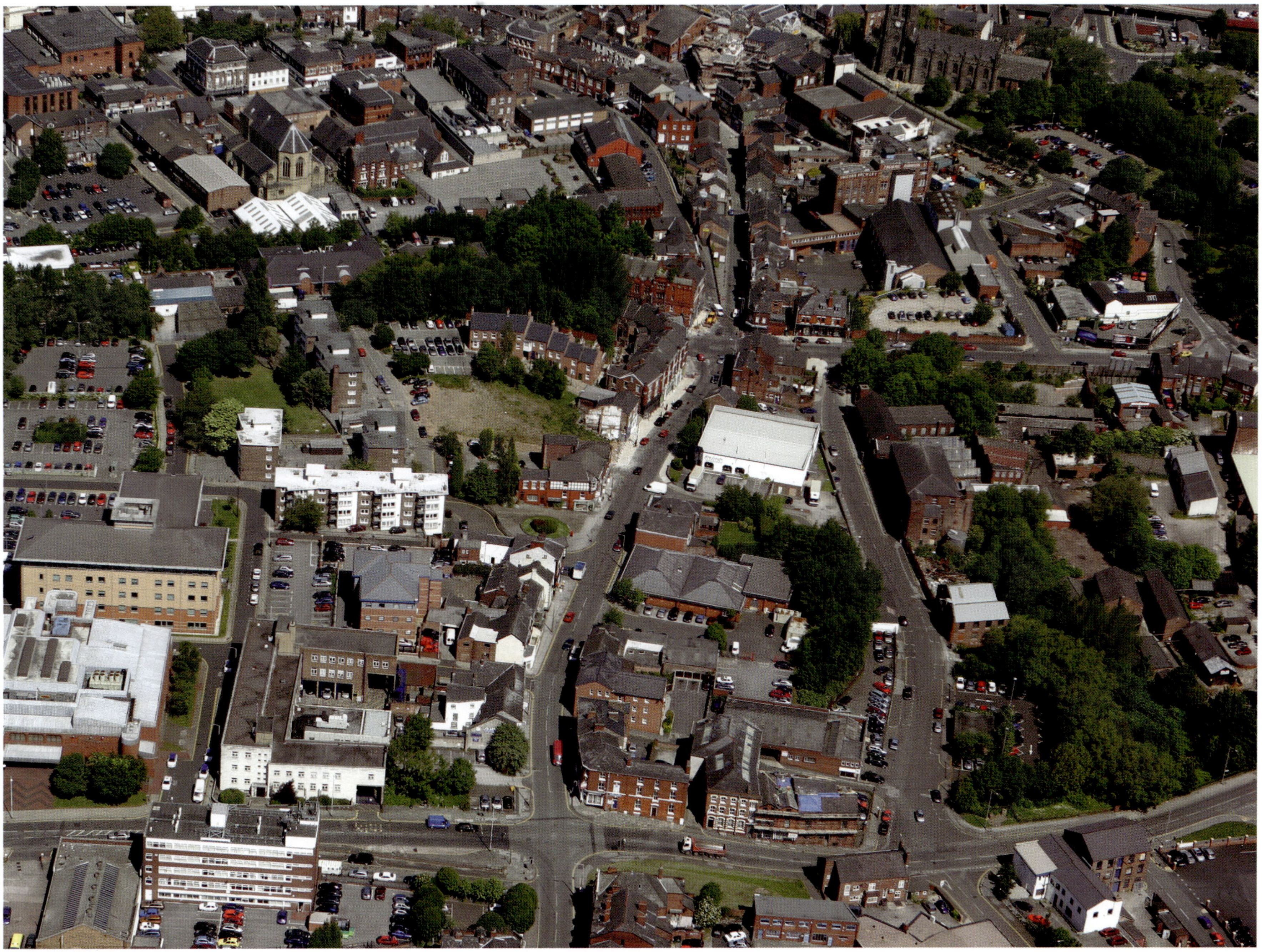

Hillgate

Continue down Little Underbank and you will reach Hillgate. Hillgate is actually three roads - Lower Hillgate, Middle Hillgate and Higher Hillgate - but is usually just given the one name. This picture shows Lower Hillgate (centre) at the crossroads with Edward Street (on the left) and Waterloo Road (on the right). Prominent in the centre of the picture is Crowther Street, where a new row of terraced houses now sits on the steep incline. The street was made famous by an LS Lowry painting from 1930 that depicted the old cramped houses that previously stood here. The painting is now on permanent display in Stockport Art Gallery. To the right is Hopes Carr. This area was the early hub of industrial activity during the industrial revolution in Stockport, with dozens of mills and factories filling the land. It was also the scene of one of the darkest days in Stockport's history, when on the morning of Sunday 4th June 1967, a British Midland Douglas DC4 aeroplane crash landed on the site, killing 72 of the 84 passengers and crew on board. The pilot, Harry Marlow, who survived, brought the plane down on the only piece of "open" land available after the plane suffered a fuel problem. Just ahead lay Stockport Town Hall, and the 4 large blocks of flats at Mottram Street.

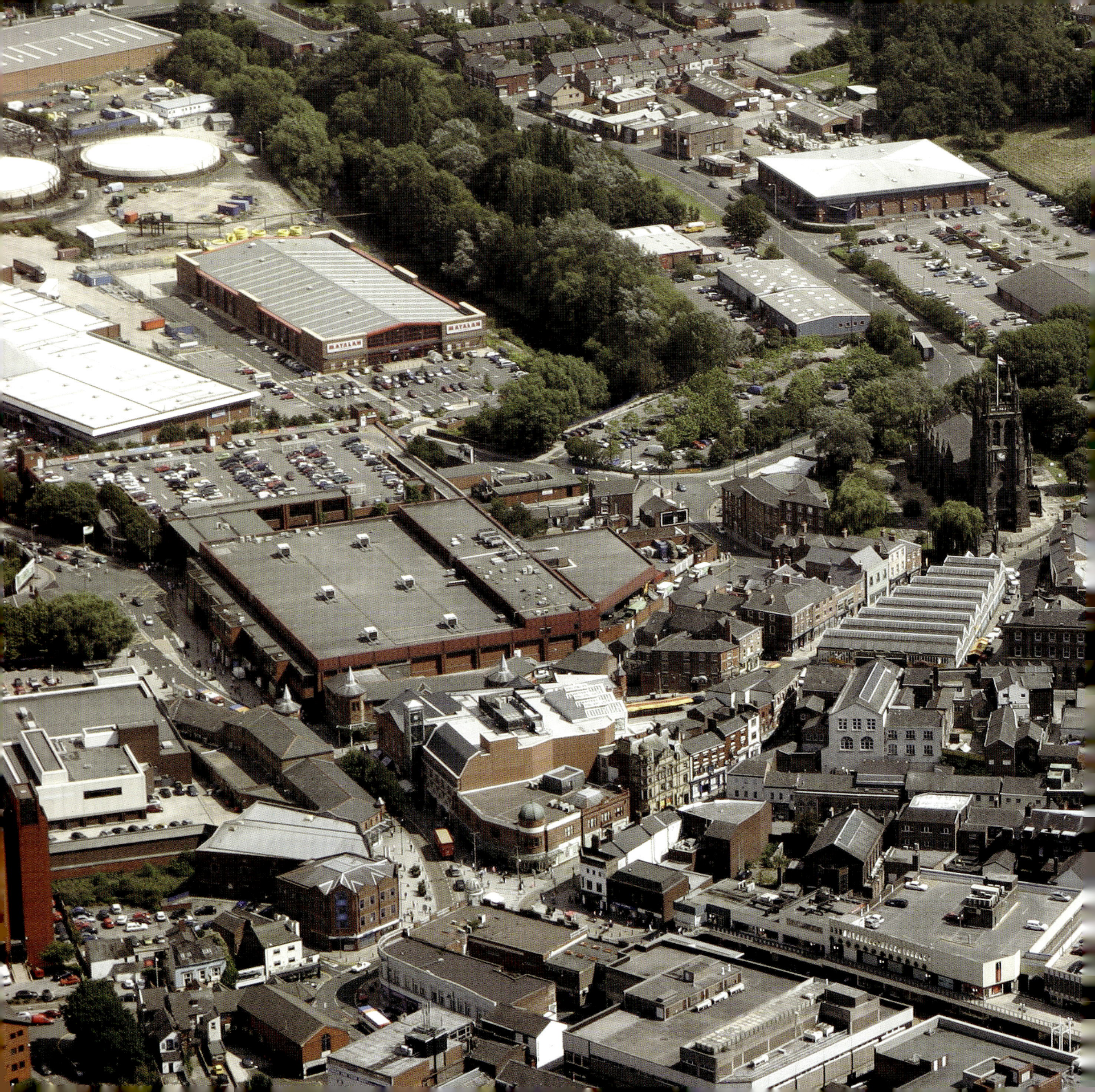
MATALAN
MATALAN

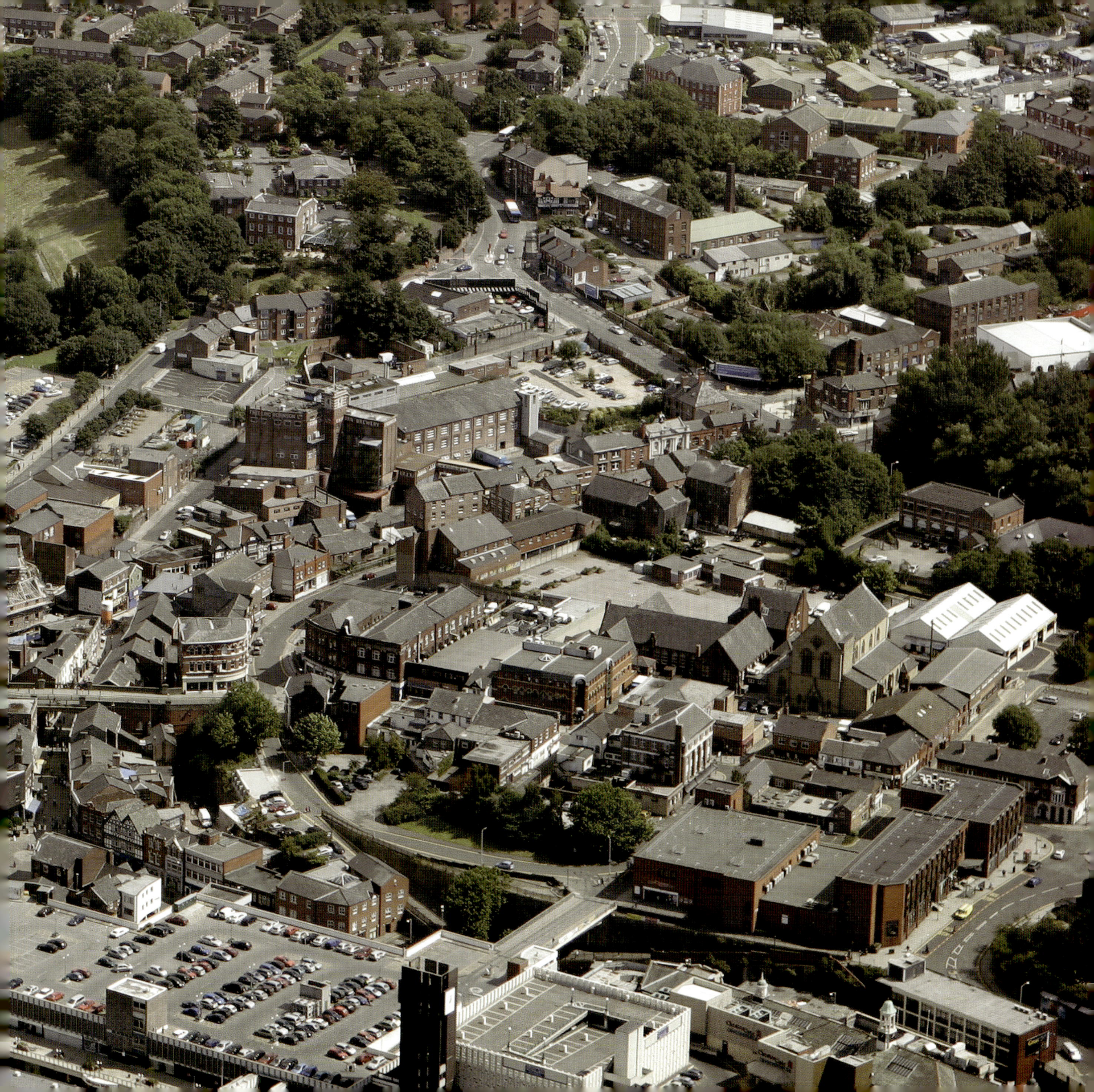

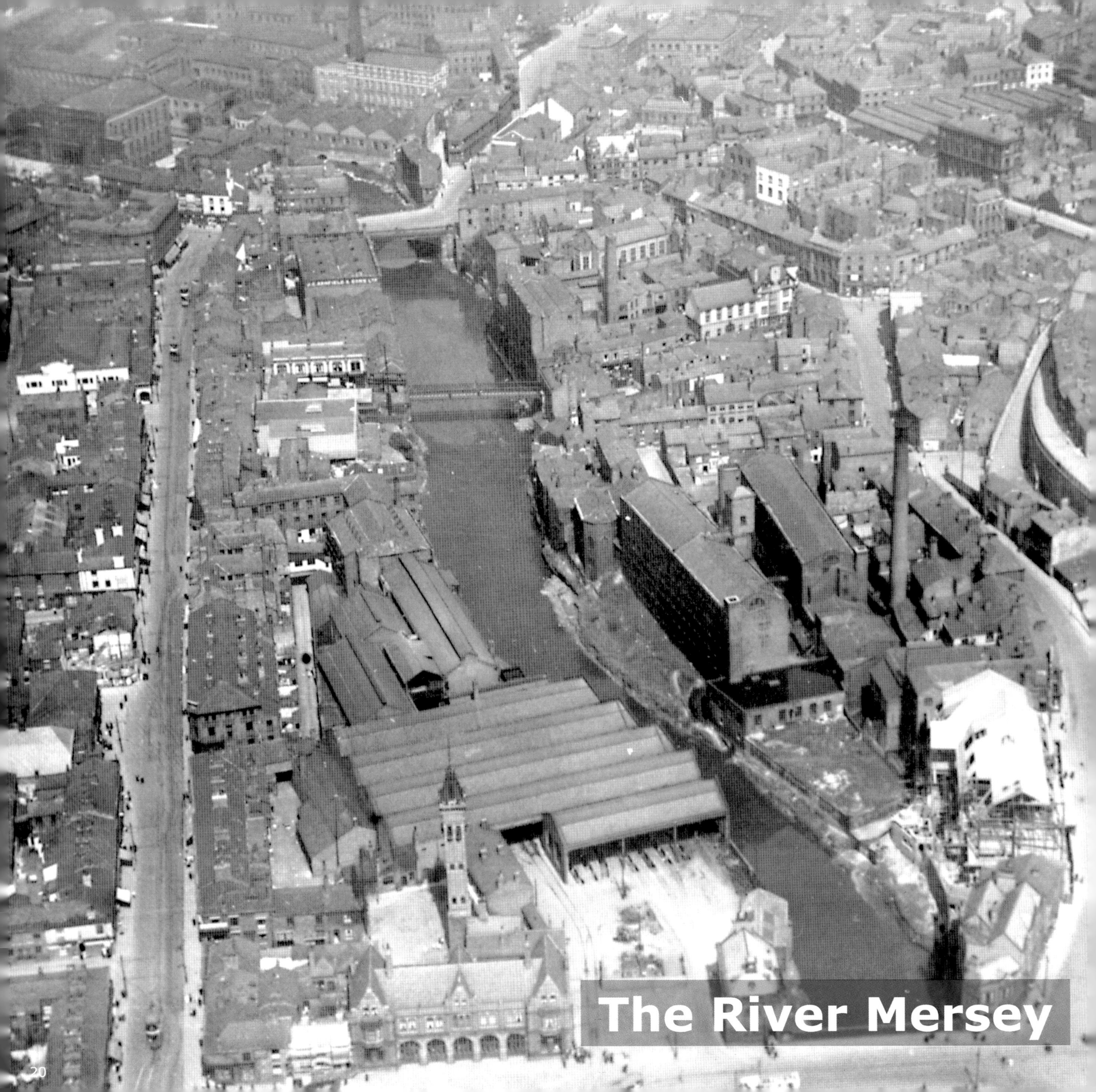

The River Mersey

The River Mersey 1926

Many people visiting Stockport will be unaware that a major river runs through its centre. Even fewer will probably know that it is one of the most famous rivers in the UK, second only to perhaps the River Thames. It is, of course, the River Mersey. The river is usually associated with Liverpool, where it reaches the Irish Sea 40 miles to the west, but the Mersey is the historic site of the first settlement in Stockport, and is the reason that the town exists today.

Look on many old maps though, and you will see that the Mersey continued along what is now considered to be the River Goyt. In 1911 the Mersey was recorded as starting at the confluence of the Goyt and the River Etherow just to the north of Marple, near Brabyns Park. In modern times, the accepted start is now the confluence of the River Tame and the River Goyt in the town centre at the foot of Lancashire Hill, just to the top left of the old image, taken in April 1926.

The name Mersey means "boundary river". It is a function that the river has performed for centuries. The river is known to have been the border between the ancient kingdoms of Northumbria and Mercia in Saxon times, and it was also the historic boundary between the counties of Cheshire and Lancashire. This boundary was changed three times during the late 19th and early 20th centuries in 1889, 1901 and 1913, in recognition of the expansion of Stockport by the addition of Heaton Norris Township (which actually took place in 1835), Reddish and Heaton Norris Urban District.

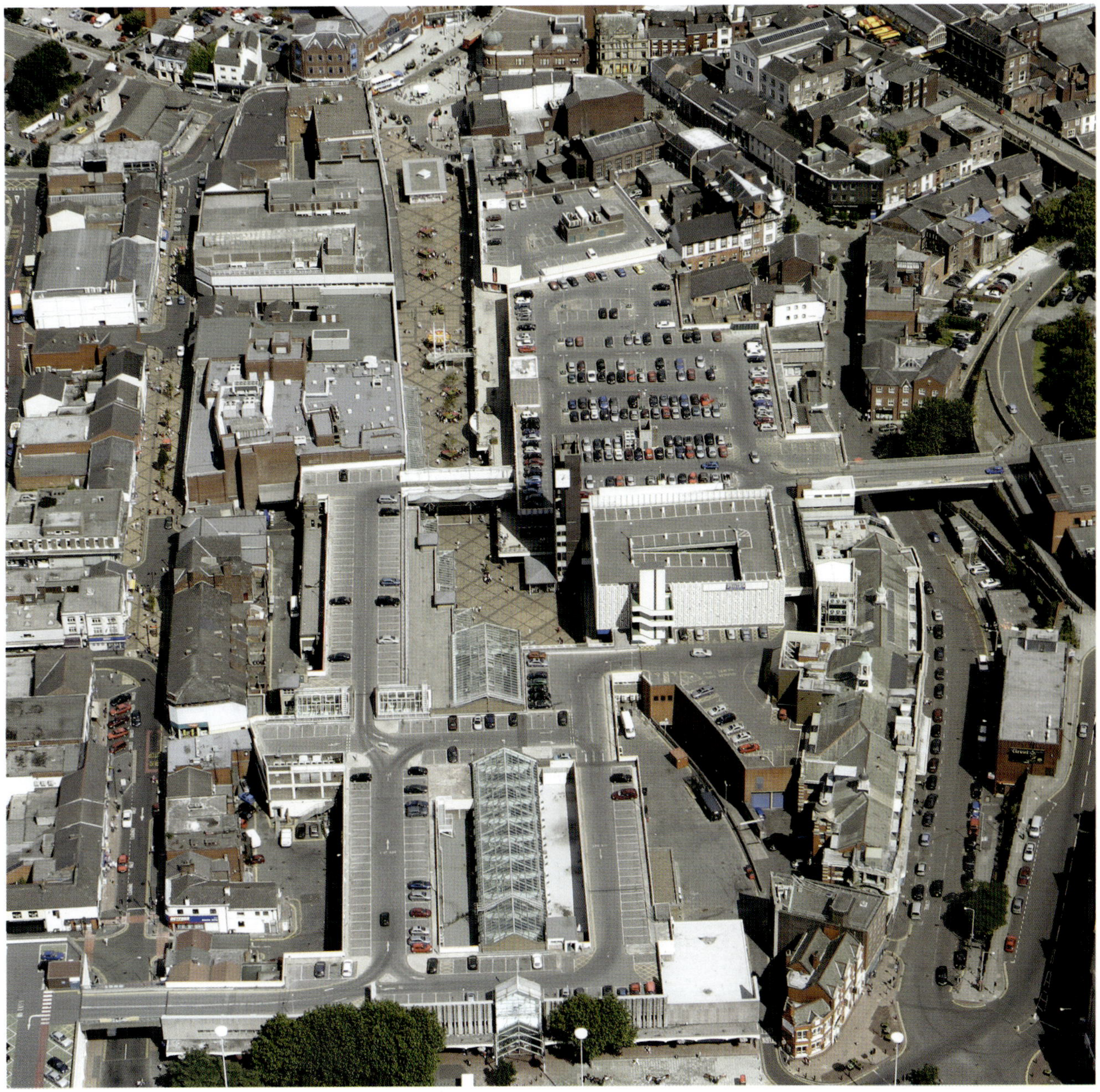

This image is the earliest known aerial photograph of the town centre. The main shopping areas at the beginning of the 20th century were on either bank of the river, on Heaton Lane (Princes Street) to the left, and the Underbanks on the right. There were no large department stores, although the new Co-operative building is seen here on the right undergoing development.

The main river crossings were at Lancashire Bridge (at the top of this picture) and Mersey Square Bridge (at the bottom). There was also an iron footbridge, crossing between Hatton Street and Deanery Way, leading to the White Lion public house on the south bank (right hand side of picture). The river would go on to became the source of the town's power during the industrial revolution, which resulted in dozens of mills, both large and small, being built along its route.

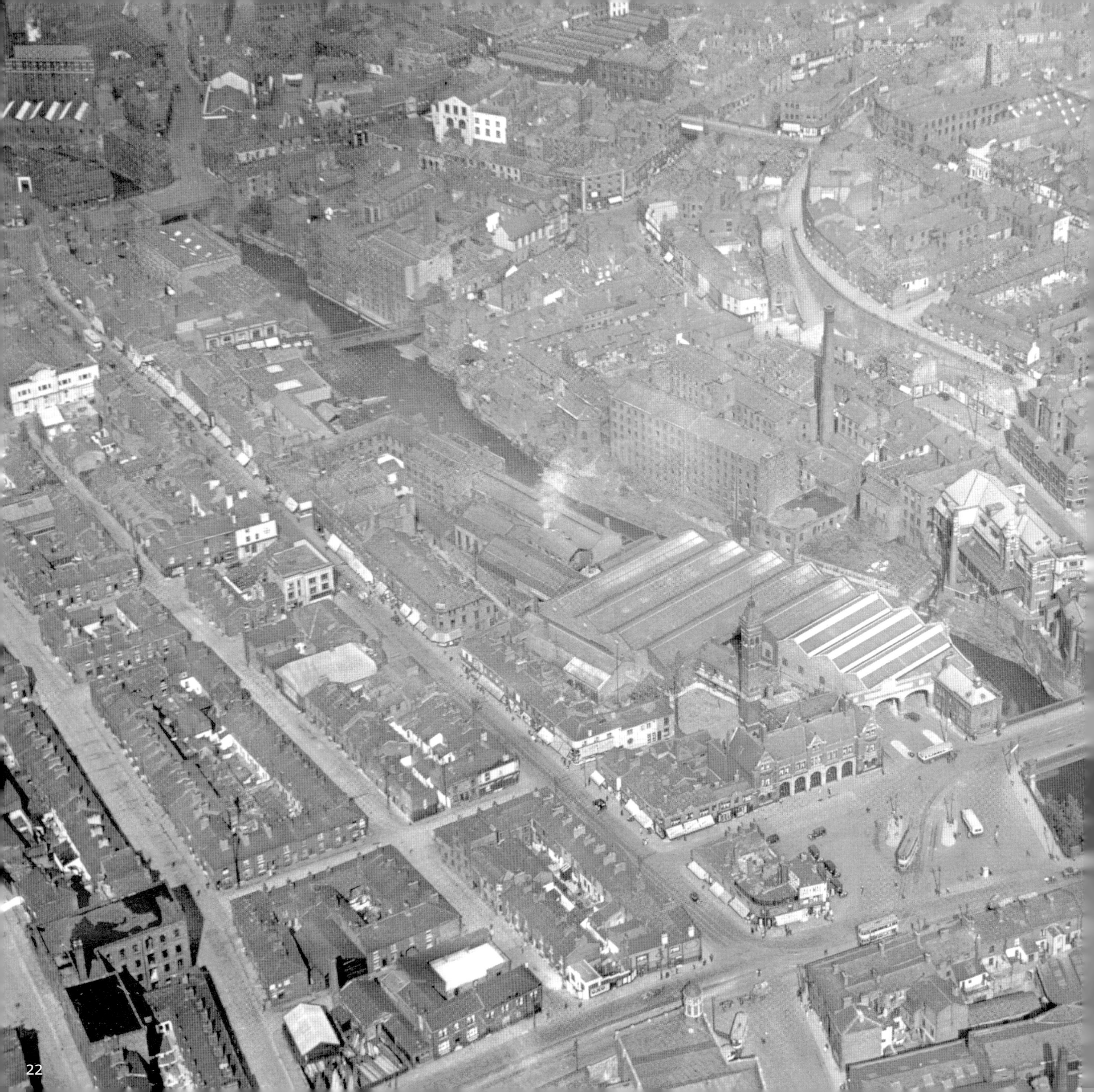

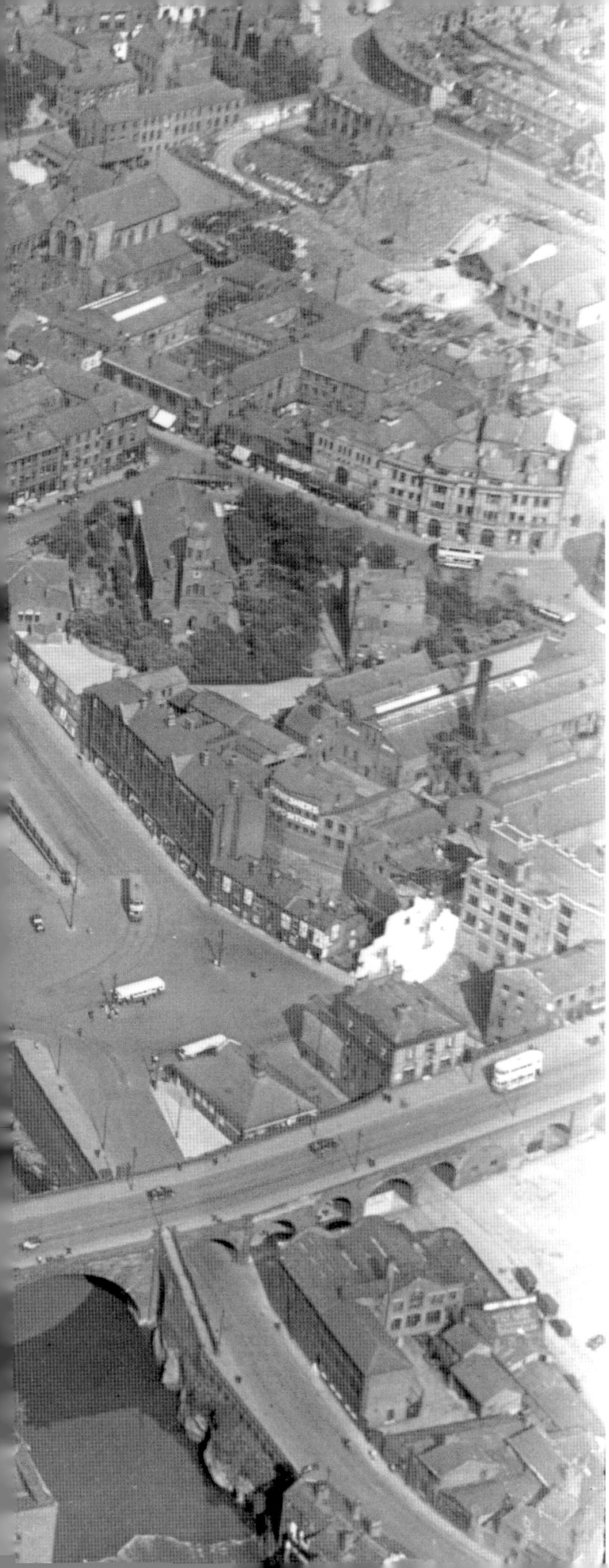

The River Mersey & Mersey Square 1931

Mersey Square was the main focal point in the centre of town in the 1930s, and it housed one of the most remarkable buildings around at the time. The Fire Station, with its impressive rescue-tower and five arched Fire Engine entrances was an imposing presence in the centre of the square. It was opened in 1902 and survived for 65 years. Mersey Square, much like today, was a busy transport hub. The old bus station was located in the square itself, just on the right of the river up against Wellington Road Bridge. The station building was extremely small compared to today, and here we can see a bus at the front of the building ready for passengers.

As well as buses, trams used to travel on the streets of Stockport. The main tram depot was the building with the multi-spanned roof to the right of the Fire Station. The number of trams and services grew to such an extent that a further depot was constructed on the site of the Heaton Lane Gasworks in 1924, in the middle bottom of the picture. Here we can see some trams entering the yard, just in front of some horse and cart on the main road. This also became the site of the main bus depot, which could hold over 100 vehicles.

The main tram stop in the square was in front of the station, where a tram can be seen passing between the two parallel paved areas that made up the stop. Look closely and you can also see a large stop with a shelter on the far side of St Peter's Church (middle right, this page). A tram has just passed this stop and is turning into Lord Street on the extreme right of the image. There is also a tram heading back towards the square at the top end of Princes Street (top left), as well as others on Wellington Road South, indicating their popularity at this time. In fact, there were so many service routes that in 1912 one of the bays of the covered market hall was removed to allow trams to make the tight turn at the Boars Head pub on the way to Offerton. The picture of the market hall on page 15 shows that there are now eight bays - the ninth was at the larger end in front of the produce hall.

Most of the streets running parallel to Princes Street have long since gone. The densely built buildings may not look very impressive, but they were of great importance as this was the major part of the Heaton Norris Township that developed after Stockport spread over the River Mersey. The whole of the area to the left of the river in this picture was officially in the county of Lancashire until 1835. Almost all of these buildings were two-up, two-down houses with not a garden or a patch of grass in site. The remnants of this township remain in the shops cited on Princes Street today, where some of the buildings date back more than 150 years. These may not survive for much longer as a new shopping development known as the Bridgefield Project has been planned for the site. Bridgefield Street is the road running next to Princes Street.

On the lower middle right is an area of gleaming white that stands out next to the darkened exteriors of the neighbouring buildings. These are the Plaza Steps linking Mersey Square with St Peter's Square. The steps were built out of reinforced concrete to try and replicate the effect of Portland stone. A new building would rise next to the steps in the following year that would completely alter the appearance of the square (see next page).

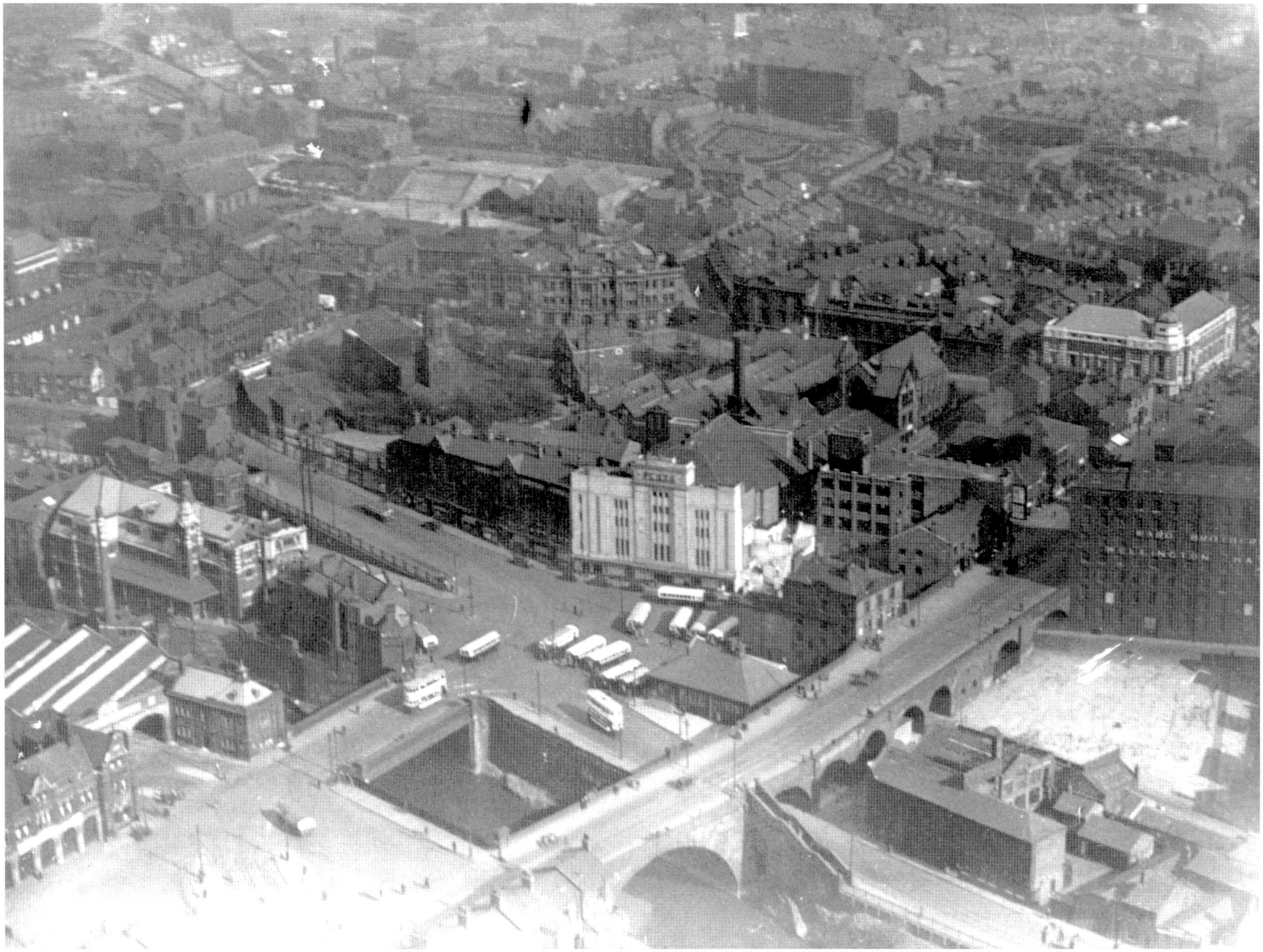

Mersey Square 1933

The biggest change to the square by 1933 was the addition of the Plaza Theatre. Opened on October 6th 1932, just a year before this image was taken, the theatre was literally hewn out of the cliff face behind, with thousands of tonnes of rock removed from the Mersey valley sides in order for it to be built. With its tiled art-deco exterior and neon sign, the building quickly became a significant landmark, providing hours of entertainment for the locals, particularly during the austere war years. Changing times, however, led to a downfall in the theatre's popularity, and it was bought by the Mecca Bingo group in July 1965. Its closure was fought by Stockport Council, but Mecca appealed to the Government and won their case. The last show was on December 31st 1966. The bingo hall closed in 1999 and in 2000 the cinema was bought by the Plaza Theatre Trust and reopened for screenings soon after. With 1200 seats (it originally had 1850) and the original Compton Organ, the Grade 2* Listed theatre is now one of the best preserved 1930s "Super Cinemas" in the UK, and plans are in hand to enhance the building further by restoring the exterior tiles and re-installing the neon size to bring it back to its full former glory.

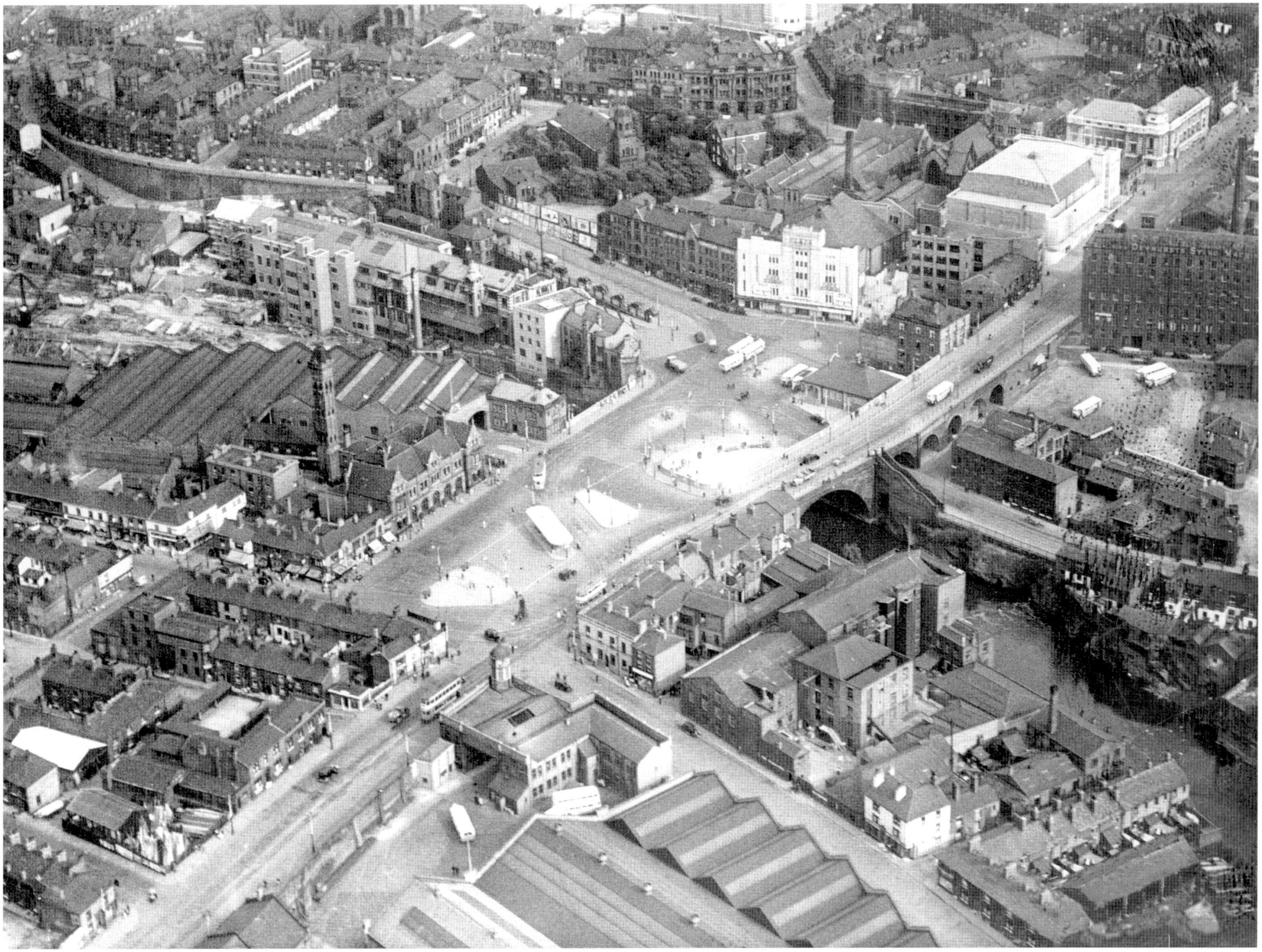

Mersey Square 1937

By 1937 major changes had started to take place in the area around Mersey Square. In the top left of the picture we can see an extension to the Co-operative building under construction that would double the size of the building. But perhaps the most noticeable difference is in the square itself. In 1935 the area between Mersey Square Bridge - itself only constructed in the 1920s - and Wellington Road Bridge was covered over. This area is now more commonly known as The Bear Pit. It was the start of a major culversion scheme that would change the centre of the town completely.

In the 1930s the number of cars on the roads had started to increase as their popularity and reductions in price led to more and more people wanting to own one. Although the total number of vehicles was nowhere near the numbers that exist today, Stockport, with its narrow winding streets, was totally unsuited to travel by Motor Car and it had started to suffer with traffic congestion. To ease the problem, a scheme was hatched to create a new route from Mersey Square to St Andrew's square.

Merseyway Road 1939

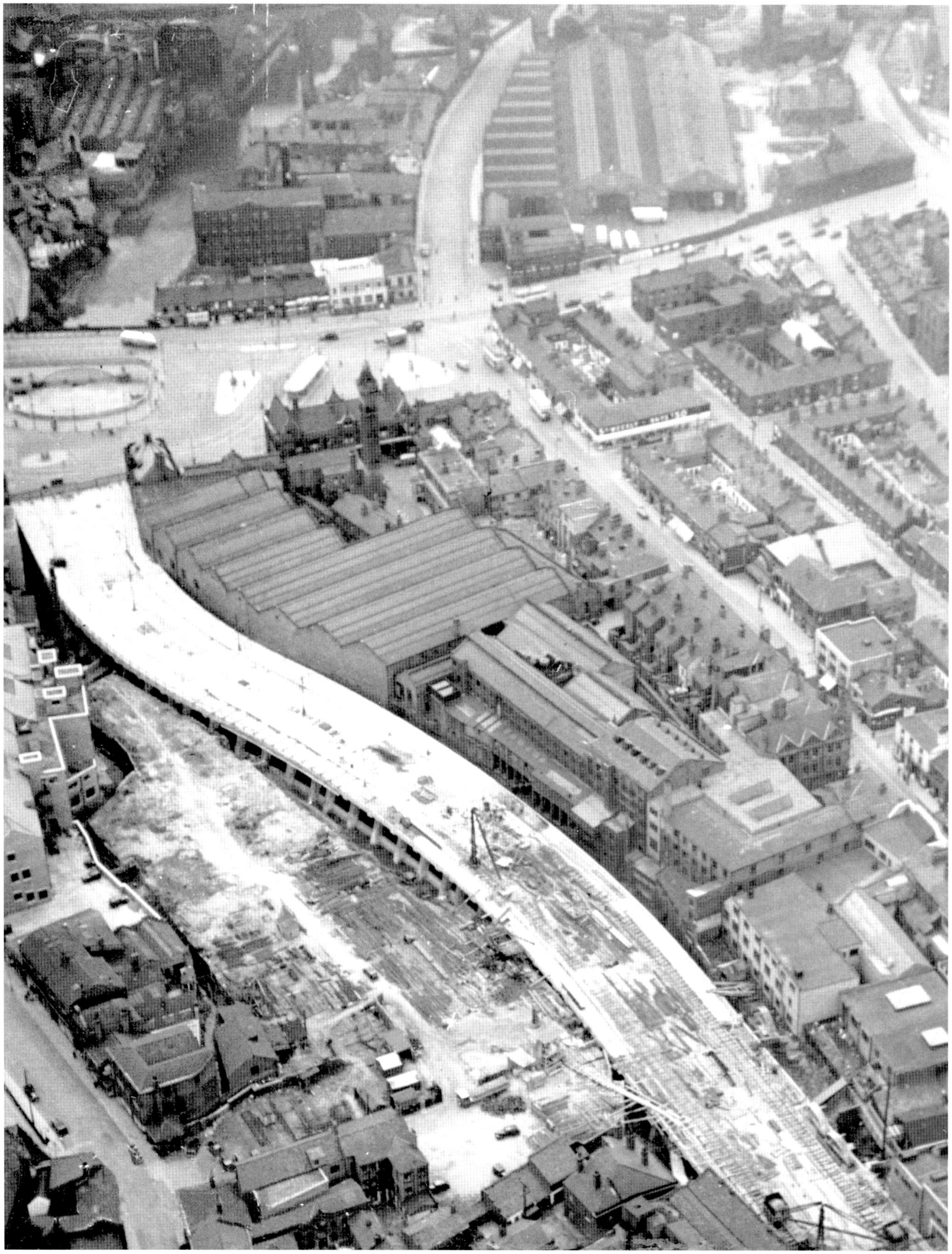

The solution to the problem of east - west traffic flow would be a create a new bypass. The road, known as "Merseyway", would be constructed over the River Mersey as it flowed through the town centre, hiding it from general view. Work commenced on the building of the road in 1937. The image taken on the previous page shows the progress that had been made on August 23rd of that year. Behind the Co-op building we can see the road under construction, but it has not yet reached Mersey Square Bridge.

By 1939, the road was almost complete. This image, taken on July 17th 1939, just weeks before the outbreak of the Second World War, shows the road nearing completion. The extension to the co-op store in the bottom left had also been completed by this time.

In modern times, the idea of covering over the main waterway through a town might not be countenanced. However, at the time the Mersey was heavily polluted, with the effluent from dozens of mills pouring into its waters daily, and there was little opposition to the loss of this stretch of the river through the town centre.

As well as providing a new route to the east, the road would help to keep the smells and pollution contained and out of sight.

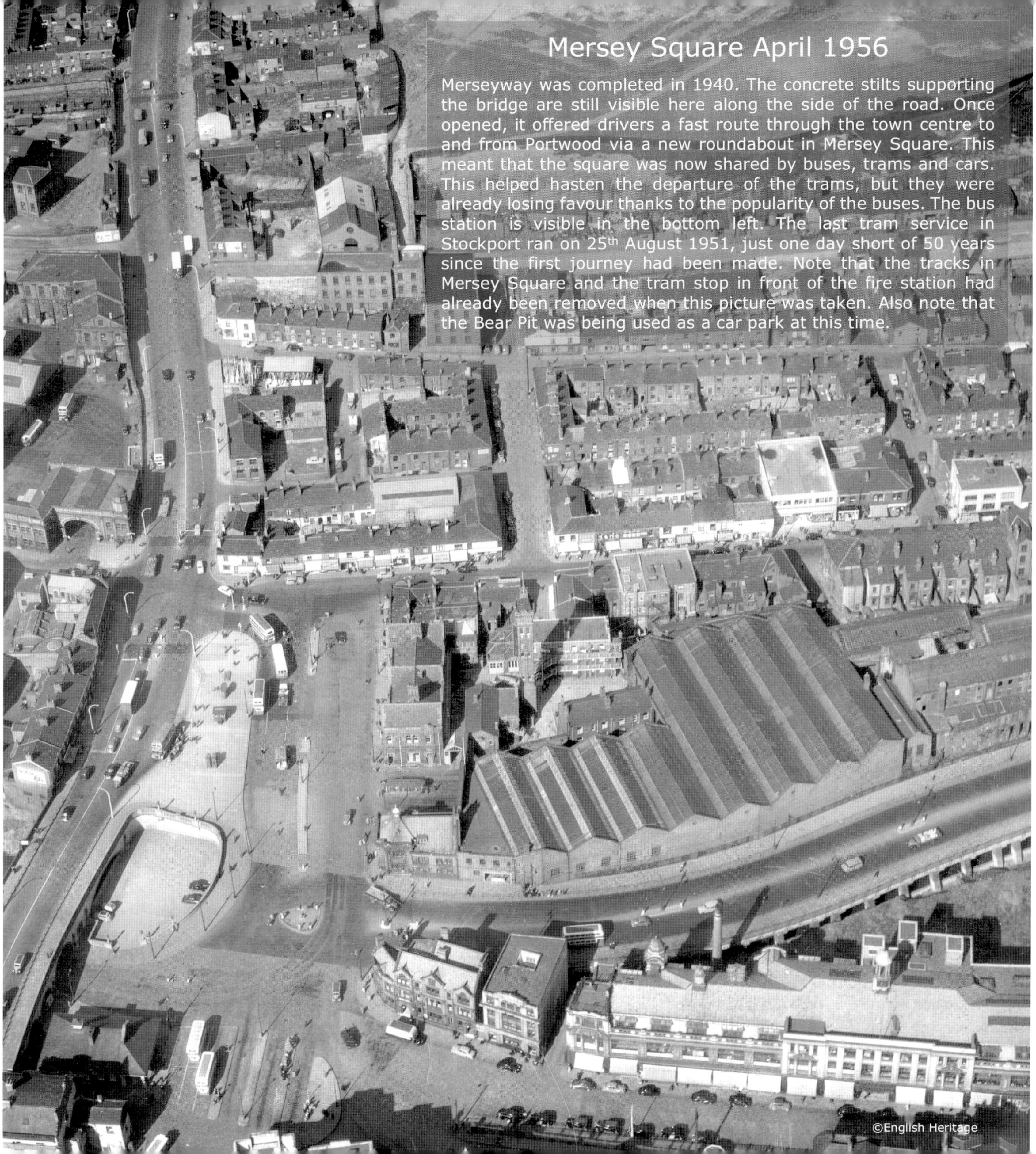

Mersey Square April 1956

Merseyway was completed in 1940. The concrete stilts supporting the bridge are still visible here along the side of the road. Once opened, it offered drivers a fast route through the town centre to and from Portwood via a new roundabout in Mersey Square. This meant that the square was now shared by buses, trams and cars. This helped hasten the departure of the trams, but they were already losing favour thanks to the popularity of the buses. The bus station is visible in the bottom left. The last tram service in Stockport ran on 25th August 1951, just one day short of 50 years since the first journey had been made. Note that the tracks in Mersey Square and the tram stop in front of the fire station had already been removed when this picture was taken. Also note that the Bear Pit was being used as a car park at this time.

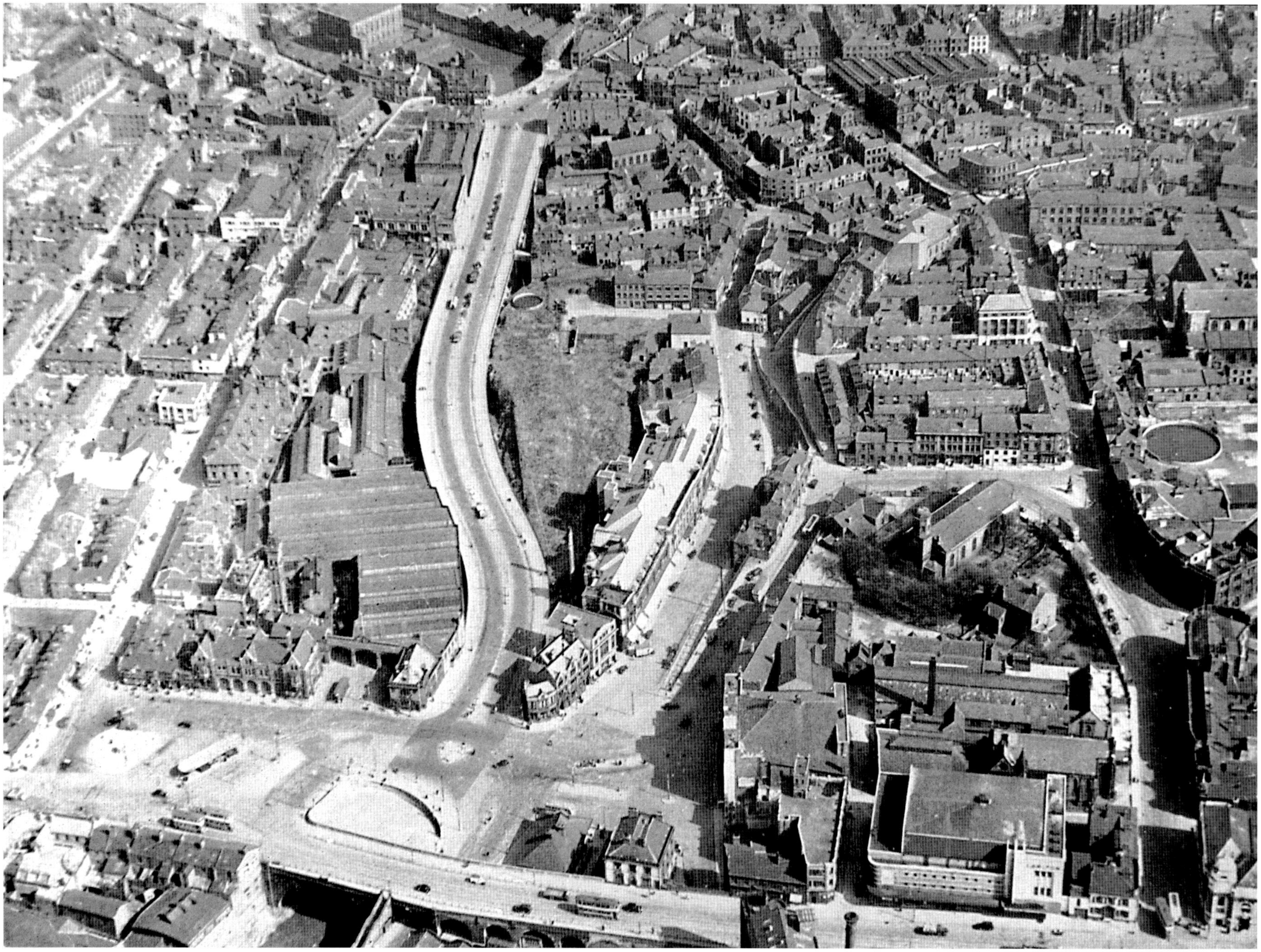

Merseyway Road 1949

This picture shows the full length of the completed road. The construction was a major engineering feat, especially for the times, and even today such a project would be a massive undertaking. The road covered over 1600 feet of the river (nearly 500m), allowing Merseyway to claim the title of second widest bridge in the world (the length is calculated from river bank to river bank). The widest bridge in the world was located just 15 miles away in Rochdale, where a similar road was built over the river Roch in the early 20th century. The new road also had greater repercussions, as it helped bring foward the demolition of many of the buildings that had lined the route of the river for decades, most notably the mills. In the picture above, many of the buildings had already gone - notice the vacant land behind the Co-op where a large 6-storey mill had stood. The road wasn't just open to vehicles. There were pavements for people to walk down its length, and this led to new department stores opening up by its side. See the image on page 48, where the Marks & Spencer store is under construction in the bottom right.

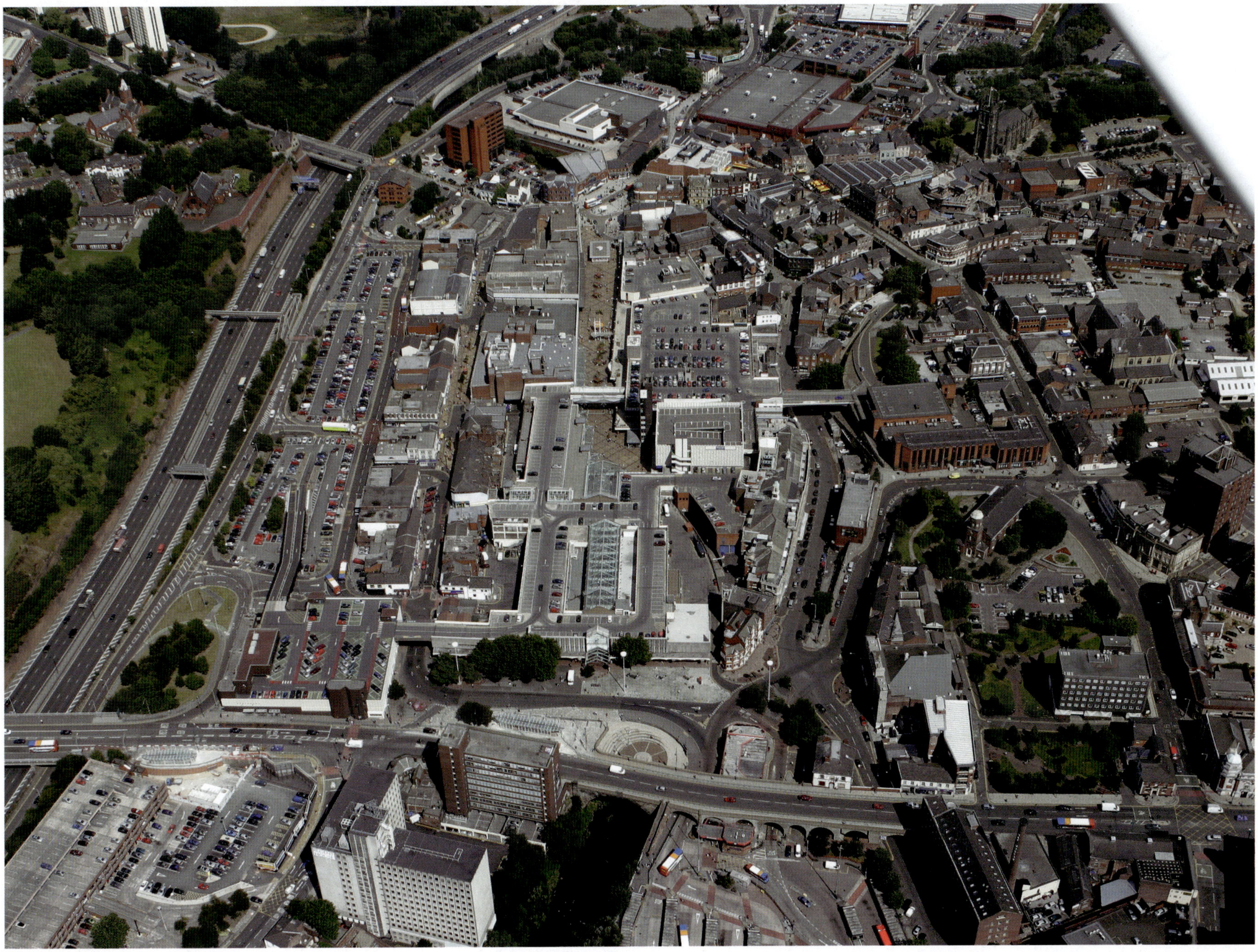

Merseyway road was closed in the 1960s when a major new shopping centre was constructed around it. The centre, known as the Merseyway Shopping Centre, was built from 1965-1970. Today, the route of the road is still clearly visible from the air, and part of it survives as an access way for service vehicles and deliveries (on the right, at the side of the front section with the glazed roof, behind the Co-op building). But where cars once roamed down its full length, pedestrians have now taken over. On the ground there is little evidence that the road was ever there, although there are a few road signs placed deliberately within the shopping centre that say "Merseyway" that give some indication as to its former use.

Mersey Square is still the main focal point of the town, but is now looking tired and in need of a revamp. Since this picture was taken it has been re-paved, but a complete overhaul is now necessary to help give the square its life and soul back and turn it into a modern public space fit for the 21st century.

Merseyway Shopping Centre 1967

The shopping centre was built at a cost of over £5 million. At the time it was one of the most modern and advanced shopping centres in the UK, and was almost as big an engineering feat as the construction of the road itself. Some of the shops along the south bank of the river (the Co-op side) are actually built on top of the road, with the weight supported at the back. The road remained open during construction, as can be seen in the image from 1967, with many cars and lorries heading towards Mersey Square. The front section of the shopping centre was completed last. This resulted in the loss of the historic Fire Station.

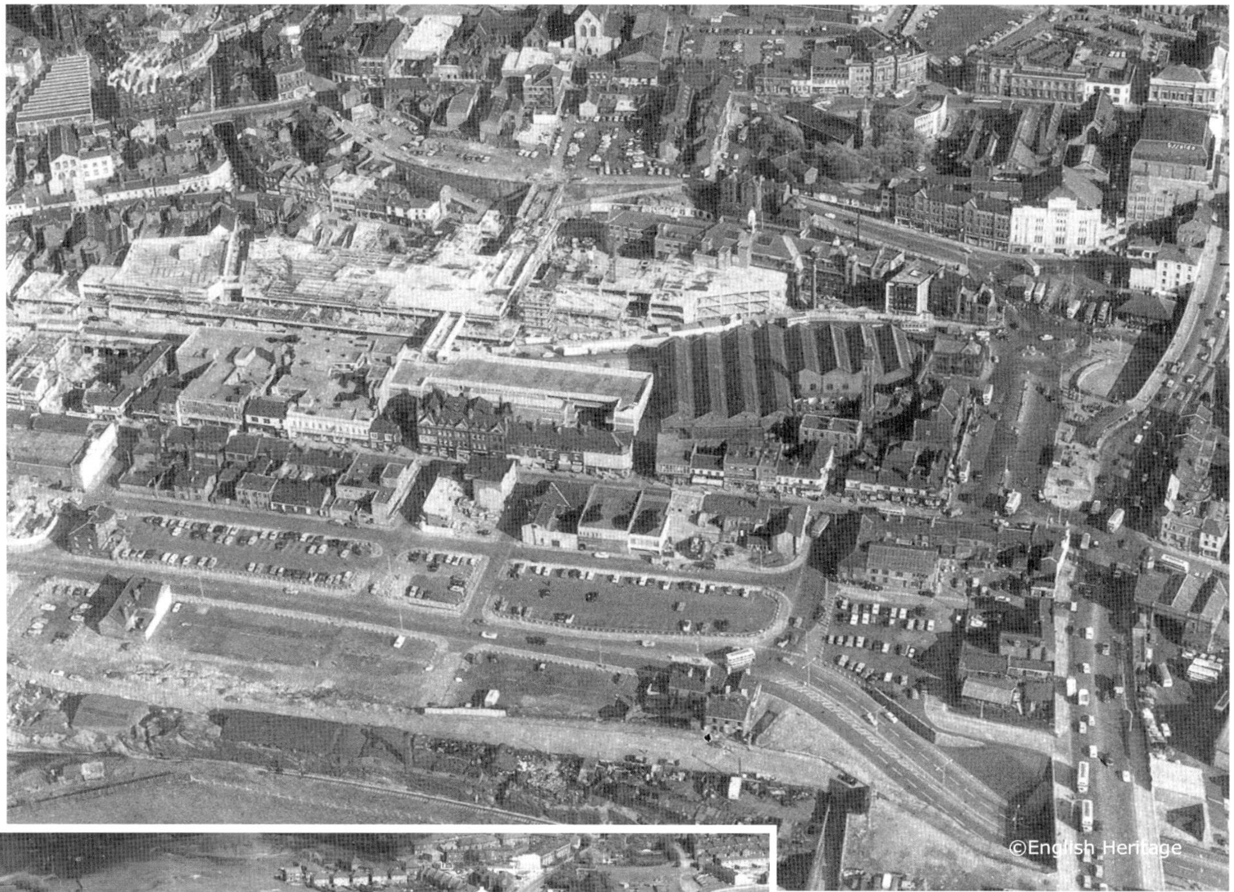

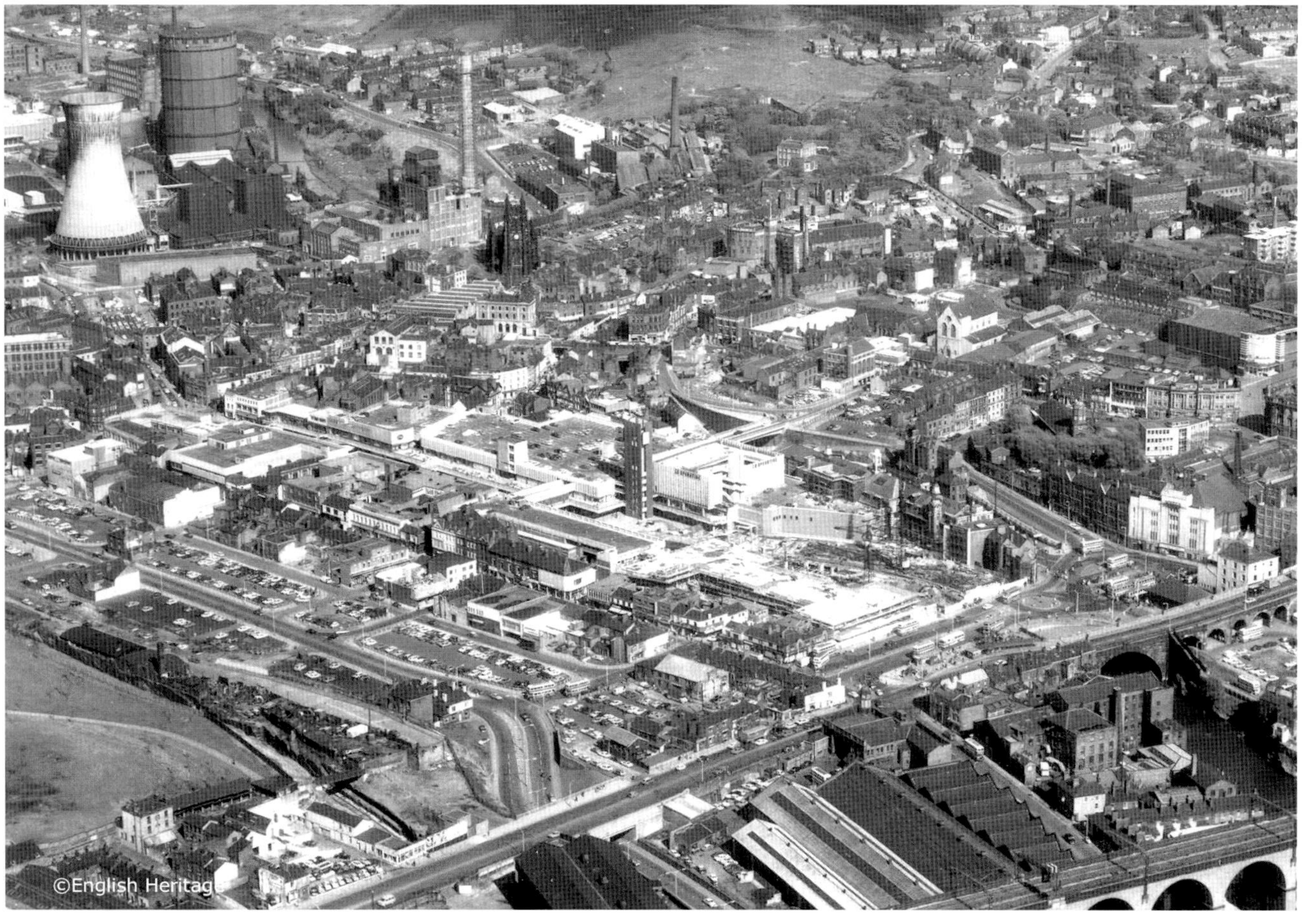

Merseyway Shopping Centre 1969

With a little more foresight and planning, the fire station would have made a superb and dramatic entrance to the new shopping centre, with shoppers entering via the archways. Sadly, this foresight was lacking, and the station was demolished and replaced with the drab, grey, concrete edifice that survives to this day, albeit with a more modern glazed entrance that was added in 1994. As if to compensate, a tall new clock tower was built in place of the station tower. Here we can see the new front section under construction after the rest of the centre had actually opened.

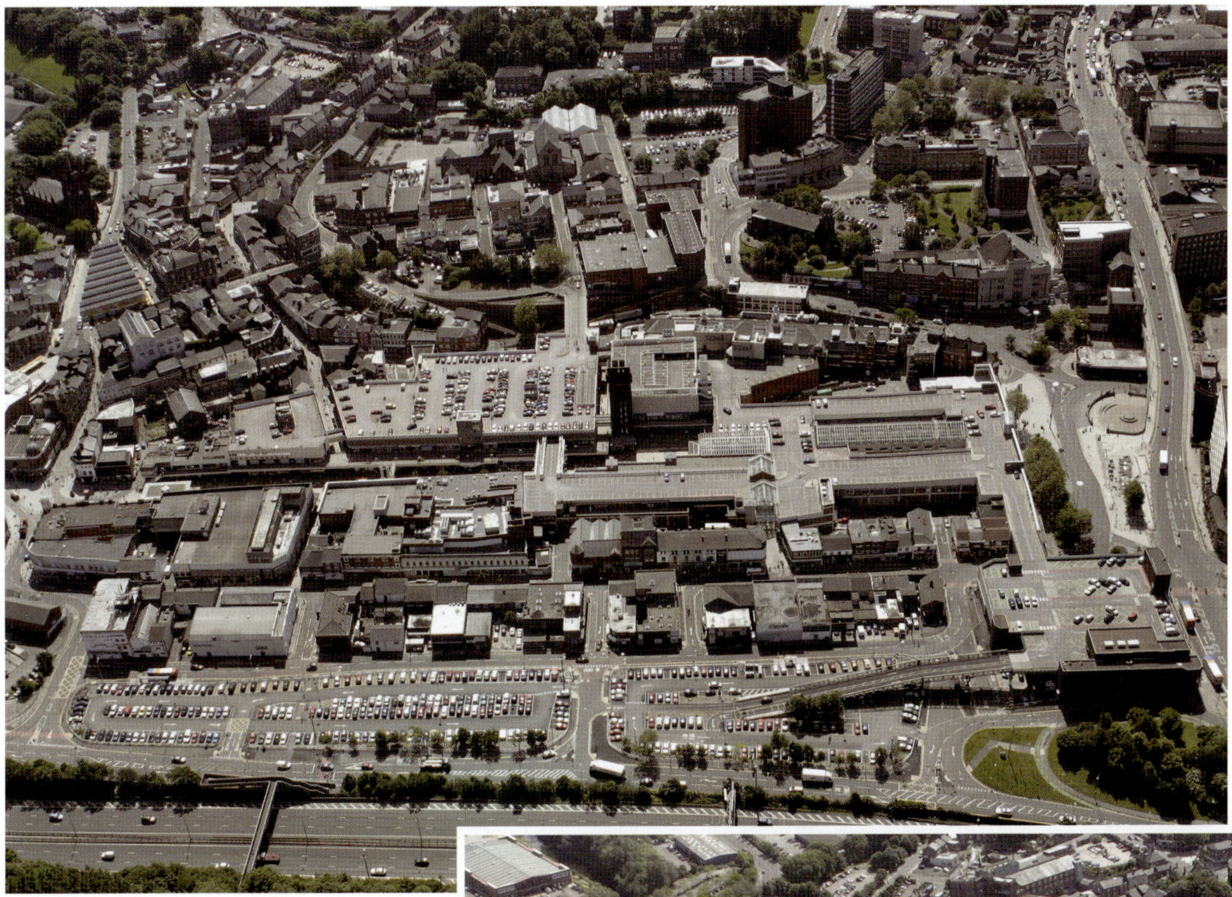

The centre has proved to be extremely popular despite its faults, and today attracts over 15 million visitors per year out of a total of 24 million who shop in Stockport Town Centre (the other main shopping areas being Princes Street, the Market Place, the Underbanks and the Peel Centre). It has remained relatively unchanged since it was built. The large Debenhams store that fronts onto the northern end of Mersey Square has probably been the biggest addition to the shopping area.

It is unlikely that the River Mersey will be uncovered at any point in the near future. Merseyway is now one of the busiest shopping centres in the UK, and to open up the river would result in the loss of the main pedestrian route, and there isn't enough space on the river banks to enable new walkways to be built.

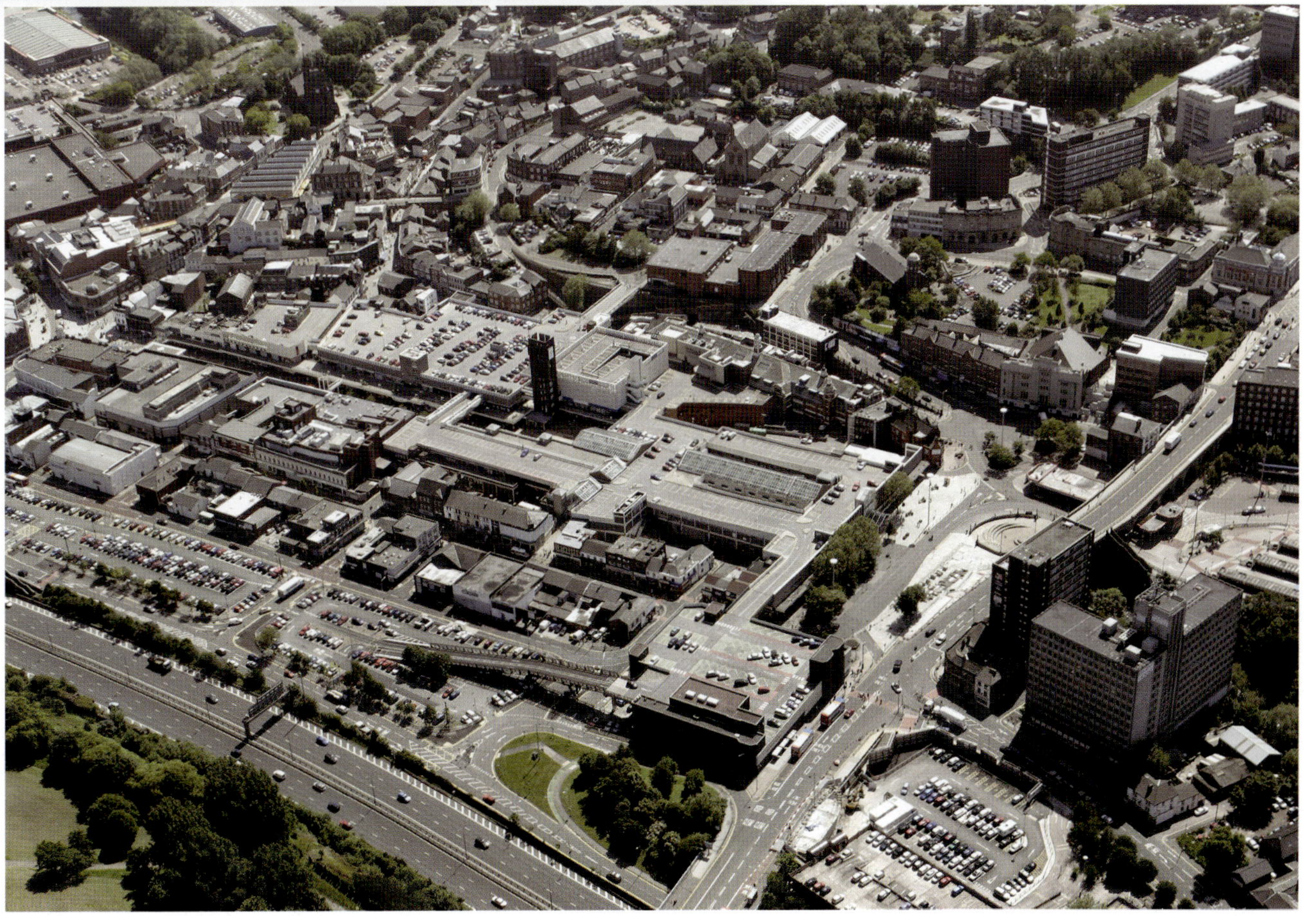

In short, to successfully open up the river you would have to completely redesign everything along its banks, and the cost of this would be far too high.

In 2007 the centre celebrated its 40th anniversary. Today, many of the people who visit will be unaware that the River Mersey is flowing onwards towards the sea, 40 feet beneath their feet, and even less will realise that they are actually walking on a road. Occasionally the shopping centre offers tours underneath the precinct, where people can see the original structure. However, if you know where to look, the original arched concrete supports that were built in the 1930s can still be seen from above ground.

The New Road

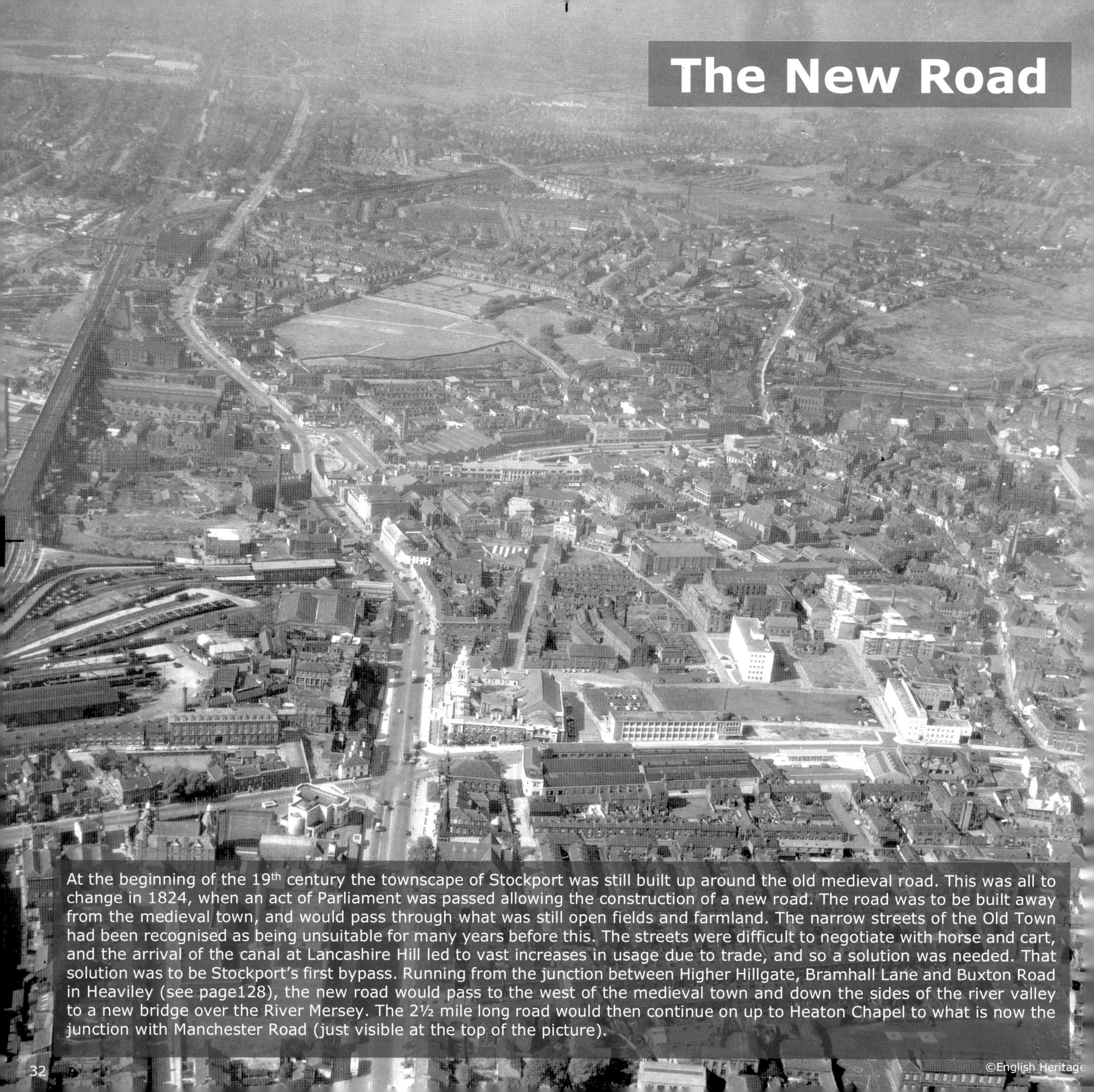

At the beginning of the 19th century the townscape of Stockport was still built up around the old medieval road. This was all to change in 1824, when an act of Parliament was passed allowing the construction of a new road. The road was to be built away from the medieval town, and would pass through what was still open fields and farmland. The narrow streets of the Old Town had been recognised as being unsuitable for many years before this. The streets were difficult to negotiate with horse and cart, and the arrival of the canal at Lancashire Hill led to vast increases in usage due to trade, and so a solution was needed. That solution was to be Stockport's first bypass. Running from the junction between Higher Hillgate, Bramhall Lane and Buxton Road in Heaviley (see page128), the new road would pass to the west of the medieval town and down the sides of the river valley to a new bridge over the River Mersey. The 2½ mile long road would then continue on up to Heaton Chapel to what is now the junction with Manchester Road (just visible at the top of the picture).

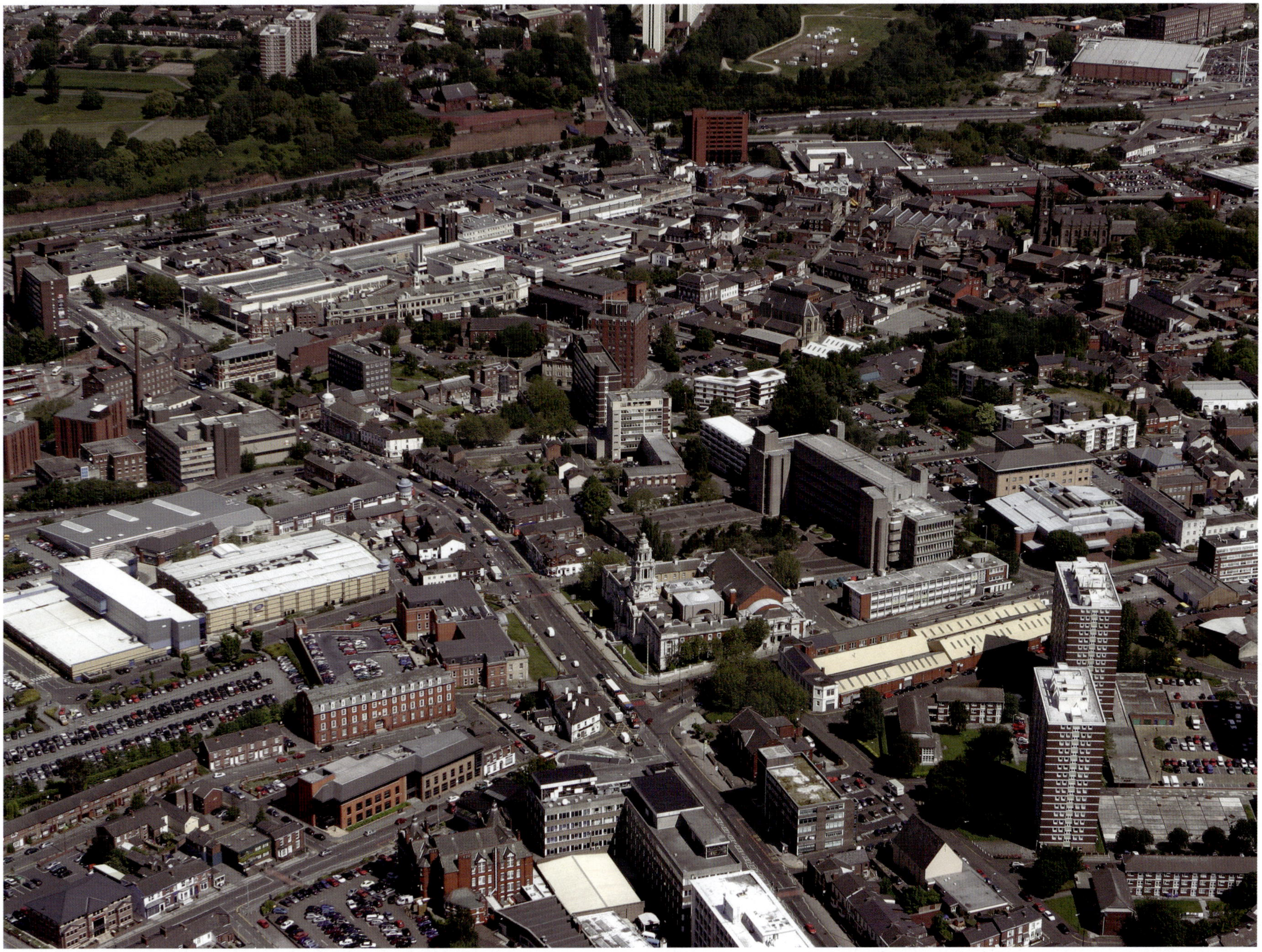

The route chosen for the road was actually one of several proposed, and was officially the "orange route". The new stone bridge in the trough of the valley contained 11 arches, with the widest arch spanning the river. Technically a viaduct, it was the precursor to the much larger viaduct that would be built parallel to it just over 12 years later. The cost of the entire scheme, including the bridge, was £36,000. The road opened on 3rd July 1826, and the occasion was marked by a huge parade, which including a procession by the workmen who had built the bypass. The road was initially written on maps as "New Road", but both the road and the bridge were eventually named after General Wellington, who had defeated the armies of Napoleon 11 years earlier. The top half of the road became Wellington Road North, and the bottom half Wellington Road South. The image opposite, taken on August 22nd 1961, clearly shows both the new road and the much narrower old road running parallel to it on the right. The new road was to become the scene of major development over the next 100 years, resulting in many grand civic buildings being built along its route. The first of these included Wellington Mill (1828), the Infirmary (1833) and the National School (1826, now demolished and the site of the town hall). The new road is now the main route through the centre of town, and its original designation as a bypass is somewhat amusing, as this road is now so busy that it probably needs a bypass of its own.

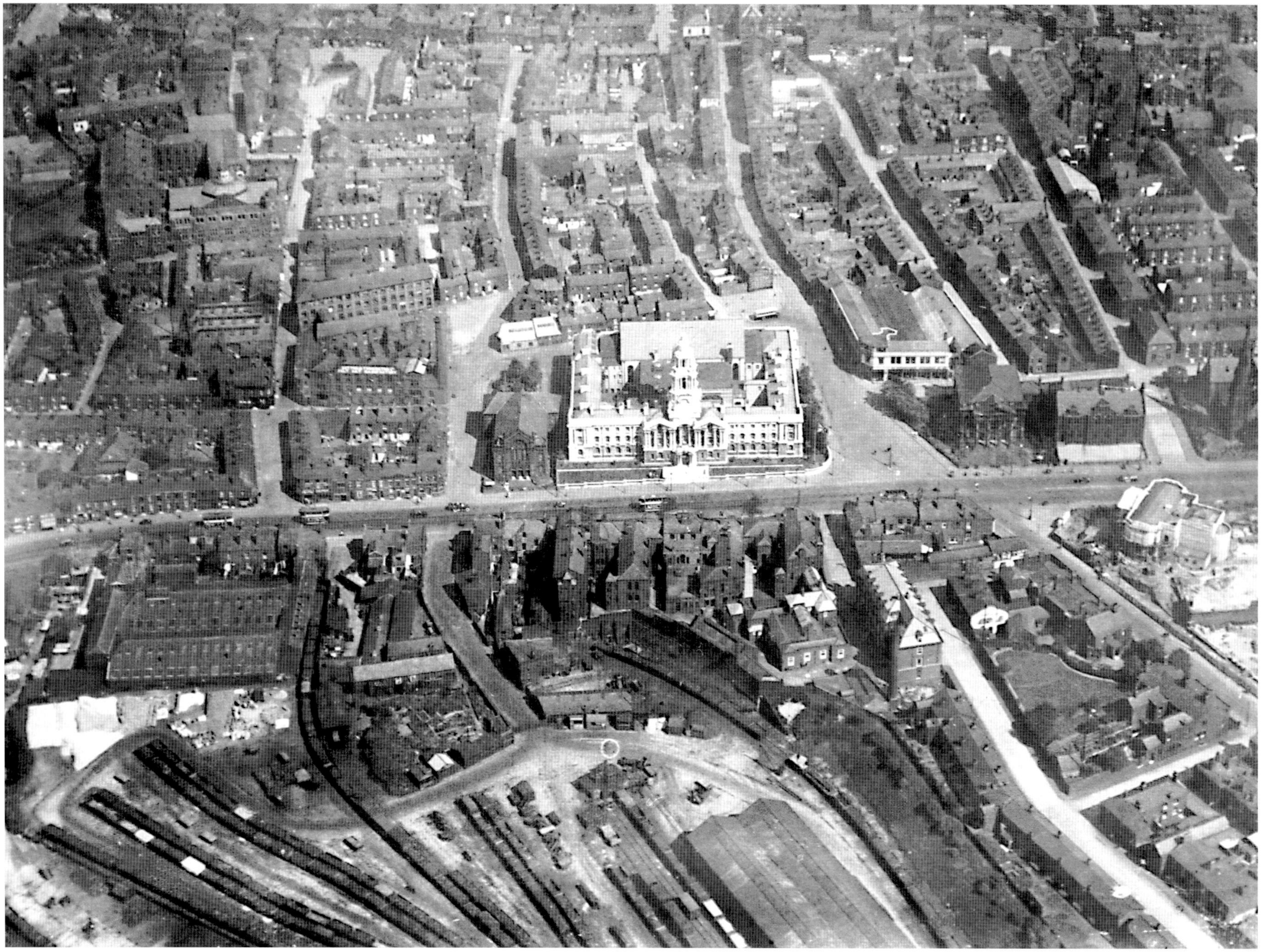

Town Hall 1933

Without doubt the most magnificent building in the town centre, Stockport town hall was designed by Sir Alfred Brumwell Thomas, who was the winner of a competition to design the new building. Built on the site of the National School, the construction commenced in 1904 and the building was officially open by the Prince of Wales in July 1908. To commemorate his visit, the part of Heaton Lane next to what is now Merseyway was renamed Princes Street, after the Prince took that route to the new building from his arrival at Tiviot Dale Train Station. Nicknamed the "Wedding Cake" due its layered tower, the Town Hall reaches a height of 130 feet and includes a magnificent Edwardian ballroom and marble staircase. There is also the original Wurlitzer organ, one of only 14 of its type remaining in the world. As can be seen in the image from 1933, the town hall was a beacon of white amidst a sea of buildings blackened by soot from years of industrial activity.

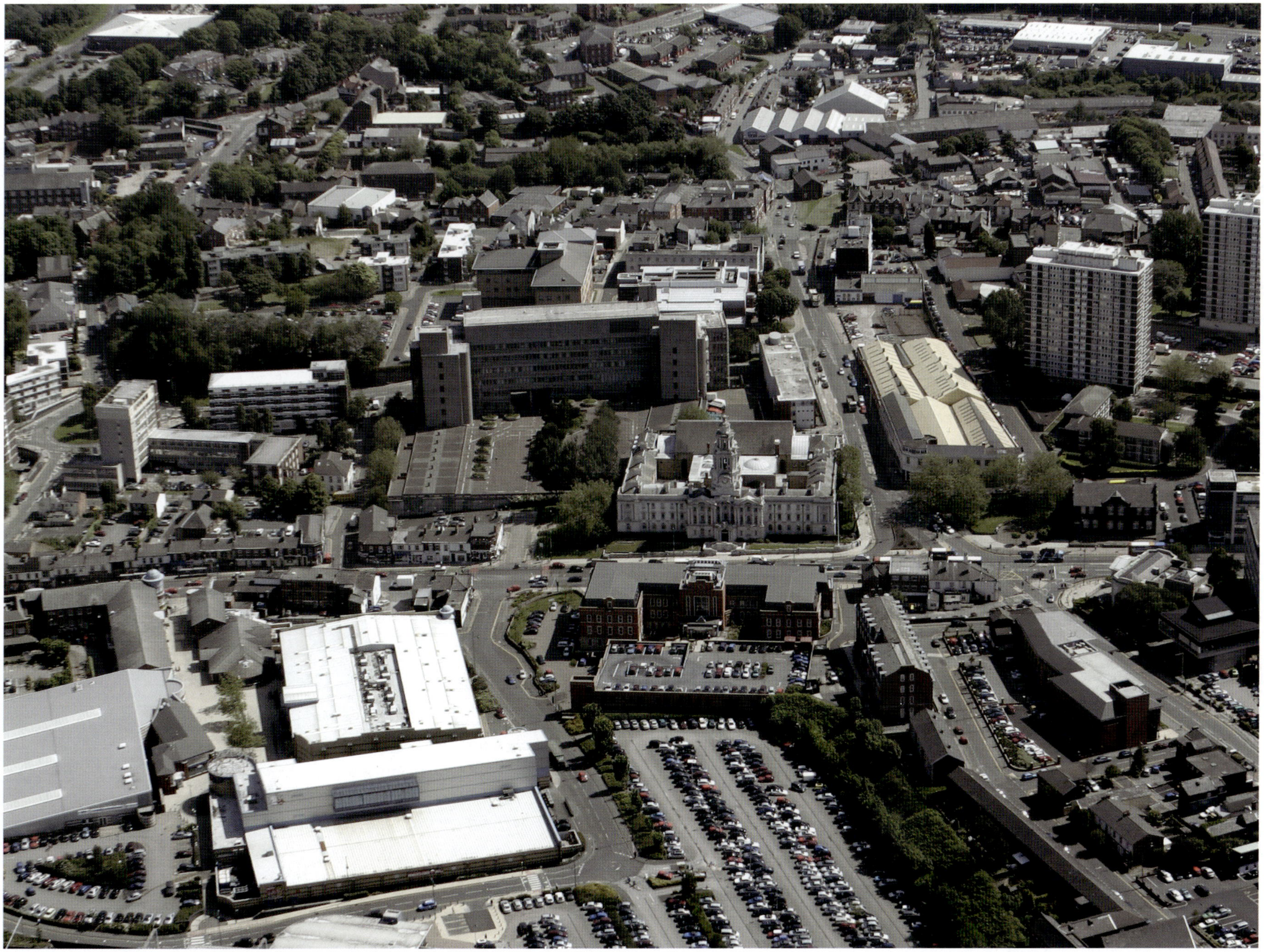

This area of the town centre has seen some of the greatest changes. In fact, with the exception of the Town Hall, almost all of the buildings on the far side of Wellington Road have gone. Of the massed ranks of terraced hoses, only those fronting onto the road remain, and all of those up to Hillgate behind have been replaced by office developments. One of these is the gargantuan Stopford House: a 1970s council office block recently made famous as the police station in the TV series "Life On Mars". The building to the immediate left of the town hall was Ebenezer Chapel. To the right of the Town Hall stood the particularly impressive Mount Tabor Chapel, The British Schools, and the Congregational Chapel (the church with the spire). Of these four, only the British Schools building survives. The site of Mount Tabor chapel, which had four large colonnaded columns and a grand stepped entrance, is now Town Hall Square. The tops of the columns from the front of the chapel - known as capitals - remain in the square as public ornaments. Today these buildings would all have been listed and the idea of demolishing them would be sacrilege. The only positive is that the open spaces now enhance the views of the town hall.

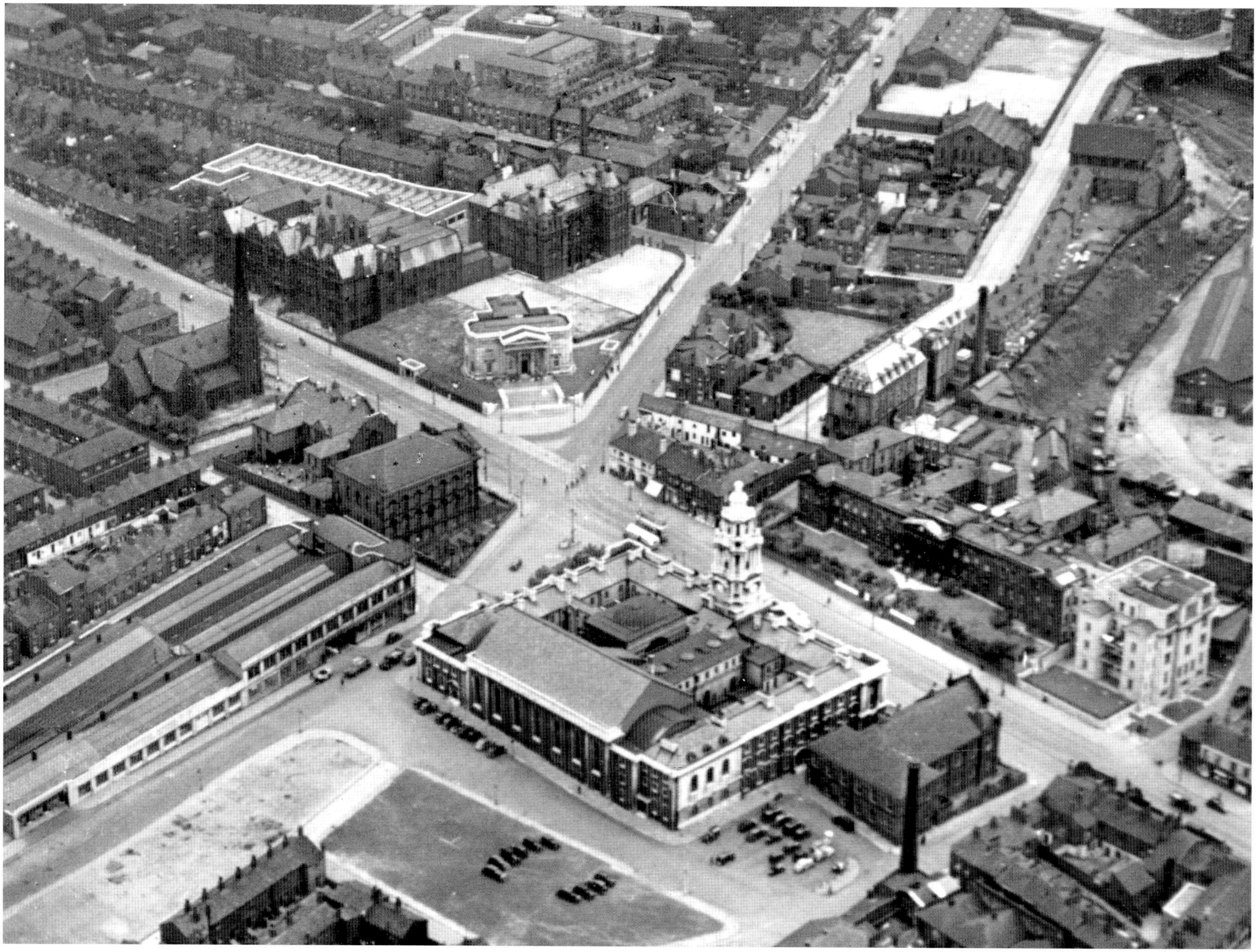

Greek Street 1939

On the corner at the junction between Greek Street and Wellington Road South is Stockport Art Gallery and War Memorial. The gallery was built on the second site of Stockport Grammar School, with the empty land at the rear showing how large the old buildings would have been. There had been plans for an art gallery on the site from 1912, but it wasn't until 1919 that work started when it was decided to combine the gallery with a memorial to the local men who had died in the First World War. The building took 6 years to complete and, like the town hall, is made from Portland Stone. Note the two bus shelters set into the walls either side of the building. These were added in around 1937 in a style that matched that of the gallery. To the left of the gallery is the modern day site of Stockport College, which back then was known as Stockport Technical School. To the rear of this is Greek Street Secondary School, which was built from 1909-10. Of the two buildings, only this one survives. The school was built to accommodate 470 boys and 290 girls, and the building is now incorporated into the modern college campus.

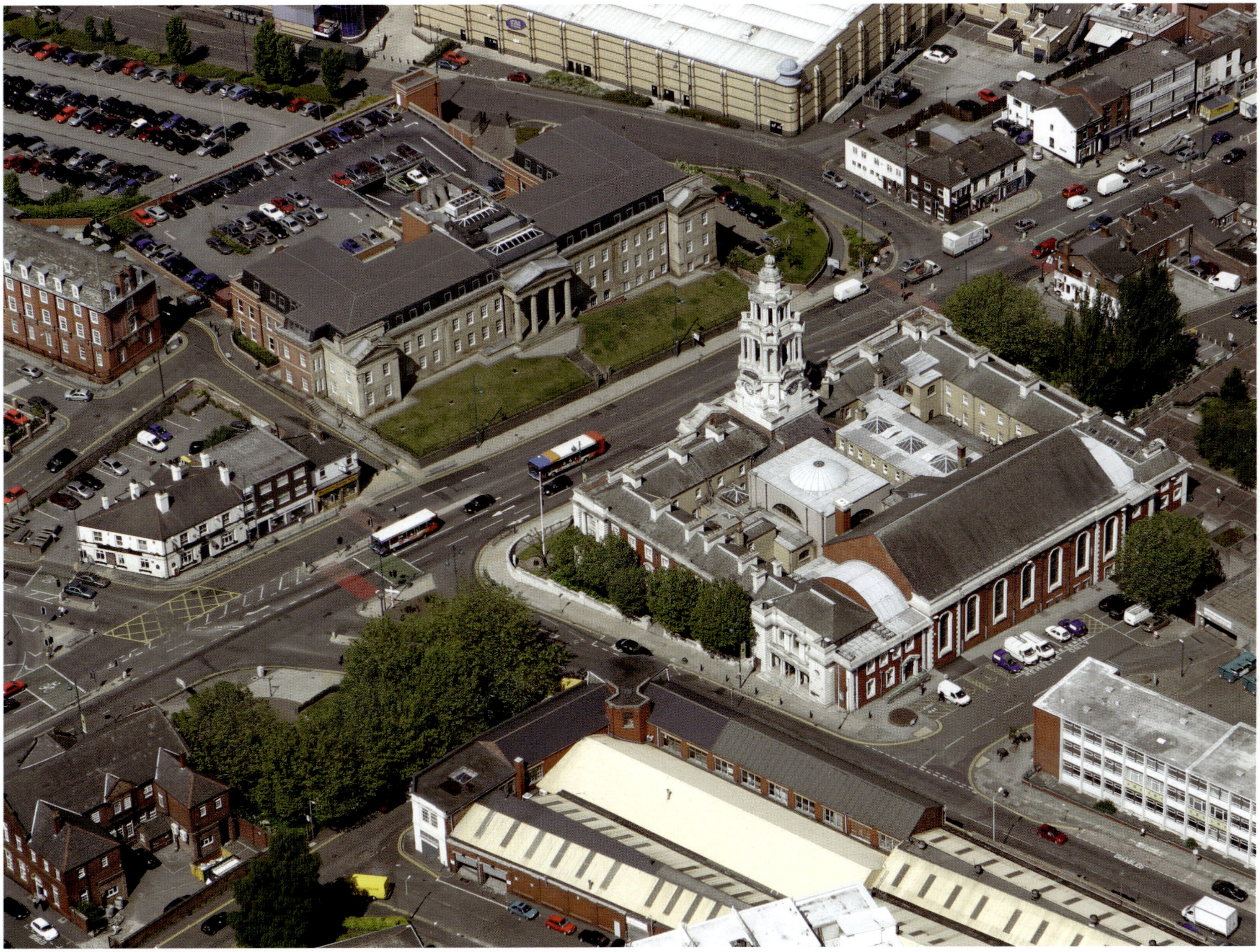

The Infirmary

The Infirmary was built from 1832-33 at a reported cost of around £5,300, all of which was raised through donations. At first it consisted of the central third of the frontage shown here, with the wings added later on when the building was extended. The south wing was added in 1870, and the wing at the north in 1898. There were further additions to the building during its lifetime both at the rear and at the sides, including the large five-storey block on the north side (the right) shown in 1939. Note that this section is much paler than the rest of the Infirmary, showing that this is one of the new sections – if it was as old as the rest, it would have turned black thanks to the industrial pollution in the air. When the new town hall was opened on the opposite side of the road in 1908 it was decided not to include chimes with the clock tower so as not to disturb the patients. The infirmary closed in 1996 when the accident & emergency department was transferred to Stepping Hill Hospital. The building was completely rebuilt at the rear with the facade retained at the front, and it reopened in 2000 as offices with the new name of Millennium House.

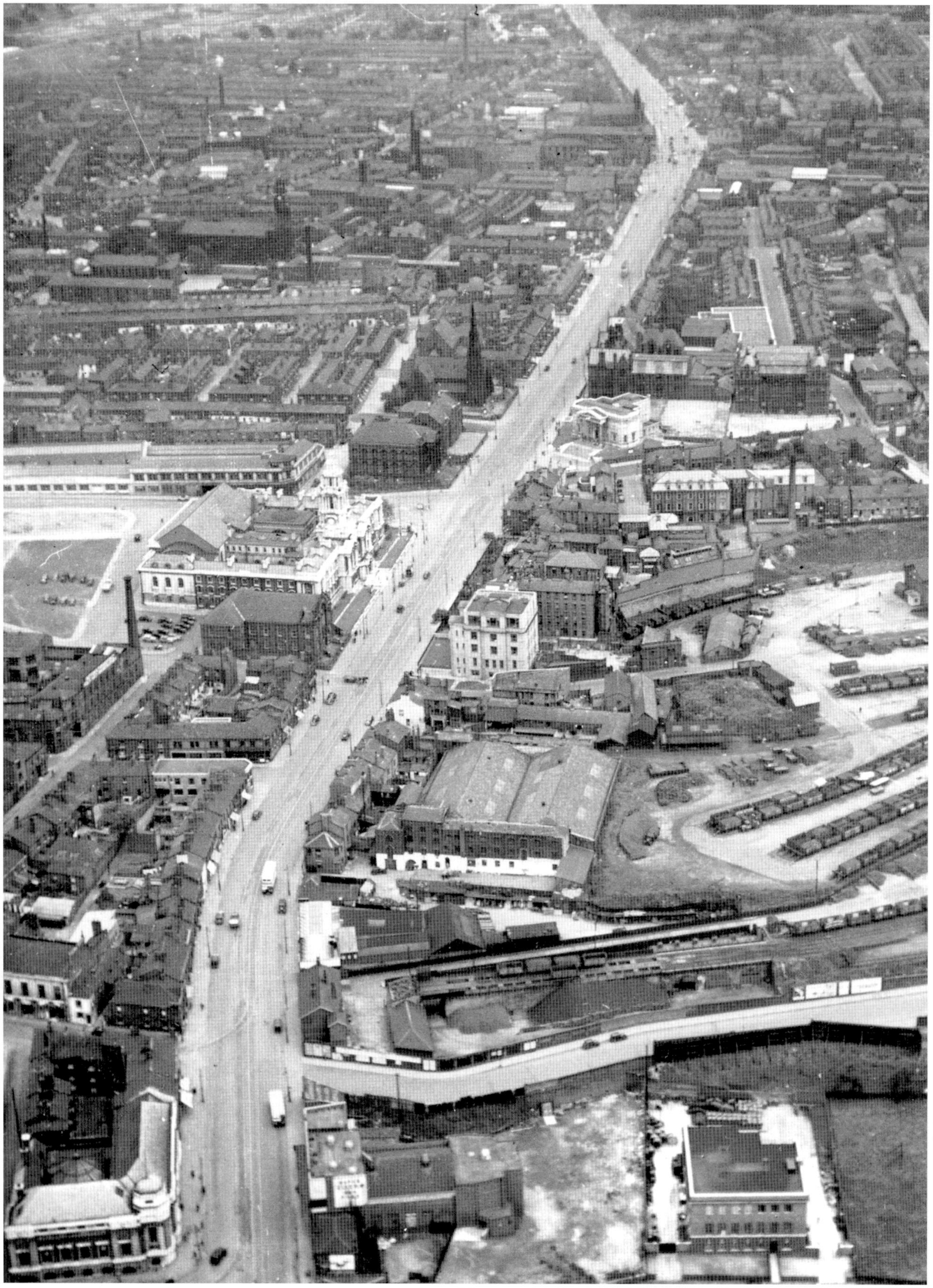

Wellington Road South 1939

This view up Wellington Road South epitomises the development of the new road. The wide boulevard was much bigger than anything that had gone before it, and it did its job very well.

As can be seen from this photograph, there is plenty of room for manoeuvre for all modes of transport, including cars, buses, trams, and Horse & Cart - Look closely in the picture and you can just see a Horse & Cart crossing the street just before Ebenezer Chapel and the town hall, heading into the coal and goods yards at Edgeley Station. Today this is the site of the Grand Central Leisure complex.

At this point the road is flanked by the many large, impressive buildings that were constructed along its route, including the town hall, Infirmary and the buildings around Greek Street. Beyond this, on either side of the road, the streets are much more densely packed, with traditional rows of cramped terraced houses intermixed with church spires and chimneys. It was these types of streets that the road was designed to alleviate in the early 19th century, but that didn't stop further development from packing the buildings in during the next 100 years.

The road remains the main route through the town centre, but the only time you will find it this empty is during the very early hours of the morning. Today the road is used by over 25,000 vehicles per day.

Wellington Mill

This impressive building was built in 1828 and designed by leading industrialist Thomas Marsland. The seven-storey mill was originally a cotton Mill, but today it is better known as home to the UK's only dedicated hatting museum, the Hatworks. The award winning museum features original hat-making machinery, a changing programme of exhibits and also has a fine collection of hats of all styles from around the world, including those belonging to famous owners. The imposing, 200-foot chimney that advertises the museum's name was added in 1860. Despite being built for cotton the building was actually used for hat making for a period when it was occupied by the Ward Brothers hat manufacturing company from 1890 to the 1930s. During this time the words "Ward Brothers Limited, Wellington Hat Factory" were emblazoned on the side of the building - see the image of Mersey Square on page 24. Next to the mill is the Garrick Theatre (bottom, left). It was founded in 1901 and moved here in 1920, becoming the UK's first amateur society to own it's own theatre.

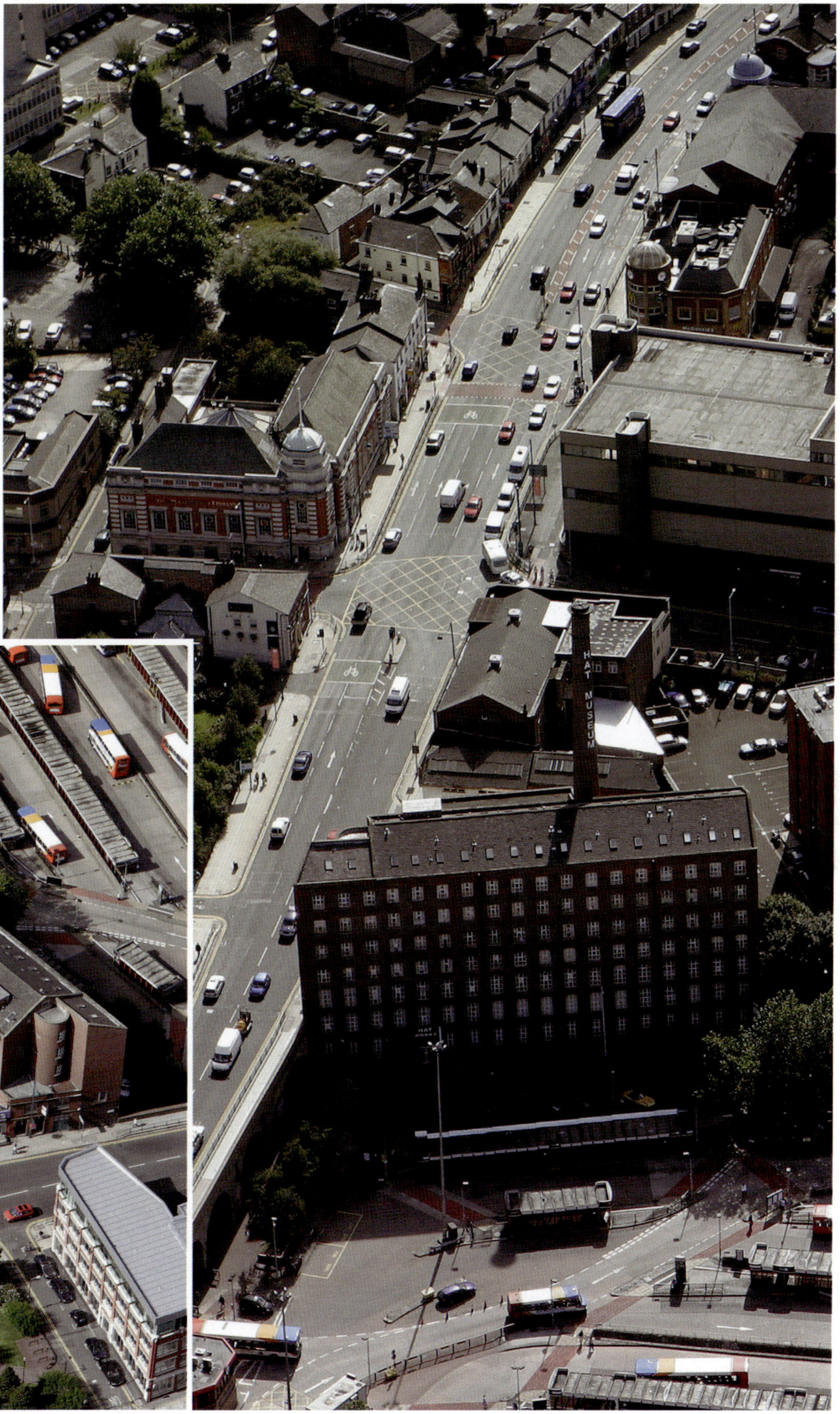

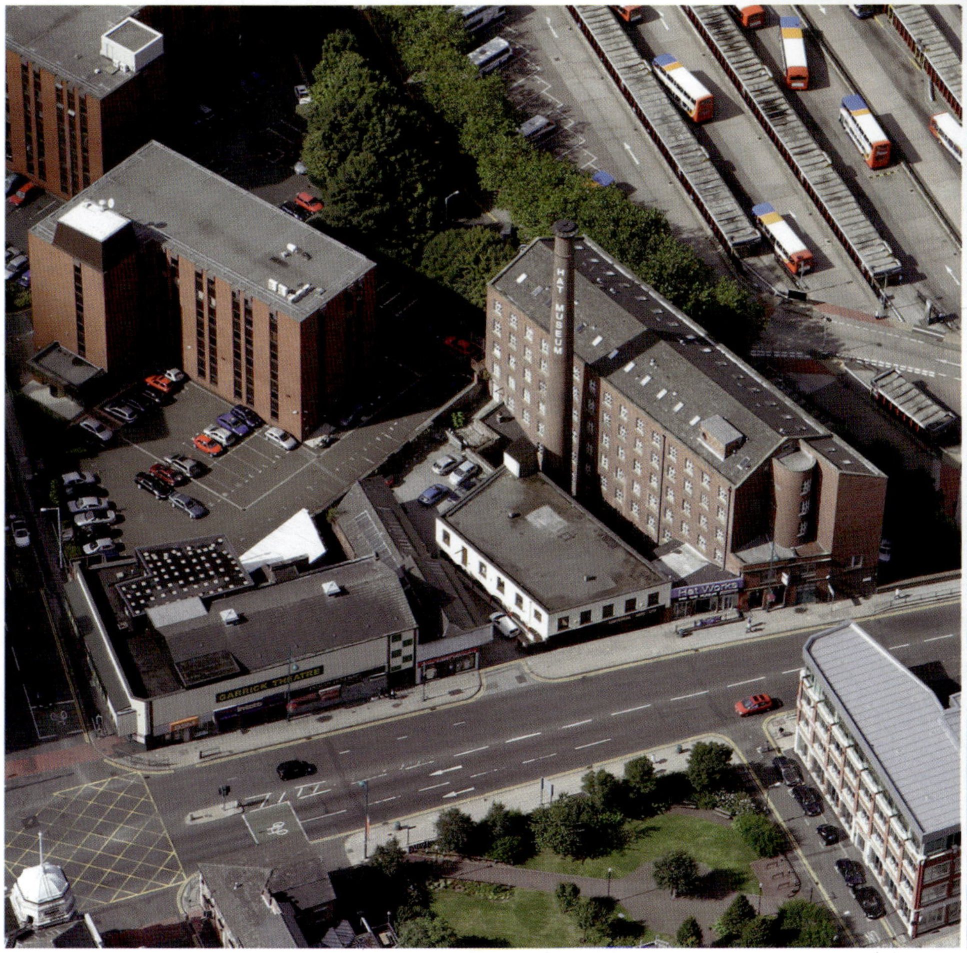

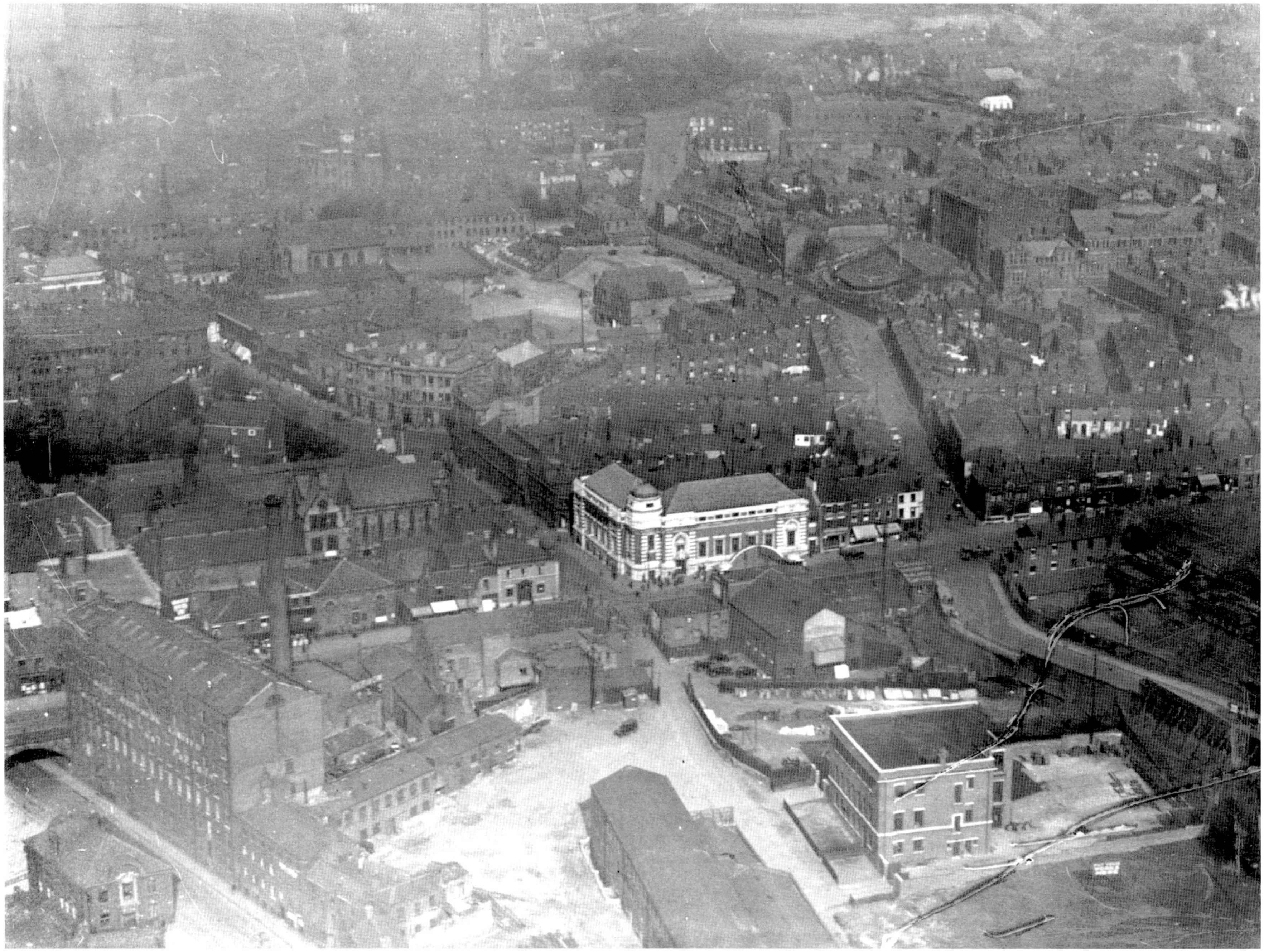

Central Library - 1933

The Stockport Central Library was constructed between 1912 and 1913 at the junction between Wellington Road South and St Petersgate, and was funded by a grant from the Carnegie Institute by American philanthropist Andrew Carnegie. The building, with its central glass-domed roof and blue tower stood out much like the town hall when this picture was taken in 1933, surrounded as it was by decades of industrial blackening. The library now is as it was when it was constructed, although it is fast outgrowing the limited space that it has inside. The building is home to the main lending library, an information library, a small hall in the basement for events, and also Stockport Heritage Library, where the old images from this book are kept. Many of the buildings surrounding this junction have been replaced. Opposite the Library stood the Super Cinema, which is now the site of the Royal Mail building. The Esoldo Cinema, to the left of the Library, had yet to be built in 1933. In the modern photograph the land is now part of a small park adjoining St Peter's Square to the rear. This land is due to be redeveloped again in the near future as an office block as part of a scheme to improve St Peter's Square.

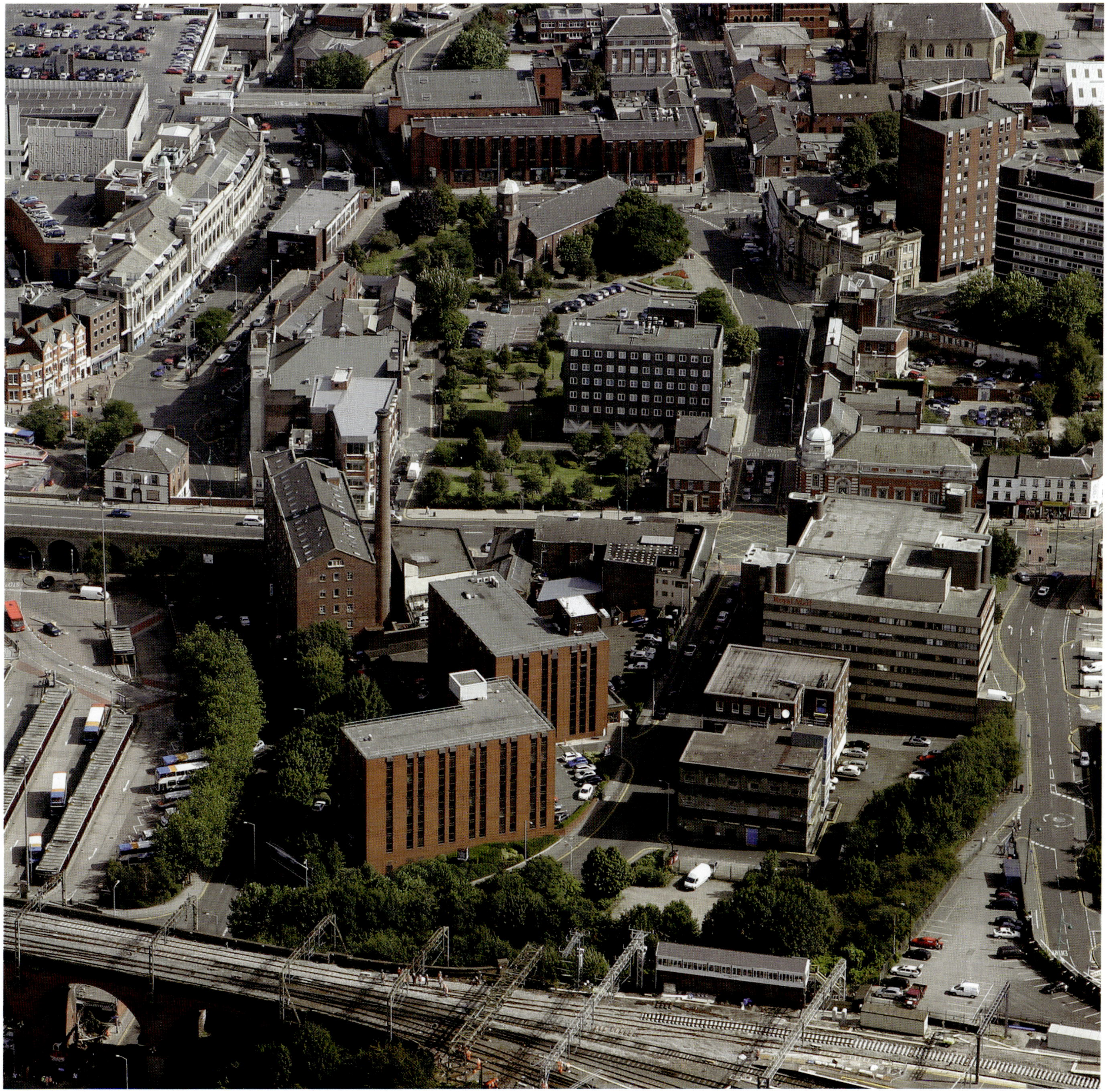
Royal Mail

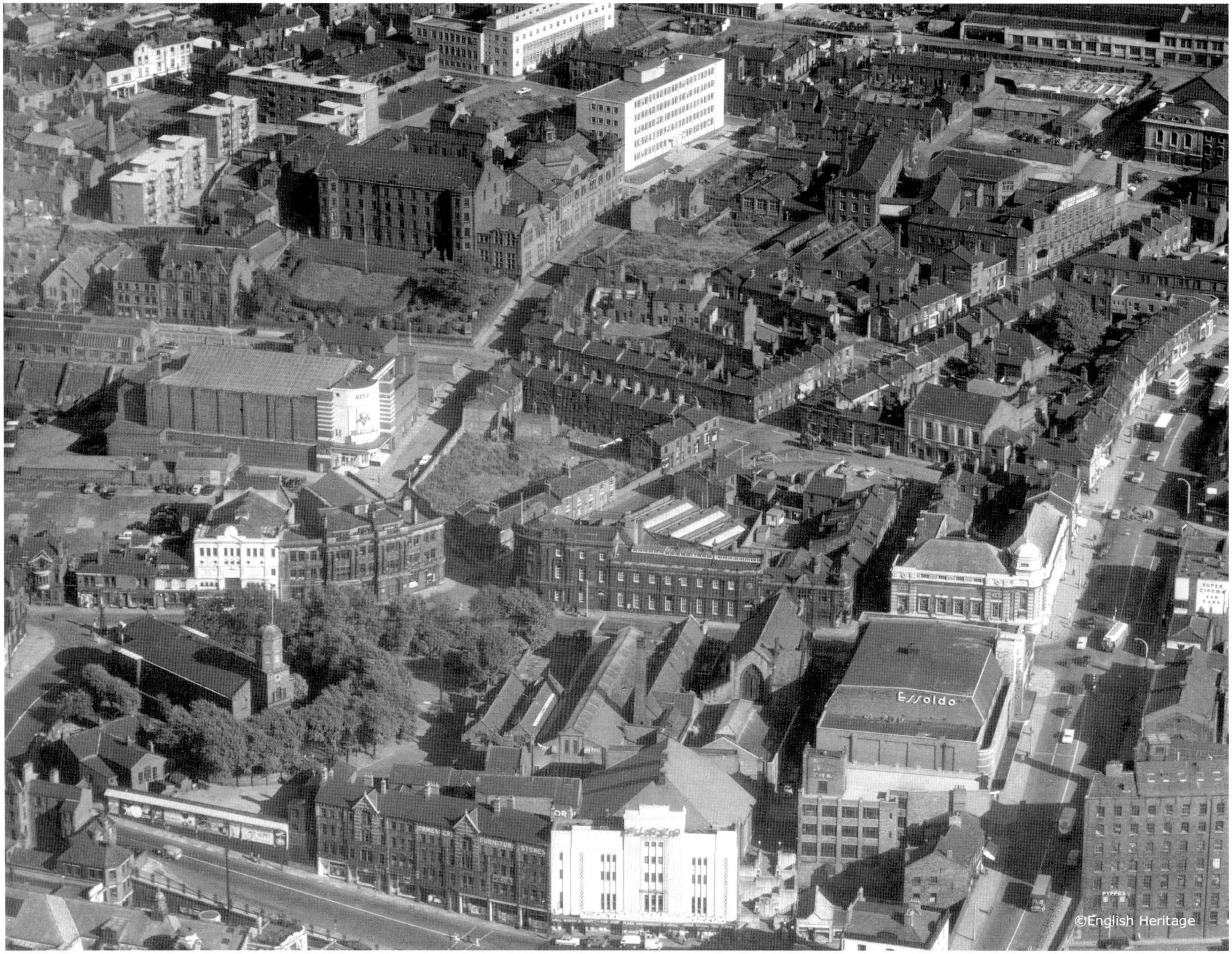

St Peter's Square 1958

St Peter's Square is the link between the Old Town and the new. Centred on St Peter's Church, the square has undergone many changes over the years, and these changes continue to this day. St Peter's Church itself was opened in 1768 and founded by William Wright. The road on which it lies, St Petersgate, was built to connect his house on High Street to the church. Notable buildings in the picture include the town's first public swimming baths (built 1858, behind the Plaza) and the Esoldo Cinema, which fronted onto Wellington Road South. Also of note is the Theatre Royal and Opera House, which is the white building directly opposite the church. Designed by Frank Matcham, the chief architect of theatres of the age, it opened in 1888 and was the place of the first ever film screening in Stockport in 1896. The theatre closed in 1957, just a year before this image was taken, and was eventually knocked down in 1962 – the result of a decrease in theatre goers due to the popularity of television. In the background can be seen the imposing four-storey facade of Stockport Sunday School.

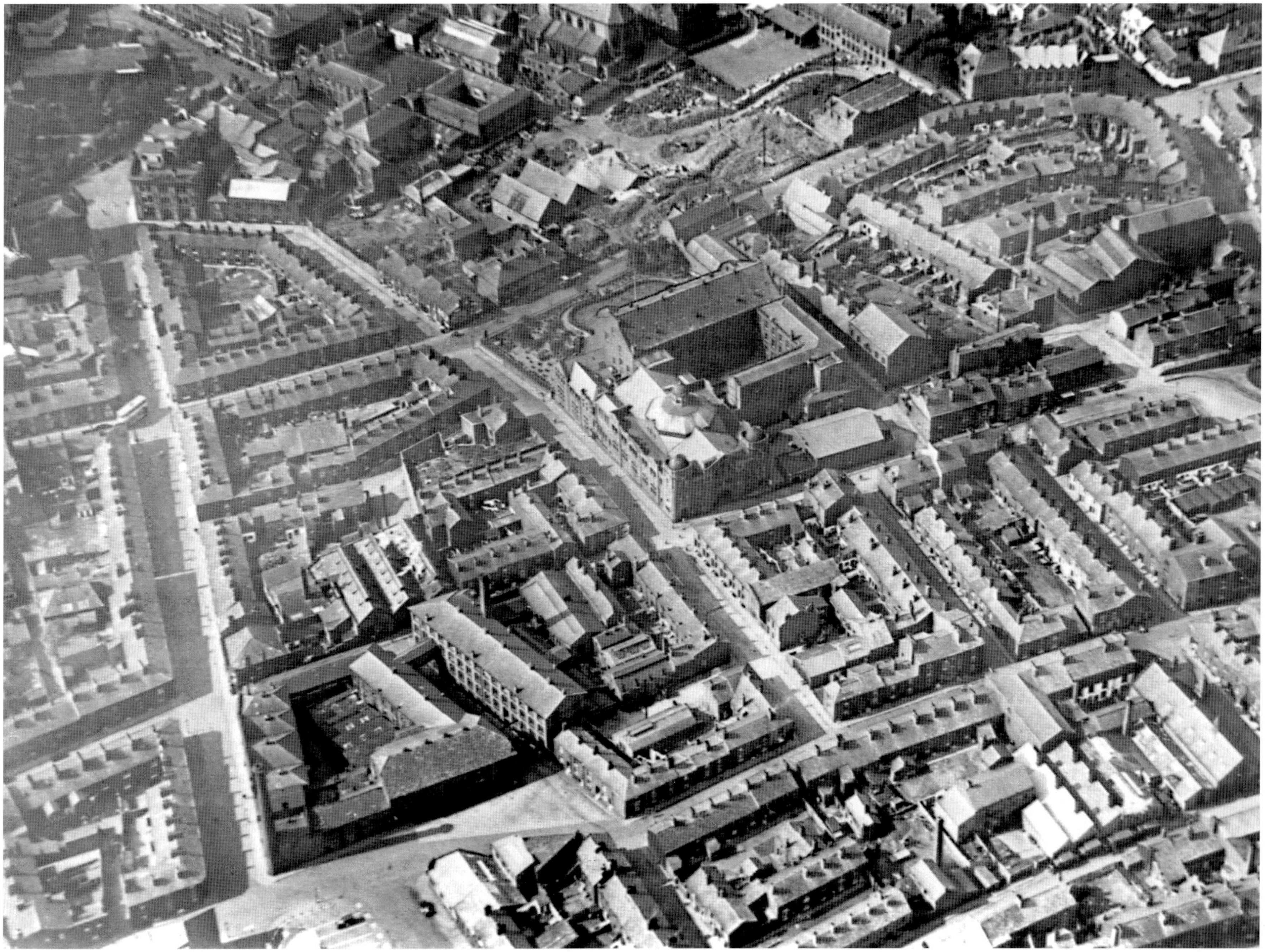

Stockport Sunday School 1939

Built from 1805-1806, Stockport Sunday School was founded in 1784 by Matthew Mayer for the intention of educating the poorest children in the town. By the turn of the 19th century the school had outgrown its buildings on Hillgate, and so work started on a new building. The impressive new school was situated on a slope next to what is now Piccadilly, and by 1825 it was said to be the largest Sunday school in the world. The building had 58 classrooms and a huge assembly room on the top floor. In 1833 the school is said to have had 5200 pupils, and in 1835 it was extended even further by the addition of a new wing (the large section with the domed roof). The building was demolished in 1970 and the site is now a car park, although the steps leading up to the building from Wellington Street survive. The road running from top to bottom on the left of the picture is Lord Street. In 1939 this road led directly to the town hall, which could be seen from St Peter's Square at the bottom. This fine promenade is now segmented. Part of the road is pedestrianised, whilst the top section next to the town hall is occupied by the car park and piazza of Stopford House. In the picture we can see a tram turning off Lord Street onto Wellington Street.

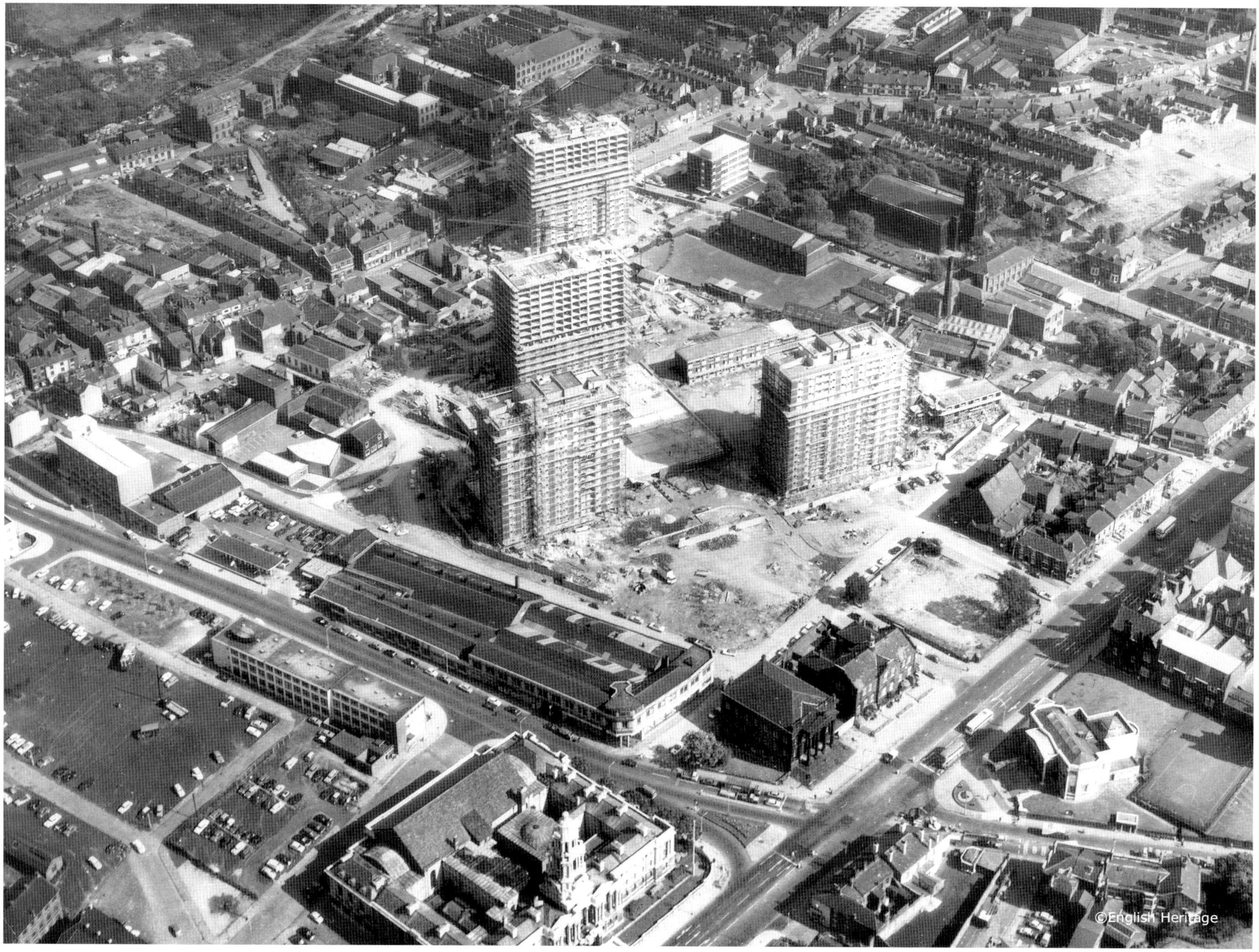

Mottram Street Flats 1965

Slum clearances became commonplace in the UK in the 1950s and 60s. Inadequate housing not fit for human habitation was rife throughout the country, and it was no different in Stockport. In order to re-house people, new homes had to be constructed, and the new building of the 1960s was the High-rise. Where previously massed terraced houses had sat around Mottram Street, four new high-rise blocks of flats were constructed in the 1960s by Stockport Council along with additional neighbouring low-rise units. This picture, taken on 17th August 1965, shows the new flats under construction. With 16 storeys each and standing at around 170 feet high (52 metres), the new buildings occupied one of the most prominent positions along the new road at the top of the river valley. Along Wellington Road South Mount Tabor Chapel is still standing, but there is now an open piece of land opposite the Technical School where the Congregational Chapel had stood.

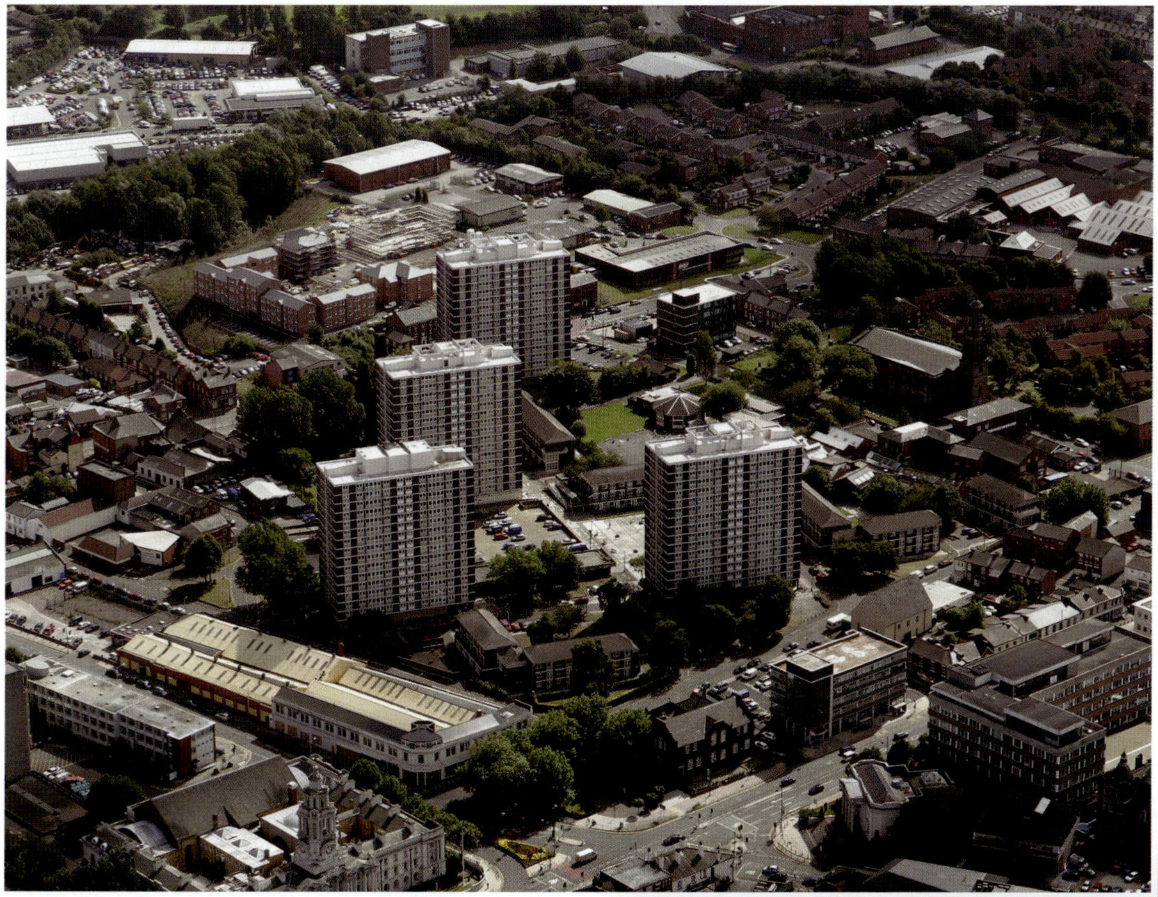

Mottram Street today has barely changed, although the familiar brown exterior of the flats could probably do with a facelift.

To the right of the flats is St Thomas' Church, with its 120-foot clock tower. Built from 1822-1825 and with 2000 seats, it was the church with the largest capacity in the area upon its opening. Its neo-classical Greek pillars at the main entrance off Hillgate make it one of the grandest buildings to have been built in the town centre. To the rear of the flats is the site of the Christy's Hat Factory. The company had been based here since 1826 after it had bought out the Worsley hat making company that was on the site. They expanded the business and built new factories on the site between 1840 and 1860. By then, it was said to be largest hat factory in England. It was also to become the last hat manufacturers in the town, and it continued to produce hats up until 1997 when it eventually closed. A new housing development is under construction on the site in the new picture.

Stockport College

Stockport College is the largest college in the town and provides further and higher education to over 18,000 students, offering courses for nearly all ages up to degree level.

The large, rather dull buildings along the main road do little justice to the main building of the old Technical School that previously stood here, but it is likely that they won't remain in their current state for long.

There is currently a major redevelopment of the grounds on the cards that will incorporate the historic former St Thomas' Hospital and Stockport Workhouse buildings at the rear. Estimated at £50m, the redevelopment will create a huge state-of-the-art town centre campus that could ultimately help the college to achieve University status in the future.

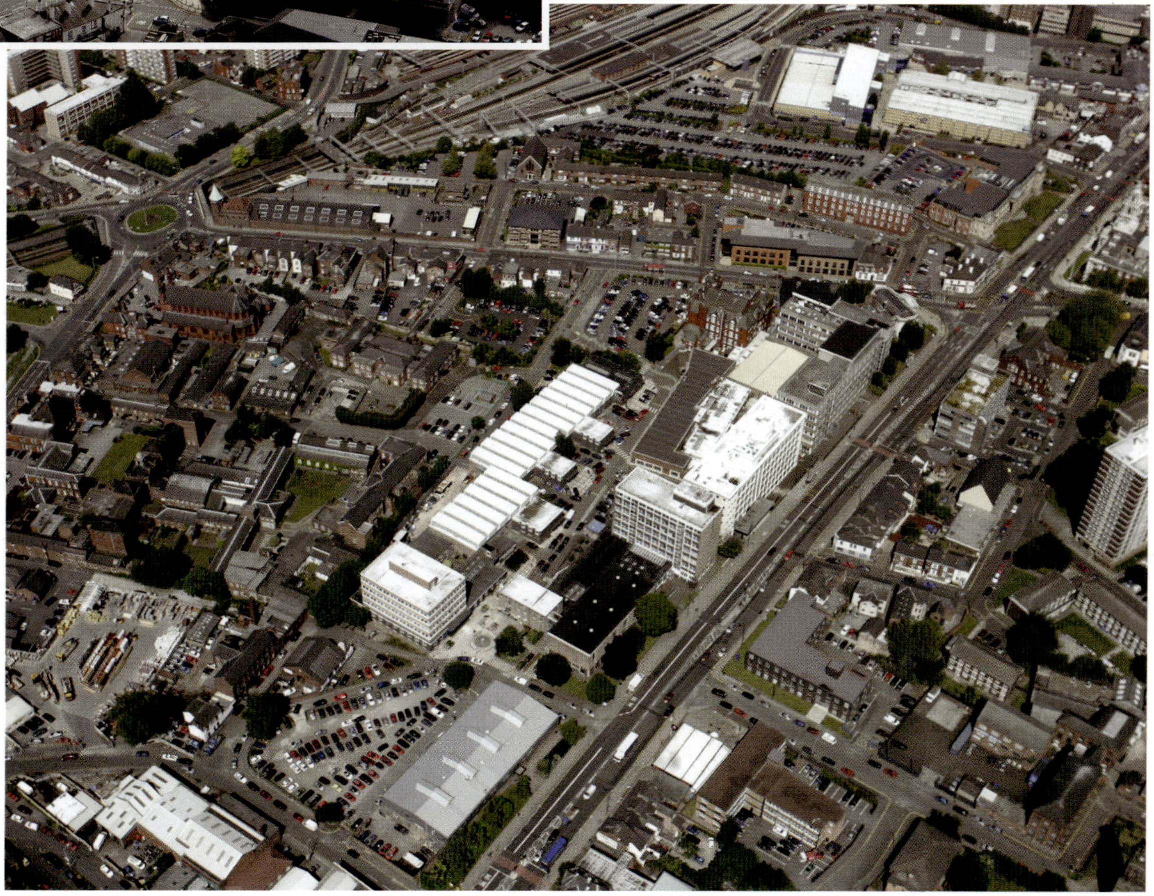

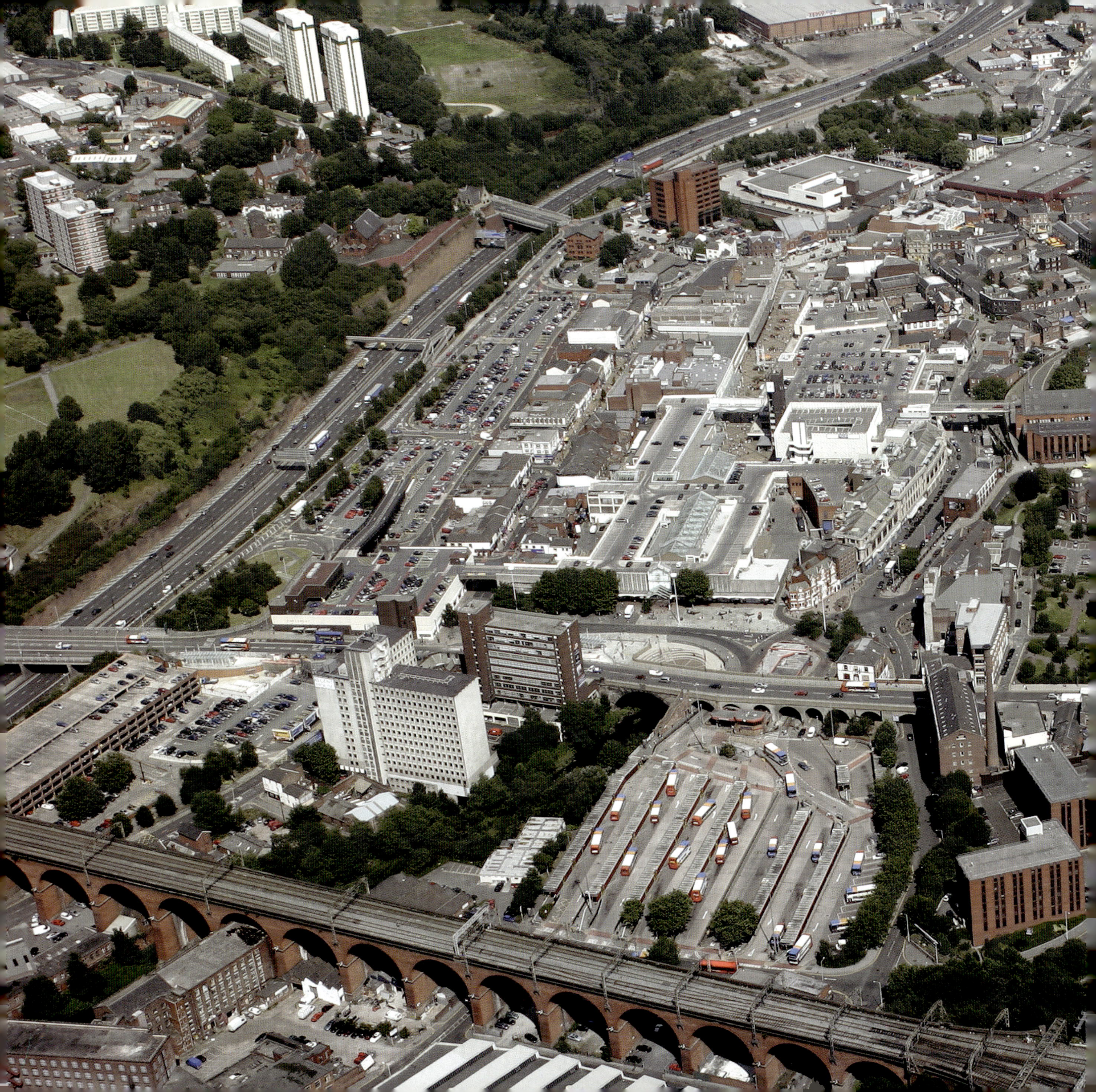

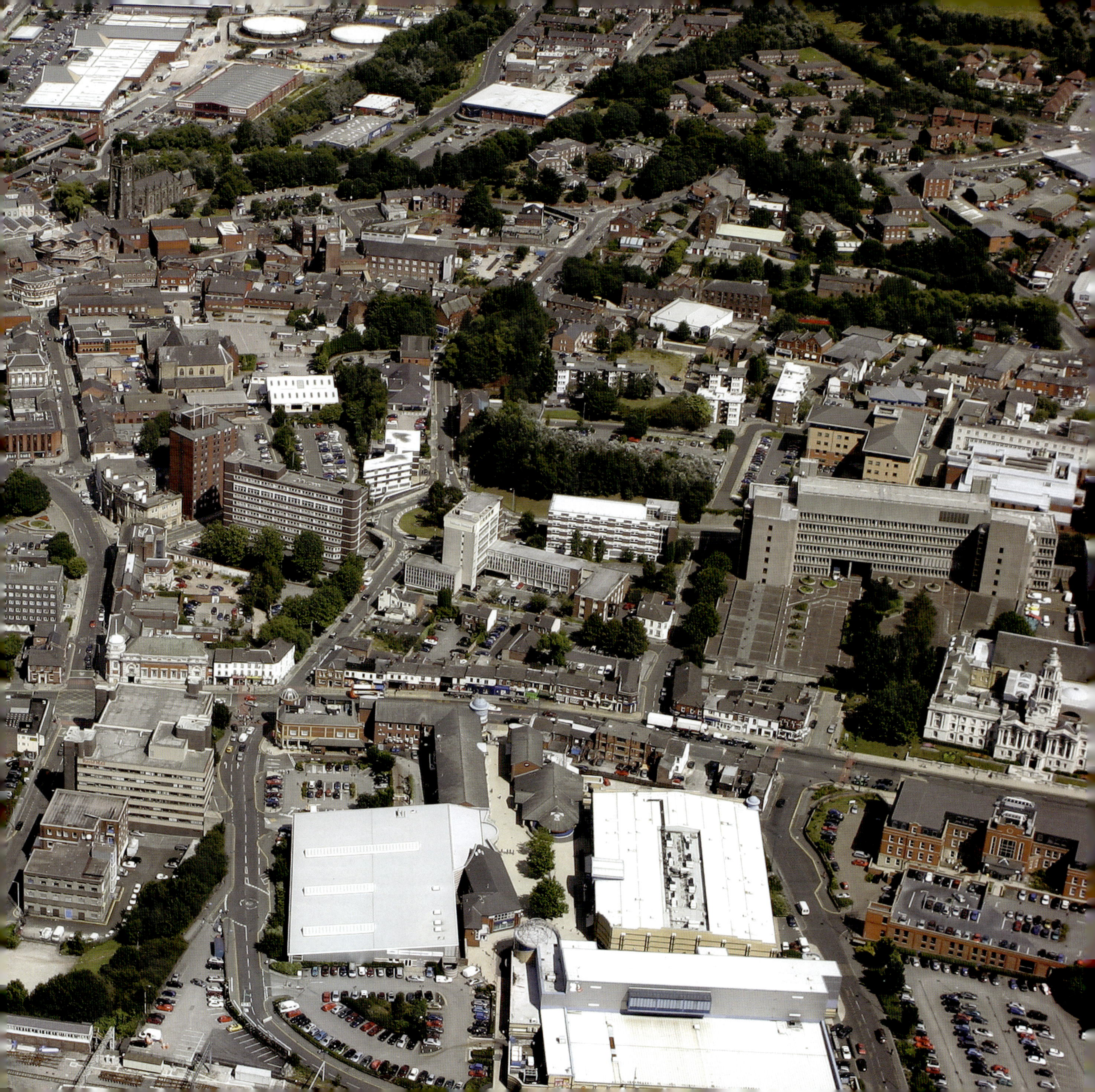

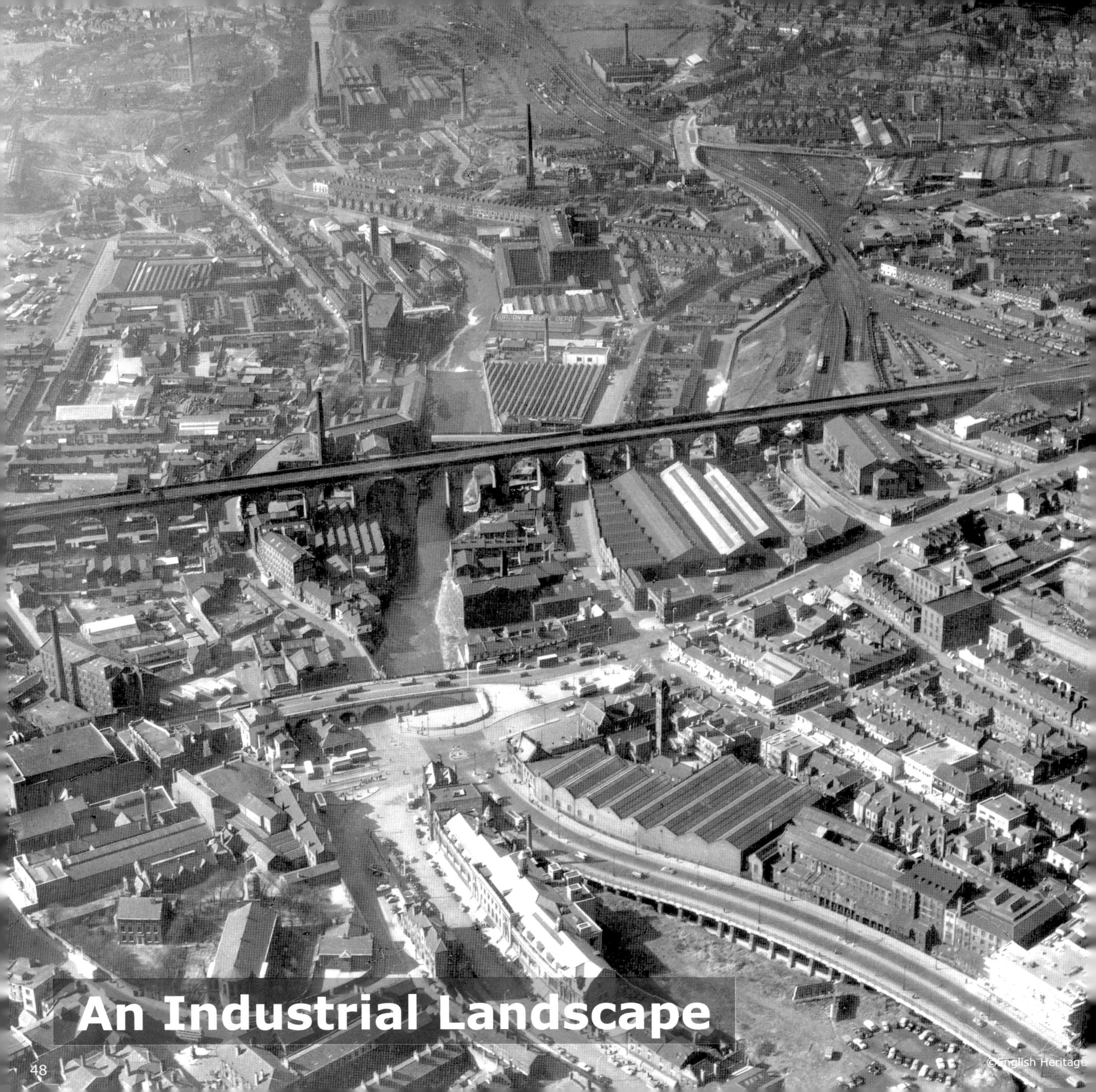

An Industrial Landscape

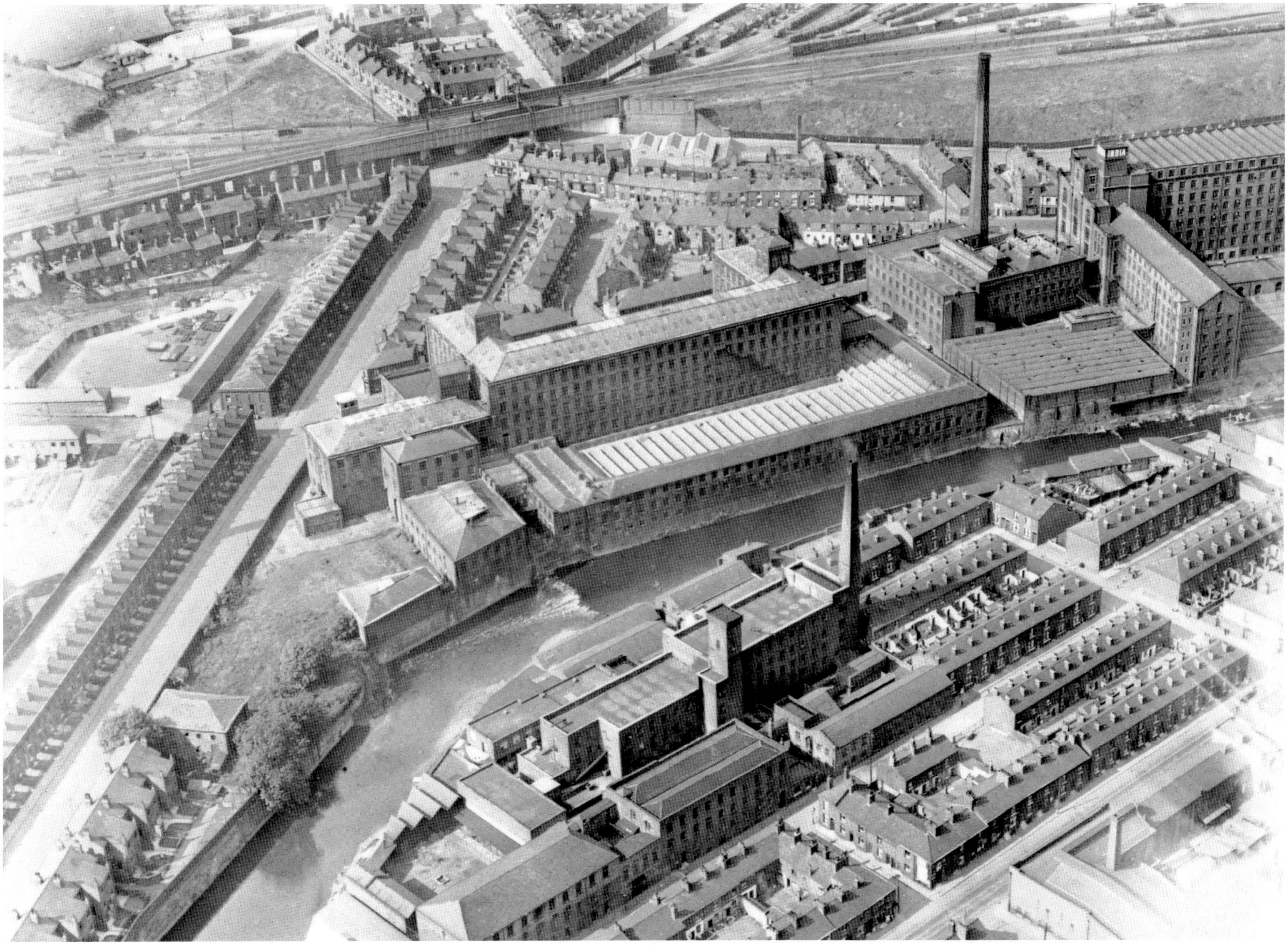

The site of smog shrouded chimneys and huge brick factories loomed large over Stockport for decades. These temples of industry were ten-a-penny in the town centre and along the waterways of its surrounding districts. There can be no doubt that the onset of the industrial revolution changed Stockport remarkably, both economically and physically. Whilst the cotton, silk and hatting industries brought wealth to the town, its new physical composition dwarfed everything that had gone before it. The image on the left, taken on June 6th 1958, shows the urban landscape that had prevailed throughout the 19th and early 20th centuries. The vast factories located along the banks of the river Mersey on the far side of the viaduct - the ultimate industrial structure in the town - clamoured for space next to row after row of terraced housing. Vast swathes of previously undeveloped land were given over to these new homes to house workers moving from the countryside. Many of these streets are now gone, having been swept away as part of the process of slum clearances and redevelopment. Areas such as Portwood, Chestergate (above in 1931) and Heaton Norris were once crammed to the brim with communities that have been lost. Many of the old mills have also long since been demolished. Having served their purpose the buildings fell into decline and became difficult to maintain. In the modern era such buildings are being converted into homes, such as in the schemes at Houldsworth Mill and Victoria Mill in Reddish, and at Wellington Mill in the town centre. There are still many mills remaining that are ripe for conversion. It is important that these buildings are preserved to protect the town's heritage and to celebrate its industrial past.

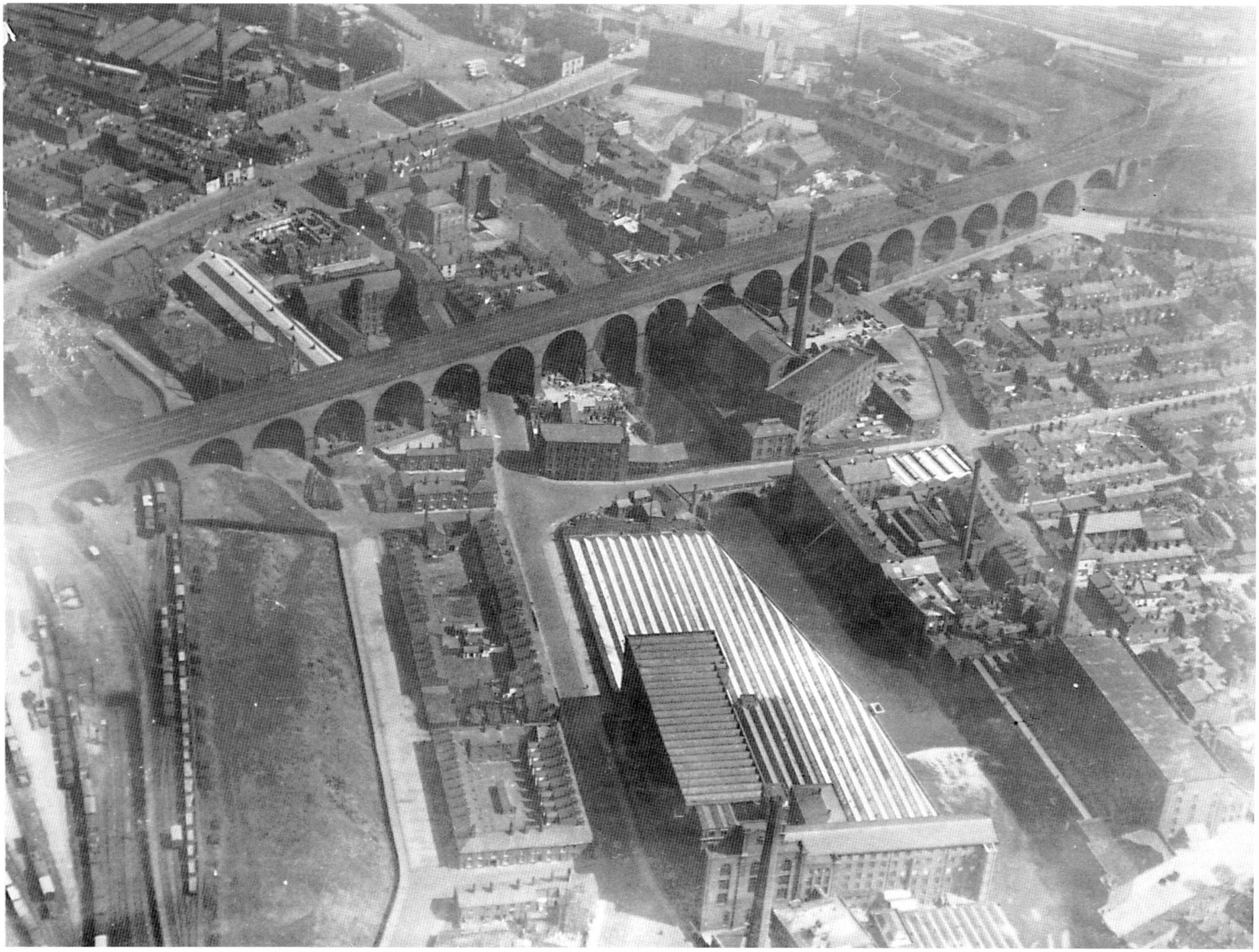

Stockport Viaduct 1927

The Symbol of Stockport, the viaduct is a spectacular feat of Victorian Engineering that dominates the town centre. Built between 1838 and December 1840, the huge structure stands a whopping 111 feet high (34m) and stretches for 1786 feet (nearly 1/3 of a mile) across the Mersey Valley. It has 27 arches (22 large and 5 small) and is constructed of over 11 million bricks. The views from the top are superb, and provide a dramatic entrance point into the centre of Stockport, especially when travelling from the north, allowing passengers to gaze over the town centre and towards the Pennines. The viaduct was built by the Manchester and Birmingham Railway Company to enable trains to reach the Midlands. Before its construction, trains had to stop at one of the two stations at either side of the valley – Edgeley Station to the south (now Stockport station) and Heaton Norris to the north (now demolished – see pages 57 & 80). The Manchester & Birmingham Railway Company set about building the viaduct to bridge the divide and enable non-stop travel, eventually all of the way to and from London.

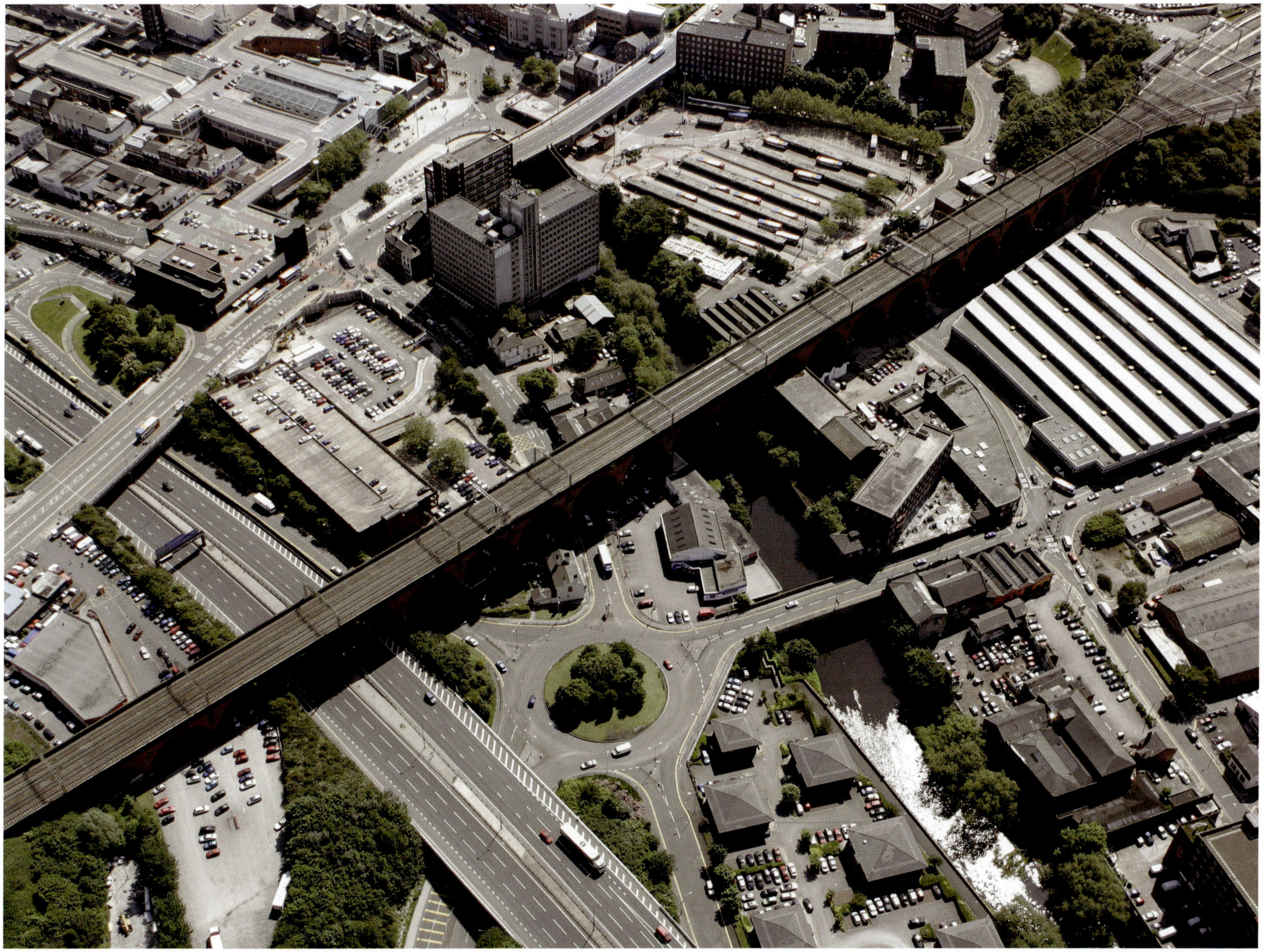

So successful was the new viaduct that it was widened from 1887-1889 to allow for a greater number of trains to cross. At first the plans were to build the new extension out of steel, but it was eventually agreed that the new section should match the original. If you stand underneath one of the great arches you can see the join today – the original is slightly wider than the extension, which is on the West side. Thanks to a somewhat prescient covenant that was issued when the viaduct was built, all trains that wish to cross the viaduct must stop at Stockport station, meaning there are no trains that just hurtle through like in many other major towns. This means that Stockport station is one of the busiest and most important in the region. This view shows that the viaduct may not have changed, but its surroundings certainly have. Only a few of the old buildings are still standing, including Weir Mill (see next page) and the Crown Inn, just above the large new roundabout in the shadow of the viaduct. Stockport town centre marks an extraordinary junction of major transport routes, all of which are captured in this photo. The M60 Motorway now passes through this area running parallel to the River Mersey, the main west coast rail line crosses the valley over the viaduct, and the A6 runs parallel to this. There is also the flightpath to Manchester Airport directly above, from where this picture was taken.

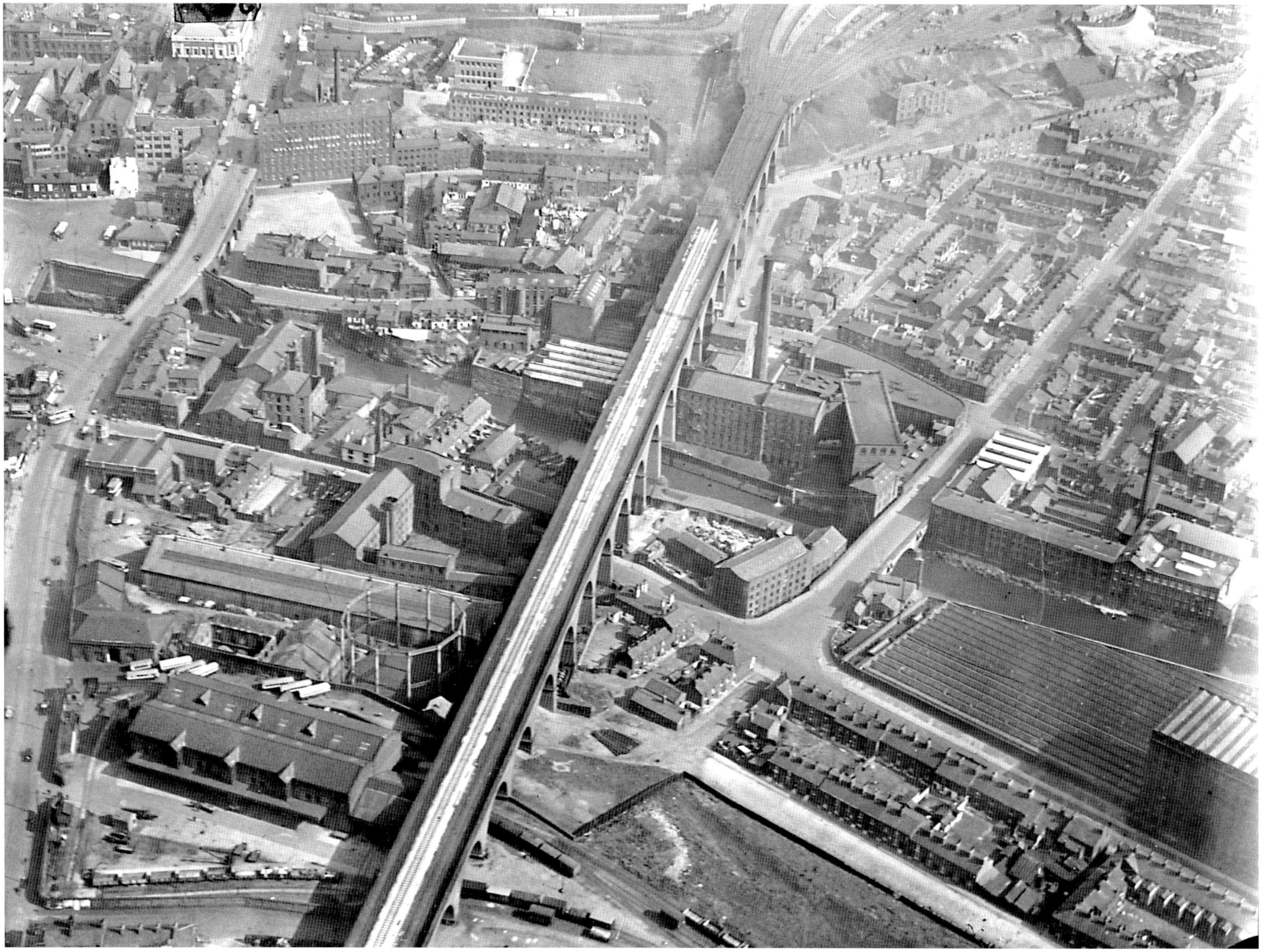

Viaduct and King Street West 1927

This image gives some indication of the highly industrial nature of the town in the early 20th century. In the centre of the picture the viaduct passes over Weir Mill on Chestergate, just off King Street West on the right. If the mill had been any taller it would no doubt have been knocked down when the viaduct was built. Weir Mill (also written as Wear Mill) was built by John Collier in 1790. It was one of two mills that he built either side of the river that shared the same weir. The mill contains the oldest surviving industrial structure in Stockport – the waterwheel shed (the section immediately built up against the bridge), which dates from around 1805. On the left of the viaduct in front of Wellington Mill is the area now occupied by the main bus station. This area was filled with buildings at the time but they had all been swept away by the late 1960s. The present bus station opened in 1980. Below this is the site of Heaton Lane Gasworks. The storage sheds were used to house buses from 1924, and several can be seen parked around the back near the frame of the gas holder. The building below this is the goods shed for the Cheshire Lines Committee Coal yard (see Georges Road – Page 57).

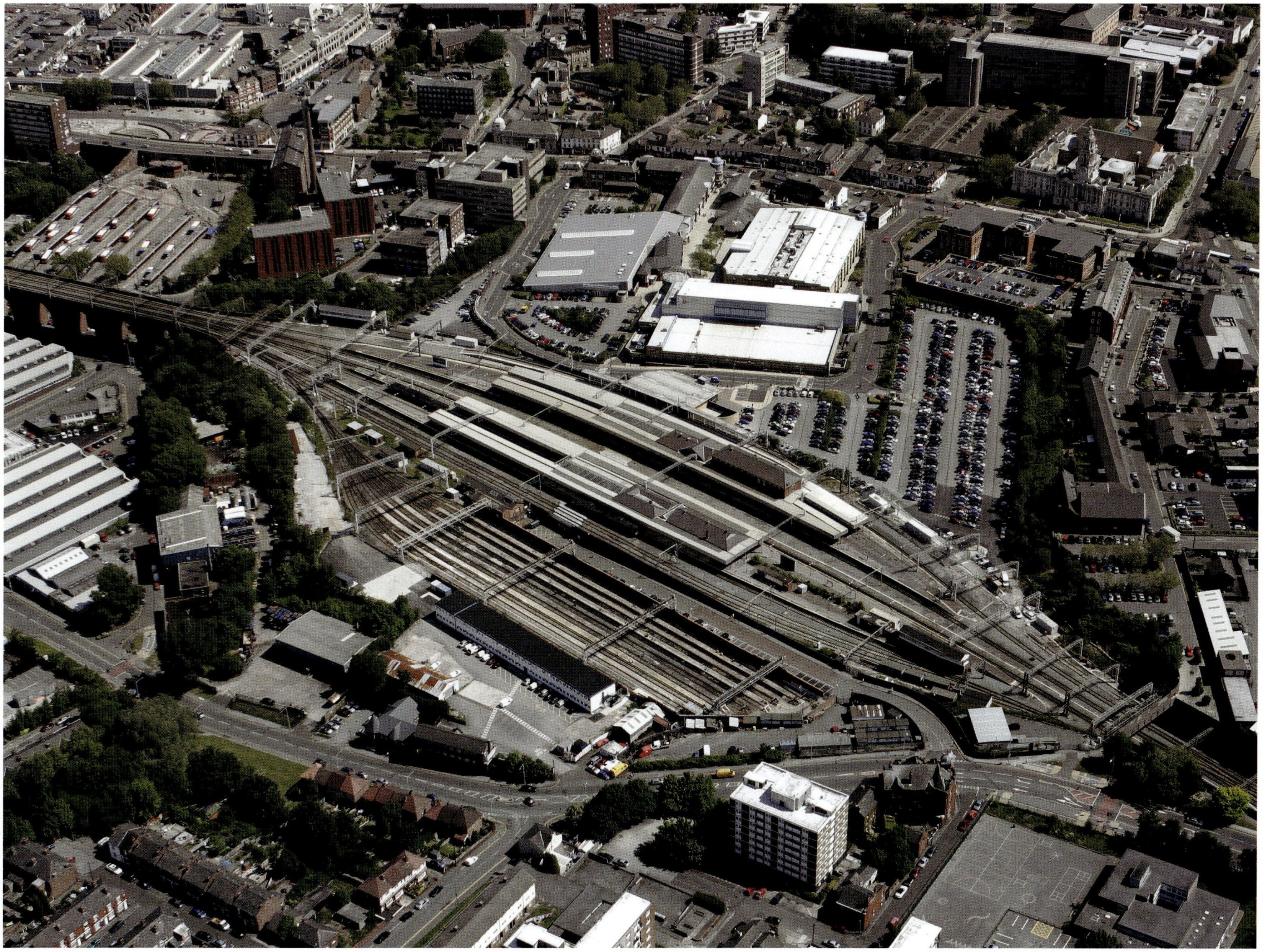

Edgeley Station

Edgeley Station is the original name for Stockport Station, and helped to distinguish it from the other large station in the town centre – Tiviot Dale station (see page 92). Edgeley never had a grand entrance or facade like so many other stations across the country (and indeed, like Tiviot Dale) but the entrance was recently rebuilt with a new glazed ticket office building to give it a somewhat more distinguished look, along with a brand new platform - Platform 0 - which has still to come into service at the time of writing. In the background is the Grand Central leisure complex, built on the site of the former coal and goods yard. The site, over 10 acres in size, was first proposed for redevelopment in the late 1980s. The new complex eventually opened in 1992, and consisted of a 10-screen cinema, Olympic sized swimming pool to replace the St Petersgate Baths, a bowling alley, and nightclubs, bars and restaurants. Sadly, the complex has started to fall into terminal decline, but a plan to breath new life into it has been proposed, with a £100 million improvement plan scheduled to start in 2008. Only time will tell if the new complex can succeed where the present one has failed, should it be built.

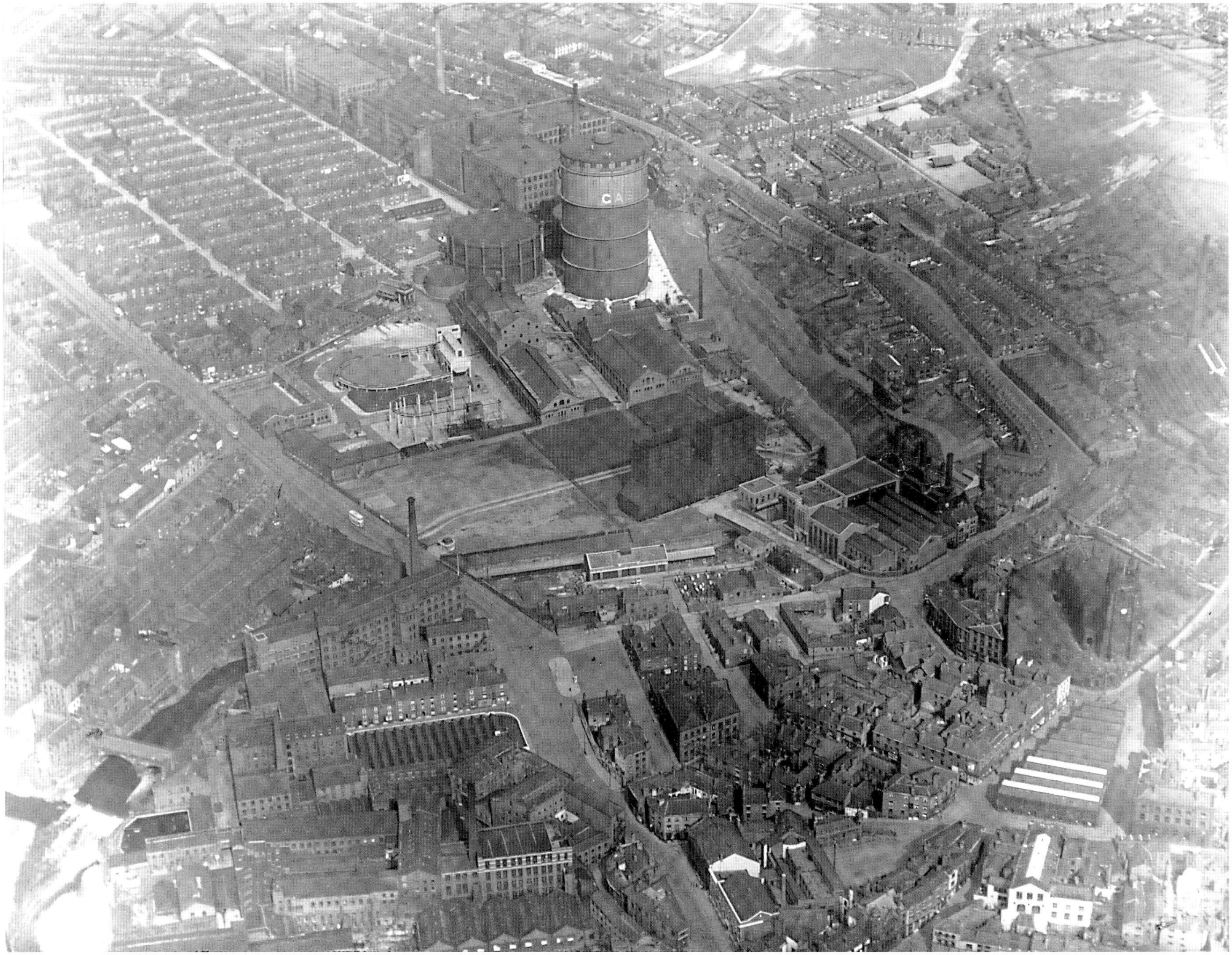

Portwood 1933

Portwood is one area that has changed almost beyond recognition. In 1933 the area was a sea of terraced houses, with the looming presence of large mills by the banks of the River Goyt always close by. Dominating the scene were also the massive gas holders of the Stockport Corporation. These were built on the site of the former Millgate Gasworks and reached a height of 253 feet (77m). These were later joined by the Millgate Power station (behind St Mary's church, on either side of the river) and also by an enormous cooling tower, which was built in 1943 (visible on page 4). The massive tower remains the largest ever structure to be built in Stockport, and rose to a height of 262 feet (80m). In the bottom left is the start of the River Mersey. Here the River Goyt (on the right) meets the River Tame (on the left) to form one of the most famous rivers in the world as it heads on its 40 mile journey to the Irish Sea at Liverpool.

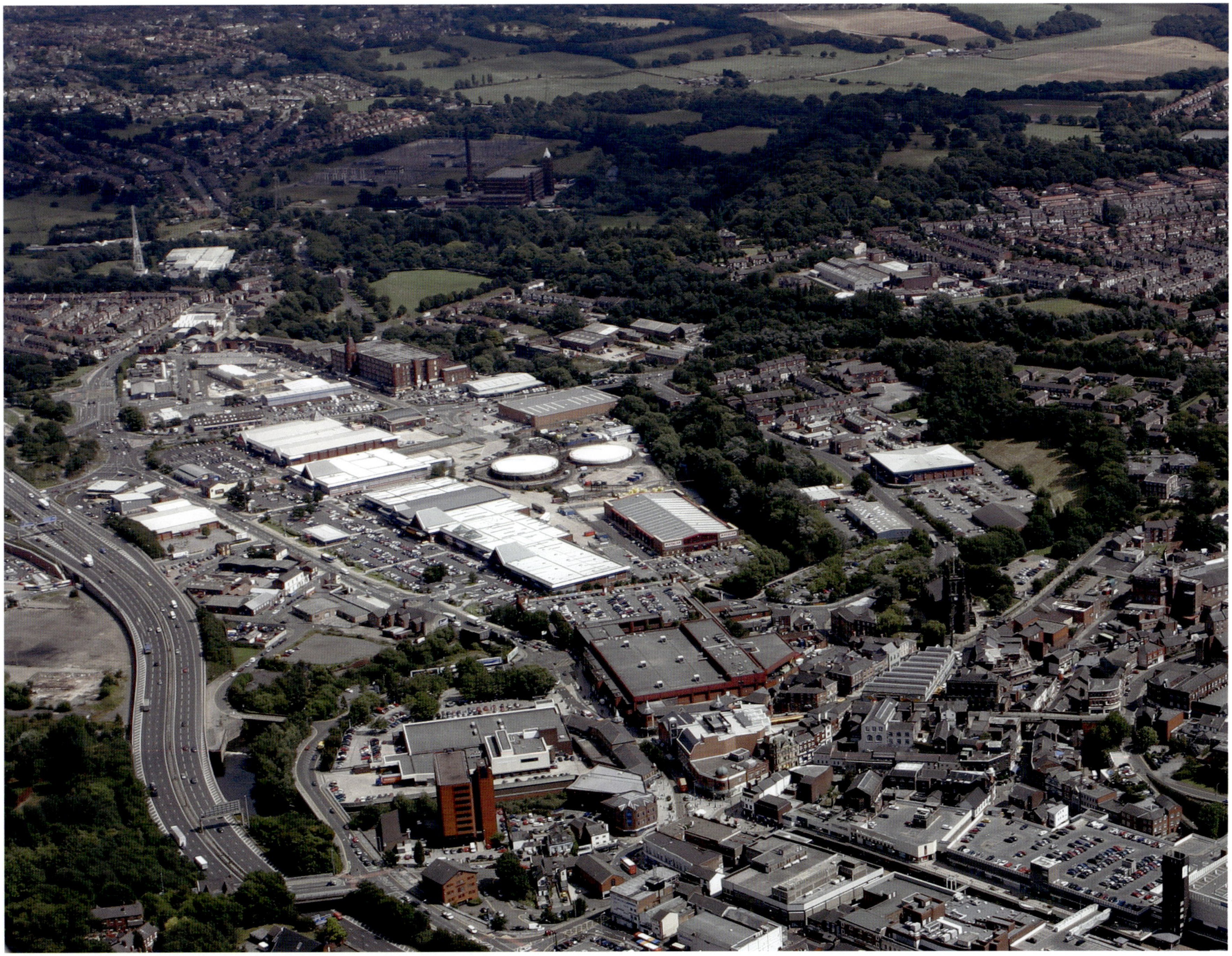

The cooling tower was demolished in 1981. Explosive charges set at the base sent it crashing down to the ground, removing what was one of the most familiar sites on the Stockport Skyline forever. Two of the gas holders of the 1930s survive, but no longer extend to the heights that they did when the first picture was taken. The larger holder has now gone. Gas has not been produced here since 1976, and the holders are just used for storage purposes. Millgate power station was knocked down in 1988, after ceasing operations 12 years previously. Today, few of the terraced houses survive, with only a handful left standing along Great Portwood Street. These are now on borrowed time if plans to construct a large new superstore are given the go ahead. The main use of the land now is as a giant retail park, known as the Peel Centre. This offers large, bulky goods shops that cannot be found in Merseyway, and is the second busiest shopping area in the town. Of the great mills, only Vernon Mill (rebuilt in 1902 after a fire) is still standing along the banks of the Goyt.

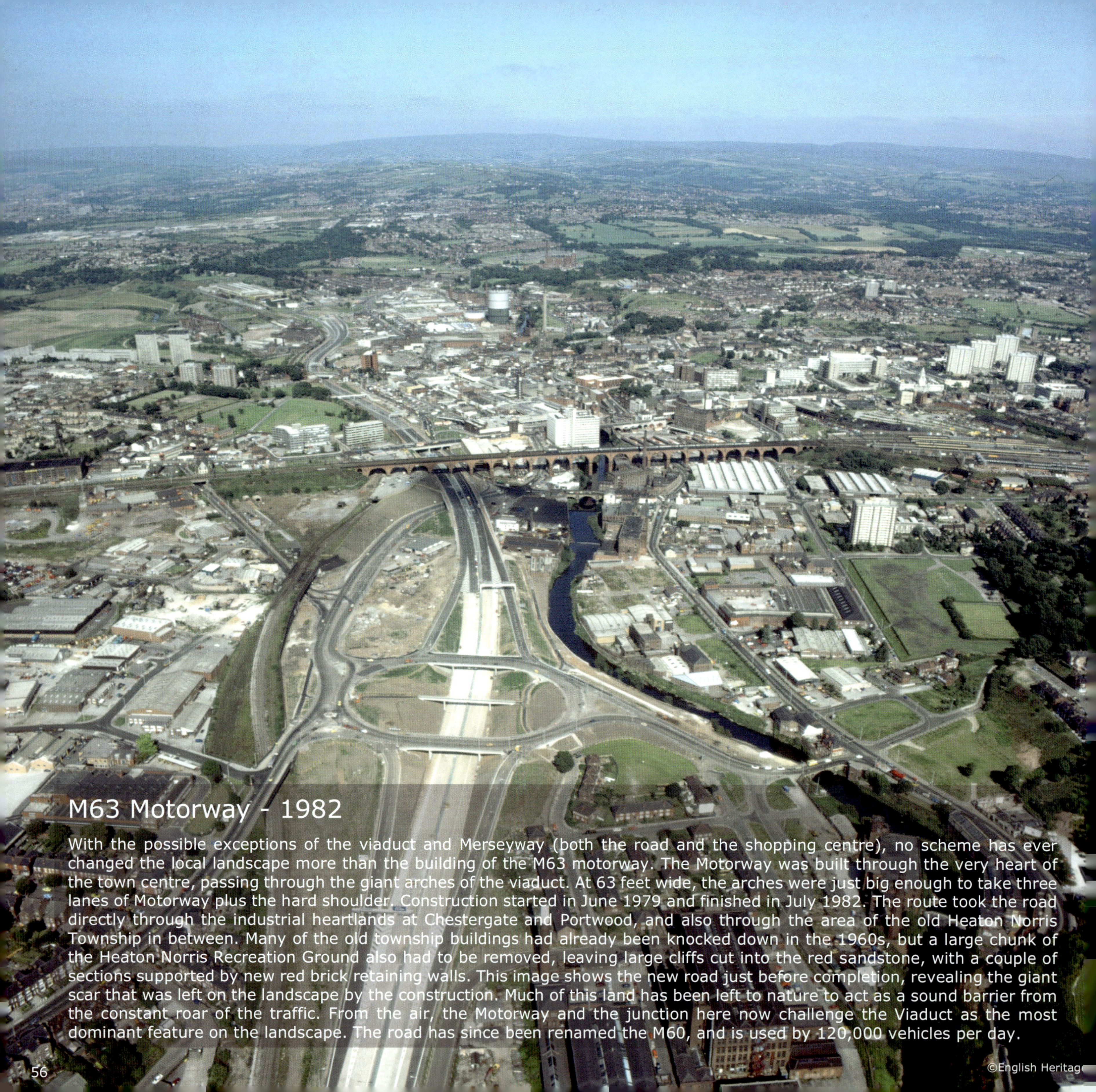

M63 Motorway - 1982

With the possible exceptions of the viaduct and Merseyway (both the road and the shopping centre), no scheme has ever changed the local landscape more than the building of the M63 motorway. The Motorway was built through the very heart of the town centre, passing through the giant arches of the viaduct. At 63 feet wide, the arches were just big enough to take three lanes of Motorway plus the hard shoulder. Construction started in June 1979 and finished in July 1982. The route took the road directly through the industrial heartlands at Chestergate and Portwood, and also through the area of the old Heaton Norris Township in between. Many of the old township buildings had already been knocked down in the 1960s, but a large chunk of the Heaton Norris Recreation Ground also had to be removed, leaving large cliffs cut into the red sandstone, with a couple of sections supported by new red brick retaining walls. This image shows the new road just before completion, revealing the giant scar that was left on the landscape by the construction. Much of this land has been left to nature to act as a sound barrier from the constant roar of the traffic. From the air, the Motorway and the junction here now challenge the Viaduct as the most dominant feature on the landscape. The road has since been renamed the M60, and is used by 120,000 vehicles per day.

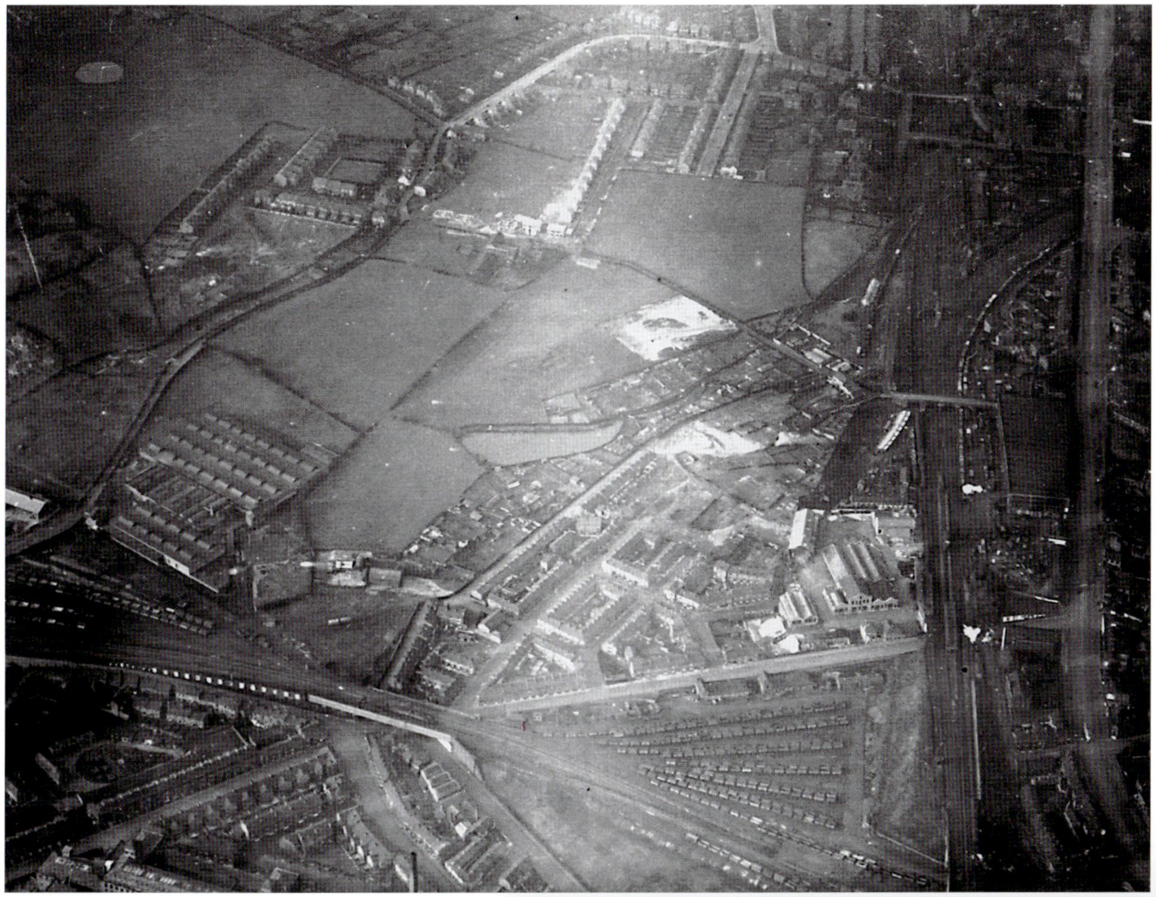

Georges Road 1934

The Georges Road area is within the old township of Heaton Norris, but due to the growth Stockport experienced in the 19th century much of this area is now within the boundaries of the town centre. This area was given over to industry, with a mixture of uses included houses for workers for the nearby mills along the Mersey. Much of it was characterised by the former railway line to Tiviot Dale, which is visible passing over the junction with Travis Brow via a bridge that also allowed entry to the Cheshire Lines Committee railway goods yards. The bridge has gone, but the supporting pillars remain as a piece of public art. The yard principally dealt in coal, which was needed to fire the furnaces of the mills to create steam. The huge number of wagons in the picture gives some indication about the massive quantities of coal that would have been needed. Also in the picture is Heaton Norris station – Stockport's first train station.

The site of Stockport County FC's first substantial ground is also in the photo. The ground was just off Green Lane in the top left of the image, on the fields between the pale circular feature and the long row of houses. These houses - on Nursery Road - are actually on the edge of the pitch. The majority of the pitch lay to the rear, running from north to south with a stand on the west side. It is now covered by Deneway Close. The club played here from 1889 until 1902, when they moved to their present ground of Edgeley Park.

The dominant features of the modern Georges Road are the large superstores of Decathlon (on the site of the goods yard) and B&Q, where previously houses had stood. The park to the rear - Bowerfold Open Space – offers superb views of the Stockport skyline and the Pennines beyond.

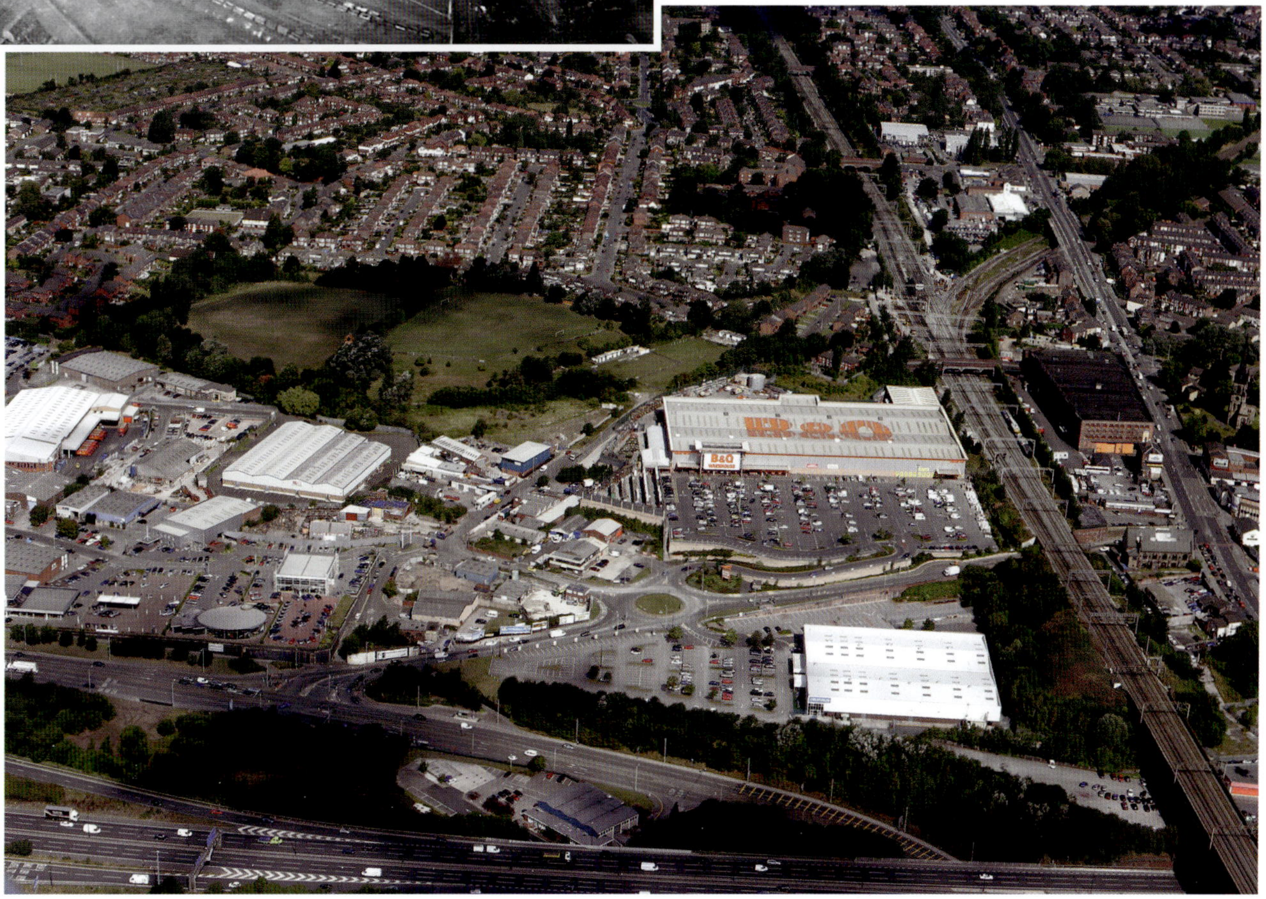

Chestergate 1927

The area around Chestergate where it meets Brinksway marks the western entrance to the town centre. Chestergate continues all of the way to Great Underbank in the Old Town, but on the western side of the viaduct the landscape was distinctly more industrial. The area was a typical mix of small houses side by side with enormous mill buildings, much as there was in Portwood. These images from 1927 show the cotton mills that lined the route of the River Mersey and the worker's houses along the side streets.

To the north of the river was the huge India Mills complex, and to the south stood Kingston No 1 Mill which still stands, although the chimney has now gone. The second picture below shows a wider angle. To the left of India Mills were Kingston No 2 Mill and the much larger Orrell's Mill, built in 1834.

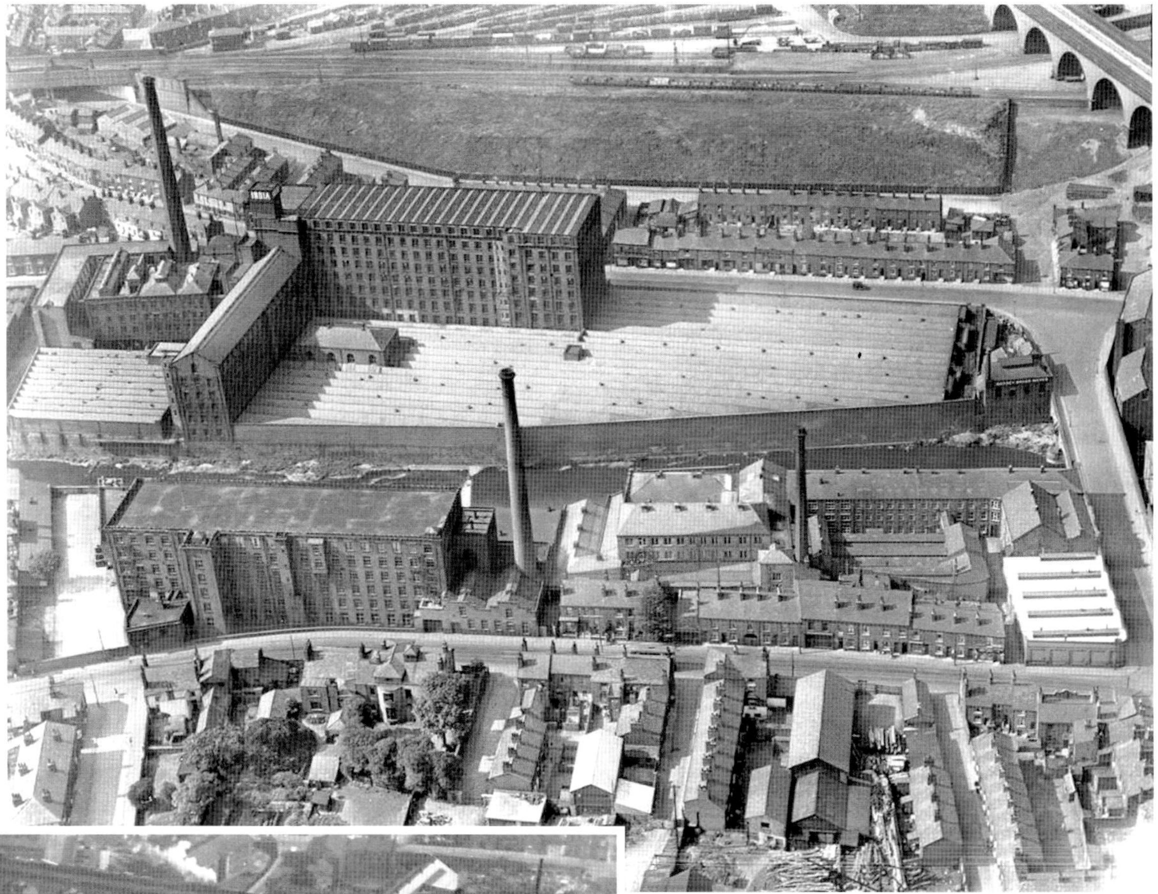

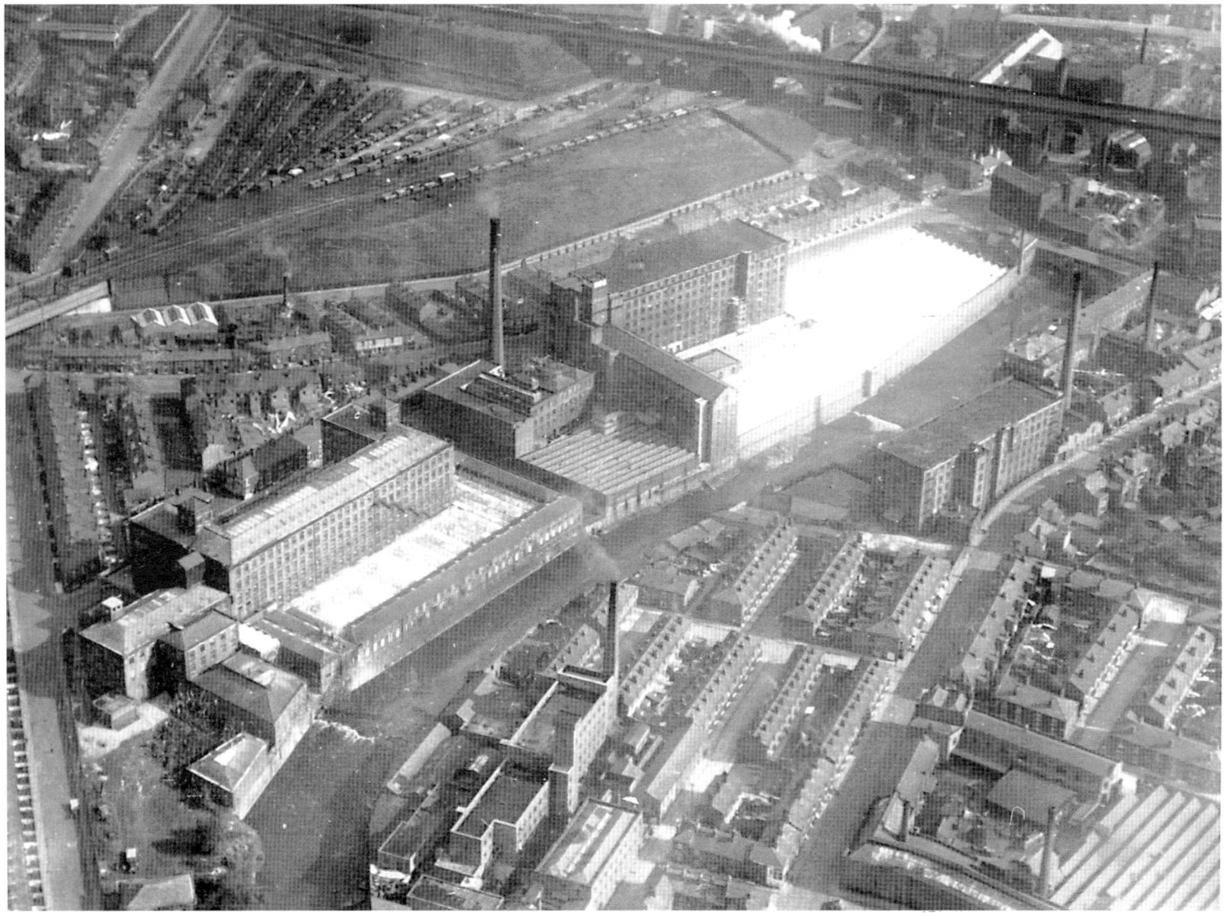

On the south bank there was also Heapriding Mill, with rows of houses between the chimney and Kingston No 2 Mill. Many of these imposing structures survived into the late 20th century, but either through neglect or redevelopment, they fell one by one.

As can be seen in the new picture on the right, this area is now occupied by low-level industrial units and is awaiting redevelopment again. Many of the structures were demolished to make way for the building of the M63 Motorway. Almost all of the houses on either side of the river are gone – just 3 survive on the south side of the Mersey on Lottery Street near the impressive Hollywood School building, built in 1896. On the right are the 12 acres of Hollywood Park - opened in 1893 - and the Hollywood Tower flats, built at the same time as its cousins on Mottram Street.

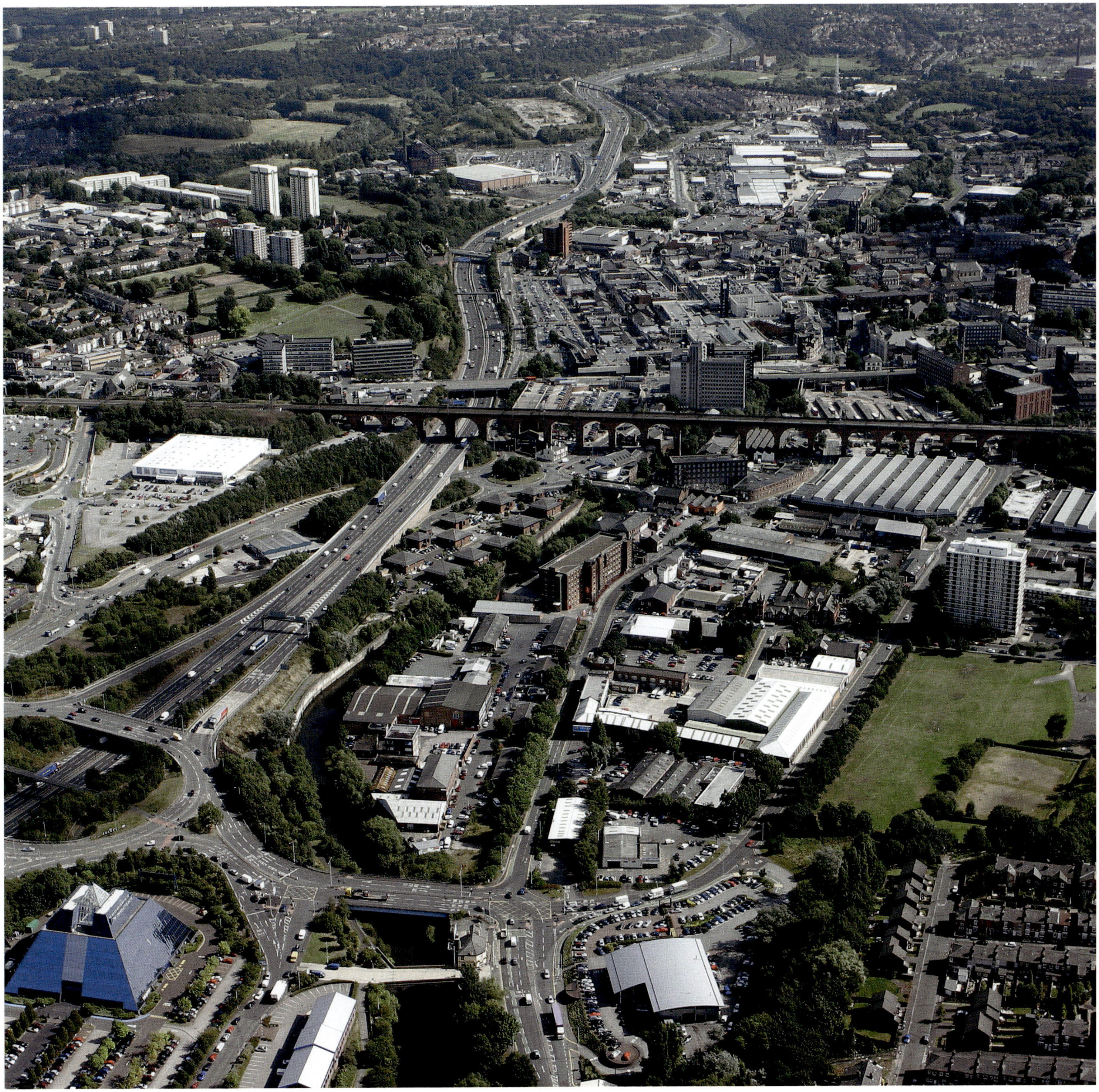

The Pyramid

At the beginning of 1989 something new began to appear on the town's landscape. It was a building far removed from anything that had ever been built before, and after its completion 3 years later it would go on to become the most iconic building in the town. The Pyramid is an office block situated next to junction 1 of what is now the M60 Motorway. It's striking blue glass exterior has made it a landmark for all who pass it on the motorway.

Originally planned as the first of 4 pyramid buildings as part of the Kings Valley development, it was the only one constructed after the firm building it went bust. Built at a cost of £15m, it's not difficult to see why. Standing 120 Feet high, the six-storey building is now arguably the modern symbol of the town, and joins the viaduct, the town hall and Bramall Hall as probably the most recognisable landmarks for those not from the area.

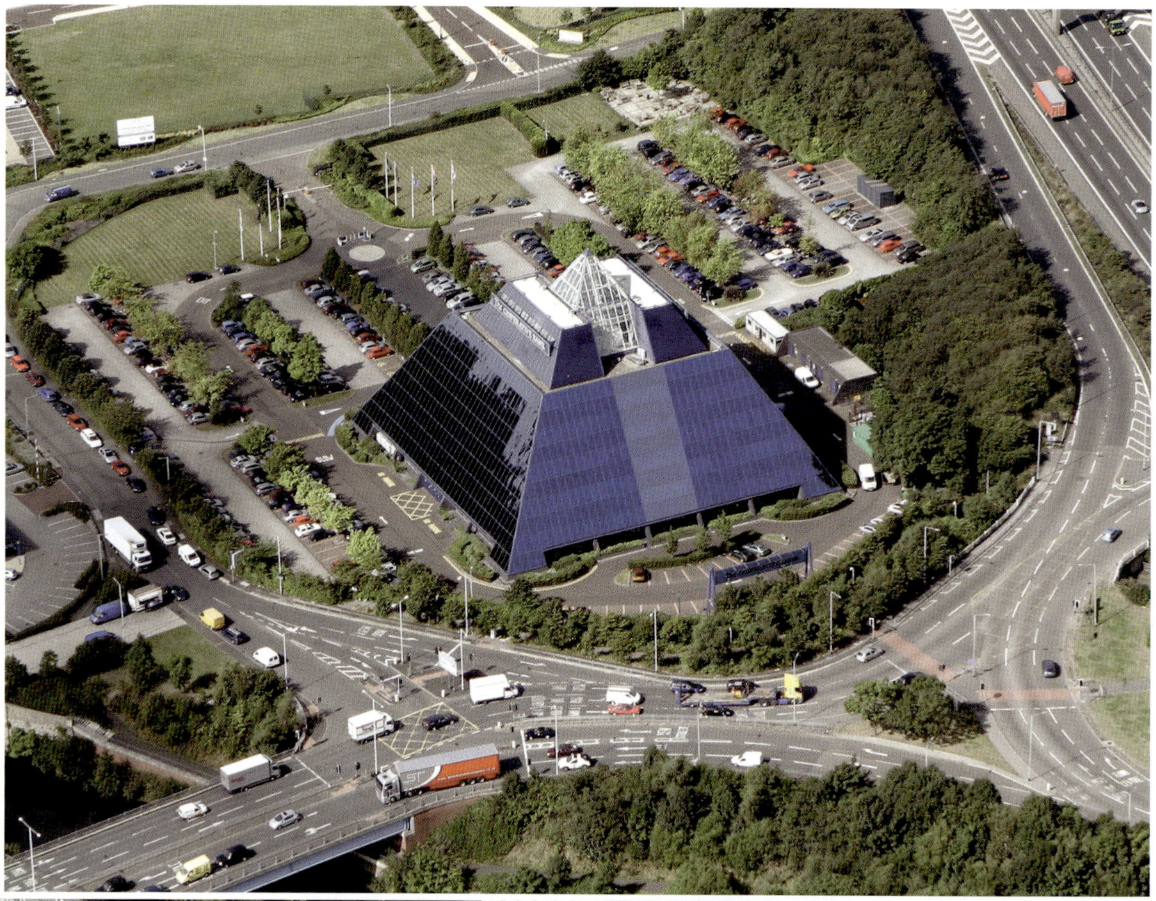

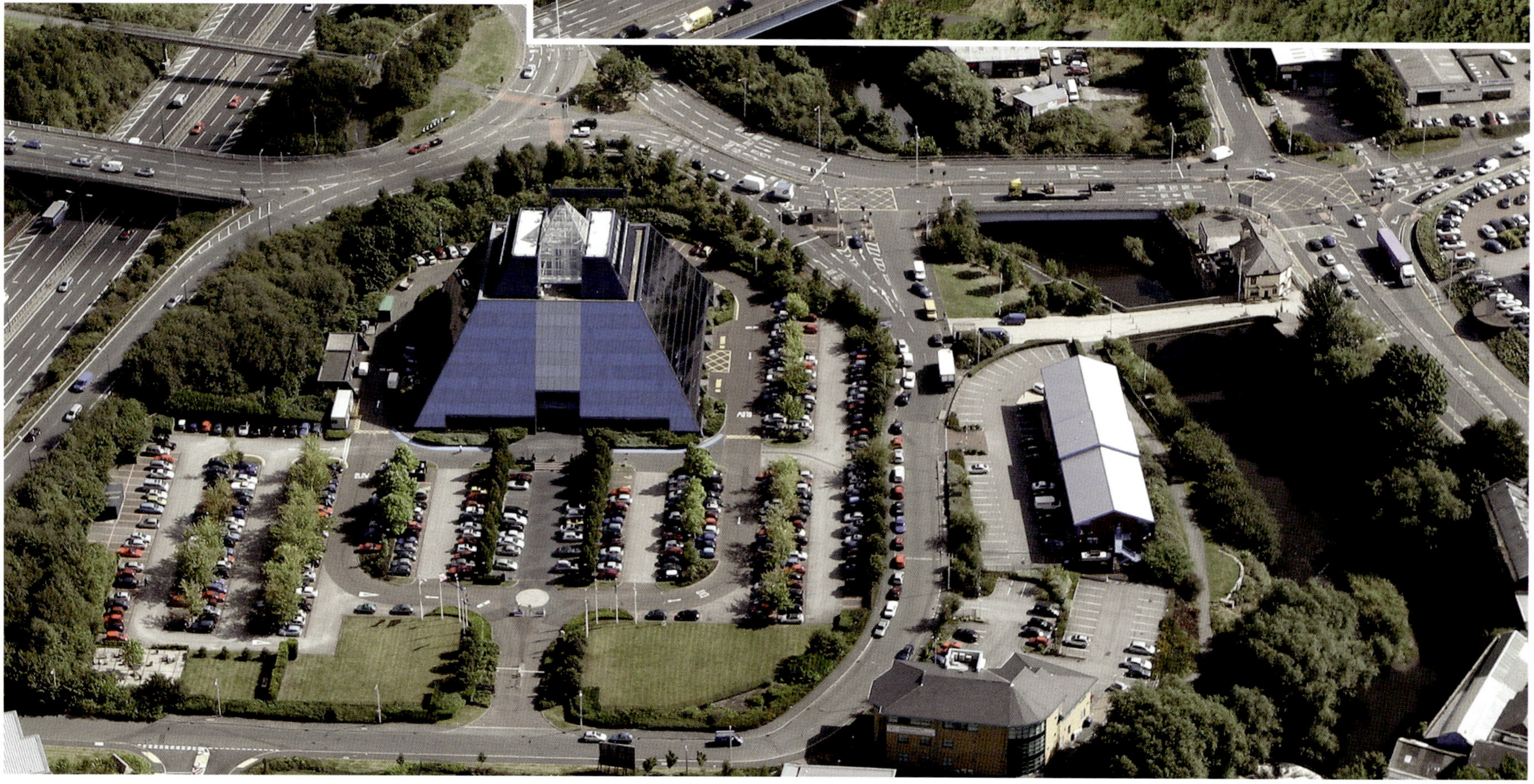

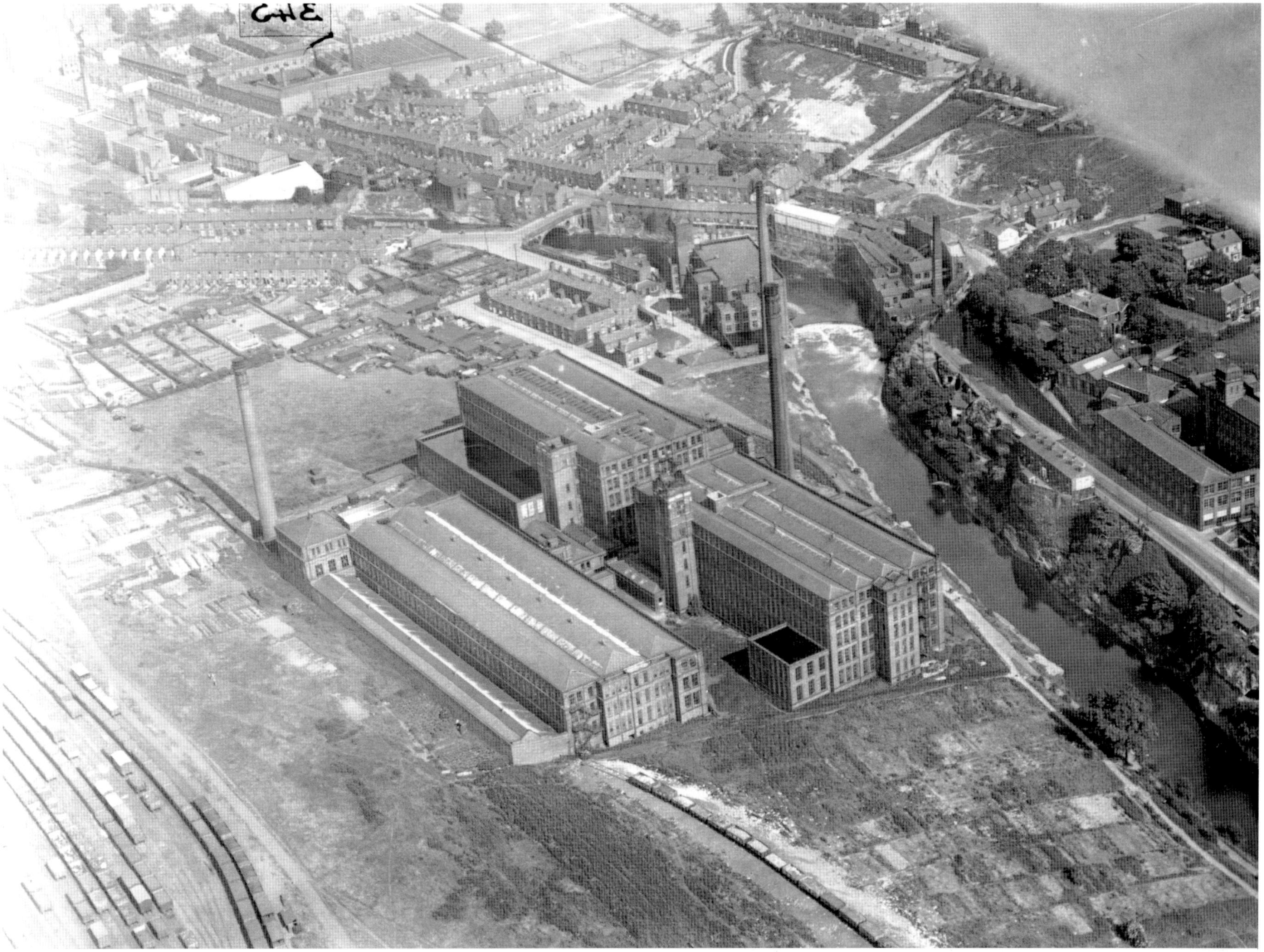

Ring Mills Brinksway 1931

Previously, the area where the pyramid now stands was housing (see image of the M63 on page 56). Before that it was home to the Chestergate allotments. The allotments can be seen in this picture from 1931. The Brinksway Mill complex, consisting of three mills built in the early 19th century, stood in the area immediately to the west of the building. It was only demolished in recent years when age finally caught up with it. This image shows the mills, along with Brinksway Bridge over the River Mersey in the background. The bridge was rebuilt in 1847 in order to widen it, and until 1992 it was the main road crossing of the Mersey here until the new Hollywood Way Bridge opened alongside it. The old bridge is now used as a pedestrian crossing. The land where the Brinksway Mills stood lay unused for several years following its demolition, but it is now being redeveloped as a new business park.

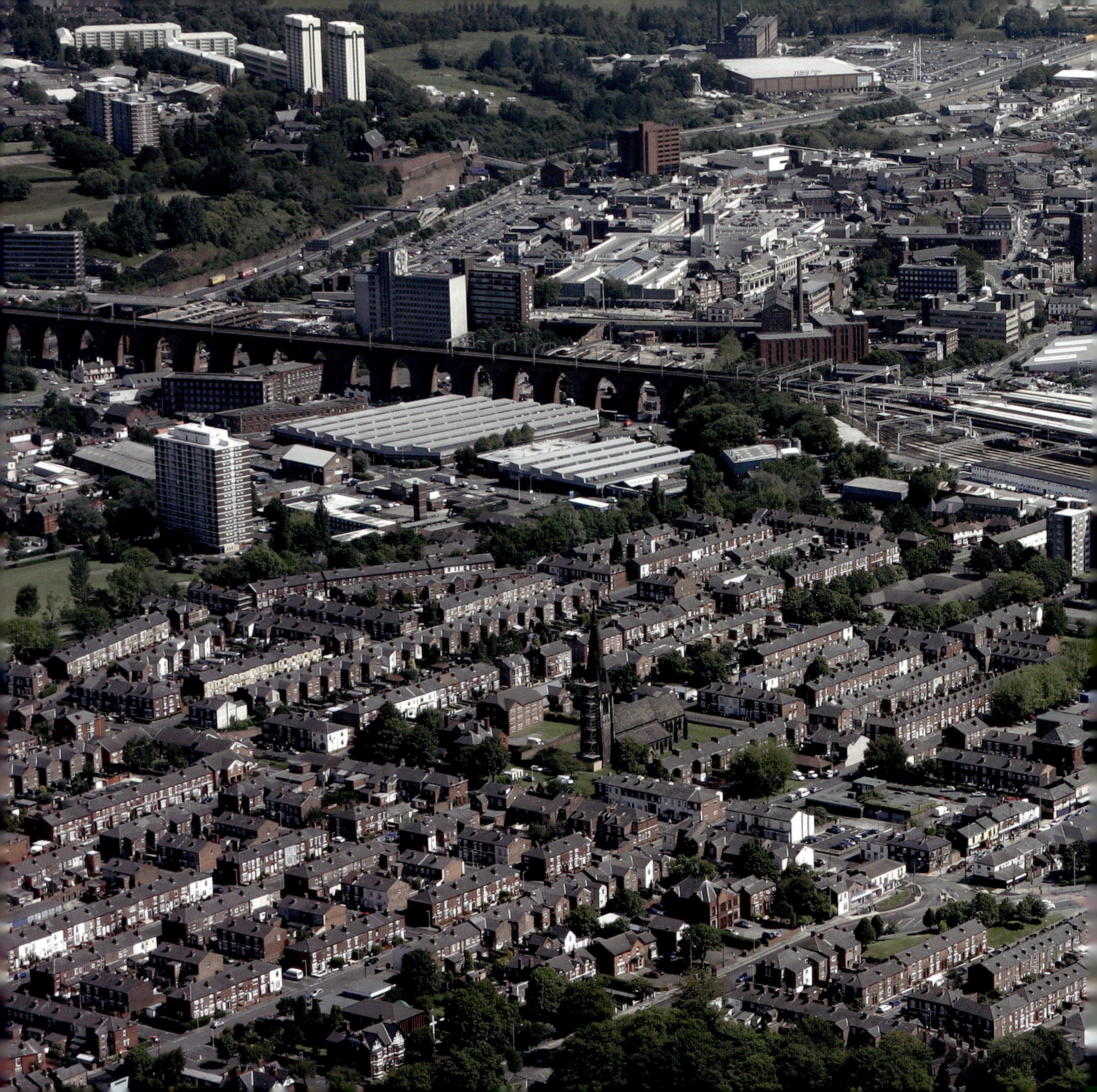

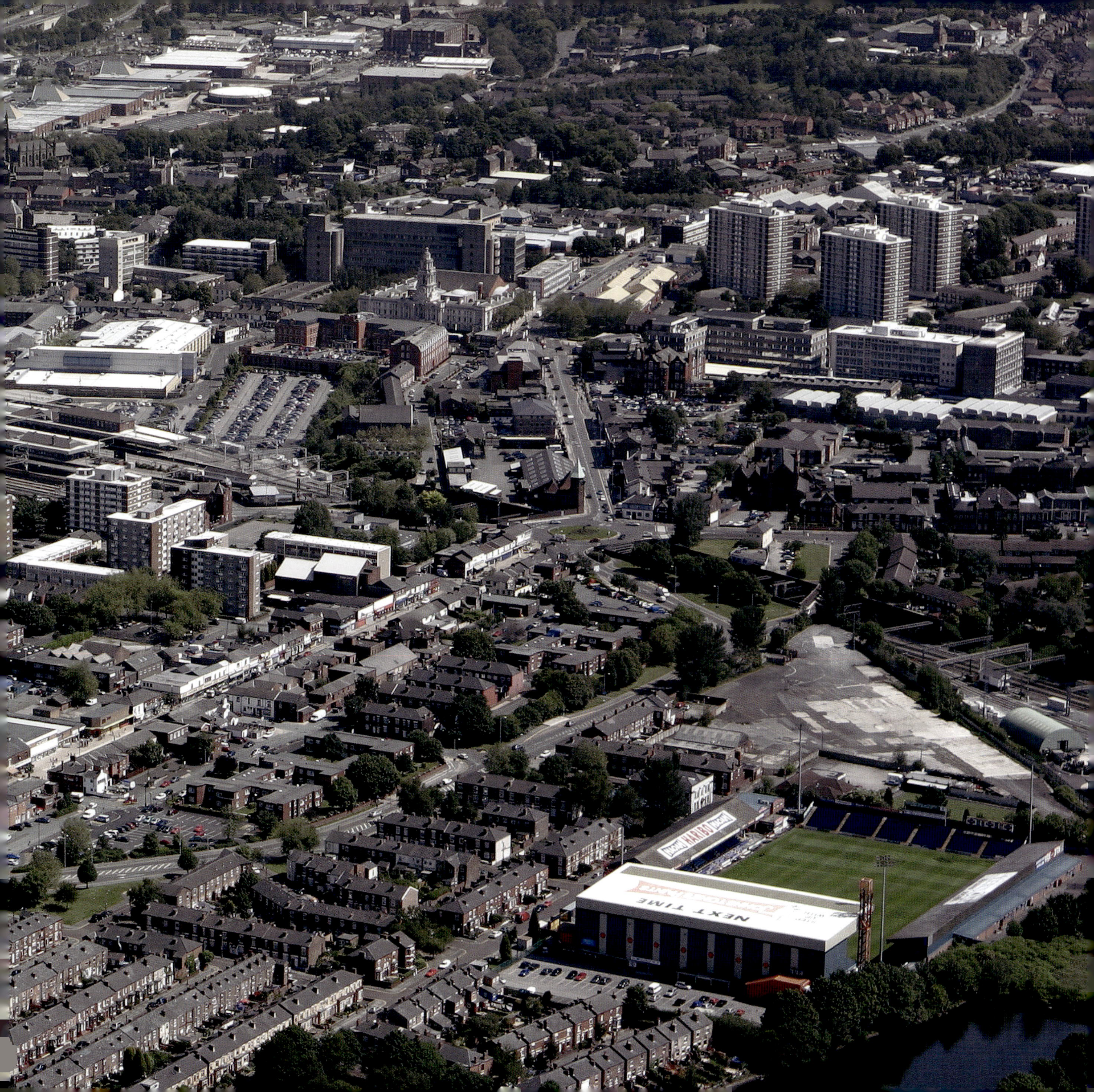
NEXT TIME

Sports Clubs

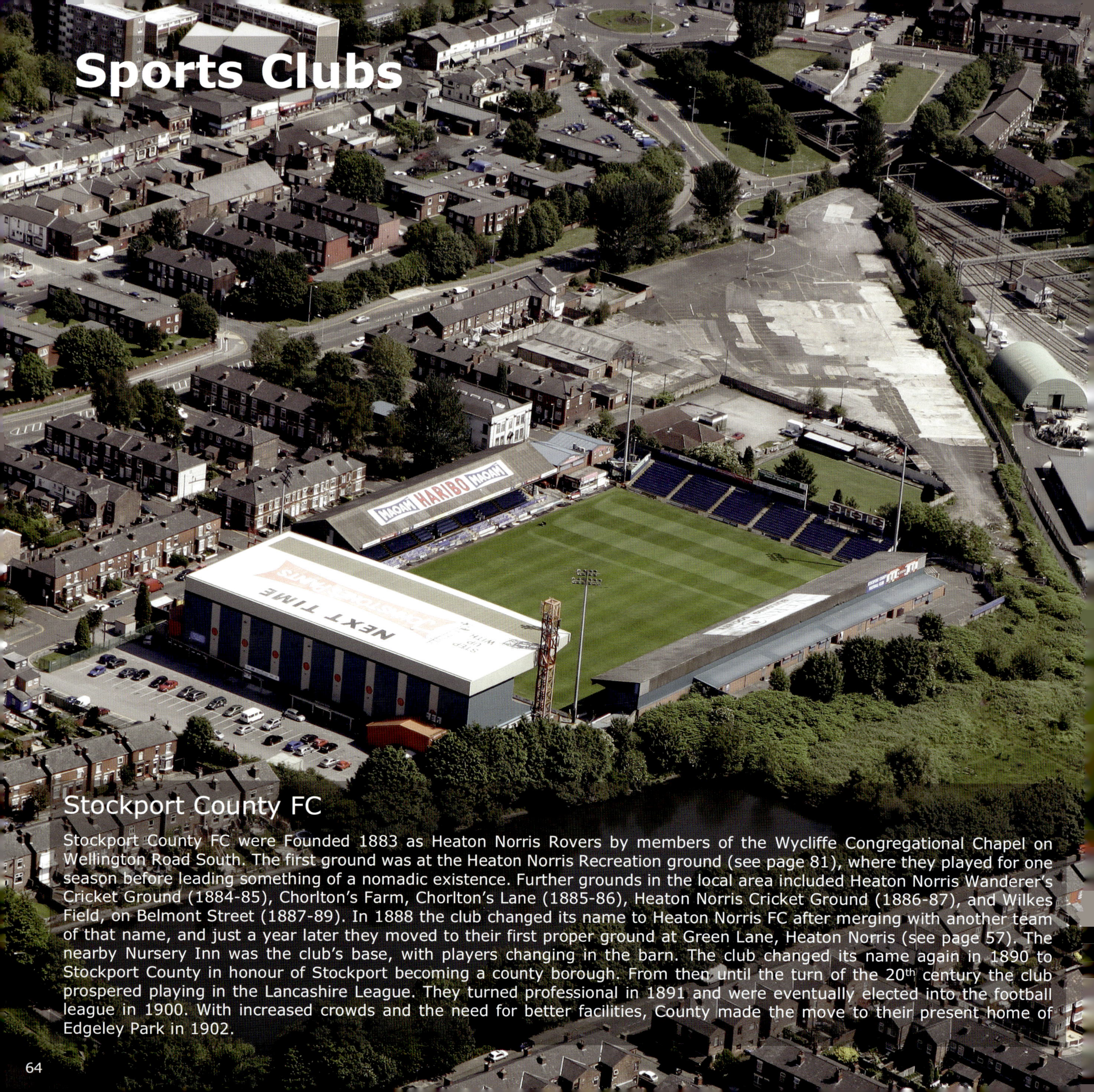

Stockport County FC

Stockport County FC were Founded 1883 as Heaton Norris Rovers by members of the Wycliffe Congregational Chapel on Wellington Road South. The first ground was at the Heaton Norris Recreation ground (see page 81), where they played for one season before leading something of a nomadic existence. Further grounds in the local area included Heaton Norris Wanderer's Cricket Ground (1884-85), Chorlton's Farm, Chorlton's Lane (1885-86), Heaton Norris Cricket Ground (1886-87), and Wilkes Field, on Belmont Street (1887-89). In 1888 the club changed its name to Heaton Norris FC after merging with another team of that name, and just a year later they moved to their first proper ground at Green Lane, Heaton Norris (see page 57). The nearby Nursery Inn was the club's base, with players changing in the barn. The club changed its name again in 1890 to Stockport County in honour of Stockport becoming a county borough. From then until the turn of the 20th century the club prospered playing in the Lancashire League. They turned professional in 1891 and were eventually elected into the football league in 1900. With increased crowds and the need for better facilities, County made the move to their present home of Edgeley Park in 1902.

Edgeley Park April 1946 & October 1956

When County moved to the ground it was already the home of Stockport Rugby League Club. The Club were founder members of the "Northern Union" (the Rugby Football League) in 1895 and once reportedly attracted a crowd of 10,000 for a home game. However, the club were to fold in 1905, leaving County as the sole tenants of the stadium. In 1904 County spent a year in the Lancashire Combination after failing to win re-election to the league following 3 dismal seasons on the pitch, but they were re-elected a year later after winning the Combination. The club has remained in the league ever since. The first major development following the club's arrival at Edgeley Park was the construction of a stand at the Pop Side, which could hold 1400 people. This was replaced in 1927 and extended to the length of the pitch in 1934. A new 500 seat main stand with offices and changing rooms on the Hardcastle Road side was built in 1913. However, an enormous fire in 1935 destroyed the wooden stand. The flames were reportedly so fierce that they melted the lead flashing on the roofs and around the windows on the houses opposite.

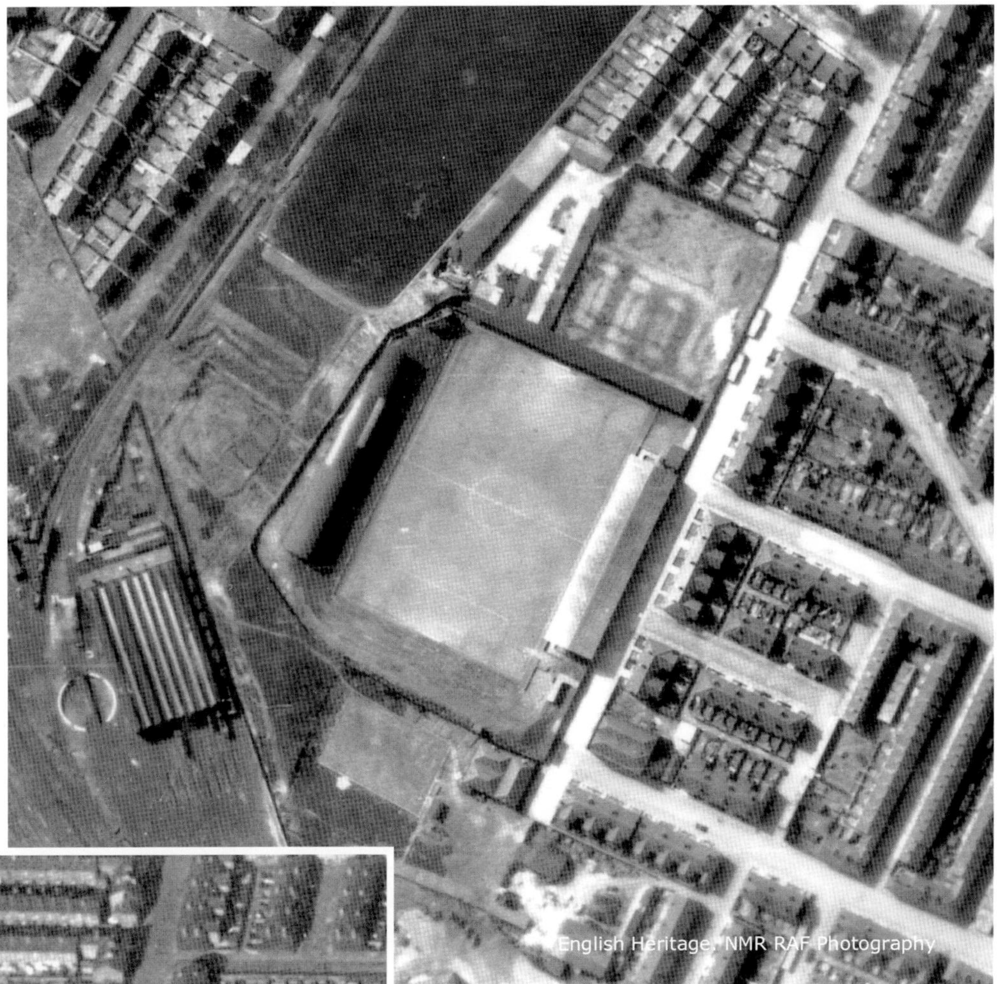

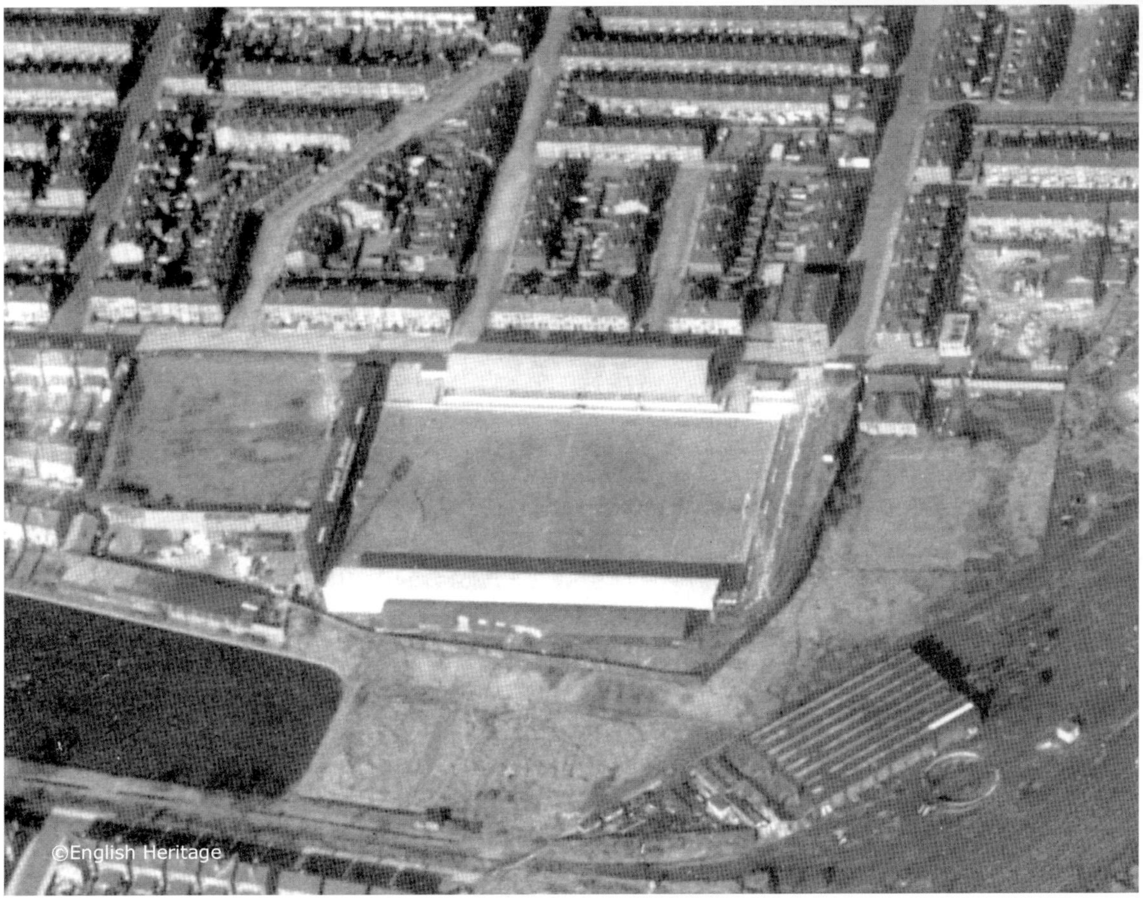

Nearly all of the club's records were lost in the fire. The replacement stand – the present main stand - was opened a year later in 1936. As can be seen from the image from April 1st 1946 (above), the ground was quite substantial, with a large uncovered terrace at the Railway End and the small wooden Cheadle End opposite. The "Pop Side" that was extended in 1934 was twice the size it is now, and featured a barrel roof over the rear of the stand. The existing roof was added to the front in 1954 (shown on the left in 1956), which is the reason why it appears so high compared to the number of rows of seats. Floodlights were installed on 16th October 1956, just days before this image was taken. A friendly against top Dutch side Fortuna '54 Geleen (Now Fortuna Sittard) saw a 3-0 defeat in front of 14,511. The Cheadle end was made all seated in 1967, until safety regulations forced its demolition in 1986.

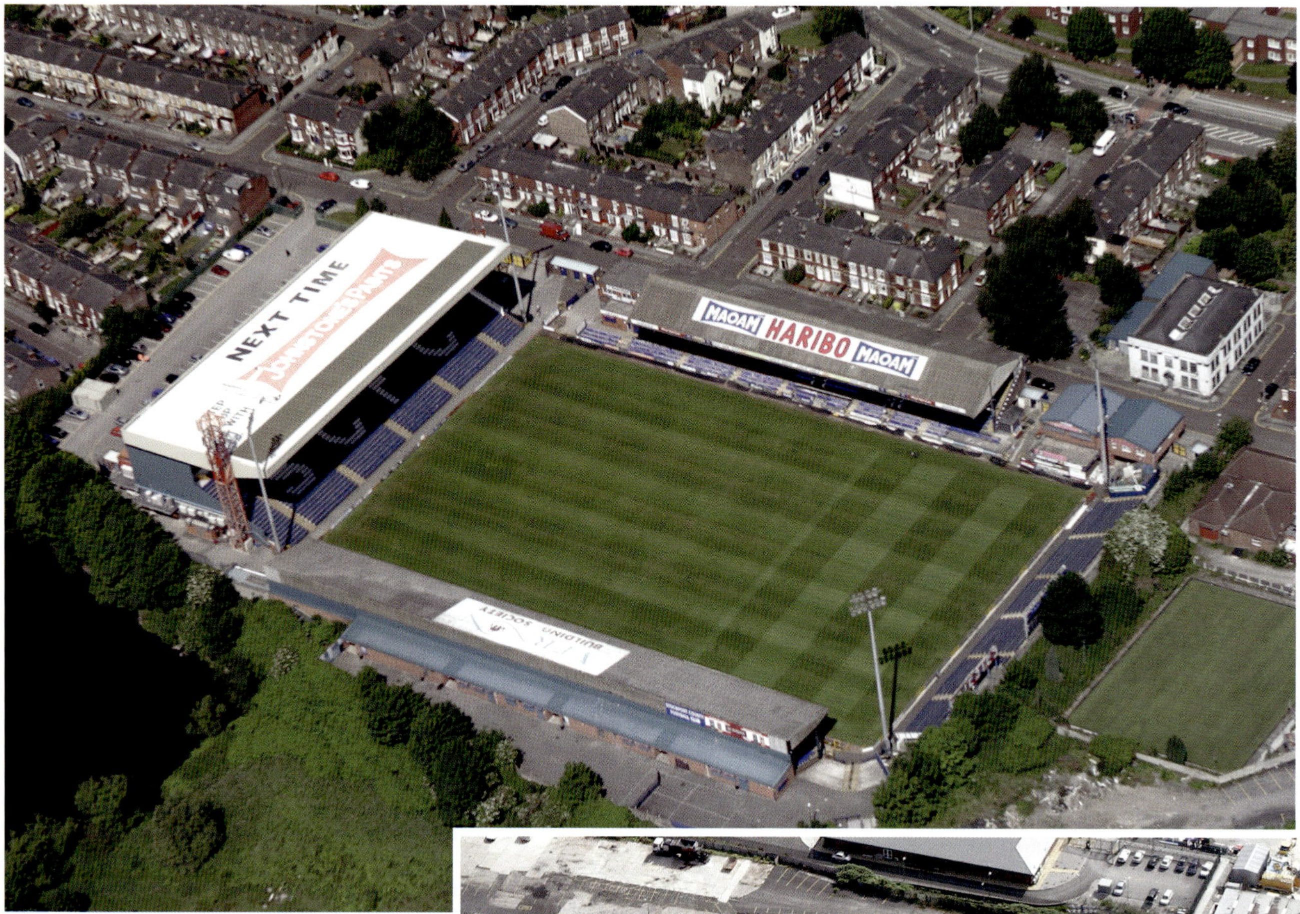

Edgeley Park

Football experienced a massive attendance boom in the 1950s, and it was during this decade that Edgeley Park saw its record attendance when 27,833 people witnessed an FA Cup 5th round defeat to Liverpool on 11th February 1950. Now all seated, the present capacity is around 10,850, which is just about right for the club as things stand.

The biggest new addition to the ground has been the new Cheadle End. The 5000 seater stand opened in 1995 and towers over the older parts of the ground. In the age of the new "Soulless Bowl" stadiums it would be a shame if Edgeley Park's more traditional comforts were lost.

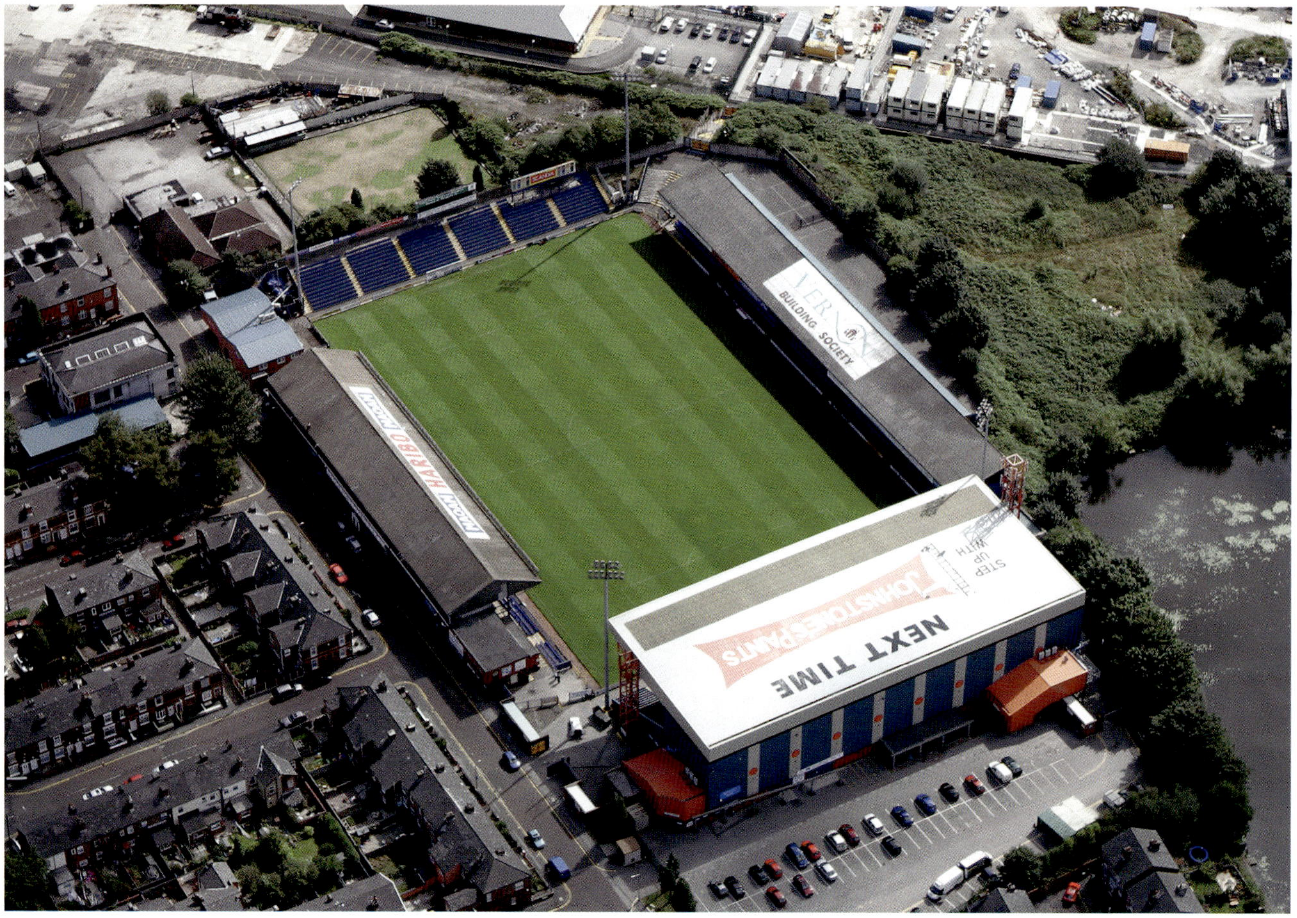

But the stadium, which was once completely isolated behind rows of terraced houses, is brimming with potential, and is probably in the best location for a stadium in the whole of Stockport. The only other site in the town that could come close to matching it is, ironically, the Green Lane Industrial estate next to B&Q, just a few hundred yards from where the club used to play. However, there is no need to relocate. There is plenty of room for expansion behind the Railway End and the Pop Side that could eventually see the capacity taken to over 30,000, if necessary. Since 2004 the ground has been shared with Sale Sharks RUFC, who currently own the ground. The SCFC Supporters Trust have plans to regain ownership in the very near future.

Woodley Sports FC

Woodley Sports FC were founded in 1970 as Woodley Athletic. Their rapid rise from the Lancashire & Cheshire League to the Manchester League to their present lofty position in non-league football has been remarkable, so much so that Woodley are now Stockport's second club having overtaken Cheadle Town. They currently play in the Unibond League and are just 4 divisions below the professional ranks.

A recent redevelopment programme led to a new "field turf" pitch being laid along with a smart new main stand. Further redevelopment of the complex has been planned, with additional training pitches and community facilities due to be built on the fields to the left of this photo that will give Woodley some of the best facilities of any non-league club in the country. The record attendance is 1500 versus Stockport County.

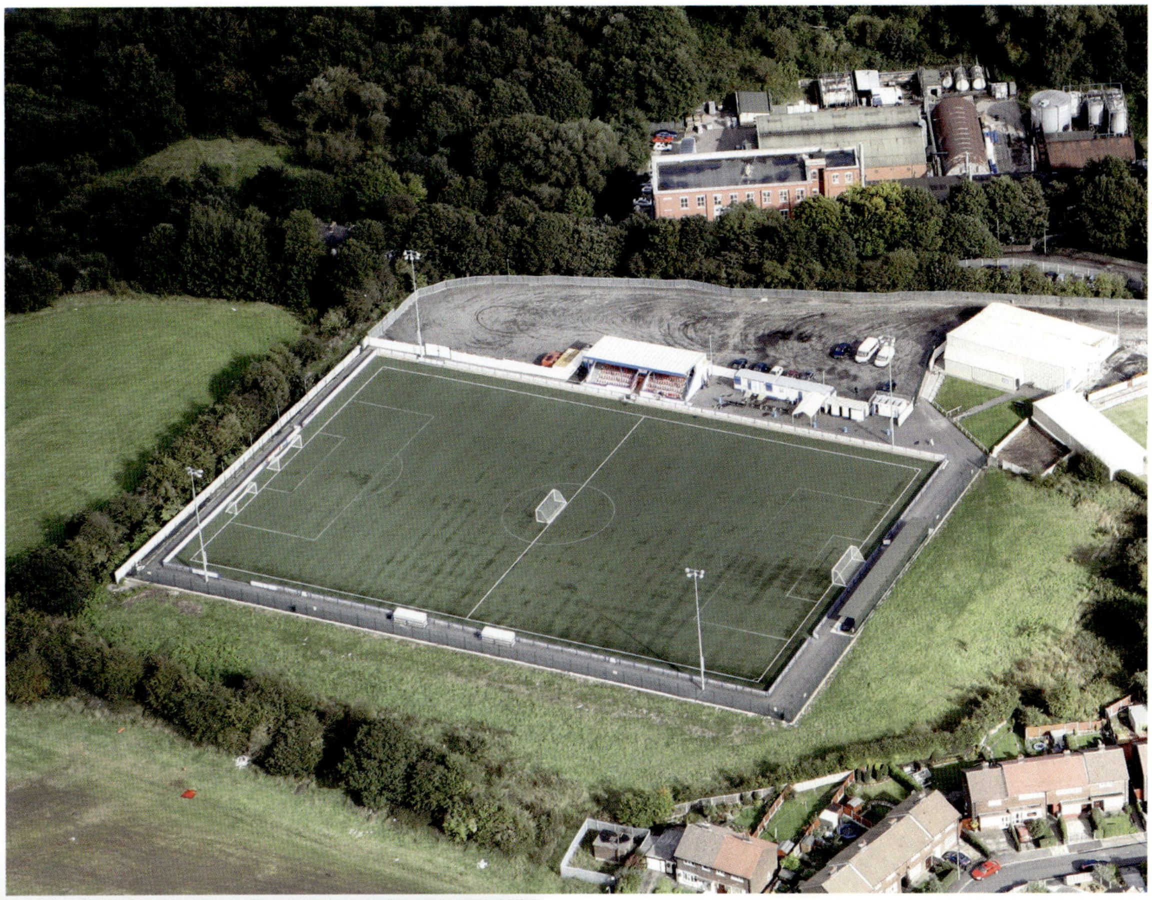

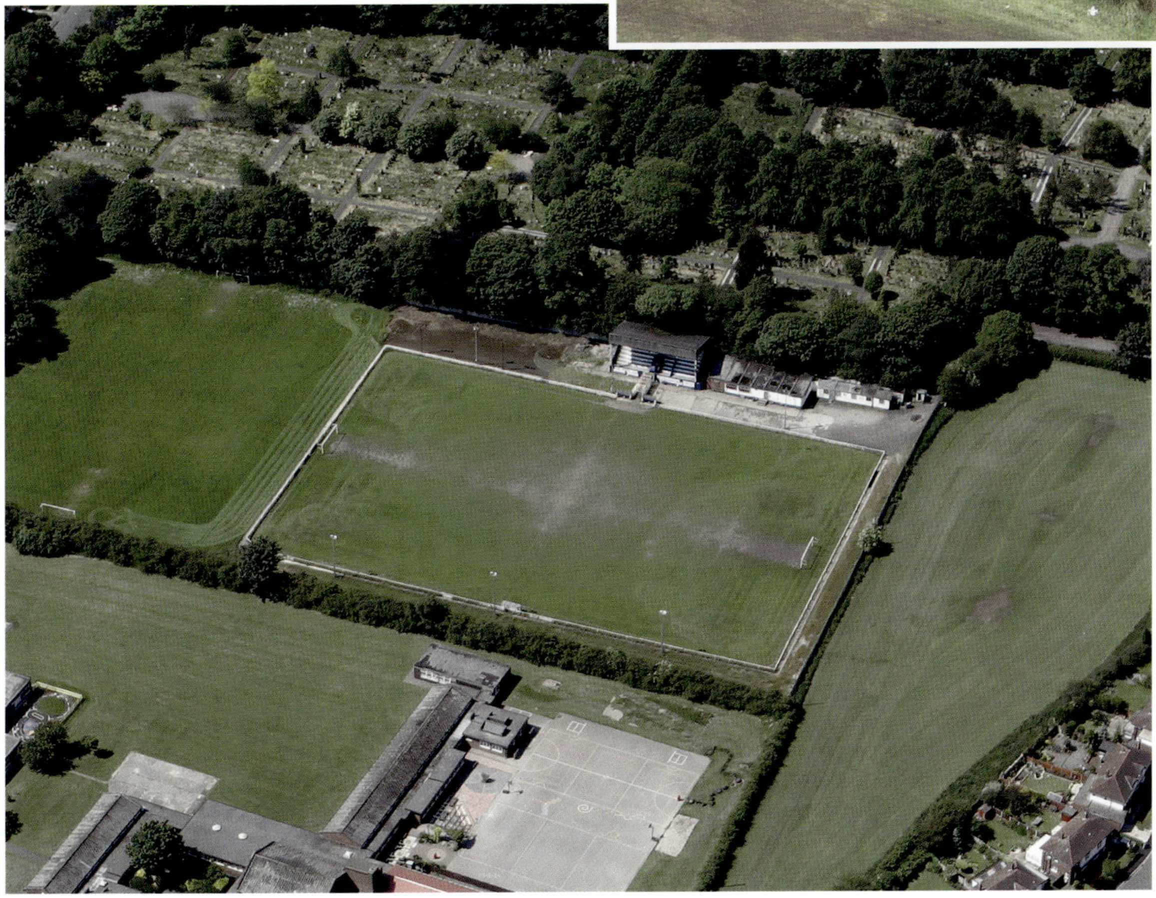

Cheadle Town FC

Cheadle Town FC were founded in 1961 as Grassmere Rovers. The club led a nomadic existence during its early years and played at both Glossop North End and Hyde United. The Park Road ground had previously been home to Cheadle Rovers FC until their demise in the 1950s. It was famously used in the 1966 world cup as a training ground for Portugal and the legendary Eusabio, and was also used by Manchester City FC for training. When the stadium became available in 1982, Grassmere won the right to move in and made the ground their own.

A year later the club changed its name to Cheadle Town and have since become well established in the North West Counties League. The record attendance at the ground is 1700 for a pre-season friendly with Stockport County in 1994, whilst 1200 people attended a match against a Man Utd XI to celebrate the arrival of the floodlights a few years later.

Linotype/Cheadle Heath Nomads FC

Cheadle Heath Nomads were formed in 1919 and play at The Heath on Norbreck Avenue. They play in the Cheshire Football League (formerly the Mid Cheshire League) at the top level of amateur football – effectively Division 11. The Nomads joined the League in 1949. Clubs in the Cheshire league, and also the neighbouring Manchester League, cannot play in the FA Cup but can enter the FA Vase if they have floodlights. In 2004 the club merged with Altrincham based Linotype FC to create a new club. Linotype had lost their ground and the Nomads needed a new team, so a merger was agreed. The Nomads, along with Stockport Georgians (see page 133), are one of two top amateur clubs remaining in Stockport. Bramhall FC (1886-1997, Lumb Lane), Grove United (1958-2001, Half Moon Lane) and Littlemoor FC (1947–2001, Ward Street) have all folded in recent years.

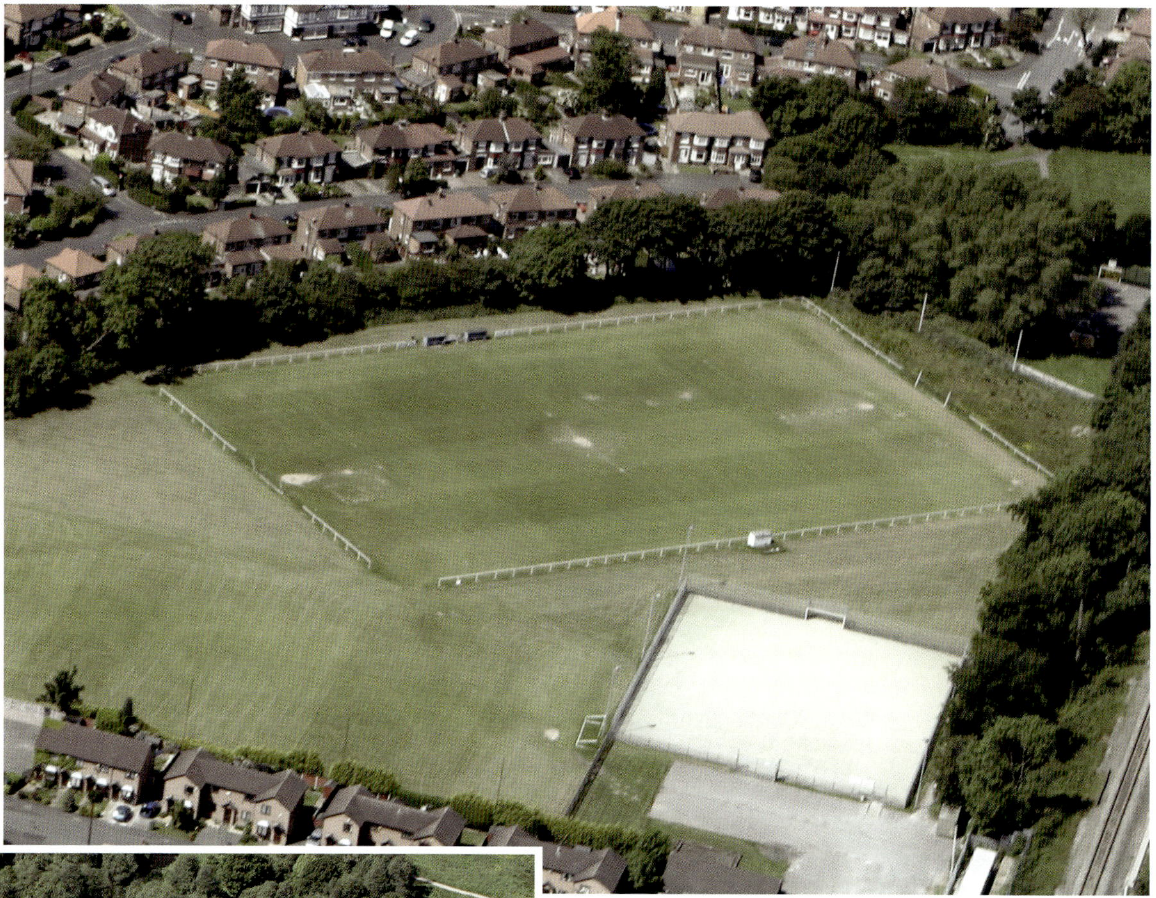

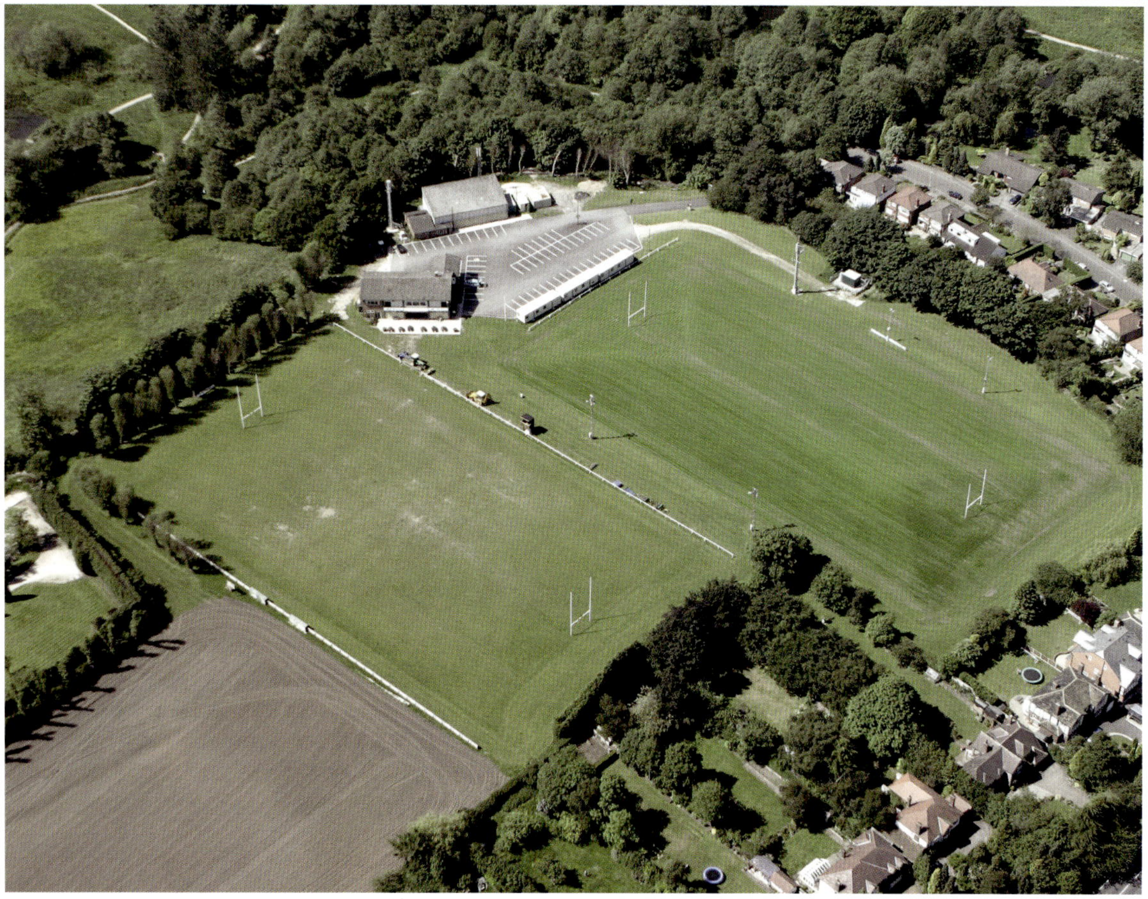

Stockport RUFC

Stockport RUFC Play at the Memorial Ground on Headlands Road in Bramhall. The club were founded in 1923 as Davenport RUFC following a breakaway from Heaton Moor RUFC (formed in 1899). Despite the name of Davenport, the club have always played in the Bramhall area. The first ground was at Grange Road, where they stayed until the outbreak of war in 1914, before the club bought 11 acres of land on Hanley Road. This was to be their home until 1964 when they moved to their present base. The new site comprised of three pitches (one of which is being re-seeded in the photo) and a new clubhouse. The ground was named in honour of 11 club members who lost their lives during the Second World War. The club changed its name to Stockport in 1992, and in recent years have enjoyed tremendous success, winning several promotions, as well as the 2006 Powergen Intermediate Cup final at Twickenham.

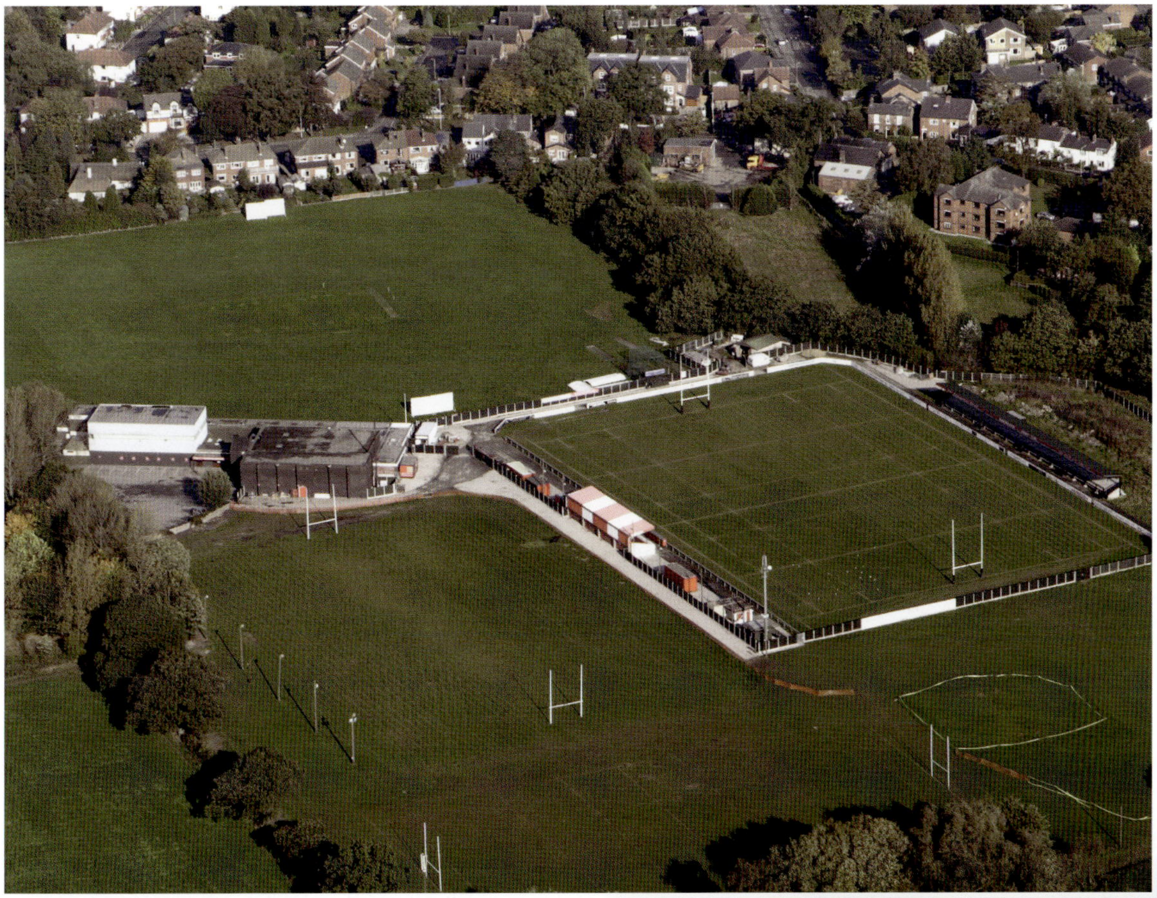

Manchester RUFC & Cheadle Hulme Cricket Club.

The 23-acre sports grounds on Grove Lane are home to Manchester Rugby Union Club, Cheadle Hulme cricket club (founded 1881) and the Grove Park Squash Club. The rugby club moved here from Chorlton, Manchester in the early 1970s. The club were formed in 1860, eleven years before the RFU even existed, making it one of the oldest rugby clubs in the world. During the 1990s the club rose through the divisions, winning 6 promotions in 10 years to find themselves in National League One - just one division below the top league. The club stayed here for five seasons before relegation down to National League Two. As such, the small but cosy stadium has developed to such as extent that it is on a par with many high level non-league football grounds, and can comfortably hold around 3000 people

Marple RUFC & Mellor FC

The sports pitches at Wood Lane in Marple are in the early stages of development, but are on the way to becoming the next major sports ground in the town. It is home to two clubs in two different sports. Marple Rugby Union Club, Mellor FC and Ridge Danyers College (now Cheadle & Marple College) teamed up to form a new association and built a new clubhouse that opened in 2000.

Mellor FC were founded in 1923 and play in the Lancashire and Cheshire Football League. This is one of the top amateur leagues and is a feeder to the Cheshire and Manchester Leagues. Many clubs have used this league as a stepping stone into semi-pro football – including Woodley Sports. There are several clubs from Stockport in this league, and the ground here in Marple is now one with a lot of potential.

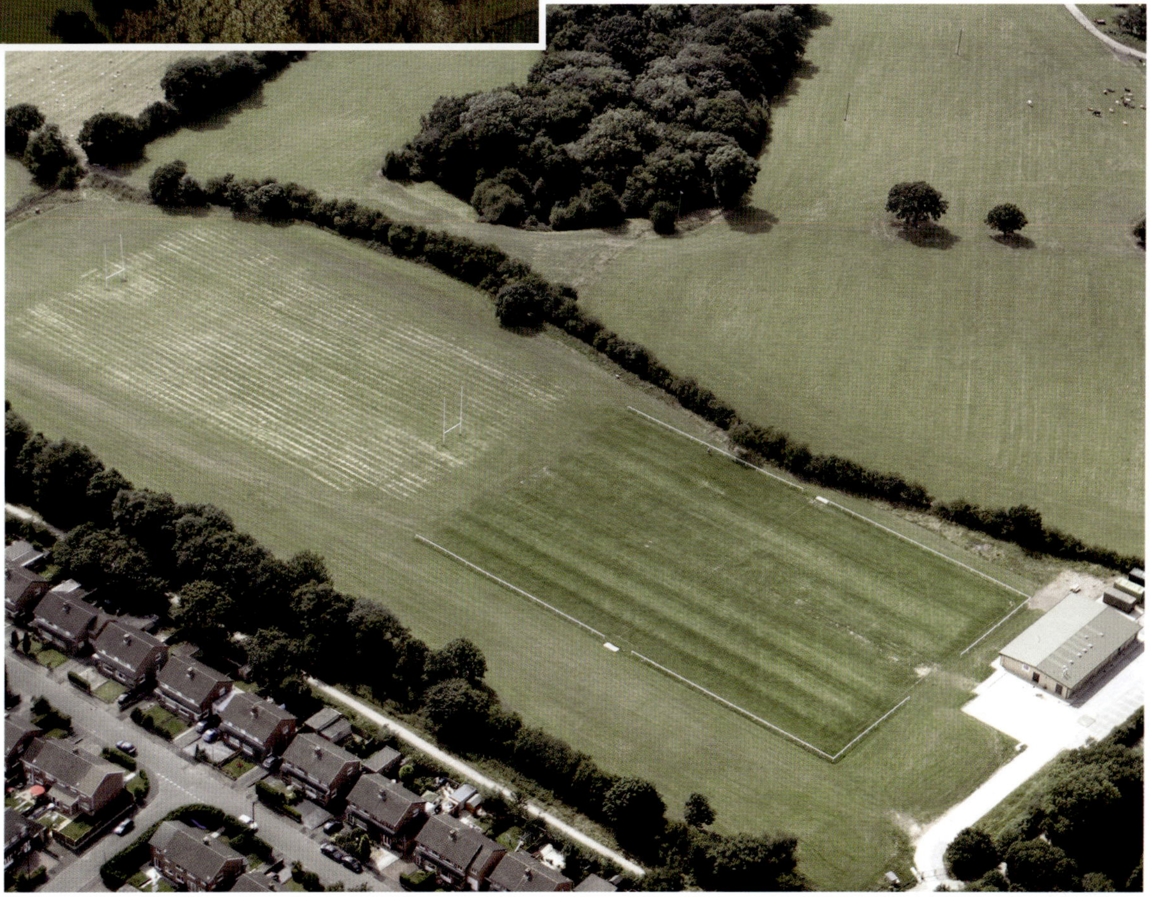

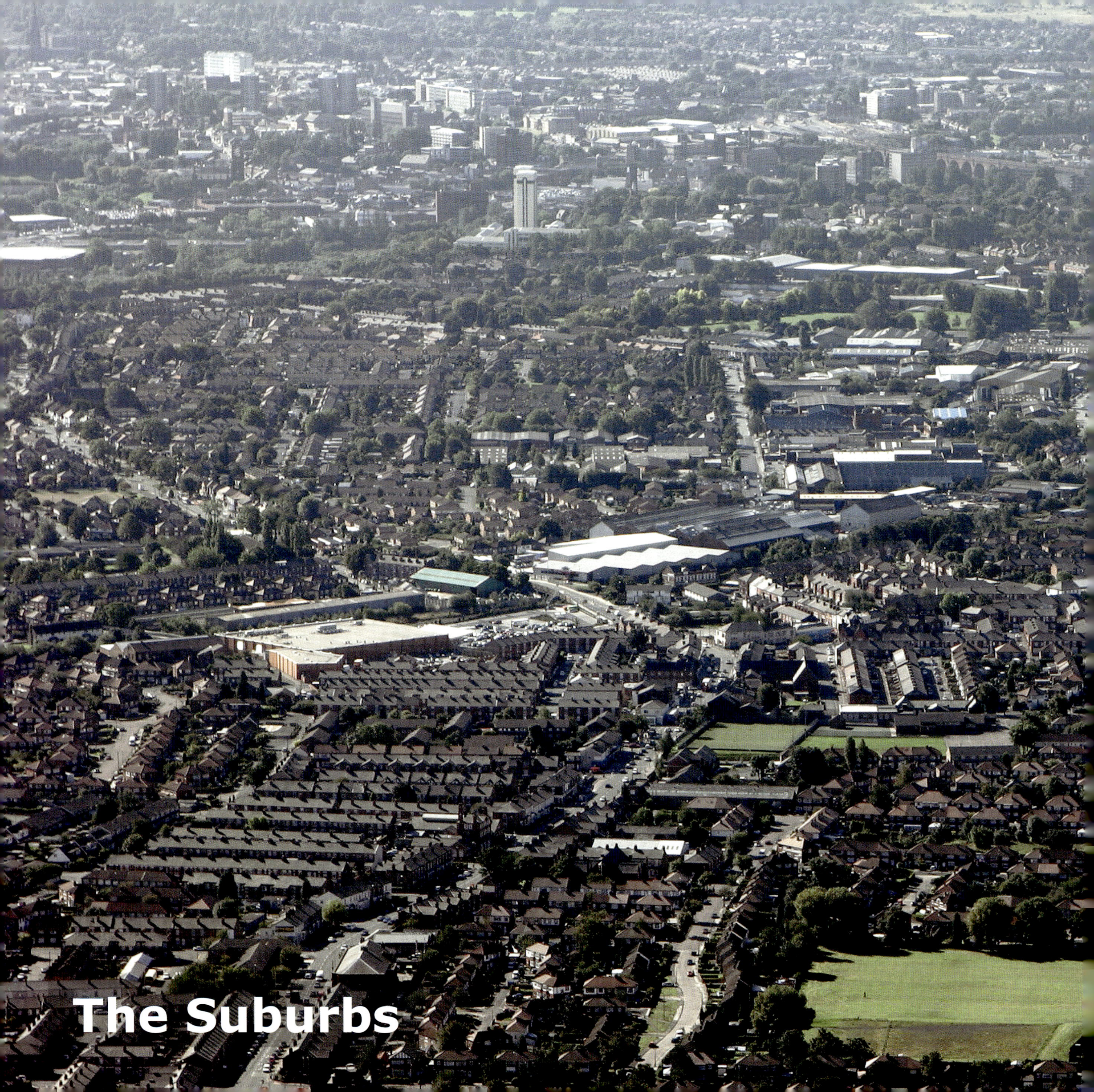
The Suburbs

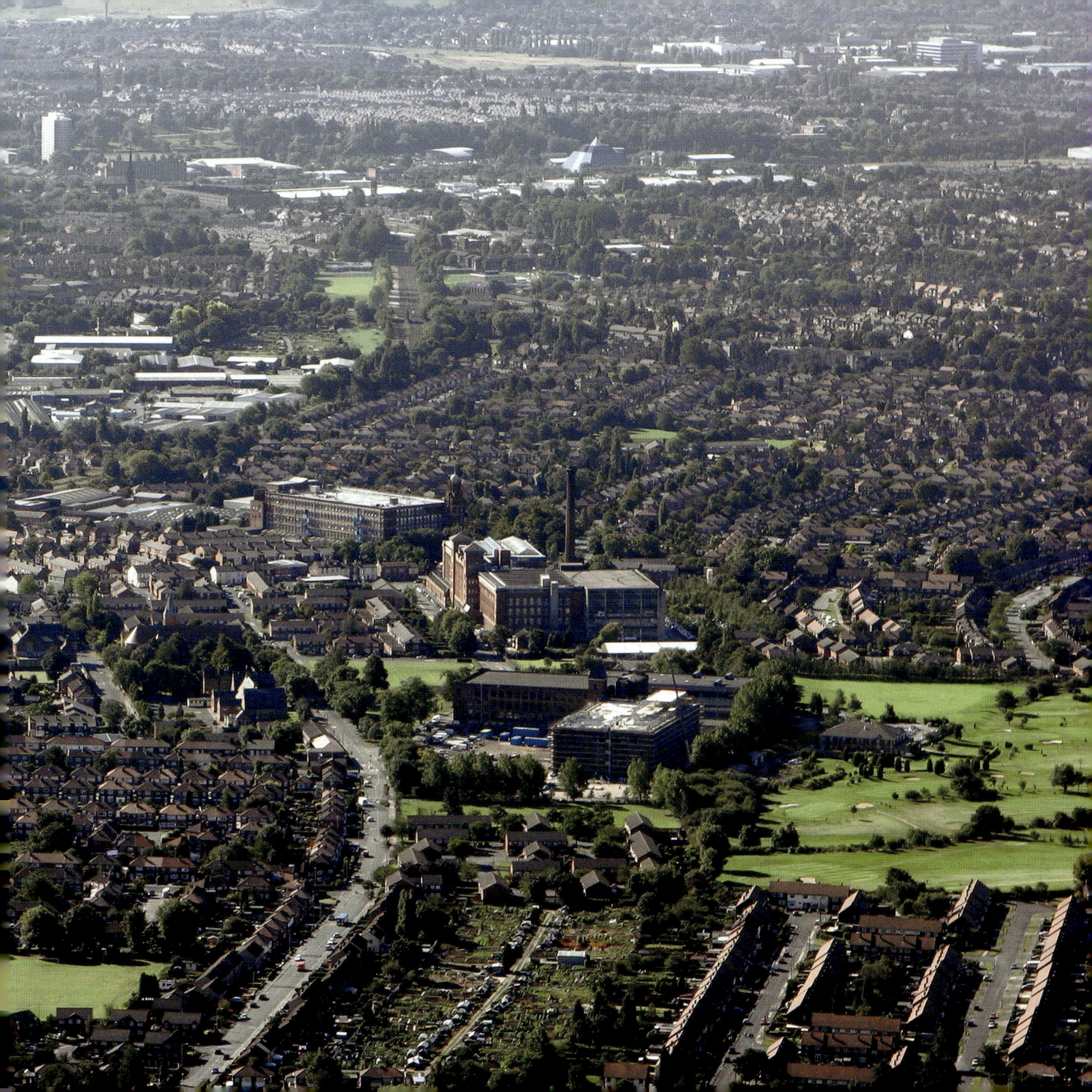

Northern Suburbs

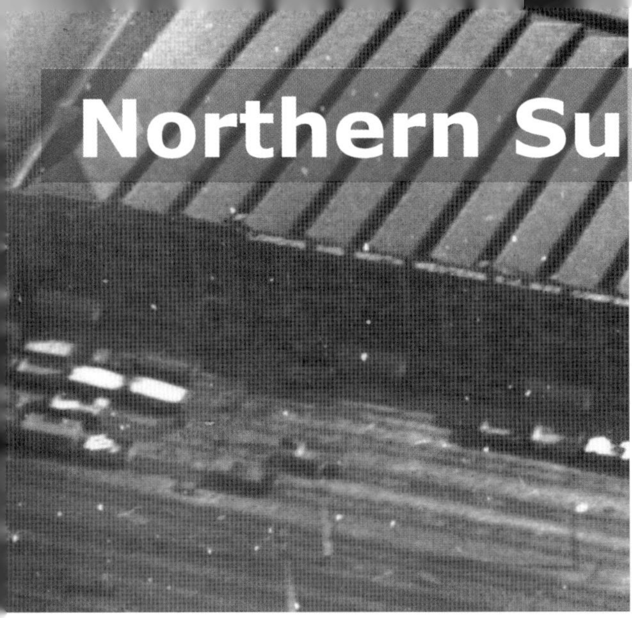
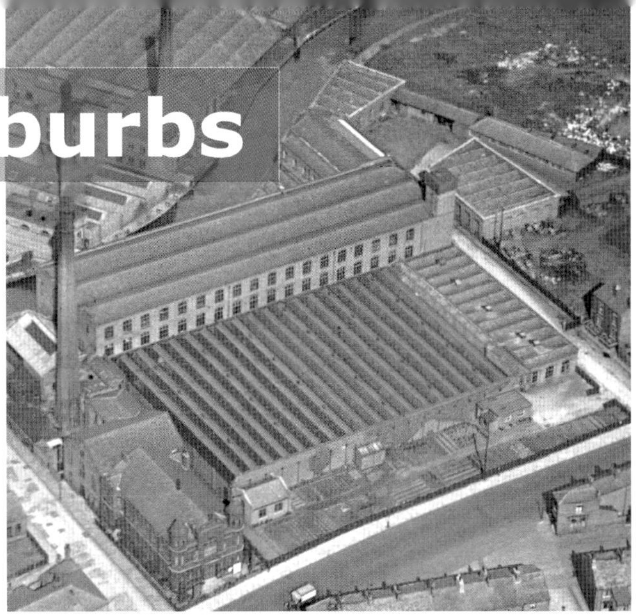
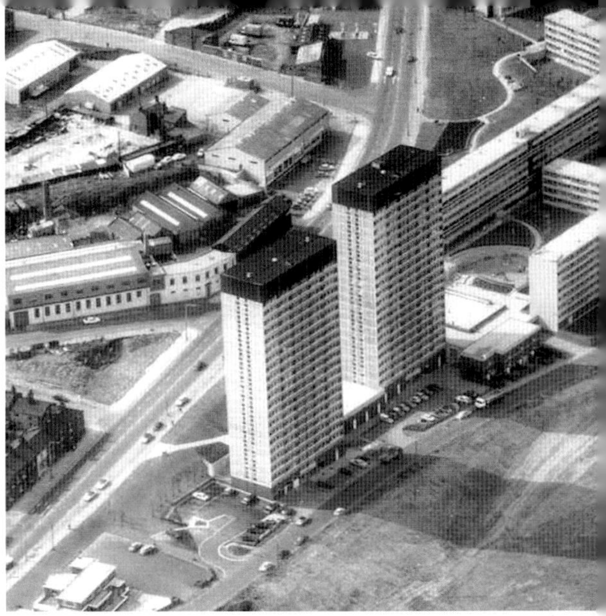
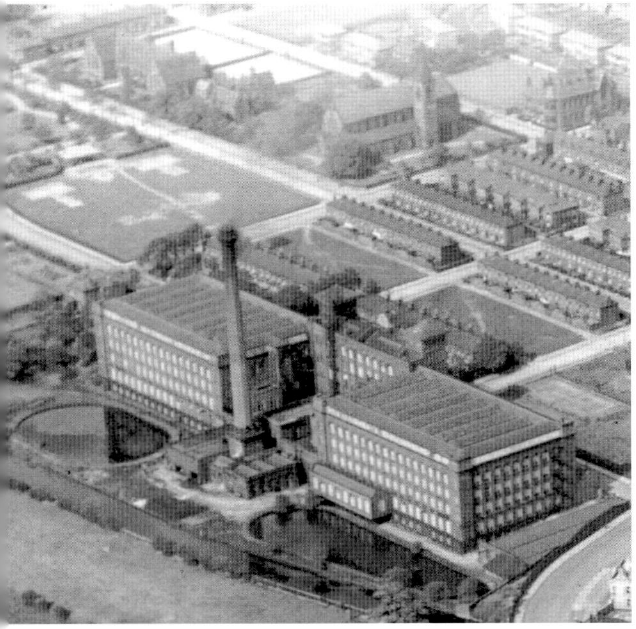
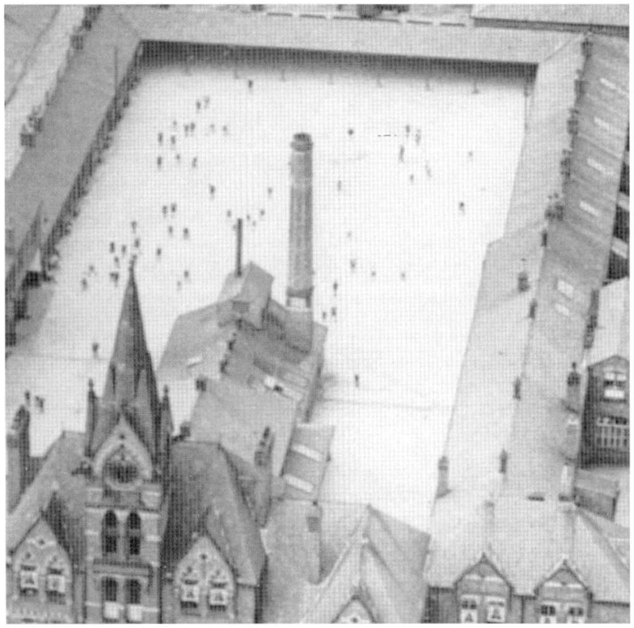
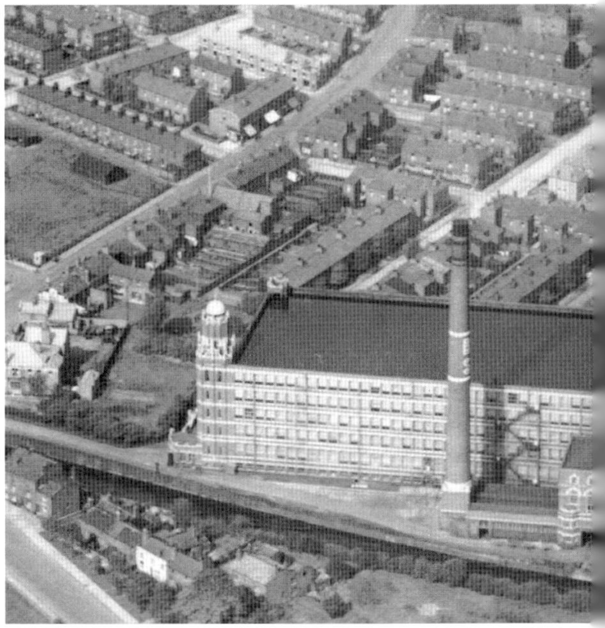
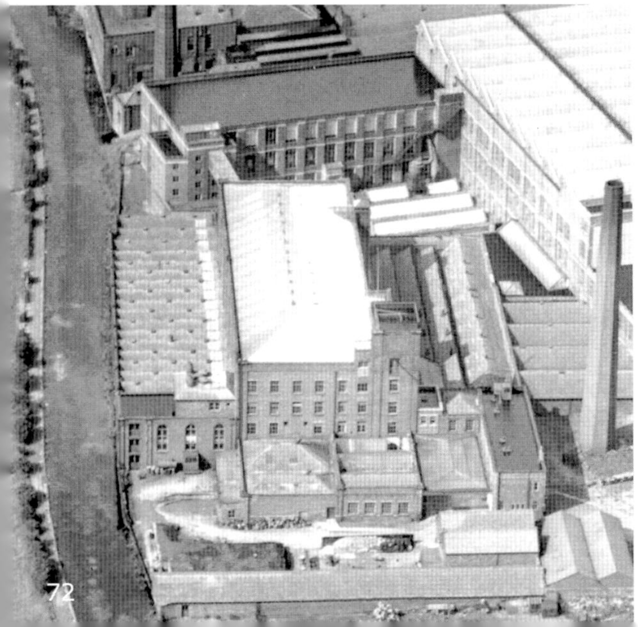
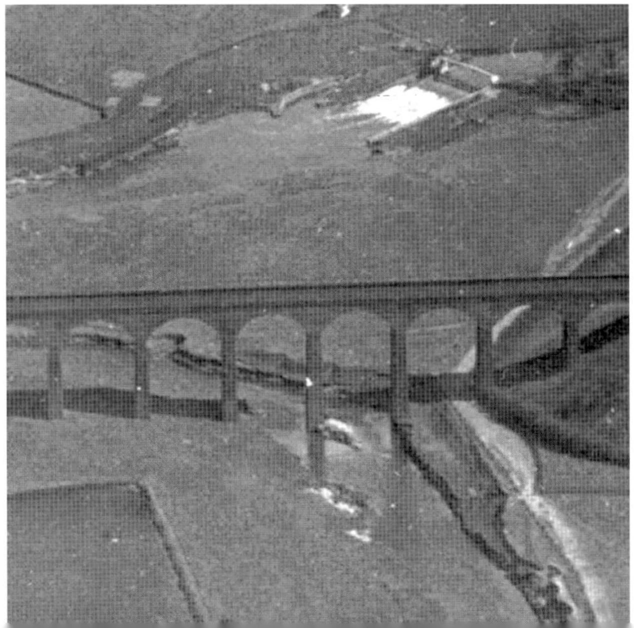
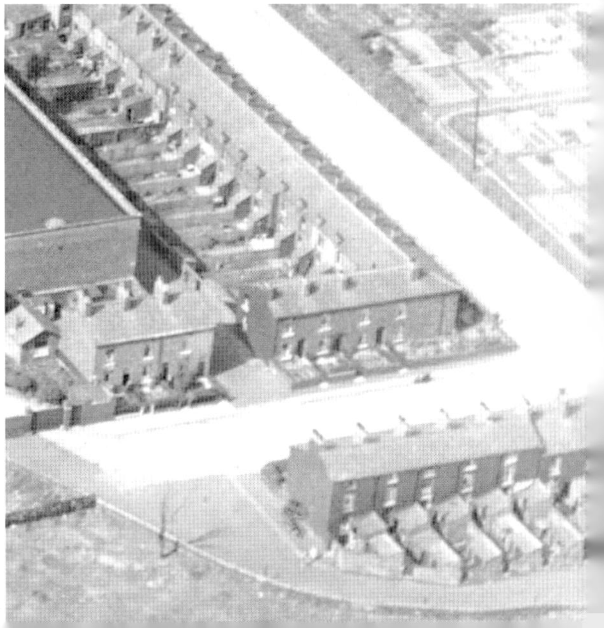

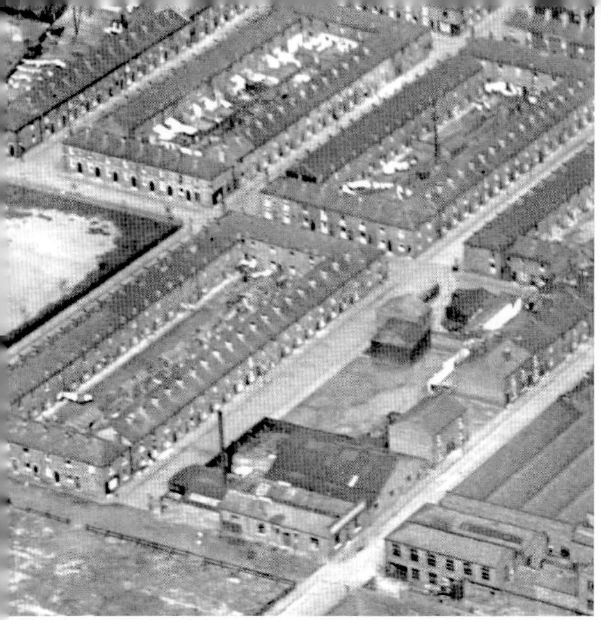
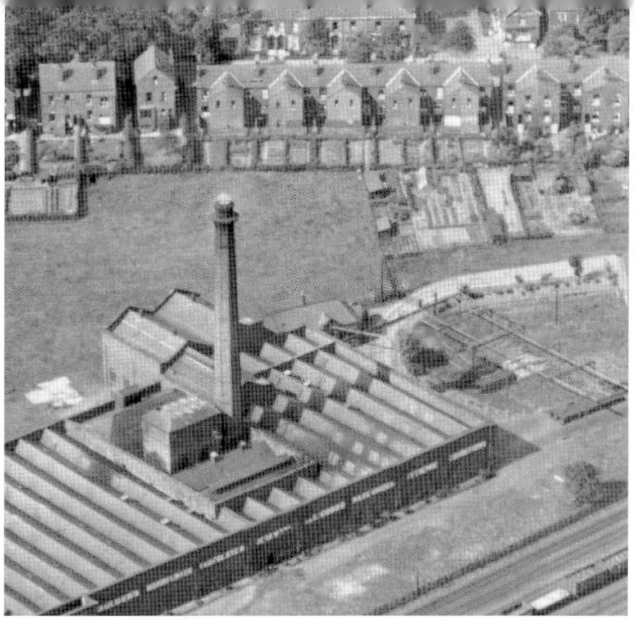
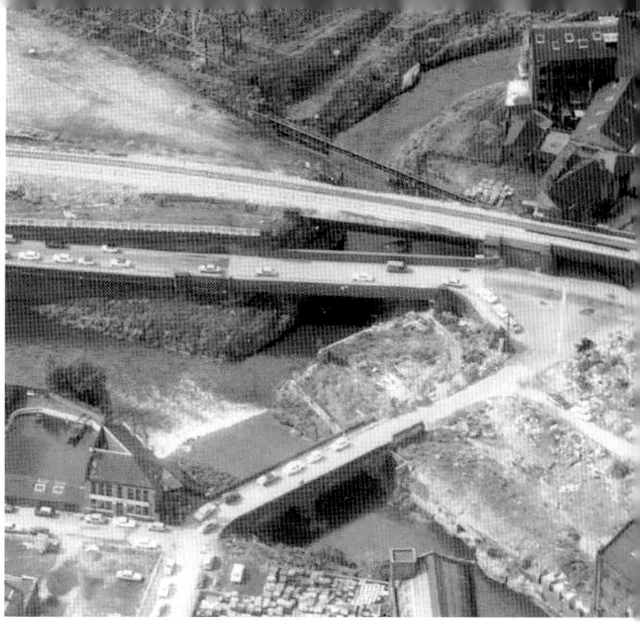

The northern suburbs contain a diverse mix of areas, including former industrial centres, well-healed districts and salt of the earth working class neighbourhoods. The northern areas are very densely populated and extremely urban, but there are still plenty of green open spaces.

From the historic township of Heaton Norris, Stockport spread over the Mersey and continued its growth north, absorbing the smaller villages up to the present border with Manchester. In places along the northwest boundary of the town, Stockport appears to merge seamlessly with Manchester, with many streets straddling the boundary where houses on one side of the road are in one town, and houses on the opposite side are in the other. However, there is still a well-defined boundary here thanks to a series of green spaces, stretching from Cringle Fields Park to the Heaton Moor golf course and the area near the Heaton Mersey Common.

The north includes the major districts of the four Heatons, with its eclectic mix of terraces and impressive Victorian villas, and the industrial suburb of Reddish, with its large mills and historic model village. There is also the large housing estate at Brinnington with its numerous tower blocks, and Lancashire Hill, which links the town centre with South Reddish.

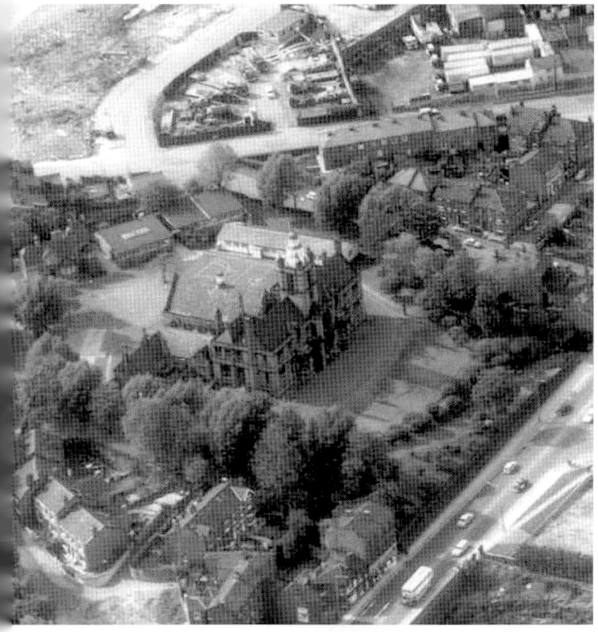
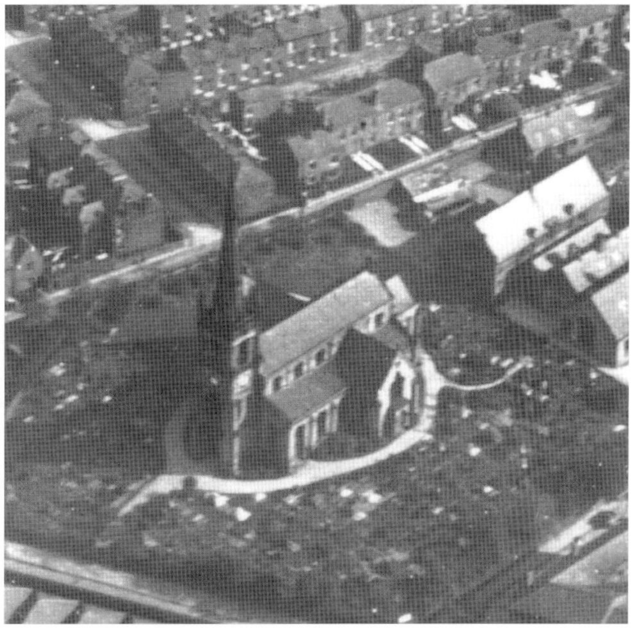
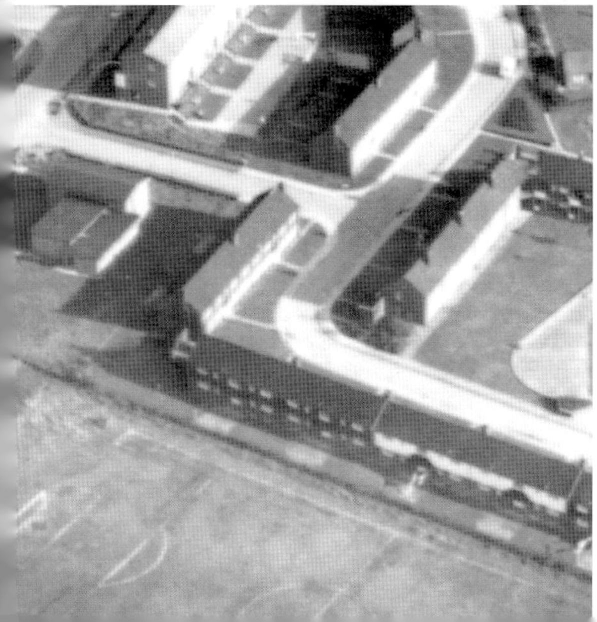
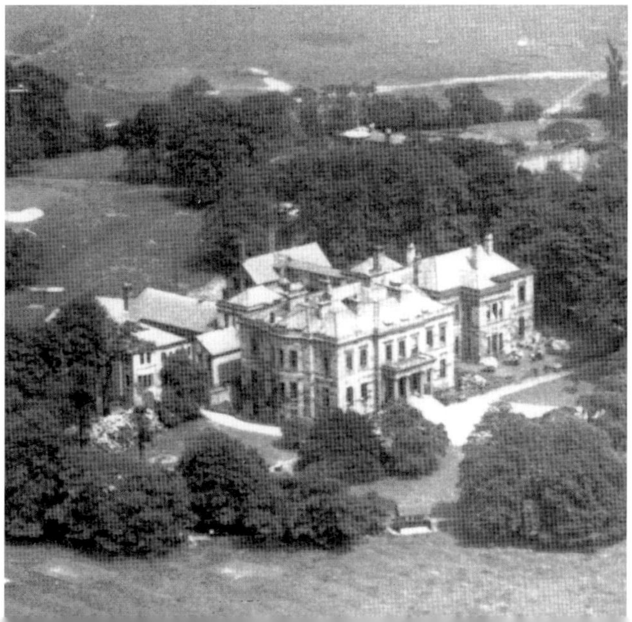

The Heatons

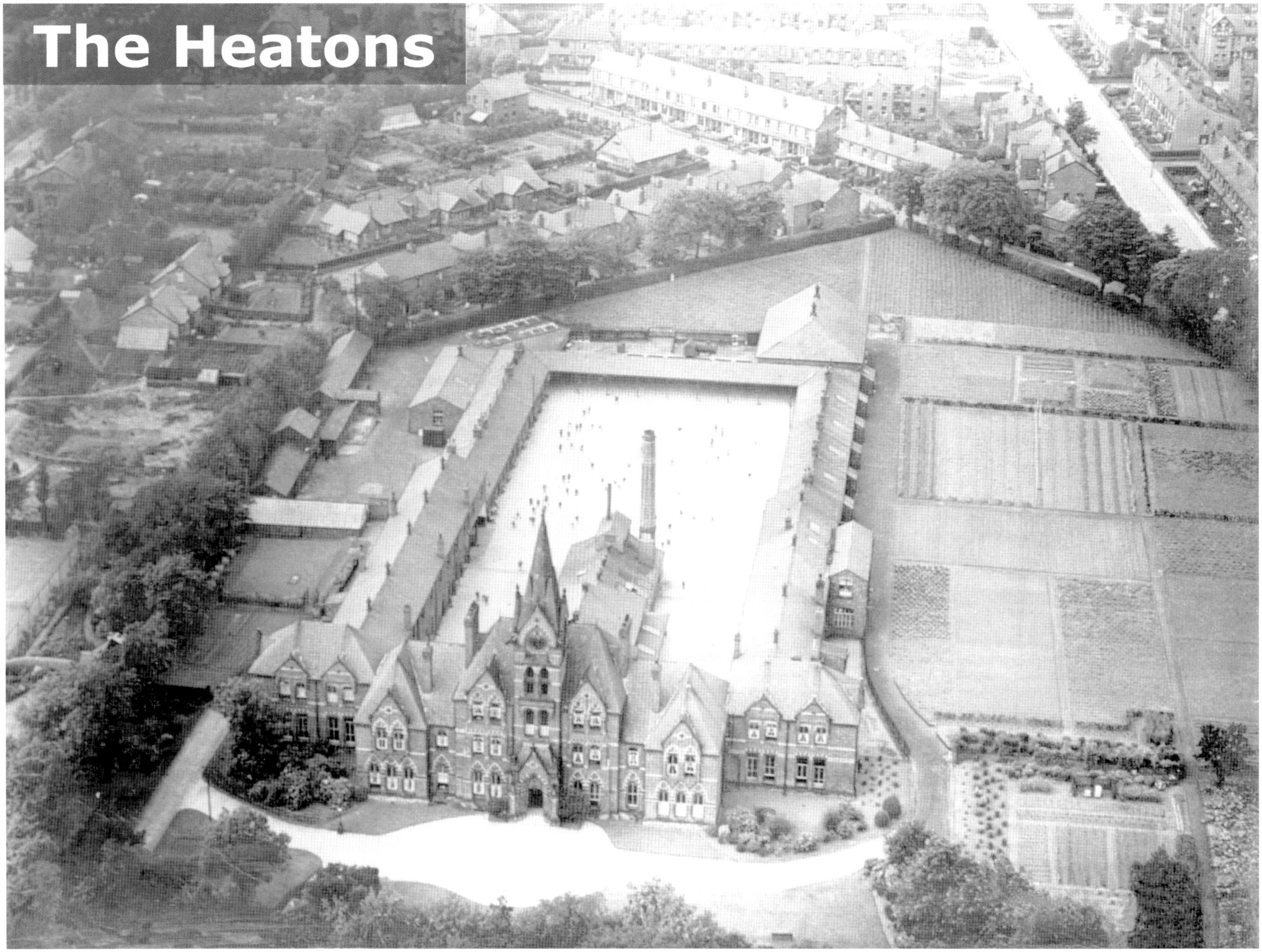

Heaton Mersey - Barnes Home Industrial School 1934

Built by Robert Barnes, Mayor of Manchester from 1851-1853, Barnes Home is one of the most striking buildings ever to have been built in Stockport. Its gothic style tower, reportedly 200 feet tall but probably less so, was visible for miles around. The building was built to educate neglected and destitute children and opened in August 1871, with Barnes donating £12,000 to the cost of the construction. It was initially intended to be a mixed school, but later became a school for boys only. Children can be seen playing in the yard of the school in the photograph. The school was situated at the top of Norris Hill on Didsbury Road, on the border between Heaton Mersey and Heaton Moor, with the tower facing the main road. The road at the top right is Moorside Road. The school closed in December 1955. Today, modern housing sits on the site, but the school is remembered by the name of the street upon which those new houses are built – Barnes Close. Barnes was also responsible for the building of Barnes Hospital in Cheadle (see page 180).

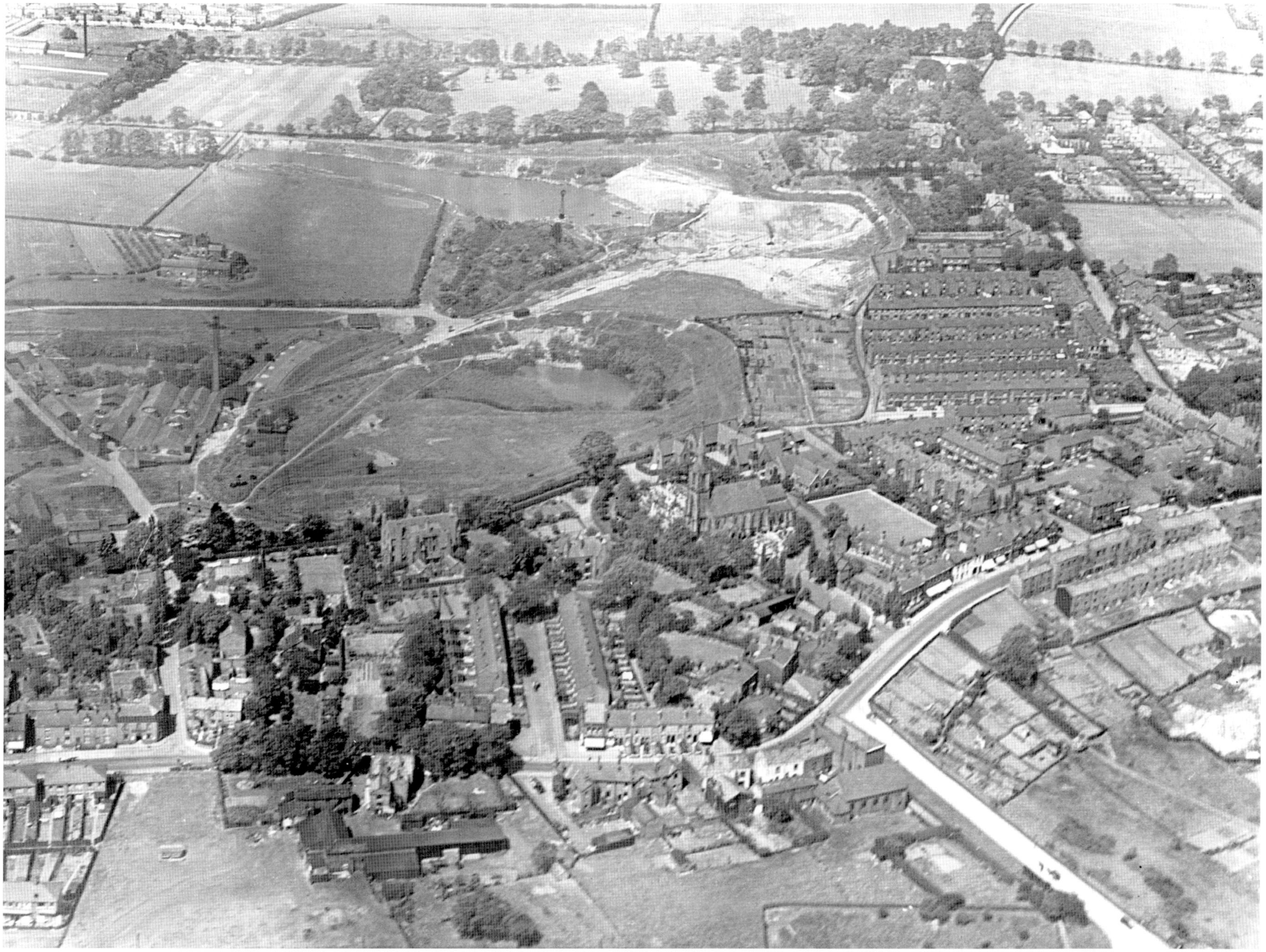

Heaton Mersey - Disbury Road 1933

Heaton Mersey was still semi-rural in the 1930s, as can be seen from the fields at the top of this picture of Didsbury Road in 1933. It wasn't to last though. New housing developments had already begun to be built at this time, and some of the newer homes can be seen here in the bottom left. In the centre of the picture is St John's Church, which was consecrated on August 26th 1850. Beyond this is Heaton Mersey Common, where a large quarry was cited in 1933. It was home to Bailey's Brickworks, who excavated the land to manufacture bricks and clay. The Quarry has since been filled in, whilst the site of the works (left of the quarry with the chimney) is now a golf driving range. The Common today is a peaceful haven amongst this busy suburb. The shops along the northern side of Didsbury Road are still there, shown on the far right. Opposite the shops is the site of the Heaton Mersey Bowl (out of picture), a venue used for sporting events, funfairs and concerts, just off Station Road on the bottom right.

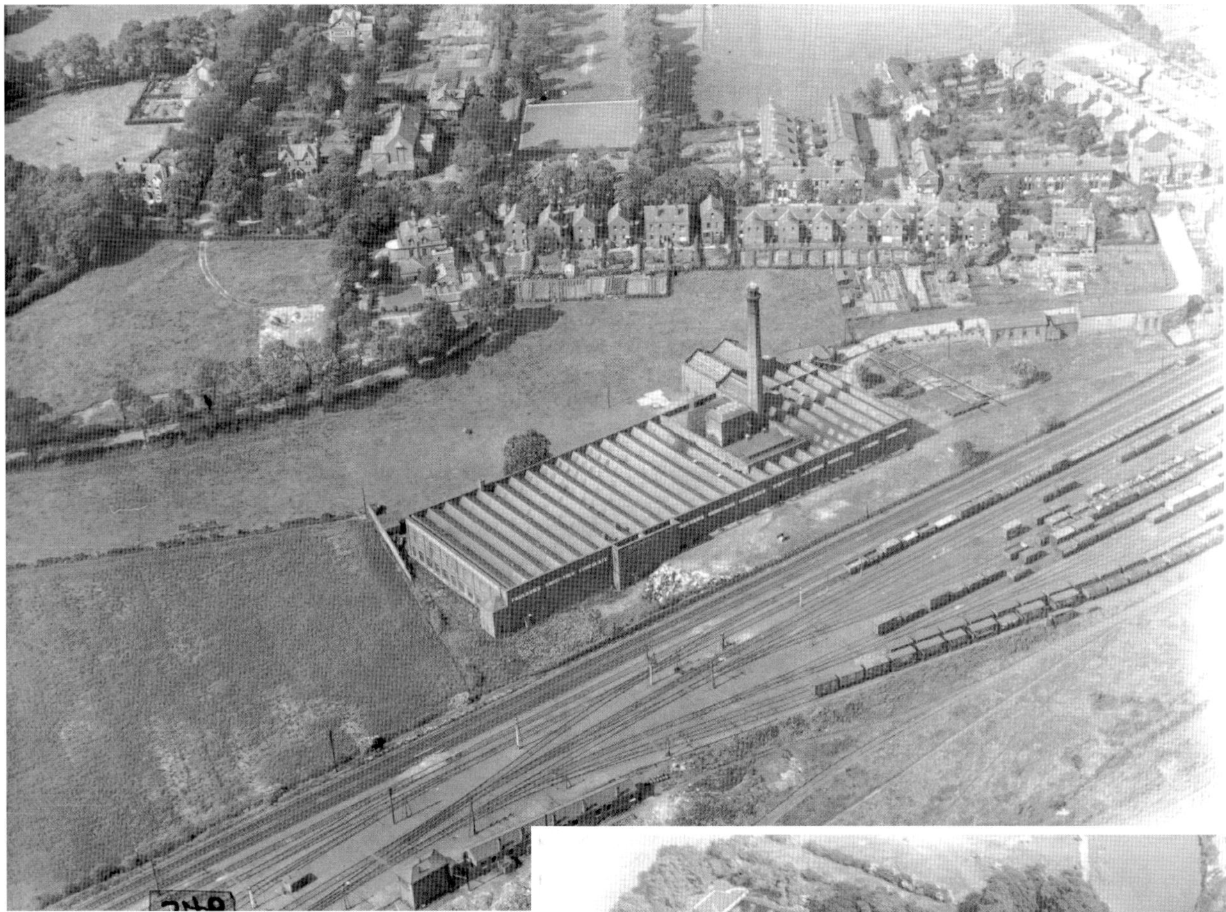

Faulders Mill
Heaton Mersey 1931

This building, built c1895, was home to the Silver Pan Fruit Preserving Factory and was cited just off Brighton Road, next to the railway yards of the Cheshire Lines Committee railway company. It later became the Squirrel Chocolate works. The white bricks on the side of the building spell out "Faulders Swiss Milk Chocolate". The road running along the width of the picture is Didsbury Road. The bowling green just to the north of the road is part of Crescent Park. To the right of this is a cricket ground, which is now under housing. The factory building still survives to this day, along with the chimney. The site of the rail tracks is now taken up by the M60 motorway, next to the Pyramid.

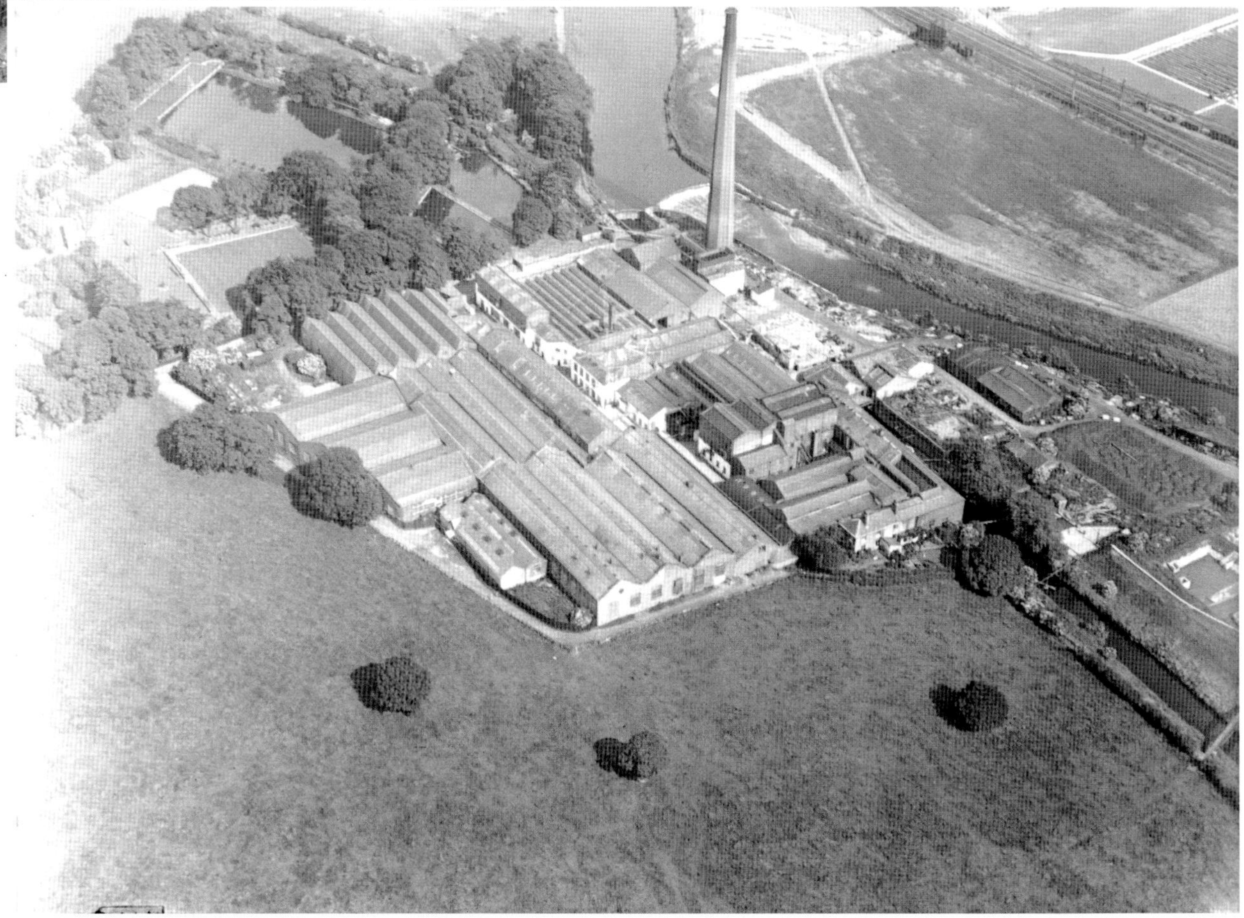

Heaton Mersey
Bleachworks 1931

The bleachworks was one of the two most important works in the Stockport area in the late 18th and early 19th centuries. The other major works was at Edgeley, and there was also one situated in Cheadle. The first recorded use of the Heaton Mersey works is in 1784. It was set up by Samuel Oldknow, who later extended the site to allow for printing and dyeing. The buildings shown here were added in 1830 by Robert Parker, who bought the factory from Oldknow. The works were situated by the banks of the River Mersey, just off Vale Road. The site has recently been redeveloped as part of Stockport's newest park - the Mersey Vale Nature Park. The 23 acres by the Mersey stretch all of the way to the edge of the Town Centre.

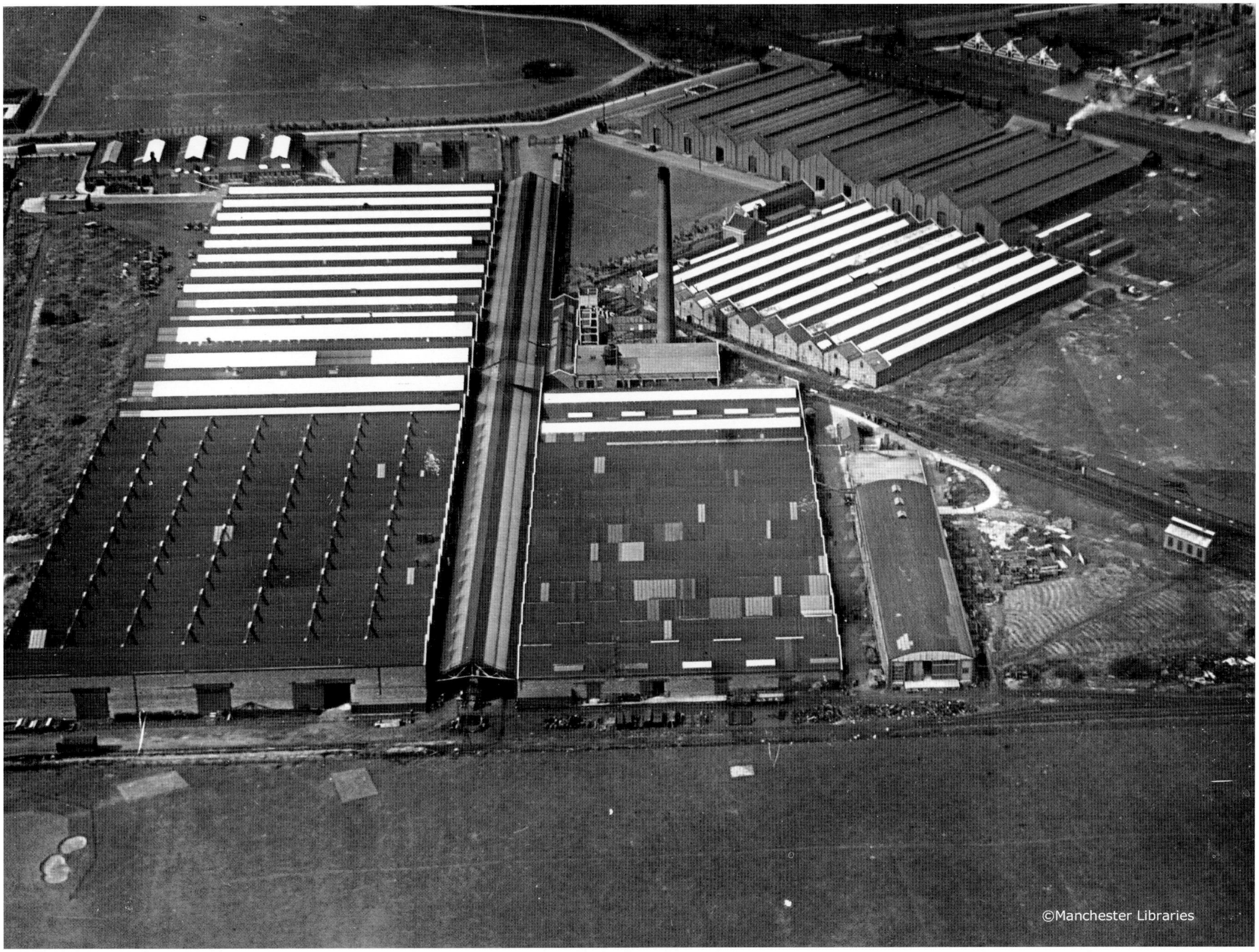

Heaton Chapel – Crossley & Willys-Overland Factory c1930

Situated just off the A6 behind the Mcvities factory and the main west coast rail line, the factory played an influential role in the production of aircraft in both the First and Second World War. Construction started on the factory in October 1917 when Crossley Motors Ltd won the right to build one of three new national aircraft factories. The factory became known as National Factory No 2 and more than 2500 people worked on the site producing de Havilland DH9 and DH10 bombers. Part of the adjacent Cringle Fields Park, just over the border in Manchester, was also used as a test airfield (on the left, out of picture). At end of the war the factory turned to car production when Crossley Motors, who had bought the factory at the end of the war, set up a partnership with Willys Overland. Production continued until 1932 when the partnership was broken due to continued losses. Crossley Motors continued alone for two more years until the factory was bought by Fairey Aviation in 1934. They produced many aircraft for the war effort, including the Battle, the Barracuda, the Firefly and the Gannet. Production stopped in 1960 when the factory closed. Note the railway lines at the bottom right, used for loading and unloading of aircraft & cars onto transporter trains.

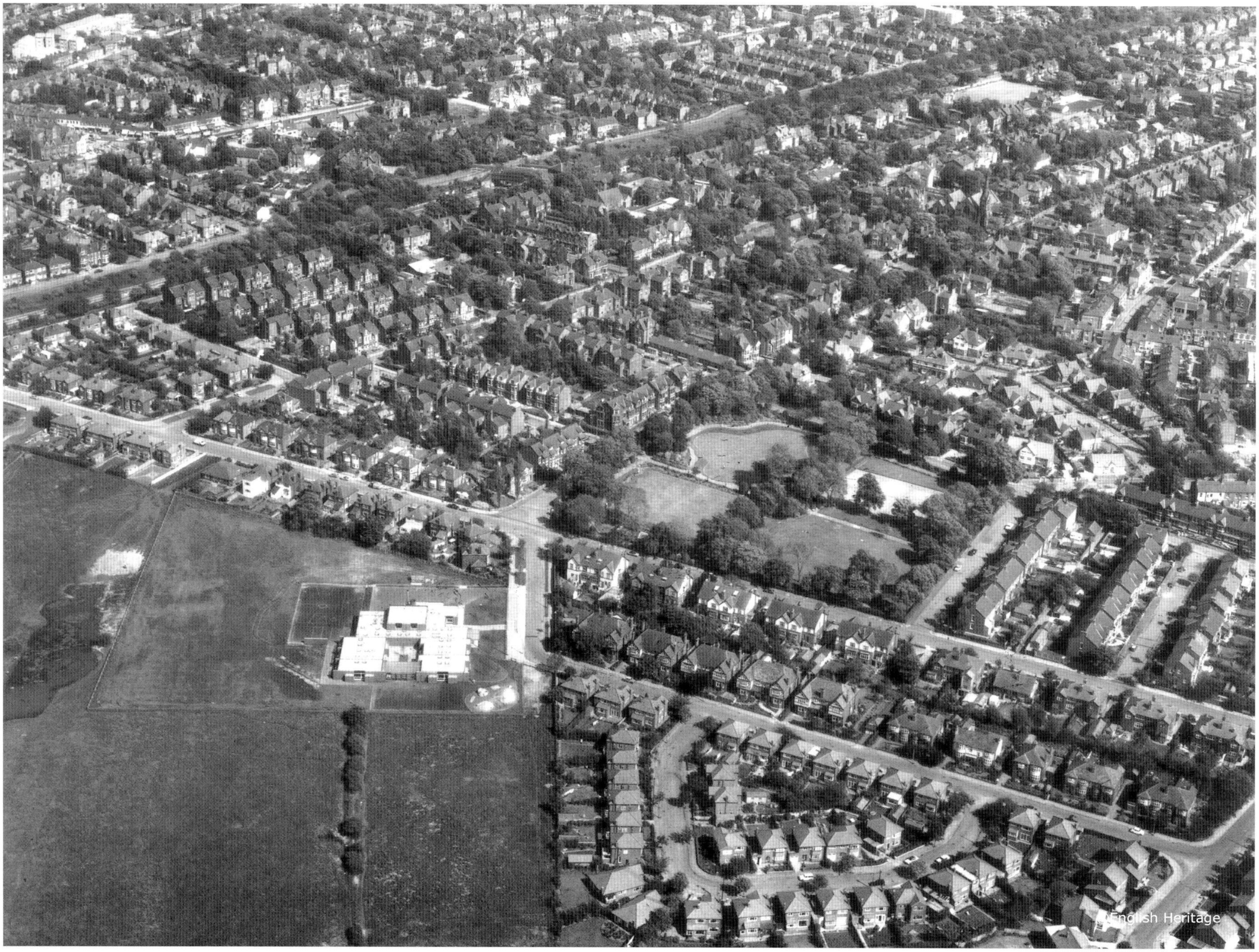

Heaton Moor 1973

Heaton Moor is a vibrant residential area synonymous with grand Victorian houses, many styles of which can be seen in this photo. The area has always proved a popular place in which to live and in recent years the property market here has been booming, buoyed by a good selection of local restaurants and bars on the village high street and good local schools. This picture is looking towards the centre of the village, which runs along Heaton Moor Road by the spire of Heaton Moor United Reform Church in the top right. Running from the middle left to top centre is the railway line, with Heaton Chapel on the other side. The land here, as the name suggests, was once moor land. The four Heatons were first known simply as "Heaton", which meant "farm on high land", reflecting its position above the valley of the Mersey. In the 12th century Heaton came under the ownership of the le Norreys family, which led to the name being changed to Heaton Norris. This was later split into four areas. St Thomas' Chapel was built by the junction of the modern A6 and Manchester road from 1758-1765, giving us Heaton Chapel. Heaton Mersey was named due to its location by the river, and Heaton Moor took its name from the moor land. There was also a Heaton Wood and a Heaton Moss.

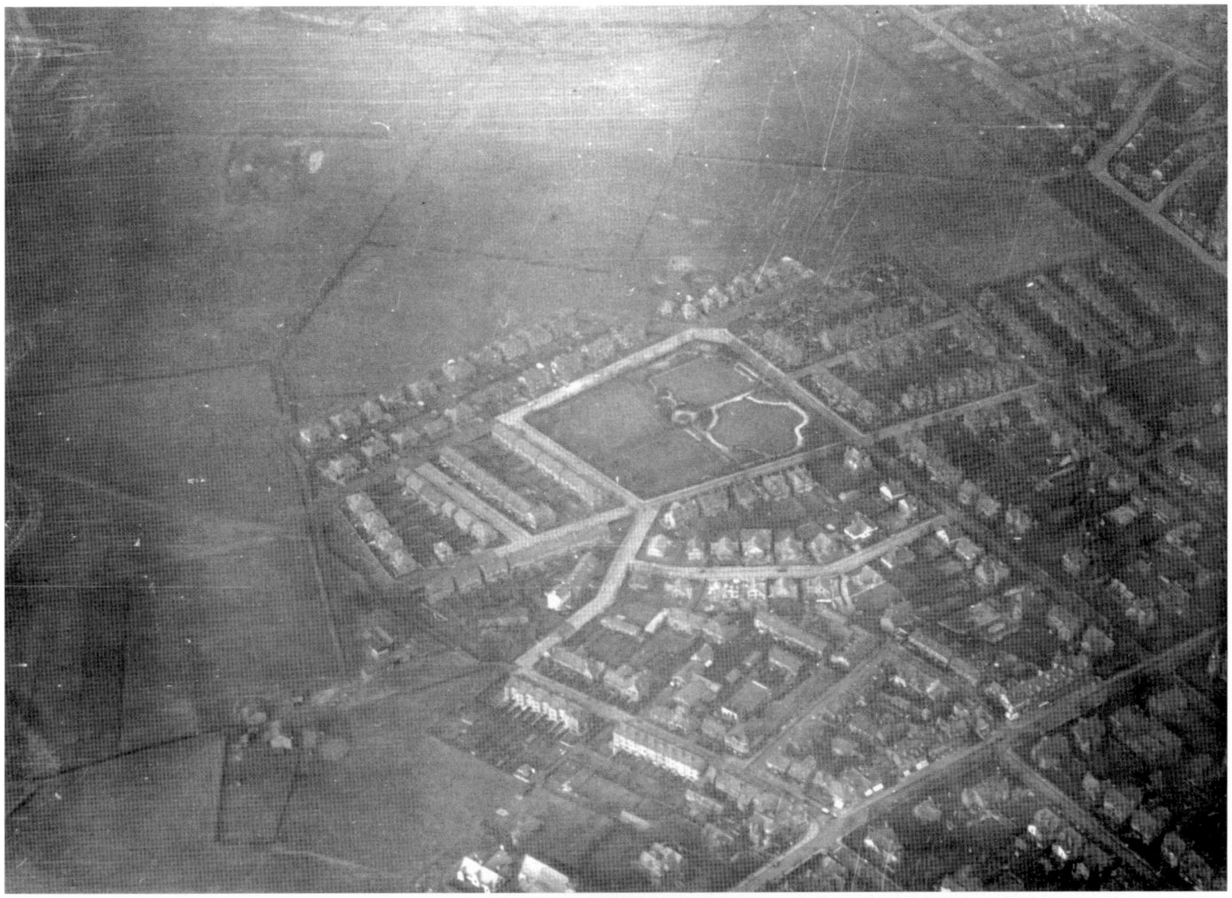

Heaton Moor Park 1934

Heaton Moor Park was laid out between 1894 & 1897 along Peel Moat Road. It was opened on July 17th - the date that Queen Victoria celebrated her Jubilee – and contains bowling greens, fine gardens and a bandstand. The original layout survives to this day, although the trees that were planted in the early years have now matured. The park is as recognisable from the image on the left as it is in the one from 1973 on the previous page. In the top left of the picture can be seen Peel Moat itself, which today is preserved as part of Heaton Moor Golf Course. The moat, which dates back to early medieval times, is something of a mystery, as there are few records of any major building ever having stood within its confines.

Mauldeth Hall 1928

Adjoining the golf course is Mauldeth Hall. Built in around 1830, it was converted into a hospital for incurables in 1882 when it was bought by the Northern Counties Supplementary Hospitals. The golf course itself was built within the hall's parkland. In 1928 the hall retained its own grounds that were separate from the course. These were mostly to the front of the building, but some bunkers can clearly be seen behind the hall on the left, showing hoe close the course was. In modern times the golf course has been extended to 18 holes and now surrounds the hall completely.

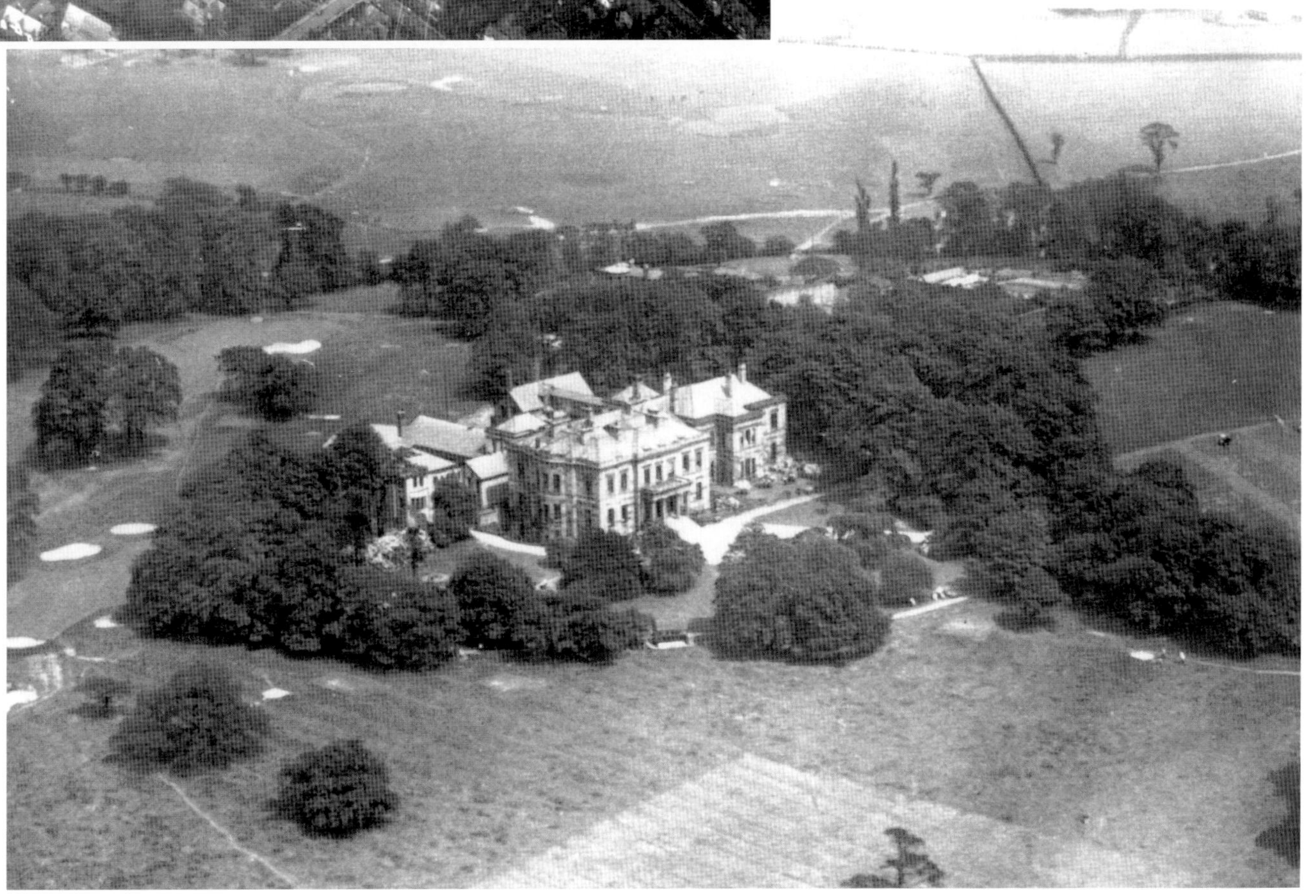

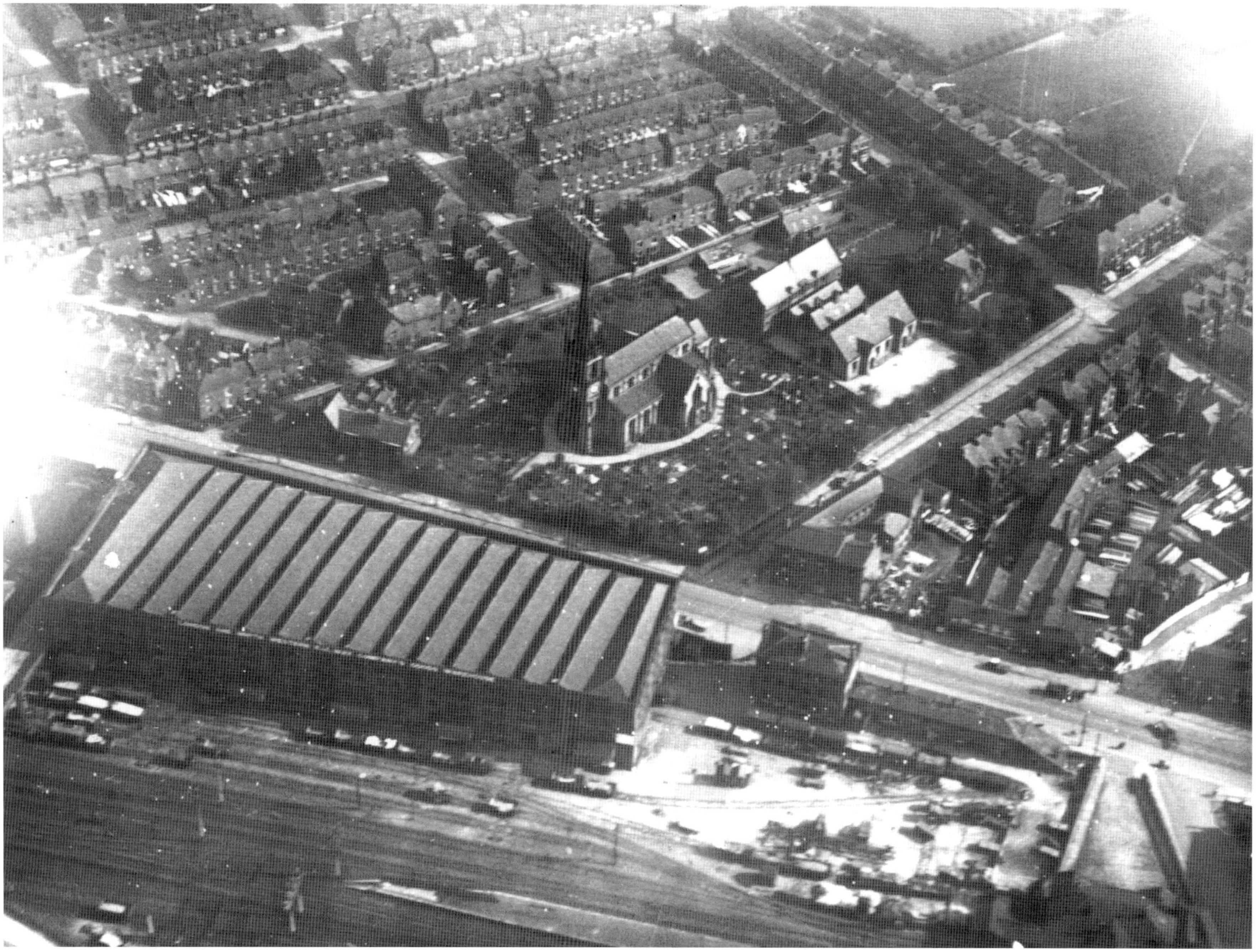

Heaton Norris - Christ Church & LNWR Goods Warehouse 1928

Christ Church and the London & North Western Railway Goods Warehouse are situated right on the very edge of the modern Stockport Town Centre. This image shows Christ Church as it had been since the building was completed in 1846. The foundation stone was laid on 29th July 1844 and the total cost was £6929. Today only the spire remains in the grounds of the graveyard.

The warehouse was rebuilt in 1877 after a fire and is also still standing. To the side of the building can be seen the railway yard that was used for bringing the train wagons up close for the loading and unloading of goods. In the bottom middle of the picture can be seen the platforms of Heaton Norris train station. This was the last stop heading south before the viaduct was built. The first service was Manchester Travis Street to Heaton Norris on 4th June 1840. Services to Crewe started on 10th August 1842 after the viaduct had opened. It survived into the 20th century, but with the much larger Edgeley station just a few hundred yards away following the opening of the viaduct, it eventually became obsolete and was closed.

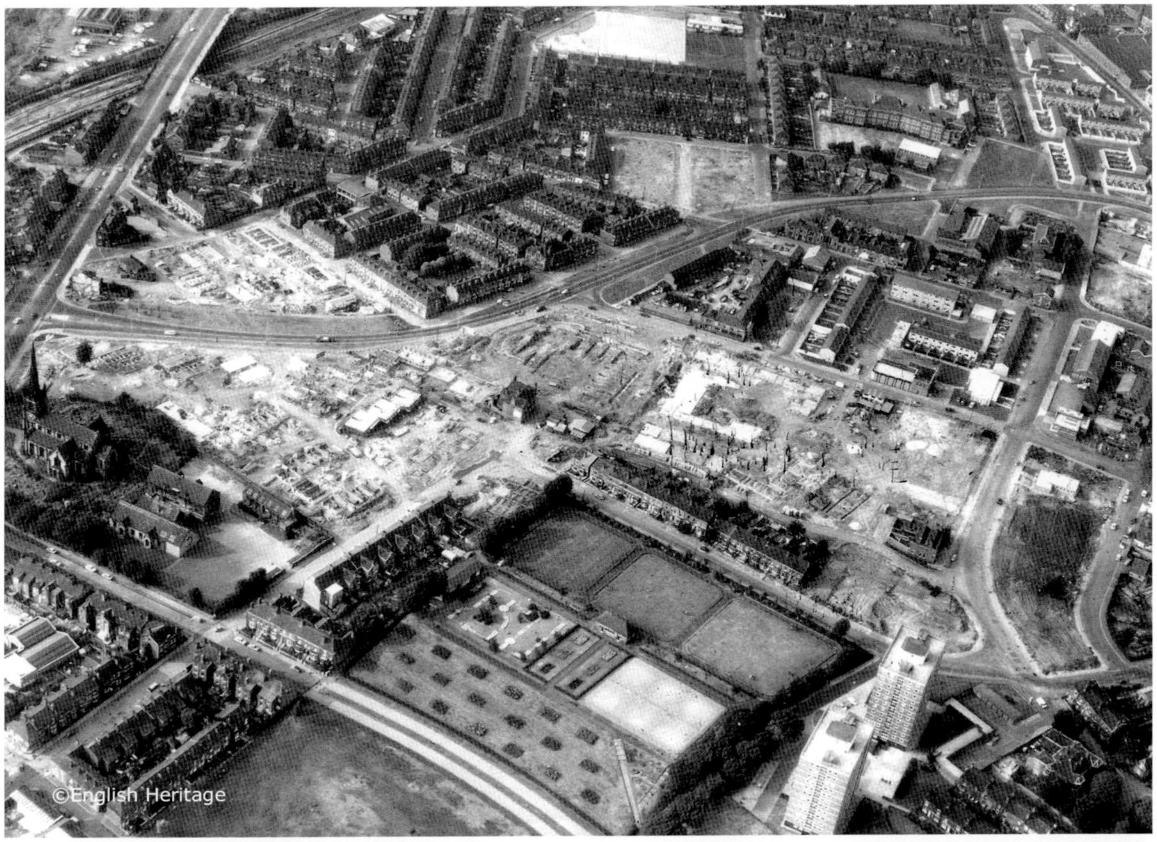

Heaton Norris
1973 & 1975

During the 1960s and 1970s redevelopment of previous slum areas continued apace, and Heaton Norris saw its fair share. The new estate by Belmont Road was built over two years from 1973. This first image shows the area after the land had been cleared, although the terraces on the opposite side of the road remained untouched. The new estate was completed by 1975 and included a small parade of shops. It backs onto Heaton Norris Recreation Ground. This park offers stunning elevated views over the town centre, both from the top near the bowling greens and lower down. The park is famous for being the first home of Heaton Norris Rovers FC, later to become Stockport County, and is now also used for the annual Stockport Civic Bonfire on Guy Fawkes Night, which attracts over 7000 people. The park opened on June 5th 1875, and at the time totalled 16 acres. Several acres were lost when the M63 was built.

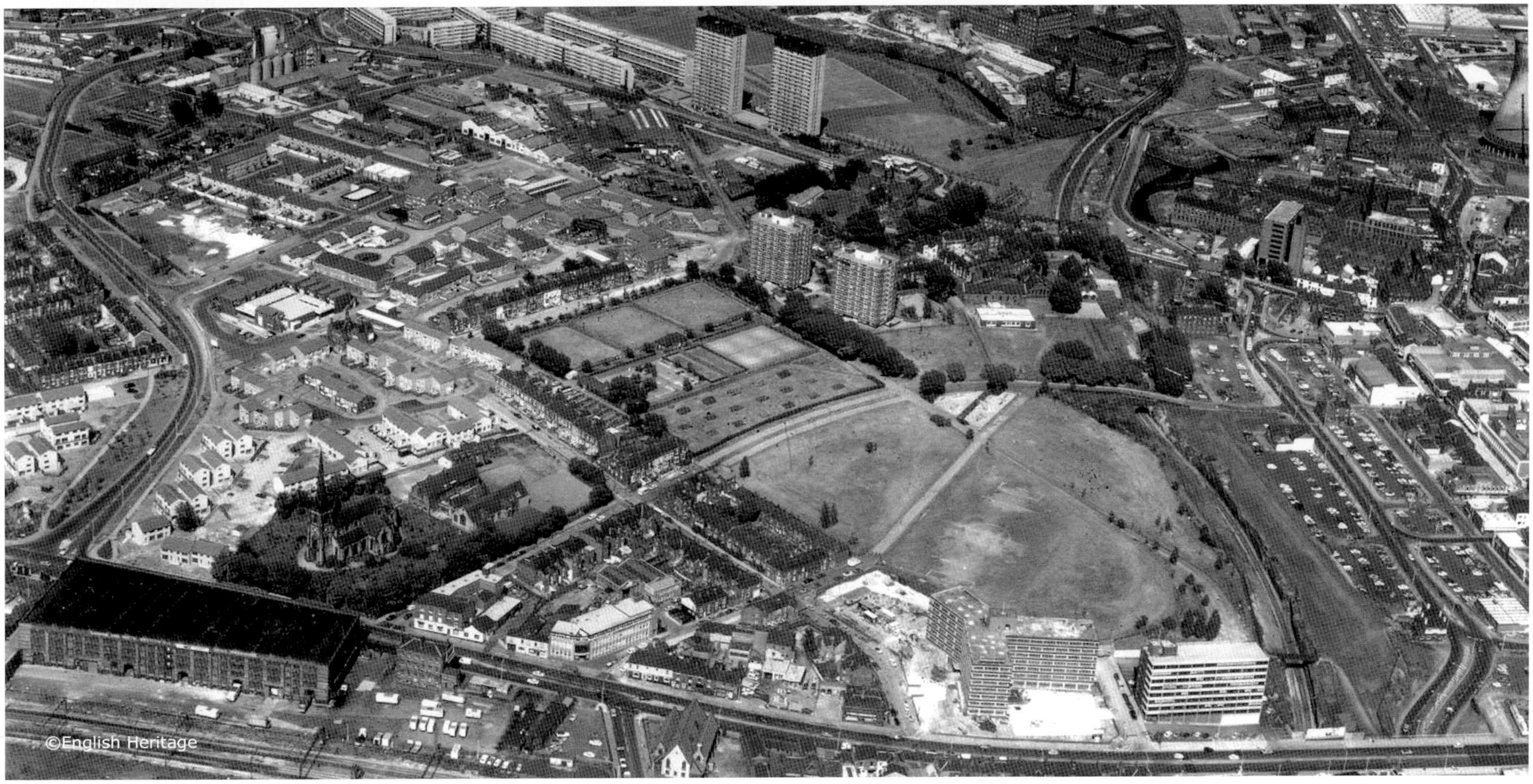

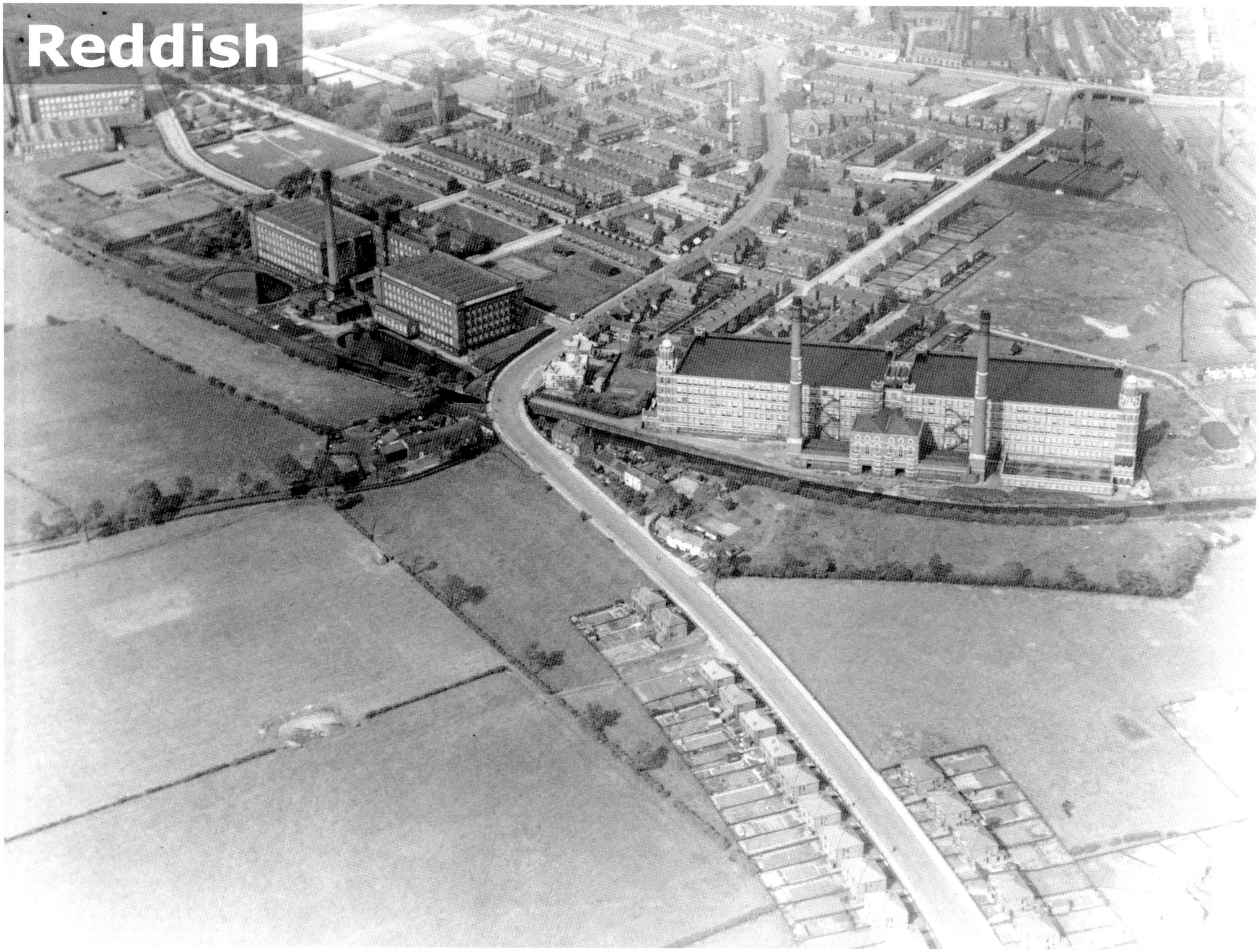

Reddish 1931

Despite the presence of the Ashton Canal, there was still very little industry in Reddish up until the 1840s. However, when the first of several large mills was constructed along its banks, things began to change. Reddish boomed, becoming a major centre for manufacturing, especially concerning cotton. Two of the largest mills built here were Houldsworth Mill (centre left) and Broadstone Mill (on the right). Unlike most other mills of the time, Houldsworth Mill was named after its founder, William Henry Houldsworth. He is the man chiefly responsible for the look of Reddish today, and his name still crops up everywhere. After his first great mill opened he set about building a community for the workers. This included houses, a working men's club (opened 1874 & designed by AH Stott & Sons), and the magnificent St Elisabeth's Church. Both can be seen just above Houldsworth Mill. The church was designed by Alfred Waterhouse, a leading architect of the day who also designed Manchester Town Hall. It was consecrated in 1883, two years after work had started on its construction, and is now Grade 1 Listed.

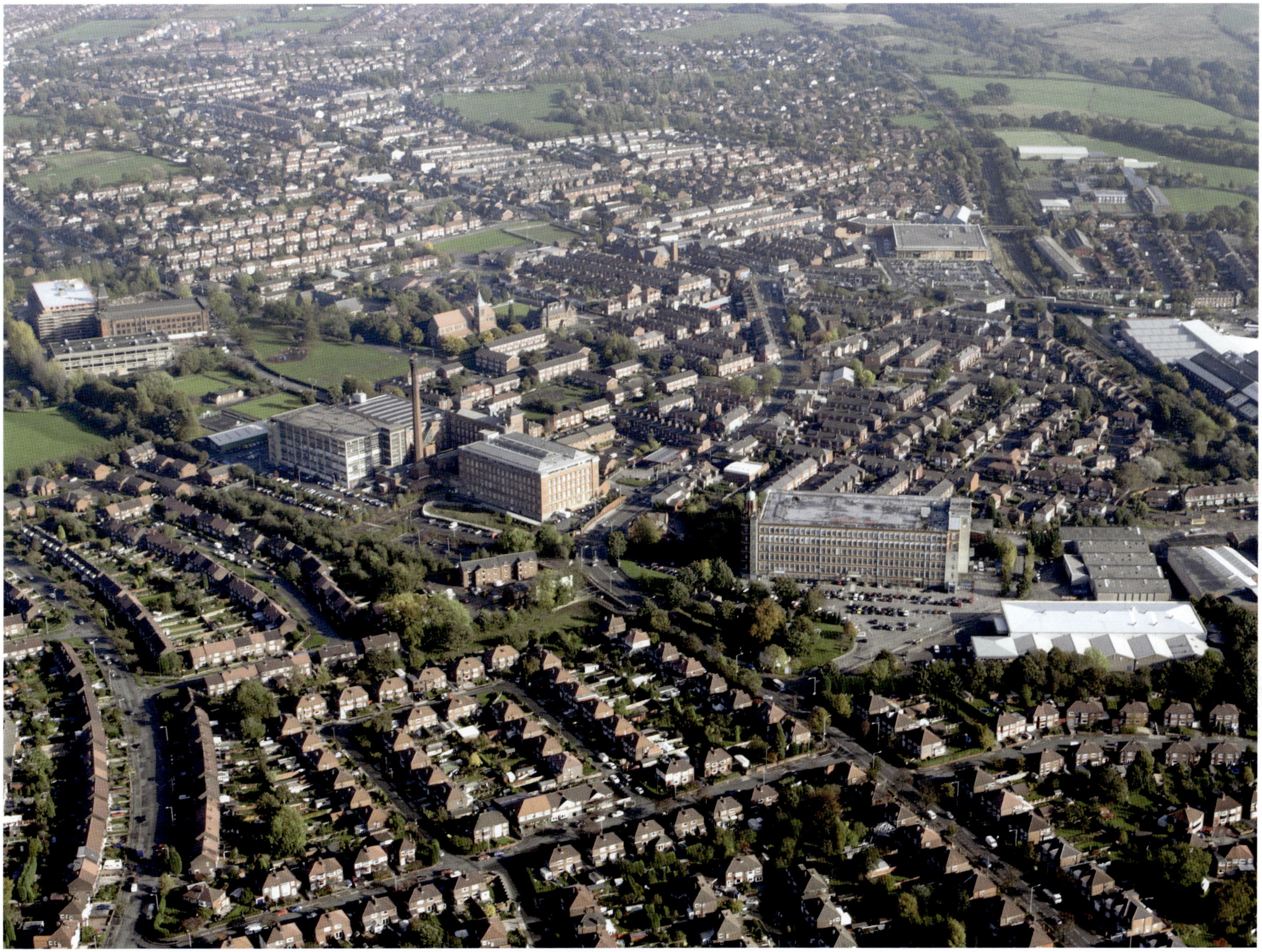

Houldsworth paid for the entire cost of these buildings himself, and today it forms part of the "Houldsworth Village" conservation area. At its heart is Houldsworth Square in the centre of Reddish, where a clock tower was erected in Houldsworth's honour in 1920, 3 years after his death. Broadstone Road, which passes between the two great mills, can be seen winding its way north towards the Square in the very centre of the village.

The scene today is instantly recognisable, with the mills still dominating the local landscape. The first signs of typical 1930s ribbon developments in 1931 (homes built either side of a new road, seen on the bottom right) were continued, and led to the old farmland being completely covered with housing that now fills the bottom of the picture. The neighbouring Victoria and Elisabeth Mills (top left of the picture) have recently been redeveloped as part of a complex of 486 new flats. Together they were originally known as "New Mill" when opened in 1874, but were later renamed. This should not be confused with the other Victoria Mill of 1845 by the Ashton Canal (see page 85)

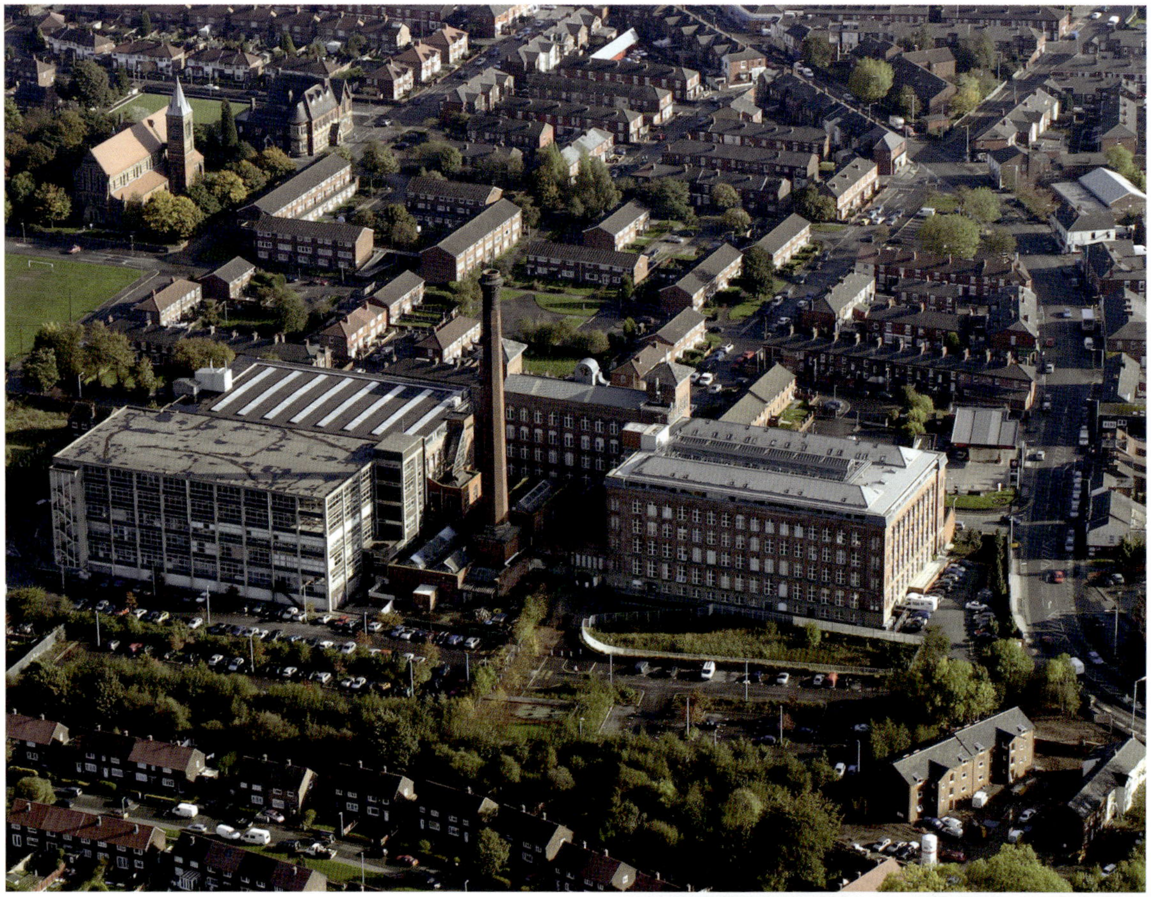

Houldsworth Mill

Houldsworth Mill was was founded by William Houldsworth and was built on previously open farmland. It was built from 1863-1865 but did not open until 1867. The mill is a "double mill" – it had a central area housing offices with the engine house to the rear, whilst the two wings contained the machinery for cotton manufacturing. The exterior of the mill features a magnificent central facade with impressive clock face above. To continue the symmetry of the building, the 110 foot chimney at the back is aligned with the clock. Also at the rear were two reservoirs for storing water to power the steam engines inside (see the image from 1931 on page 82).

It has now been redeveloped as a business centre, and also includes an indoor shopping centre, although the hideous looking carbuncle that has been added to the rear of the building could do with being removed.

Broadstone Mill

Broadstone Mill is now only half the building it once was. Like Houldsworth Mill, it was a double mill with two symmetrical wings and a central engine house, but now only the northern end of the building remains. When it was opened in 1907 after four years of construction it was the largest cotton spinning mill in the world and housed 262,500 spindles. The record was to last for only a year, as a larger mill was opened in Middleton in 1908.

The Mill was designed by AH Stott & Sons who were responsible for many of the other large mills in the area. Cotton production ceased in 1959 when the mill closed. Today, the remaining half of the building is still in use, and houses business and retail premises

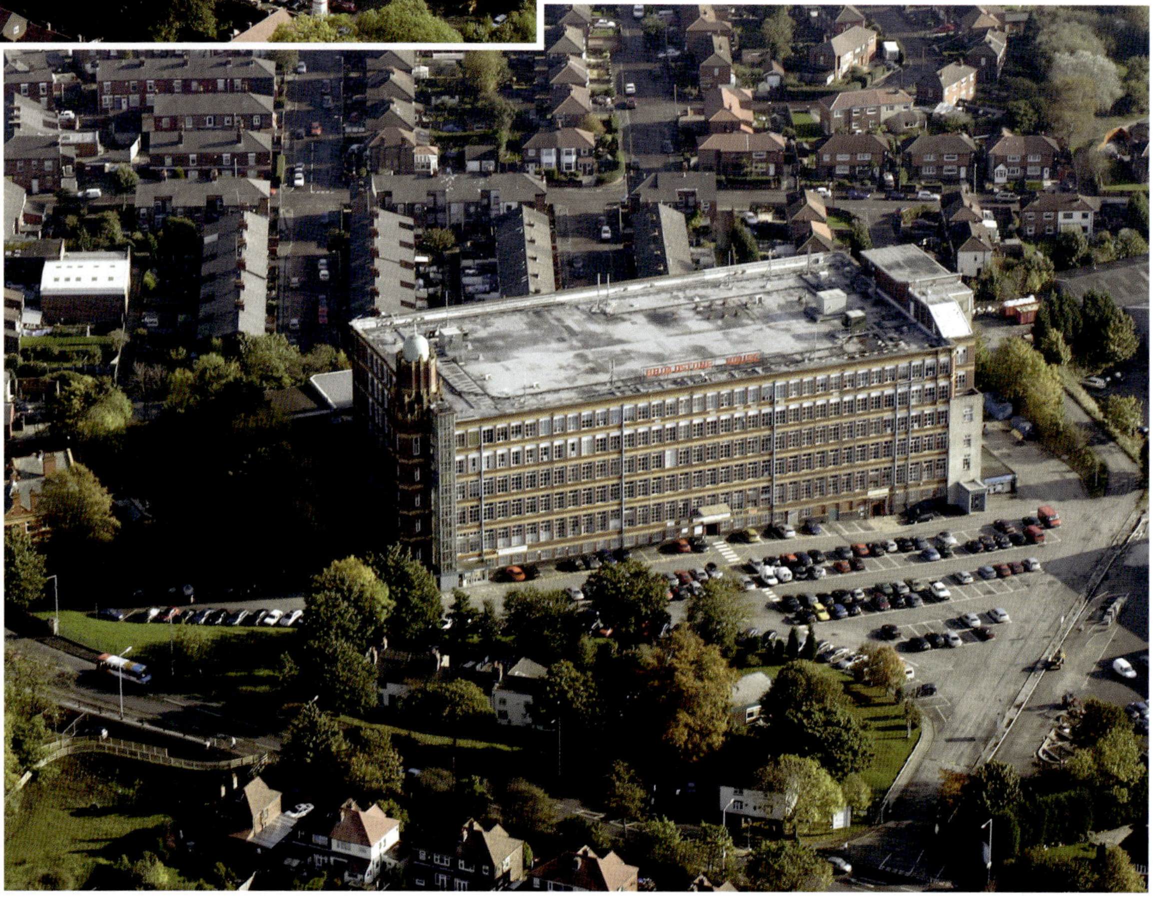

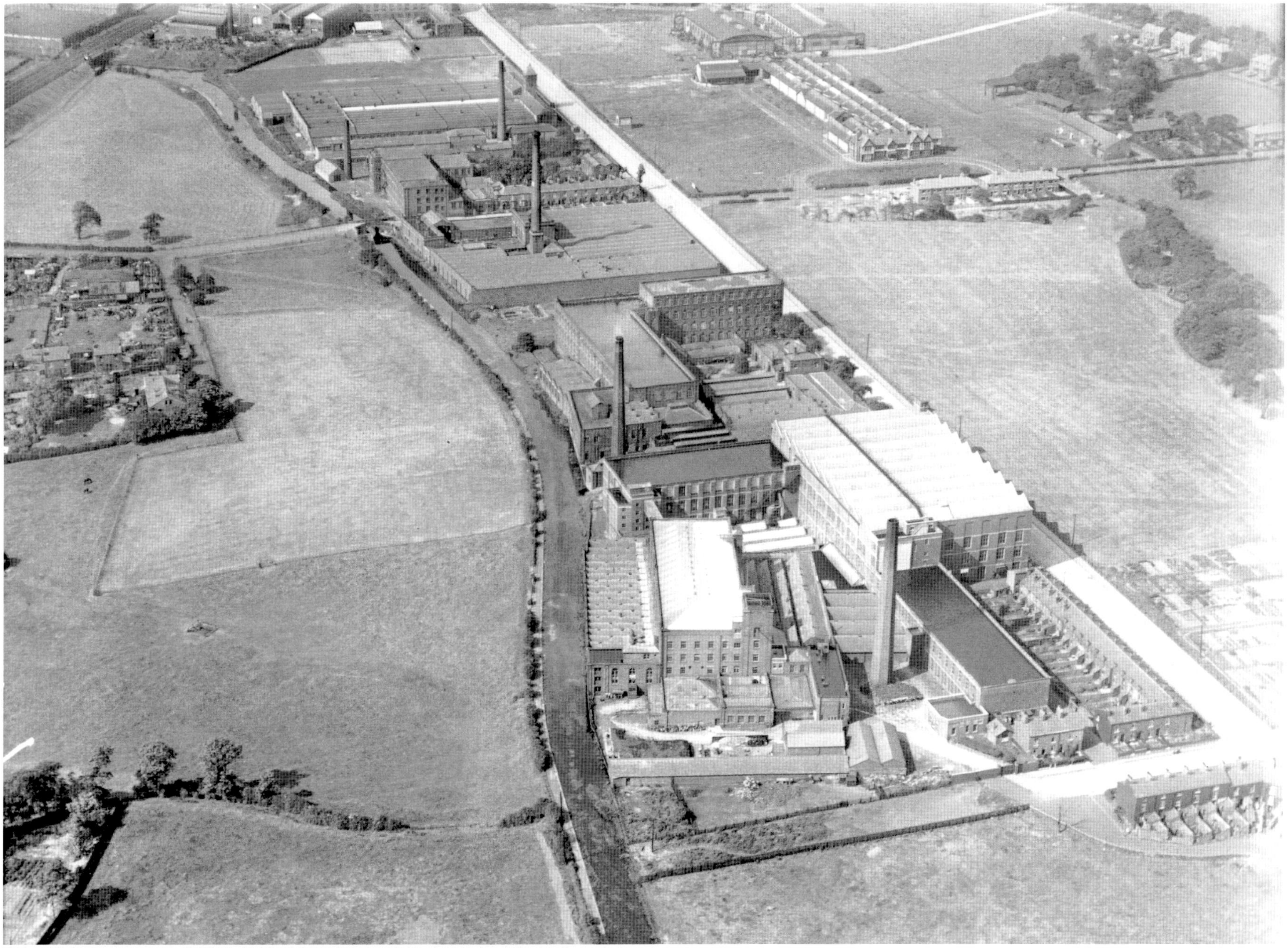

Ashton Canal 1931

The Stockport arm of the Ashton Canal was proposed in 1793 when permission was sought from parliament to build the new branch. It opened in 1797, although it was not completed until a year later. A few small factories were built along its sides, but it wasn't until the Gregg family built their first mill here that Reddish began to experience serious growth. In 1845 Robert Hyde Gregg and his brother John built Victoria & Albert Mills on what is now Gregg Street. They were the sons of Samuel Gregg, who had built the mill and community at Quarry Bank Mill in Styal. Samuel had bought large chunks of farmland in Reddish by the 1830s, but it wasn't until after his death in 1834 that the first mills were erected here. Other mills soon followed, including Hannover Silk Mill in 1865. From bottom to top, we can see the Albert Mill complex, Hannover Mill, Spur Doubling Mill (opened in 1907, this was a rarely seen single storey mill, almost like a large shed) and finally the four-storey Victoria Mill, on the far side of the bridge over the canal. The low level building at the very top of the picture with the tower along Gregg Street was the home of the Manchester Guardian's Printing Works (now known simply as the "Guardian"), built in 1899. Greg Street today is still an industrial area, though only a few of the buildings seen here remain.

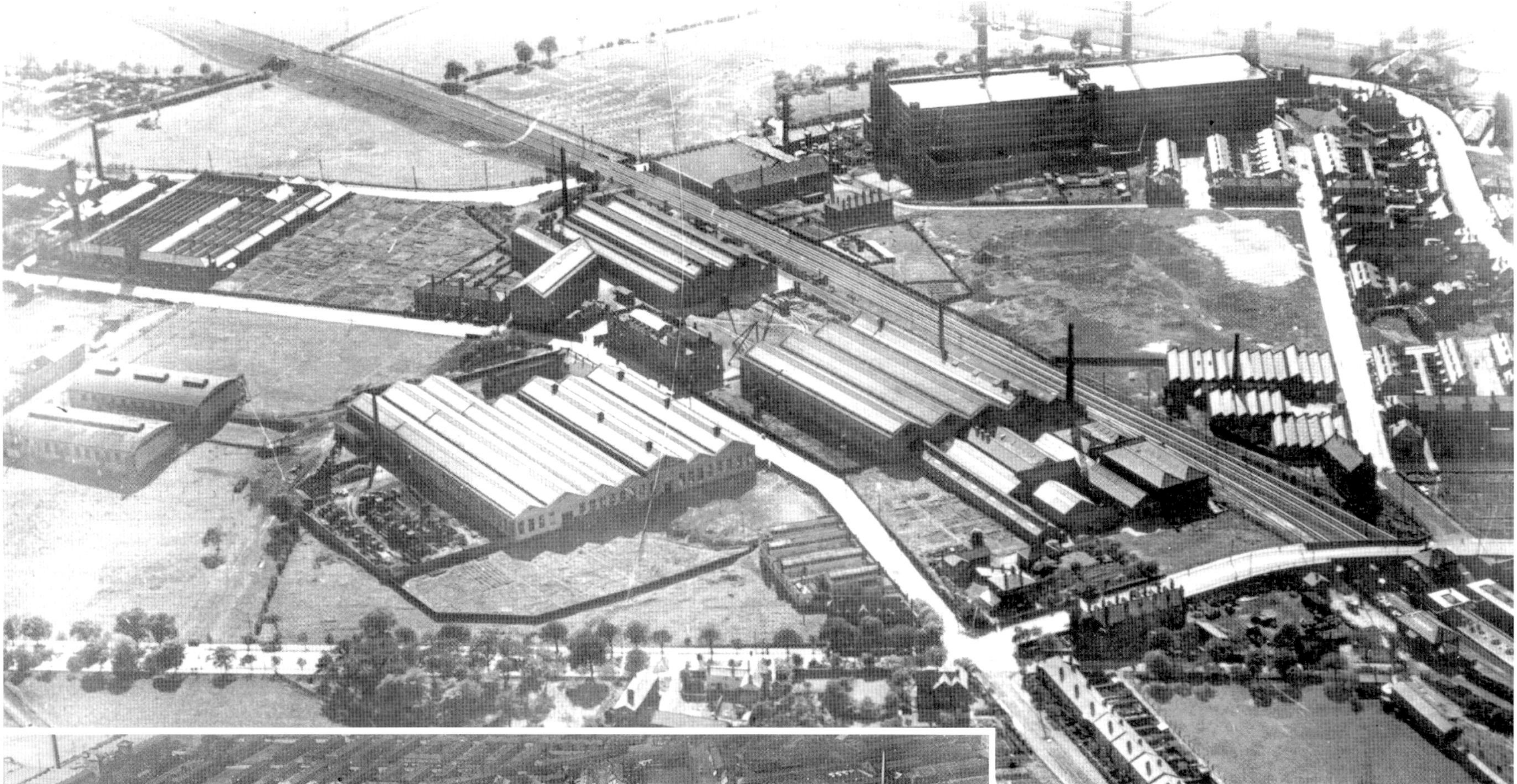

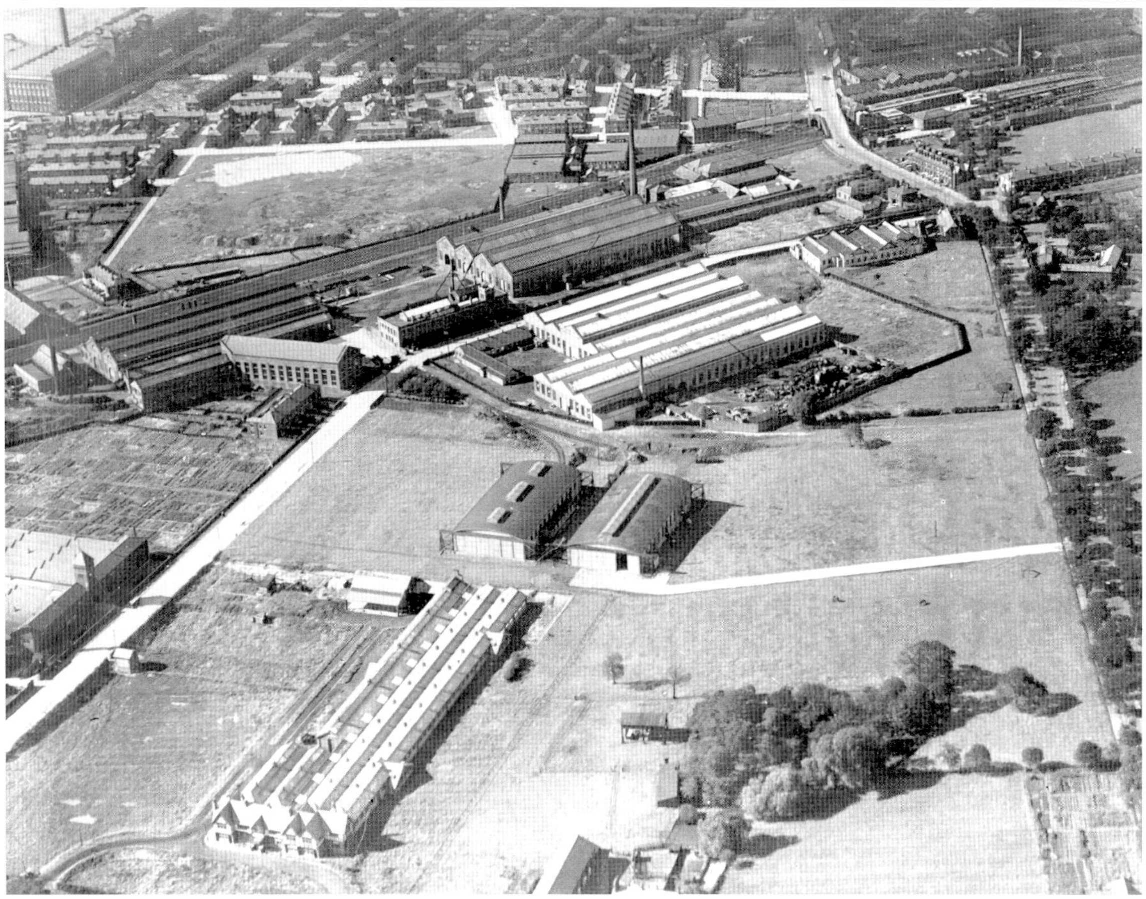

Reddish Station 1934

Reddish's growth was also helped by the arrival of the railways. Reddish Station (bottom right, main picture and top right, small picture) was opened in 1849 just south of the centre of the village, and immediately became the focus for new development. It was later renamed as Reddish South when a second station was opened to the north in 1875. Reddish was also the terminus for one of the first tram services in Stockport, which travelled from Mersey Square to Reddish Green from 1902. The buildings seen here around the northern end of Gregg Street were built as a direct consequence of the railway's development. The units either side of the street were home to Craven Brothers Engineers, who moved to the site in 1900. They were one of the leading manufacturers of cranes and machine tools for the railway industry - hence the need to be by the tracks - and employed close to 1500 people. The site closed in 1970.

Reddish Vale Viaduct 1928

With its 16 Arches, Reddish Vale Viaduct is the second largest in Stockport. Built in 1875 to carry the Hope Valley Railway Line, the viaduct straddles the River Tame as it flows through Reddish Vale Country Park, just to the east of Reddish village. Little appears to have changed since the first image was taken in 1928, but look closely and you can see that there were still several houses standing that were constructed during the industrial use of the site. The ponds were constructed in the 19th century to supply water to two mills that stood by the river. Reddish Vale Country Park (next page) extends right up to Stockport town centre along the path of the River Tame to where it meets the River Goyt. The park was opened in 1985, and contains a massive 398 acres of parkland, along with a nature reserve and butterfly park. On the left can be seen the familiar tower blocks of Brinnington.

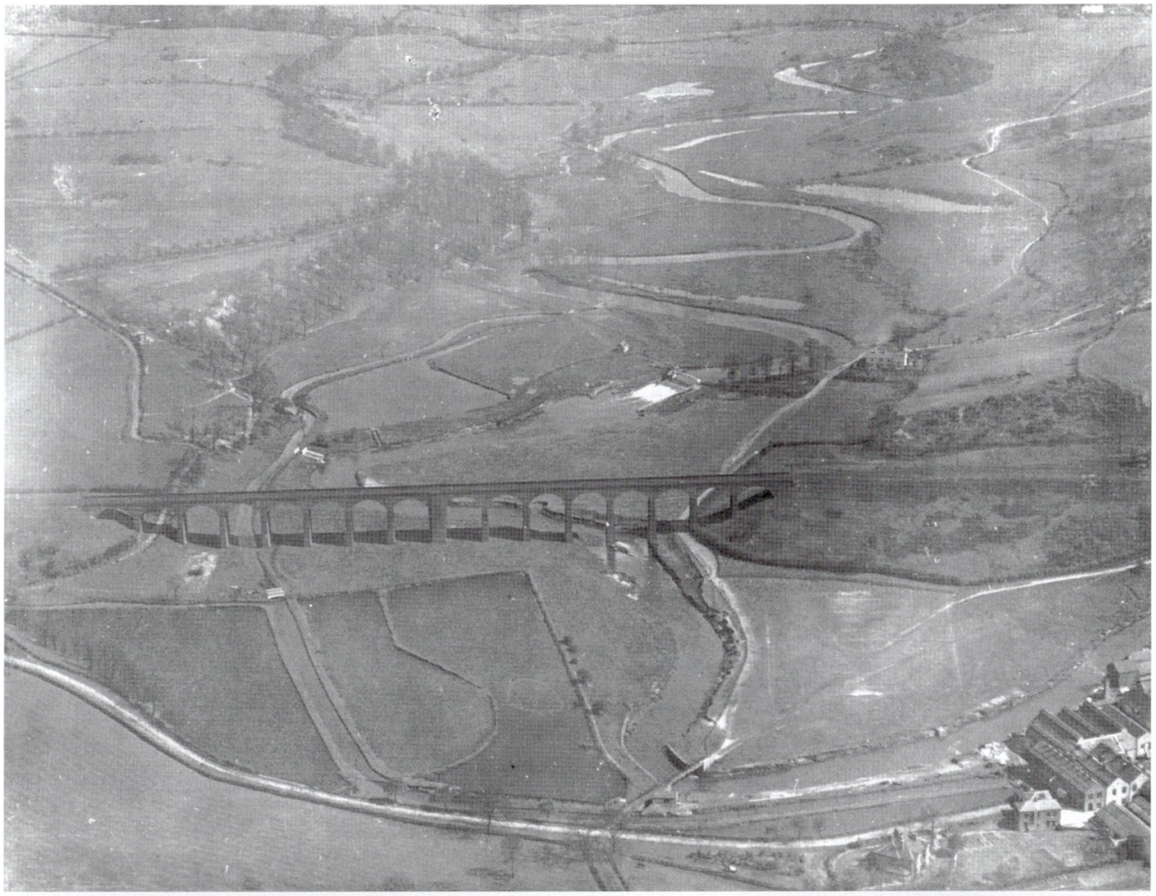

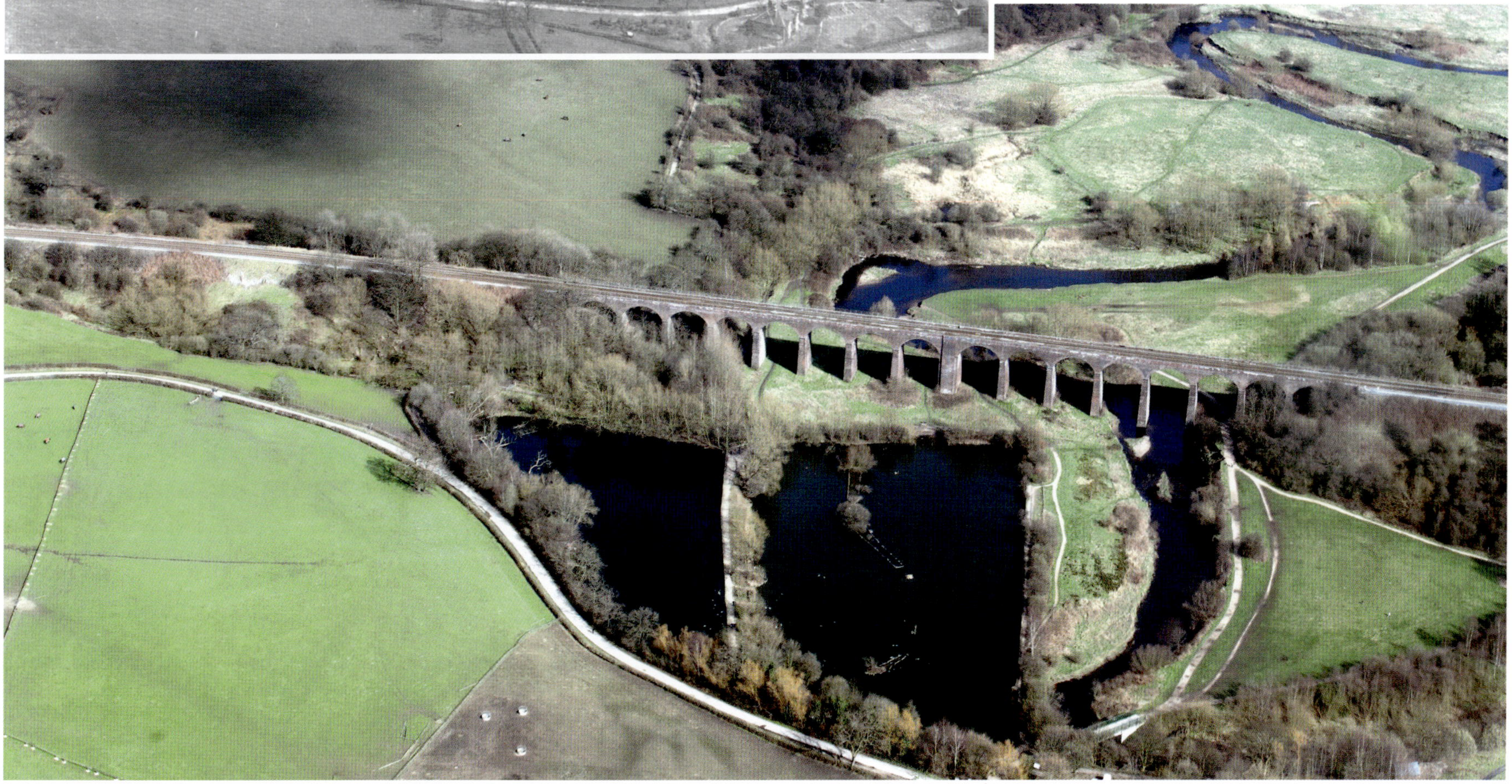

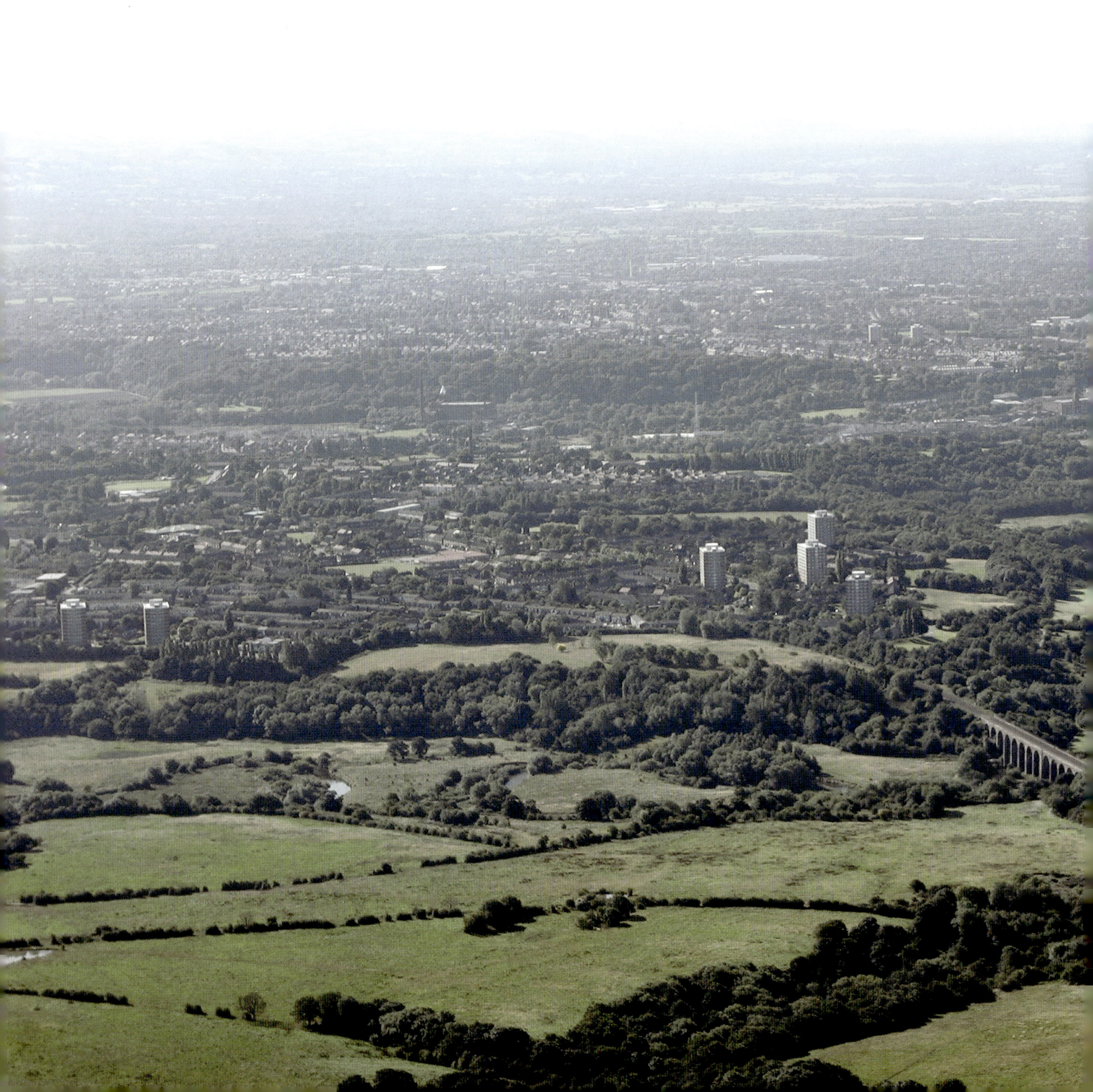

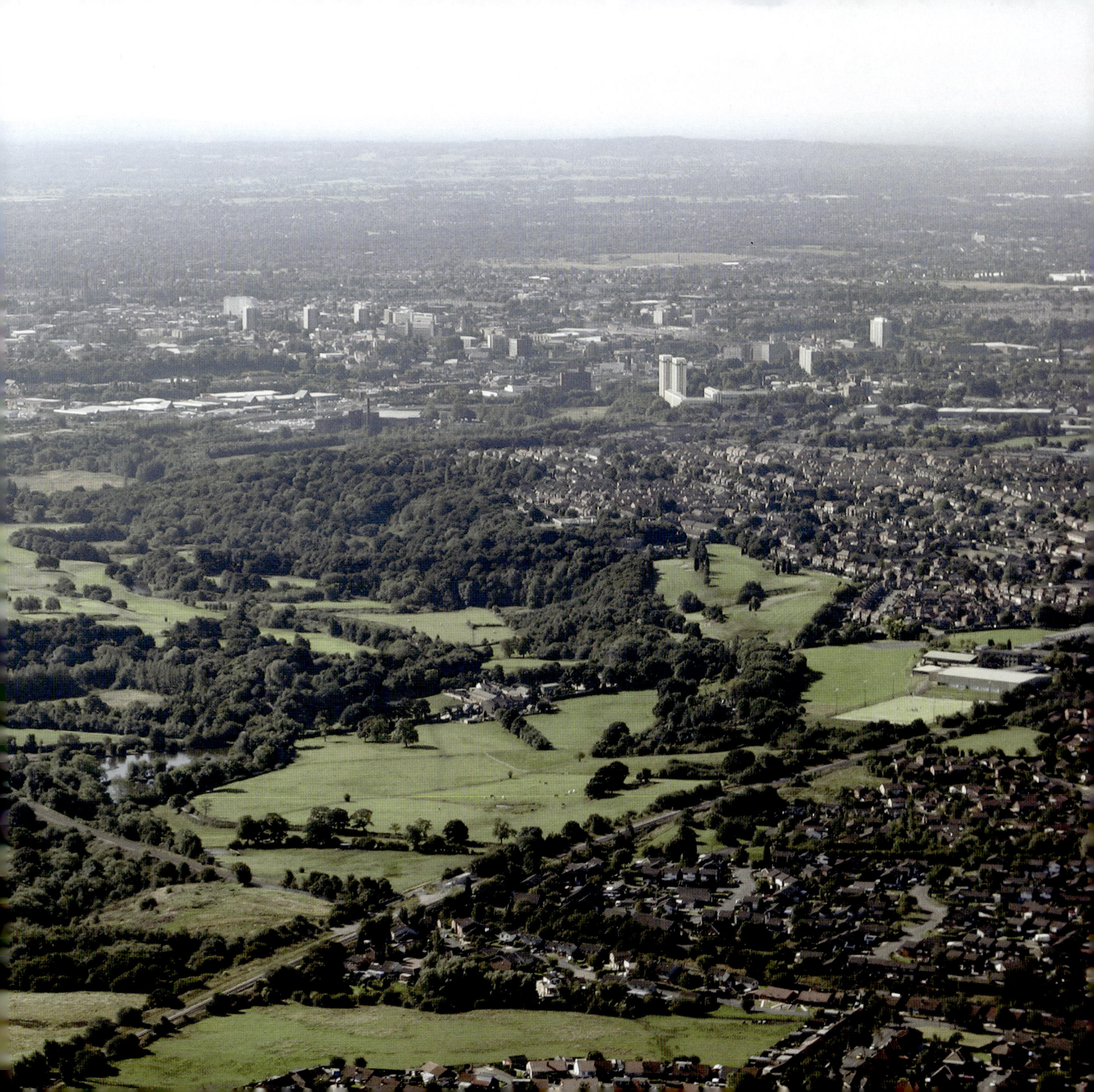

Brinnington

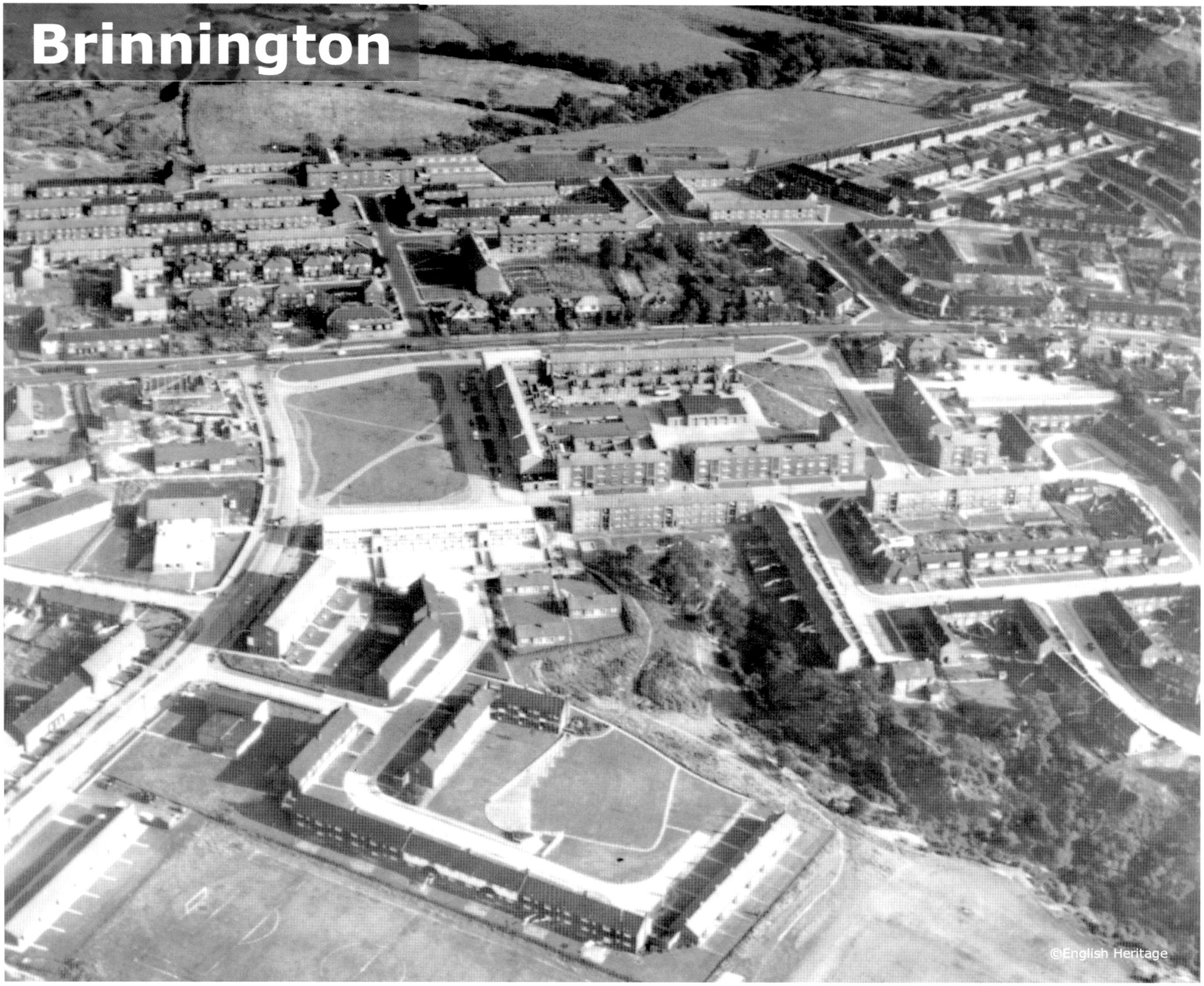

Brinnington 1964

Brinnington is now a large council-built housing estate, but was once a place where the landed gentry resided. Due to its elevated position, Brinnington was home to many fine, large houses in the 18th and 19th centuries that allowed for excellent views over the centre of Stockport. The land for the new estate was purchased from Bredbury & Romiley UDC in 1952, with construction starting soon afterwards. The massive new estate is shown here in 1964 just after completion, looking towards the "Top Shops" on Brinnington Road. The seven tower blocks have recently been re-clad, and are now painted white. The top shops were demolished in 2006 as part of a new development and replaced with more modern units with flats above.

Lancashire Hill

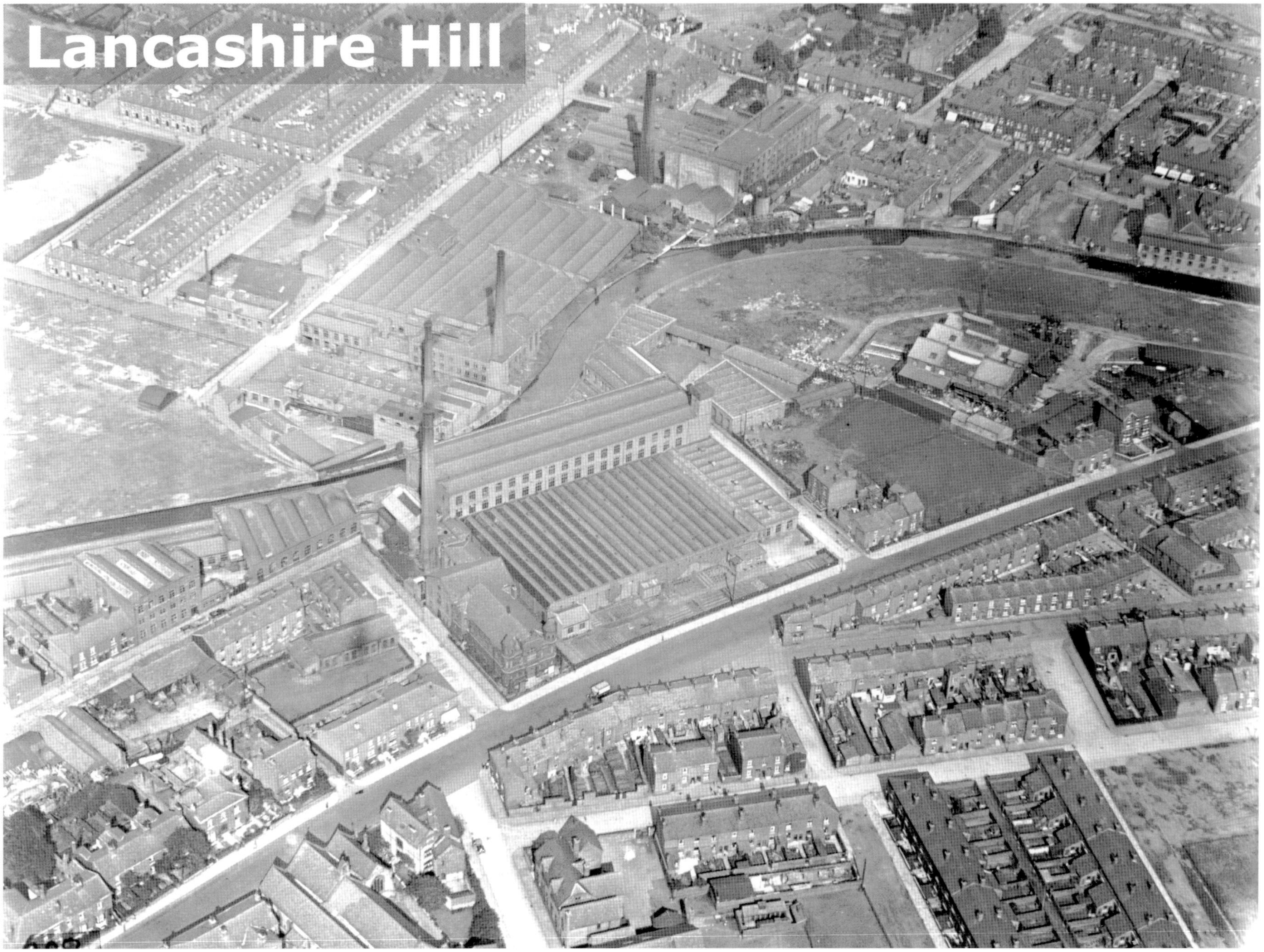

Lancashire Hill 1931

Lancashire hill marks the connection between South Reddish and the town centre. The terminus of the Ashton Canal was located here, close to the Albion Flour Mill. The Mill, which is still fully functional and producing flour to this day, was originally built in 1820 but was extended in 1893 after a fire destroyed the neighbouring Park Corn Mills. In the centre of the image is Rivett's Mill. This was home to Thomas Rivett Ltd, who produced cotton. To the left of the factory is the Lancashire Hill Ropery. The Ashton Canal can be seen snaking around the back of the building towards the basin on the opposite side of the road (out of picture). The canal finally closed in 1962 and was filled in. The route can still be traced along most of its length, and there are plans to try and resurrect the canal and bring it back into full working order. The Manchester & Stockport Canal Society has been set up to try and achieve the aim. On the far side of the canal, running from left to right are Bankside Mill, Coronation Mill, and Bankfield Mill. The main road running through the picture is is Manchester Road, with Stockport town centre to the right. This site is now occupied by a retail park on the north side of the Lancashire Hill roundabout, but Rivett's mill is still visible in the image from 1971 on the next page.

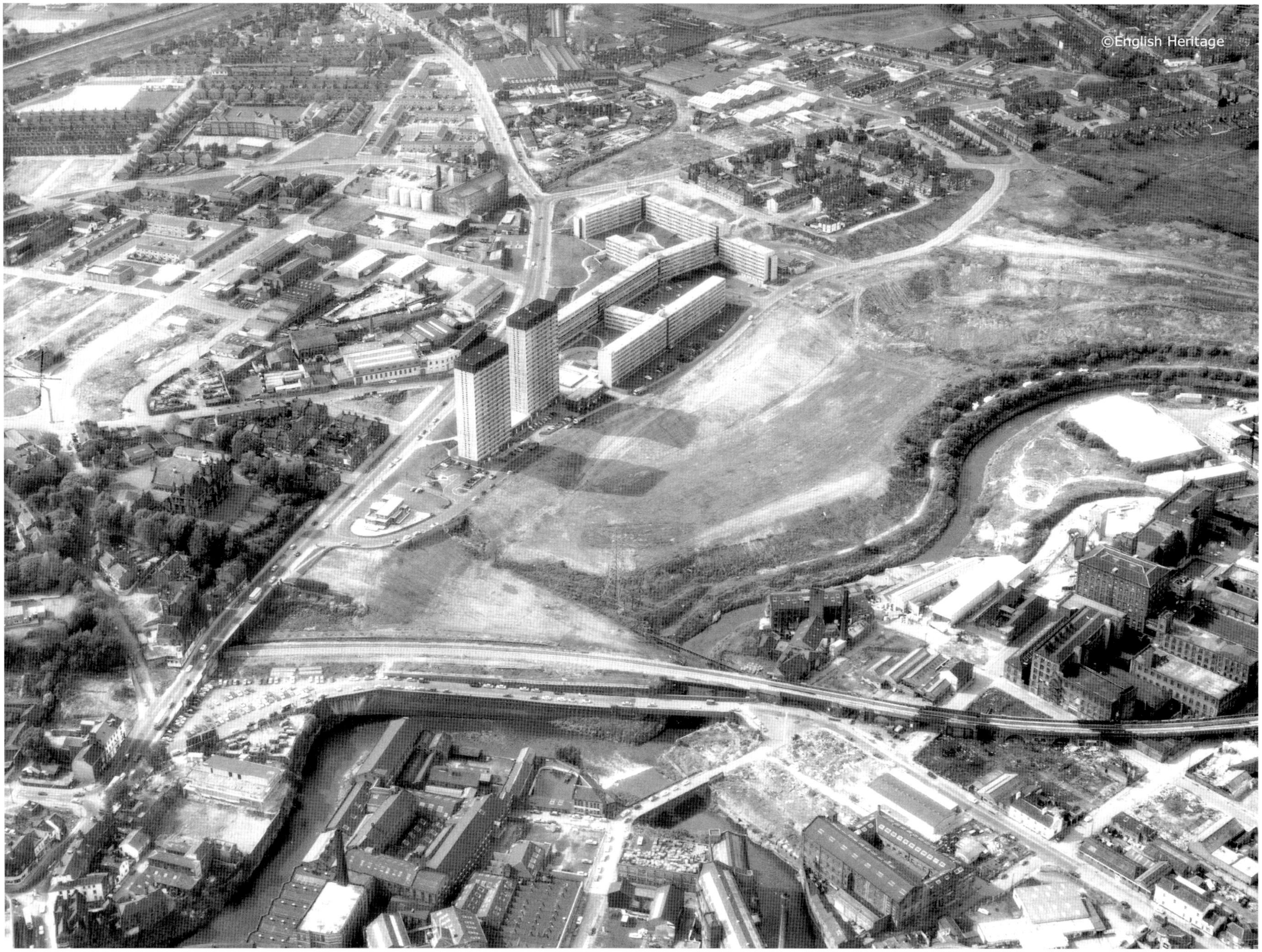

Lancashire Hill Flats 1971

Lancashire Hill flats were constructed in 1969 and consisted of two tall, multi-storey blocks and some smaller blocks of adjacent flats. Pendlebury & Hannover Towers, as they are known, were the tallest multi-storey buildings in the town, rising to a height of 200 feet (61m) and with 22 floors each. Below them can be seen the remains of Tiviot Dale station. The station had a superb multi-arched facade and was extremely well placed for the developing Stockport town centre. But as the importance of Edgeley station continued to grow with more and more trains using the direct route over the viaduct, Tiviot Dale eventually found itself being left aside. The station opened in 1865 on the site of the Spring Vale Printworks as part of the new C.L.C. line from Portwood to Altrincham. Portwood station, just beyond the site of the new Tesco superstore (bottom right), was closed on 1st September 1875 due to it being too close to the new station, but remained in use as a goods yard. The death knell finally sounded for Tiviot Dale when the Cheshire Lines Committee decided to close the station in 1967, and it was demolished a year later. The line remained open for freight until the 1980s.

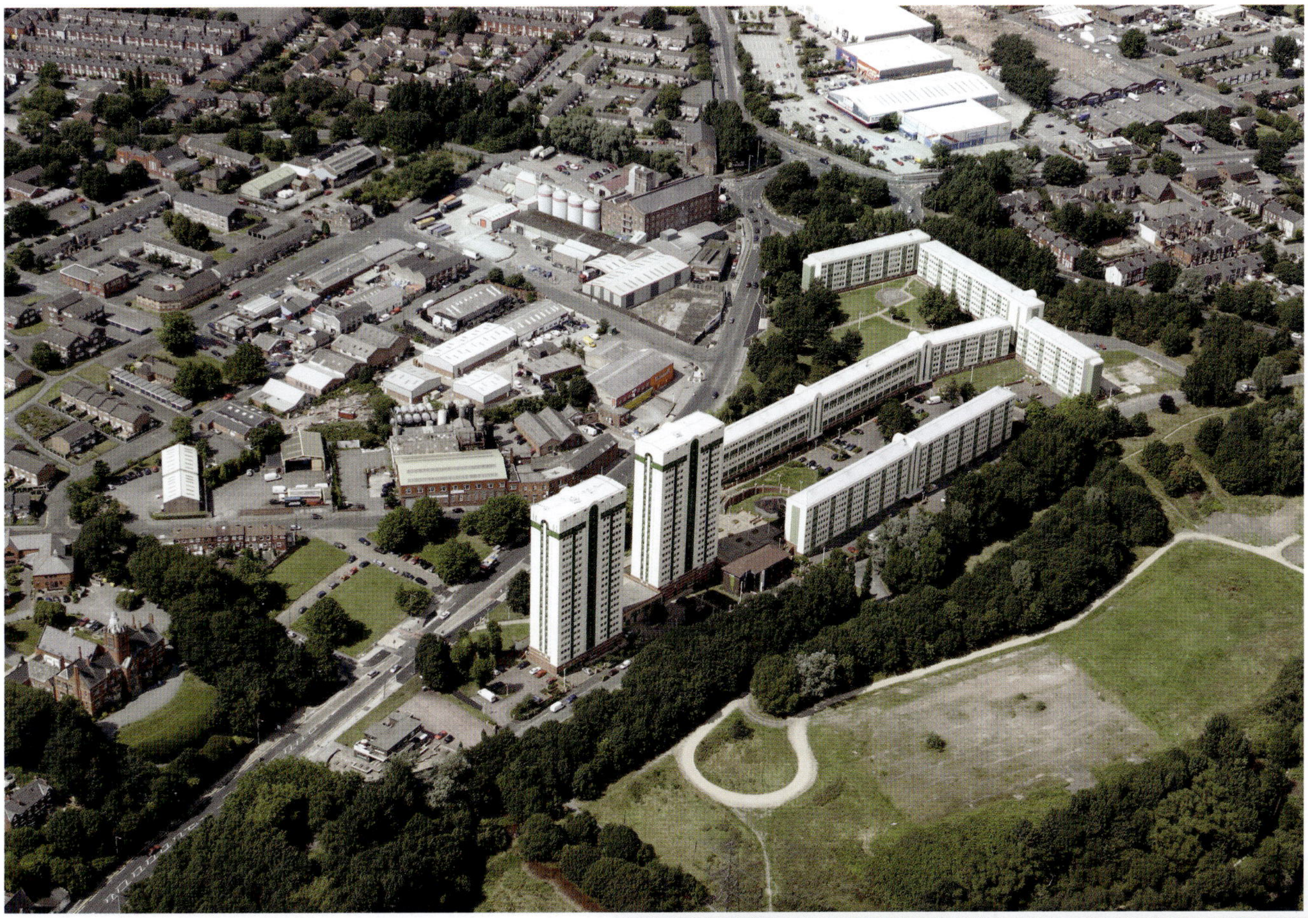

Today most of the site of the station is underneath the M60 Motorway, but there is still evidence of the station hidden amongst the undergrowth on the north side of the road. The north platform and some of the railway sleepers can be found, as well as the remains of the bridge over the river.

The Lancashire Hill flats look a little different now from when they were first built. In the last few years they have been rather fetchingly re-clad in white with green stripes, replacing the more grim-looking, grey exterior that they once had. Although they may not be regarded as luxury flats, the views they have over the town centre, towards the Pennines and the Cheshire plain are superb.

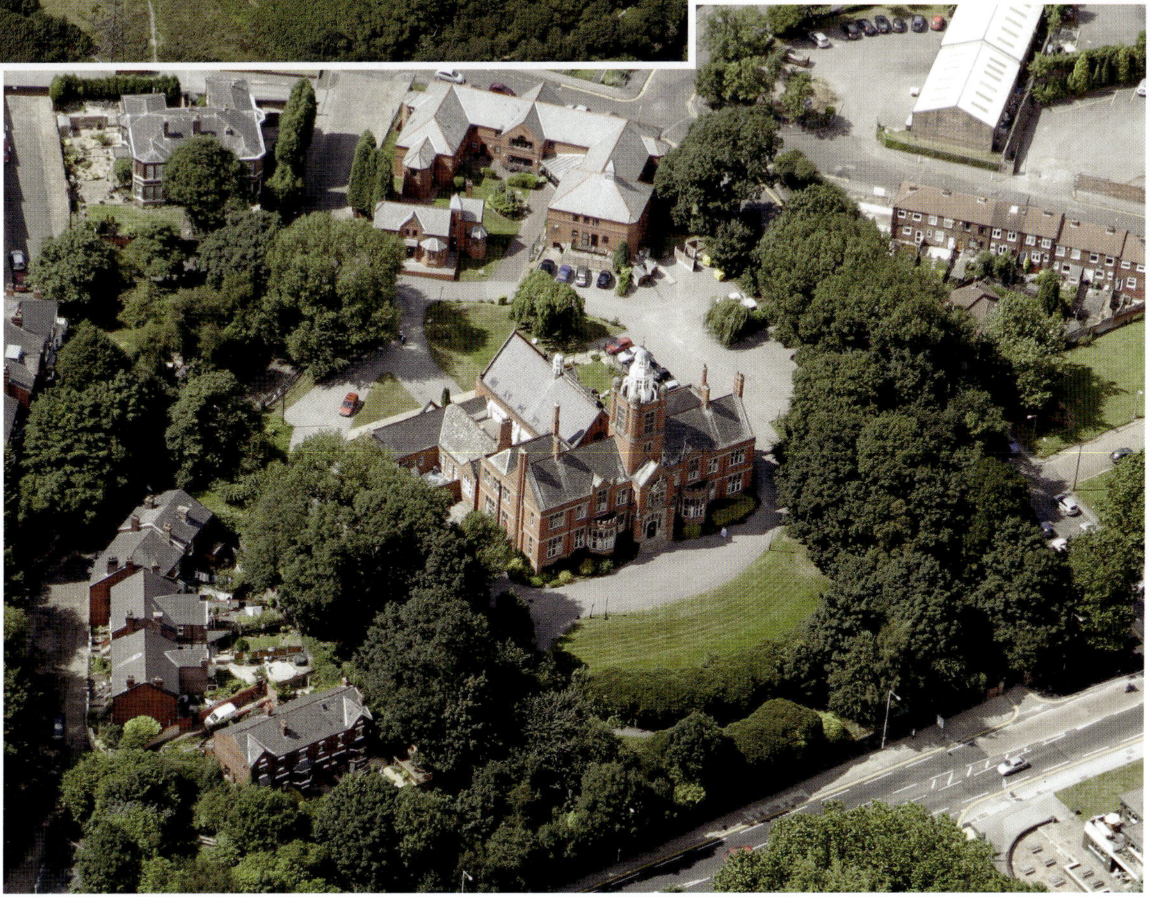

Pendlebury Hall & Dodge Hill

Pendlebury Hall is a superb, Grade 2 listed building that was built from 1881-1882 and features a 98 foot tall central tower. It was founded by Ralph Pendlebury, a former mayor of Stockport, who left £100,000 for the building's construction. Originally used as an Orphanage, the building was also utilised as a Red Cross hospital during World War Two. It is now a care home. The hall is situated on Dodge Hill, which was once the main route down the valley to Lancashire Bridge and still features the original 16th century cobbles. The land here was named after the Dodge Family, famous for its descendants who founded Dodge City in the USA. The hill was one of the locations for air raid shelters in Stockport during the Second World War. These have been bricked in, but are still clearly visible. The area is now protected as part of the Dodge Hill Conservation zone.

Eastern Suburbs

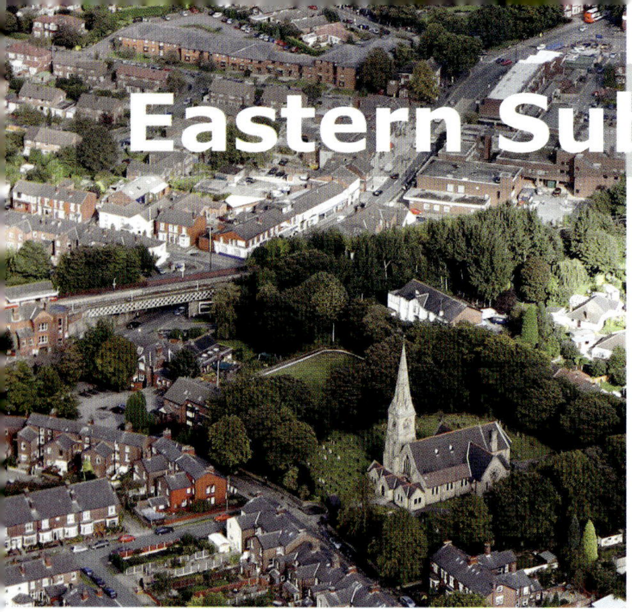
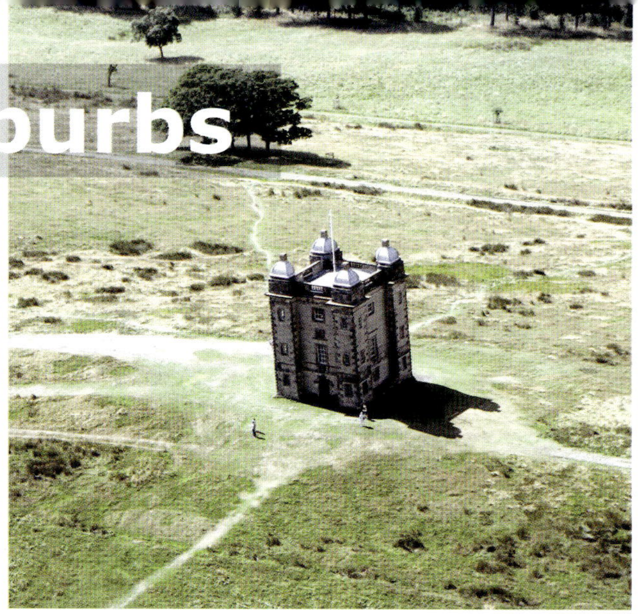
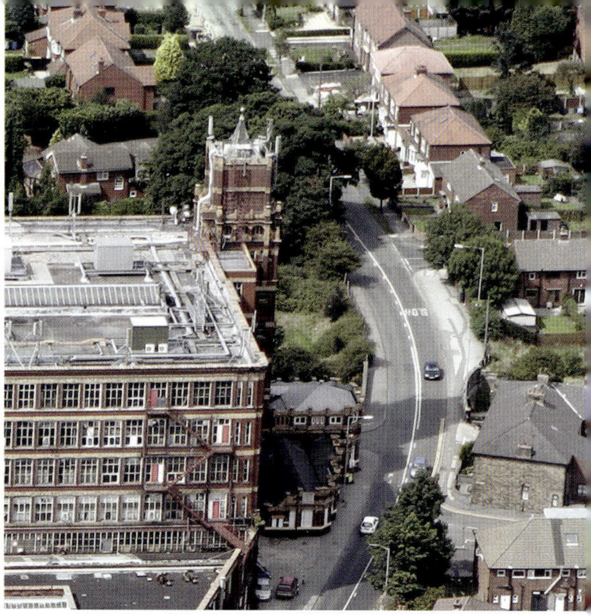
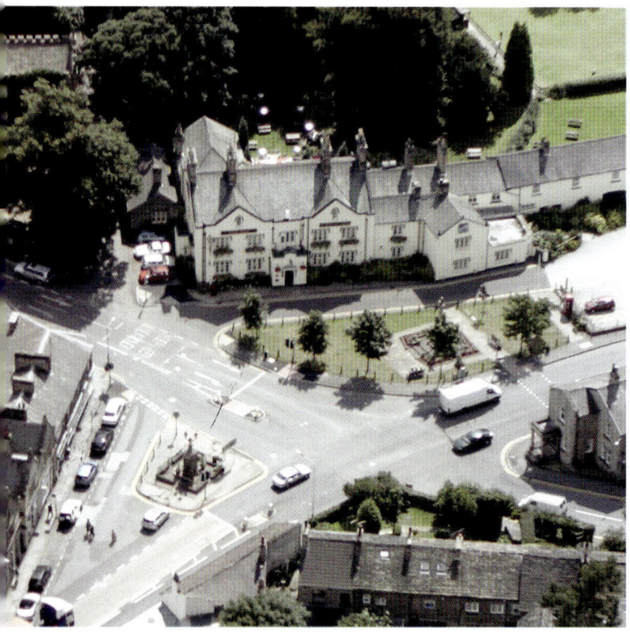
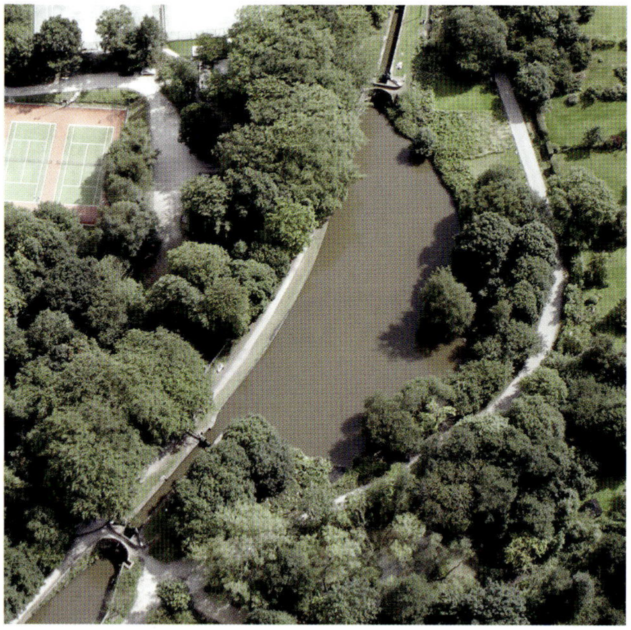
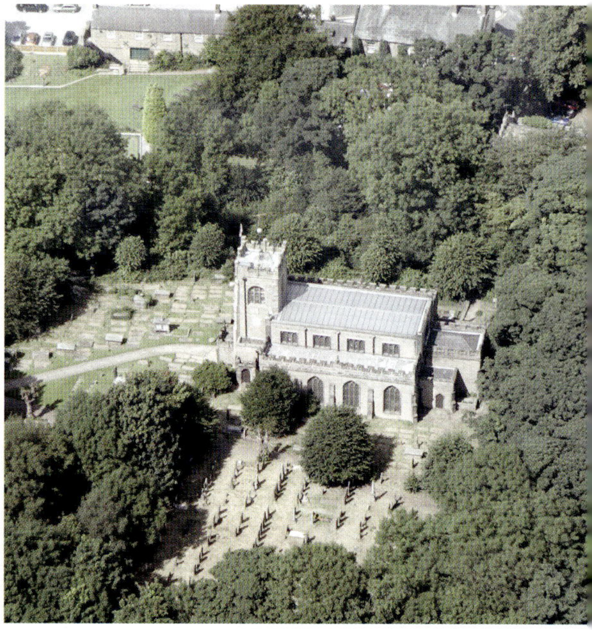
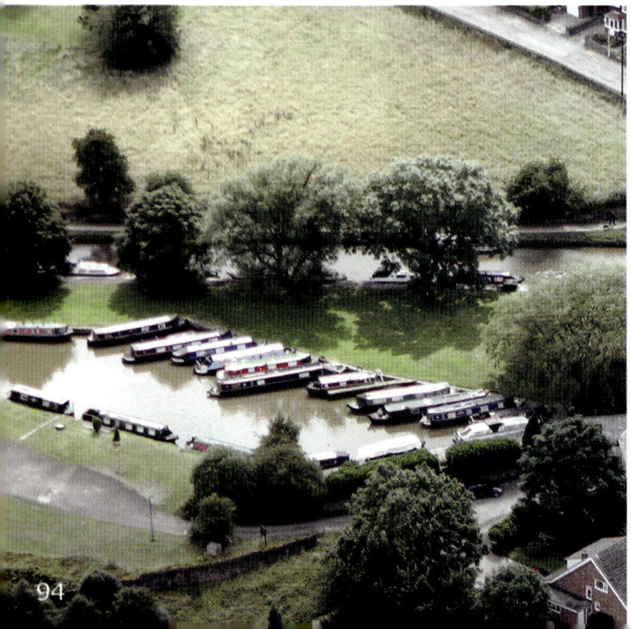
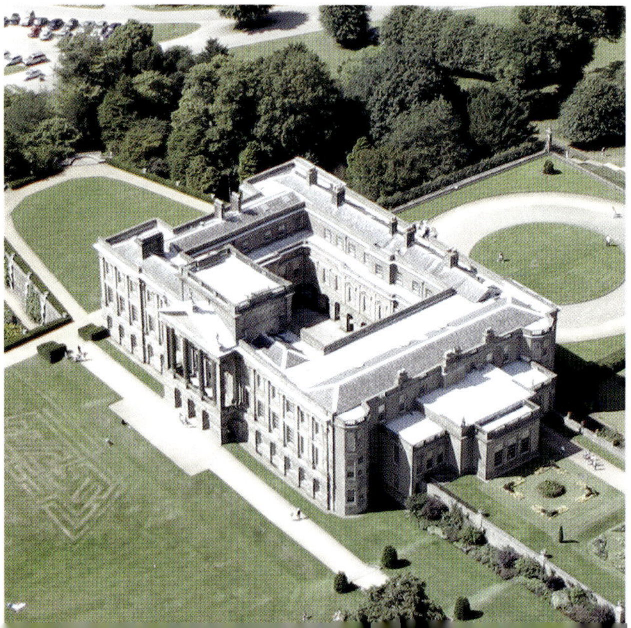
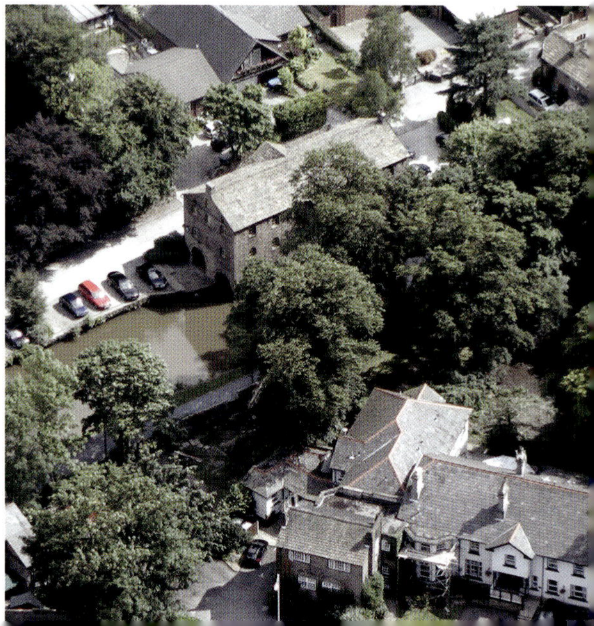

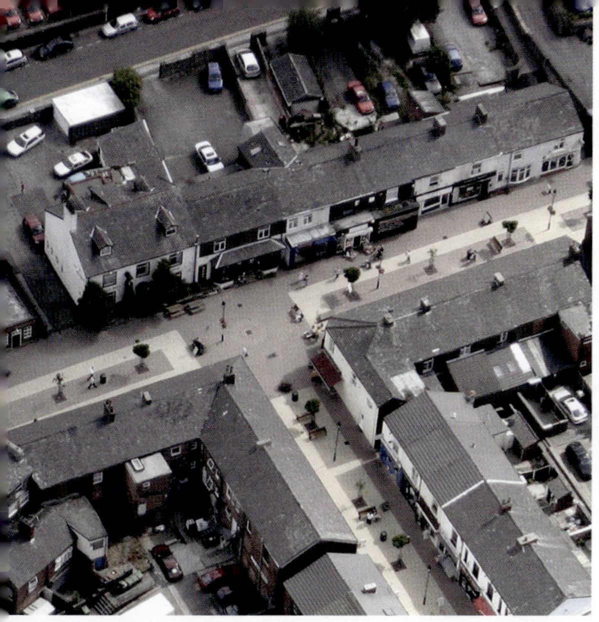
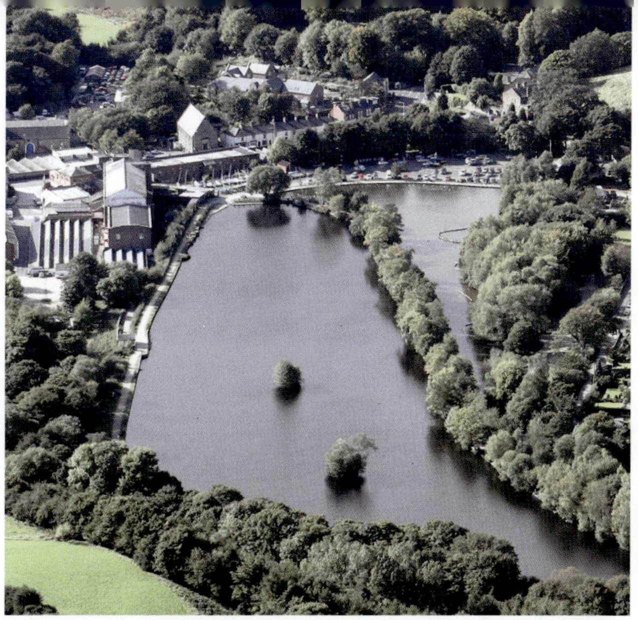
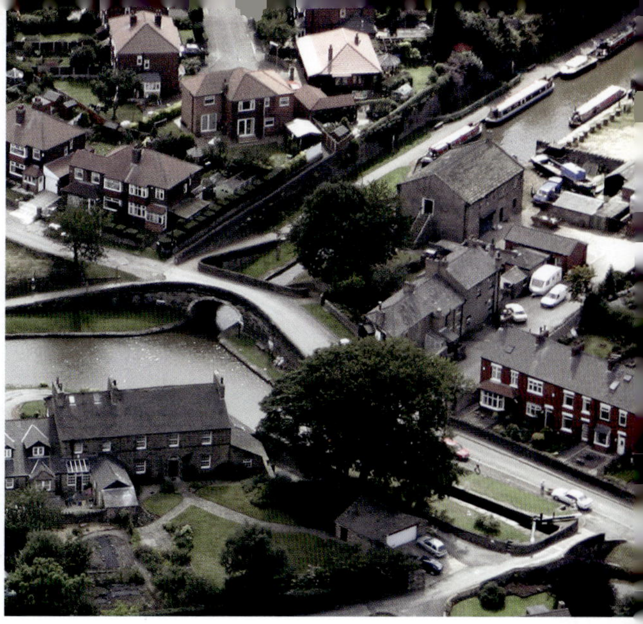
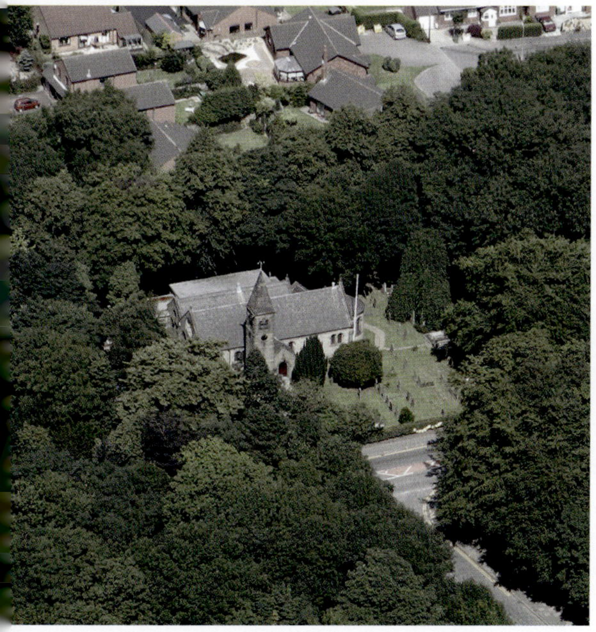
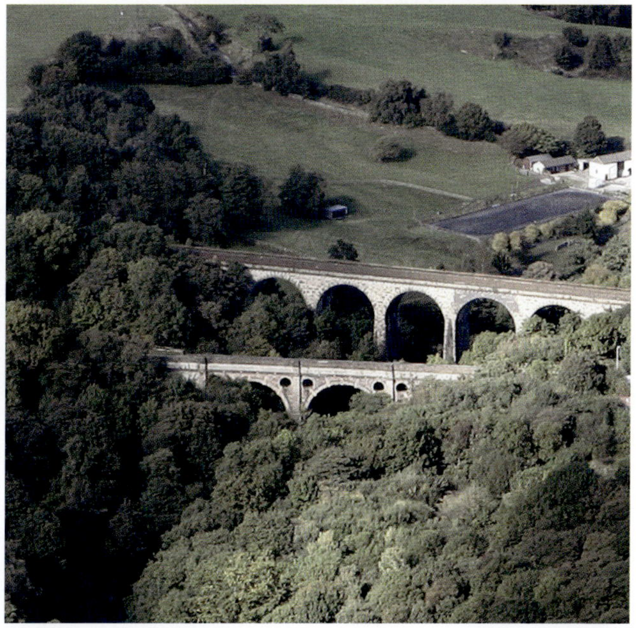
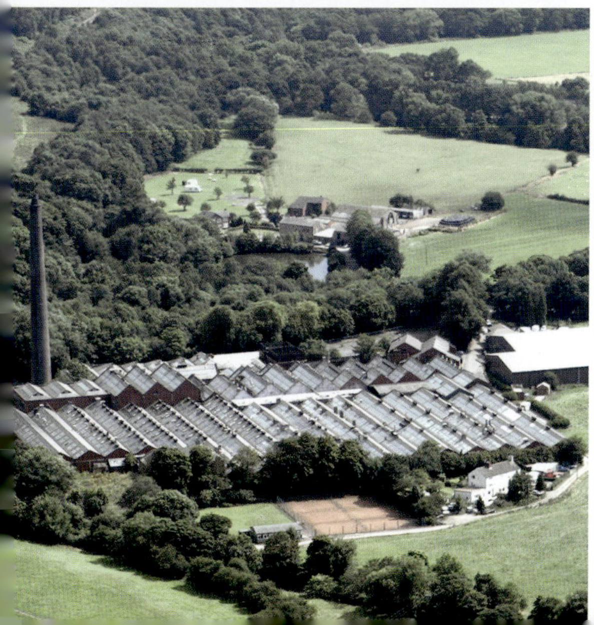
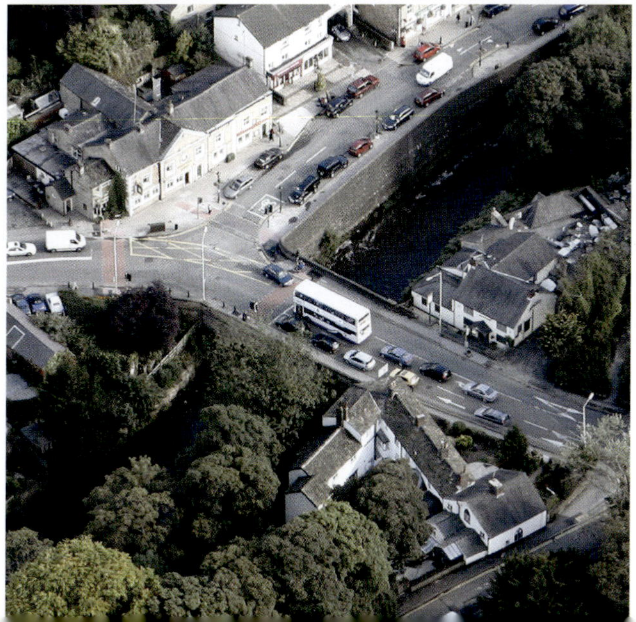

The eastern suburbs mark the gateway to the countryside and the Peak District. The area becomes increasingly rural extremely quickly as you head east, particularly around Marple as you approach the foothills of the Pennine Mountains. The densely packed residential areas begin to give way to smaller villages separated from each other by the river valleys that make up the picturesque landscape. The valleys have served as protection from the onslaught of urban sprawl, and today the area includes some of the finest countryside within Stockport's borders.

From Bredbury adjoining the eastern end of the town centre where the landmark Pear Mill sits, you reach the railway suburbs of Woodley and Romiley, with its impressive church and bustling high street, before heading out to the mill village of Compstall. To the south lies Marple, with its attractive parks and popular waterways, and nearby is the charming village of Marple Bridge. The small settlements of Mellor and Strines occupy elevated positions offering stunning views. On the A6 as you start to head out of Stockport and into the High Peak lie the larger villages of High Lane and Disley. Next to Disley are the glorious surroundings of Lyme Park, with its historic hall and 1400 acres of parkland and woodland.

Bredbury

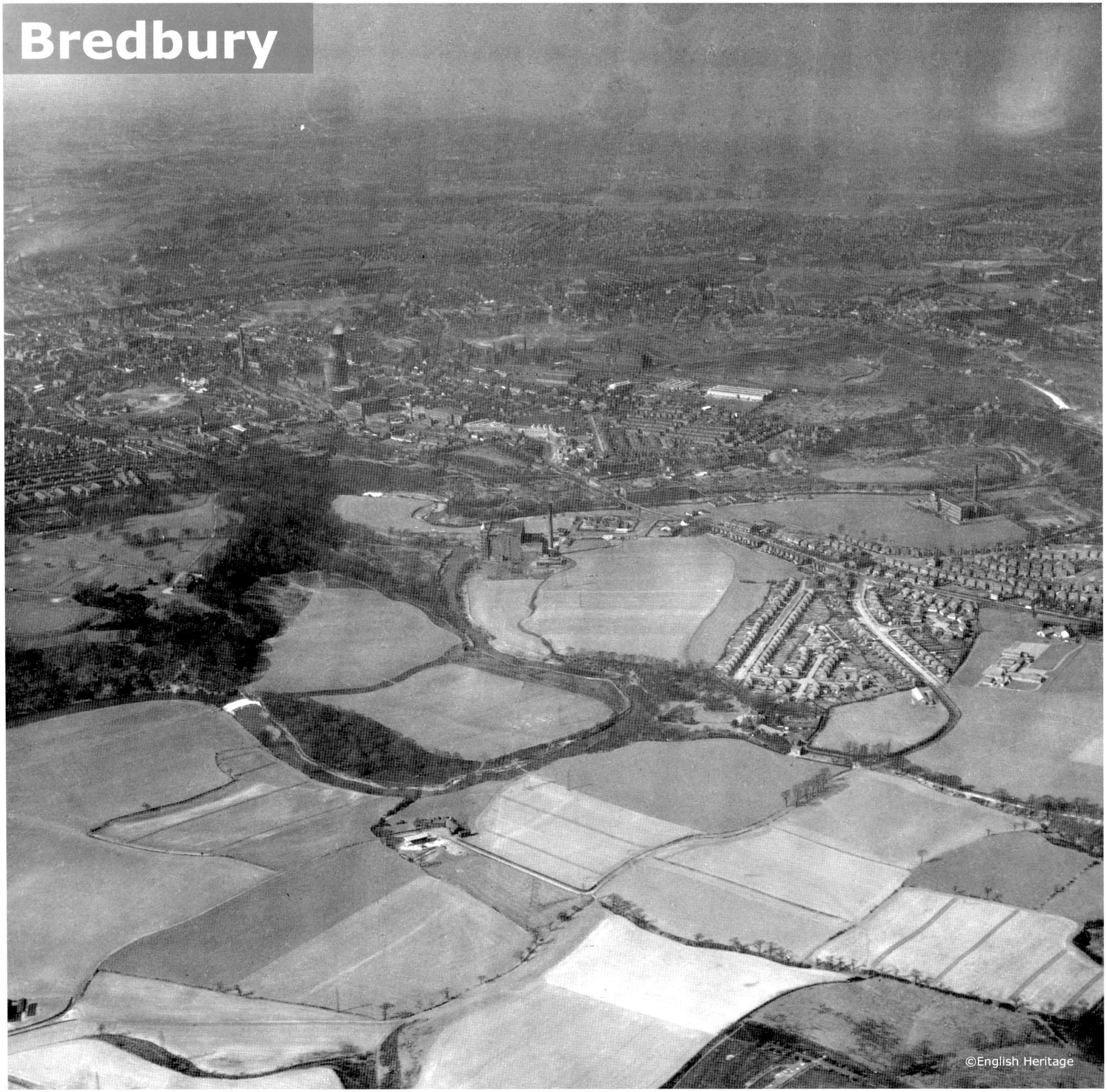

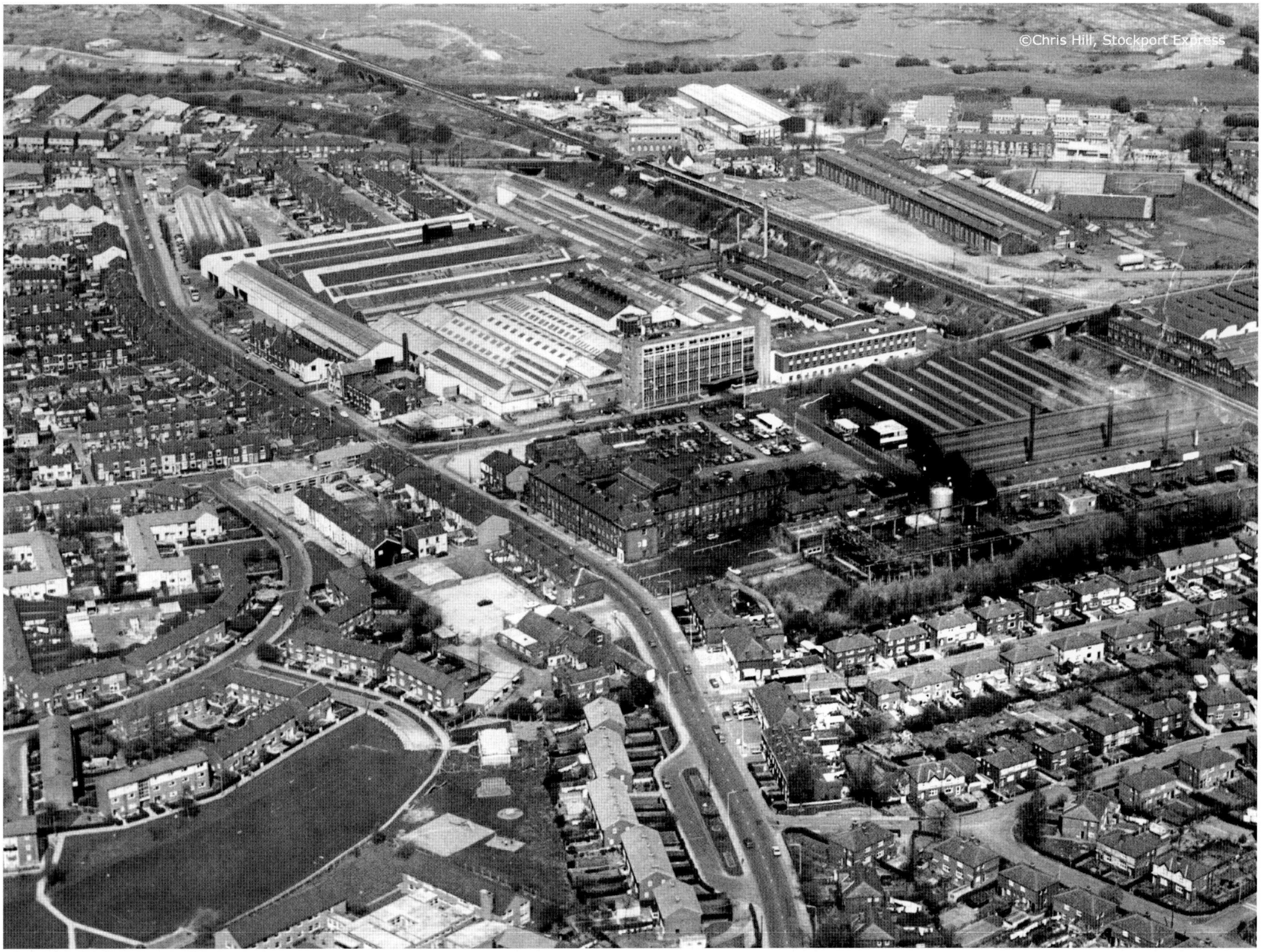

Bredbury 1956 & 1980

The photo on the left, taken from high above the Goyt valley in April 1956, is looking back towards Stockport town centre with Pear New Mill in the centre. Built from 1908-1912, the mill was built on the site of Pear Tree Farm, which helps to explain the reason for the adornment atop its tower – an enormous white copper pear. It is one of the most decorative of the large mills in Stockport, and there are also smaller pears at the top of each corner of the building. It was designed to be a double mill like Broadstone Mill in Reddish, but only half of the mill was ever constructed. On the east side of the building, which we can see in this photo, there is a large blank wall where the extension would have gone. If it had of been constructed it would have made the mill the one of the largest in the world. Further east, Bredbury steelworks on Bents Lane (above) was a major manufacturing presence in the town. Seen here in 1980, the steelworks closed just three years later and the area was redeveloped for housing. Now there is little evidence that the works were ever there. In the background can be seen Bredbury Station.

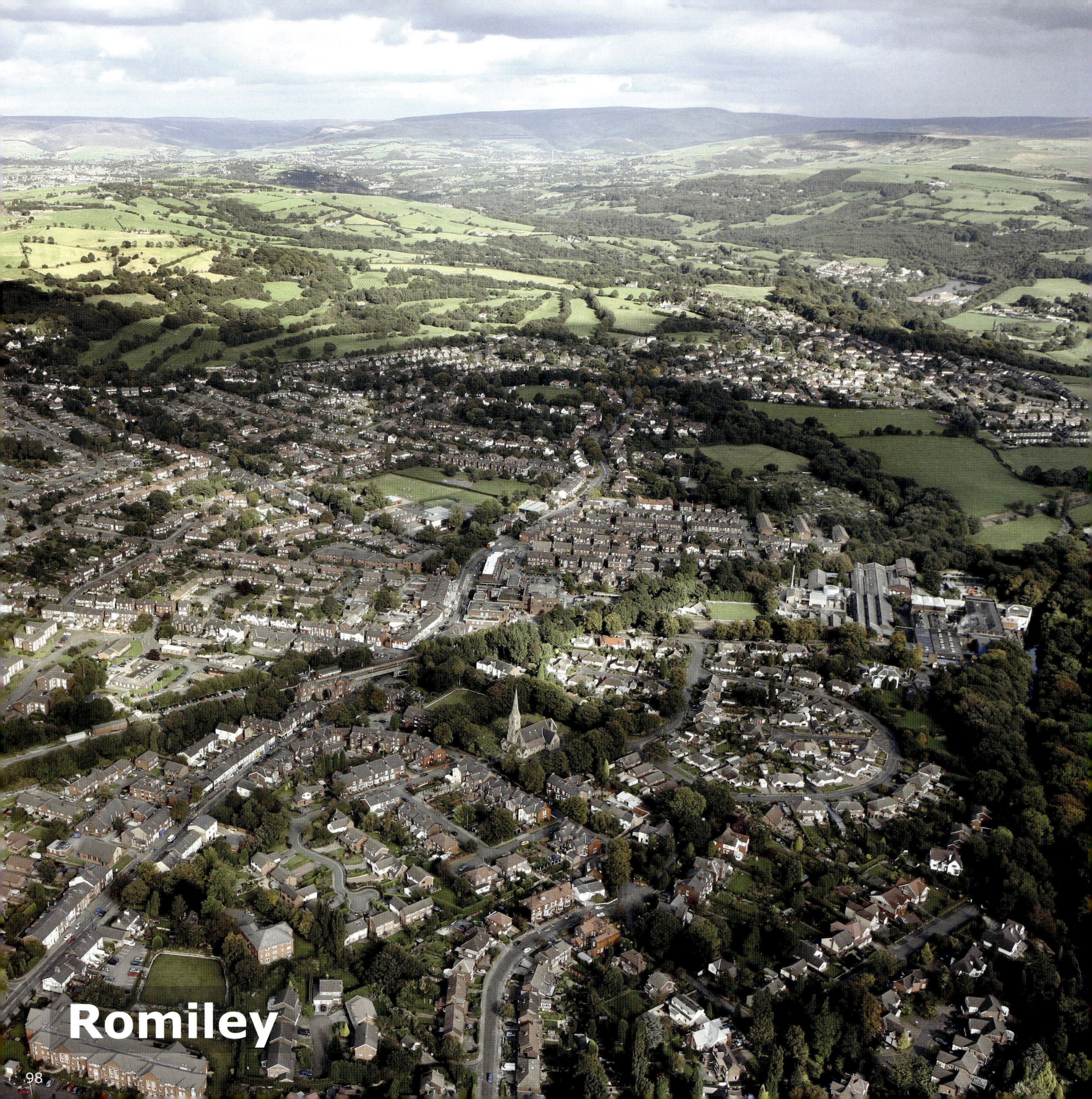

Romiley

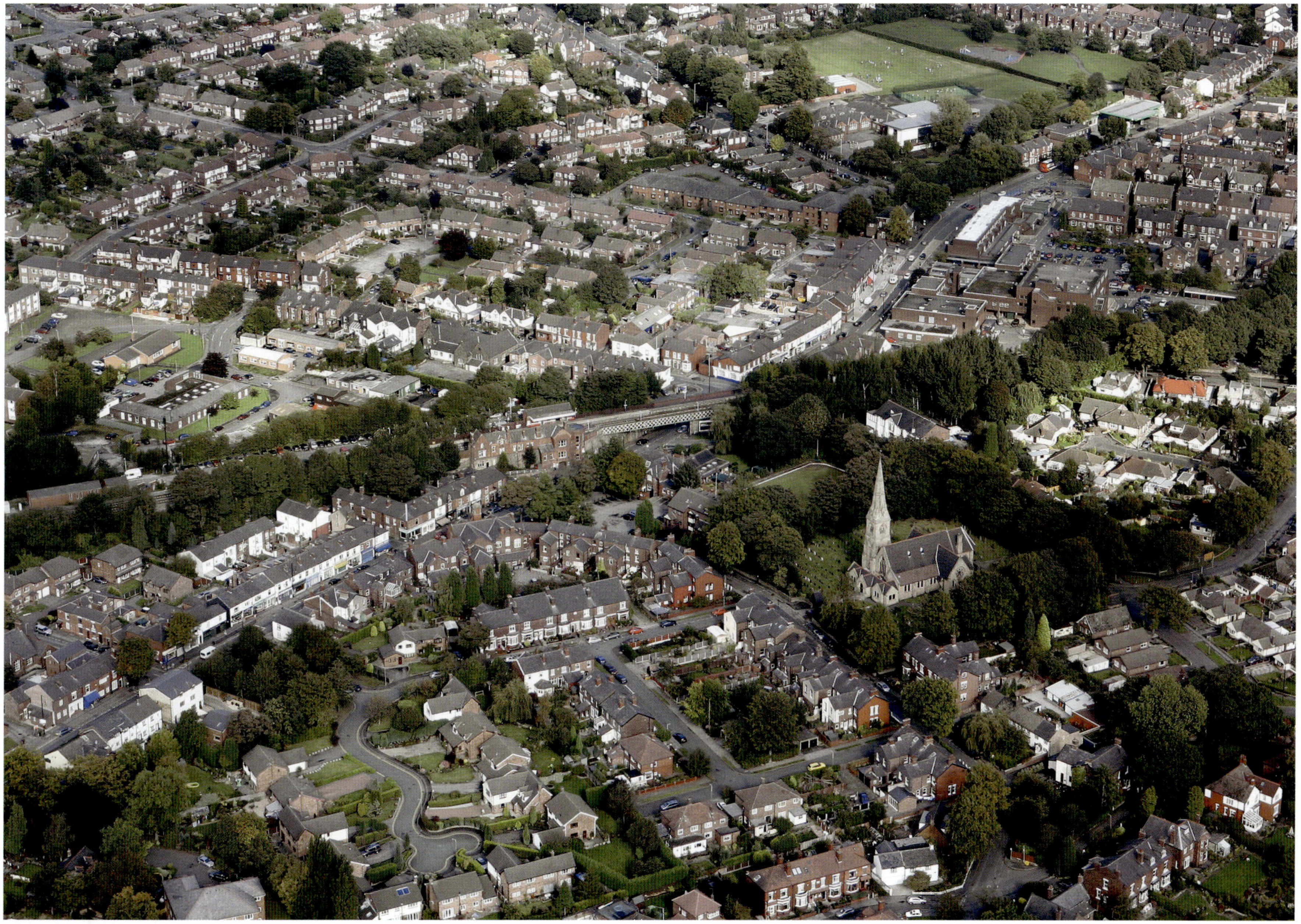

Romiley High Street

Romiley is primarily a railway suburb, but was recorded in the Domesday Book as Rumelie. It was not until the mid 19th century when the station was built that the village began to truly develop. Developments had started following the completion of the Peak Forest Canal, which passes through the west side of the village. The growth in industry linked to the canal was sufficient enough for the Manchester, Sheffield and Lincolnshire Railway Company to construct a grand new station there in 1862 as part of the new line to New Mills. The impressive terracotta brick station frontage with ornate stone detailing, seen here next to the railway bridge, make the station one of the most eye catching and historically important of the smaller stations in Stockport. The arrival of the railway signalled Romiley's arrival as a true railway suburb and turned it from a rural backwater into a place where people wanted to live. So successful was the station that a new line was added to Stockport Tiviot Dale in 1875, increasing the village's popularity and resulting in more and more people moving into the area. The most notable building in the village is the magnificent St Chad's Church. The Grade 2 Listed Church was built from 1864-66 and designed by architect J. Medland Taylor. Today the church forms the very centre of the Romiley Conservation area, protecting the historic buildings that were erected immediately after the arrival of the railway, including the station, St Chad's Cottages and other many other houses constructed at the time. Further down the high street in the top right is the Romiley shopping precinct and the Forum Theatre, which opened in 1971.

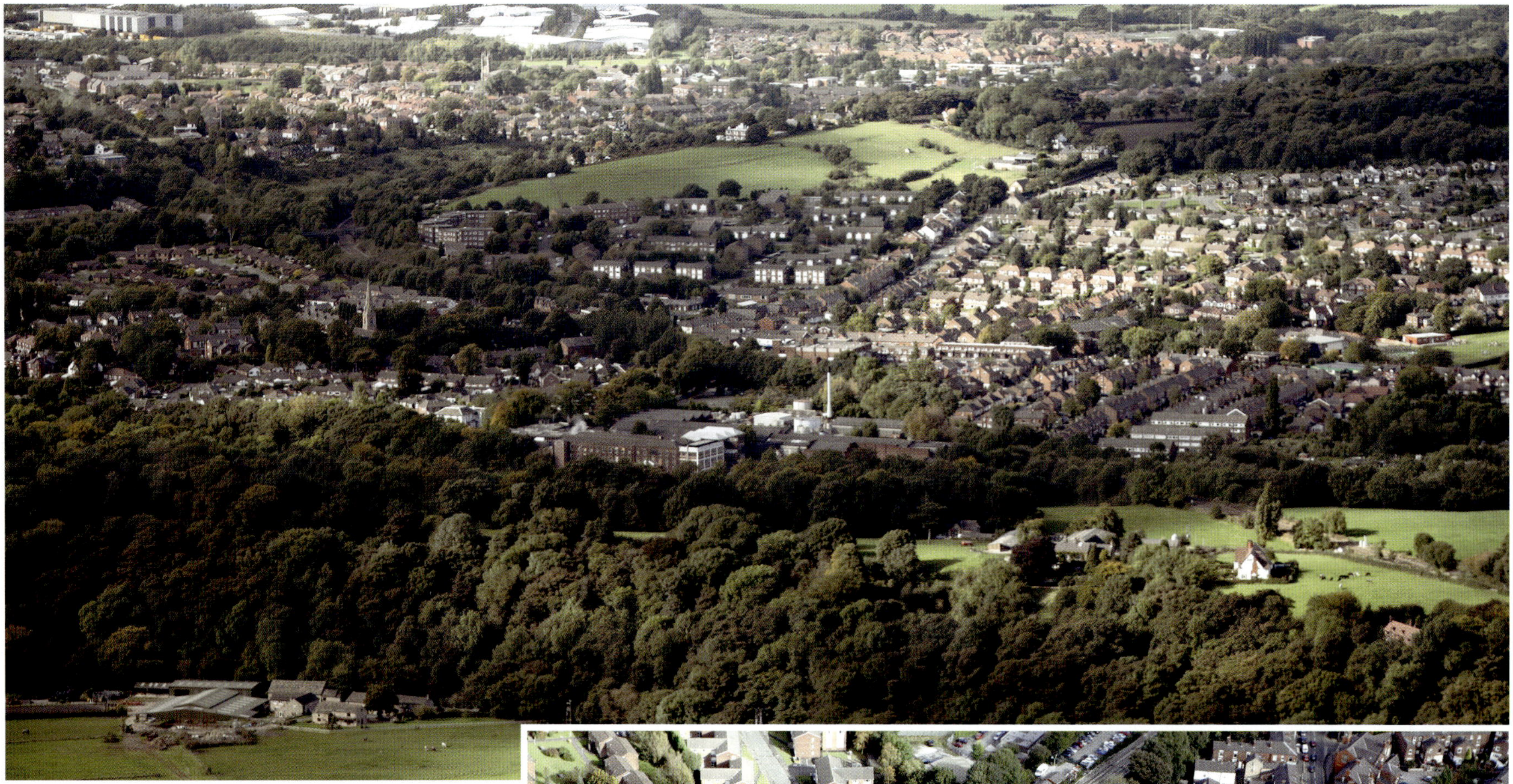

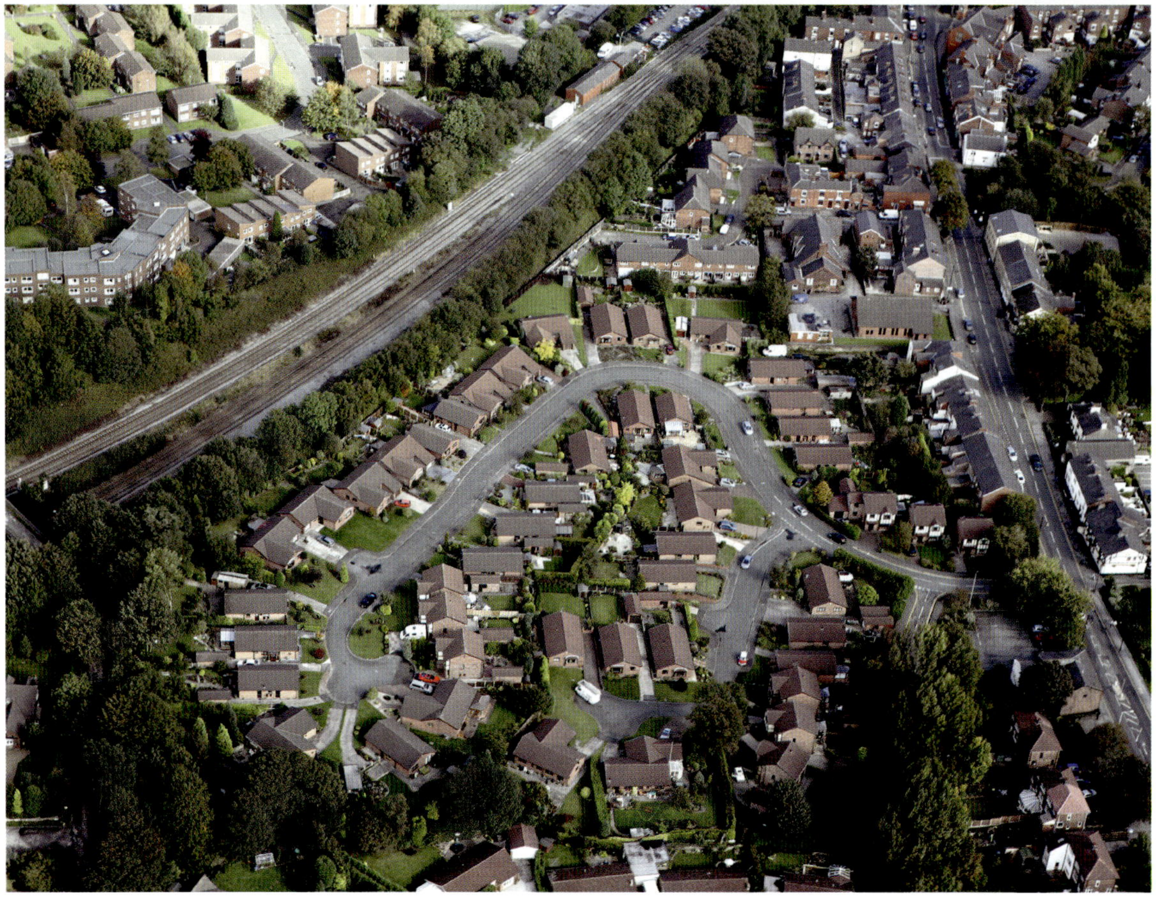

Oakwood Mill

One of the earliest and most notable buildings constructed in Romiley after the arrival of the Peak Forest Canal was Oakwood Mill. The mill was built alongside the canal to the south of the village in the mid 1830s by Ormerod Heyworth. He later built himself a grand mansion – Oakwood Hall – high above the banks of the Goyt in 1845. The mill was originally used for cotton, but production later transferred to paper. The mill is still standing by the banks of the canal, and can be seen peeking up above the trees in the picture above. There have been plenty of additions to the site during the course of the 20th century, but the original brick chimney no longer remains. In its place is modern white equivalent.

On the right are houses on Hill Rise, just off the main high street. Behind them is the 1875 rail junction to Tiviot Dale station.

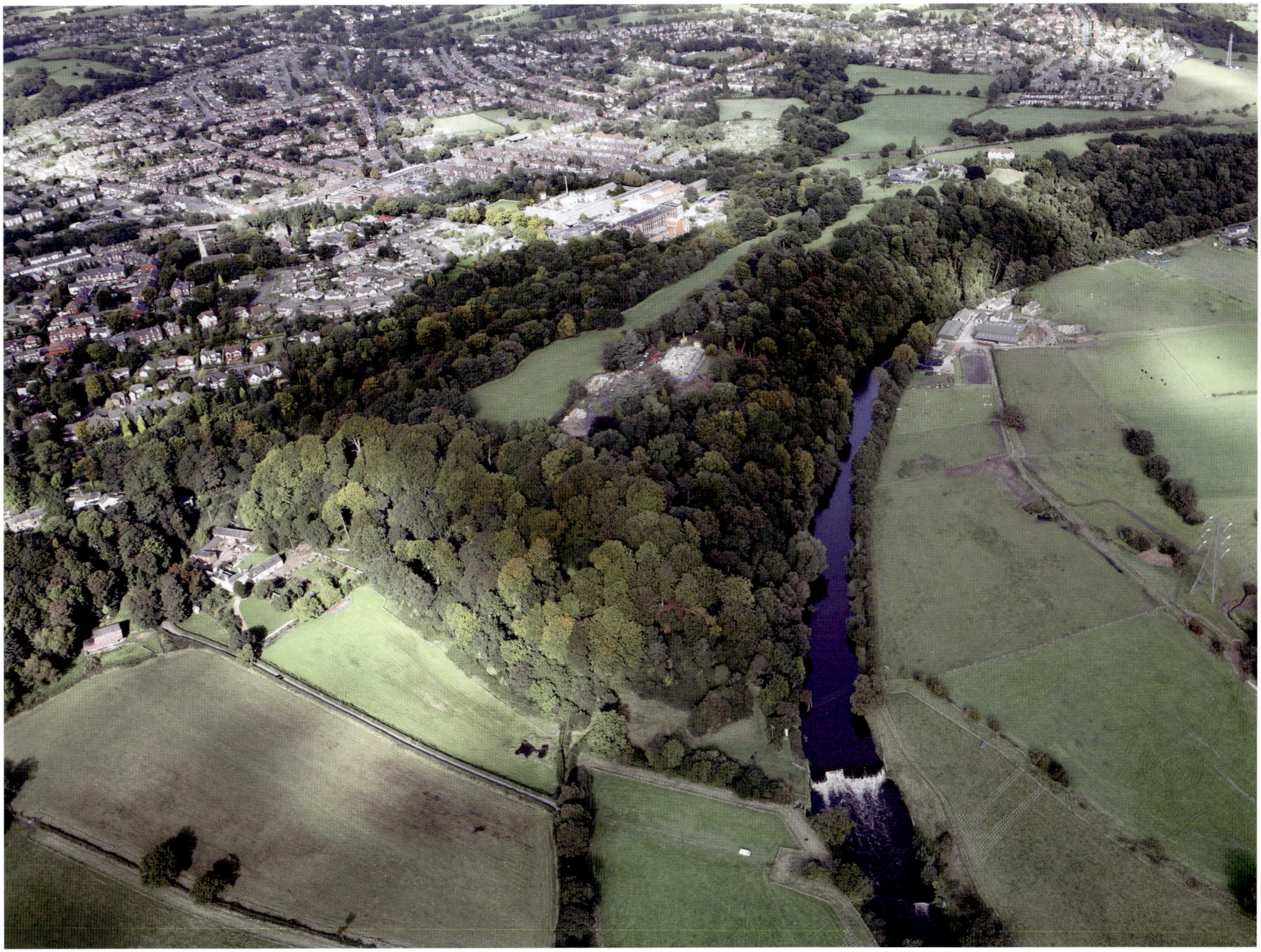

Chadkirk Country Park

Chadkirk Country Park along the banks of the River Goyt is home to one of Stockport's hidden treasures - Chadkirk Chapel. This beautifully restored 14th century chapel is situated in the quaintest of surroundings and boasts a superb walled garden amongst the 60 acres of parkland. It is claimed that a chapel was founded here by St Chad of Northumbria (635-672), who stopped here to worship as part of his work as a missionary to convert the people of Mercia to Christianity (the name "Chadkirk" means "the church of Chad" - "Kirk" being an old English dialect term for a place of worship). However, this may simply be a legend, and a more likely explanation is that the chapel would have been dedicated to his name. The Chapel and the gardens are visible just below the trees on the left. The chapel is the narrow white building.

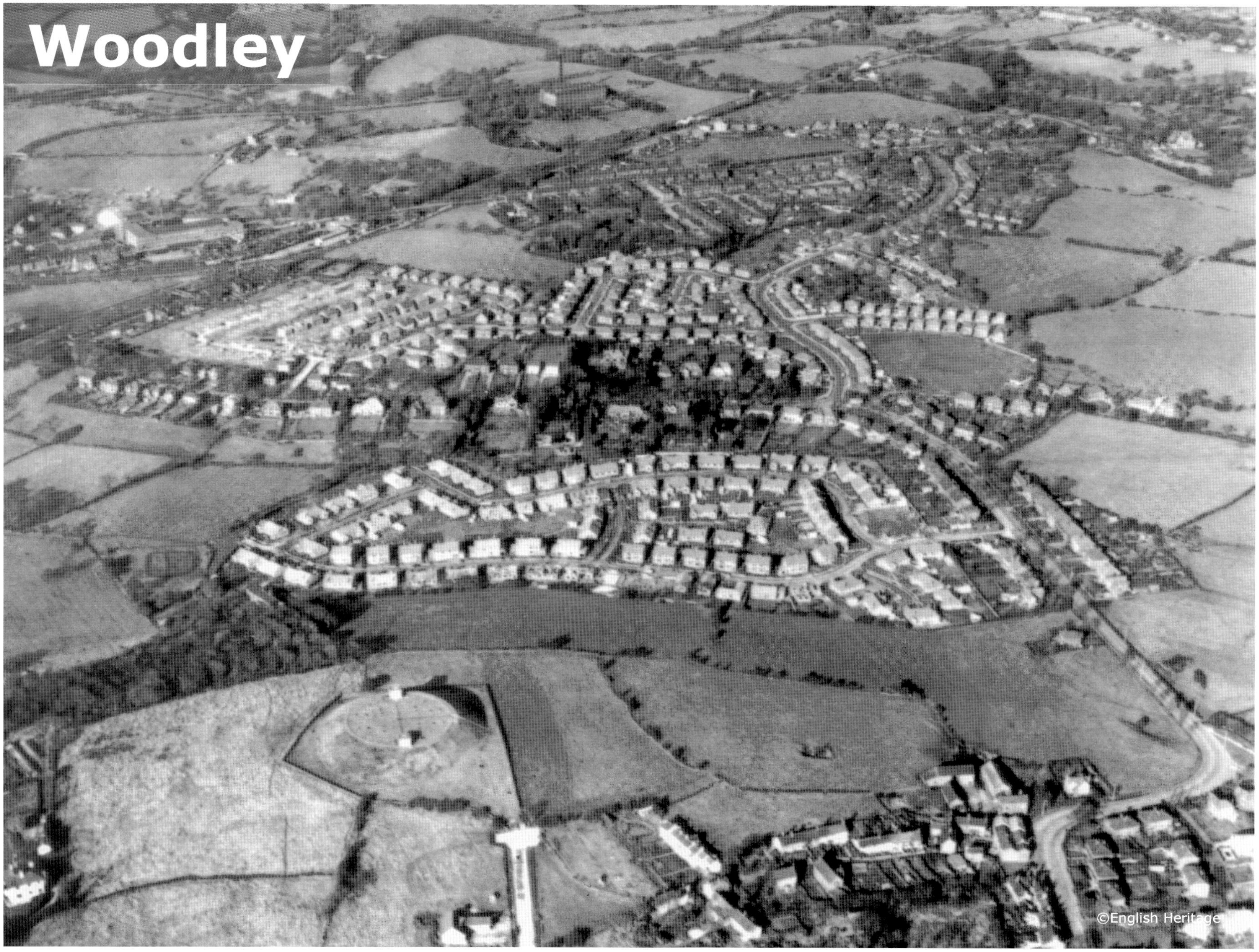

Woodley 1960

Woodley is one of the most easterly suburbs and is bounded by the River Tame to the north. The picture from 1960 shows the residential area between the station and Greavefold. The strange, circular mound in the bottom left of the picture is Greavefold Reservoir, which is a large covered reservoir, camouflaged in green grass to make it less prominent on the landscape. The Peak Forest canal runs through the centre of the village, passing underneath the main road. In the modern picture we can see Hyde Road looking towards Woodley Station in the centre of the picture. The main railway line in Woodley opened in 1862 after work had started in 1858. The junction seen branching off to the left was added from 1860-1863 as part of a new line that went to Portwood Station. It would eventually reach the new Tiviot Dale station in 1865. Woodley station was also the terminus for one of the first tram routes from the centre of Stockport in 1902. The service was so successful was that it was quickly extended eastwards to Hyde.

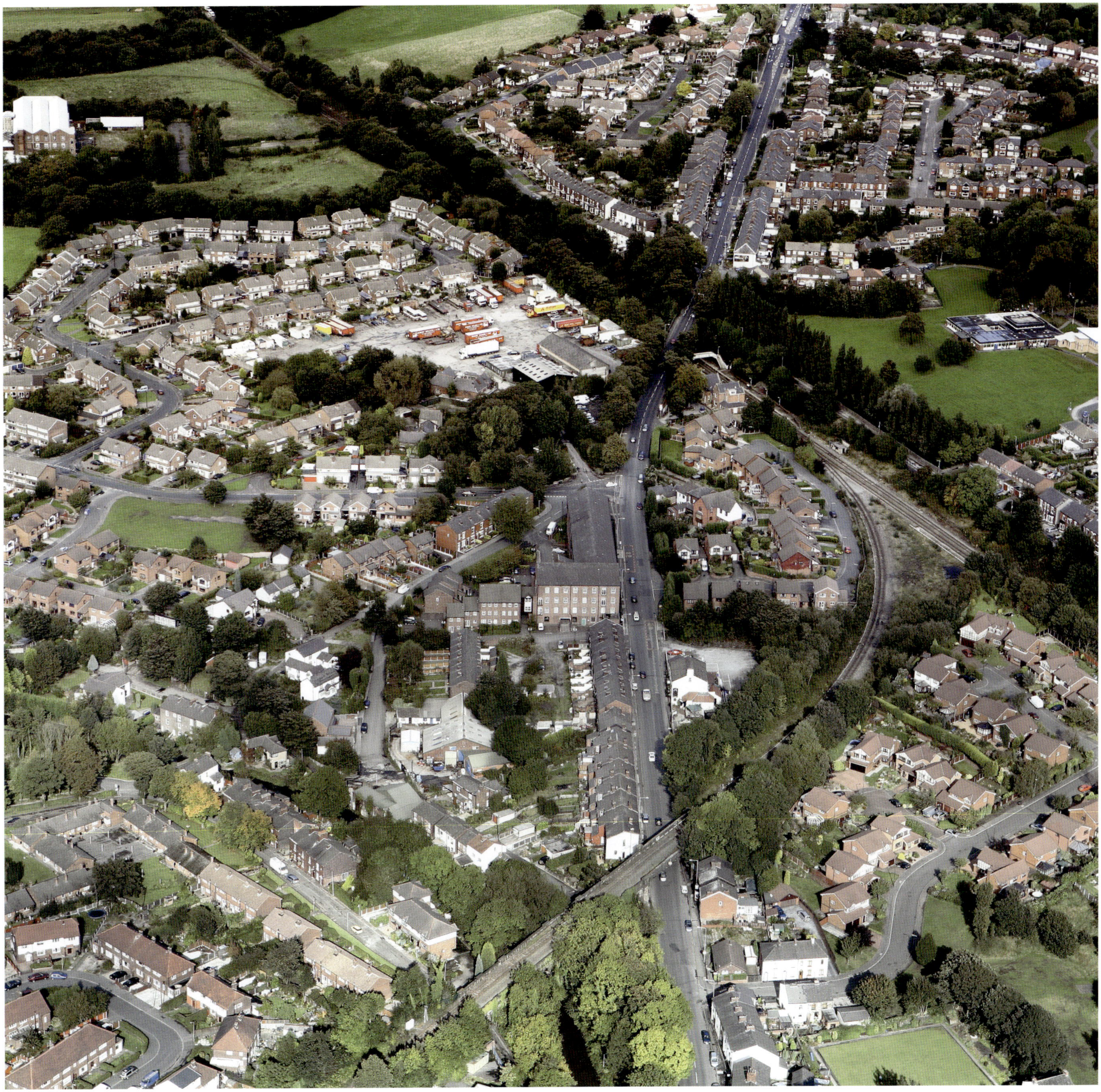

Compstall

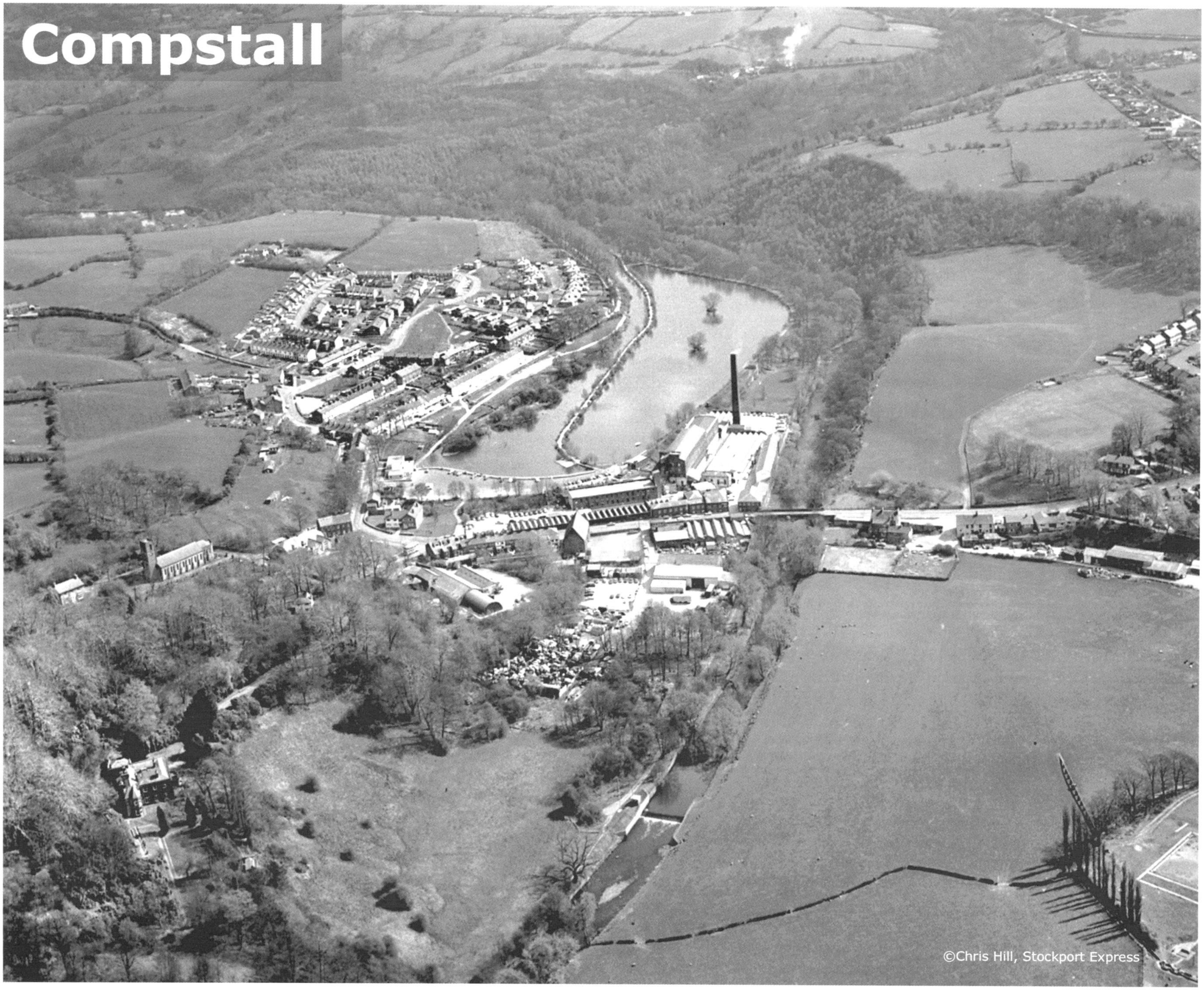

Compstall 1980

The village of Compstall was constructed by George Andrew from around 1820. He founded a mill here for the purposes of cloth manufacturing and finishing, and the village grew around the industry. Water for his mill was taken from the River Etherow and pooled into the two large reservoirs seen in these pictures. A great weir was built on the river, and a huge water wheel, 50 feet in diameter and 17.5 feet wide - the largest in the country at that time - was added in 1838. As the village developed, further facilities were added. The first houses went up from 1820-1824, a new school opened in the mid 1830s, and an Athenaeum (a place for learning, such as a literary club) followed this in the early 1860s.

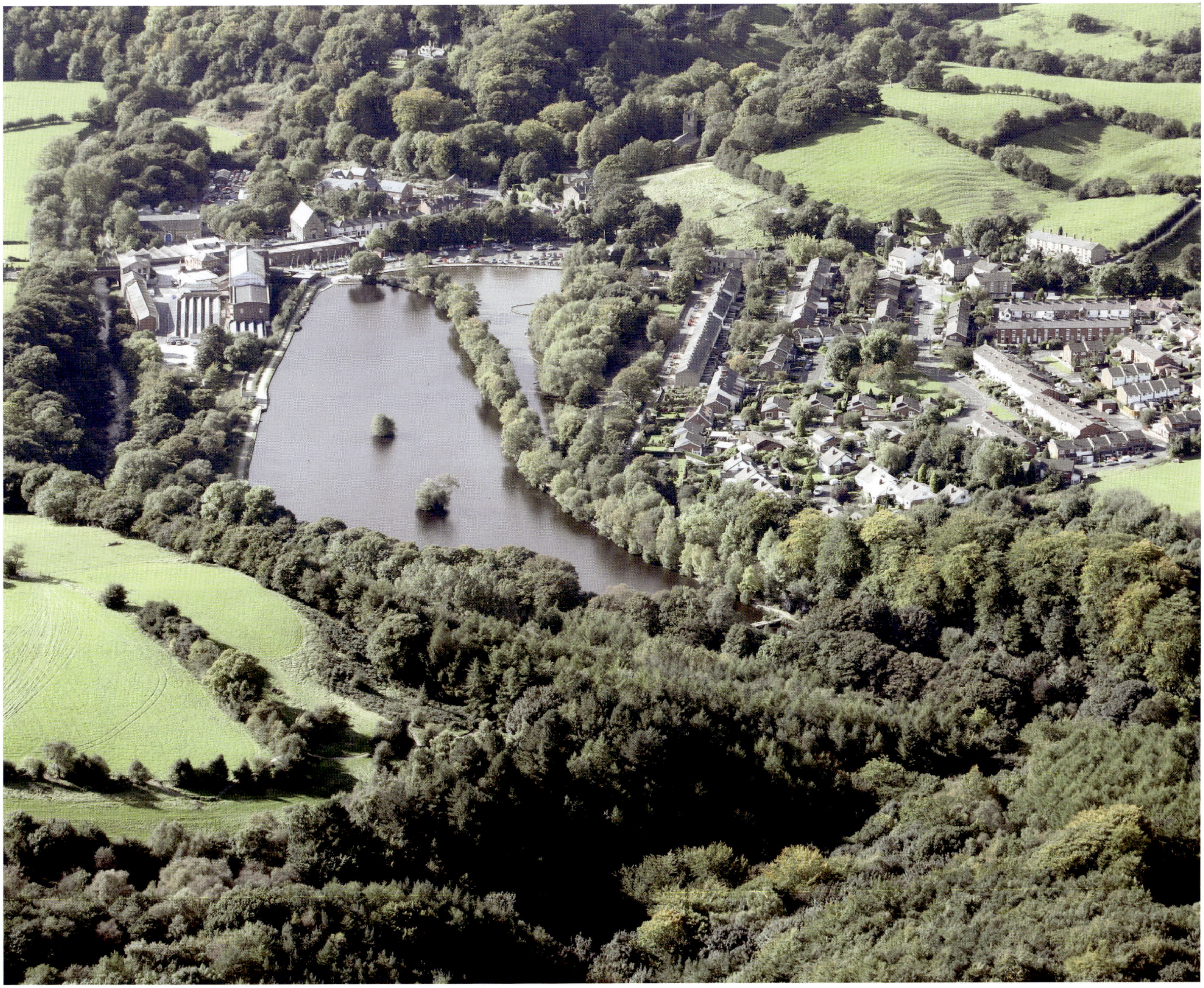

Looking in the opposite direction, not much appears to have changed in the village since the image from 1980 was taken. The mill chimney has been demolished, but the village is still very similar to how it would have been in the mid 19th century. In the hill amongst the trees is the listed St Paul's Church, built from 1839-1841 (on the right, above, and on the left on the previous page). Also visible at the back of the 1980 image is Etherow Country Park (bottom of the modern picture). The park first came into being in 1965 and contained the land between the village up to the weir. This total was extended in the late 1980s when Ernocroft Wood was purchased, and the park now extends to an area of 240 acres, with woodland walks and a nature reserve. The reservoirs are now used as boating and fishing lakes.

Marple

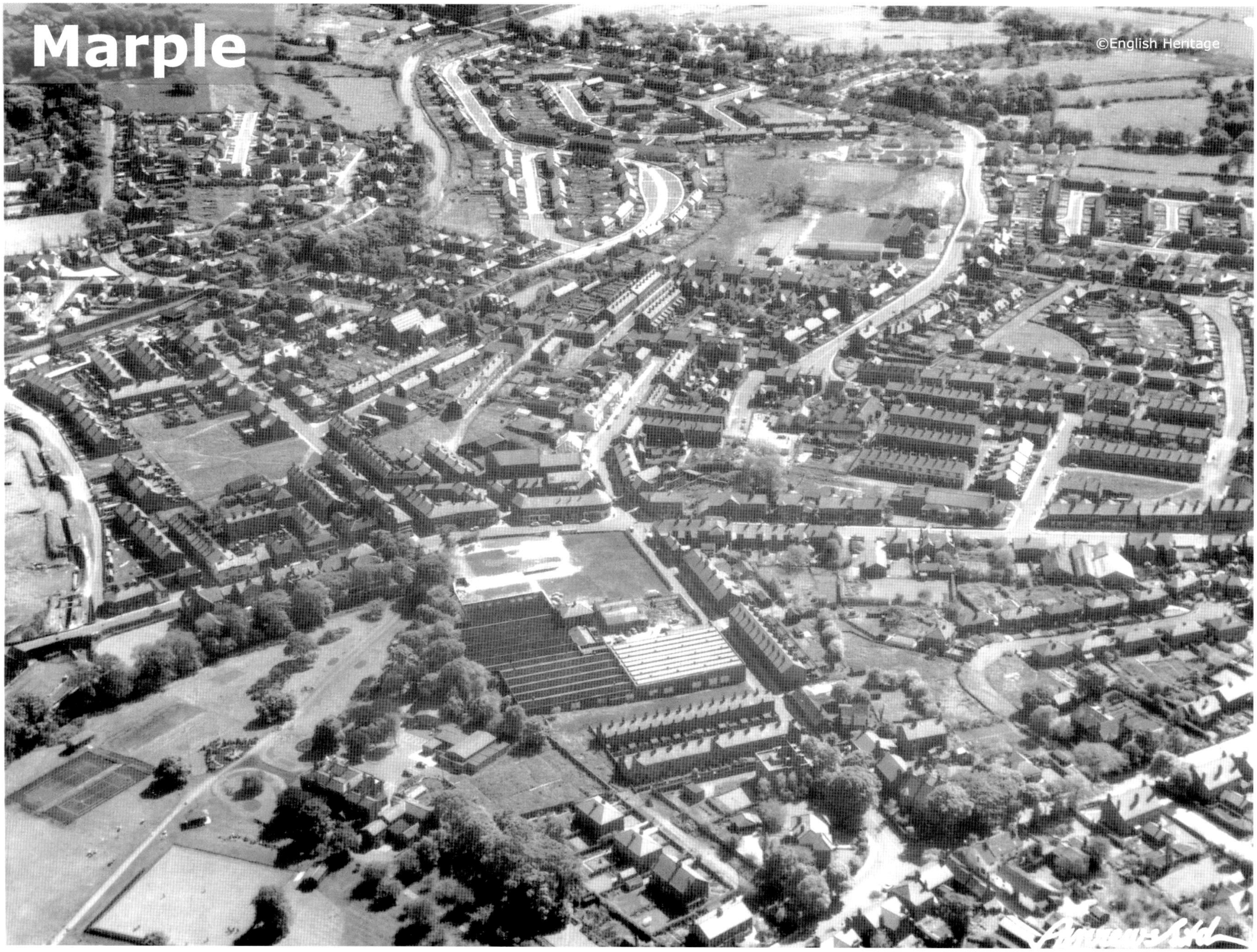

Stockport Road c1957

The village of Marple sits at the edge of the Peak District, with the hills beyond within easy reach. Its position overlooking the Goyt Valley makes it a most attractive area in which to live. It is the presence of this valley to the east, and also of the steep sided Torkington Brook to the west, that has prevented the village from being swallowed up by the growth of suburbia during the late 19th and early 20th centuries. This natural barrier, albeit a small one, has allowed Marple to develop a look and feel all of its own. This is notable in the housing stock, where the principal building material is just as likely to be stone as it is brick. The core of the village is based around the Stockport Road area, shown above from the late 1950s. The bare patch of land in the middle of the picture is the site of Hollins Mill, a building that used to dominate the village centre. The mill opened in 1830 opposite Market Street, and even had its own short arm of the Peak Forest Canal through Memorial Park, on the left. This was filled in during the 1950s but the route can still be traced. The mill complex was extended several times, but the main building was demolished in 1957, just before this picture was taken and a year after the factory had closed. On the site now is a supermarket and a row of shops, known as The Hollins precinct.

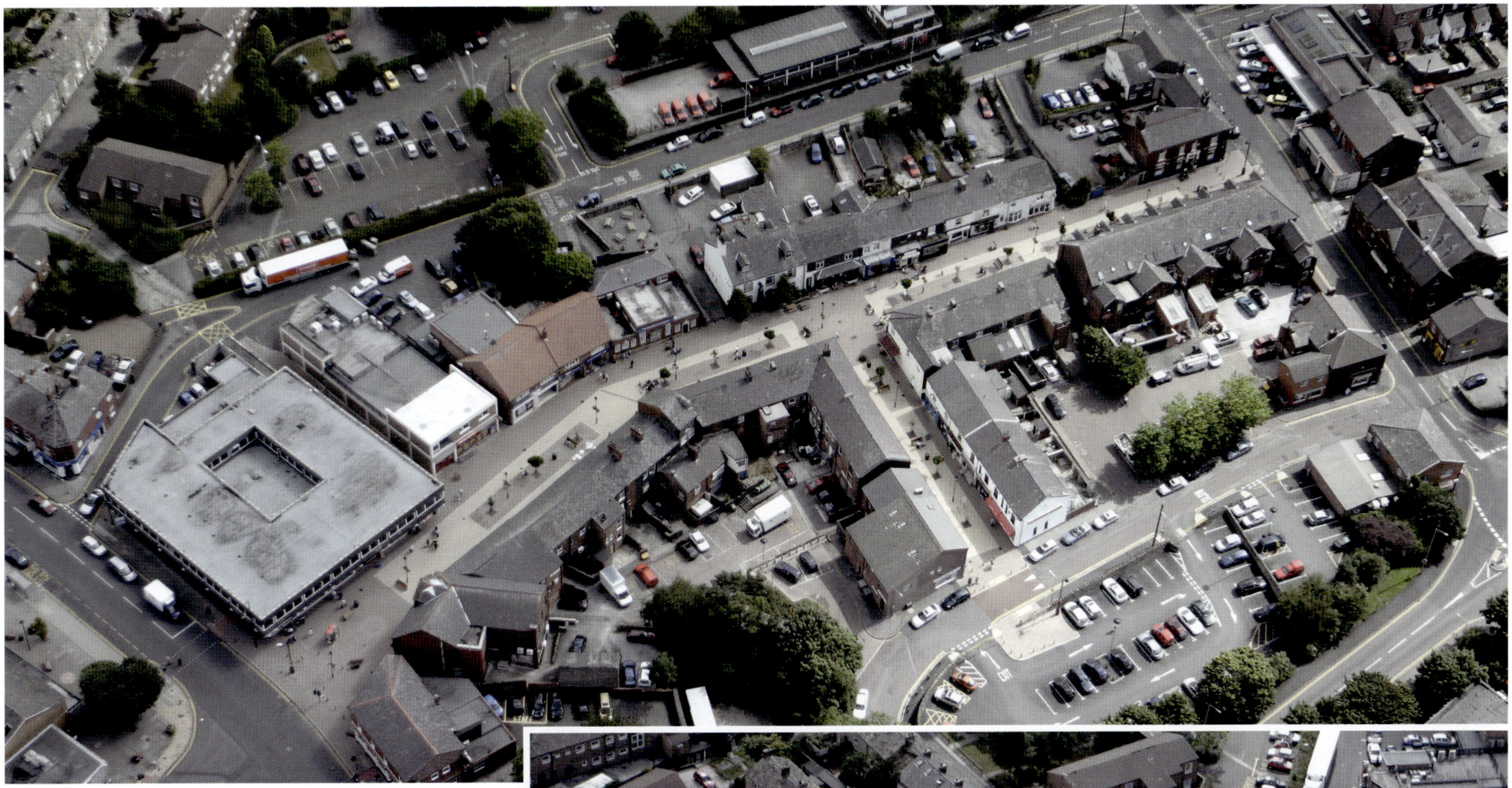

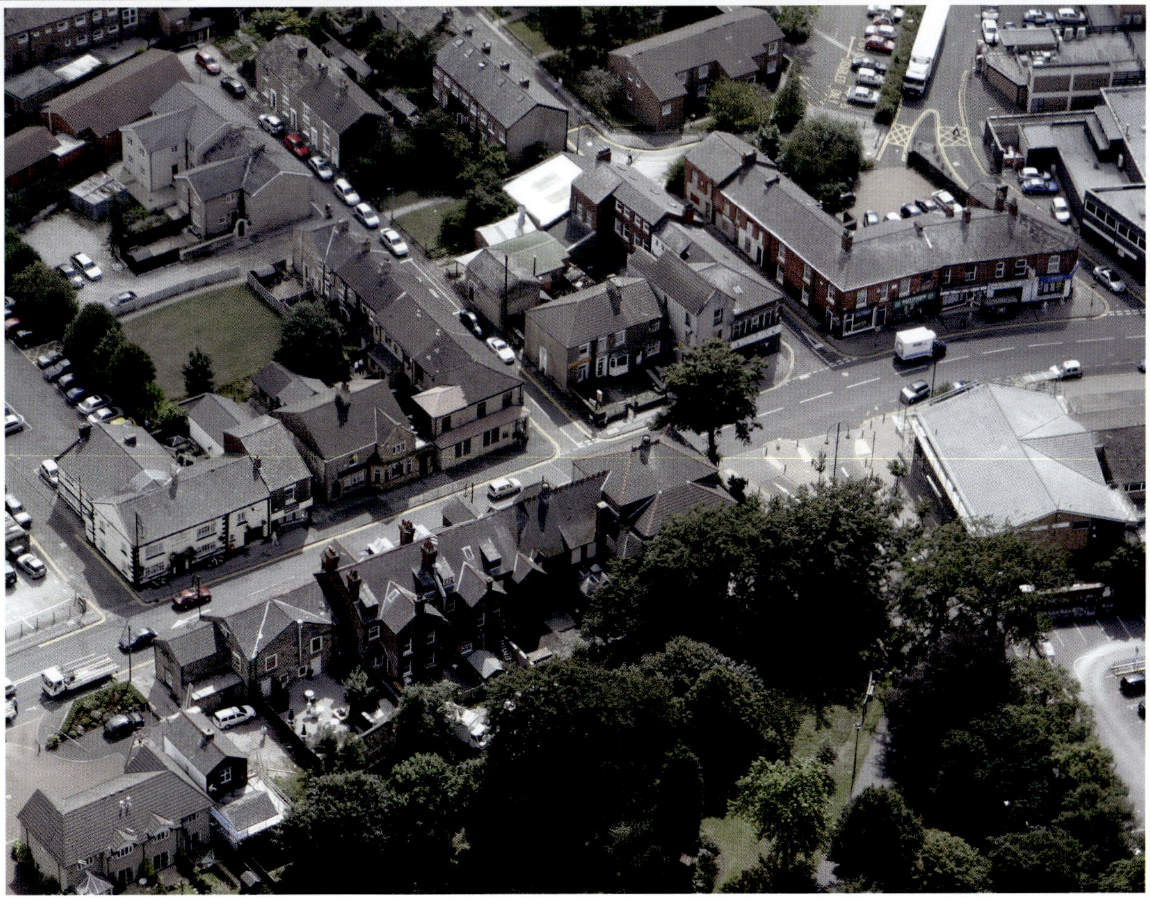

Market Street

The main shopping street in the village is Market Street. The street used to be open to traffic, but is now pedestrians only. The name of Market Street is perhaps something of a misnomer, as Marple has never held a regular market. In the late 18th century Samuel Oldknow had a 3-storey building built on his land in Marple with the intention of using it as a market hall. He petitioned parliament for an Act to allow the market to take place, but this was refused on the grounds of it being to close to the market in the centre of Stockport.

Opposite Market Street is the Regent Cinema on Stockport Road. Sadly, this is now the last remaining independent cinema in Stockport after closure of the Savoy in Heaton Moor. The cinema has just one screen, and can seat 285 people. To the right of the cinema is the entrance to Memorial Park.

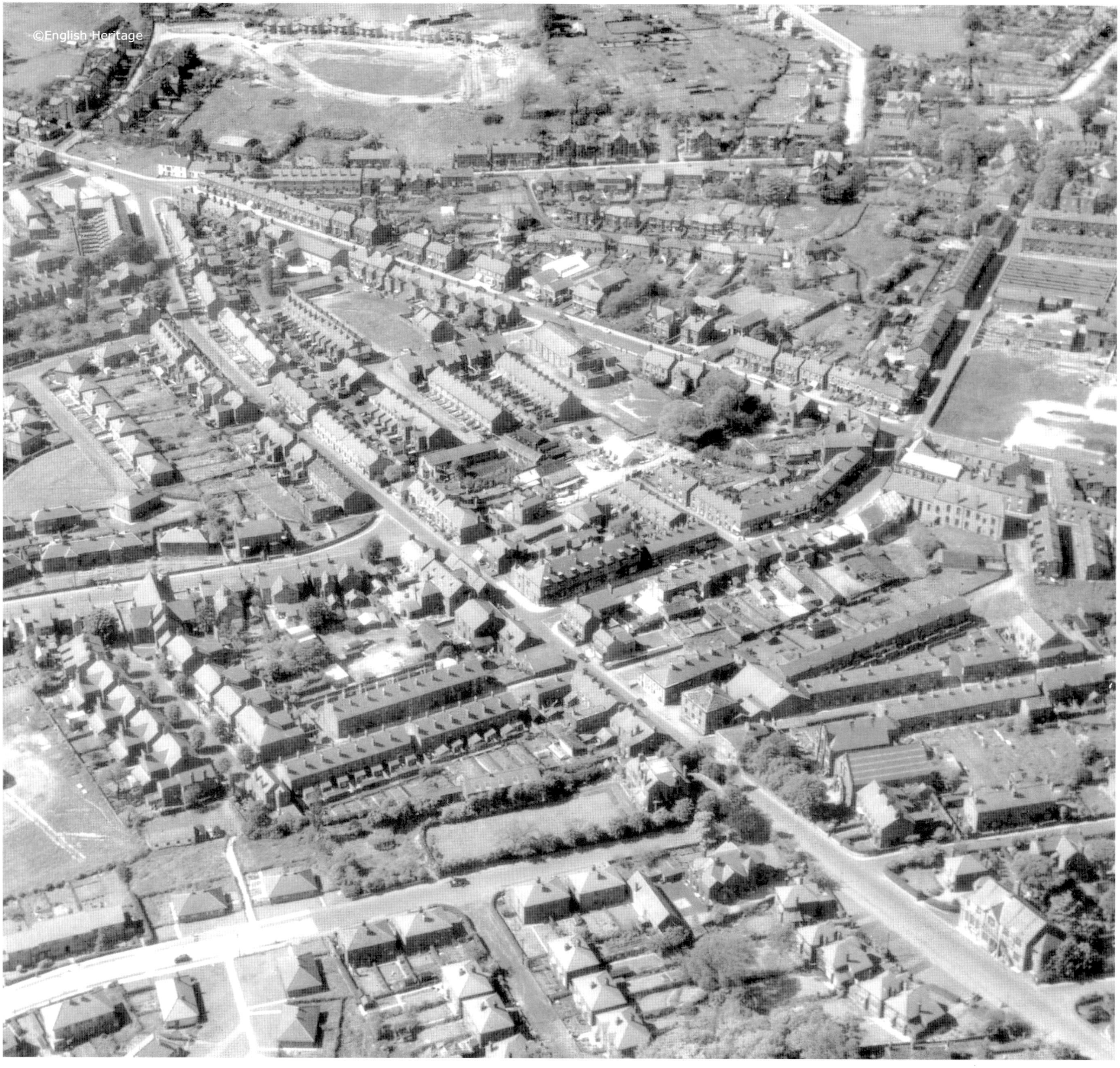

Looking towards Market Street (centre of picture) c1957

Memorial Park

The Memorial Park was built in honour of the men of Marple who lost their lives in the First World War. The land was given by the local Carver and Barlow Families and it opened in 1922. The park's setting in the centre of the village could not be better. Not only are there excellent facilities for play and relaxation, but the local library, health centre, police station, scout hut and citizens advice bureau are located within it's borders. The park also has stunning views over towards the Peak District and Marple Bridge.

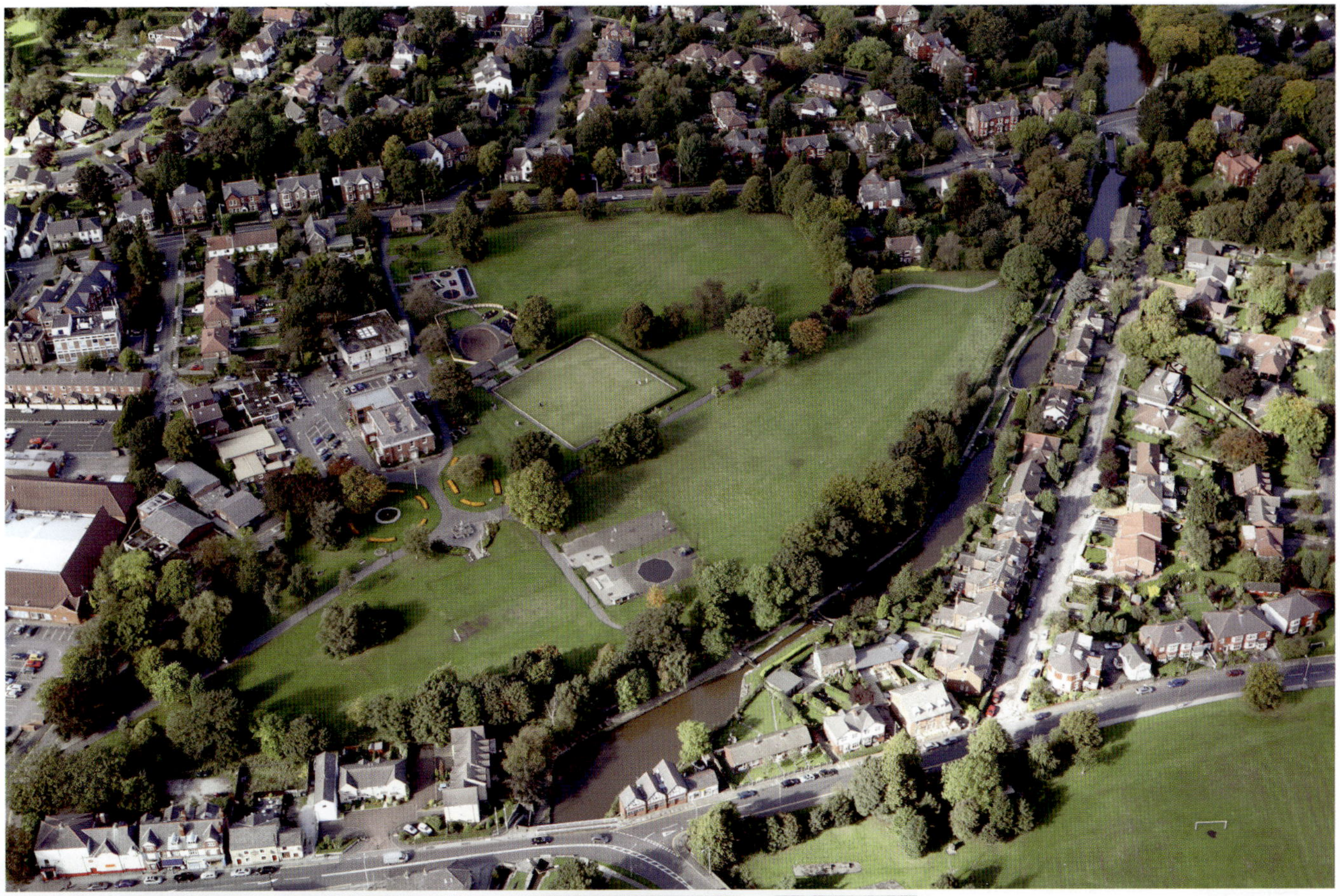

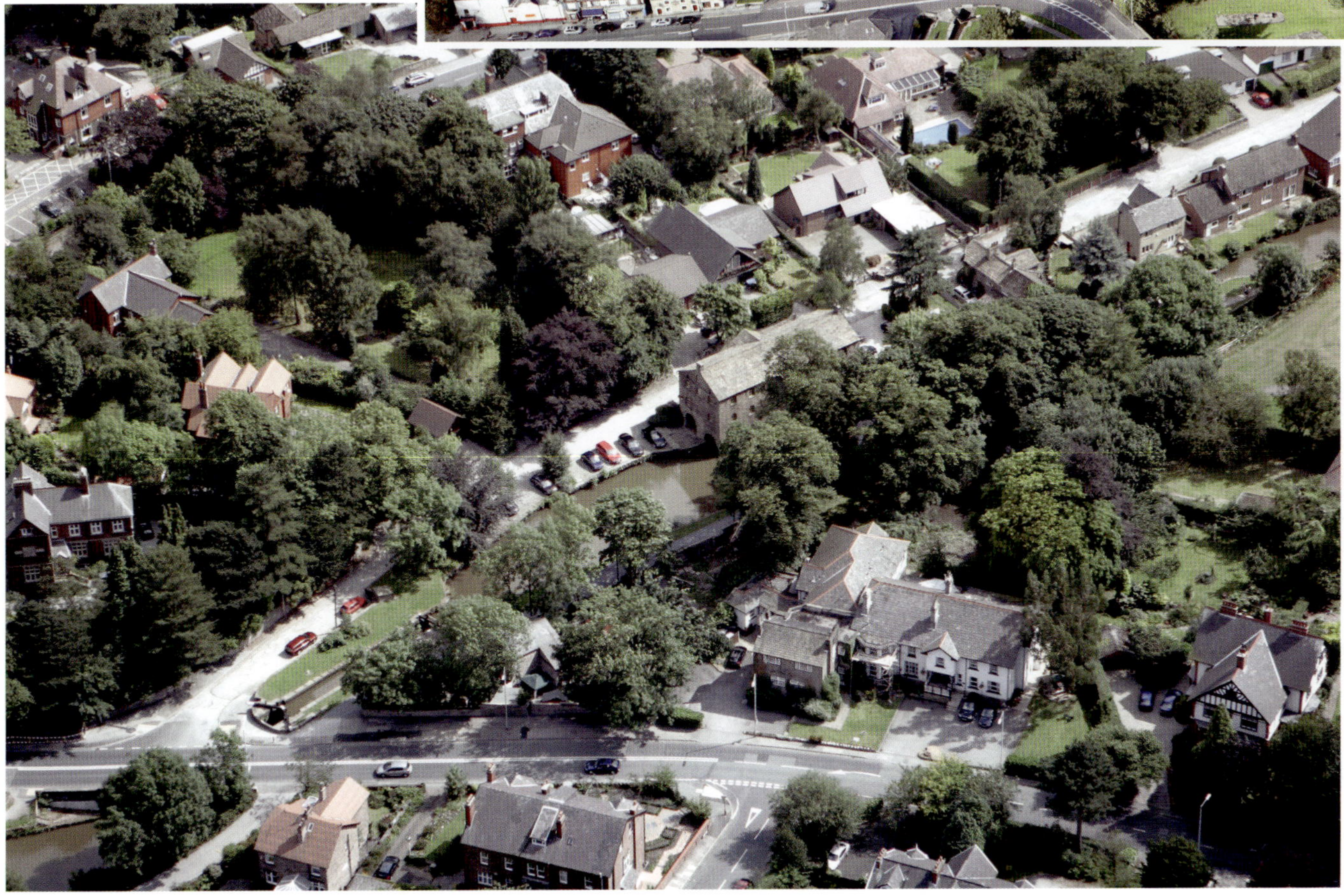

Oldknow's Warehouse

Samuel Oldknow was one of the leading industrialists in Stockport in the 18th century. Among the many mills that he built was the enormous Mellor Mill. He had a grand house along Hillgate in the centre of Stockport behind where the Mottram Street flats are now. It has recently been refurbished and converted into flats. This fine warehouse was used for storing and drying grain that was transported along the Peak Forest Canal route. The building has now been restored and is used as offices.

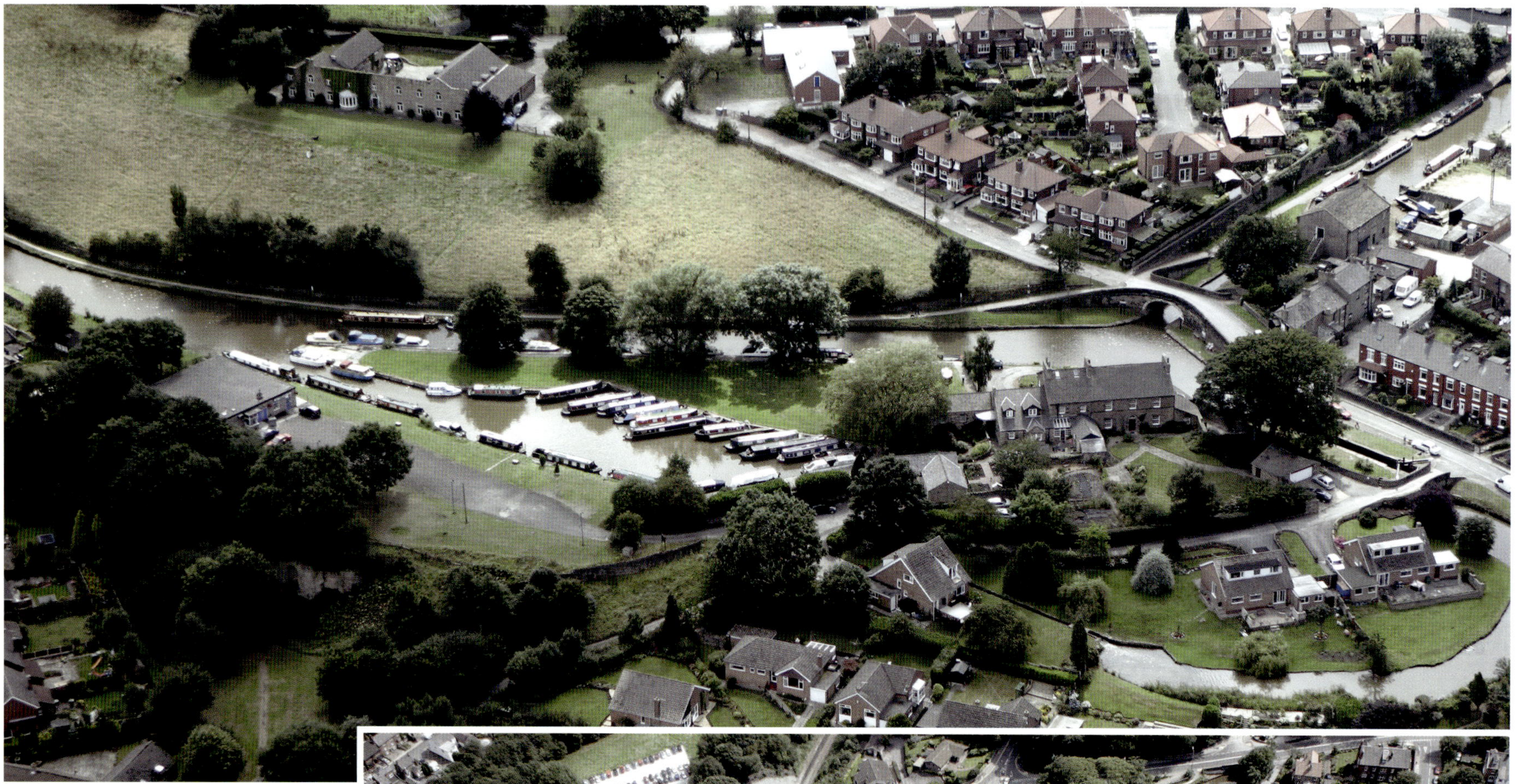

Marple Canal Locks

Marple is most famous for its system of canal locks. In total there are 16 locks, rising 209 feet to the "Top Lock" – number 16, over a distance of almost one mile. Here we are looking down upon lock number 12 running parallel to Marple Station. The canals are popular with holiday makers and for those making day trips into the Peak District. Further up the Locks is the Marina (above), situated at the junction of the Peak Forest Canal (coming in from the left) and the Macclesfield Canal (from the top right). The Macclesfield Canal was opened in 1831.

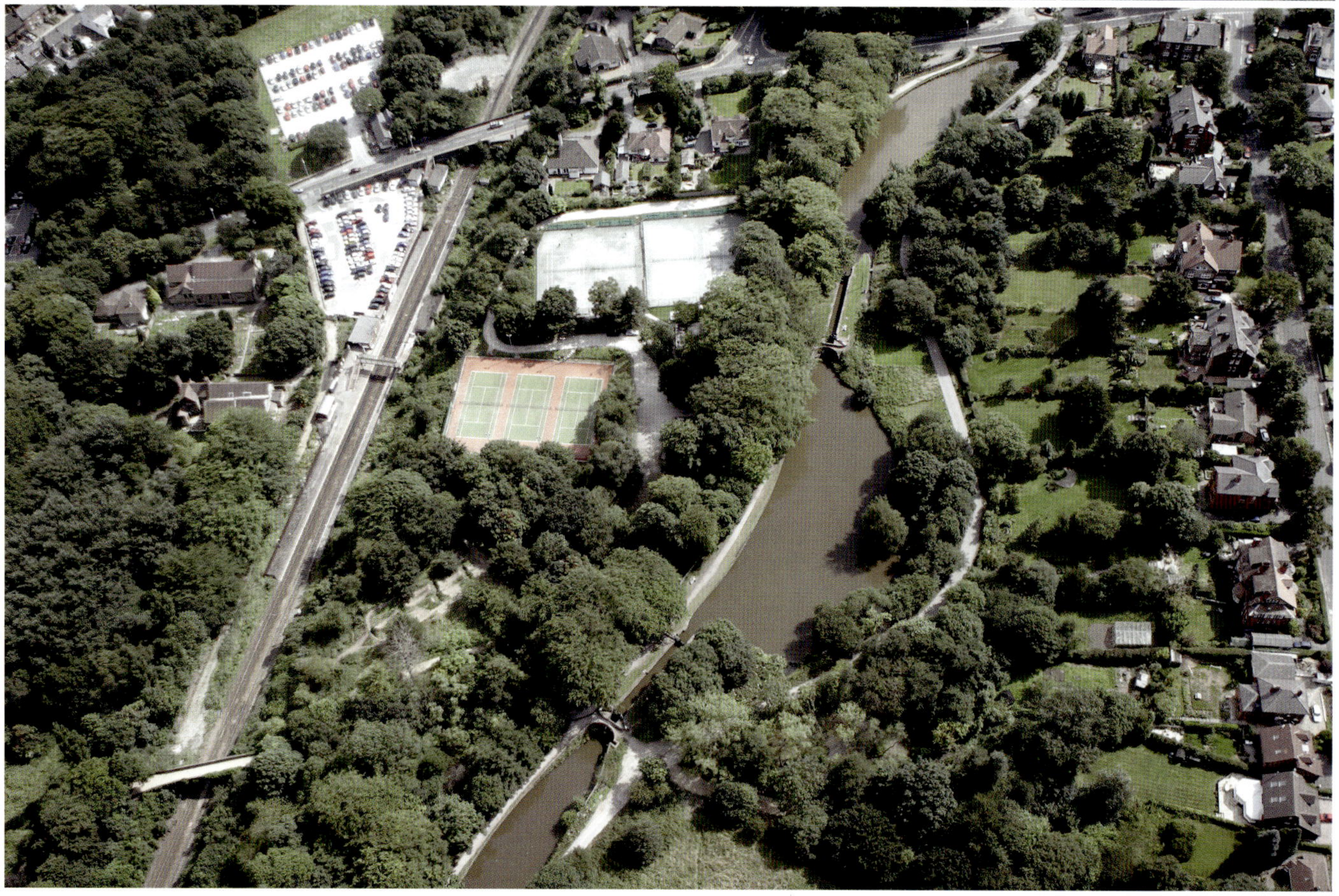

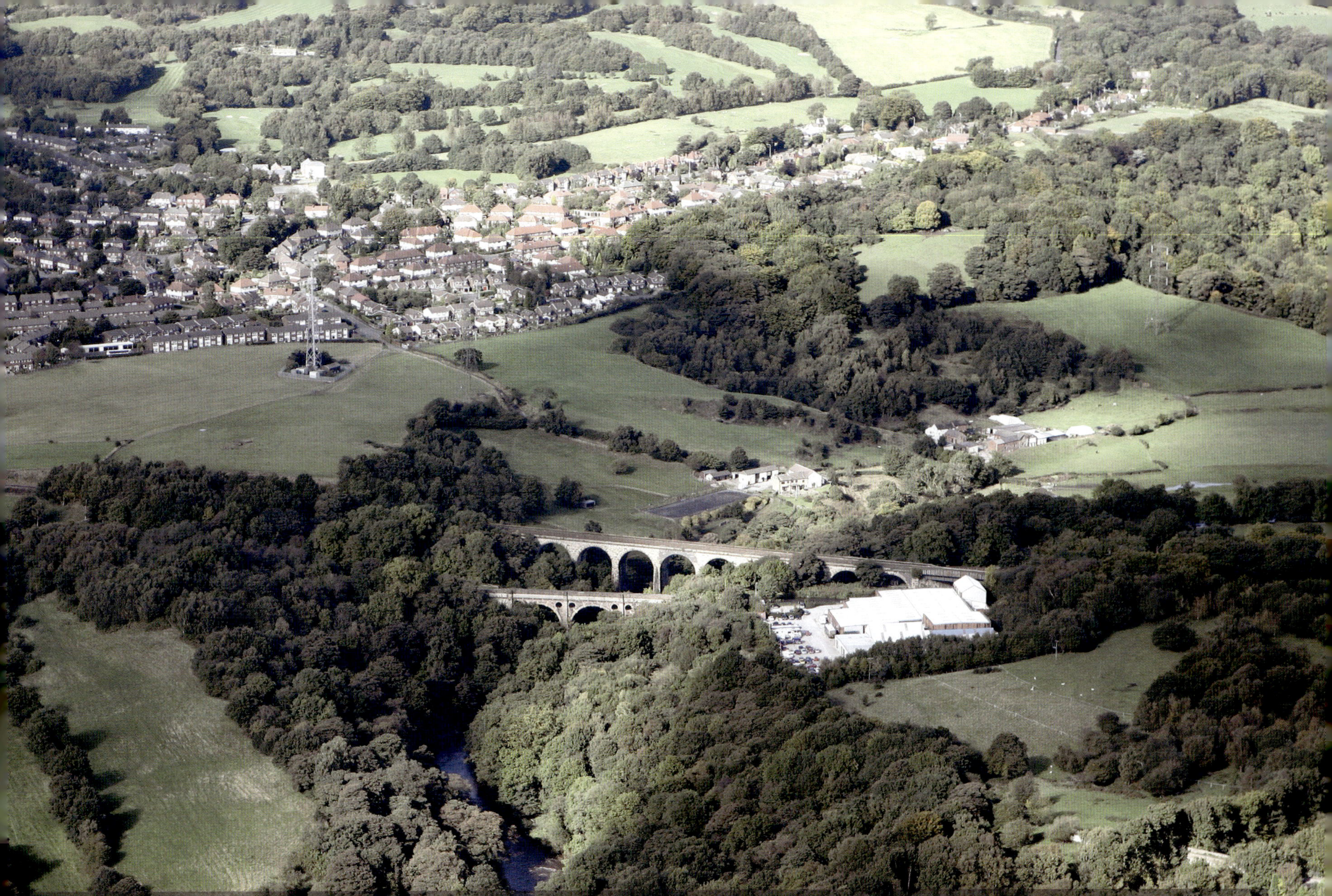

Marple Aqueduct & Viaduct

Marple aqueduct and viaduct span the valley of the river Goyt to the north of the village. The aqueduct sits 97 feet above the valley floor and is 309 feet long, whilst the viaduct behind reaches a height of 120 feet. Work started on the aqueduct in May 1794. The bridge would allow the Peak Forest Canal to continue over the valley on its journey towards Romiley. It was designed by Benjamin Outram and Thomas Brown, who were the chief engineers on the construction of the Canal. It took seven years to build but was finally completed in 1800. Seven men lost their lives as a result of the construction. The neighbouring railway viaduct was built 65 years later in 1865. Despite being much larger, it only took a year to build, showing the rapid improvements in construction techniques in the 19th century. Also, no-one died during the construction of the viaduct, which has 12 stone arches compared to the aqueduct's 3. Note the circular openings above the arches on the aqueduct. These were included to help strengthen the structure whilst lessening its weight. The aqueduct had fallen into disrepair by the early 1960s, partly due to frost damage, but thanks to a concerted campaign to restore it by local people, British Waterways and the local council agreed to pay for its restoration. The aqueduct is now a Grade 1 Listed Monument. In years gone by it was possible to take dramatic photographs from the river valley below, showing both of the structures in all of their glory. Nowadays they are obscured by trees, making it difficult to get a good shot, but this image does them both justice, showing the spectacular setting above the valley sides with the river running below.

Canal Pounds c1957

Despite being surrounded by water, from canals to rivers and streams, sometimes the flow of water in Marple stops. This picture shows one such time when the canal pounds by the marina had run dry. A pound is the area of water between locks used for storing water to avoid too much fluctuation in its levels. These particular pounds are "side pounds", which branch off at the side, unlike most of the other pounds on the canal that just have a wider section between each lock (see the image of Lock 12 on page 110). Note the narrow boat stuck in the mud in the last pound on the right. The junction with the Macclesfield Canal is just visible on the lower left. Compare it to the modern picture of the marina on page 110. There are now houses on the land in between the pounds.

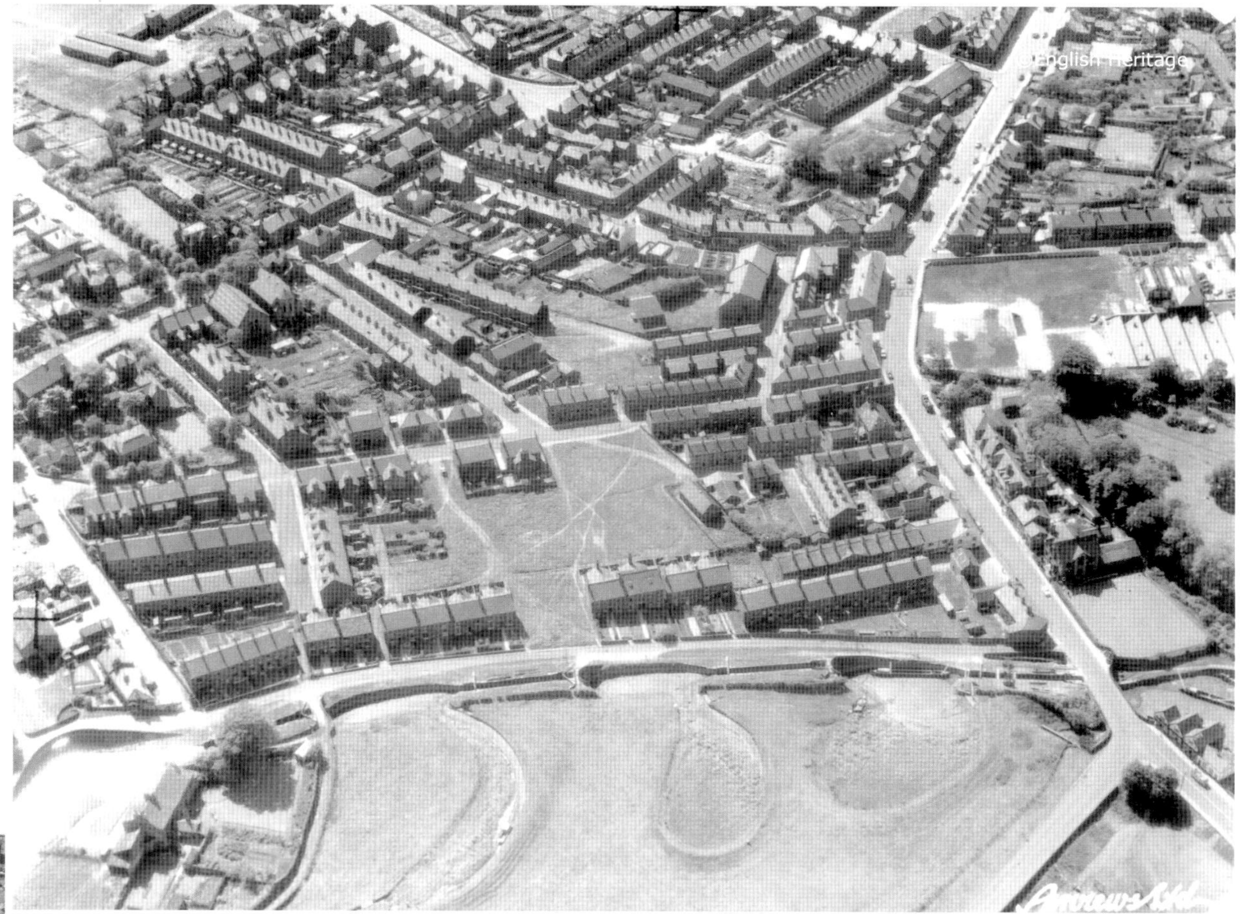

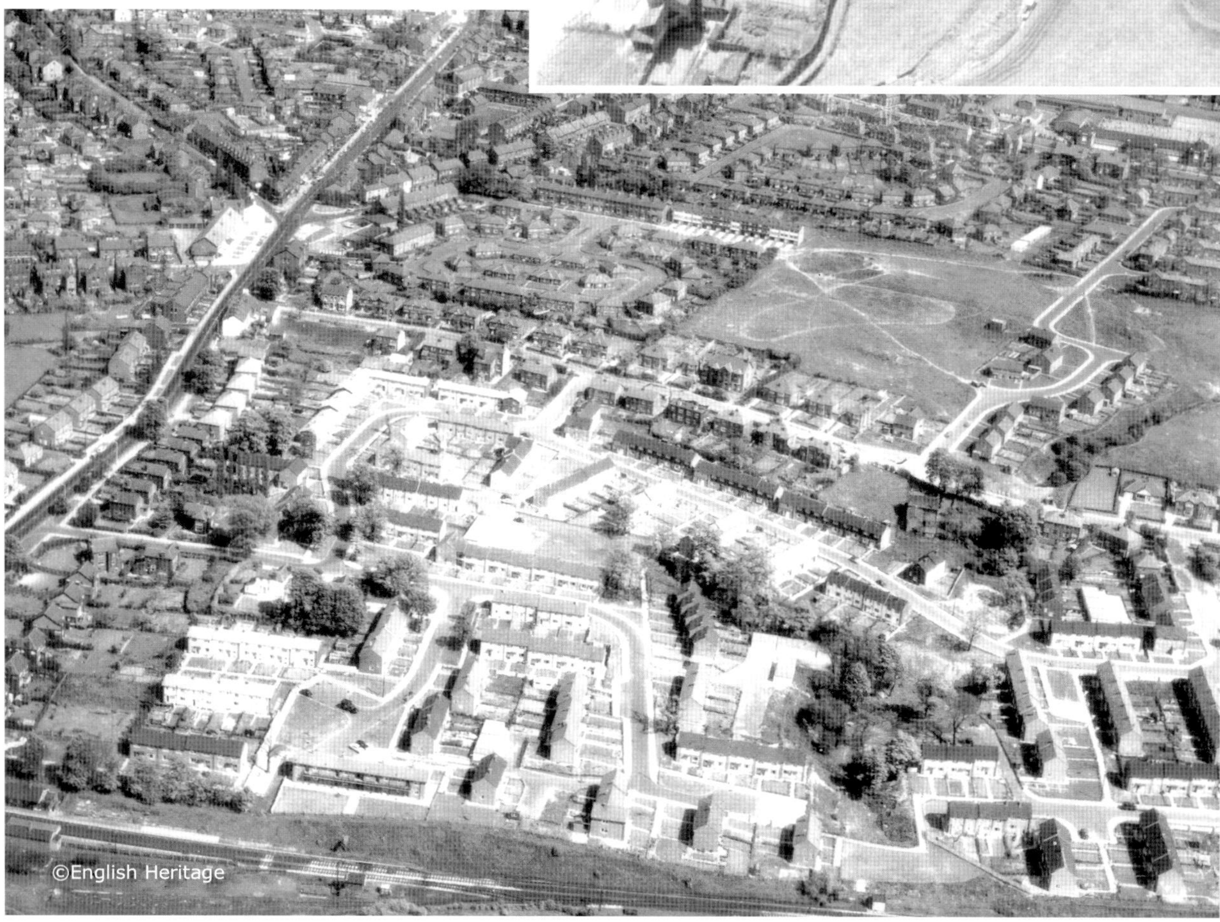

Rose Hill Estate c1960

Marple experienced the same growth as the other major districts during the inter and post war years, with many new homes and estates built. One such new estate was the overspill estate for Manchester City Council on Rose Lane. This was one of 7 such estates to be built in Stockport, with the intention being to re-house people whose own homes had become unfit for habitation. This picture shows the estate recently after completion in the early 1960s. This was a typical infill development of the time, making use of land that was already bordered by older housing. On the bottom left is Rose Hill Train Station. This is now the end of the line, as the track heading south to Macclesfield has become a nature walk known as the Middlewood Way.

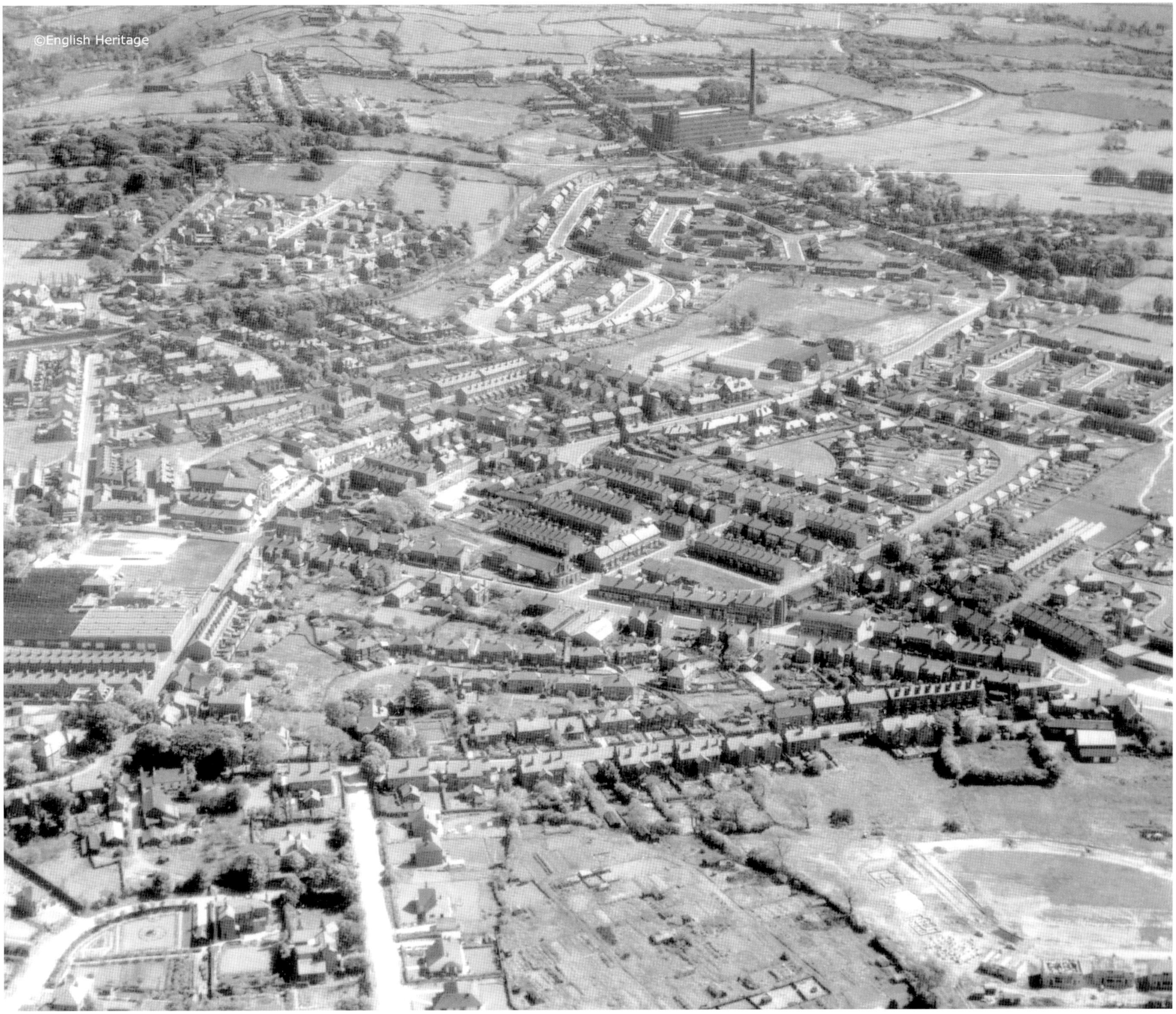

View towards Hawk Green c1957

In the distance can be seen the towering presence of Goyt Mill in Hawk Green. Hawk Green was a small hamlet on the southern edge of Marple but thanks to the residential growth it is now attached to the rest of the village. Beyond Hawk Green the area is still fields, and this picture gives some indication of how close Marple really is to the countryside. On the lower right can be seen some more new housing being built on Norbury Drive next to the allotments.

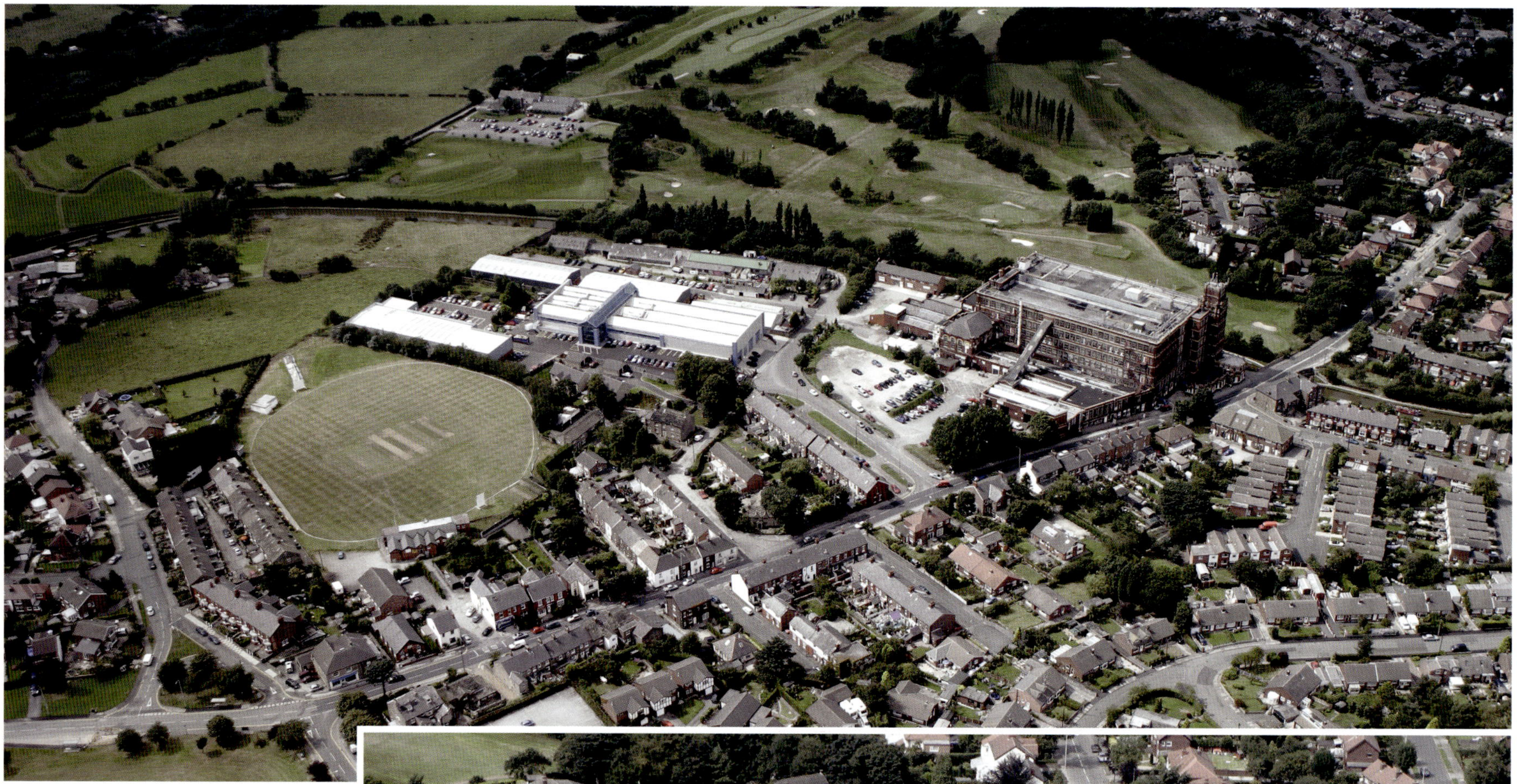

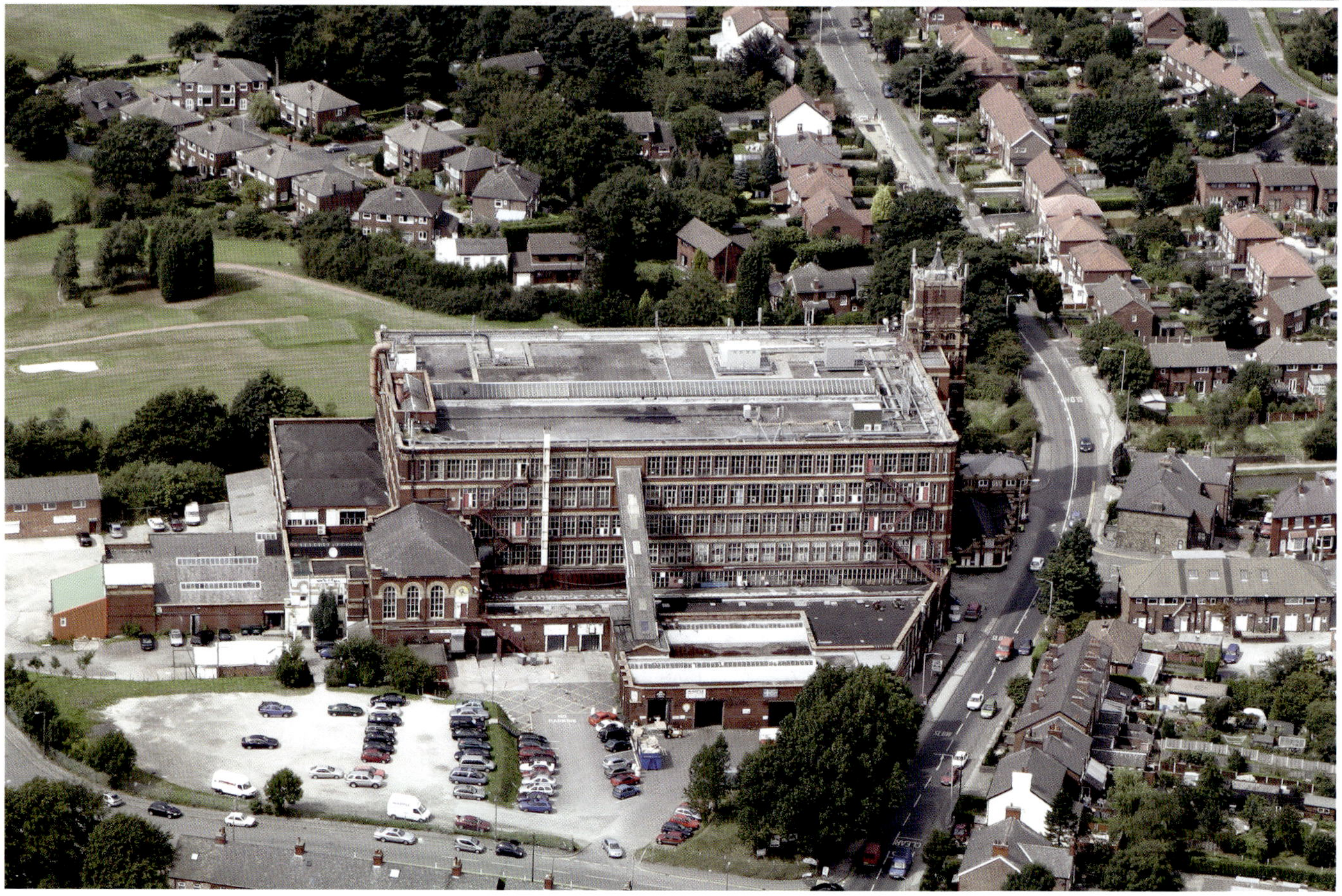

Hawk Green

Hawk Green is dominated by the imposing six-storey Goyt Mill. This former cotton mill on the banks of the Macclesfield Canal was designed by AH Stott & Sons in 1905. It closed in 1959 after the government offered subsidies to firms leaving the textile industry. This was the same reason for the closure of Broadstone Mill in Reddish.

The chimney was demolished in the 1980s, but the mill is now occupied once again and has been turned into a business centre which is now home to over 80 businesses. To the left can be seen Hawk Green Cricket Club, and to the rear is Marple Golf Course.

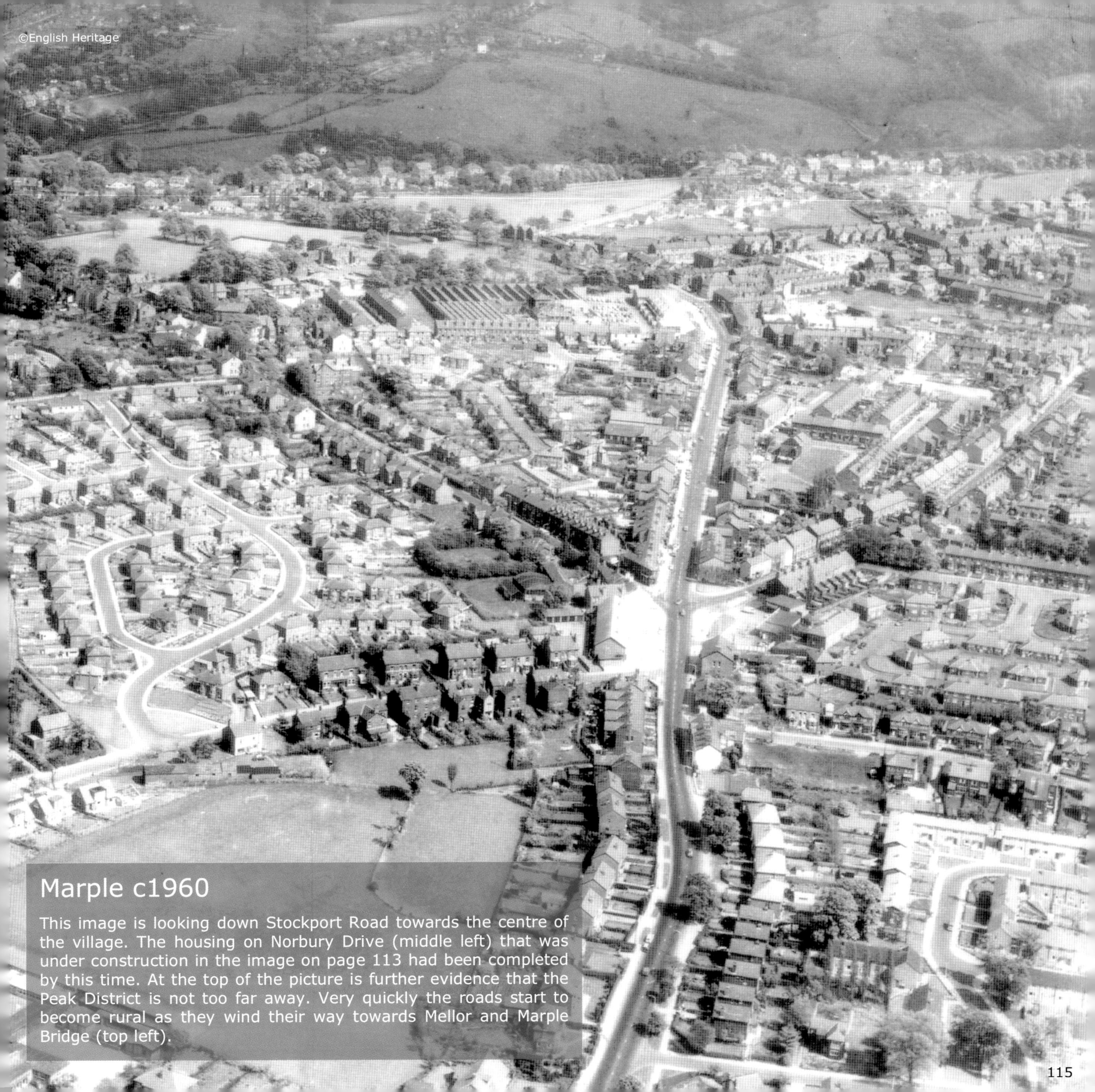

Marple c1960

This image is looking down Stockport Road towards the centre of the village. The housing on Norbury Drive (middle left) that was under construction in the image on page 113 had been completed by this time. At the top of the picture is further evidence that the Peak District is not too far away. Very quickly the roads start to become rural as they wind their way towards Mellor and Marple Bridge (top left).

Marple Bridge - Town Street

Town Street is the main street in the charming village of Marple Bridge, so named because of the 19th century bridge to Marple over the River Goyt. The beautiful setting by the side of the river only enhances its picture postcard attractiveness, along with the character stone built Georgian houses that are prevalent in its small streets. But things are not always as picturesque or peaceful as they appear. From 1845 up until 1976 Marple Bridge was home to a large gas works at the northern end of the village, and in 1991 part of the wall along the banks of the river collapsed, leaving a 30-foot drop to the water below. Town Street was closed to traffic for over a year while the wall was restored. The village is also home to the 90 acre Brabyns Park, which was originally the estate of Brabyns Hall and features an historic iron bridge from 1813. The entrance to the park is opposite the car park at the bottom of the facing page.

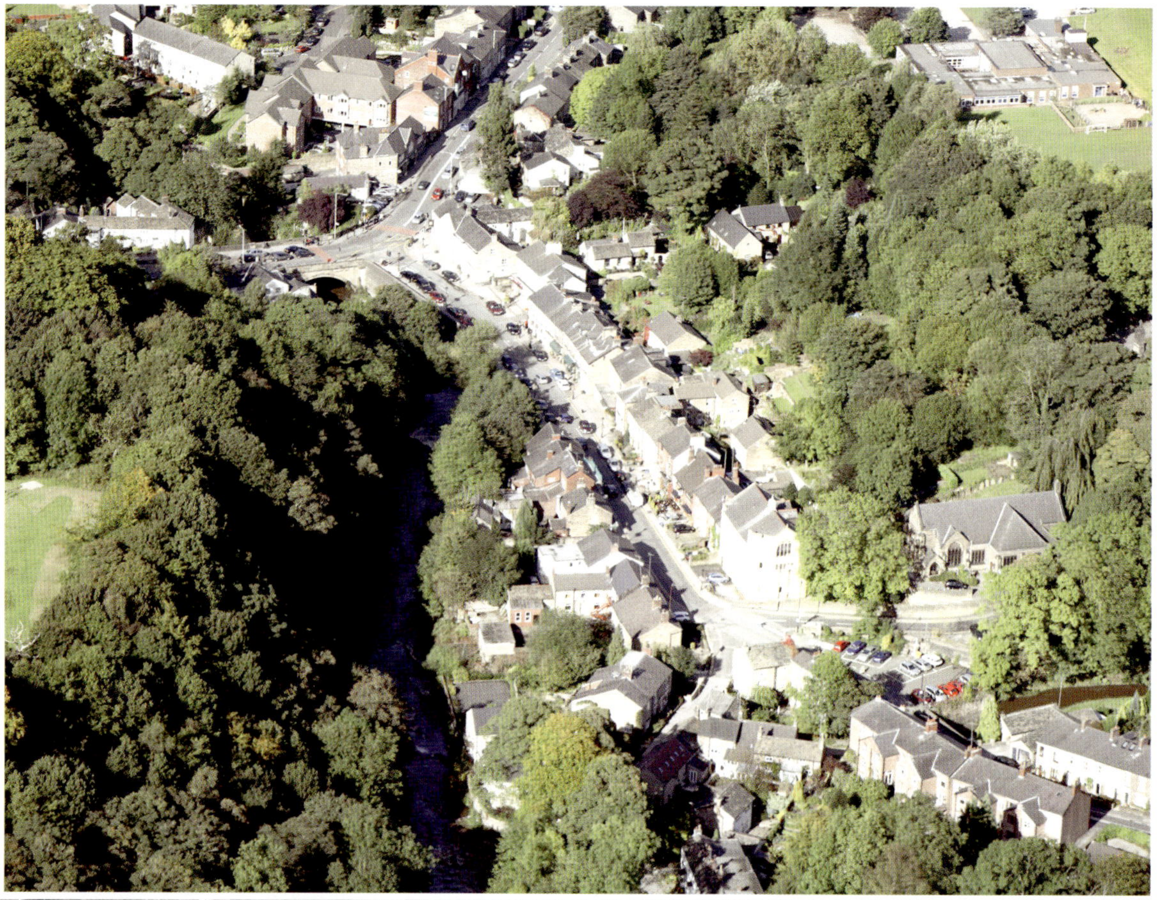

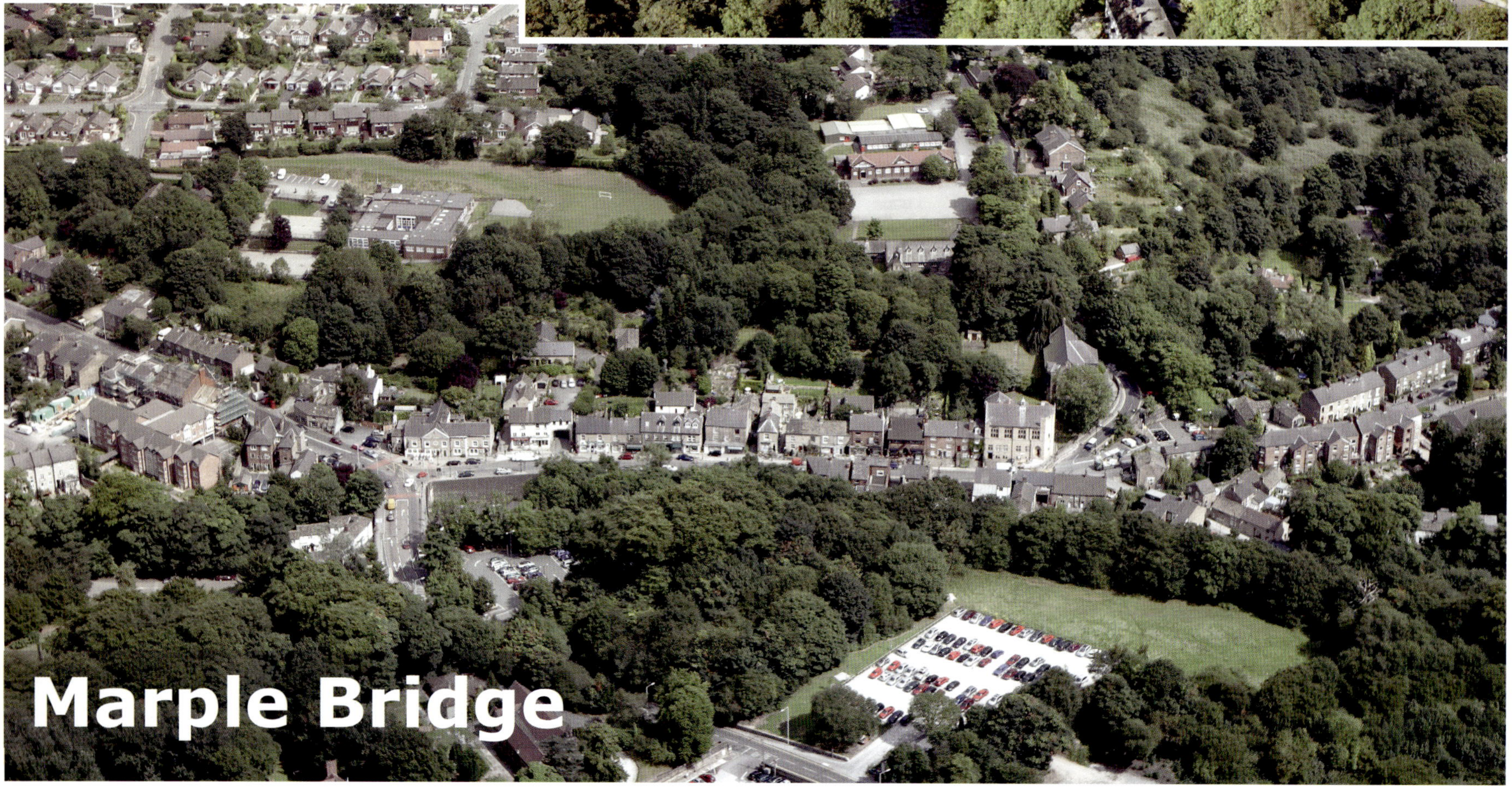

Marple Bridge

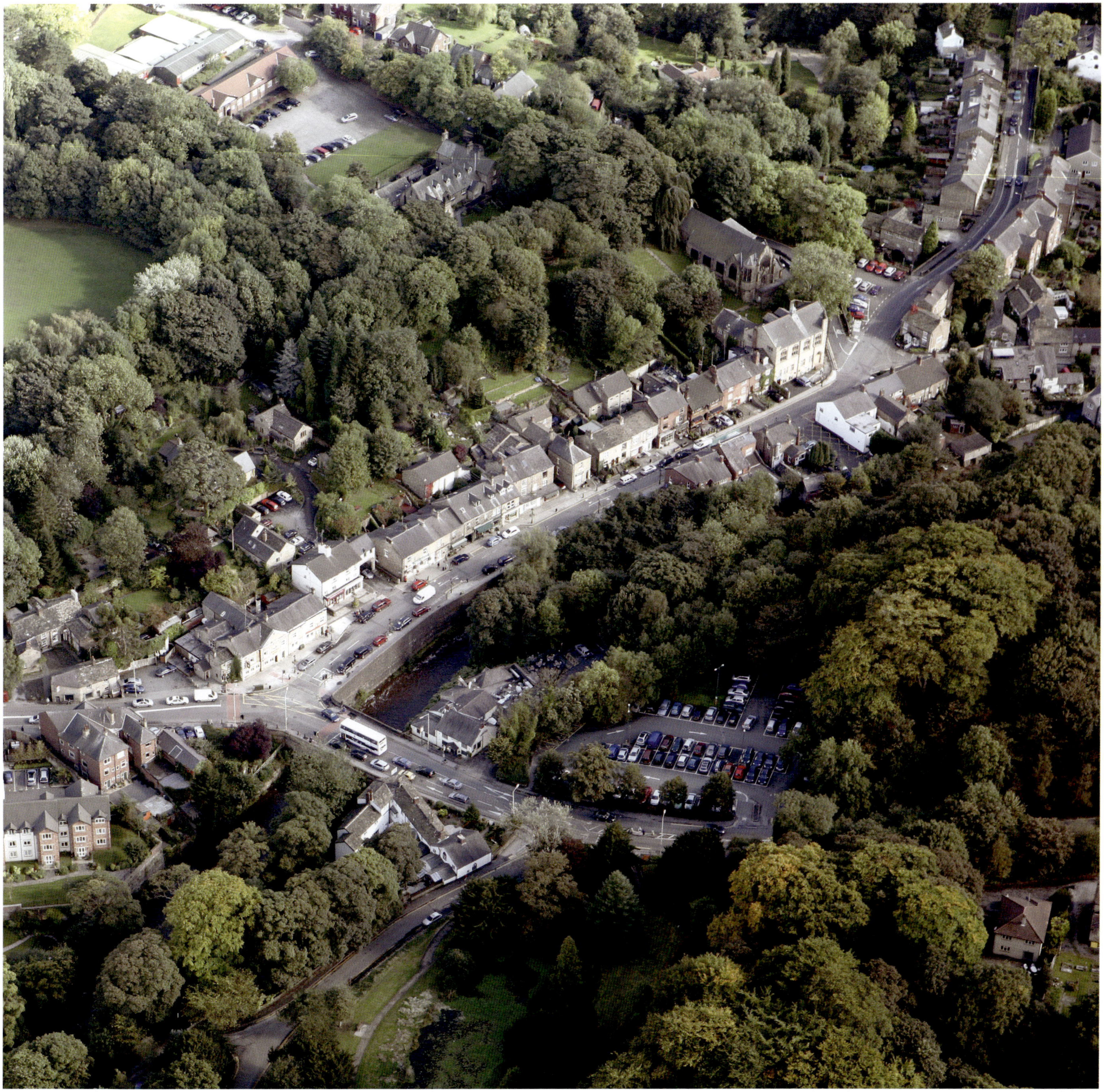

Mellor

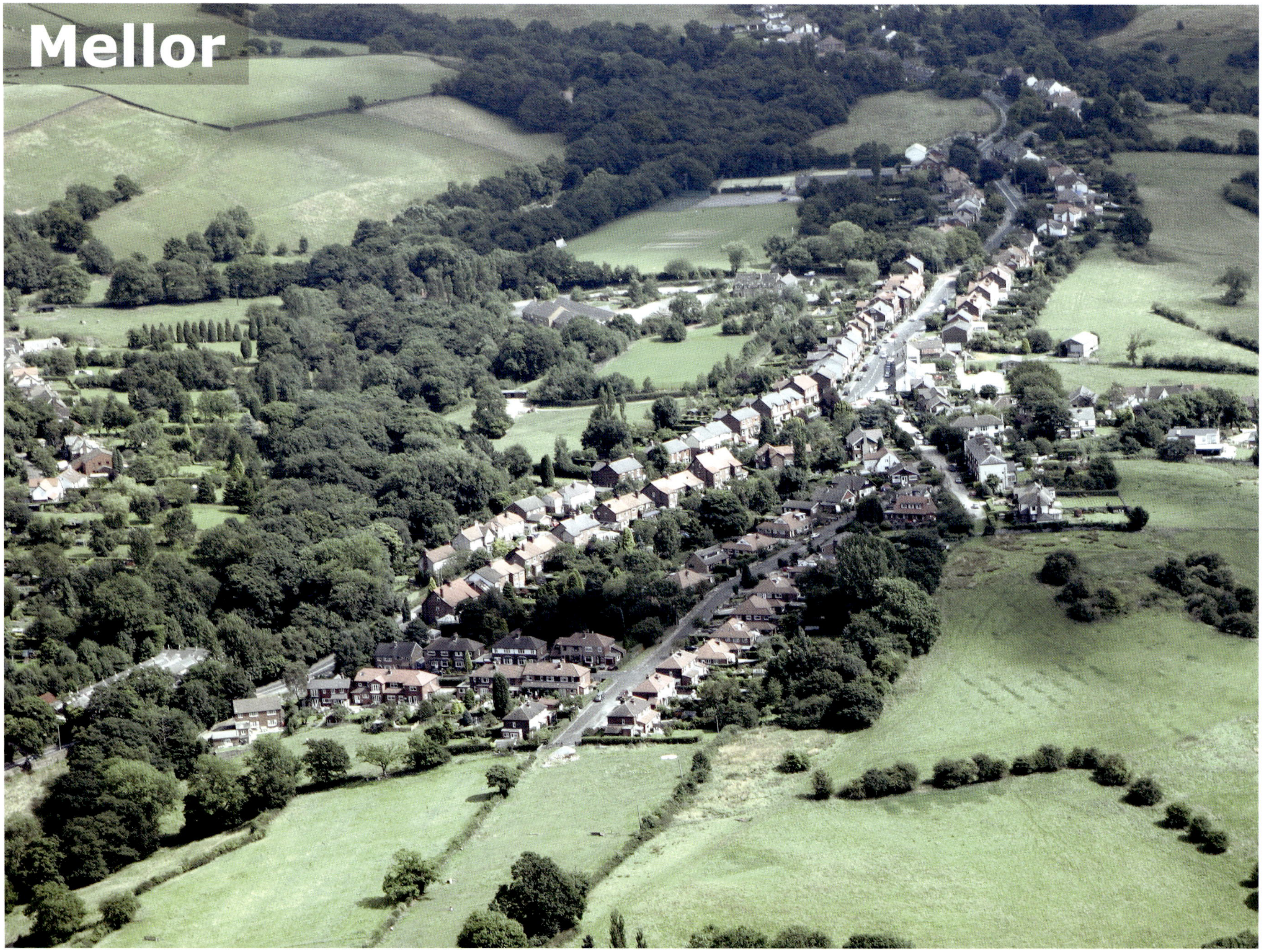

Mellor - Longhurst Lane

Mellor, along with the township of Ludworth, used to be in Derbyshire. It was transferred to Cheshire in 1936 when it became part of Marple Urban District. Set high up in the hills, the village is genuinely rural, and its elevated position has tremendous views looking back across Stockport. The usually quiet village has attracted a lot of attention in recent years due to the discovery of a medieval fort around the local vicarage. To help research and catalogue the site, the Mellor Archaeological Society was set up and now holds an annual dig. Many fascinating items have been uncovered including artefacts such as spearheads and arrowheads, the likes of which have not been found anywhere else in the area. This picture is looking towards Mellor Sports Club along Longhurst Lane. Mellor was also the site of one of the largest mills of its day. Built by Samuel Oldknow, it opened in 1792 and stood 6-storeys tall and 210 feet long. Two large reservoirs were built to provide the mill with water for power. Steam power was not introduced until as late as 1860. The mill continued in operation until November 1892 when it was destroyed in a disastrous fire. Remnants of the building still remain, most notably the reservoirs. These were renamed as Roman Lakes in Victorian times and have been used for leisure ever since (see facing page).

Strines

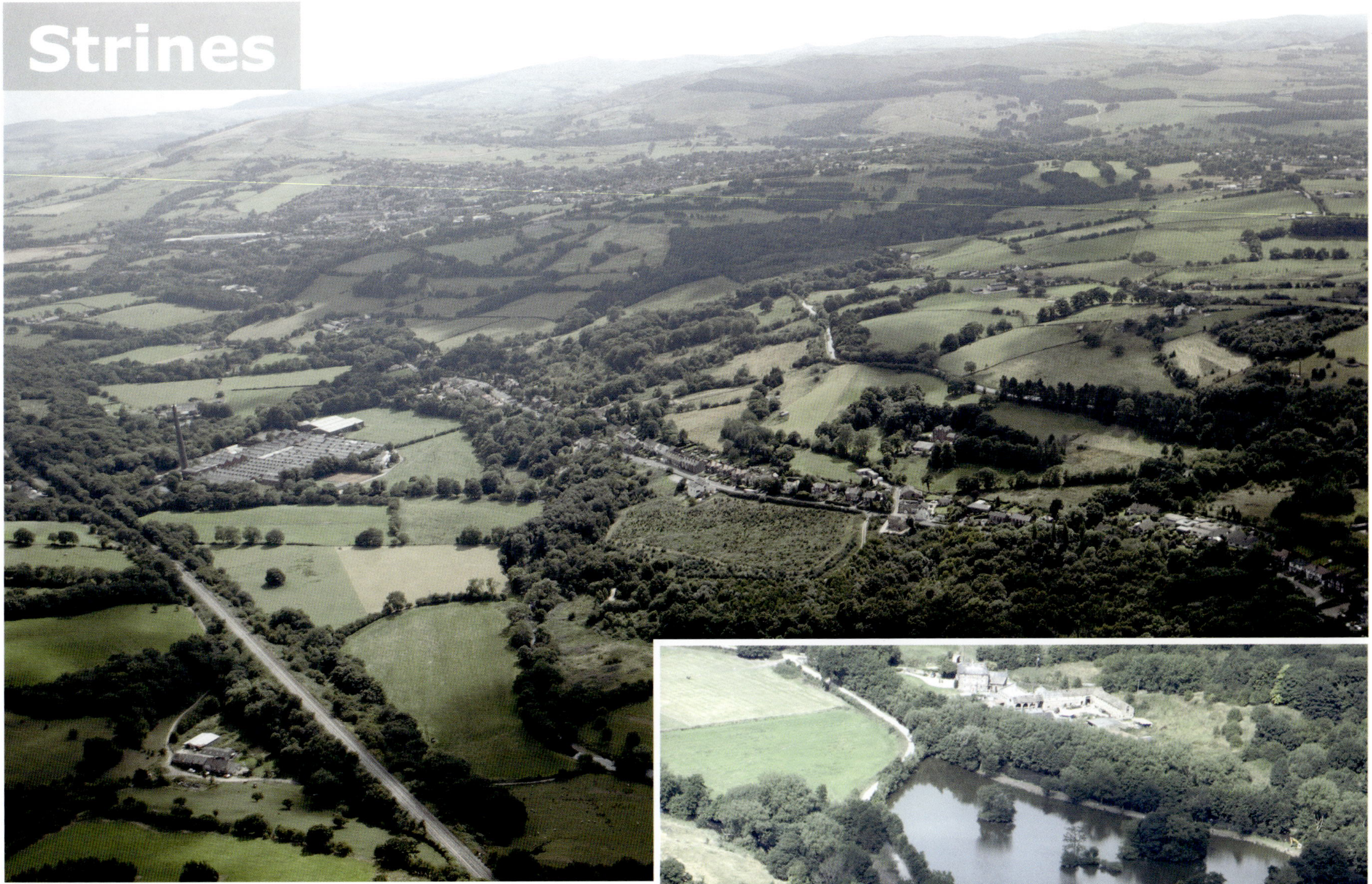

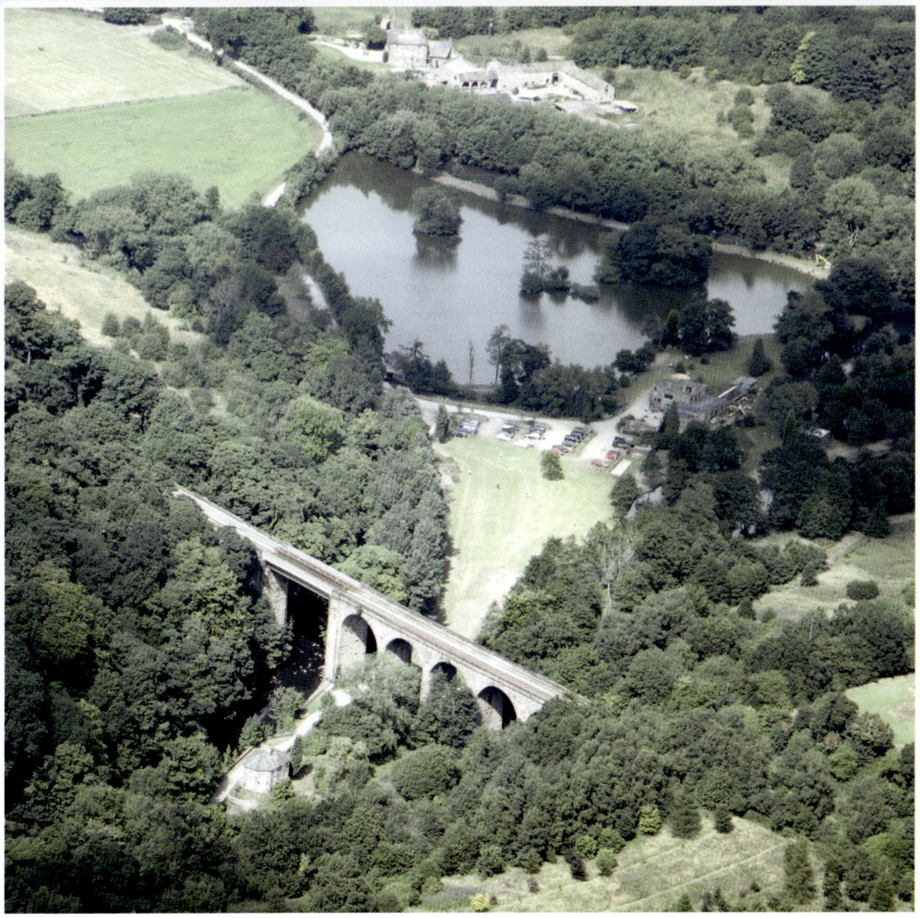

Strines

The small community at Strines is situated just down the canal from Marple. The village was previously dominated by the huge printworks and its impressive chimney, seen here on the left. The buildings dated from around 1925 but a printworks had been based closed to here since the late 18th century, specialising in calico printing. The owner of the factory, Thomas Henry Neville, purchased Bramall Hall for his son Charles as a wedding present in 1882. The buildings and the 240 foot chimney were demolished in January 2007 to make way for a new housing development on the site. In the background can be seen the village of Disley. The railway line to New Mills can be seen on the left. Just off the bottom of the picture is the Strines viaduct (right), which carries the track over the valley of the River Goyt, 89 feet below. To the rear of the viaduct is Roman Lakes, the site of Mellor Mill.

High Lane

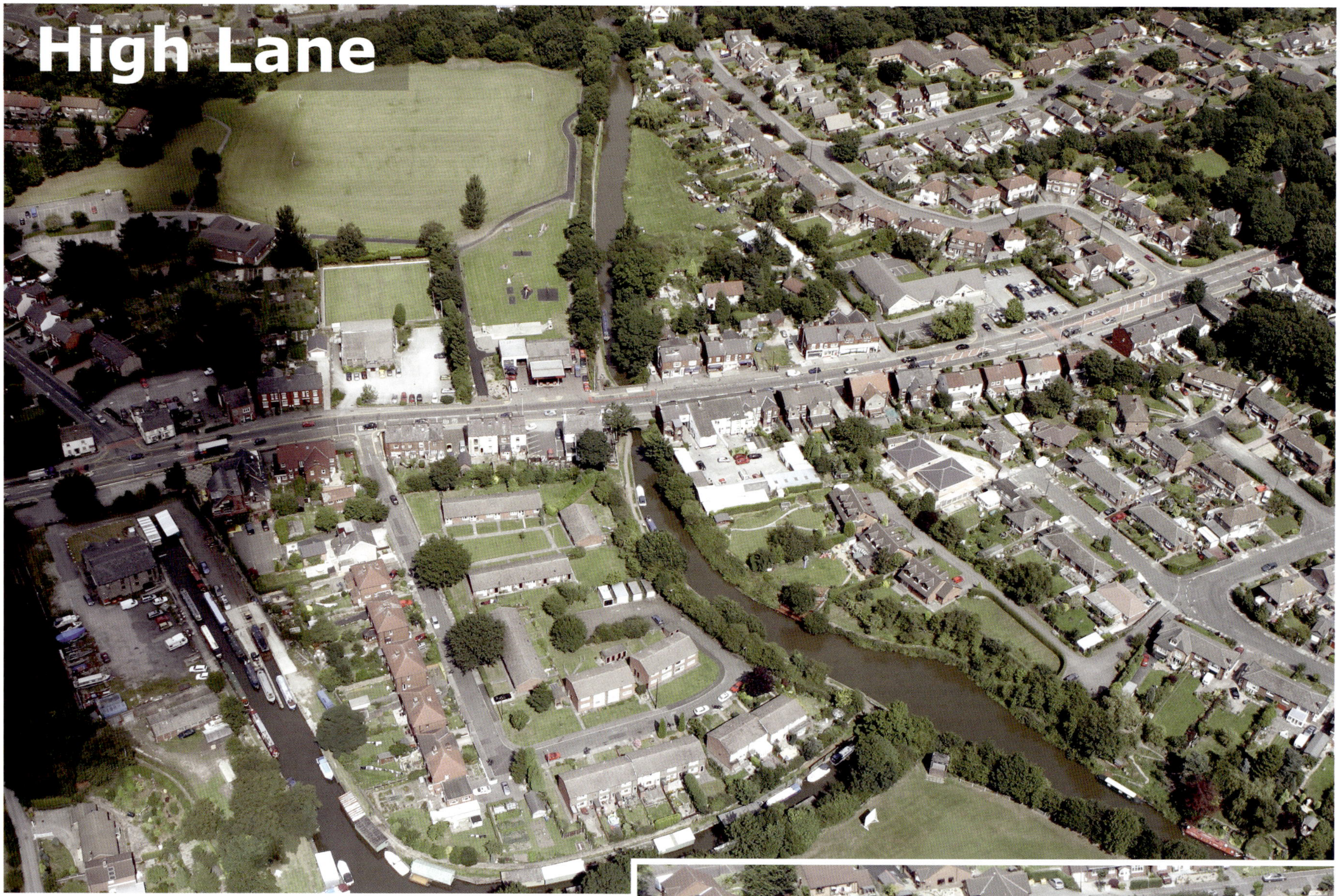

High Lane

High Lane is quite a large commuter village built around the busy A6, and the centre of the village can be seen here. The small marina in the photo is home to the North Cheshire Cruising Club, which is accessed through bridge 12 on the Macclesfield Canal, on the right. The club was founded in 1943 and was the first cruising club on the entire canal system in England. It has moorings for 52 boats.

Just to the right of the main photo further down the A6 is the site of St Thomas' church (right). The church dates from 1851 but was not consecrated until 1859. It has long had the nickname "the church in the trees" for fairly obvious reasons, but the trees are now so big that it is becoming difficult to see the church or even the tower from afar.

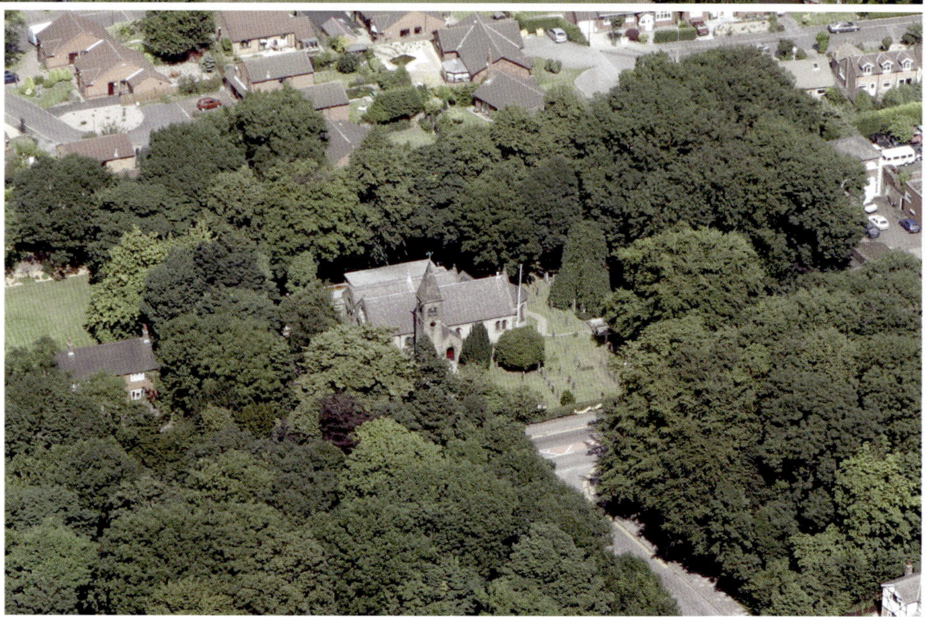

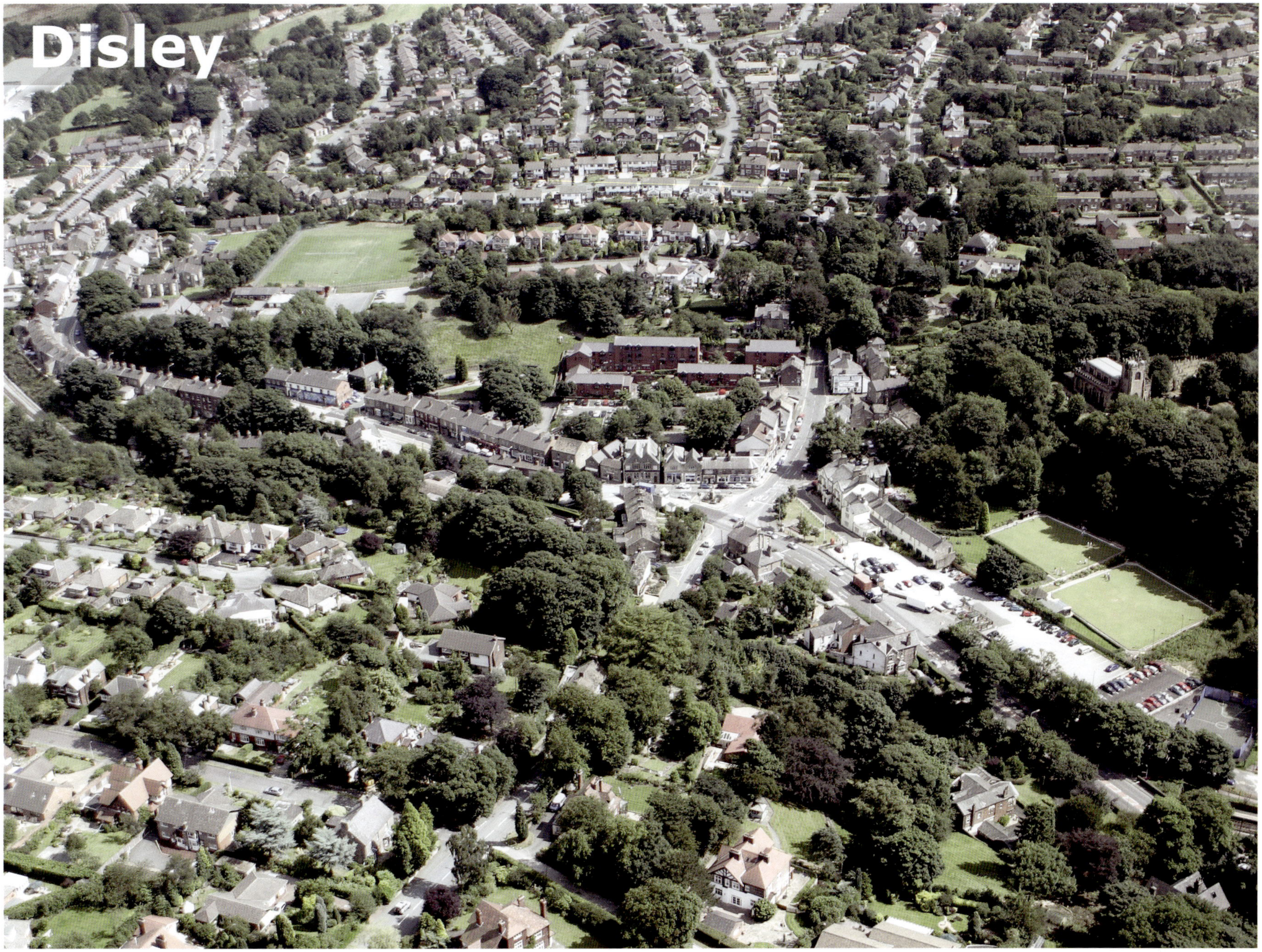

Disley

This delightful Cheshire Village is situated next to Lyme Park and is right on the border with Derbyshire. Disley was a traditional coaching stop on the road from London. Its Anglo-Saxon name was Dystiglegh or Dystelegh, which meant a "windy settlement". The Ram's Head pub is the most recognisable building in the village. It is recorded as being here as early as around 1650 when it was used as a lodge belonging to the Lyme Park estate. The current building dates from about 1840. The pub, situated on Fountain Square just off Market Street, later became an important coaching stop on the route to Buxton and back. The fountain itself is now situated on a mini-roundabout just by the main road. It was given to the village in 1834 by the Orford family. St Mary's Church is a superb Grade II* listed building situated on a bluff overlooking the village (on the right). It was founded by the fifth Sir Piers Legh of the Lyme family between 1527 and 1558 but was rebuilt from 1824-1835. Only the tower and the nave ceiling were retained from the original building.

Lyme Hall

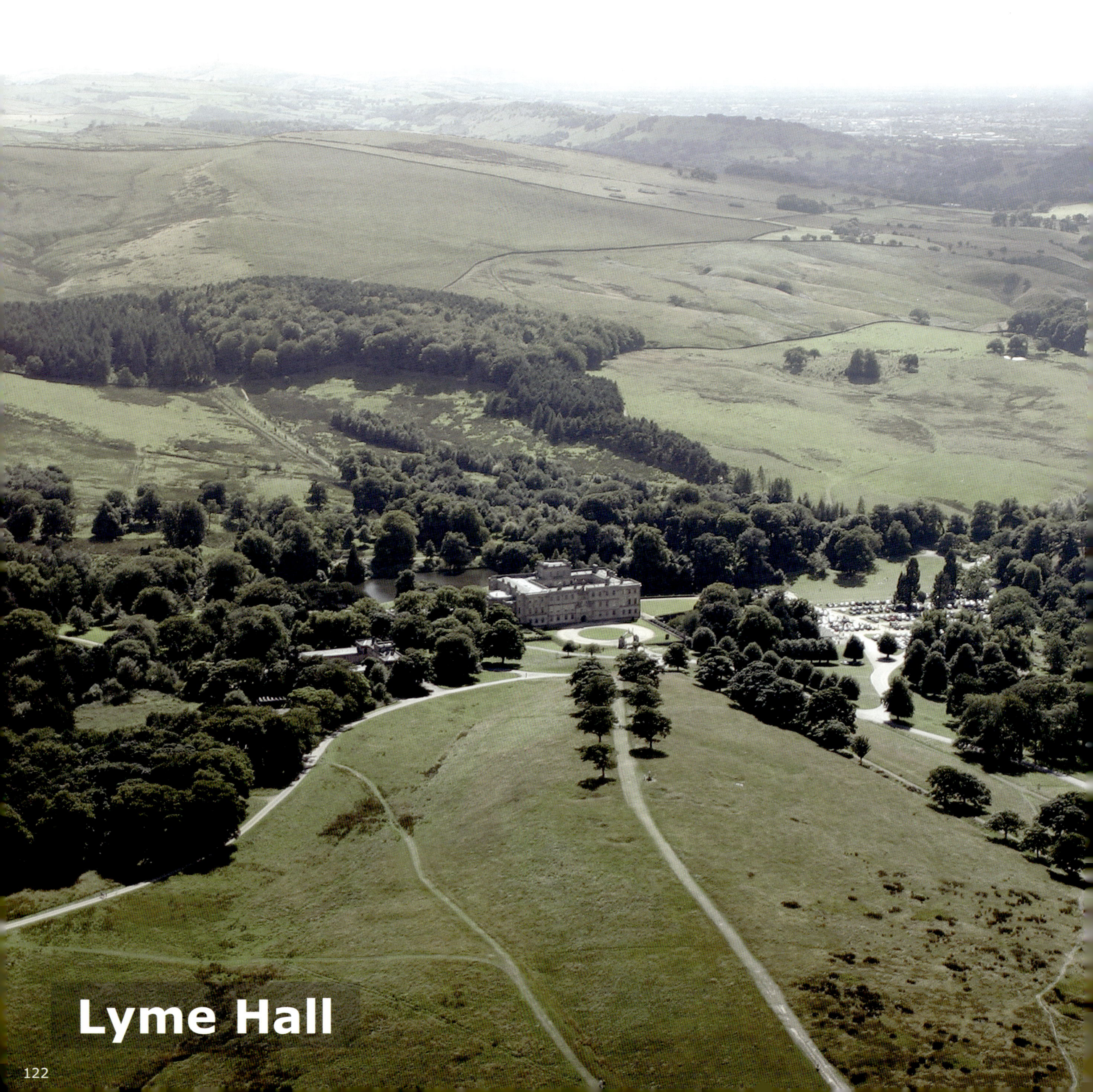

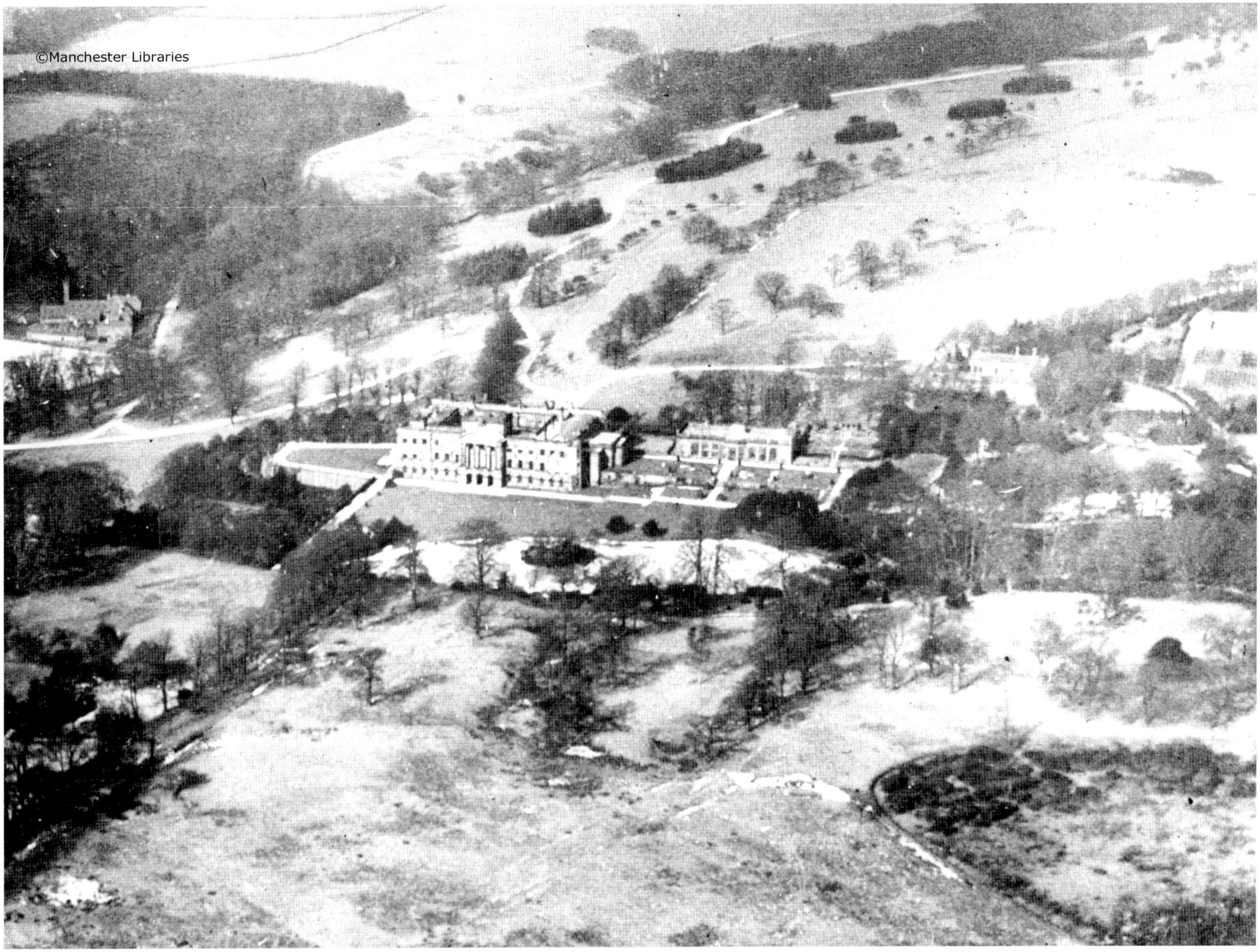

Lyme Hall c1928

Lyme Park is an historic deer park covering over 1400 acres of Cheshire countryside. At its centre is the magnificent Lyme Hall. The original hall was built in Tudor times but the present Italianette look was created in the early 18th century when it was extended by the Venetian Architect Giacomo Leoni, making it the largest house in Cheshire. It was home to the notable Legh family for almost 600 years. The gardens of the actual house extend to around 16 acres, and include a magnificent Dutch Garden, Orangery and a maze, which can be seen cut into the grass on the next page. There is also a fine lake to the rear of the hall. It was this lake that helped lead to the hall becoming internationally famous following the filming of the BBC's adaptation of Jane Austin's "Pride & Predjudice" in 1995, when it was used as "Pemberley", the home of Mr Darcy. The most famous scene was when Mr Darcy was seen emerging from the water after taking a swim.

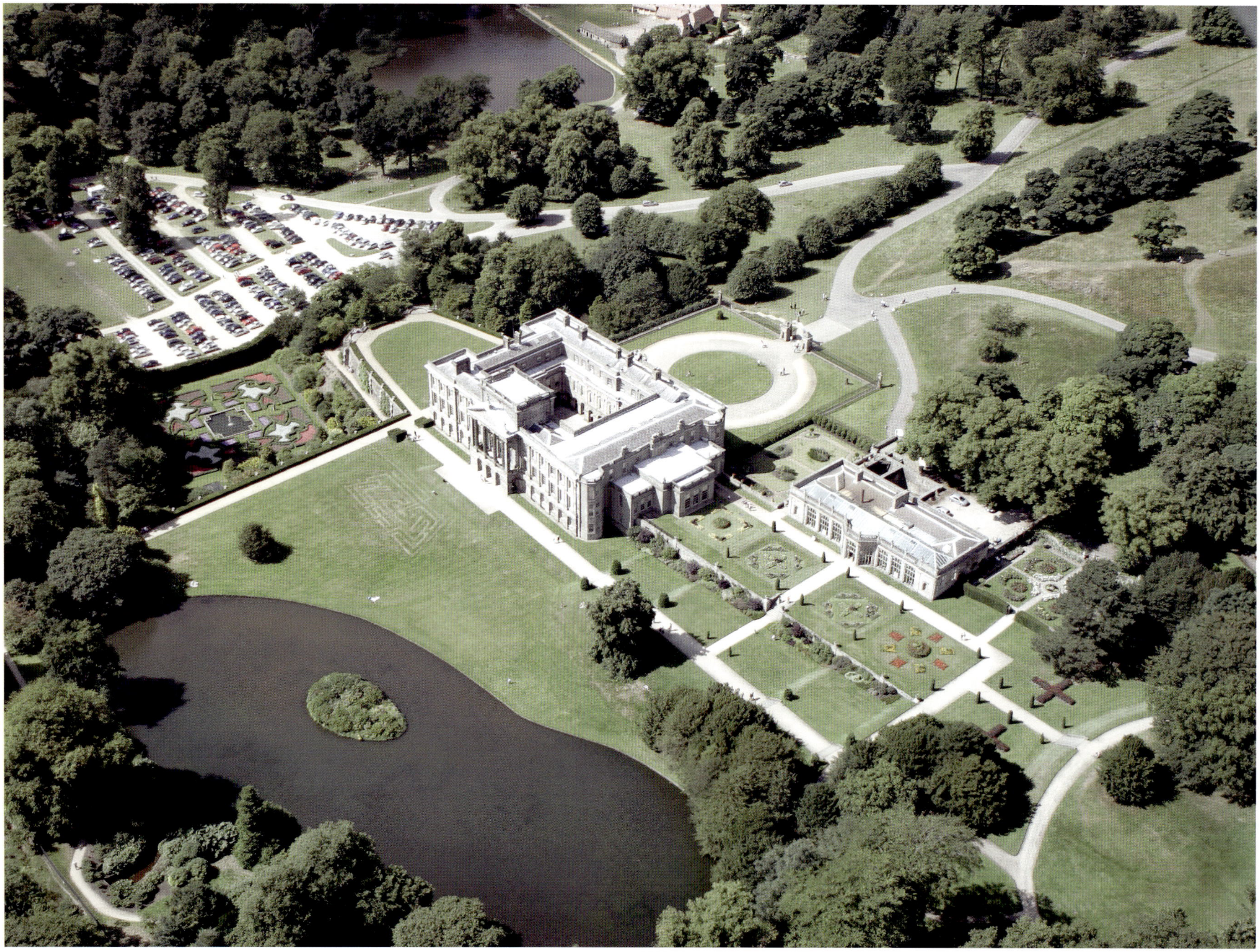

For a time the reservoirs within Lyme Park were used to supply the burgeoning Stockport population with water. Originally water was taken from the River Goyt, but increasing pollution meant that the supply was becoming dangerous to use, and the supply was taken from Lyme from 1863. But as the population continued to increase, more and more water was needed, and eventually new reservoirs were built for Stockport further down the Goyt Valley in Derbyshire. Kinder reservoir was constructed from 1903-1912, and Fernilee Reservoir near Whaley Bridge was built from 1932-1939. A second reservoir was built at Fernilee in the 1960s. The park and hall ceased to be a private residence when they were offered to the National Trust by Lord Newton. The trust was able to accept the offer with the support of the Stockport Corporation, who agreed to lease the hall and open it up to the public, with visitors allowed in from June 1947. In 1994 the Trust took sole ownership of the park, although it is still part funded by Stockport MBC today. On a hill to the east of the hall is the Cage (top left, opposite page). The Cage was a hunting lodge and was built around 1524. It was later used to lock up poachers that were discovered trespassing on the grounds. It later became the house of the Park Keeper, and was also used as a house until the 1920s. It was recently restored back to its original splendour.

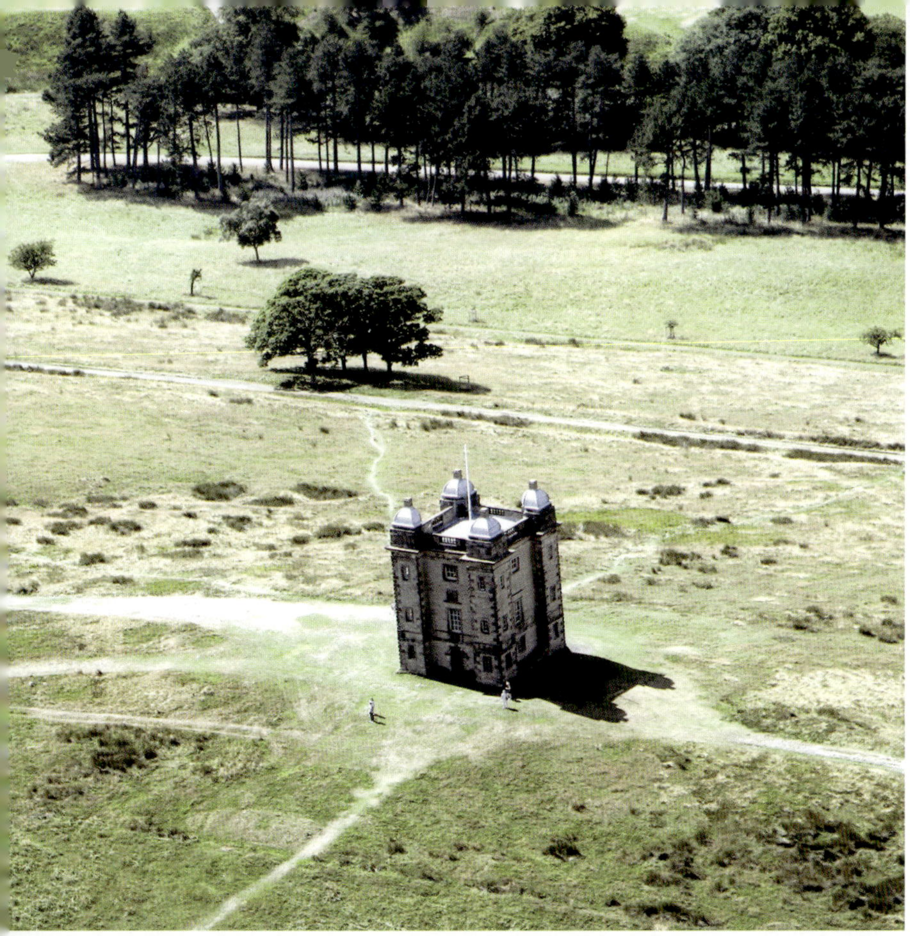
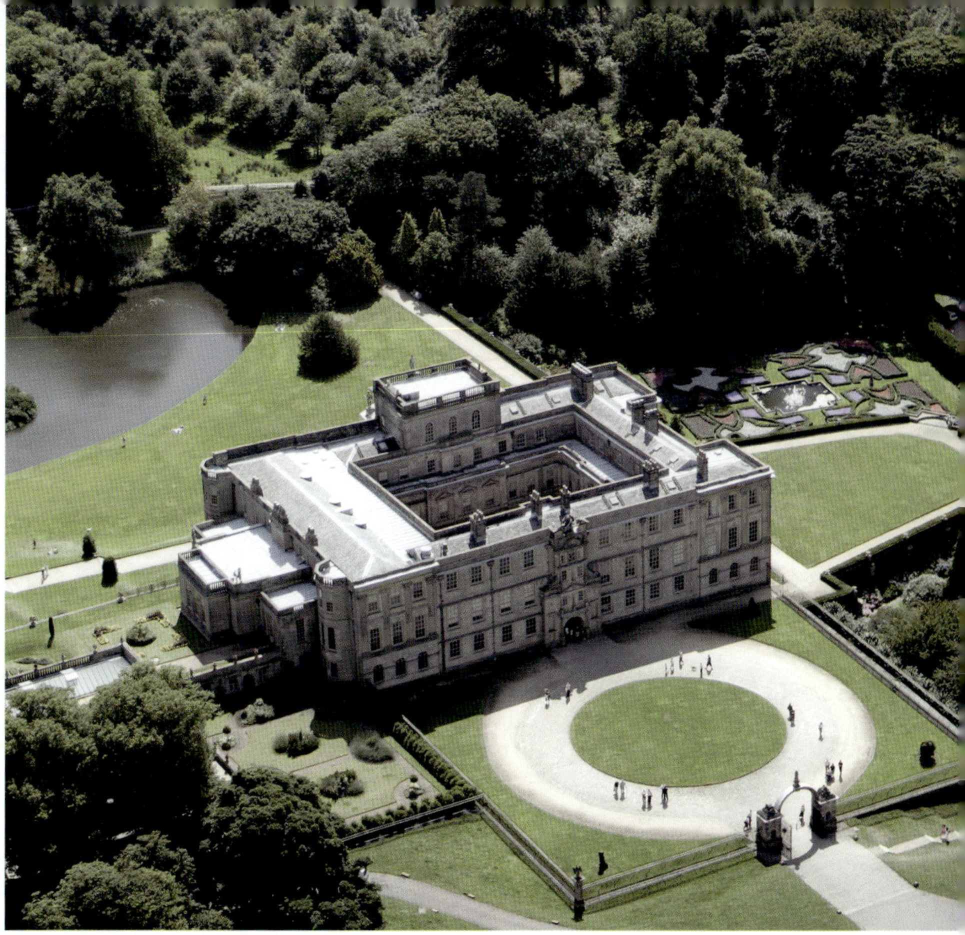
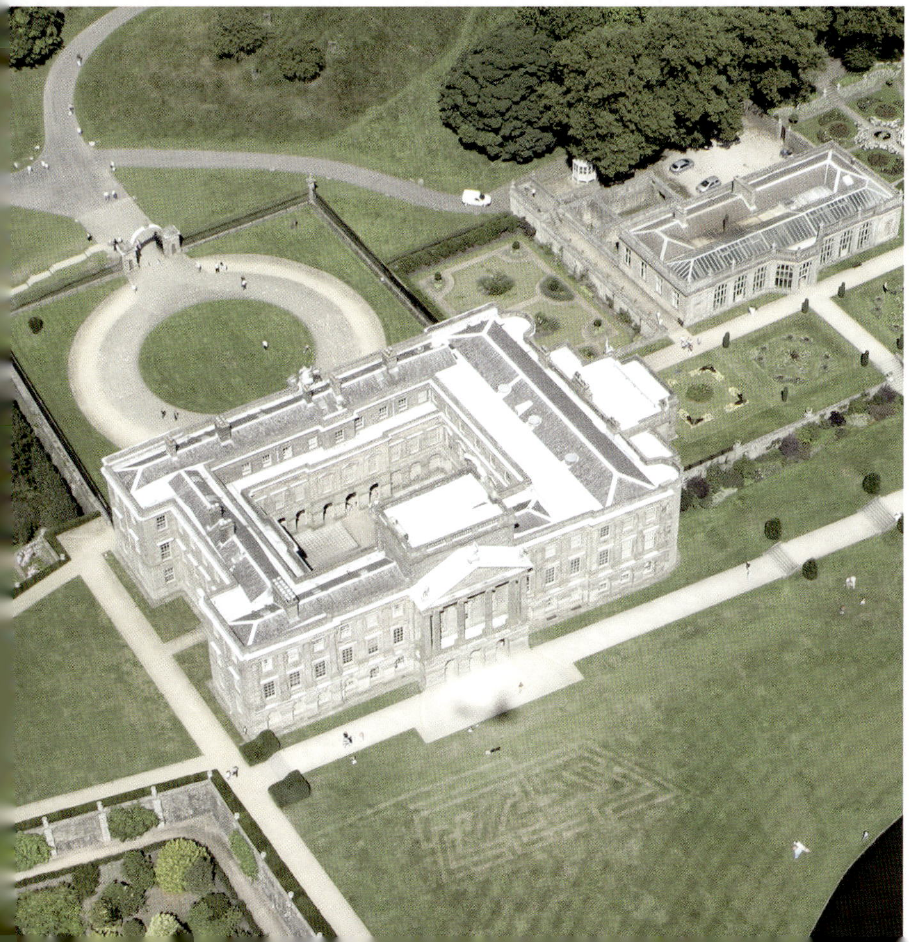
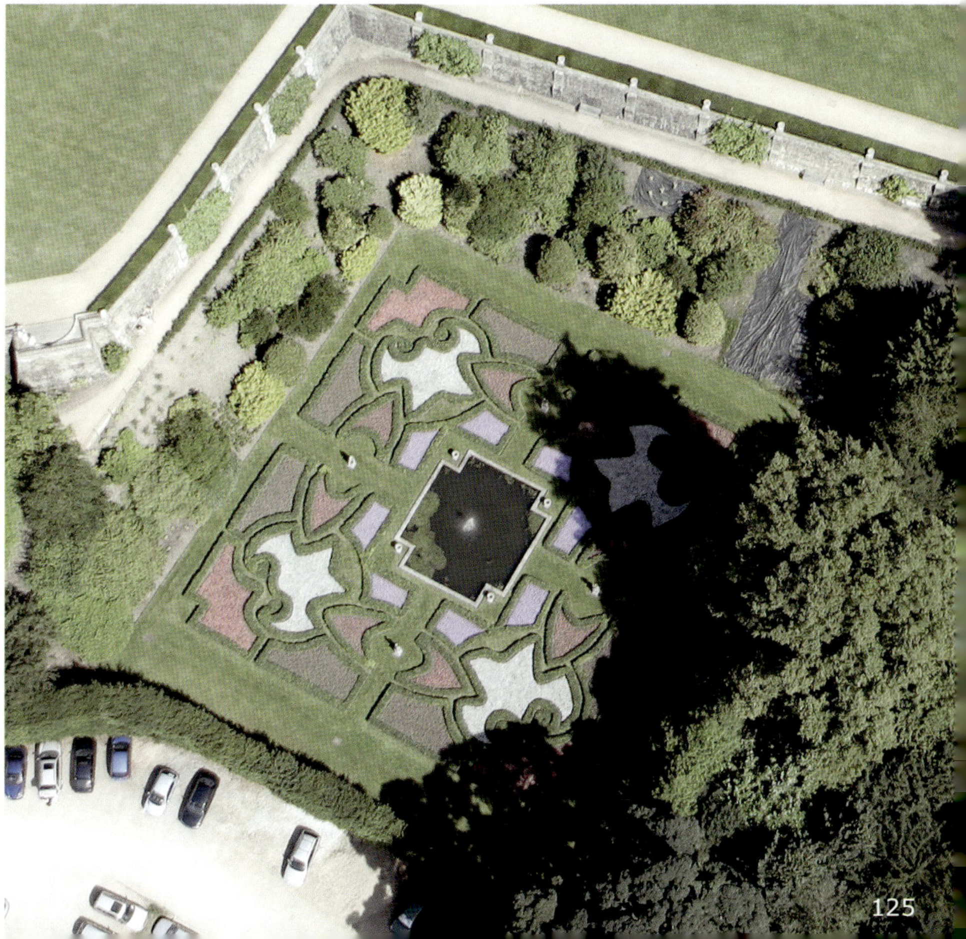

Southern Suburbs

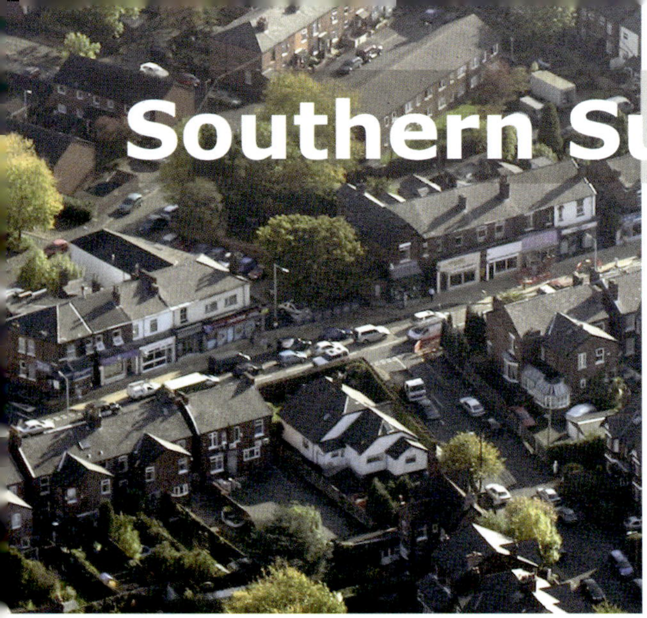

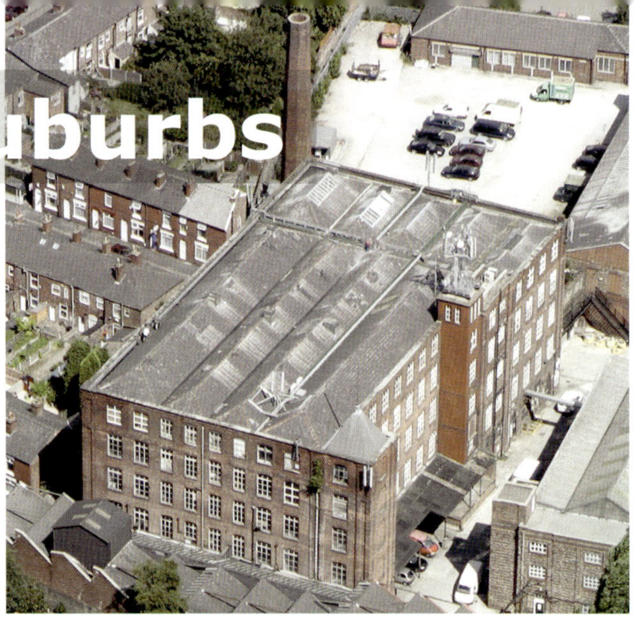

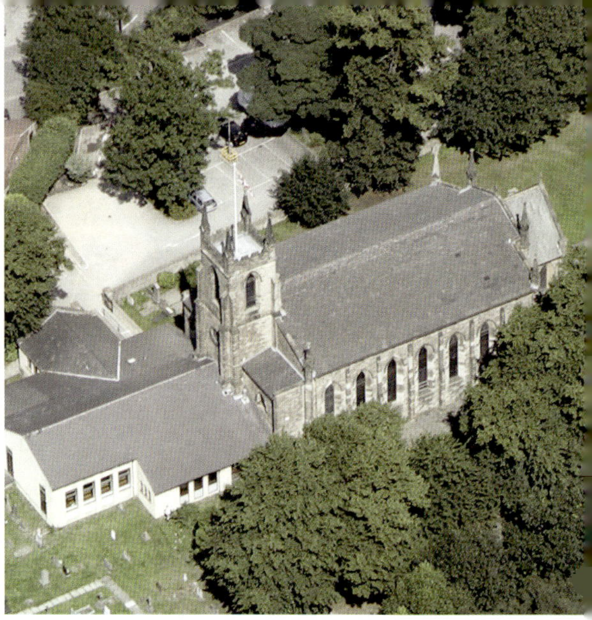

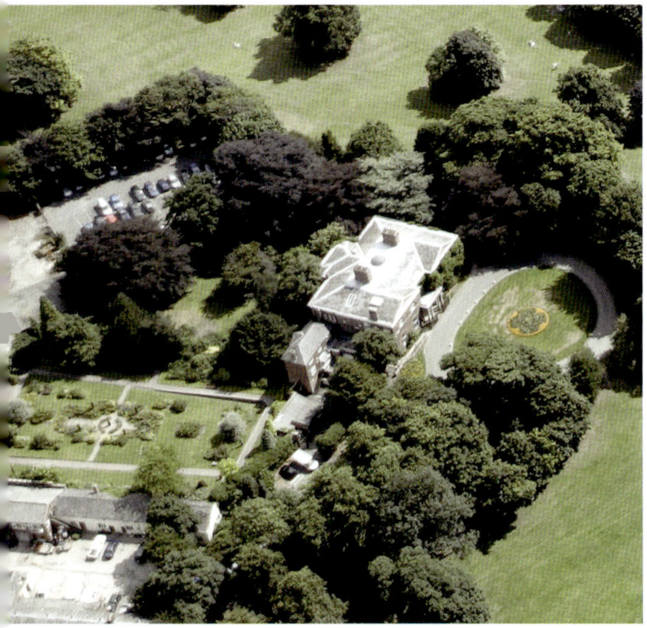

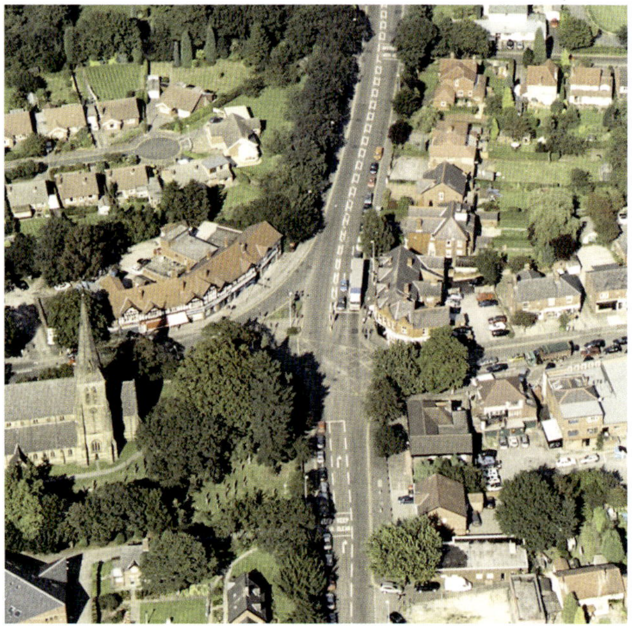

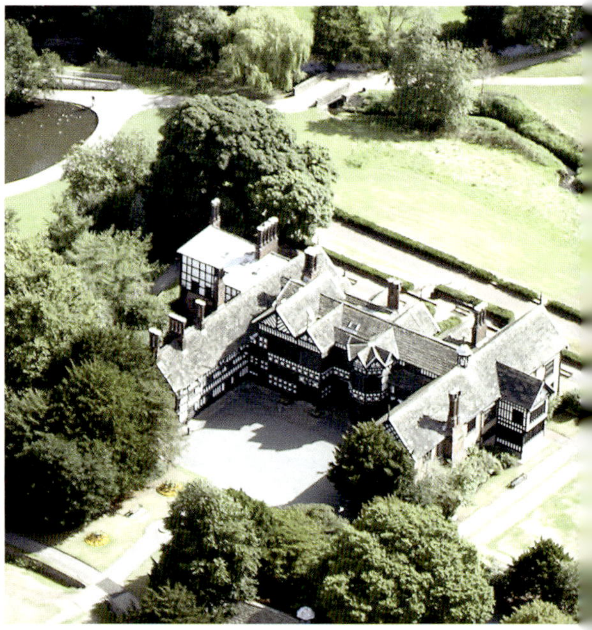

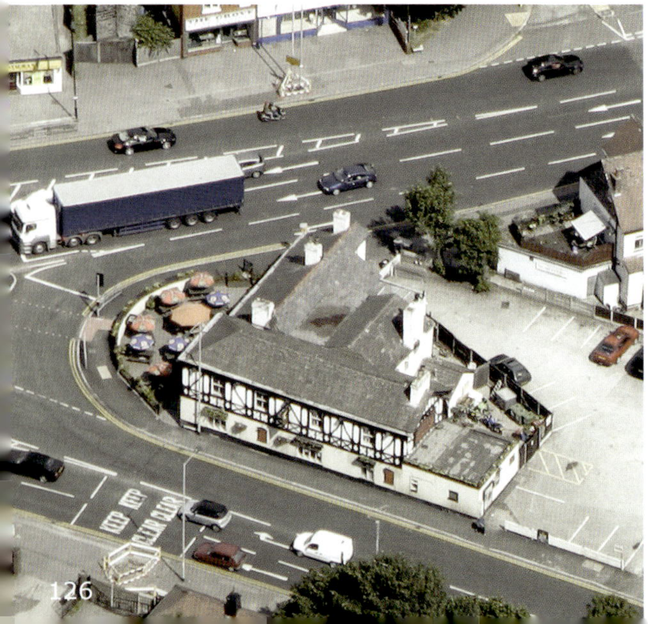

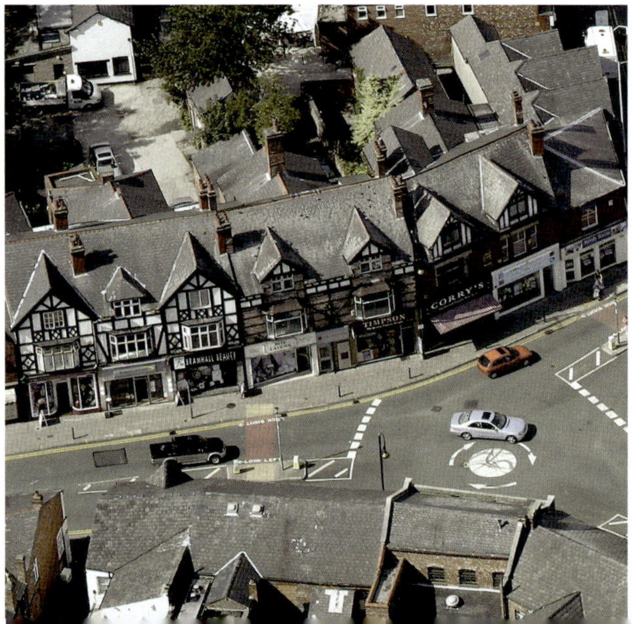

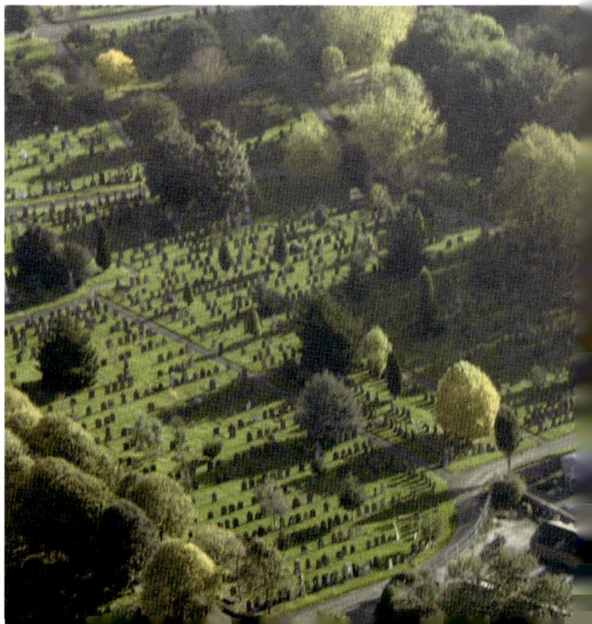

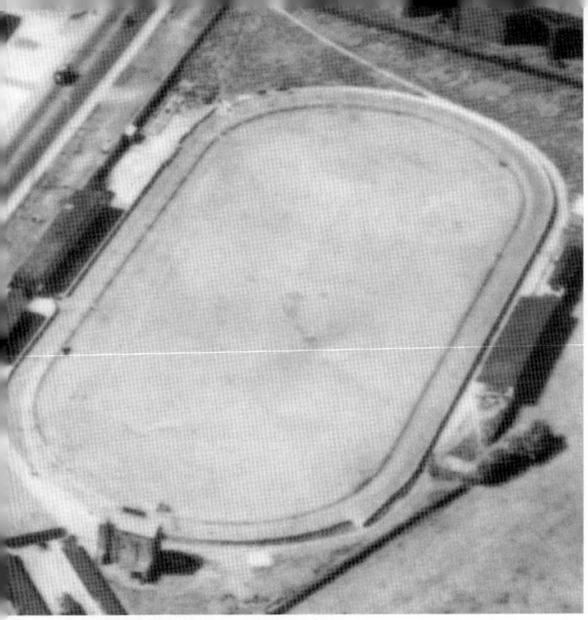

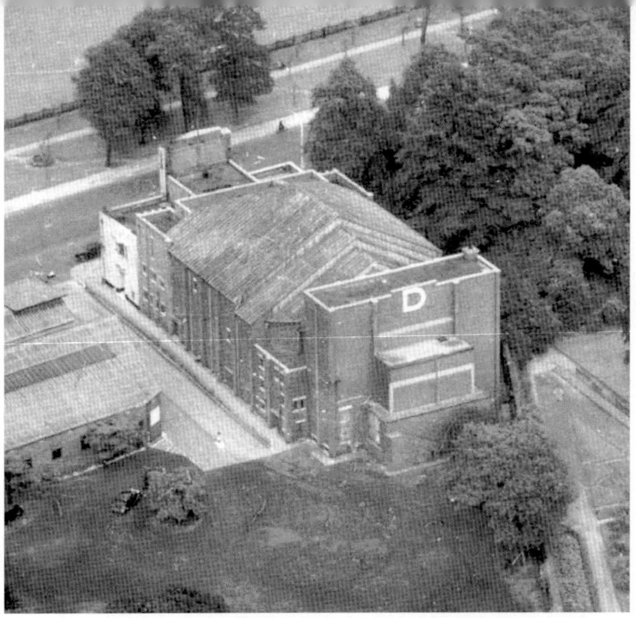

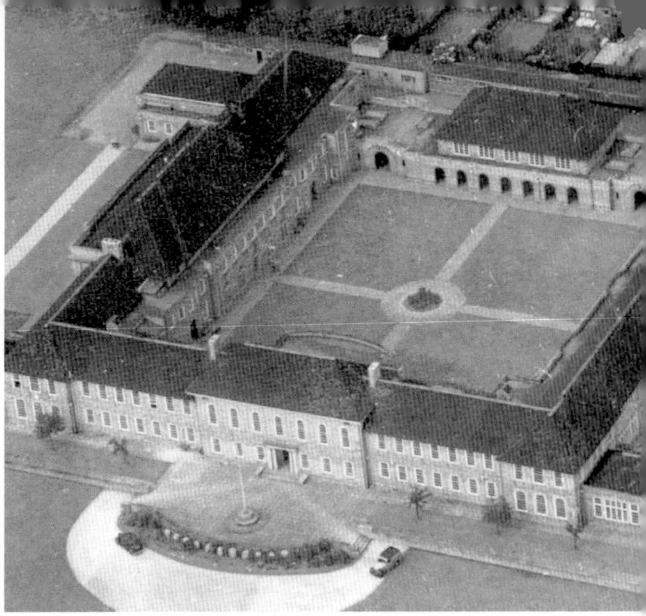

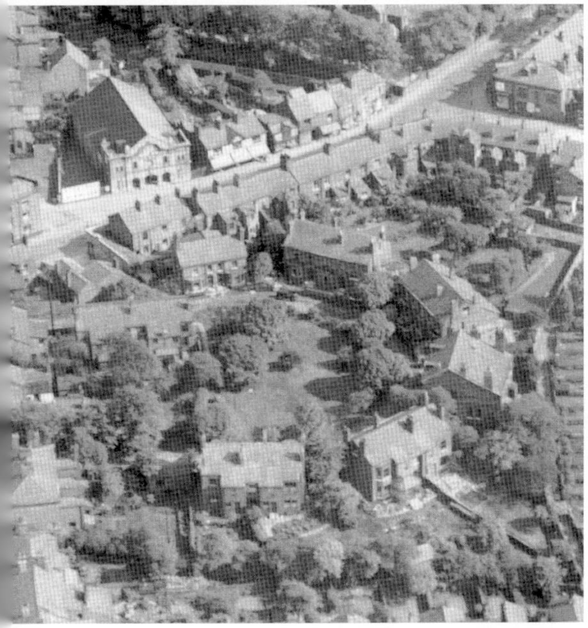

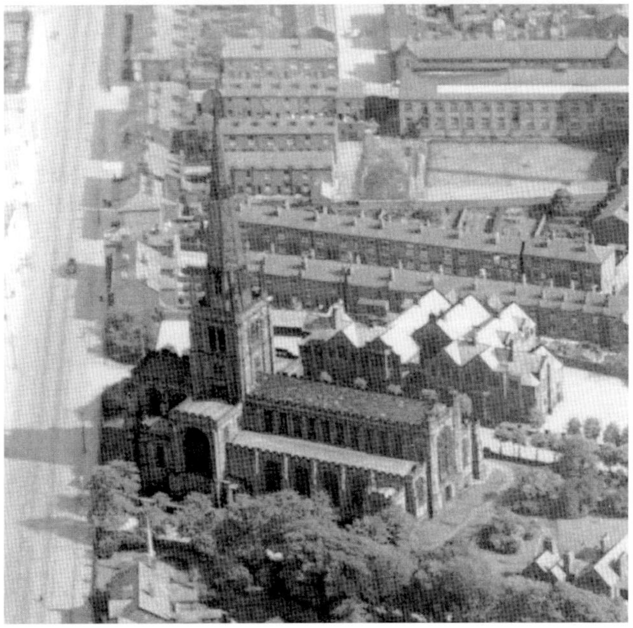

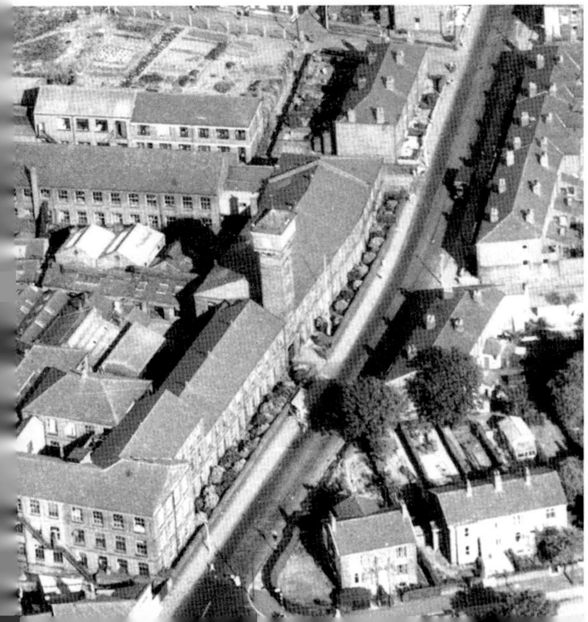

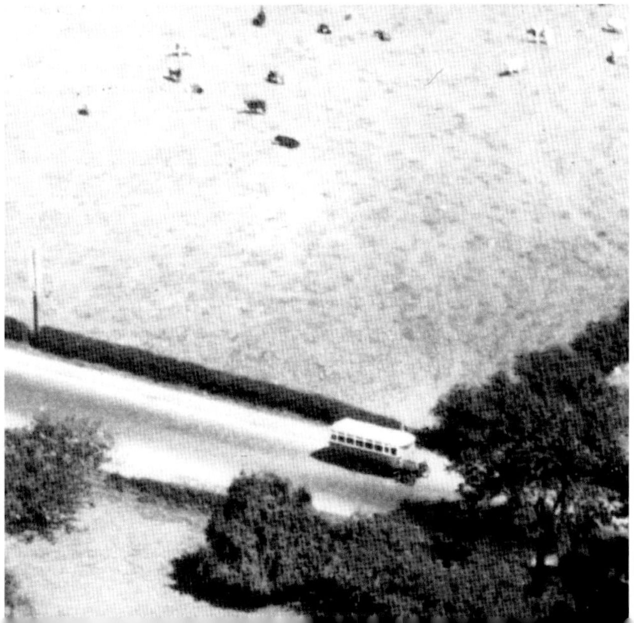

The suburbs to the south change from a mix of true inner city neighbourhoods interspersed with areas of Victorian and Edwardian villas, to areas containing grand detached residences with large gardens and large price tags.

To the immediate south are the districts of Heaviley, Cale Green and Davenport, all closely intertwined but each with a distinctive atmosphere of their own. Heading beyond Davenport, Woodsmoor developed with the housing boom of the 1930s, when the semi-detached was king. The importance of the A6 through Stockport can be seen in the districts situated along its length, including Great Moor, with its mixture of terraces and notable school buildings, and Hazel Grove, which is the very embodiment of a linear village built along a busy traffic route.

To the west of Hazel Grove is the highly regarded neighbourhood of Bramhall. It is here that you will find one of Stockport's treasures – the magnificent medieval Bramall Hall. As suburbia starts to dwindle and the countryside takes over there is the small village of Woodford with its large aerodrome. The runway points directly to Poynton, a popular commuter village with an attractive centre that sits at the very edge of the Cheshire Plain.

Heaviley

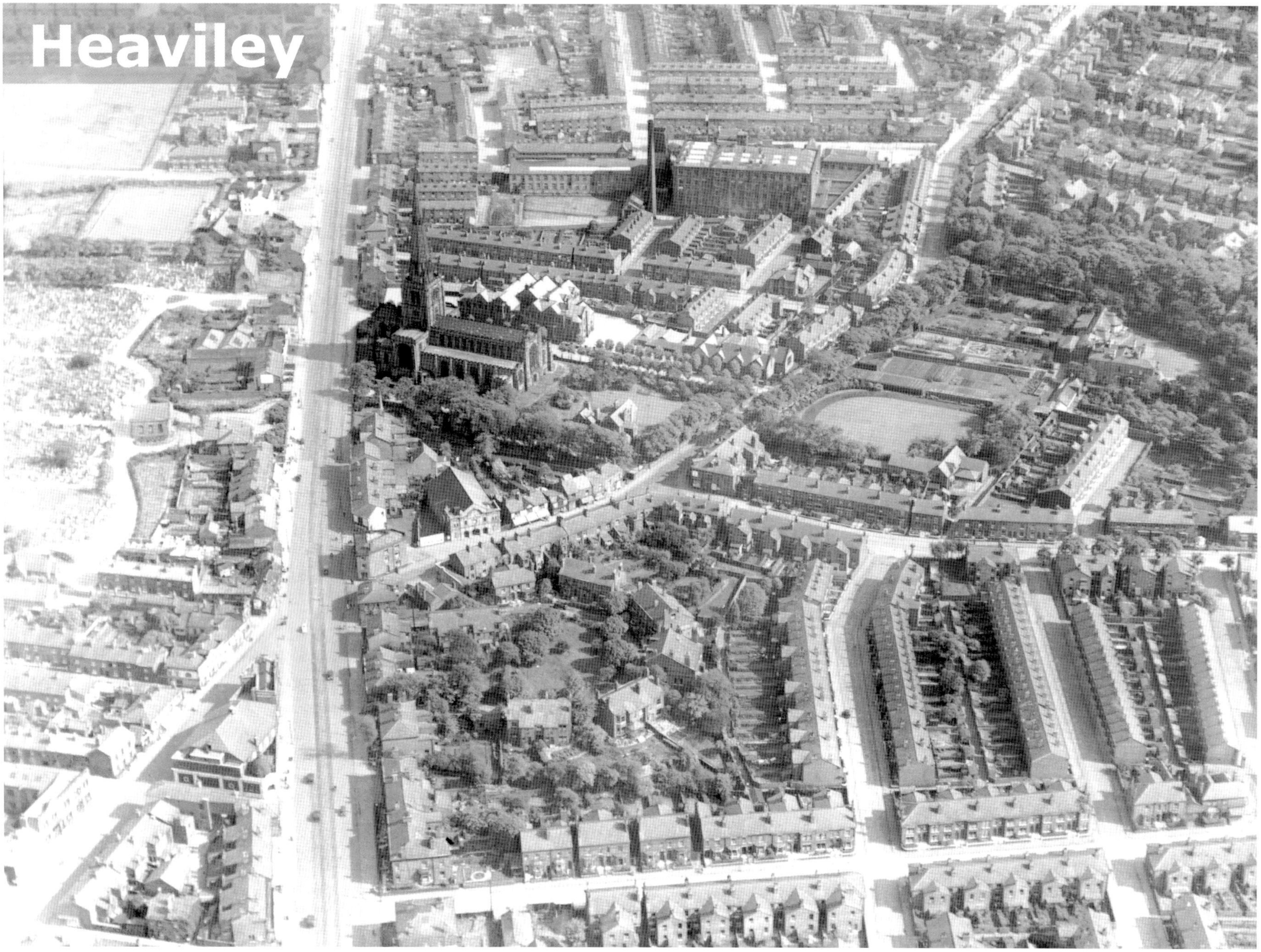

Heaviley 1931

Unlike many of Stockport's districts, Heaviley developed around a turnpike road (a road with a toll gate where you had to pay to be allowed to pass) and not a railway station. The toll was situated at the historic junction between Hillgate (bottom left) and Buxton Road (top). The "New Road" – Wellington Road South (bottom) was added later from 1824-1826. Before this Hillgate continued straight on to Bramhall Lane (right), which remained a country lane for many years. This is the reason for the rather odd shape of the junction today. This important junction saw rapid development in the 19th century, and many historic buildings are still located there. Two notable landmarks were built right at the junction itself (to the left of the main road). These were the former Wellington Picture House (the lower building) and a branch of the Manchester and County Bank (the upper building), which opened in 1917. On the left of the image is Stockport Cemetery. It was laid out in 1836 and opened two years later. 148 burials took place in the first year. Also of note is the large house now known as Heathfield Hospital (middle right). This was formerly a private residence of the Carrington Family, who owned a hat factory in Cale Green, and was built c1850.

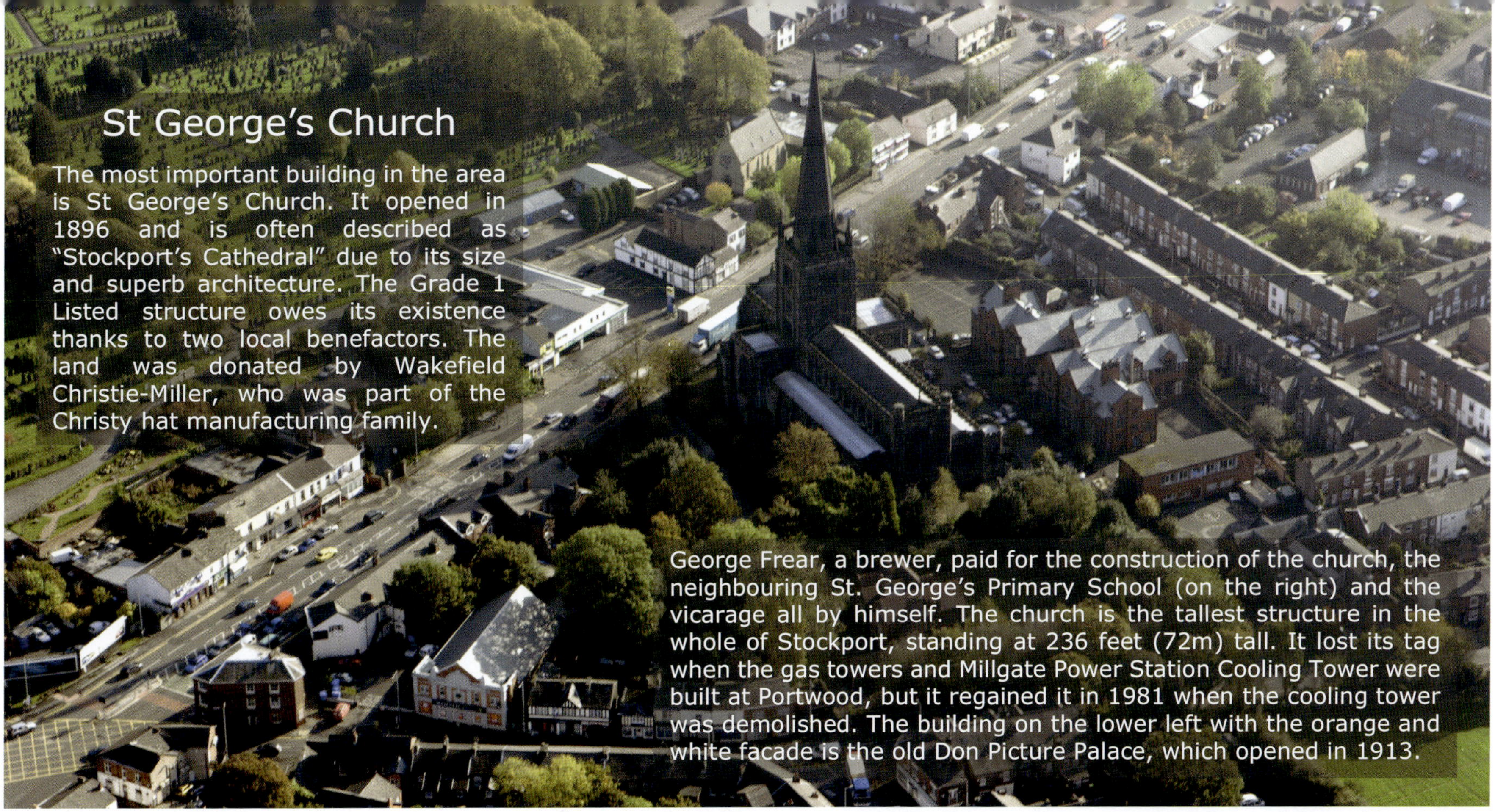

St George's Church

The most important building in the area is St George's Church. It opened in 1896 and is often described as "Stockport's Cathedral" due to its size and superb architecture. The Grade 1 Listed structure owes its existence thanks to two local benefactors. The land was donated by Wakefield Christie-Miller, who was part of the Christy hat manufacturing family.

George Frear, a brewer, paid for the construction of the church, the neighbouring St. George's Primary School (on the right) and the vicarage all by himself. The church is the tallest structure in the whole of Stockport, standing at 236 feet (72m) tall. It lost its tag when the gas towers and Millgate Power Station Cooling Tower were built at Portwood, but it regained it in 1981 when the cooling tower was demolished. The building on the lower left with the orange and white facade is the old Don Picture Palace, which opened in 1913.

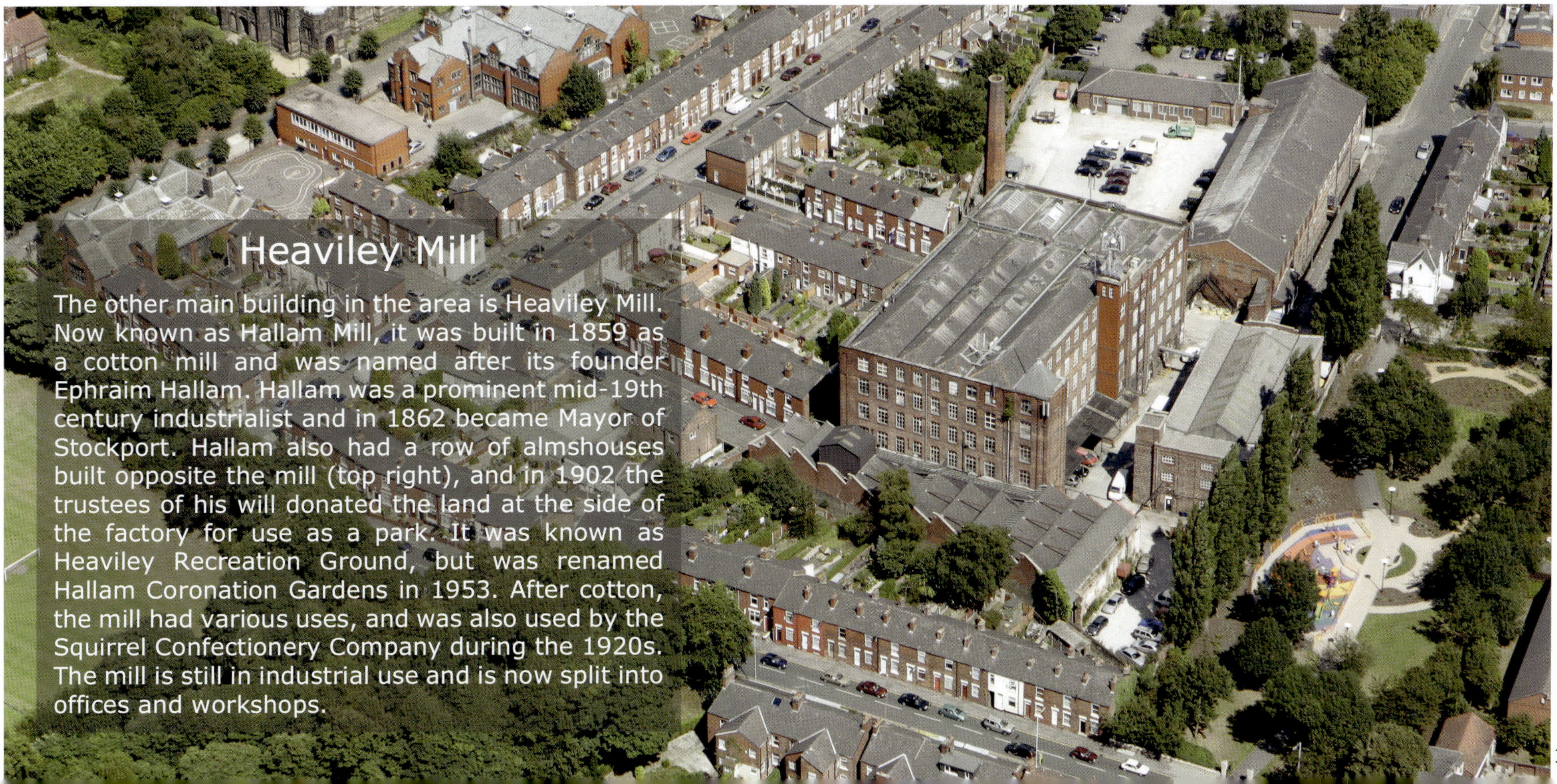

Heaviley Mill

The other main building in the area is Heaviley Mill. Now known as Hallam Mill, it was built in 1859 as a cotton mill and was named after its founder Ephraim Hallam. Hallam was a prominent mid-19th century industrialist and in 1862 became Mayor of Stockport. Hallam also had a row of almshouses built opposite the mill (top right), and in 1902 the trustees of his will donated the land at the side of the factory for use as a park. It was known as Heaviley Recreation Ground, but was renamed Hallam Coronation Gardens in 1953. After cotton, the mill had various uses, and was also used by the Squirrel Confectionery Company during the 1920s. The mill is still in industrial use and is now split into offices and workshops.

Cale Green

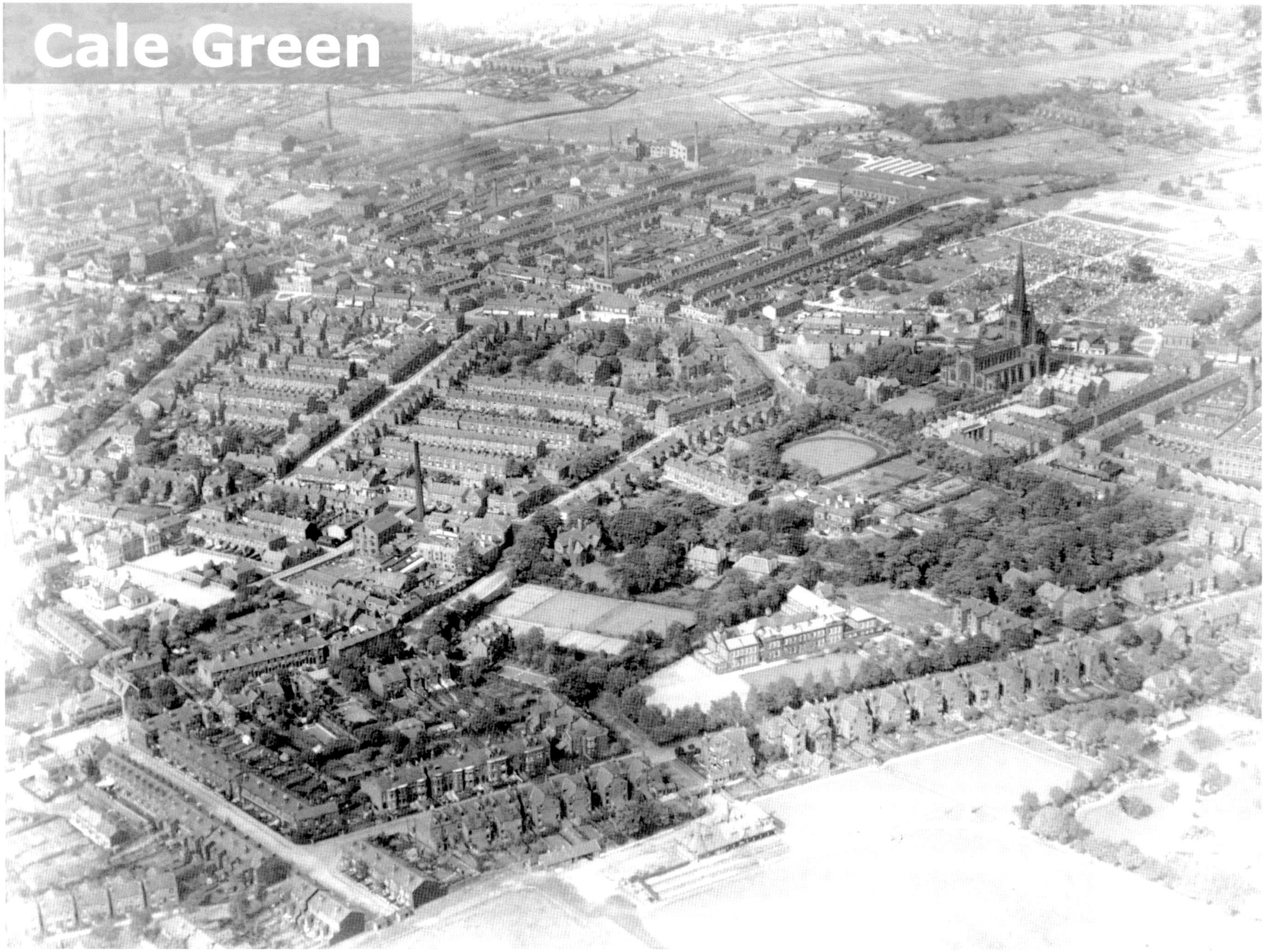

Cale Green 1931

Cale Green Park (bottom right) is a fine Victorian park that was laid out the end of the 19th century. It was given to the people of Stockport as a gift from Henry Bell, a former mayor of Stockport, and is now a major part of the Cale Green conservation area, which includes the impressive Hillcrest Grammar School building on Beech Road (centre of old picture, left on the new picture). To the left of the park are the grounds of Stockport Cricket Club & Stockport Lacrosse club (founded 1875), also on Beech Road. The cricket club play in the Derbyshire and Cheshire Cricket League. They moved to the ground in 1883 after it was also donated by Henry Bell on the grounds that the club contributed towards the cost. Stockport is the centre of UK Lacrosse, with four of the top teams in the county. Mellor, Stockport, Heaton Mersey and Cheadle all regularly challenge for the top honours in the game, and in 2005/06 finished in the top four places in the northern Premier Division, in that order. Cheadle Hulme (1893), Norbury (1908) and Poynton also have long standing clubs. At the time of writing the Stockport Lacrosse Club are currently League Champions. On the middle right of the new picture is Davenport high street.

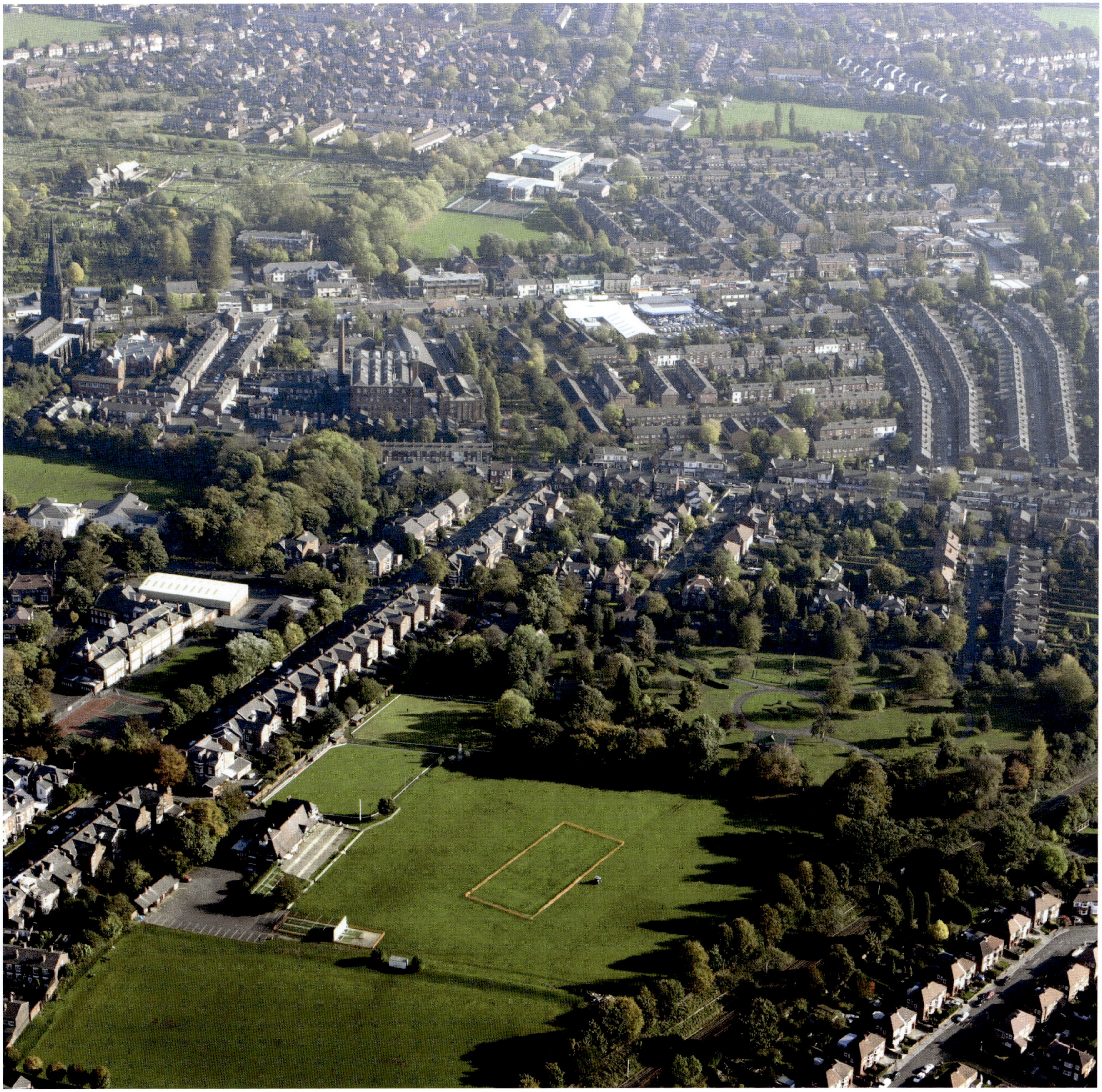

Davenport

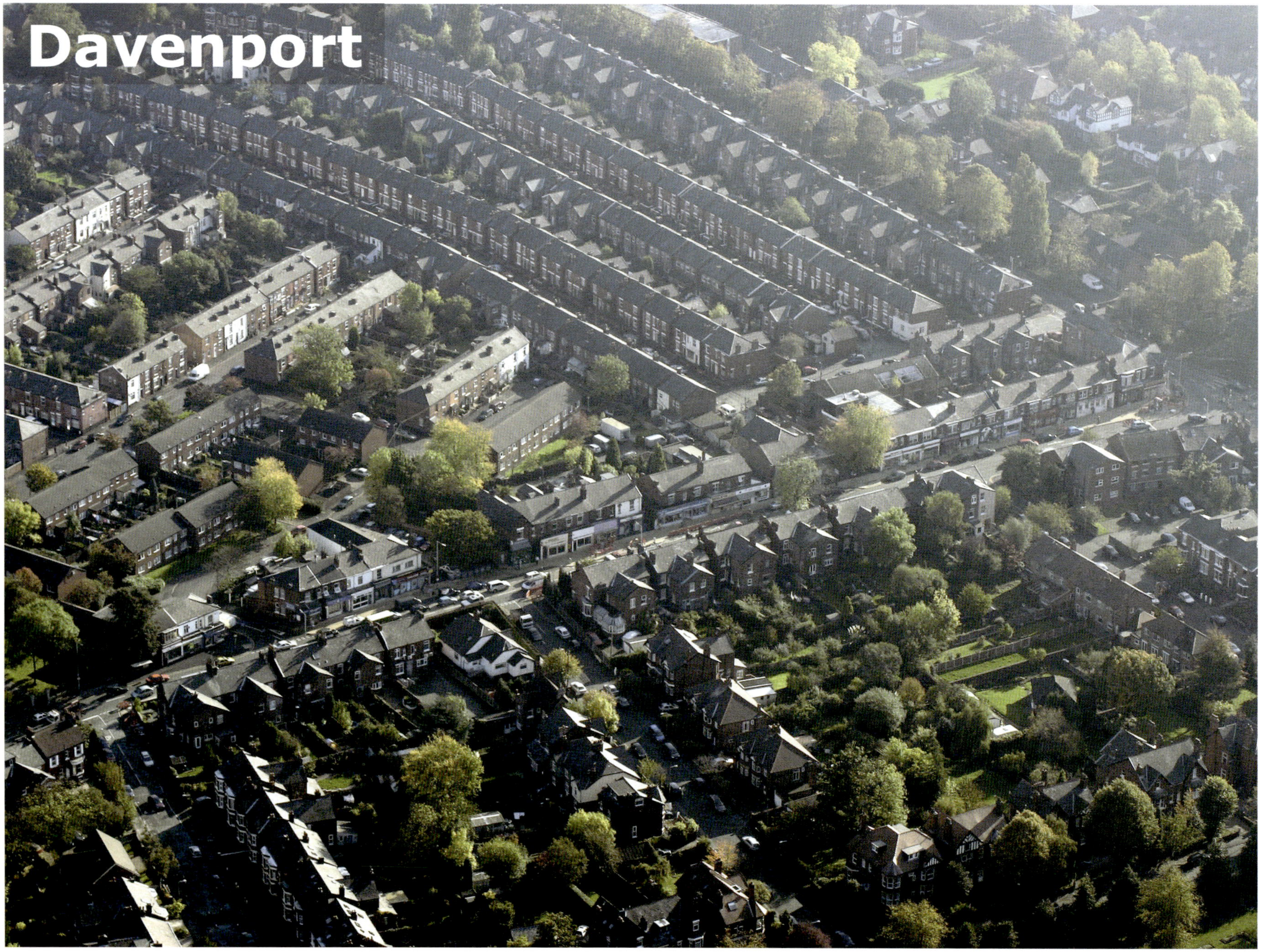

Davenport High Street

Davenport today is a very pleasant area, with an attractive mix of Victorian terraced houses and grand Victorian and Edwardian Villas, as well as a popular high street on Bramhall Lane (above). It was named after the important Davenport Family, who resided at Bramall Hall for many years. The land in which the village sits was an undeveloped part of the Davenport's estate until the mid 19th century until a new railway line led to the opening of Davenport Station. Once the station had opened it did not take long for new houses to follow. These were mostly large villas, and were home to many of the industrialists who had become rich due to Stockport's booming industries. Davenport remained a place of executive-style housing for many years, particularly by Kennerley Road, visible in the top right of the photo. Here there is a wonderful gated area of impressively large detached Villas known as Davenport Park, just off Davenport Village Green. The terraces of the working classes did not follow until later in the century. Today, this distinctive split can still be seen. The terraces shown here are to the east of the high street, whilst the larger houses are on the opposite side and to the south.

Woodsmoor

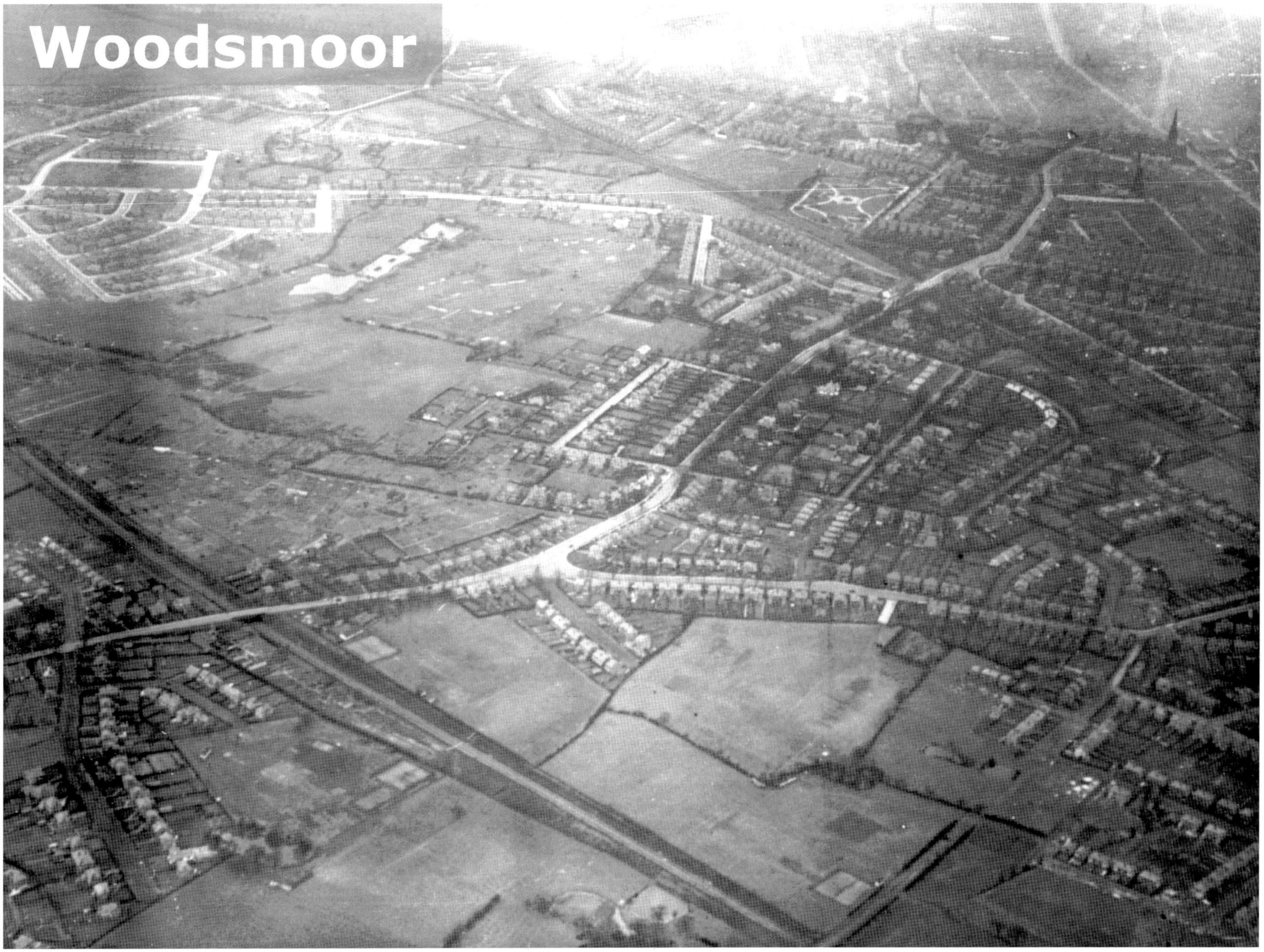

Woodsmoor 1934

Woodsmoor was an ancient area of moss land to the south of Davenport. Today it is a residential district, and this image from 1934 shows the area as it was developing, with new infill streets being added to earlier ribbon developments. Woodsmoor is also the site of the newest train station to be built in Stockport; Woodsmoor station opened in 1989 just down from Davenport Station. Davenport and the layout of Cale Green Park are visible at the top of the image, and on the left can be seen new estates being laid out in Adswood. In the bottom right is the site of Stockport Georgians FC's ground at Cromley Road. The pitch can just be made out between the railway line and the dark square of the adjacent cricket pitch, home to Stockport Georgians Cricket Club. Part of this pitch is now the club car park, and part is under housing, and there is a new cricket pitch to the left of the football ground. Georgians play in the Manchester League and were formed in 1908 by members of St George's Church. The club merged with local side Adswood Amateurs in 1987 and immediately won the Manchester League Premier Division title, as Adswood had done in 1986. The club also won the championship in 2002. The ground today has a small covered terrace behind the west goal, a club house and an all weather training pitch, and has the potential for further development.

Great Moor

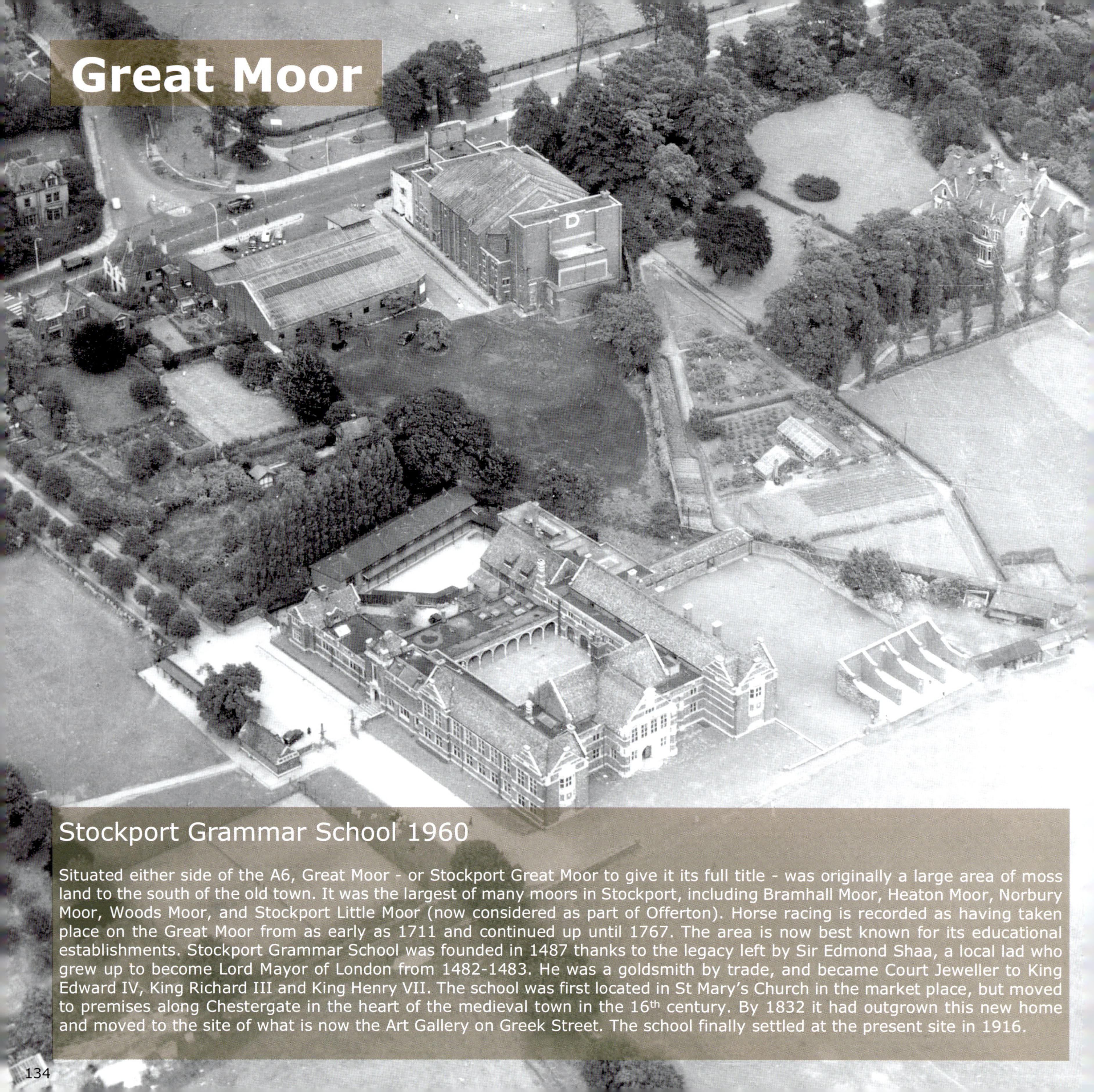

Stockport Grammar School 1960

Situated either side of the A6, Great Moor - or Stockport Great Moor to give it its full title - was originally a large area of moss land to the south of the old town. It was the largest of many moors in Stockport, including Bramhall Moor, Heaton Moor, Norbury Moor, Woods Moor, and Stockport Little Moor (now considered as part of Offerton). Horse racing is recorded as having taken place on the Great Moor from as early as 1711 and continued up until 1767. The area is now best known for its educational establishments. Stockport Grammar School was founded in 1487 thanks to the legacy left by Sir Edmond Shaa, a local lad who grew up to become Lord Mayor of London from 1482-1483. He was a goldsmith by trade, and became Court Jeweller to King Edward IV, King Richard III and King Henry VII. The school was first located in St Mary's Church in the market place, but moved to premises along Chestergate in the heart of the medieval town in the 16th century. By 1832 it had outgrown this new home and moved to the site of what is now the Art Gallery on Greek Street. The school finally settled at the present site in 1916.

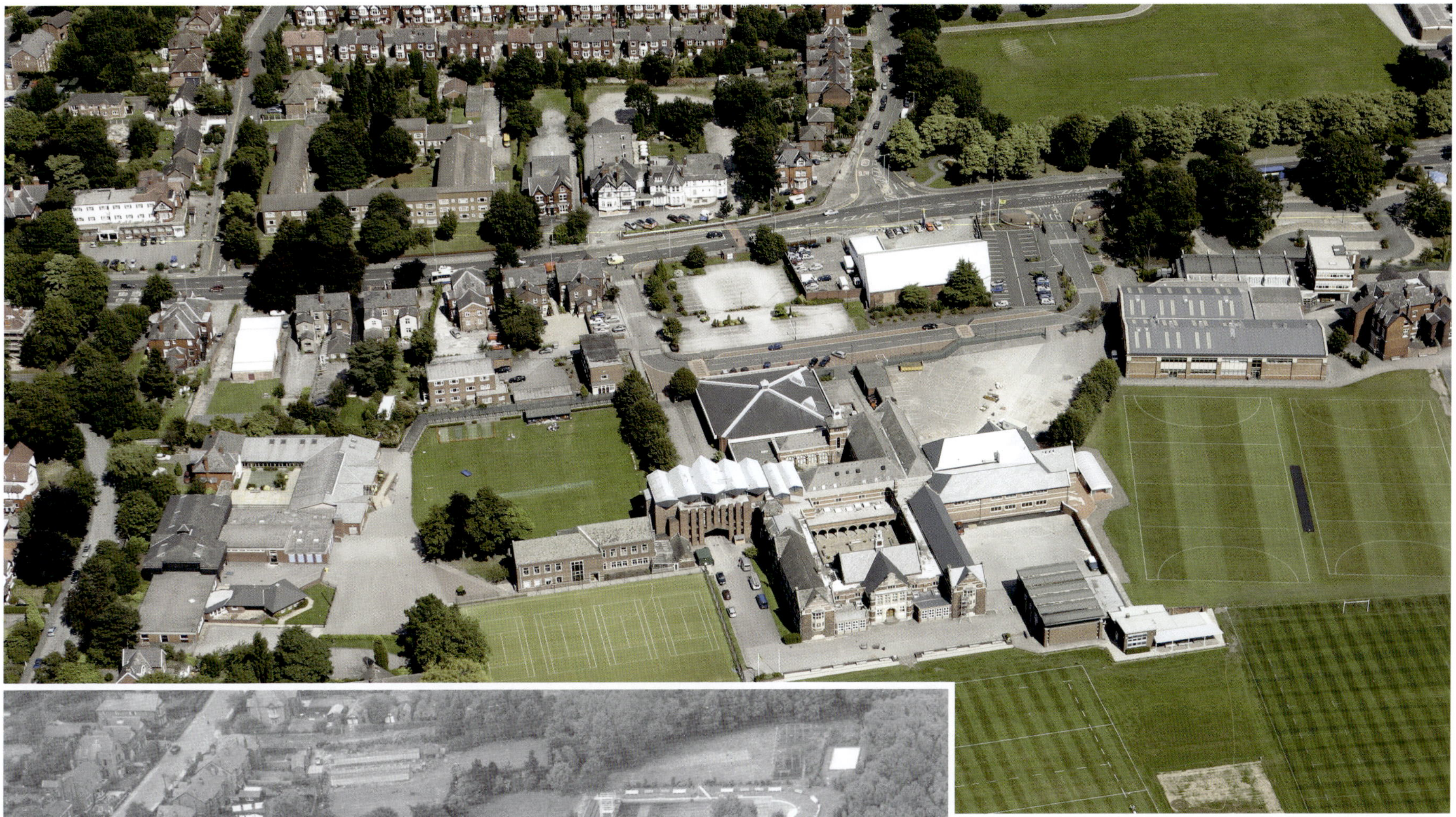

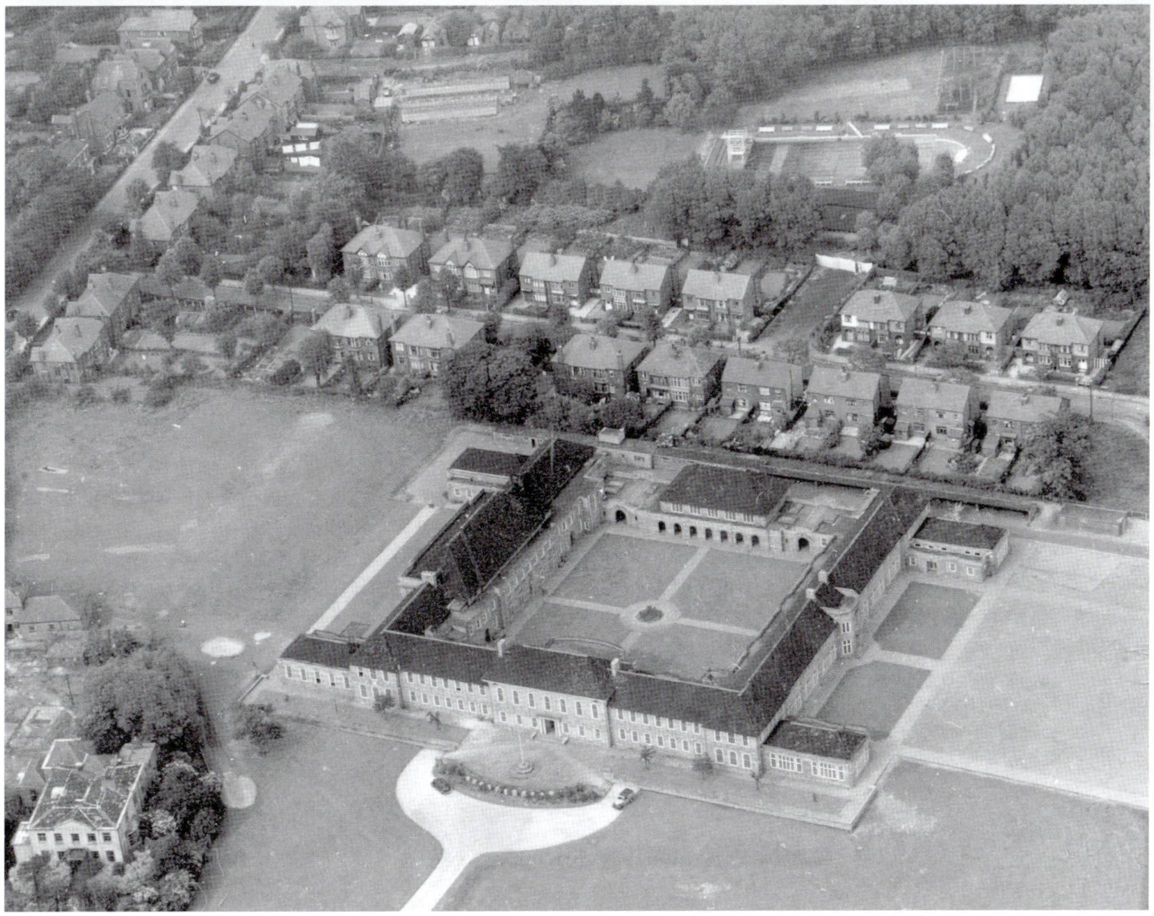

Also in the picture is the Davenport theatre. The theatre opened on 17th June 1937 and had seating for 1750 people (500 in the balcony, and 1250 below). The theatre was also used as a cinema, and in the 1972 the restaurant was converted into a second small screen seating 180. The cinema was also used as a set in the film "Yanks" in 1979. Sadly, and to the shock of many locals, the theatre was demolished in March 1997. The land was redeveloped as part of the schools grounds and is now merely a car park.

On the opposite side of the road is Stockport School (left, also 1960). This secondary school opened in 1938 and features an impressive facade facing the main road. To the rear of the school was the site of the Blue Lagoon Swimming pool. This was an open-air pool that had 1m, 3m and 5m diving boards. The site has been filled in and has been redeveloped as houses.

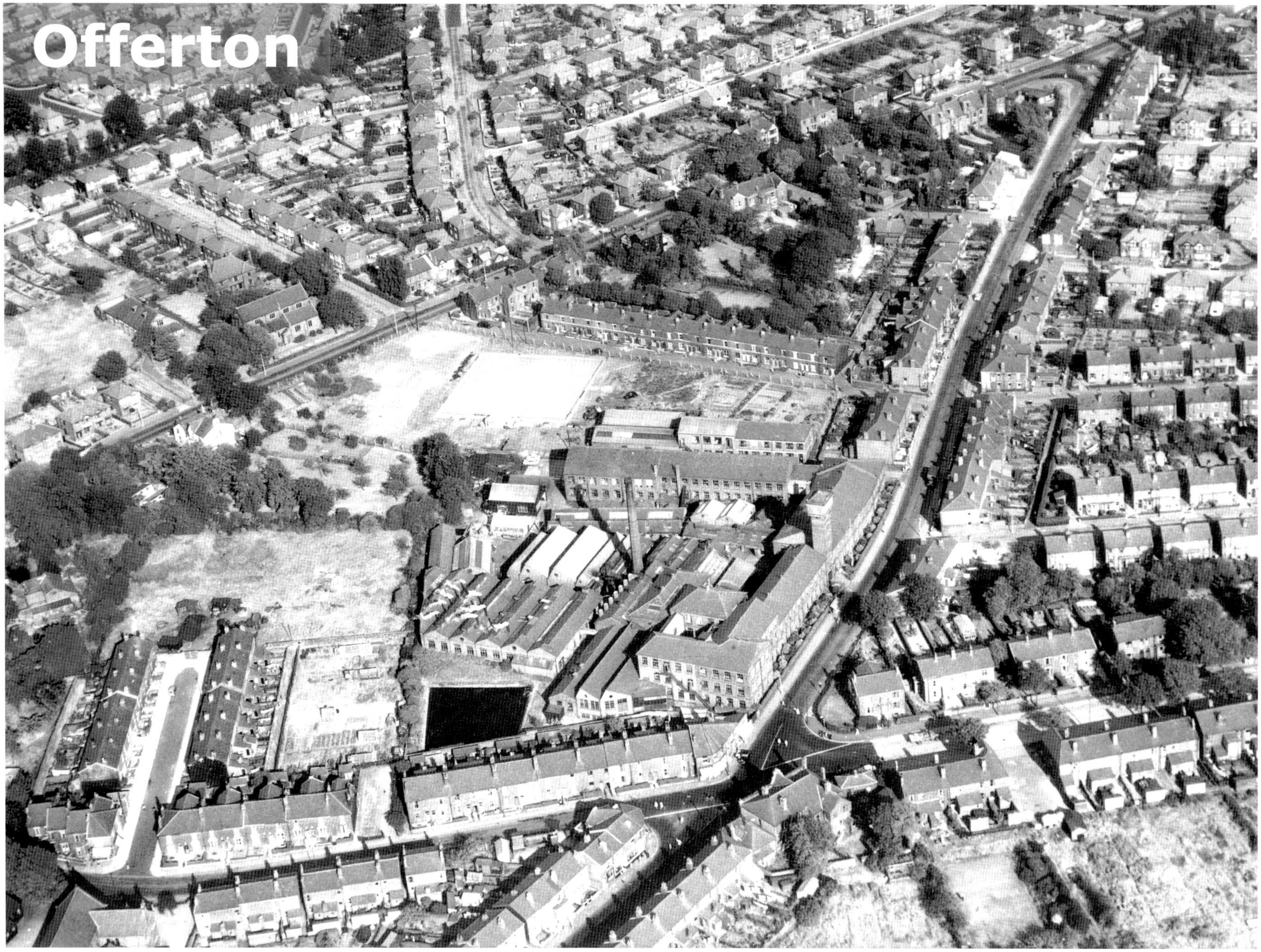

Battersby Hat Factory - Hempshaw Lane 1960

Battersby & Co Ltd's hatworks, seen here in 1960, was founded in Stockport in 1865. The company moved to a site on Hempshaw Lane in 1886, where this impressive looking factory with its imposing 7-storey central tower was built. The company continued to make hats up until 1966 when they merged with 3 other companies. This included local firm Christy's, and also the two largest hat manufacturers from Denton – Moores and Wilsons. The new company was called Associated British Hat Manufacturers Ltd. But eventually the hatting industry fell into decline and the decision was taken to revive the name of Christy's. Later, the factory became the first home of the Hat Museum from around 1995. This was only a temporary arrangement until the new premises were ready in Wellington Mill. The building now forms part of the Offerton Industrial Estate and is still a prominent landmark on the Offerton skyline, with the name of Battersby writ large at the top of the tower for all to see. It is no longer the tallest building in the area though, as just three years later work started on two new 12-storey blocks of council flats just a few hundred yards away.

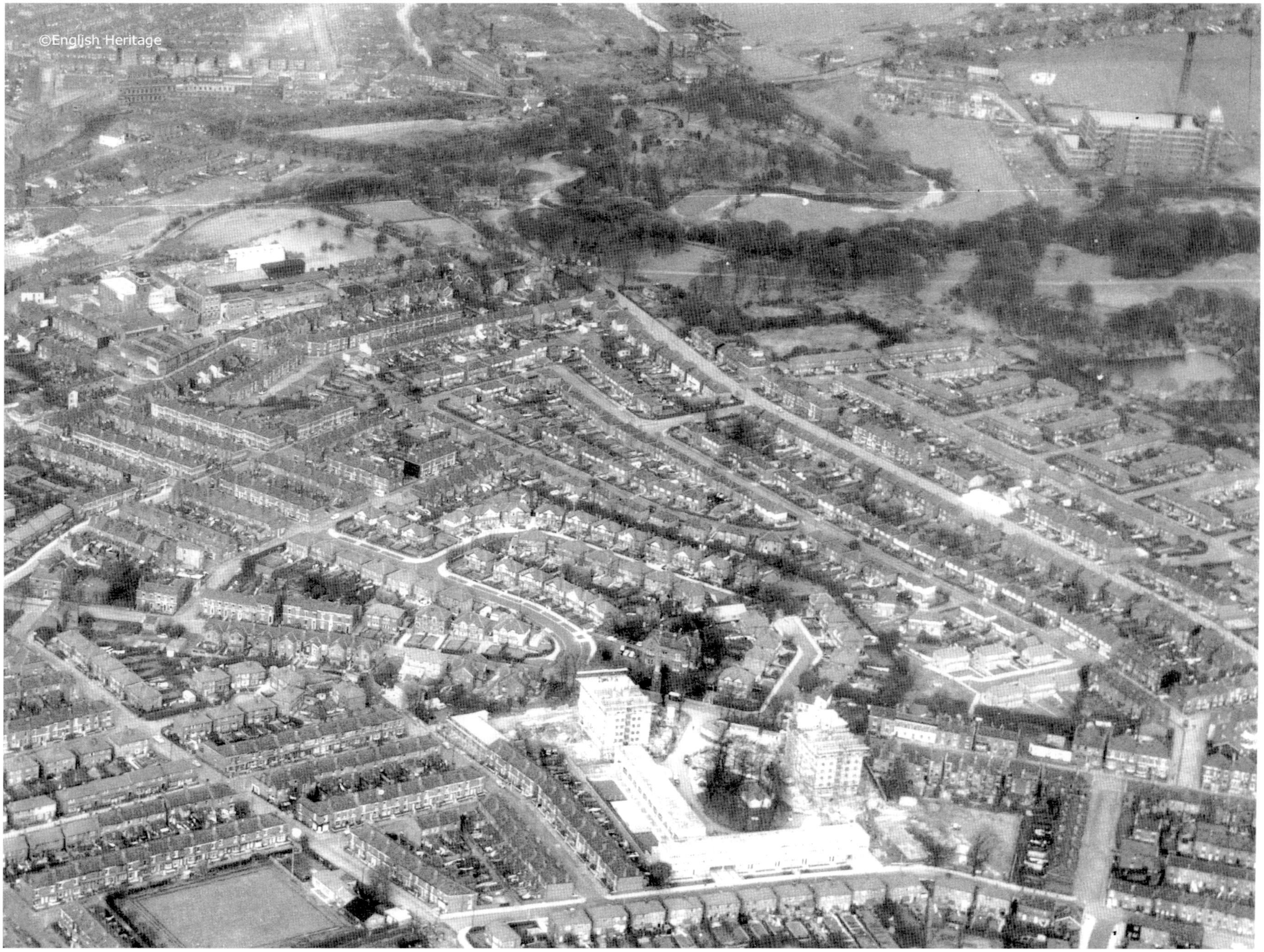

Offerton 1963

This image taken on October 21st shows the new flats - Voewood and Beaver House - part-way through construction just off the main road (Hall Street). In the background in the centre of the picture is Vernon Park & Stockport Museum, and on the right is Woodbank park, just before Pear New Mill. Vernon park was Stockport's first public park. It was opened on Monday 20th September 1857 on farmland that was previously known as "Stringer's Field". The land was offered to the Stockport Corporation in 1844 by Lord Vernon. It was already used for leisure and was regarded as a local beauty spot due to its wonderful setting by the Goyt valley. Work to create the sculpted park that exists today did not commence for several years. When it did open, an estimated 30,000 people were present to witness the occasion. The Stockport Museum building opened in October 1860 and was paid for by the town's two MPs, James Kershaw and John Benjamin. The building was an instant success, and a new wing was added in 1866. It was also the home of the Free Library until 1875 until it moved to the Hen Market. Vernon Park itself proved to be so popular that a tram service from Mersey Square was opened in 1901. In recent years the whole park has been restored to its Victorian splendour, including the historic bandstand, thanks to a grant from the Heritage Lottery Fund.

Hazel Grove

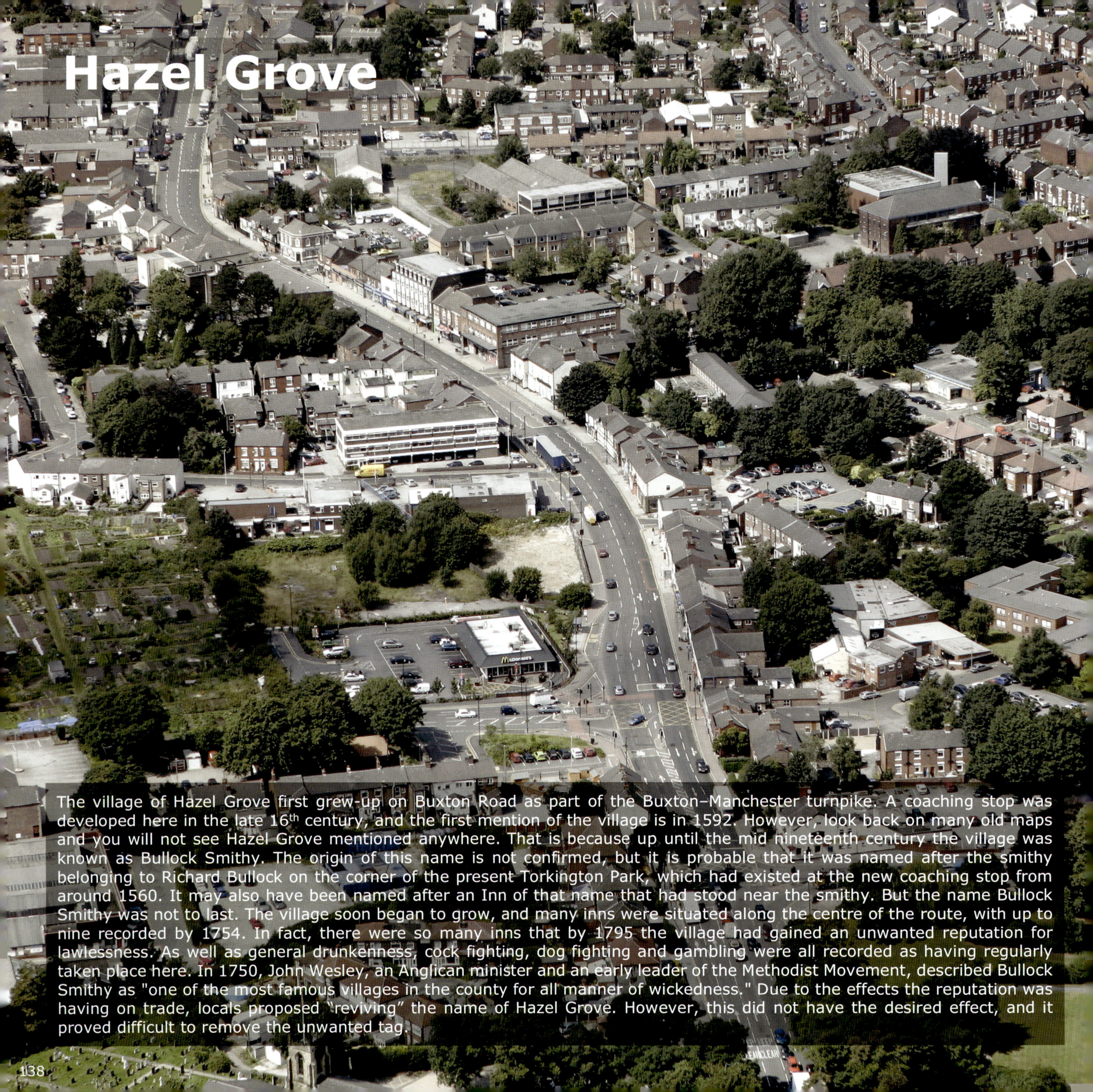

The village of Hazel Grove first grew-up on Buxton Road as part of the Buxton–Manchester turnpike. A coaching stop was developed here in the late 16th century, and the first mention of the village is in 1592. However, look back on many old maps and you will not see Hazel Grove mentioned anywhere. That is because up until the mid nineteenth century the village was known as Bullock Smithy. The origin of this name is not confirmed, but it is probable that it was named after the smithy belonging to Richard Bullock on the corner of the present Torkington Park, which had existed at the new coaching stop from around 1560. It may also have been named after an Inn of that name that had stood near the smithy. But the name Bullock Smithy was not to last. The village soon began to grow, and many inns were situated along the centre of the route, with up to nine recorded by 1754. In fact, there were so many inns that by 1795 the village had gained an unwanted reputation for lawlessness. As well as general drunkenness, cock fighting, dog fighting and gambling were all recorded as having regularly taken place here. In 1750, John Wesley, an Anglican minister and an early leader of the Methodist Movement, described Bullock Smithy as "one of the most famous villages in the county for all manner of wickedness." Due to the effects the reputation was having on trade, locals proposed "reviving" the name of Hazel Grove. However, this did not have the desired effect, and it proved difficult to remove the unwanted tag.

In 1836 a second "revival" of Hazel Grove was held, and since that time the name of Bullock Smithy has not been used. The origins of "Hazel Grove" are also uncertain. It was claimed to be an ancient name, but the closest matches are for an area known as "Hessel Grave", which is recorded on map of 1674 near High Lane. It may also have referred to the large number of Hazel Trees that existed in the area. The Hazel Grove Inn, now known as the Grove Inn, was opened in the 1790s, showing that the name had been in use somewhere. The change of name was finally ratified on 26th September 1836 when a large celebration took place to mark the occasion. Around 6,000 people are recorded as having taken part, and this celebration is something that has been repeated every 50 years since. The next one is due in 2036.

London Road 1934

In modern times London Road is synonymous with one thing – traffic jams. Not a day goes by without a chock-a-block build up of vehicles through the centre of the village. Back in 1934 (right) there were no such problems with traffic. Here we are looking at London Road by the junction with Commercial Road, running from left to right at the bottom of the picture. The village has always had a long, linear appearance since its first inception, and this is clearly visible today by the length of the rows of shops on either side of London Road. The area is still waiting for the Stockport north-south bypass to be built to alleviate the problem, 62 years after first being proposed, and 35 after detailed plans were drawn up. The factory in the middle right is now the location of the Sainsbury's supermarket, and in the top left is Stepping Hill Hospital.

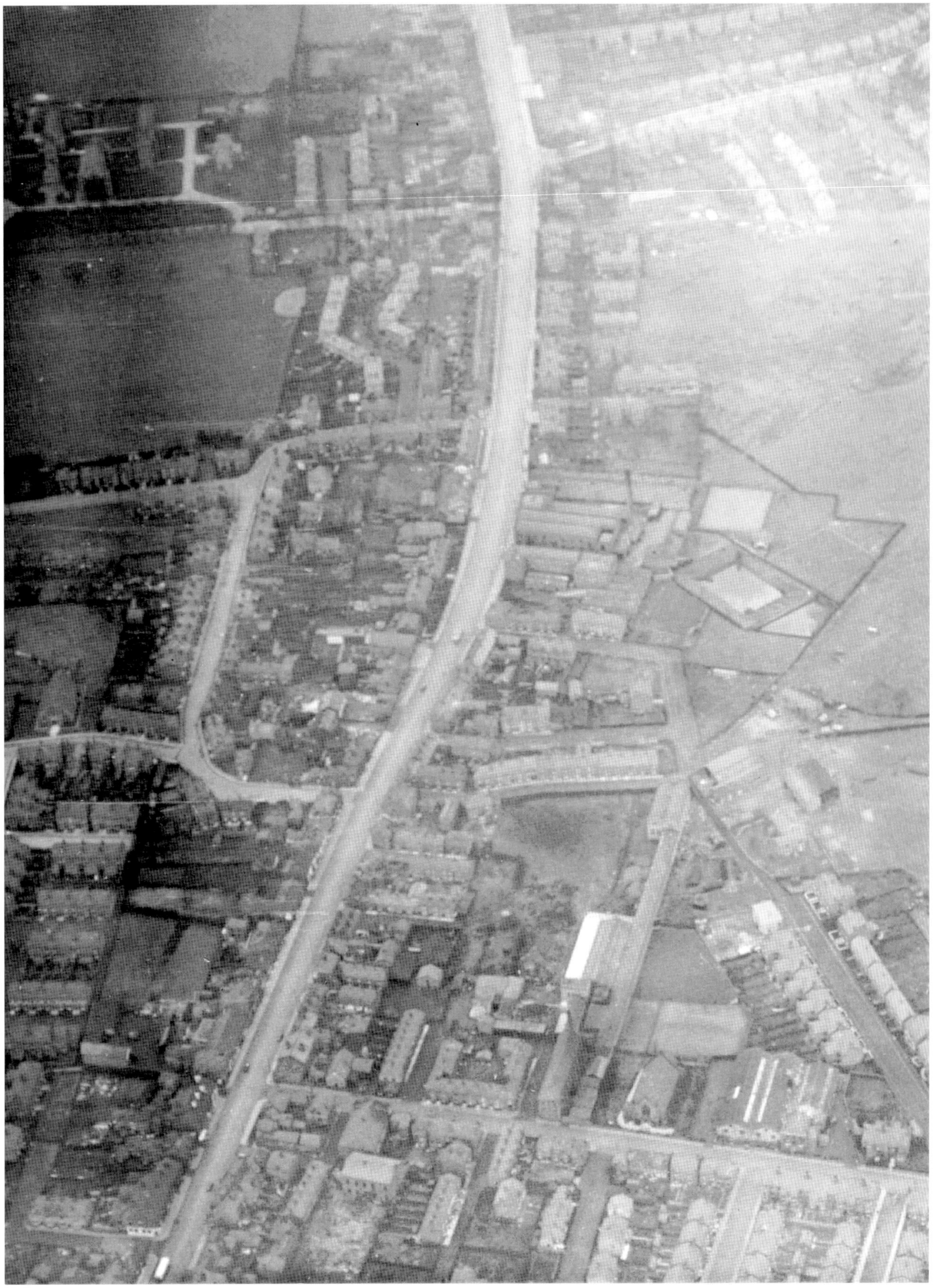

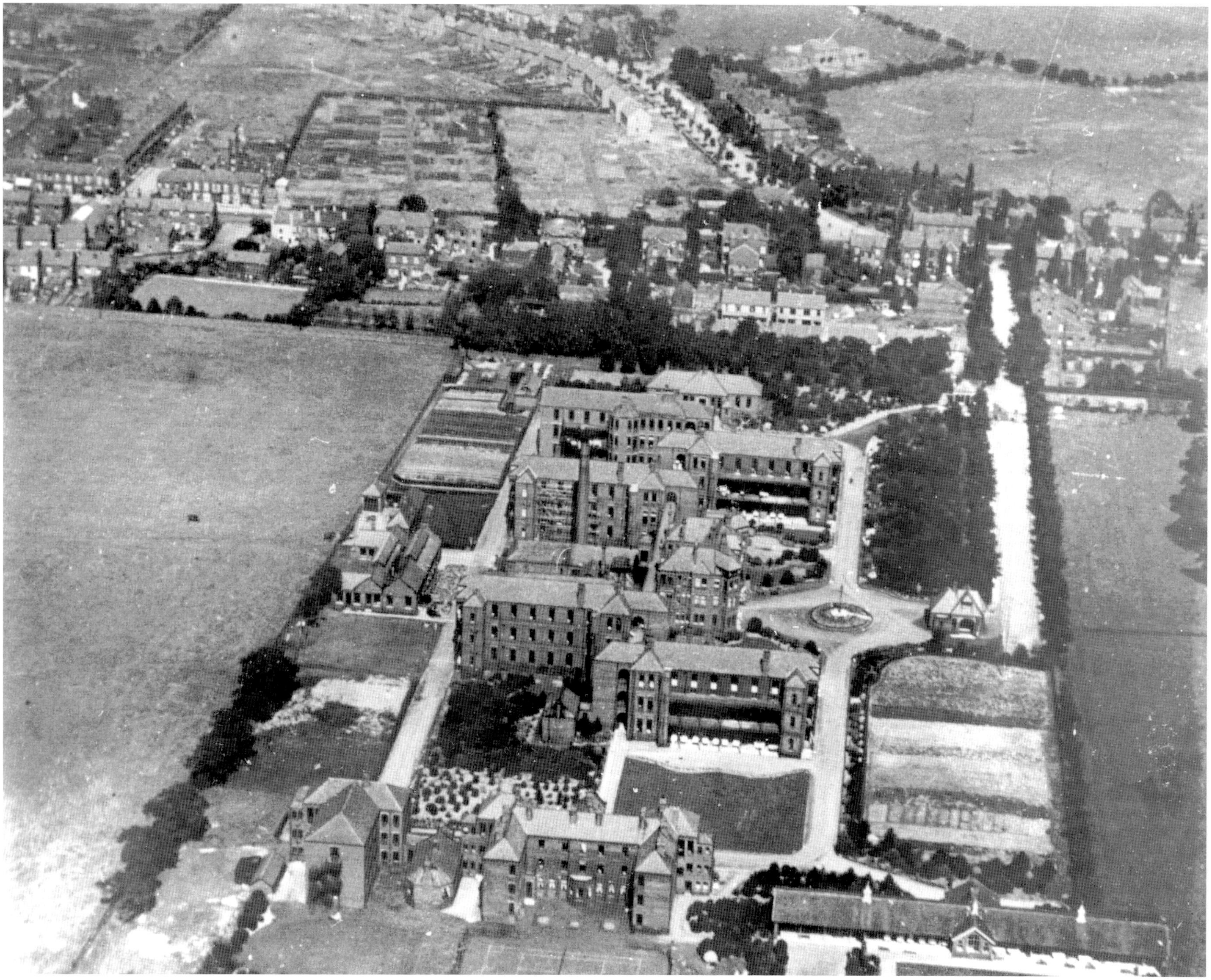

Stepping Hill Hospital 1928

Stepping Hill is Stockport's main hospital and was opened in 1905 on what had been farmland. It is situated off Poplar Grove, on the right, near the junction with Dialstone Lane, which can be seen at the top of the picture as it arches away towards Offerton. The new hospital was built far from the industrial centre of Stockport enabling patients to receive treatment away from the smog and pollution of the early twentieth century. The hospital consisted of the buildings seen here in 1928 and these are still standing, although they have been swamped by new developments. The hospital now covers an area over five times the size of the original footprint, and the developments are continuing to this day, as shown by the construction taking place in the photograph. Since the closure of the Infirmary in 1996 all of the town's main NHS facilities have been based here.

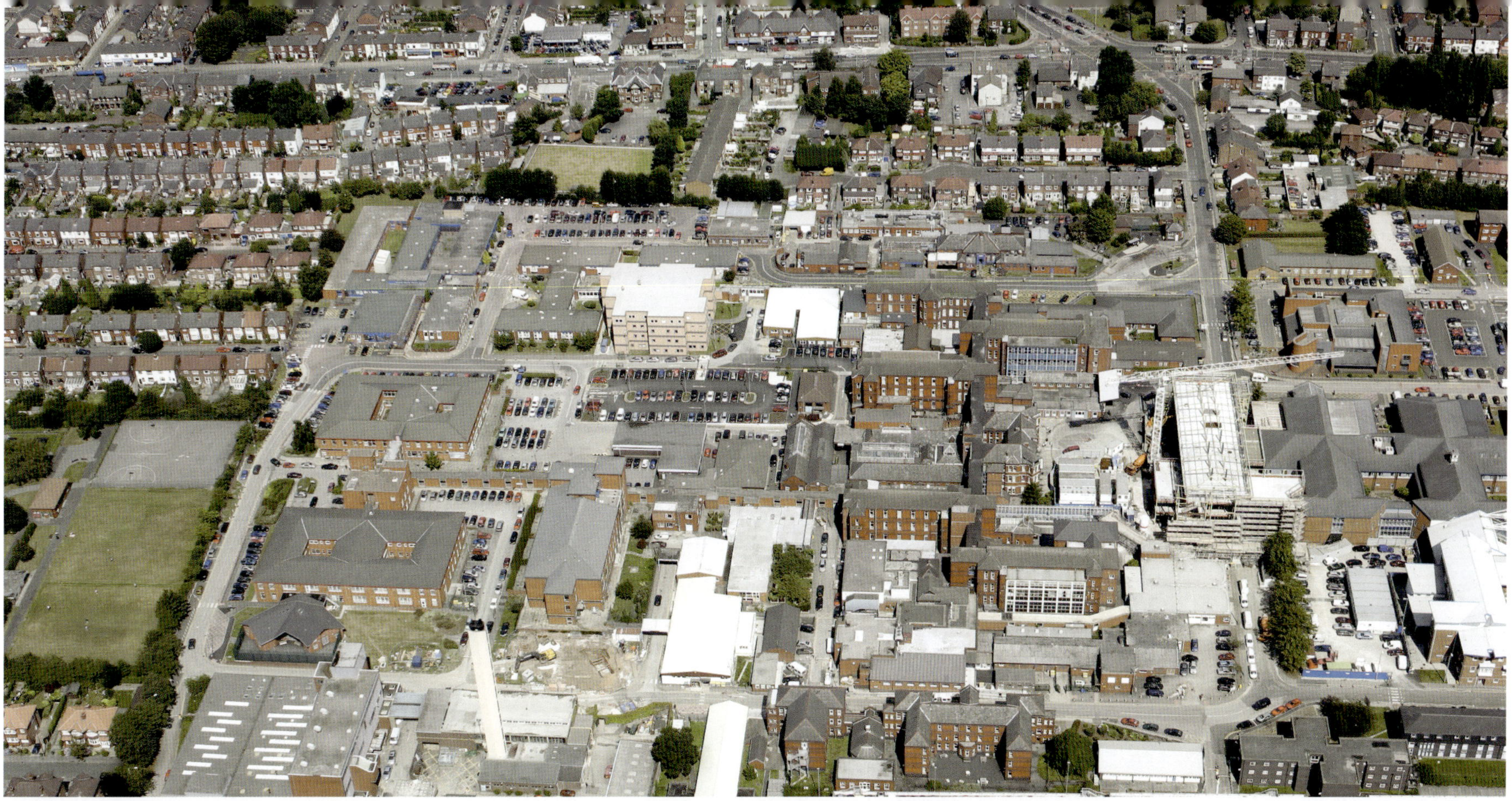

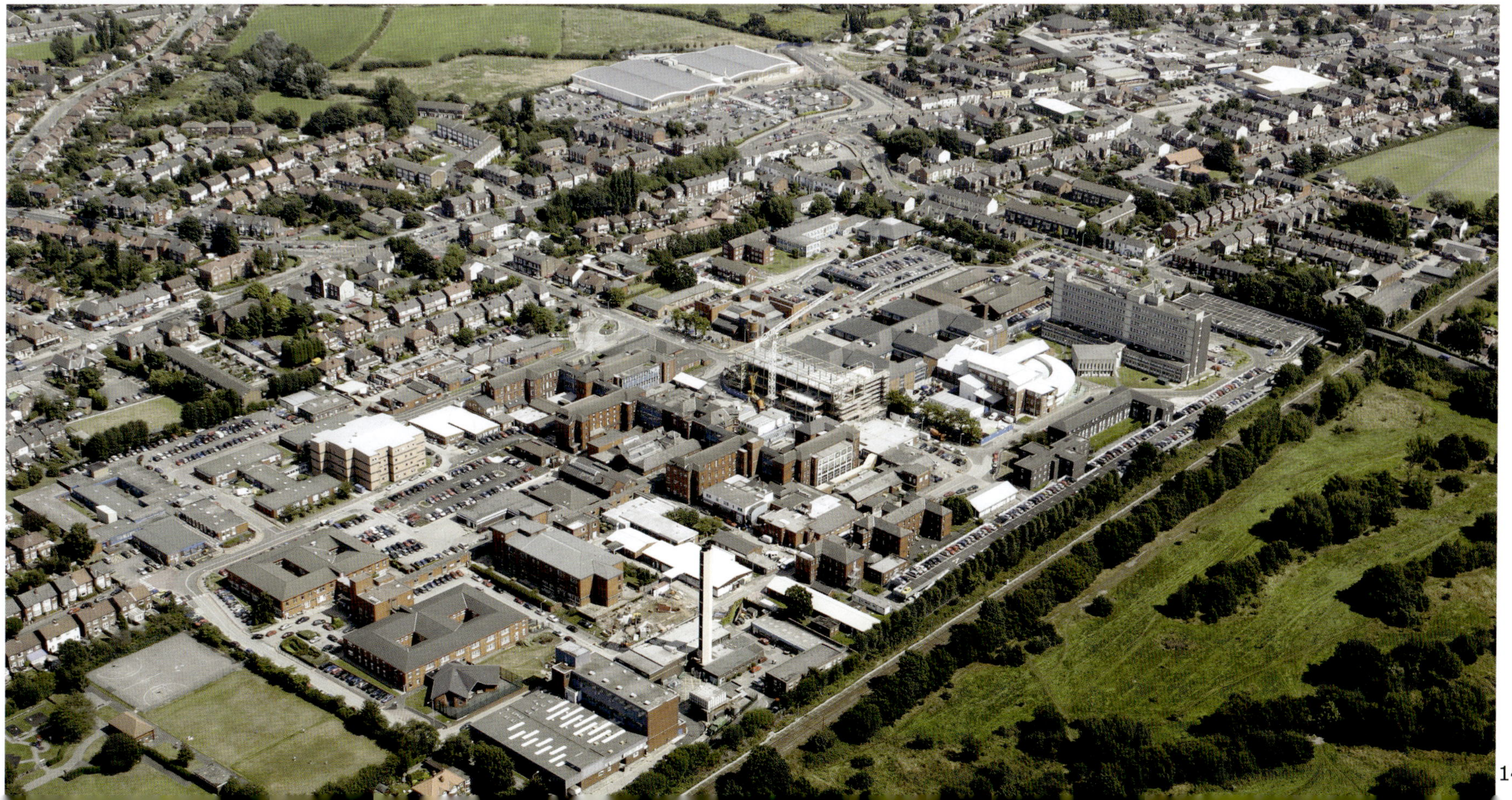

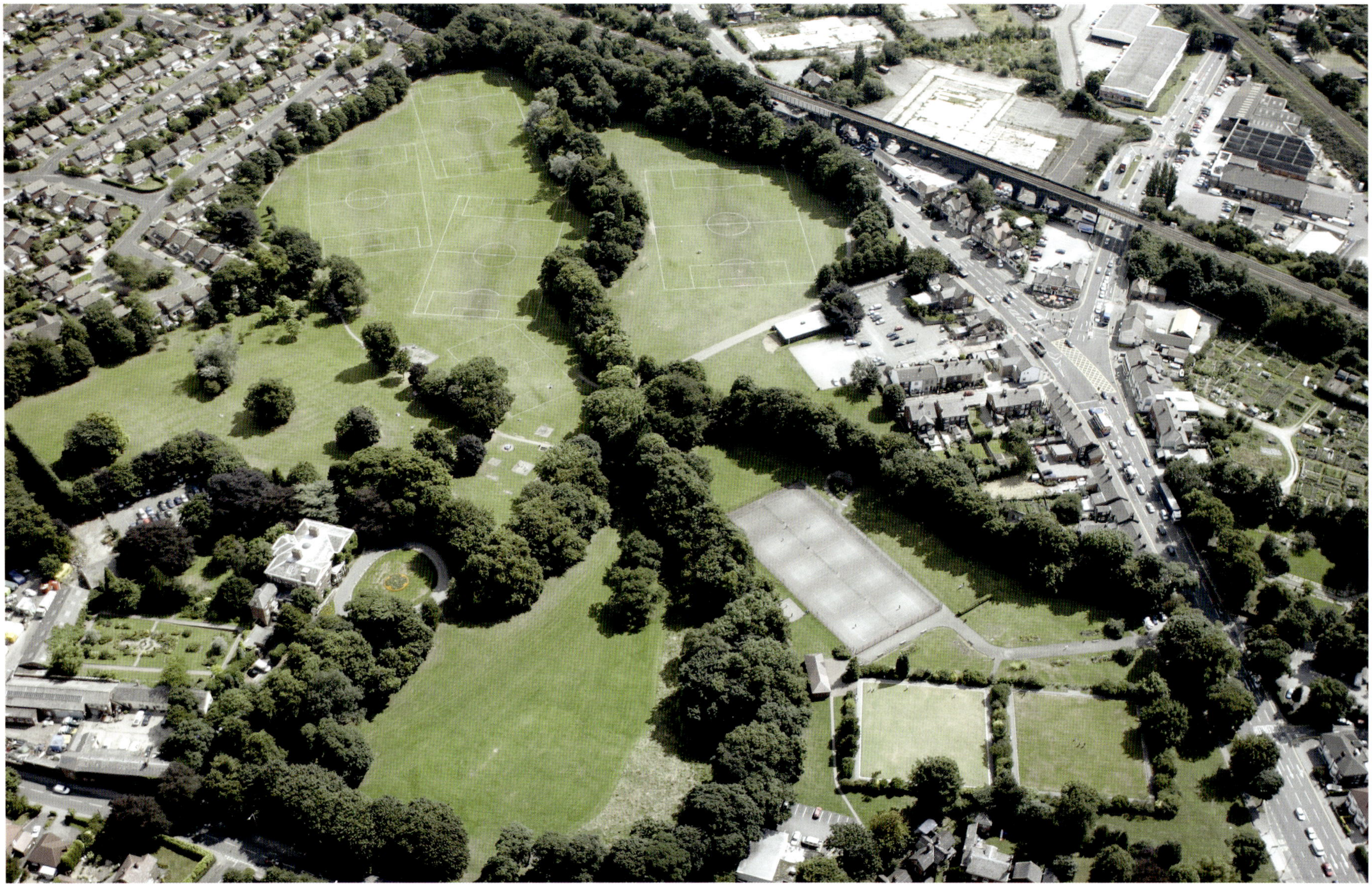

Torkington Park

The wonderful Torkington Park occupies a prominent position on the A6 opposite the Rising Sun public house. On the left can be seen Torkington Lodge. The Lodge is a Grade II Listed Georgian mansion that was home to the Legh family of Booths, near Knutsford. Its elevated position gave it great views over the entire estate, but these views are now obscured by the mature trees. The lodge was purchased in 1935 by Hazel Grove & Bramhall UDC and was used as council offices, a role that it still performs today. At the same time the estate became the public park, covering a total of around 34 acres. On the left to the rear of the Lodge is the Secret Garden; a hidden walled garden with splendid floral displays where people can sit and relax in peace.

St Thomas' Church & Rising Sun Public House (opposite page)

St Thomas' Church, also known as Norbury Parish Church, lies just off the A6 opposite the northern end of Torkington Park. It was built from 1831-1833. The mayor of Stockport, J.K. Winterbottom, laid the final stone on May 13th in front of a crowd of 6,000. The church was officially consecrated a year later.

The Rising Sun is a well-known landmark at the junction between Macclesfield Road and Buxton Road. The pub is recorded as being there in 1754. In 1898 a fountain was erected outside called the "Jubilee fountain". It is recorded as featuring "2 metal cups for humans, 2 troughs for horses and 4 for dogs", but it was later demolished when the junction was changed.

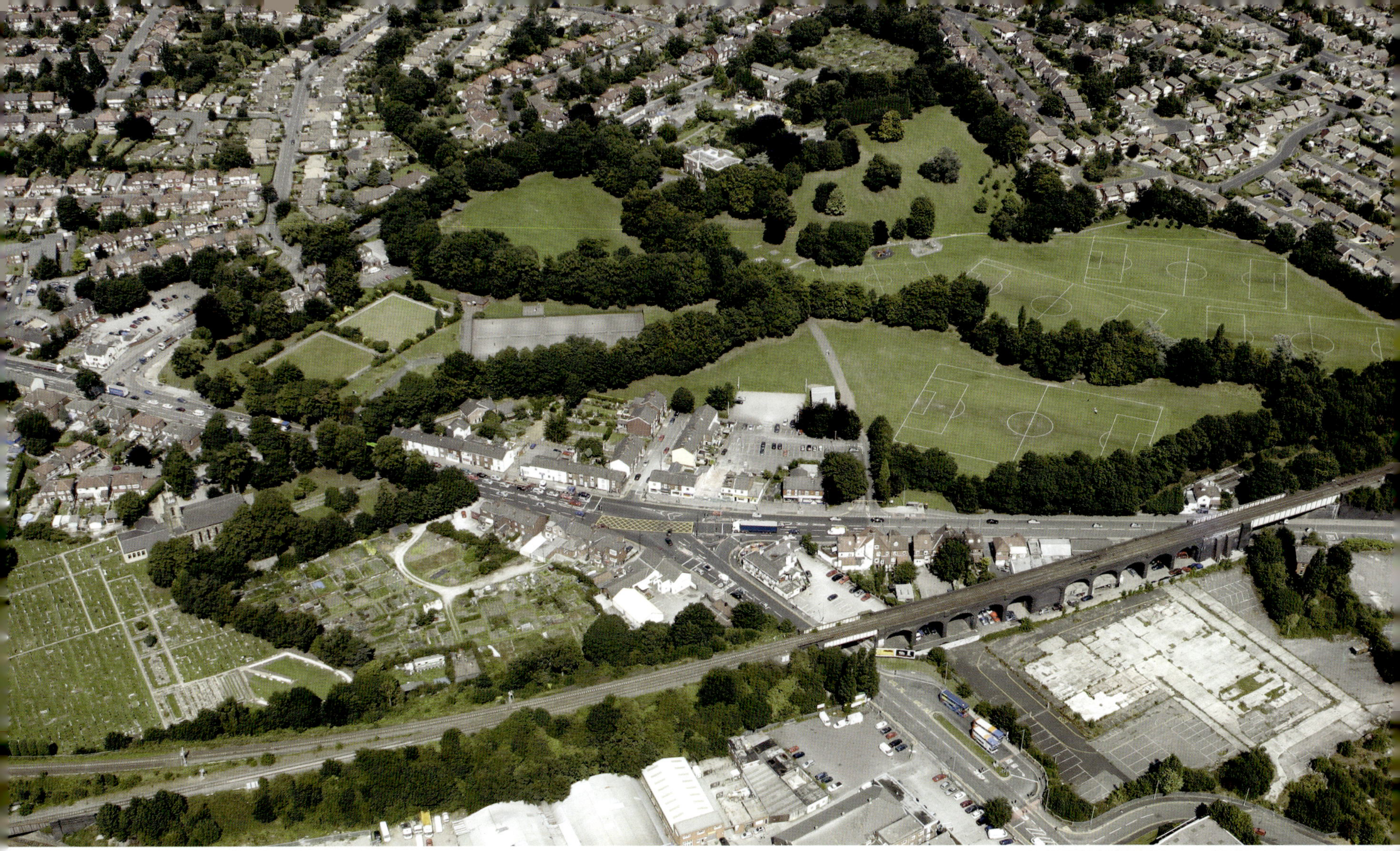

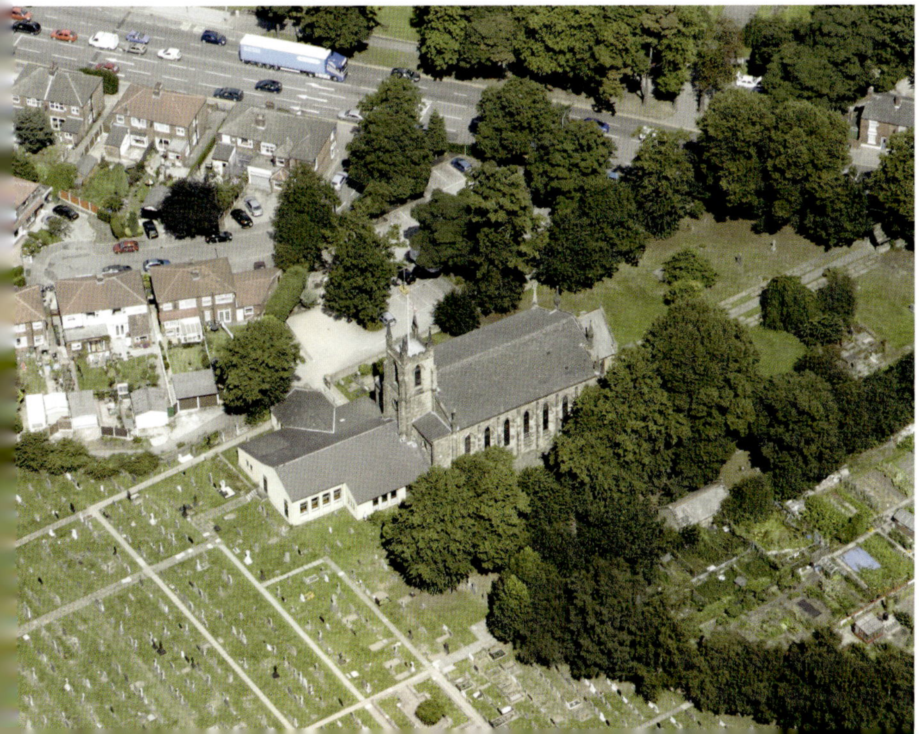

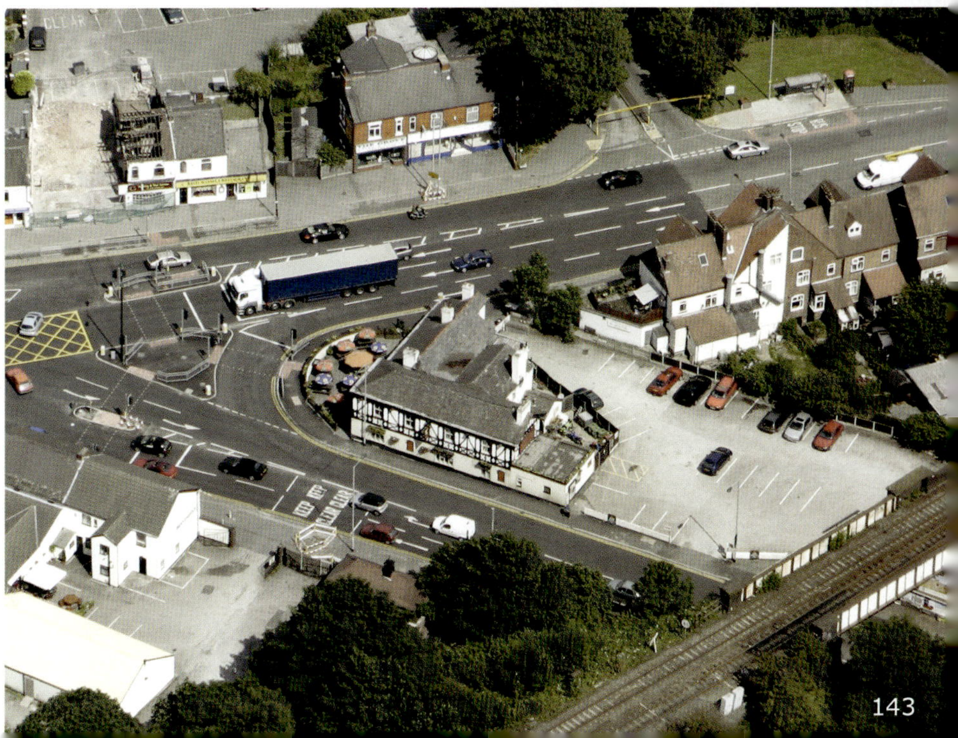

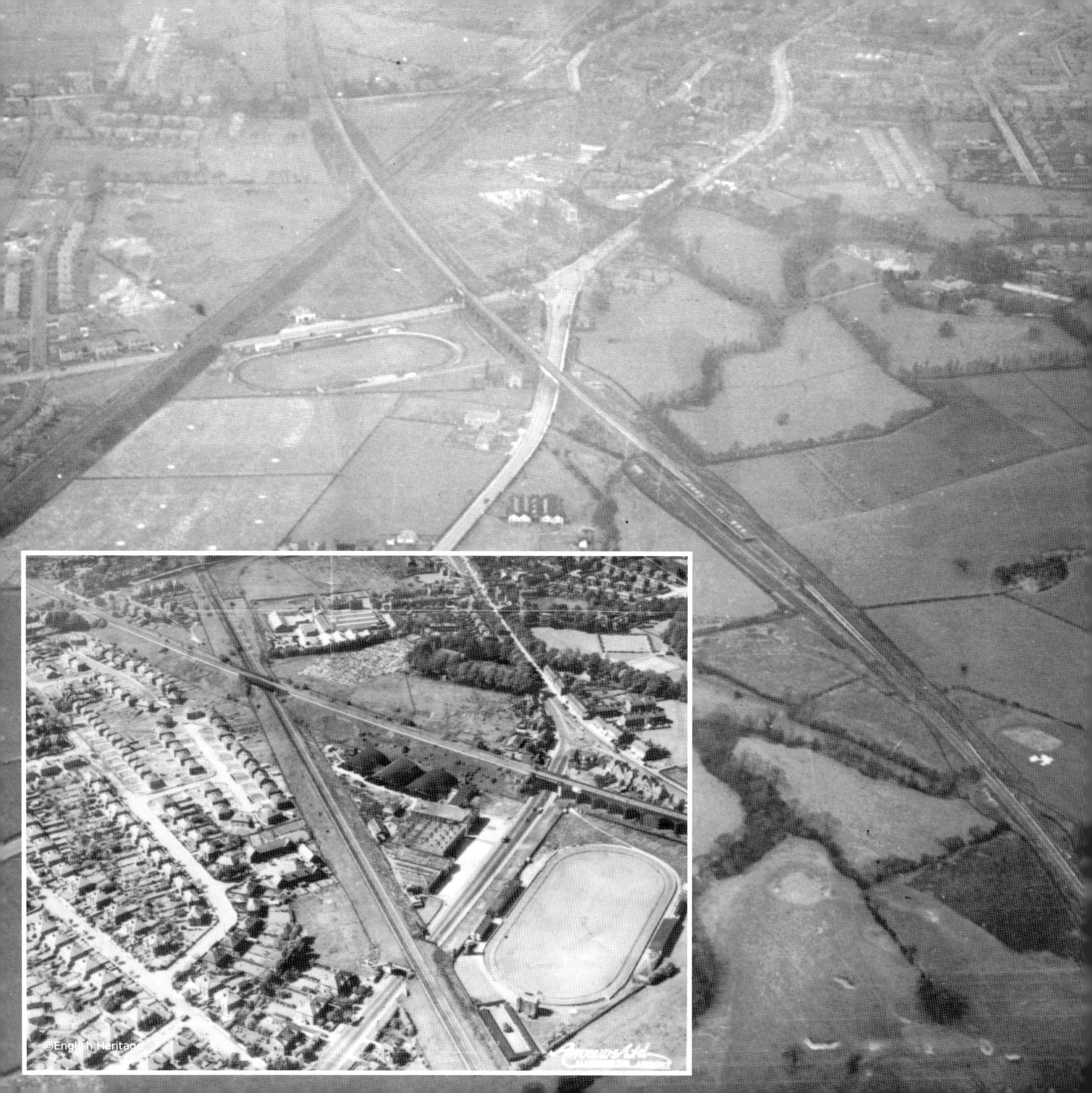
©English Heritage

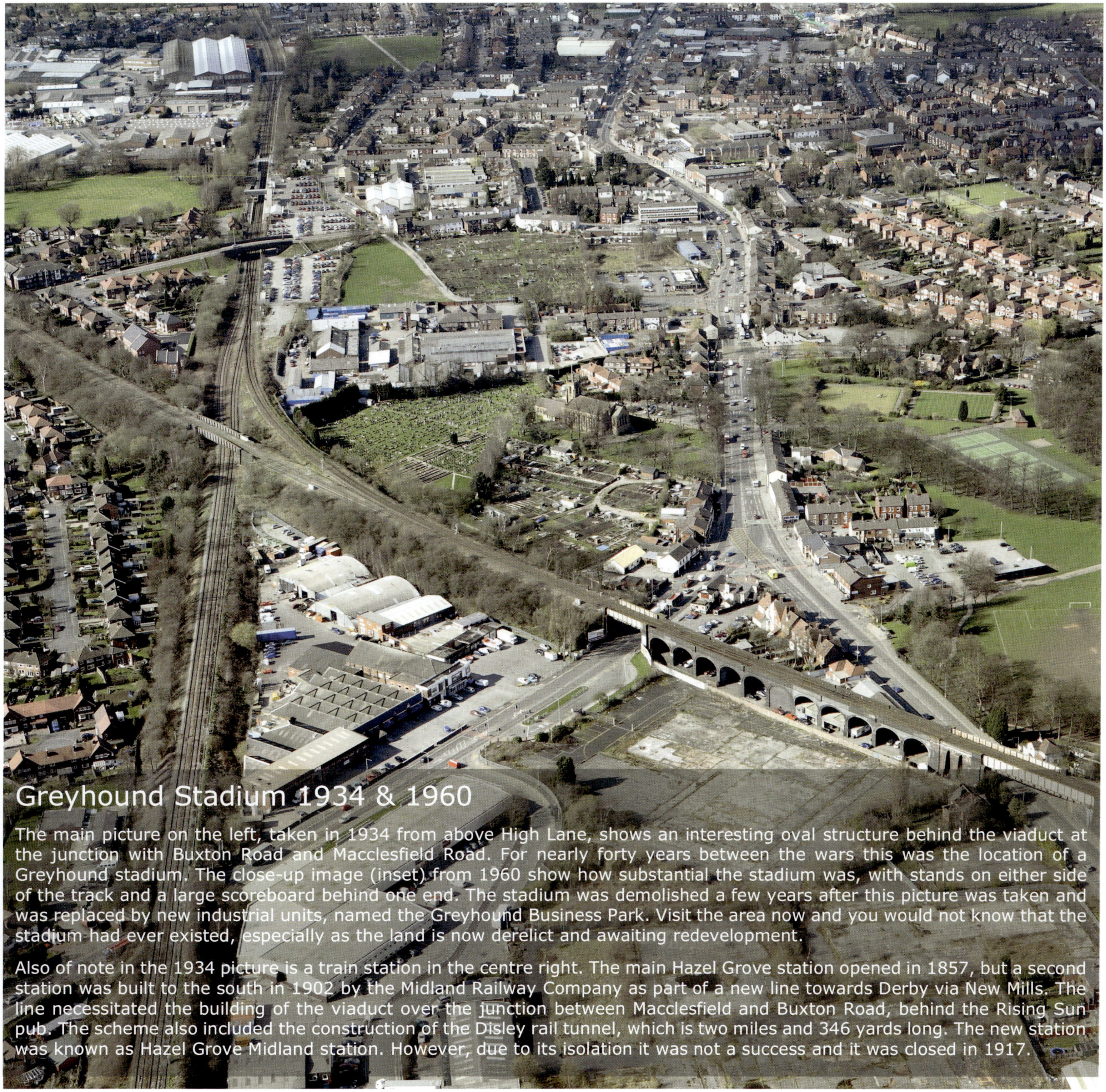

Greyhound Stadium 1934 & 1960

The main picture on the left, taken in 1934 from above High Lane, shows an interesting oval structure behind the viaduct at the junction with Buxton Road and Macclesfield Road. For nearly forty years between the wars this was the location of a Greyhound stadium. The close-up image (inset) from 1960 show how substantial the stadium was, with stands on either side of the track and a large scoreboard behind one end. The stadium was demolished a few years after this picture was taken and was replaced by new industrial units, named the Greyhound Business Park. Visit the area now and you would not know that the stadium had ever existed, especially as the land is now derelict and awaiting redevelopment.

Also of note in the 1934 picture is a train station in the centre right. The main Hazel Grove station opened in 1857, but a second station was built to the south in 1902 by the Midland Railway Company as part of a new line towards Derby via New Mills. The line necessitated the building of the viaduct over the junction between Macclesfield and Buxton Road, behind the Rising Sun pub. The scheme also included the construction of the Disley rail tunnel, which is two miles and 346 yards long. The new station was known as Hazel Grove Midland station. However, due to its isolation it was not a success and it was closed in 1917.

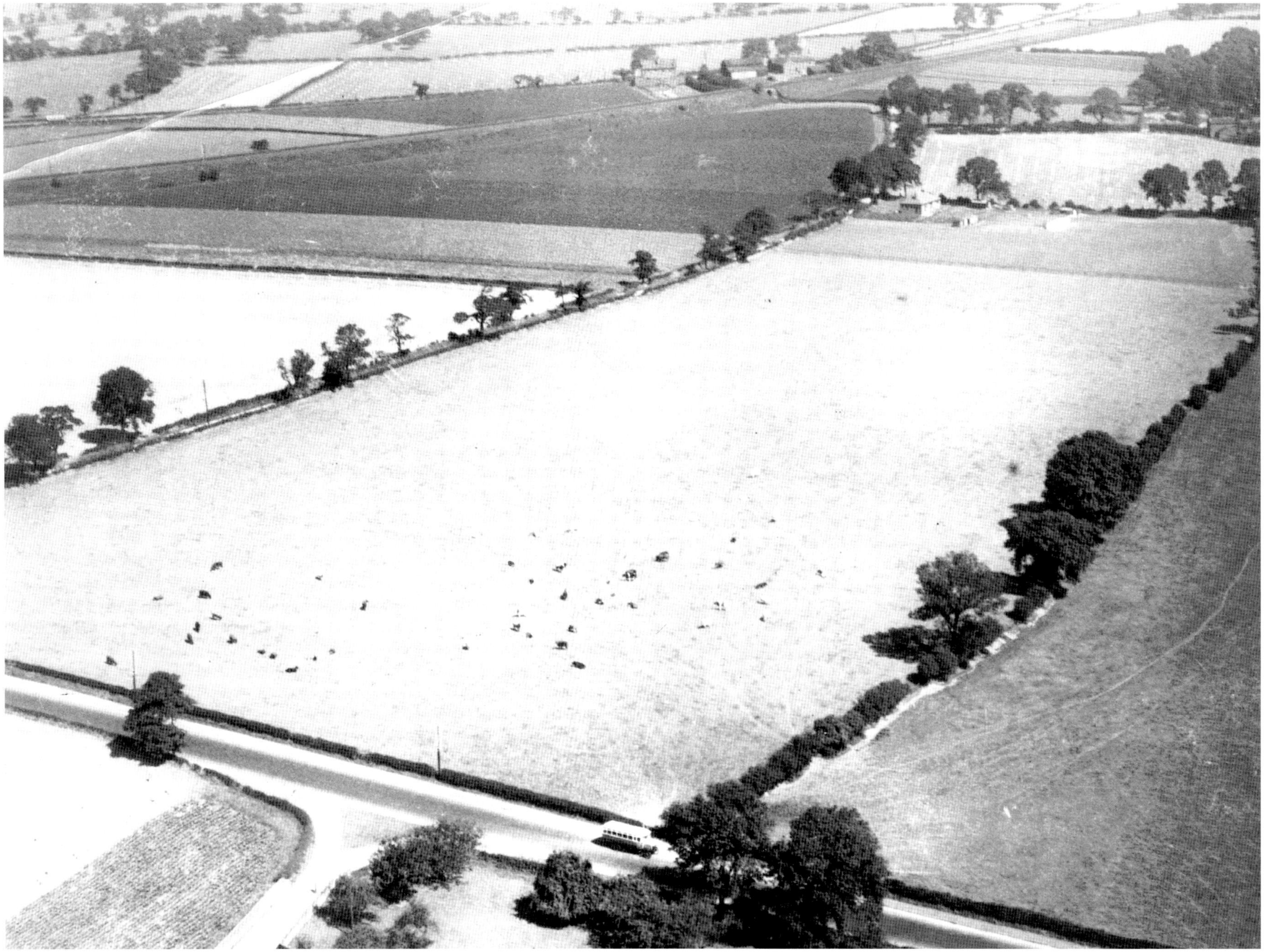

Old Aerodrome – 1933

The fields in the picture were licensed as an aerodrome from 1923-1927. The length of the field would have made it perfect for both landing and take-off of the aircraft of the day, which did not require long strips and hard surfaces. The picture was taken from above Norbury Hall on Macclesfield Road (the road at the bottom of the old picture is the entrance to the hall). This is just south of where the Greyhound Stadium was located, and in the background can be seen the railway line running to the main Hazel Grove station. This was part of the Stockport, Disley & Whaley Bridge Railway that opened in 1857. In the centre of the picture is Mill Lane which heads towards the line and a tunnel under the track. Today, the land has been developed and is covered with housing, but the shape of the old fields is still noticeable in the layout of the streets. Mill Lane still runs towards the railway line in the centre of the new picture. Look very closely and the farmhouse at the top of the Lane on the other side of the railway track is still visible. On the bottom left of the new picture is the Fiveways shopping parade.

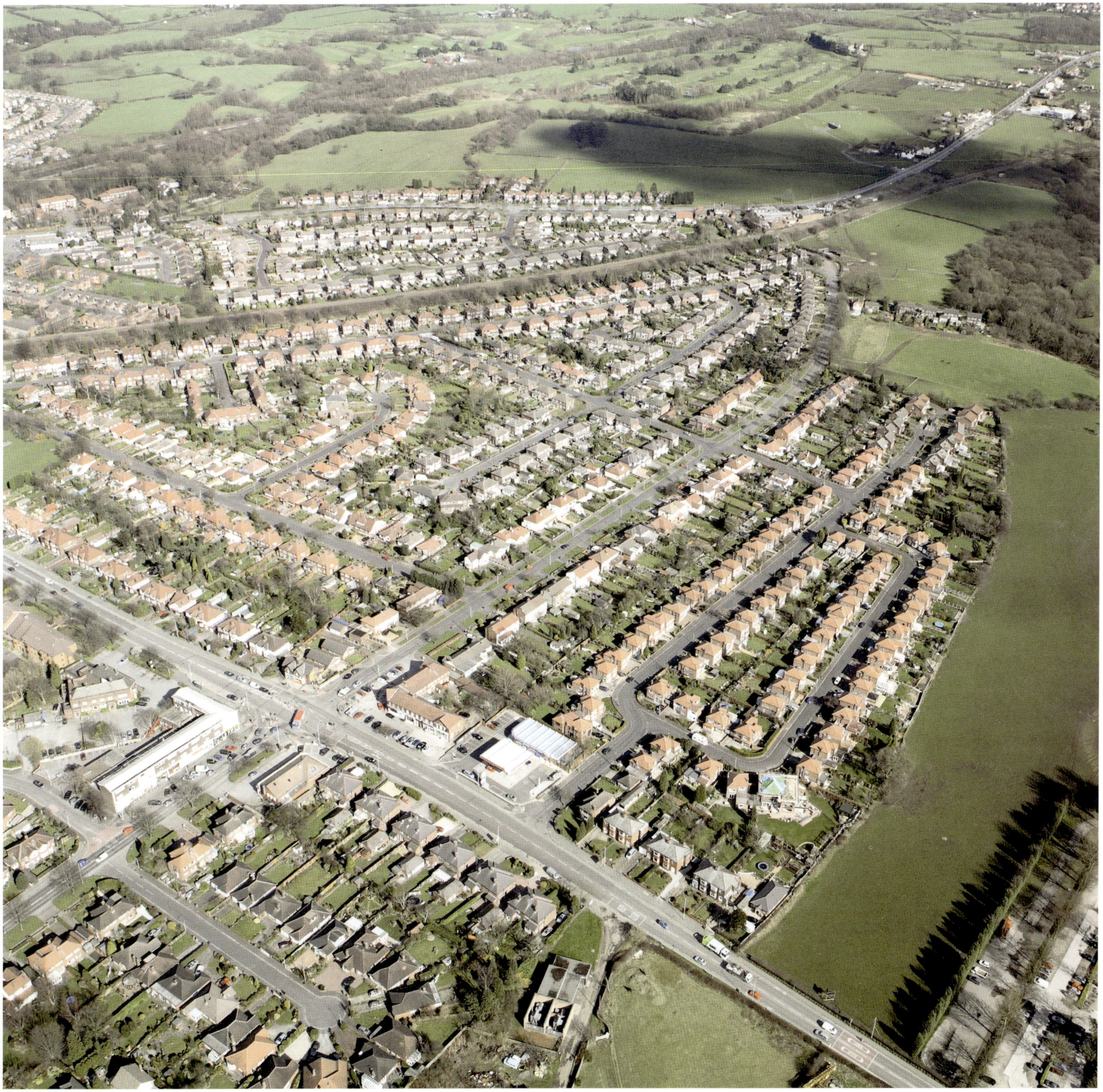

Bramhall

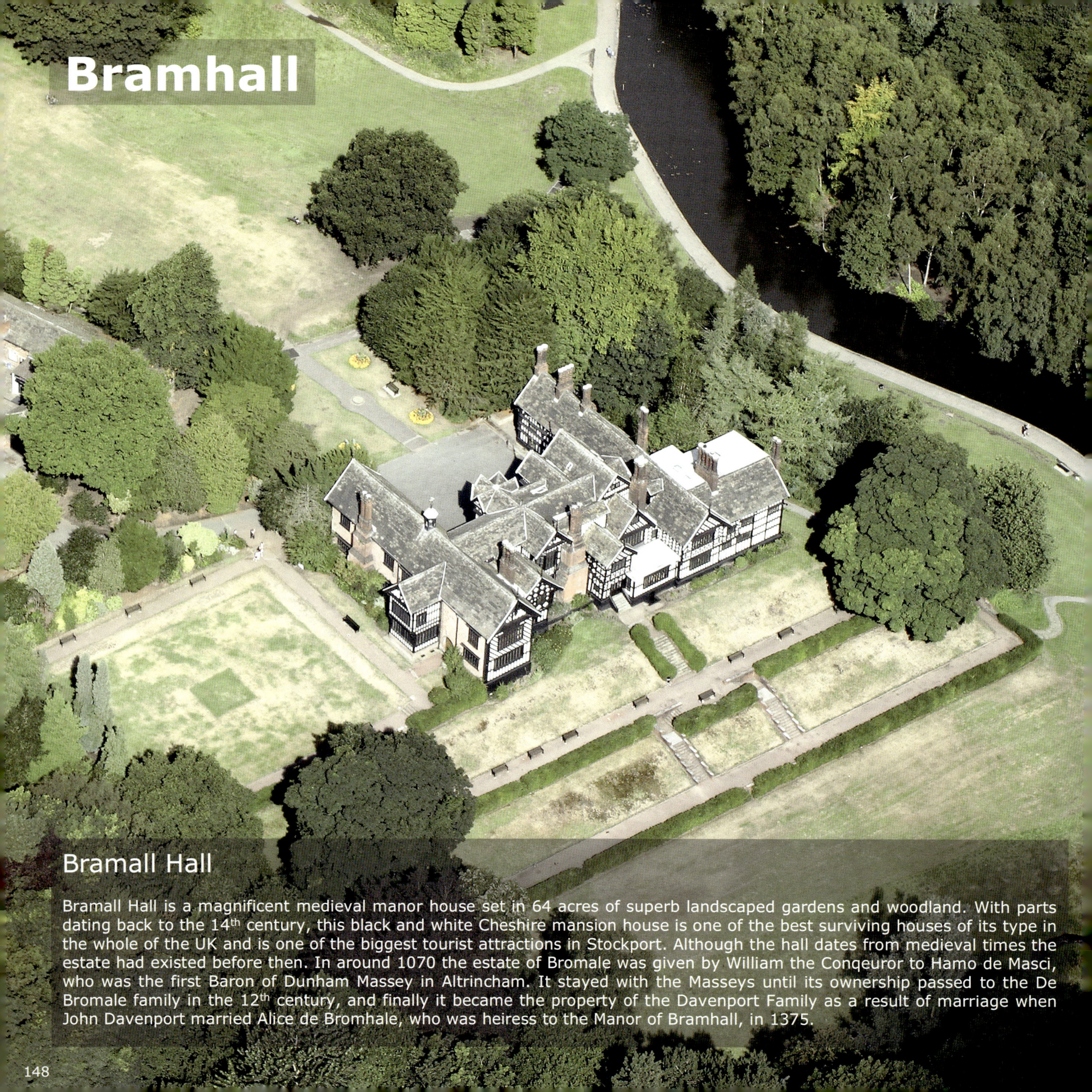

Bramall Hall

Bramall Hall is a magnificent medieval manor house set in 64 acres of superb landscaped gardens and woodland. With parts dating back to the 14th century, this black and white Cheshire mansion house is one of the best surviving houses of its type in the whole of the UK and is one of the biggest tourist attractions in Stockport. Although the hall dates from medieval times the estate had existed before then. In around 1070 the estate of Bromale was given by William the Conqueror to Hamo de Masci, who was the first Baron of Dunham Massey in Altrincham. It stayed with the Masseys until its ownership passed to the De Bromale family in the 12th century, and finally it became the property of the Davenport Family as a result of marriage when John Davenport married Alice de Bromhale, who was heiress to the Manor of Bramhall, in 1375.

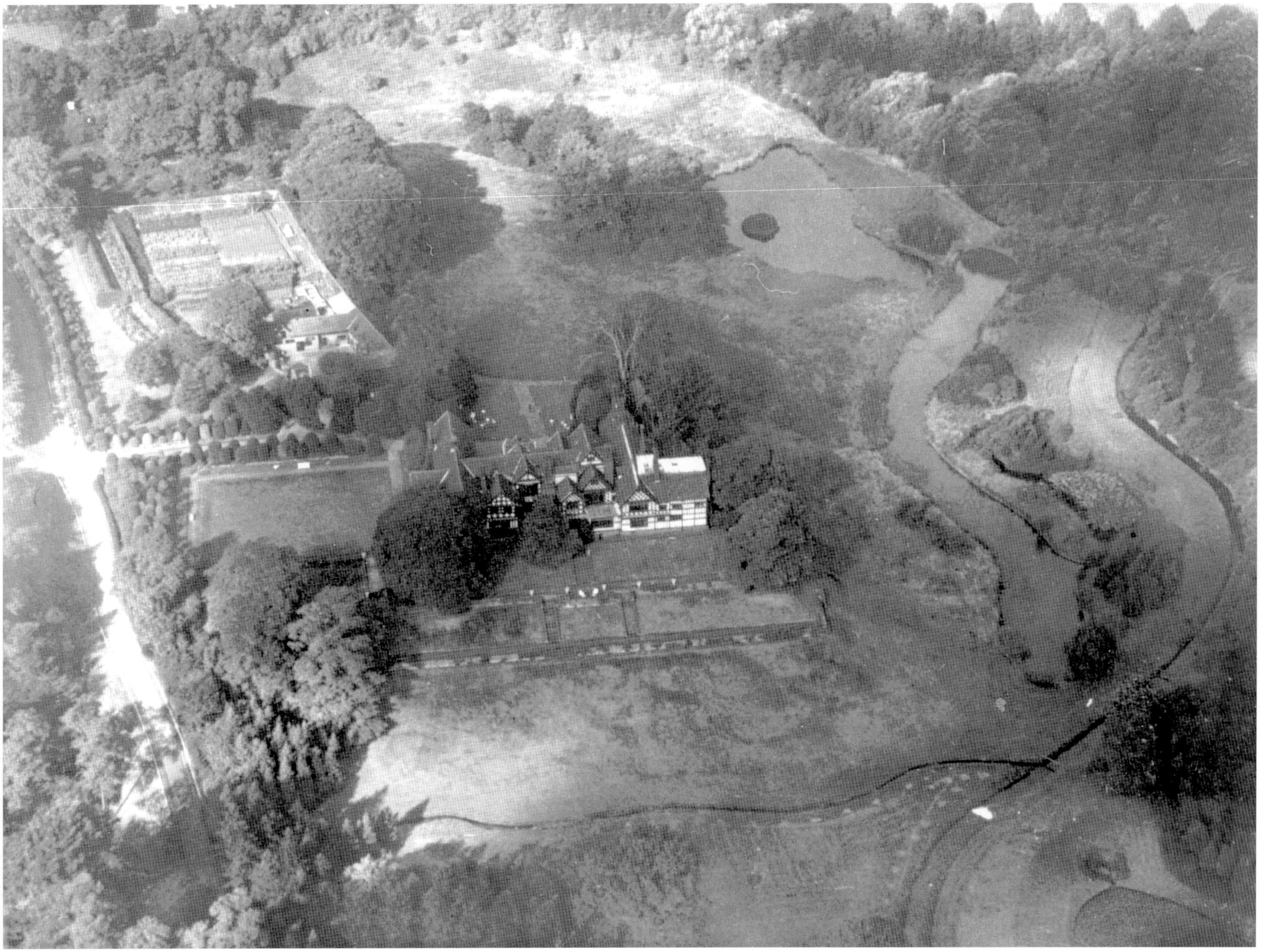

Bramall Hall 1928

It was around the time of the Davenports taking ownership that the first sections of the current hall were being built. The centrepiece of the building was the Great Hall, which until 1590 was open to the elements. Other features included the 15th century banqueting room, a chapel and a ballroom. As well as being a residence, the grounds were originally a deer park, much like at Lyme Hall, and would have been extensively larger than today. This land would have been woodlands like most of the remaining grounds. Evidence that the park was used for hunting is shown by the presence of a "ha-ha", which is the sunken ditch at the front of the hall that kept animals within the park and away from the house, clearly visible along the bottom of the above picture.

The hall remained the property of the Davenport family for over 500 years until 1877. In that year it was sold to the Freeholders Company Ltd of Manchester, a newly established property company with intentions of selling off plots of the estate for housing. Six years later it was bought by Thomas Neville of Strines Printworks as a wedding present for his son, Charles.

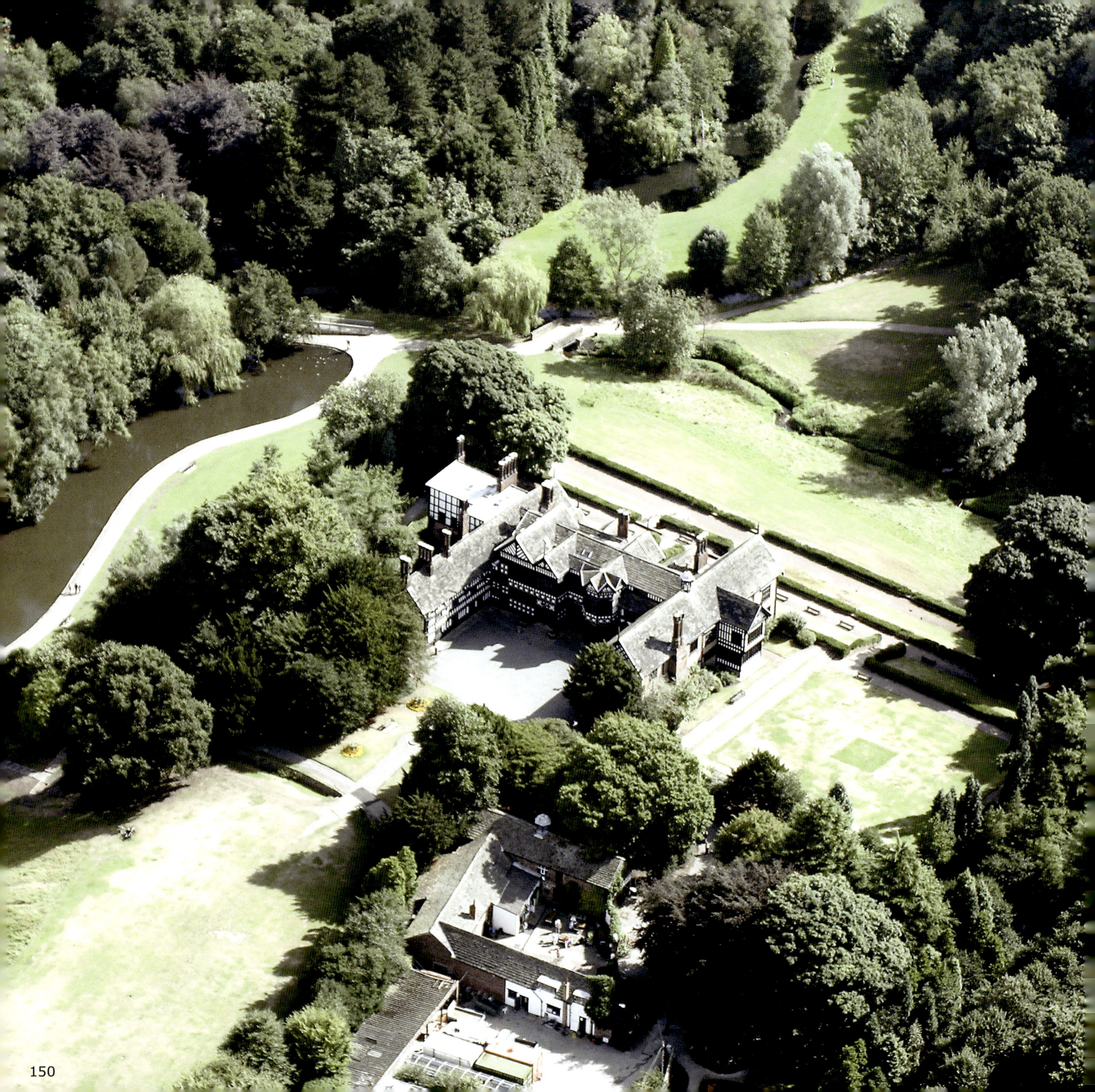

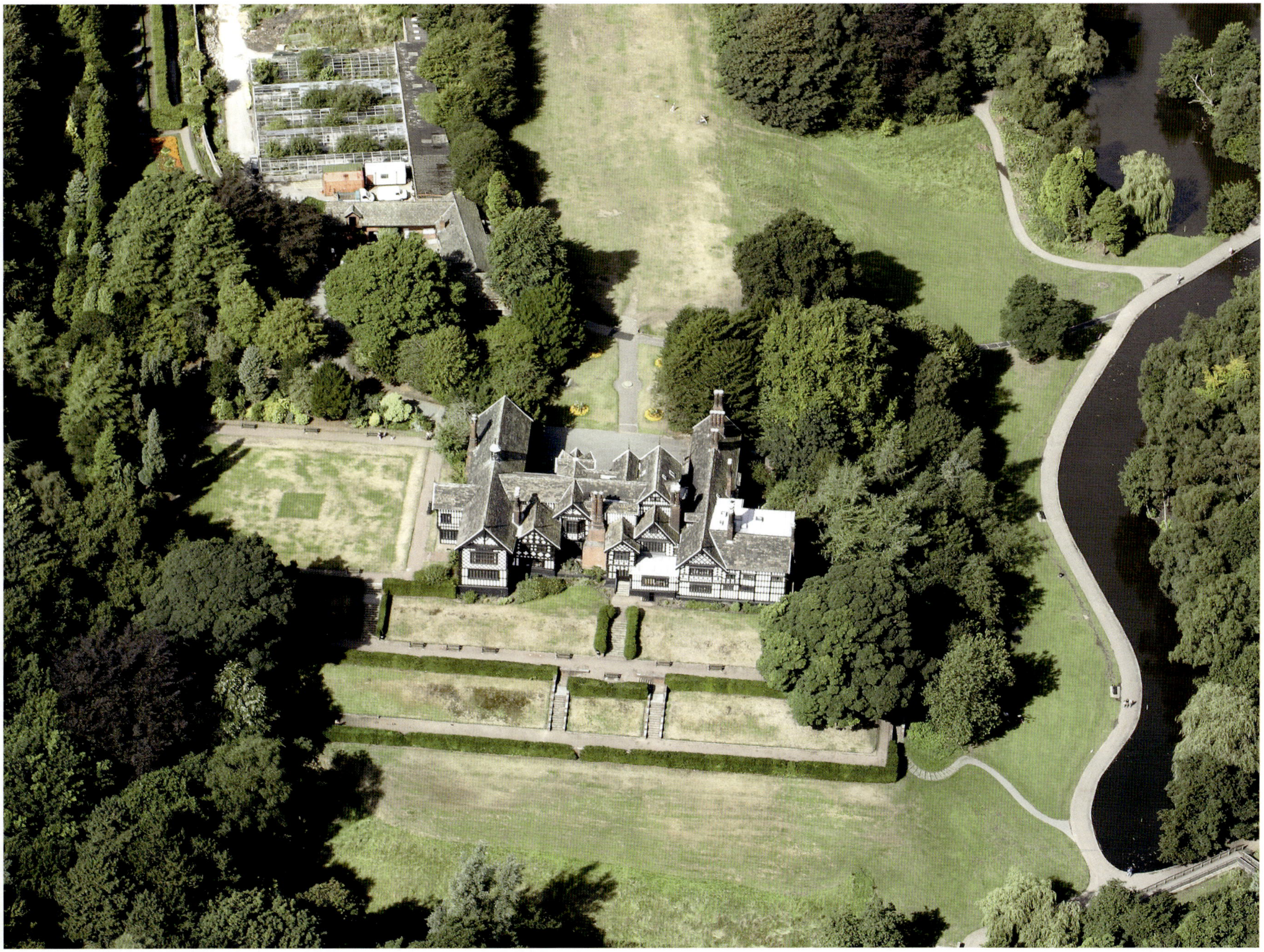

It was thanks to Charles Neville that the Hall underwent a great period of restoration. It was he who added the impressive Victorian fireplace that now stands in the drawing room, and he also created the ponds within the hall's grounds when he altered the course of the Lady Brook in the 1890s. It is also because of Neville that the extra "h" in Bramhall was dropped from the hall's name. It is claimed that he chose to spell it as "Bramall" because it was closest to the original medieval name, and also because it was his preference. In 1925 Neville put the entire estate up for auction. He proposed dismantling the building and selling off the fittings if a buyer could not be found. The Stockport Corporation made a bid for the building but it was rejected, and after no bidder reached the reserve price the future seemed bleak. The hall was saved by John Davies, the president of Manchester United FC, who agreed to purchase the hall and its grounds in a private sale. He lived in the hall with his wife until his death in 1927. His widow sold the hall to Hazel Grove & Bramhall UDC in 1935, with the aim being to open the hall up to the public. The first visitors were allowed access in April 1936, and the grounds were opened up as a public park. Today the hall and the park have barely changed since 1928, save for a few trees. Together they attract thousands of visitors a year from far and wide who wish to sample the hall's history and see its breathtaking scenery.

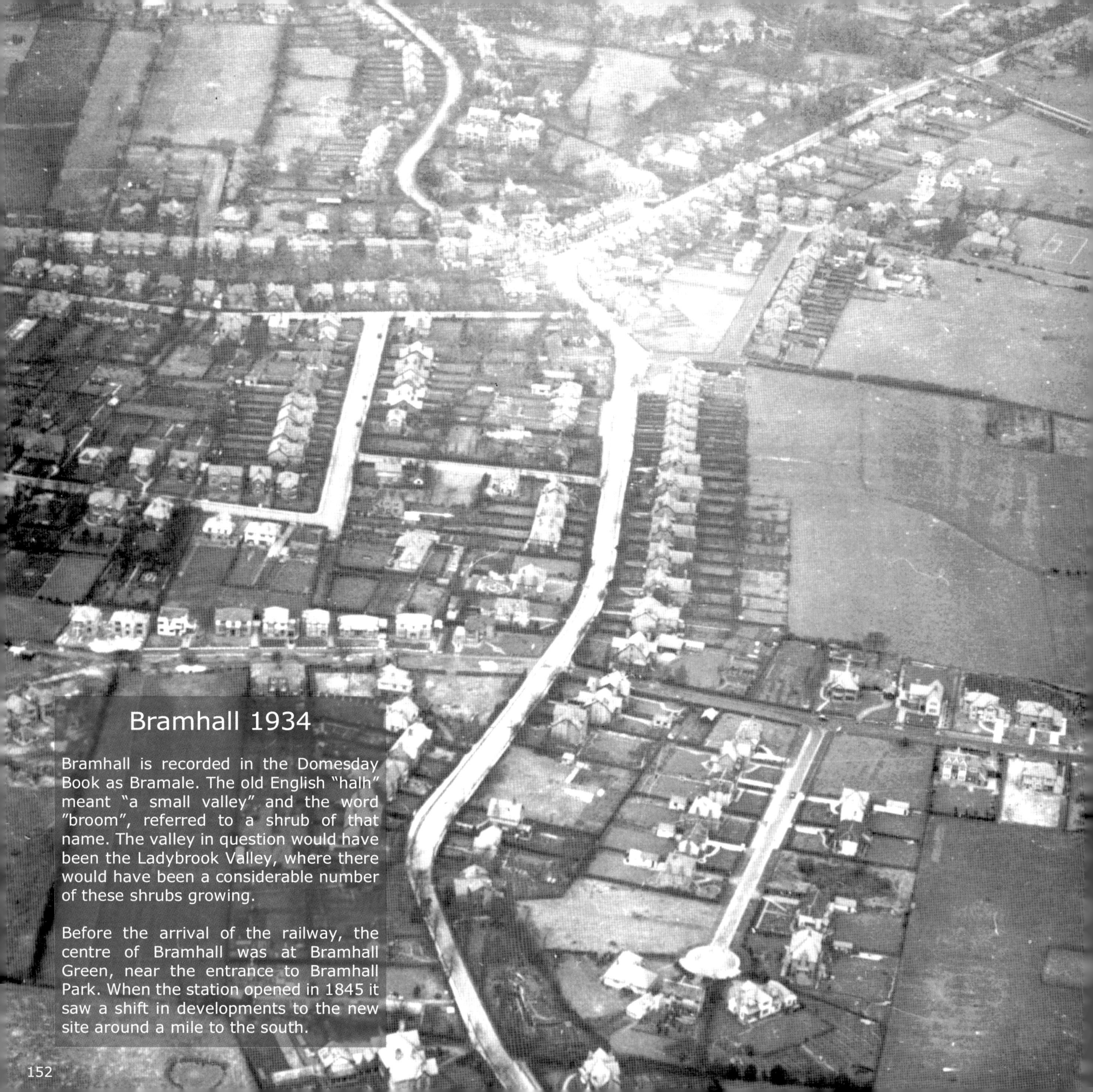

Bramhall 1934

Bramhall is recorded in the Domesday Book as Bramale. The old English "halh" meant "a small valley" and the word "broom", referred to a shrub of that name. The valley in question would have been the Ladybrook Valley, where there would have been a considerable number of these shrubs growing.

Before the arrival of the railway, the centre of Bramhall was at Bramhall Green, near the entrance to Bramhall Park. When the station opened in 1845 it saw a shift in developments to the new site around a mile to the south.

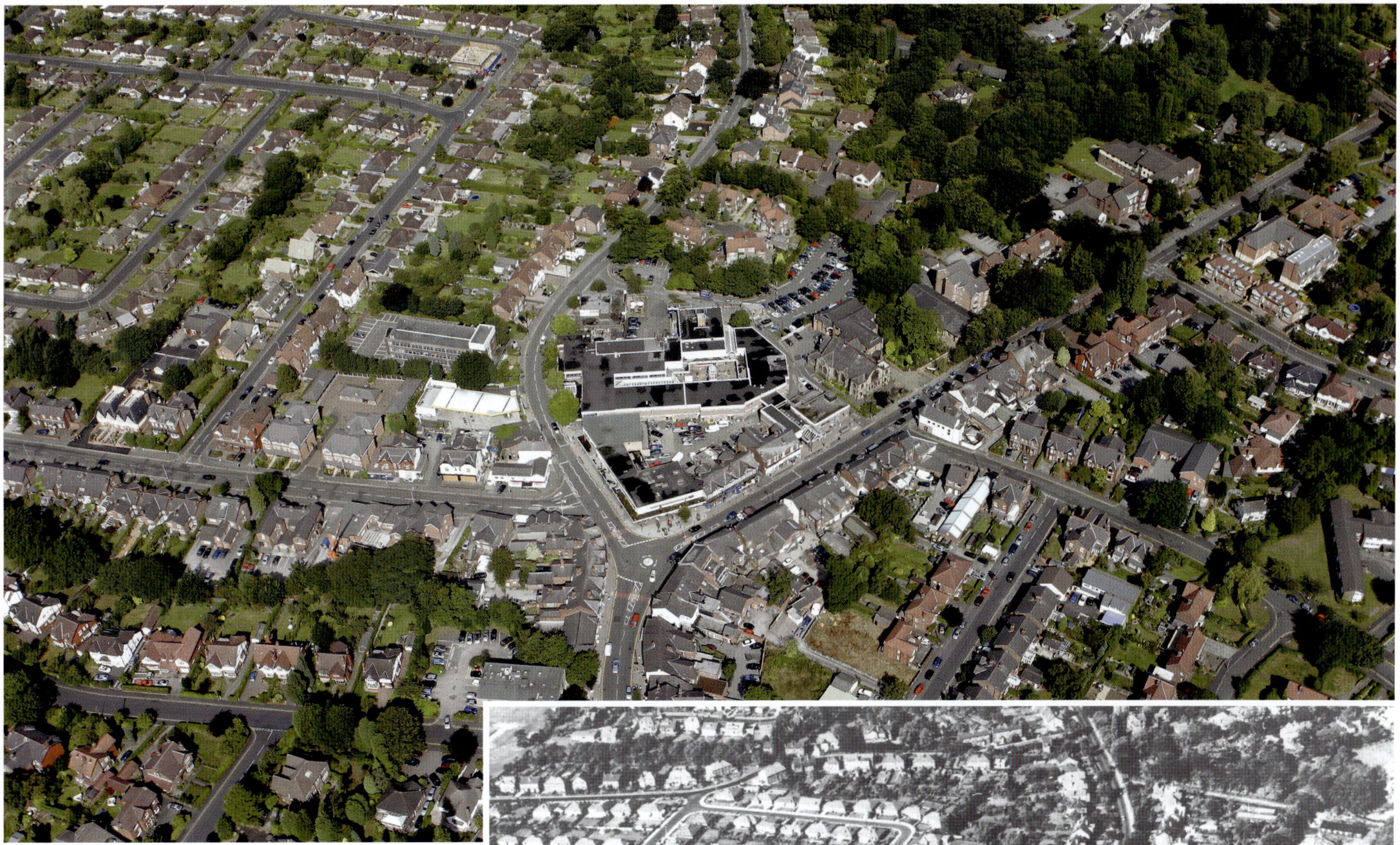

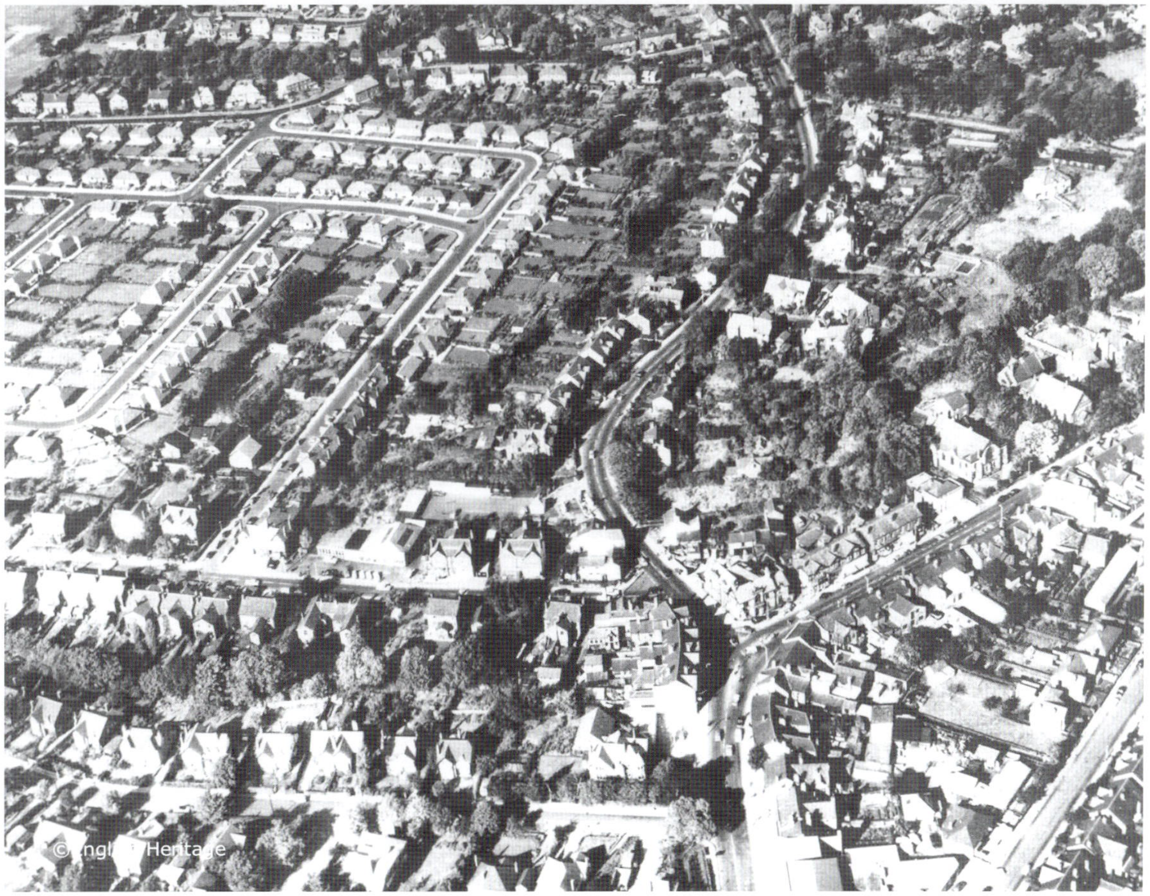

Bramhall 1966

These series of images provide a good insight into how the village has developed. In 1934 much of the centre of the village was still very open. By 1966 there had been more in-fill developments, with new housing along the roads leading off the main roads. The centre of the village was almost as it was 32 years previously, although now there was a larger amount of traffic.

The biggest change since 1966 has been the addition of the indoor shopping precinct, known as The Bramhall Square Shopping Centre. The precinct's construction required the demolition of some of the buildings that had fronted onto Bramhall Lane South (heading right in the picture) and Ack Lane East (heading up).

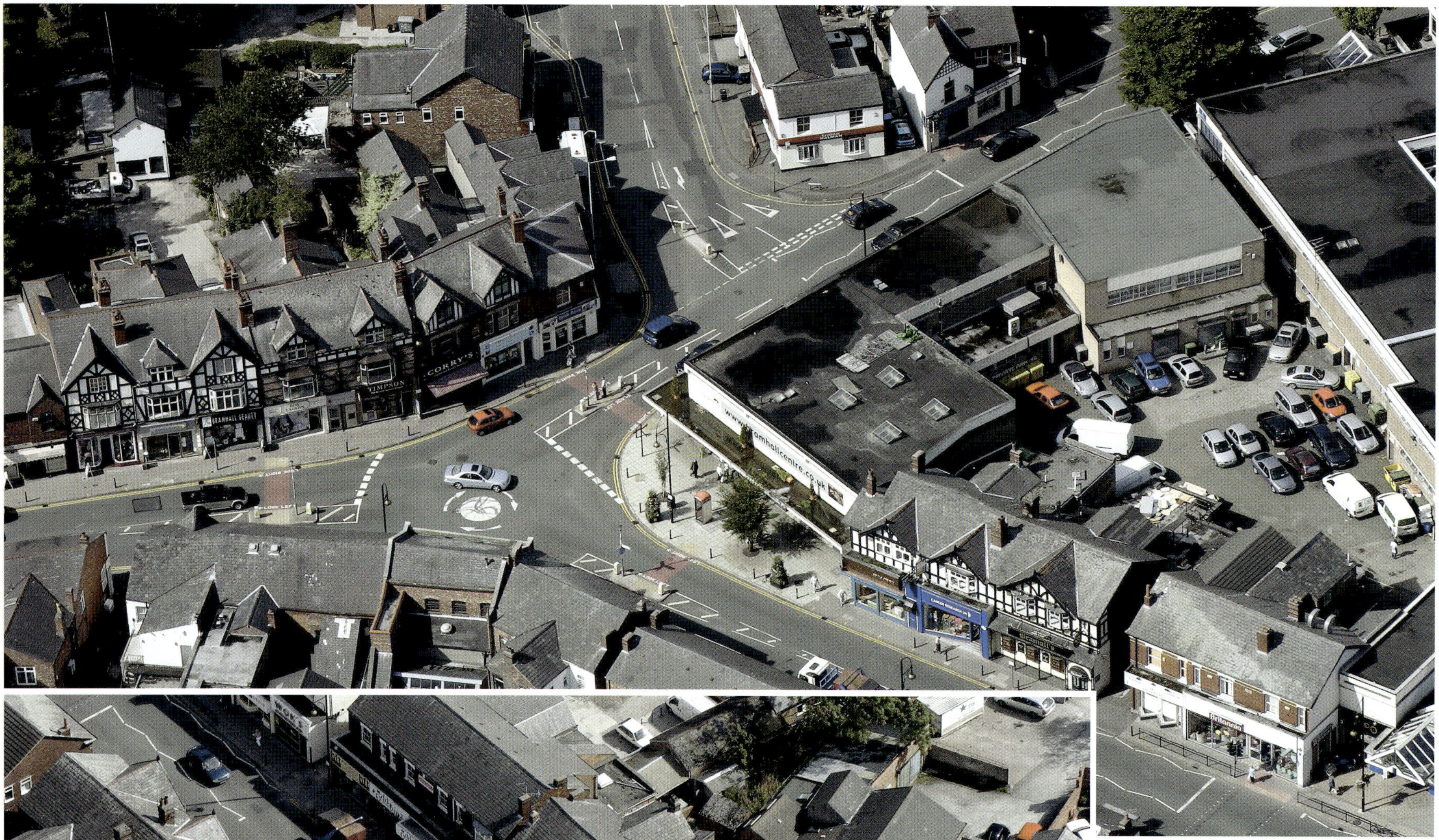

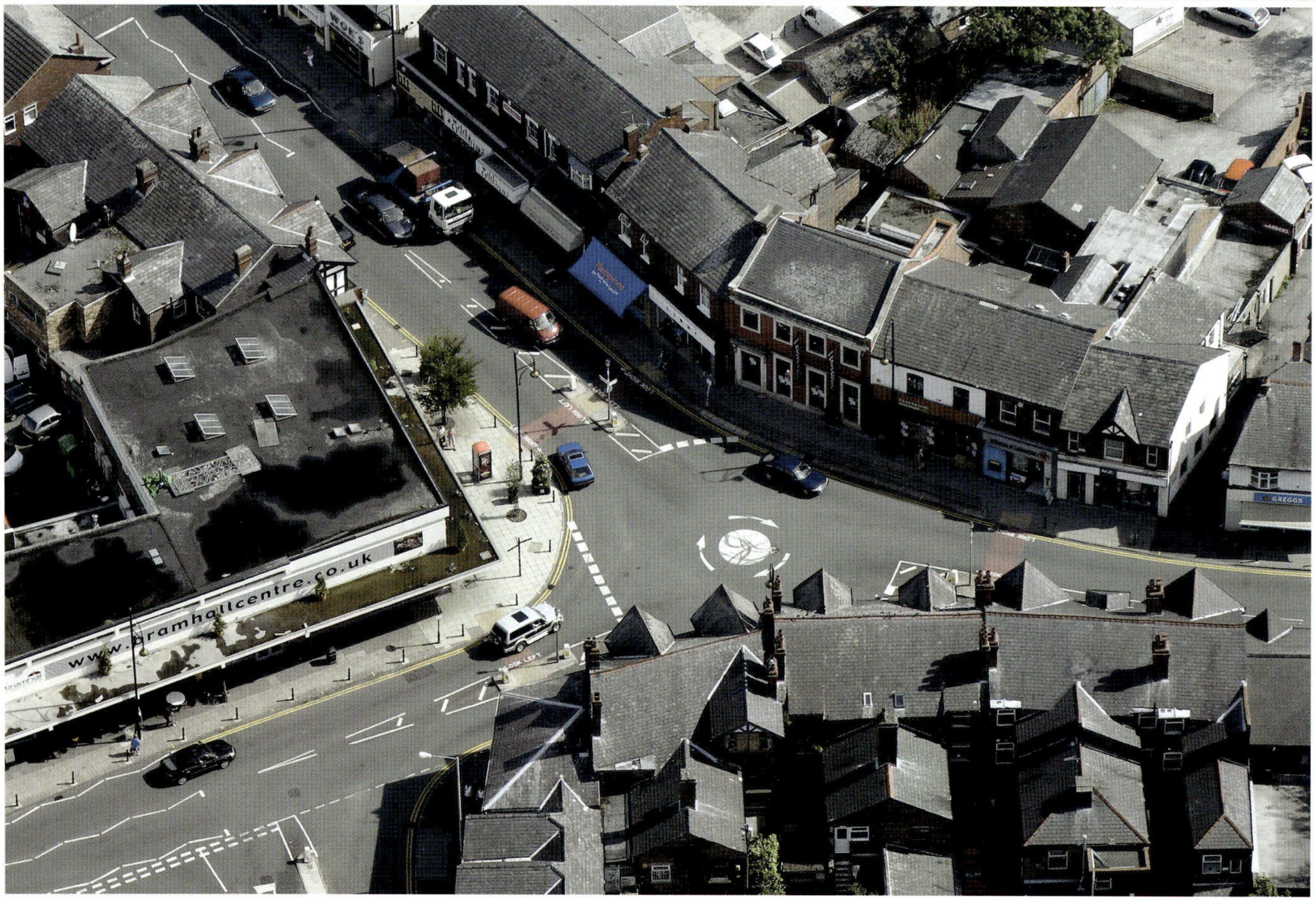

Bramhall Village

The modern village of Bramhall has a reputation for posh shops, chic boutiques & wine bars, but it still manages to maintain a welcoming Cheshire village feel.

Much of the village is still made up of the late 19th and early 20th century buildings that have been the mainstay of the shopping area. These mock Tudor buildings are representative of the style of the era, with similar buildings also present in Cheadle and in the Old Town around Great Underbank.

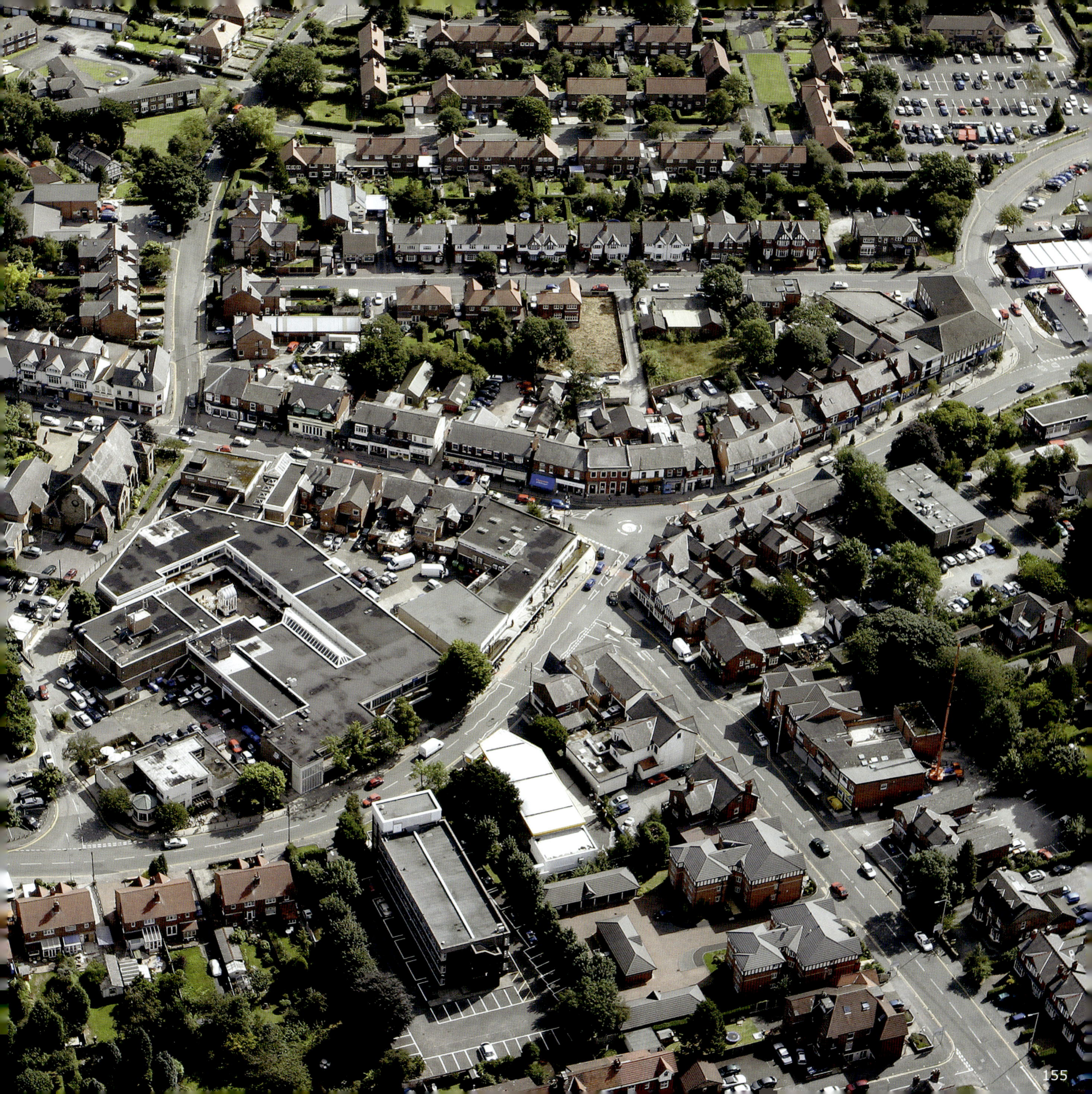

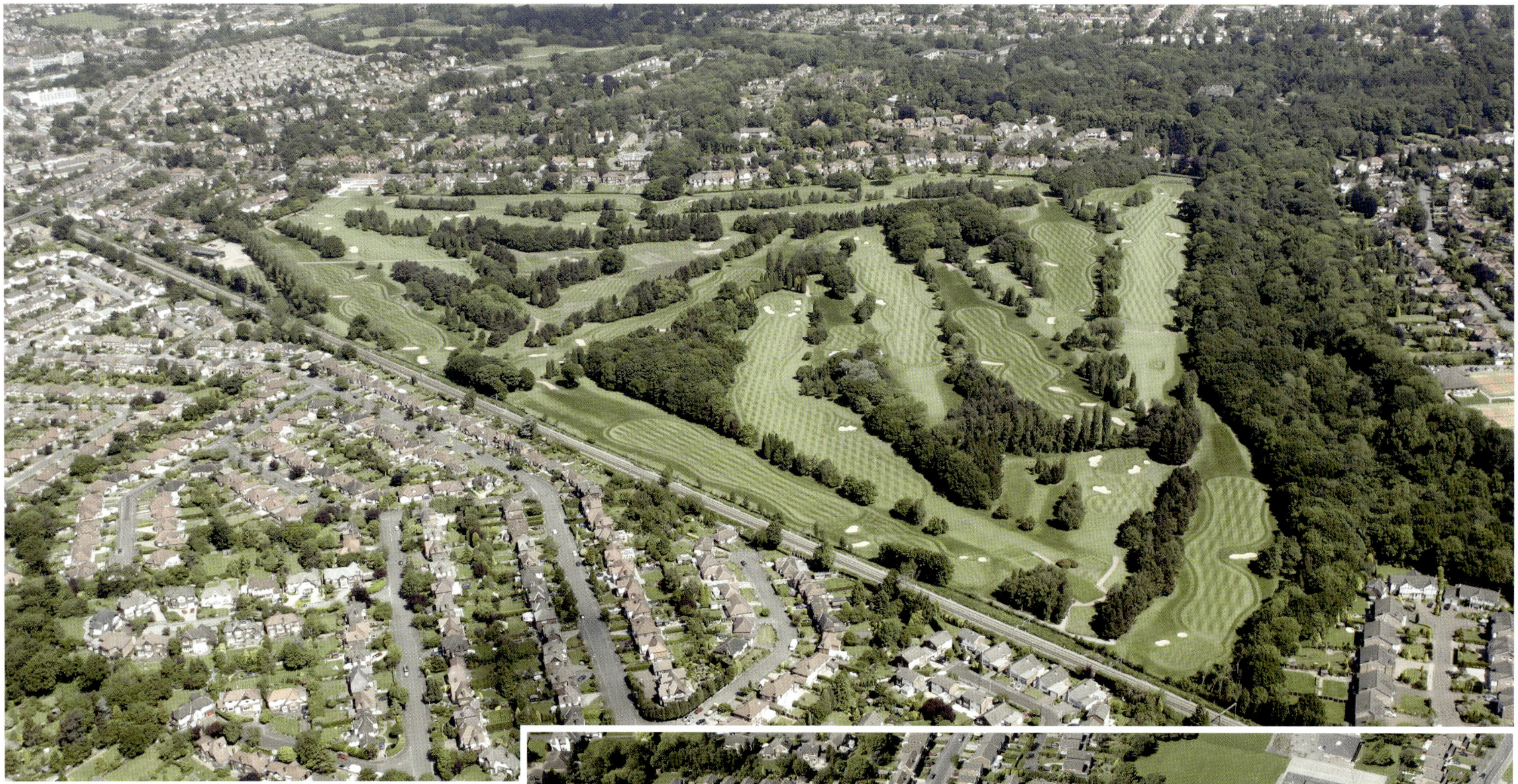

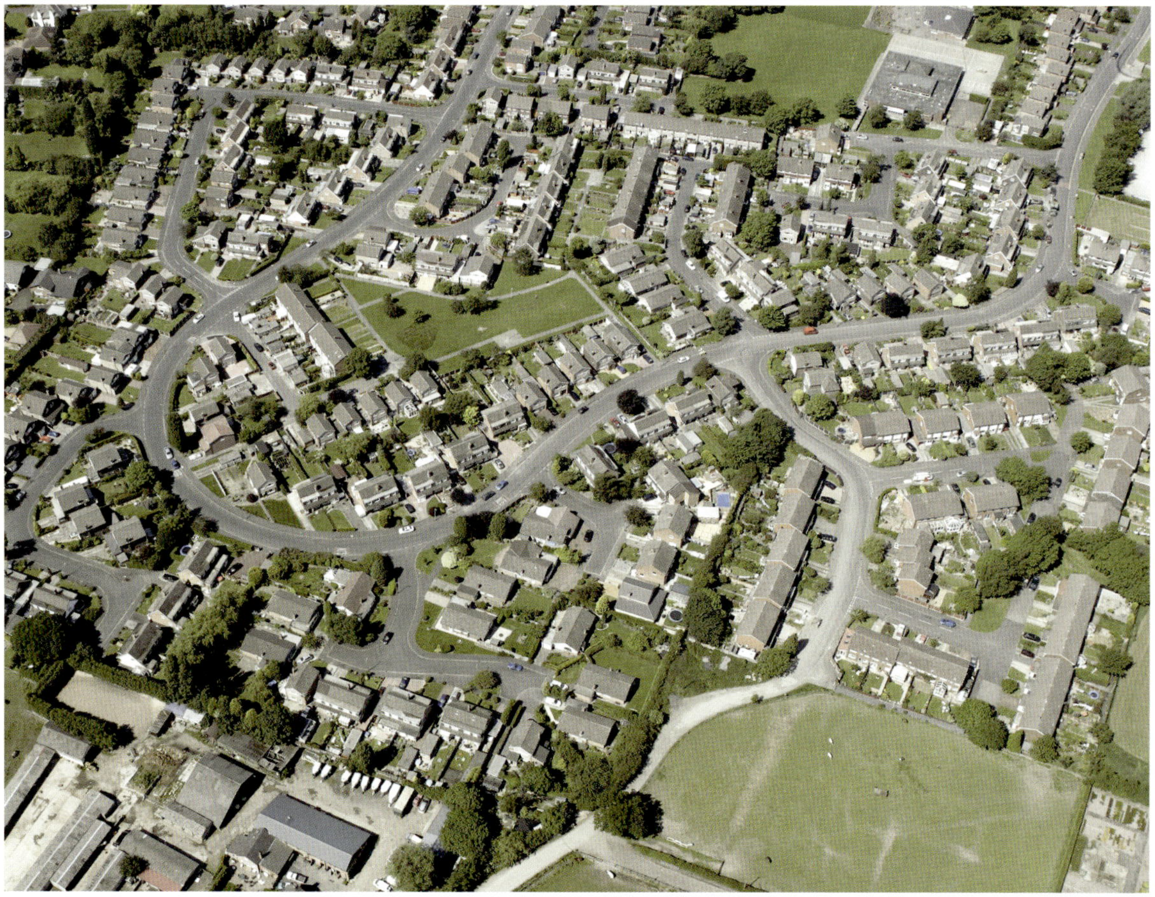

Bramhall Park Golf Course

At one point the land of Bramhall Park Golf Course would have been woodland that was part of the grounds of Bramall Hall (top right). One remnant of that woodland remains to the right of the course, known as the Carrs or Carrs Wood. The Carrs is a protected belt of green belt land running along the Carr Brook, a tributary of the Ladybrook that joins up with the larger river in Bramhall Park. Bramhall is renowned for being a place of large, executive housing and is a much sought after place to live. The average house price is higher than anywhere else within Stockport and it is not uncommon for larger houses to exchange hands for more than seven figures. The areas around the golf course and either side of Bramhall Park in particular always command large prices. But the village isn't just comprised of mansions, and there are many other popular areas for families, such as the estate around Dairygound Road, shown on the right.

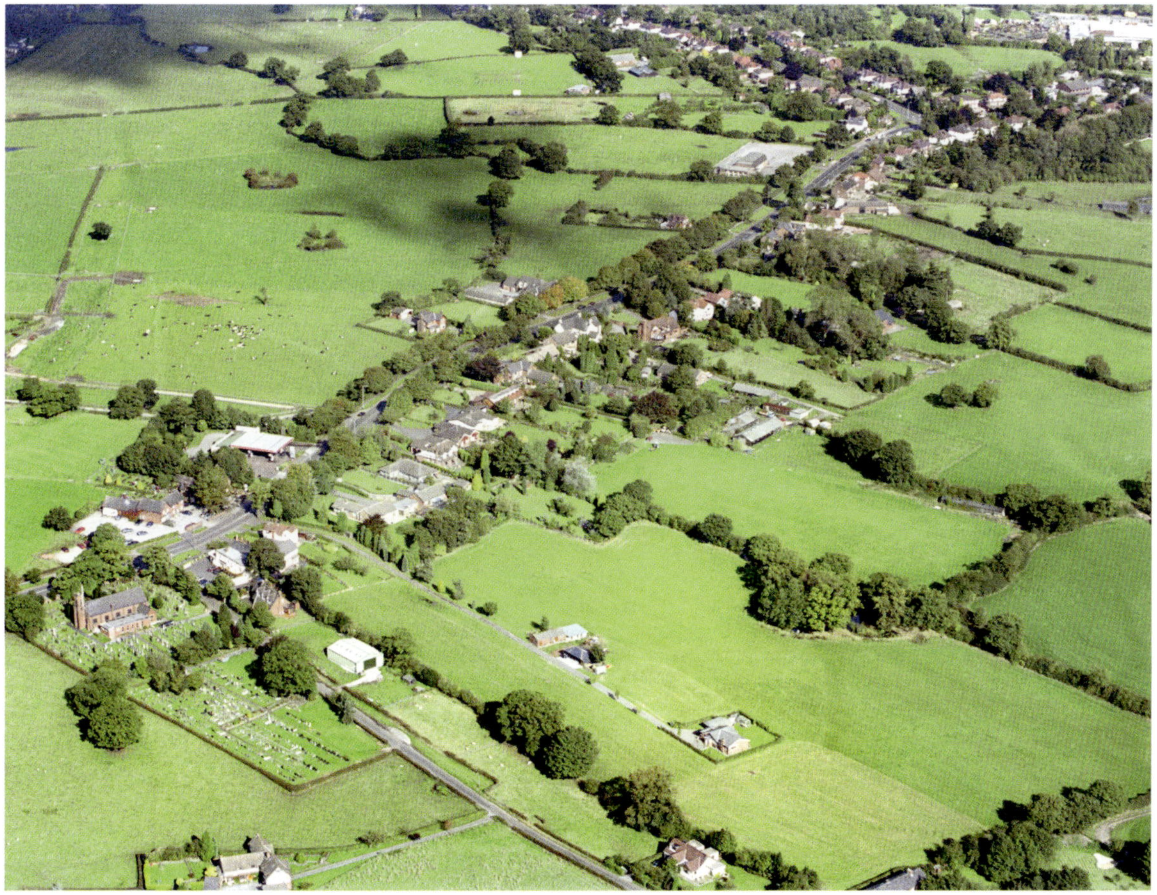

Woodford

The small village of Woodford lies to the very south of Stockport. This image of Chester Road shows the very rural nature of the area. In the bottom left of the picture is Christ Church, which was completed in 1841.

The village is dominated by the presence of the Woodford Aerodrome (below) with its enormous aircraft factory. The Aerodrome was opened in 1924 by the Avro aviation company, who moved to the site from Alexandra Park Aerodrome in Manchester. The new site was to be the birthplace of many famous aircraft over many decades of production. During the Second World War Avro built "The Manchester" here. The plane originally had 4 Rolls Royce "Vulture" Engines, but these were not a success. When they were replaced with 4 Rolls Royce "Merlins", a new plane was born and re-christened as the Lancaster Bomber.

The first test flight took place on 9th January 1941, and the plane would go on to become one of the most iconic aircraft of the age, most notably after its efforts during the famous "Dam Busters" Raid in 1943. Other famous planes have included the Vulcan Bomber (one of which is on display by the runway) with its distinctive "Delta Wing" shape (the same as the Concorde) and the Nimrod. Avro became part of British Aerospace in 1971, and are now known as BAE Systems. The Aerodrome also used to host the annual Woodford Air show.

The first show took place in 1968, but in later years it was reduced to a biannual event. In excess of 90,000 people attended the shows, which was the second largest in the UK and featured flights from aircraft ranging from the Vulcan to the Concorde, as well as spectacular displays from The Red Arrows. The end finally came in 2001 when the show was scrapped due to the appalling weather that usually accompanied the event and the increasing costs of staging the show.

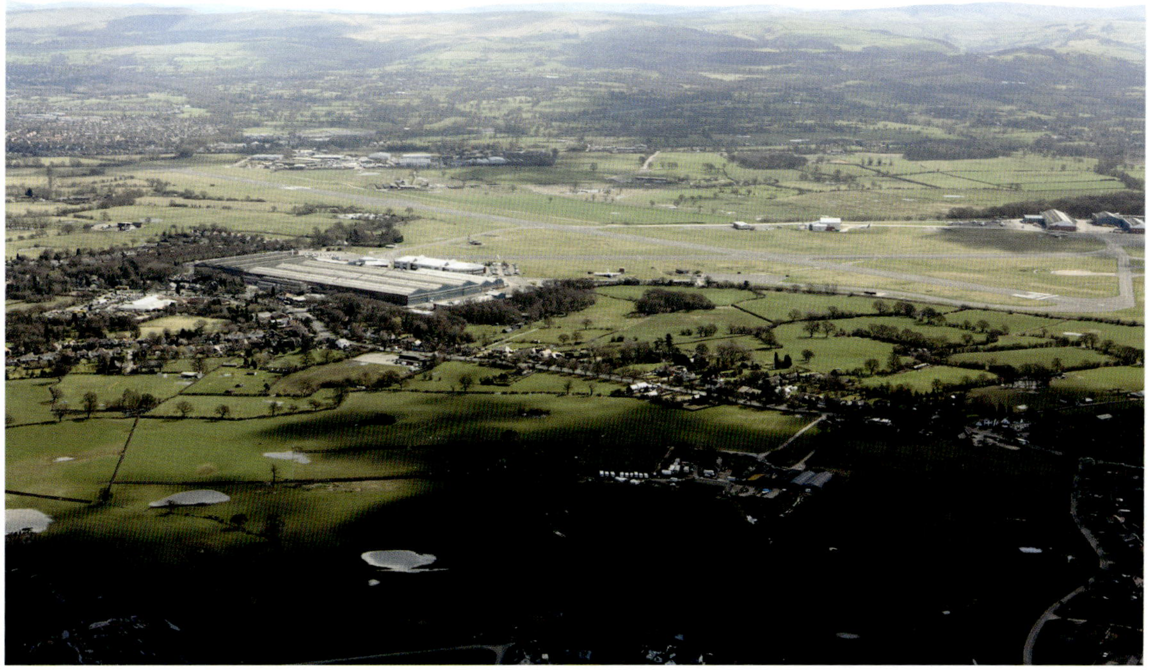

Poynton

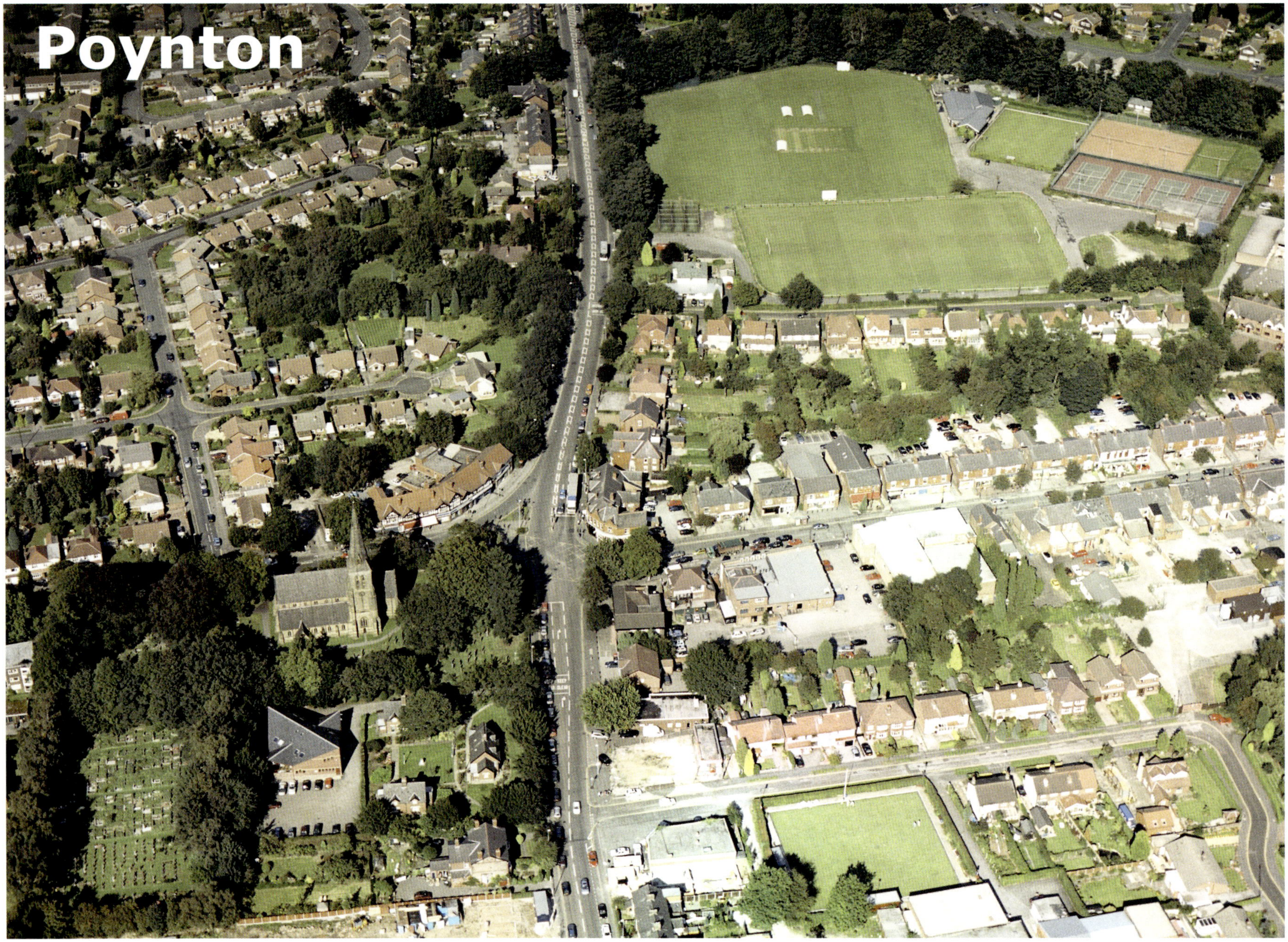

Poynton Village Centre

The village of Poynton has managed to retain its appearance of a traditional Cheshire village. Officially it is now in the Borough of Macclesfield, but historically it has been associated with Stockport for centuries. Poynton is first mentioned in 1289 when it was part of the Barony of Stockport. The Manor of Poynton was just one part of the Barony that contained most of the historic Townships that make up the major Stockport districts today. Poynton remained under the ownership of the Lords of the Manor up until 1920. The manor had belonged to the Warren Family up until as late as 1826 when Lady Warren Bulkeley, the last surviving member of the family and daughter of the last male, Sir George Warren, died. She left the estate to Lady Vernon of the Vernon Family, and they held on to Poynton until 1920 when it was sold for the last time. This image is looking at the centre of the village, with the magnificent St George's Church the centrepiece. The church was consecrated on February 1st 1859, but the steeple wasn't added until 1886. In the top right are the grounds of Poynton Sports Club on Park Lane, including the grounds of Poynton Cricket Club and Poynton FC. The football club were formed in 1893, when it was known as Poynton Amateurs Football Club. They currently play in the Cheshire Football League alongside Cheadle Heath Nomads.

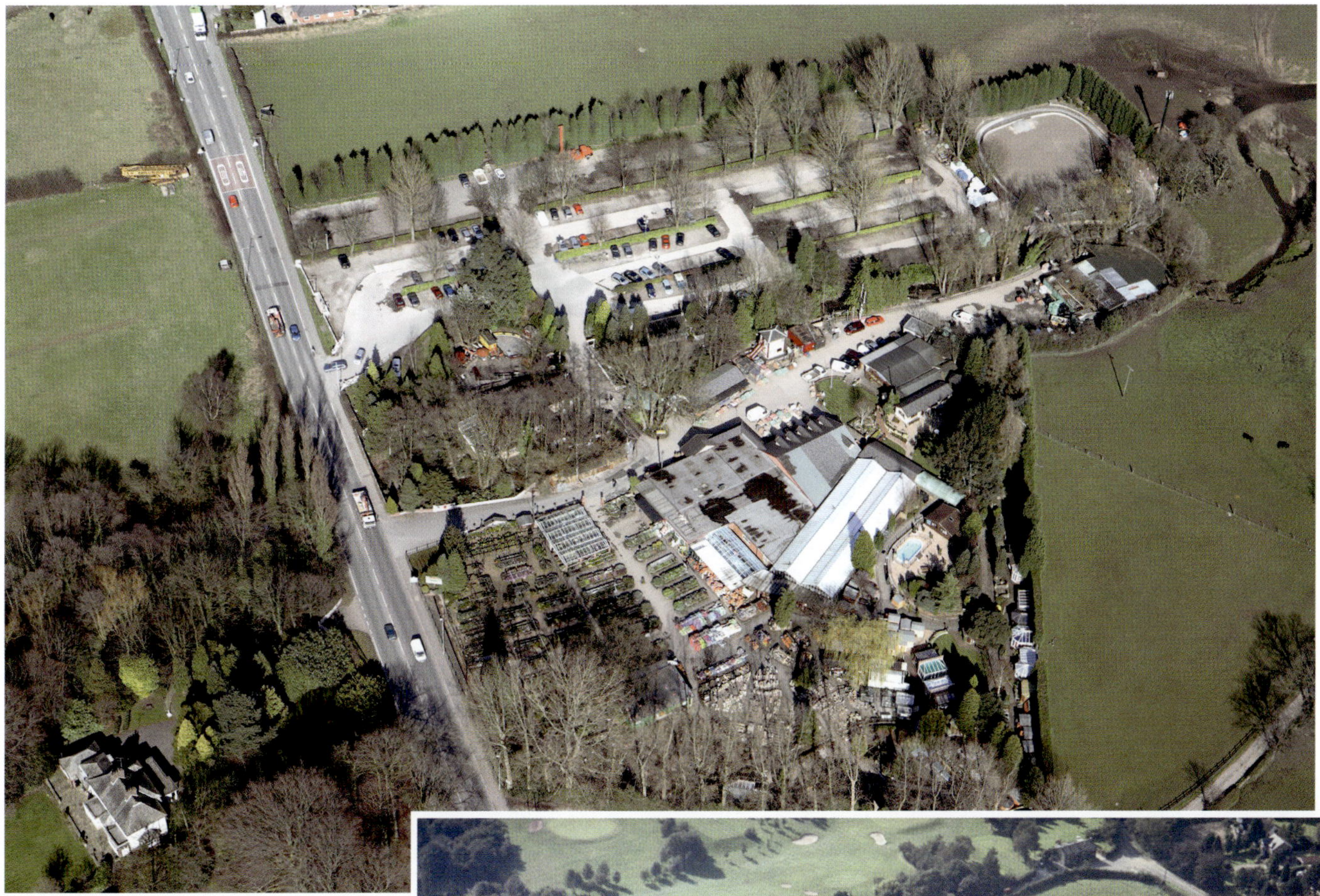

Brookside Garden Centre

The Brookside Garden Centre is a well-known landmark just south of the boundary with Hazel Grove. It is one of the largest and best-stocked garden centres in the area, but is also famous for its miniature railway. The railway extends for half a mile on a 7¼" gauge track, and has five locomotives (three steam and two diesel powered). The track has its own station and many interesting features, including a turntable and a 65-foot tunnel under the main entrance road. The track runs around the perimeter of the entire site.

Higher Poynton

Higher Poynton (right) is a small hamlet to the east of the main Poynton village by the side of the Macclesfield Canal. Here we are looking at Carleton Road to the north of the centre, close to the equally small hamlet of Middlewood. The tree-lined route passing under the bridge at the bottom of the picture is the Middlewood Way, the nature trail that runs from Rose Hill train station in Marple to Macclesfield. In the top left can be seen Davenport Golf Course.

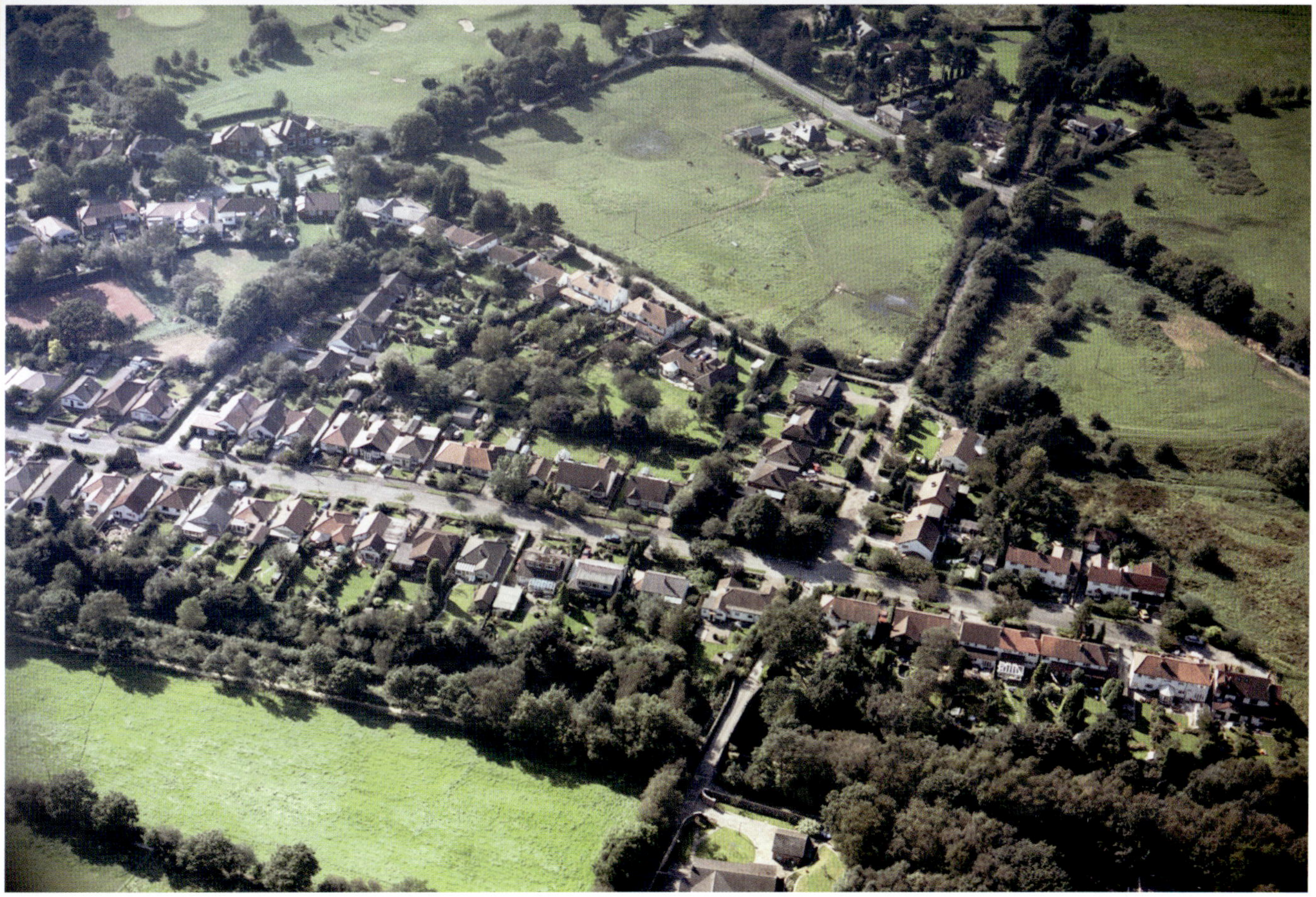

Western Suburbs

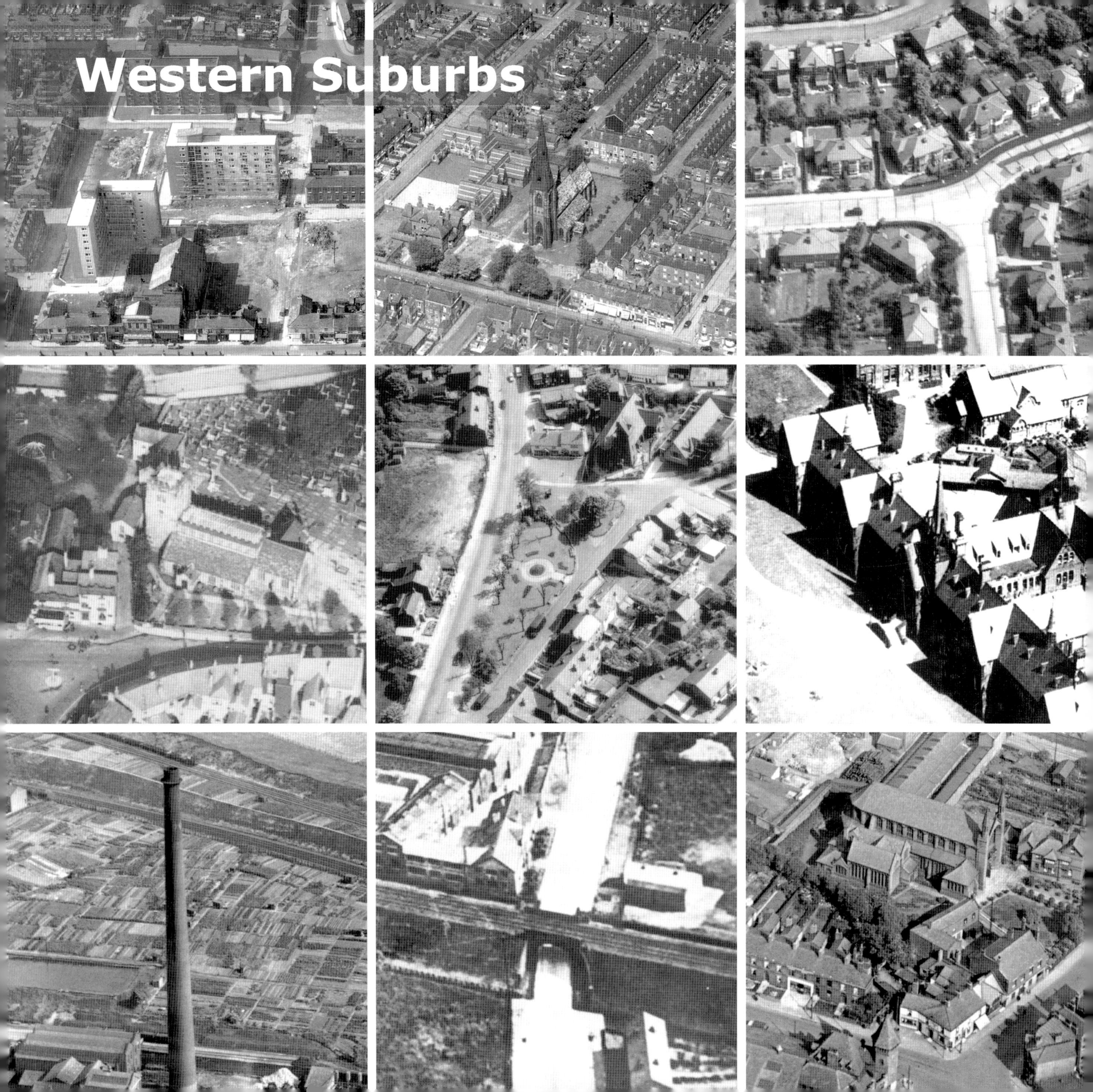

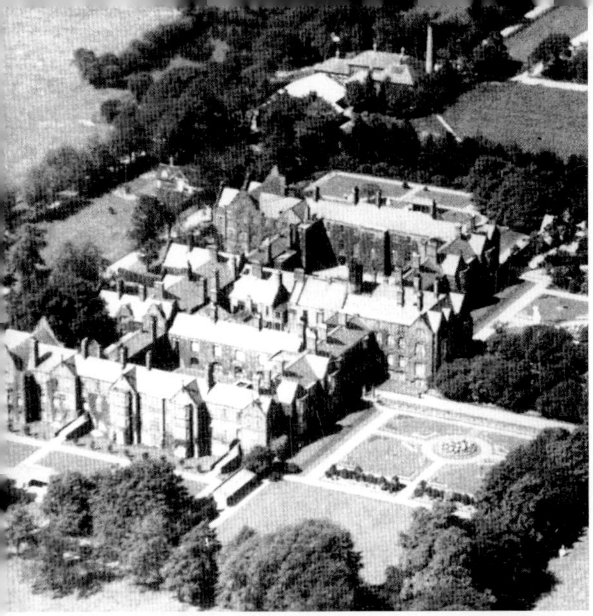

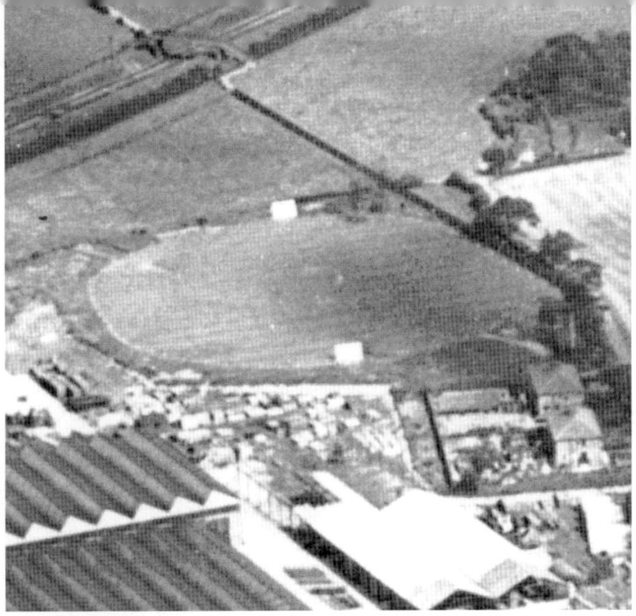

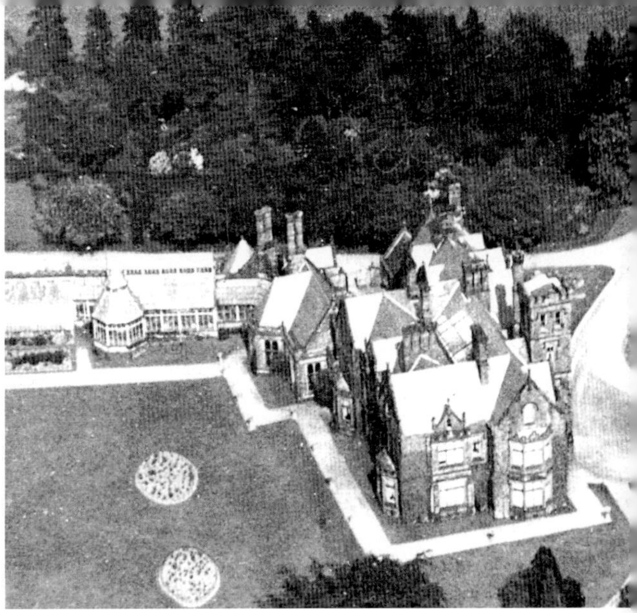

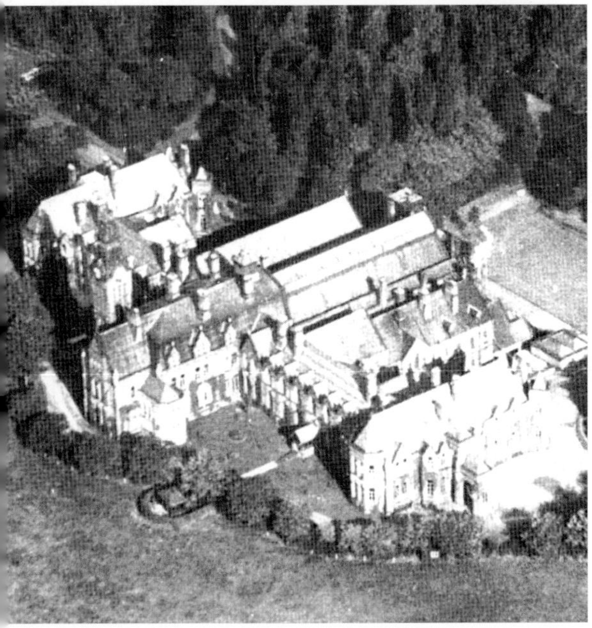

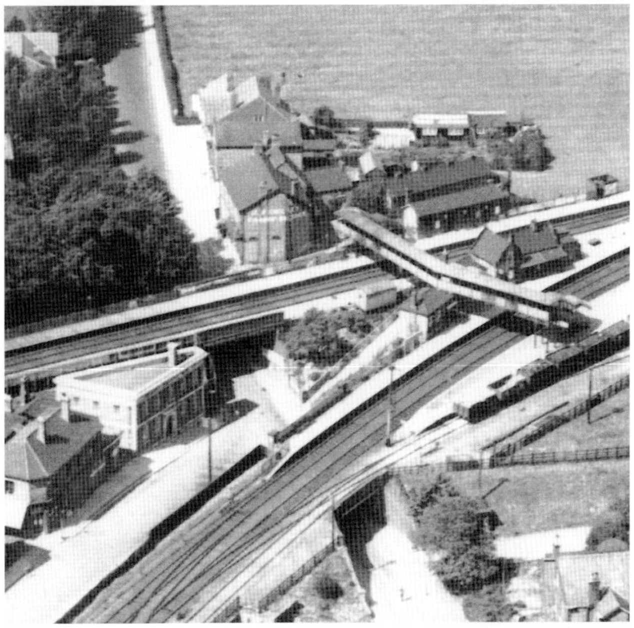

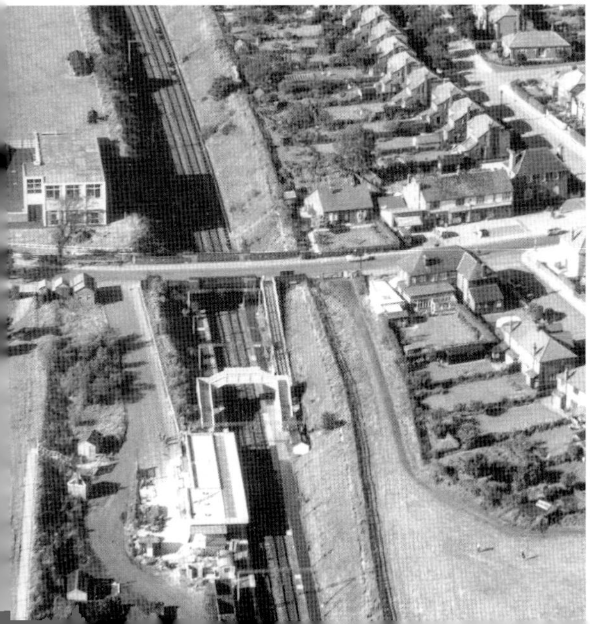

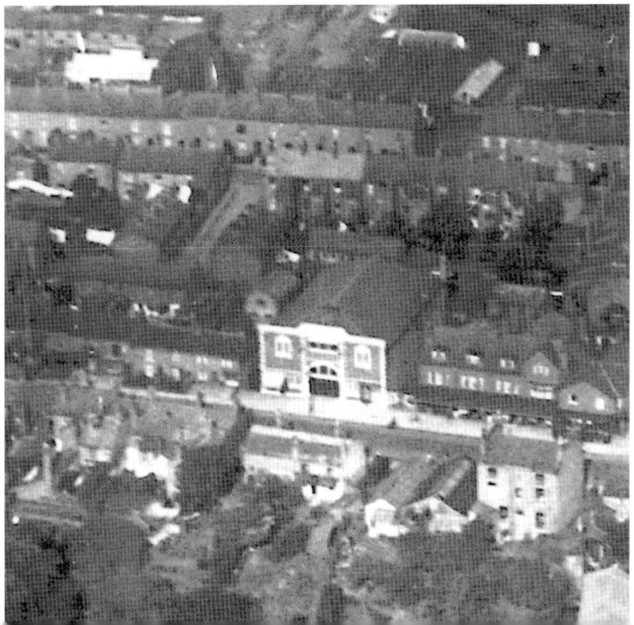

The western suburbs feature some of the most historic settlements in the town, including the major areas of Cheadle, Cheadle Hulme and Edgeley.

Edgeley is a true working-class suburb right on the edge of the town centre, seemingly made up of terraces, terraces and more terraces. However, there are also many areas of peace and solitude with historic buildings dotted amongst the landscape. To the south of Edgeley is Adswood, now an up and coming residential area experiencing new growth. West of Edgeley is Cheadle Heath, with a real mixture of residential, industrial and retail buildings.

Cheadle is a village of significant historical importance and is a highly desirable place to live, with an attractive high street and many pleasant parks and residential streets. South of here is the popular village of Cheadle Hulme, which was still fairly rural for much of the early 20th century but experienced massive growth in the 1930s and 1950s.

On the western edge are Gatley and Heald Green. Once combined as the township of Stockport Etchells, these neighbourhoods have managed to retain their village atmospheres and are popular residential areas.

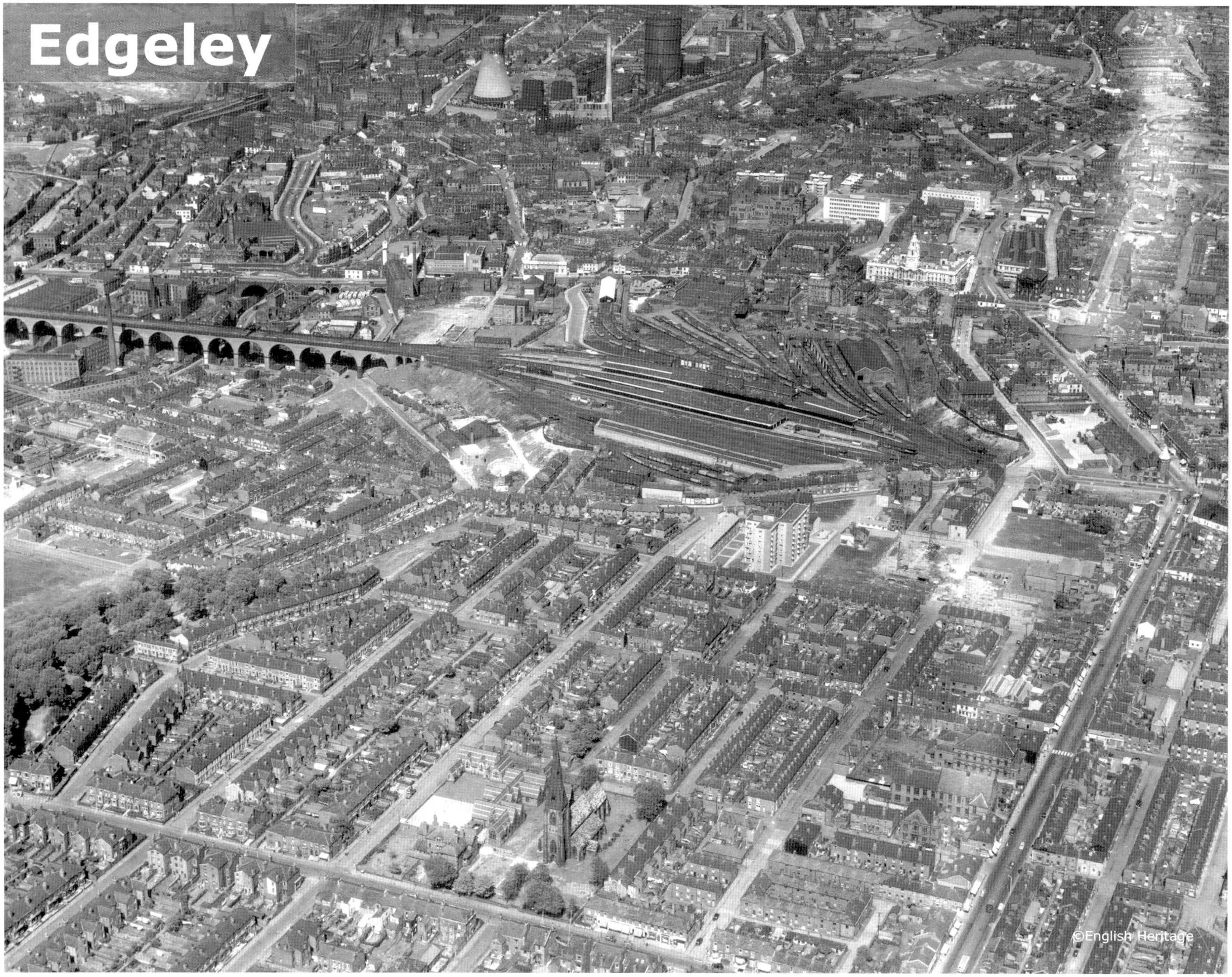

Edgeley 1958

Edgeley is the epitome of a working-class inner-suburb born out of the industrial age. The popular image is of street after street of high density terraced housing, but there are also many quaint little nooks and crannies that offer something different. Edgeley's proximity to Stockport town centre saw it grow rapidly following the industrial revolution, but up until the 18th century it remained as mostly farmland. The name of Edgeley can be traced back as far as the 13th century, when it was often written as Eddyshelegh. The name means "Leah at an enclosed park", where Leah meant wood, or clearing in a wood. Looking at this picture, it is difficult to imagine that historic settlement that would have been here for so long. The area's growth took off after the building of Edgeley station in 1843, and within a few years it was firmly attached to the ever-expanding town centre. As industry boomed in Stockport the area became home to more and more people, leading to the building of the terraced houses that now fill the streets.

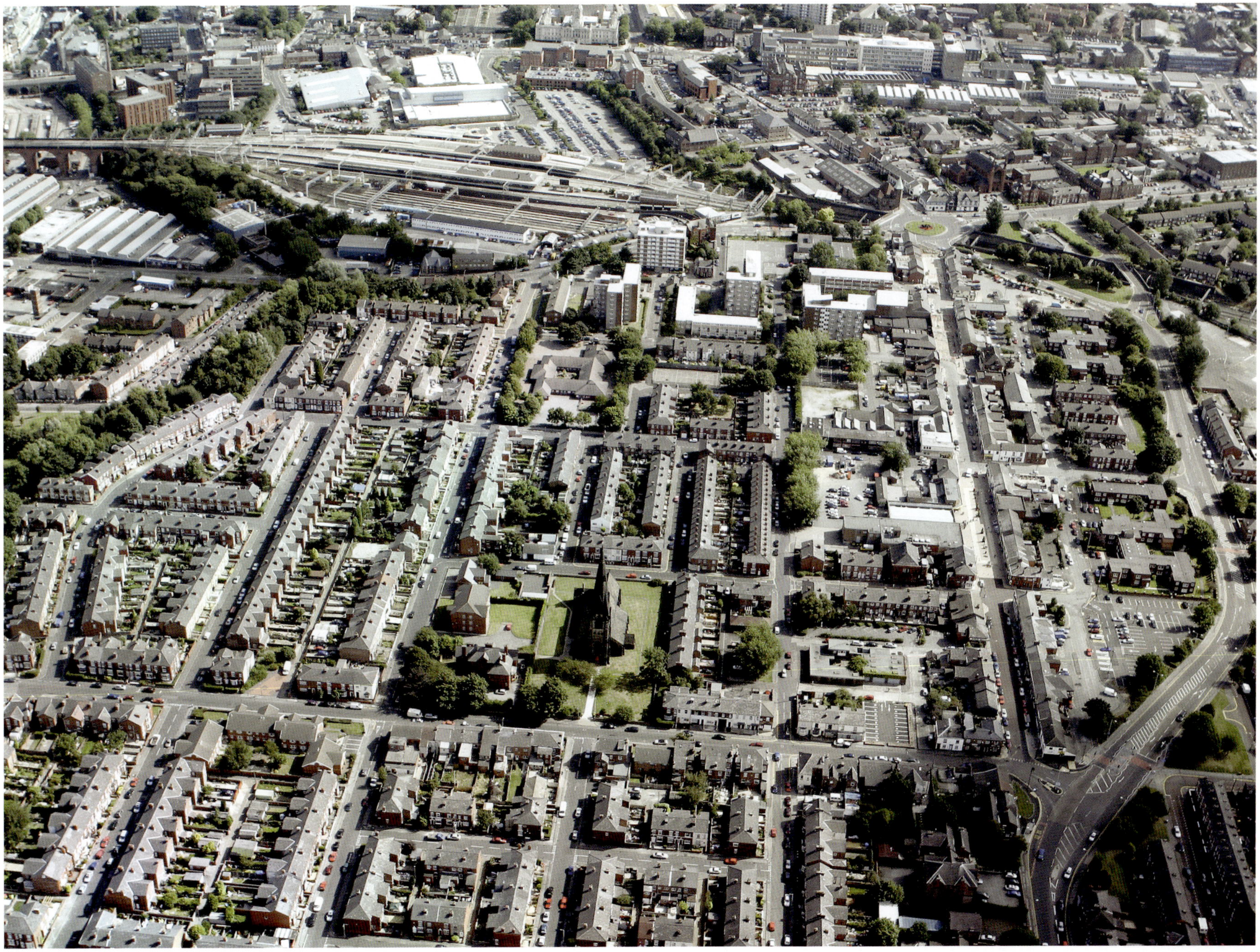

Most of the houses date from the 1890s-1920s, with some earlier additions remaining. The houses were built on a large grid-pattern on a scale not seen anywhere else in Stockport. The image from 1958 of the northern half of Edgeley shows the compact nature of the houses, and also how close the suburb is to the centre of town. On the left the houses continue down King Street West alongside Hollywood Park. This area is now home to the large bus depots, as well as the Hollywood Towers block of flats (see the image in the section on Chestergate on page 59). In between the houses is the unmistakable spire of St Mathew's church (bottom middle). The church was founded in 1844 and built on the site of the Brinksway Chapel, but has now been surrounded for well over a hundred years. The new image taken nearly 50 years later shows the relatively few changes that have occurred. With the exception of the cars and satellite dishes and the occasional new building such as the school and the 1950s flats, the two pictures could have been taken at the same time. Castle Street is Edgeley's main shopping street (above, right). It is now pedestrianised, but was once the main route for traffic heading into the town centre. The shop fronts back then had a traditional village feel about them, with canvas covers over most of the entrances. Mercian Way (above, extreme right) was built in the early 1980s as a bypass to prevent traffic congestion at the junction between Castle Street and Shaw Heath.

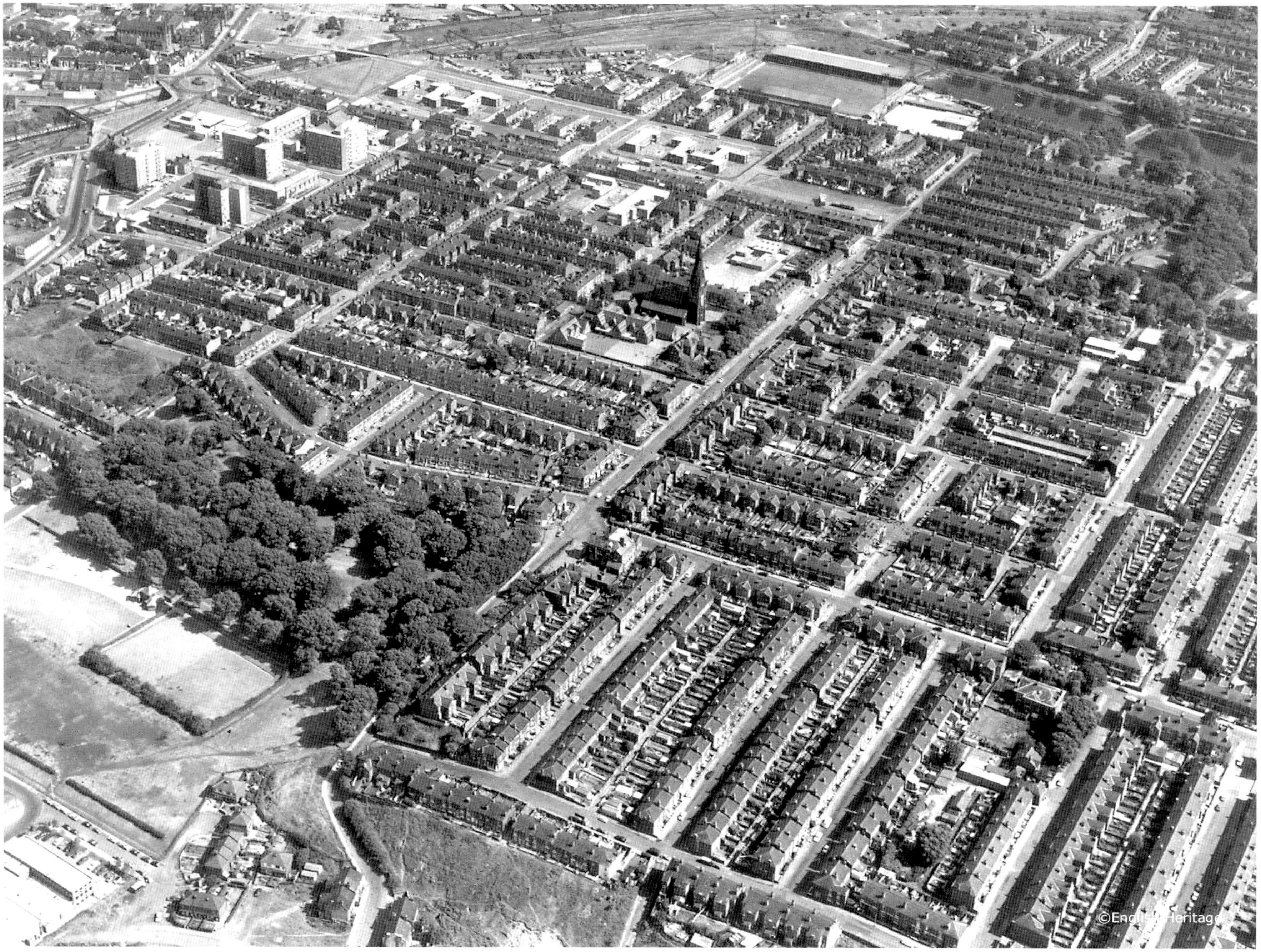

Edgeley 1973

Castle Street has perhaps lost some of its lustre since the opening of Mercian Way, as there is now less passing trade, but match-day trade from Stockport County and Sale Sharks games helps to sustain many of the local retailers. The building of the bypass, added to the previous construction of new flats along the route in the 1970s, resulted in the demolition of many houses. This picture shows the new low-level flats that were built close to Edgeley Park stadium at the top of the picture. Compare this to the image on page 7 which gives an indication of the number of homes that were levelled. One plus point from the demolition of the houses and the creation of Mercian Way was that it led to a general opening-up of the area, allowing greater access to the stadium that had previously been tucked away from the main road down narrow streets.

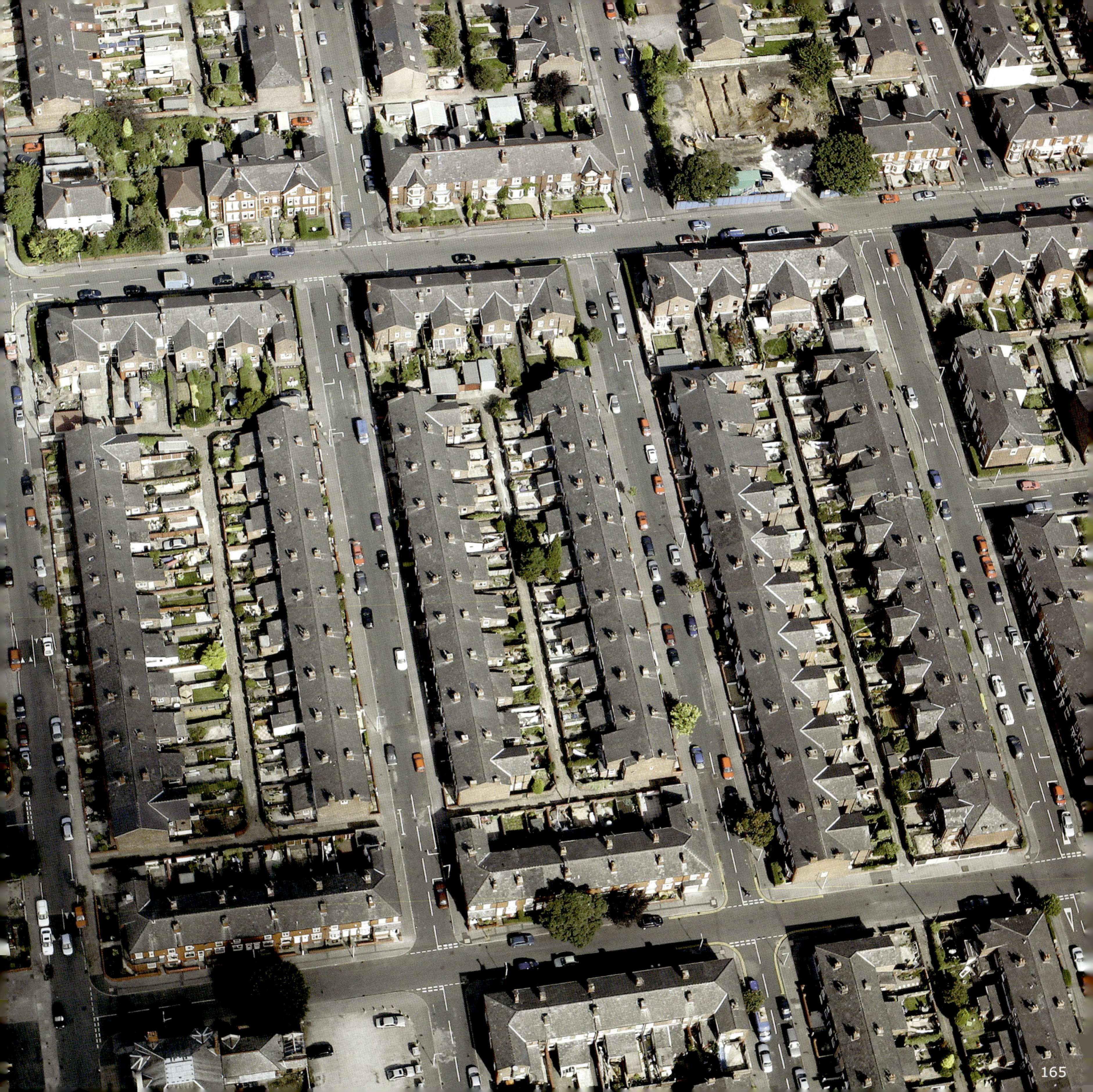

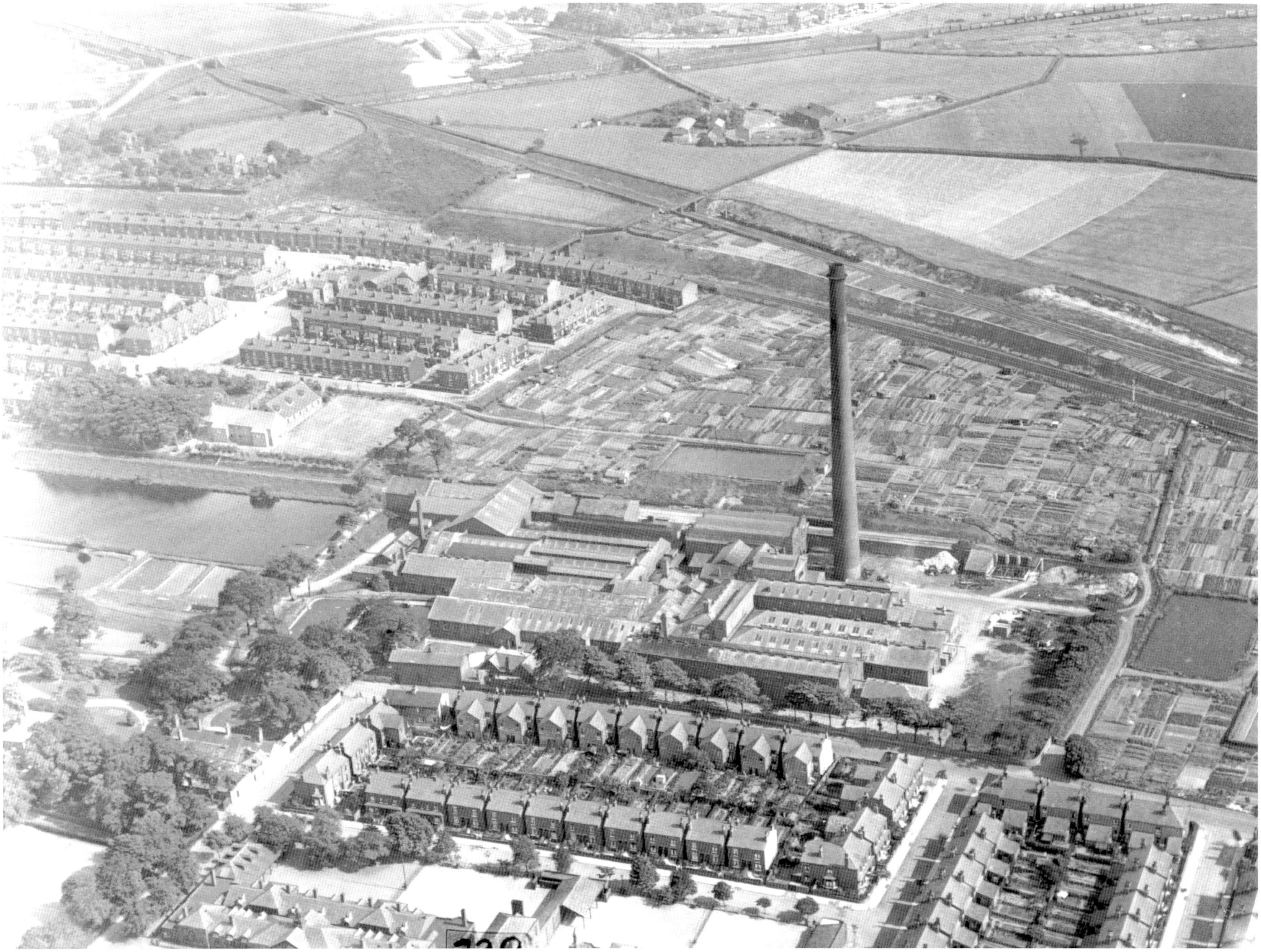

Edgeley Bleachworks 1931

Edgeley Bleachworks was started by William Sykes and his partners in around 1792 for the purposes of dyeing cotton. He became sole owner of the enterprise in 1795 at around the time that he took possession of his new home, Edgeley House. Unlike the Heaton Mersey Bleachworks, the Sykes factory prospered and was a major presence in Stockport for decades to come. Water for the works was initially taken from a small stream – the Edgeley Brook - but Sykes had two large reservoirs built in around 1850 in order to store the water needed. The reservoirs survive, but the factory has gone. It closed in 1986 after nearly 200 years of service and was demolished. The site was filled in and became housing, but the area around the reservoirs was bought by the council and landscaped to become a new park. Combined with the adjacent Alexandra Park and the smaller Edgeley Park, the area now offers some of the best parkland in the town. Alexandra Park was formerly the gardens of Edgeley House. The Stockport Corporation bought the grounds in 1900 and it opened as the park soon after. The new image on the right shows the park today, looking in the opposite direction. The bleachworks was on the left of the first reservoir, on the new road known as Sykes Meadow.

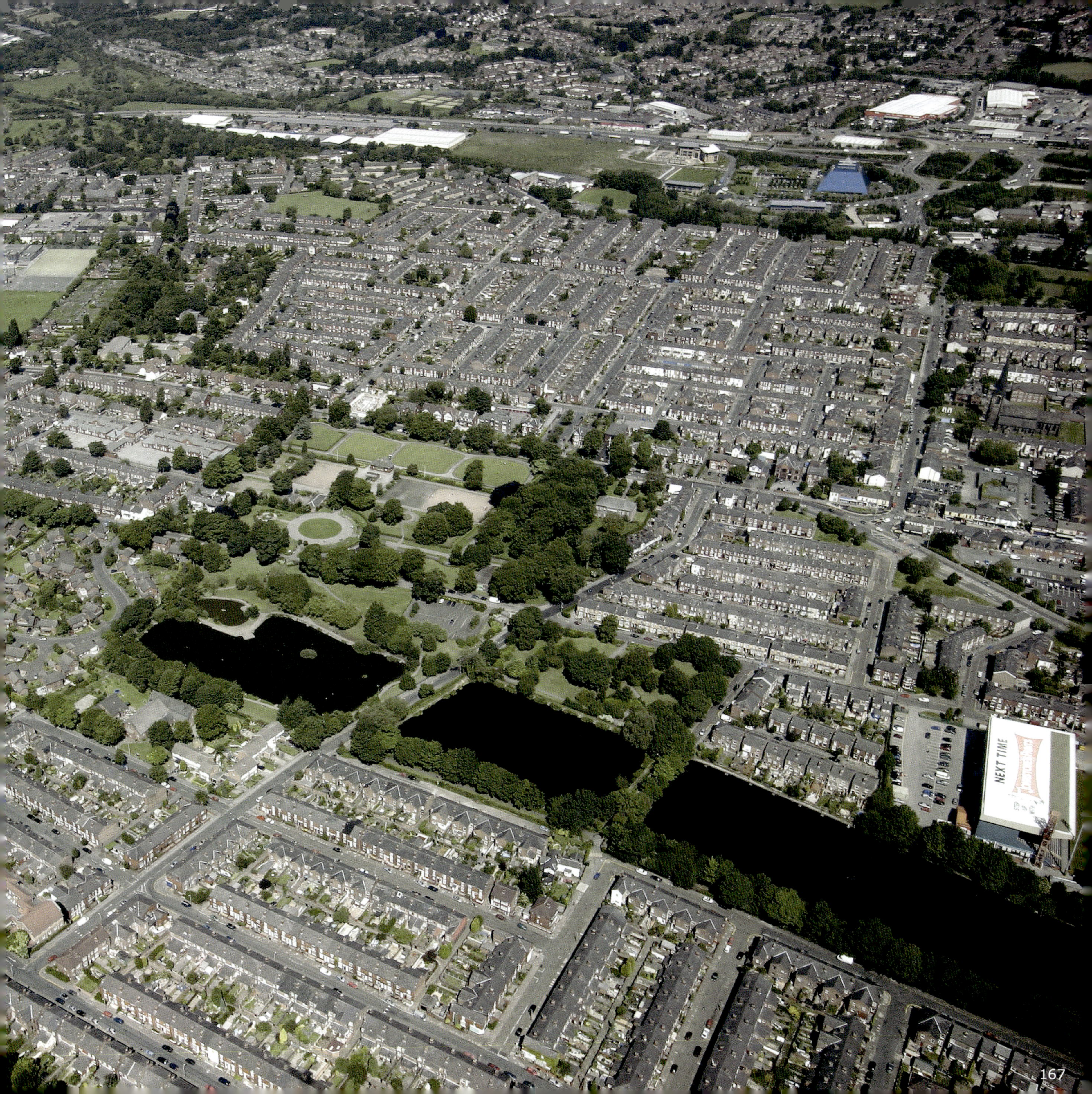
NEXT TIME

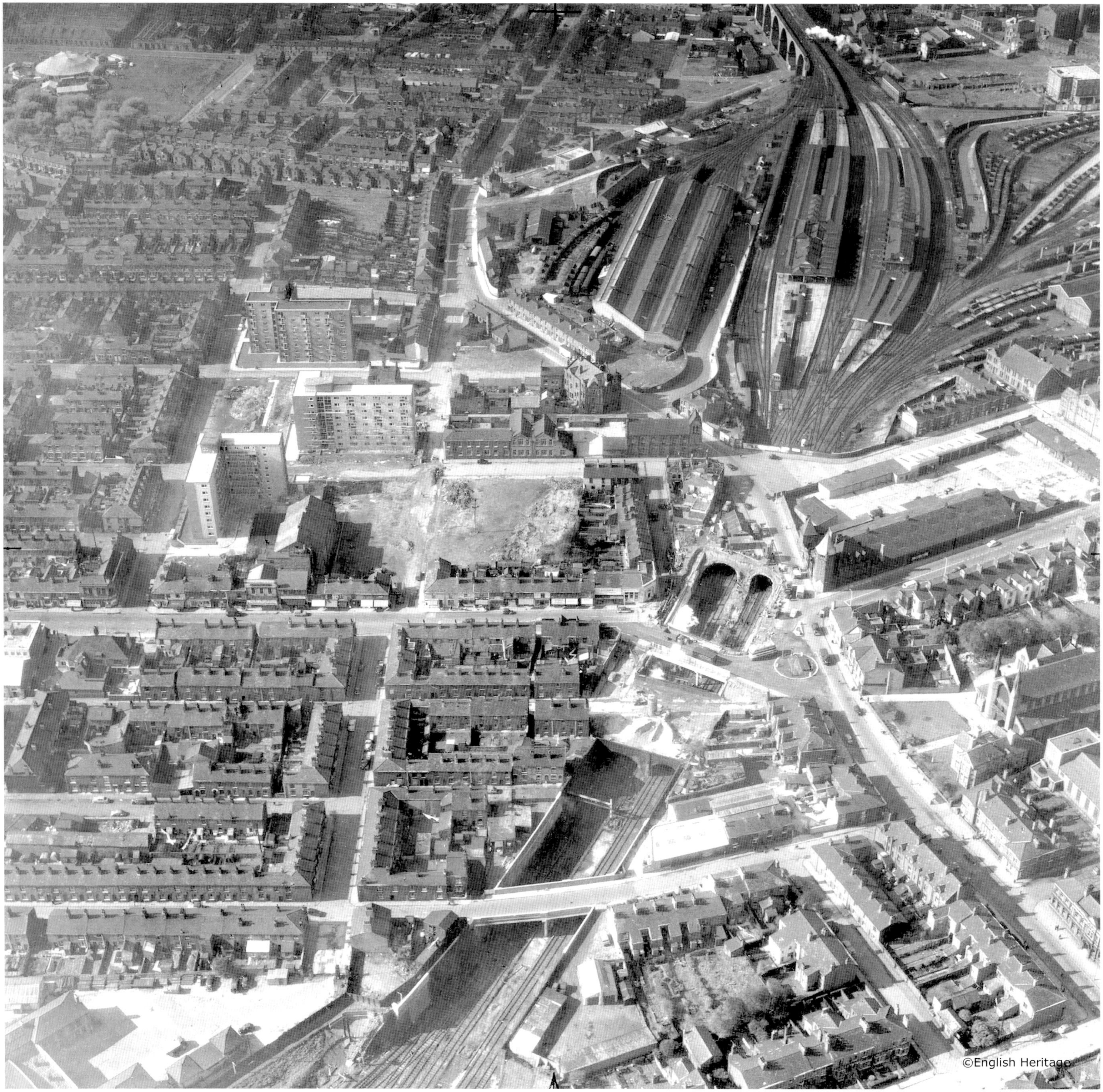
©English Heritage

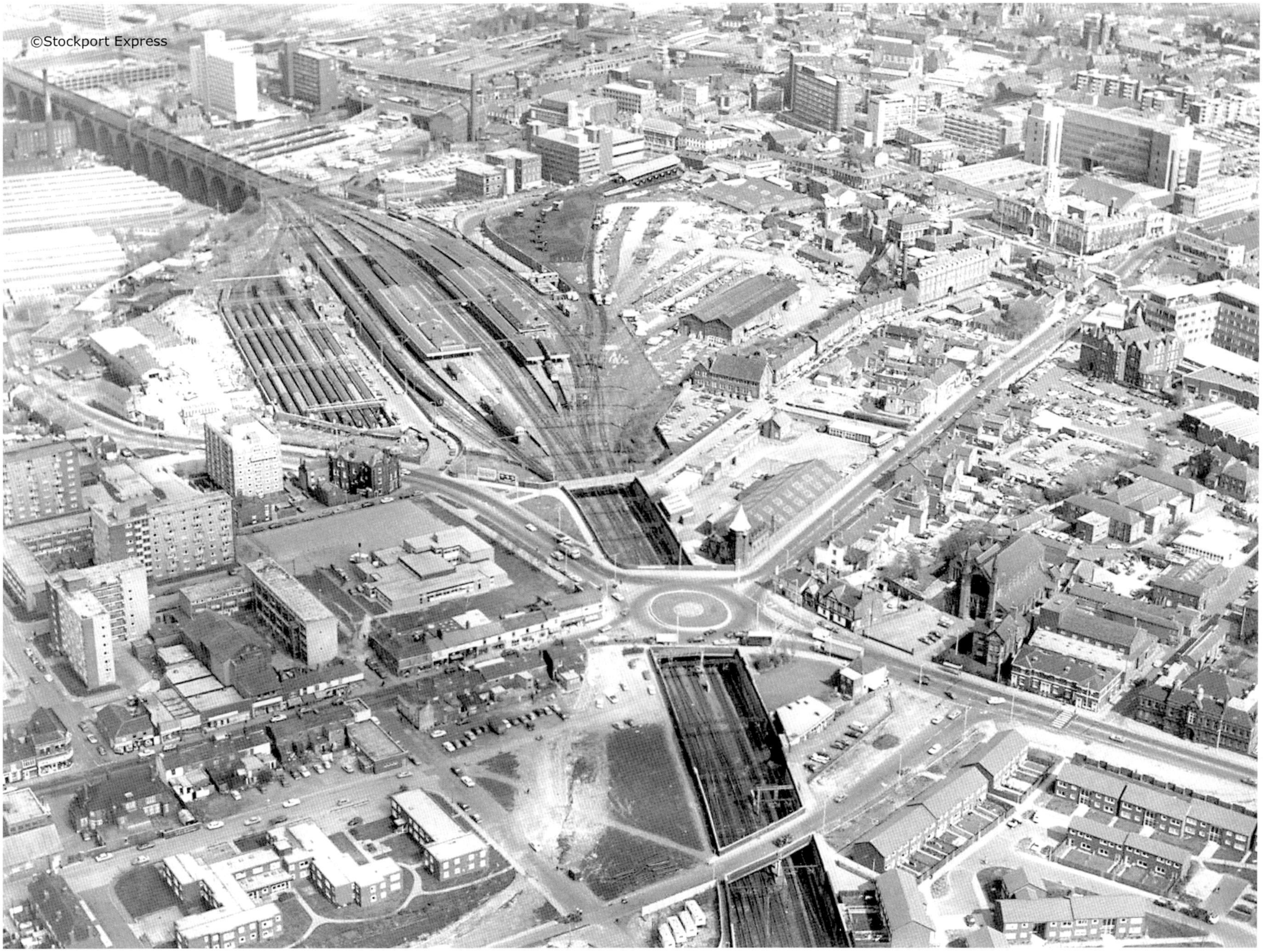

Castle Street & Shaw Heath 1959 (left) & 1980

The first signs of slum clearances were taking place in Edgeley in the late 1950s with the building of new mid-rise flats, seen here nearing completion and also during construction in the picture from 1958 on page 162. Also evident is the replacement of the brick-built bridges over the main railway line to the south of Edgeley Station. This was the start of the construction of the large new bridge that doubles as a roundabout at the junction with Shaw Heath (bottom right, near the small roundabout) just by the Stockport Armoury building (the building with the conical spire, middle right). Note also the big top in Hollywood Park (top left). The park was the site of the annual Stockport Fair for over 70 years until 2002.

In the above image from 1980 the new roundabout is complete and preparations are ongoing for the construction of Mercian Way leading off the roundabout. A large scar can be seen taking shape on the ground in the bottom middle of the picture, following the route of where the new road would be built.

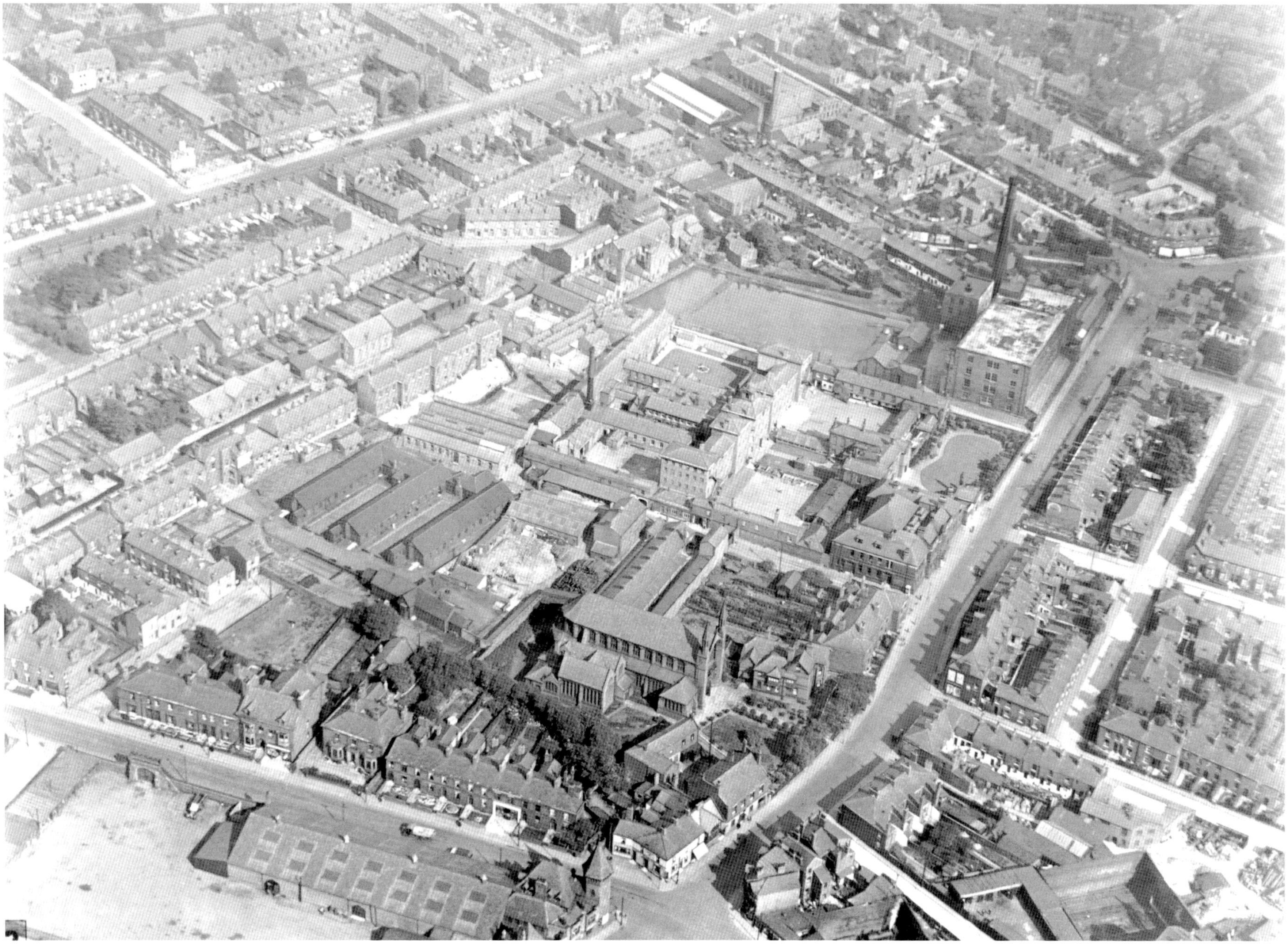

Shaw Heath 1931

Along Shaw Heath there are several historic buildings situated right on the edge of Stockport town centre. The Armoury Building (bottom left) was built from 1861-1862 for the Stockport Volunteer Rifle Corps. It was opened by Mayor Robert McClure on 25th April after the £5155, 19s 6d needed for its construction was raised by public subscriptions. The polygonal shaped Tower is topped-off by a steep sided green spire and is now home to the Territorial Army. Just above from the armoury is the stunning red-brick Church of Our Lady & The Apostles. The church was founded in 1799 but was rebuilt in 1905. Next door to the church is the Site of St Thomas' Hospital, which was previously the Stockport Workhouse. It opened on December 25th 1841 to house the poor of the town and replaced the previous workhouse that was situated on Daw Bank. In 1948 the site became Shaw Heath Hospital and was later renamed as St Thomas' Hospital. The site has now been earmarked for redevelopment as part of the new town centre campus for Stockport College. One major change has already occurred, though. Shaw Heath Mill, a former wool-spinning mill dating from around the 1890s, was demolished in 2007 after part of the roof and northern wall collapsed following fierce storms. The effect has been to open up previously unseen views of St George's Church in Heavily, but there is no doubt the general feel of the area has been changed forever. Note the large reservoirs behind the main mill building.

Adswood

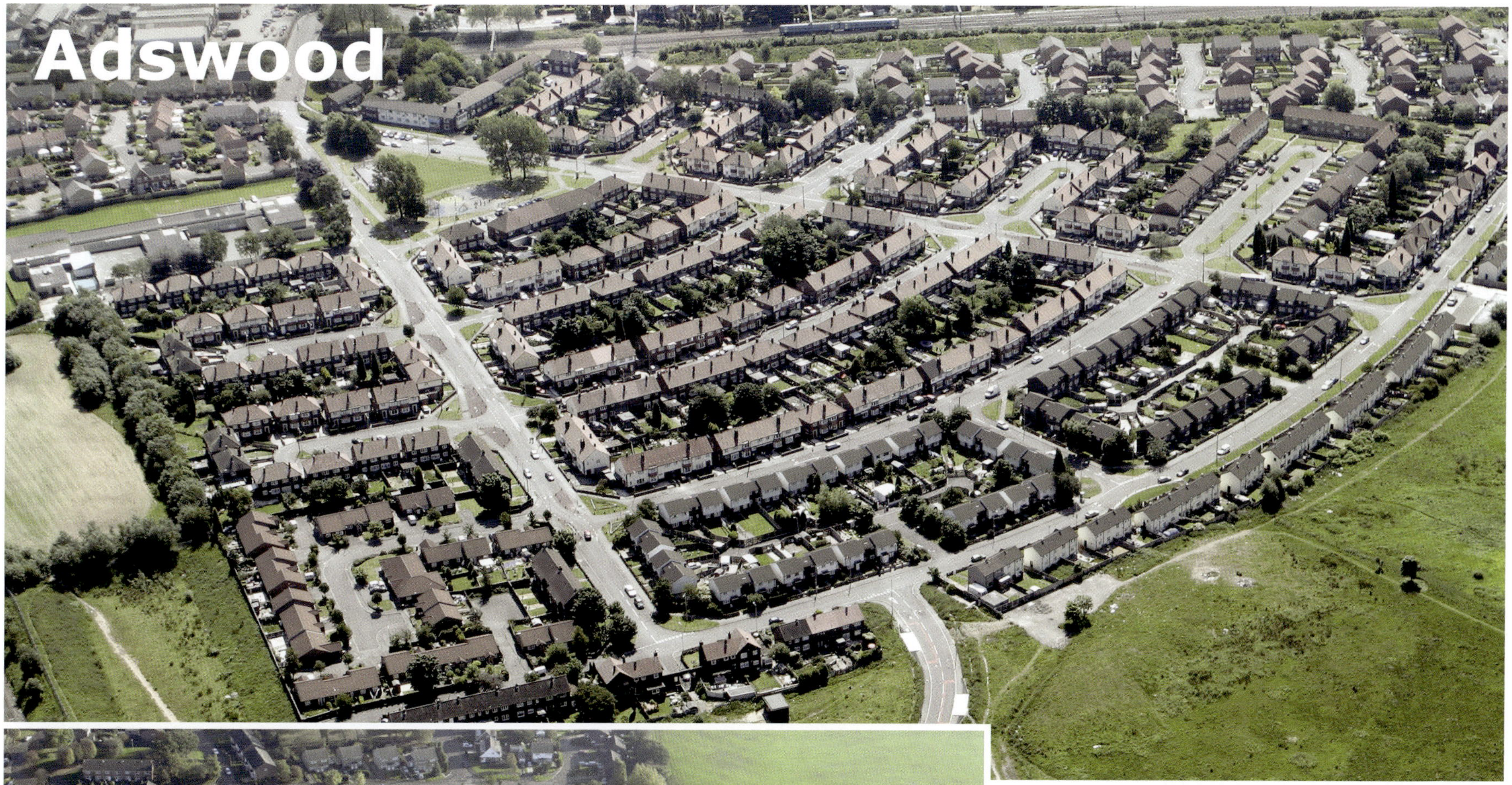

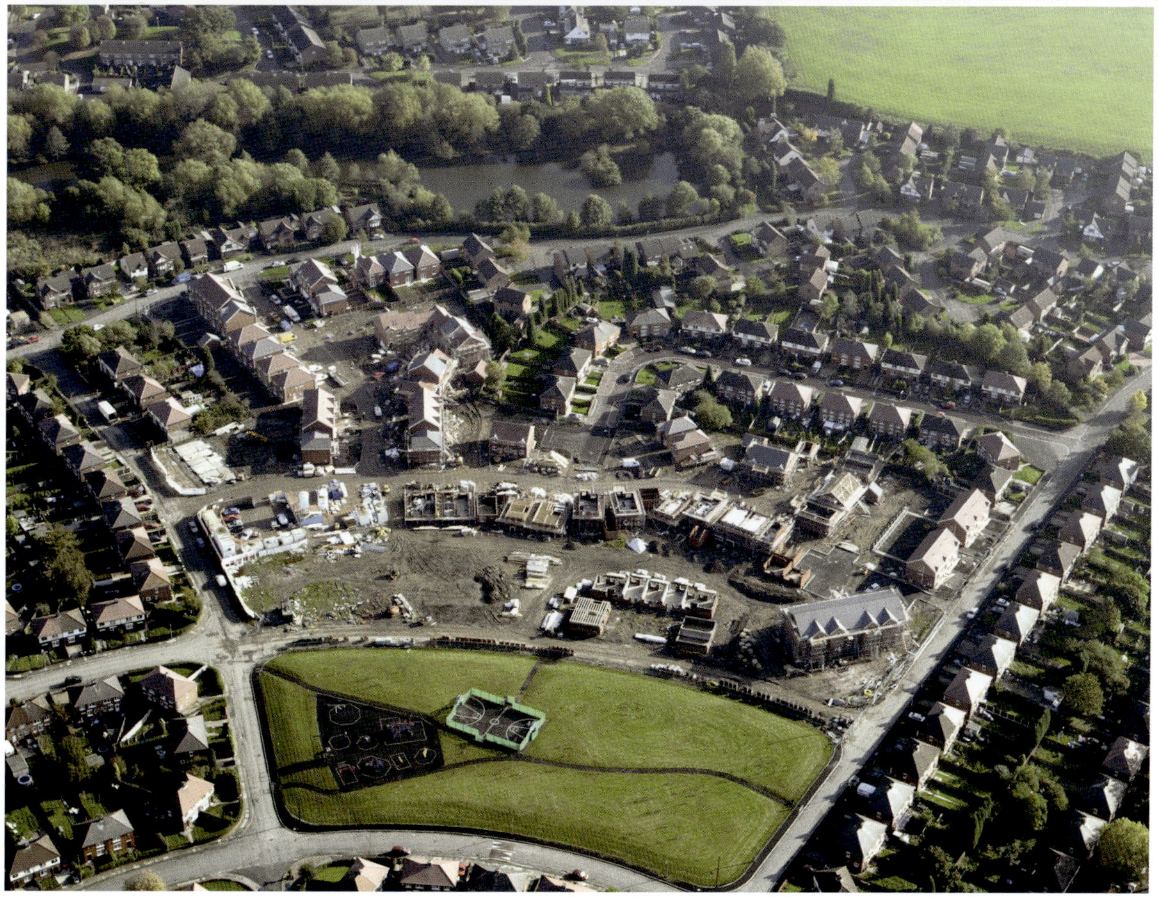

Adswood

The name of Adswood is probably derived from the term "Adder's Wood". When the area was wooded it was reportedly home to many adder snakes, and over time the name was shortened to Adswood. Adswood today is a residential area with a mix of social and private housing. The first council-built estates were begun in the 1920s and more followed in the 1930s and 1940s (see the picture of Woodsmoor on page 133). The large Bridge Hall estate (above) wasn't built until the 1950s. The land was once home to the Bridge Family of Stockport, who were first recorded in 1282. They built their family manor house in Adswood, and called it Bridge Hall. The last surviving section was demolished in the 1930s. Adswood continues to grow in popularity, as shown by this new development (left) near Rostrevor Road. Compare this to the image on page 133 and you will see there was a golf course to the side of the fish ponds back in 1934.

Cheadle Heath

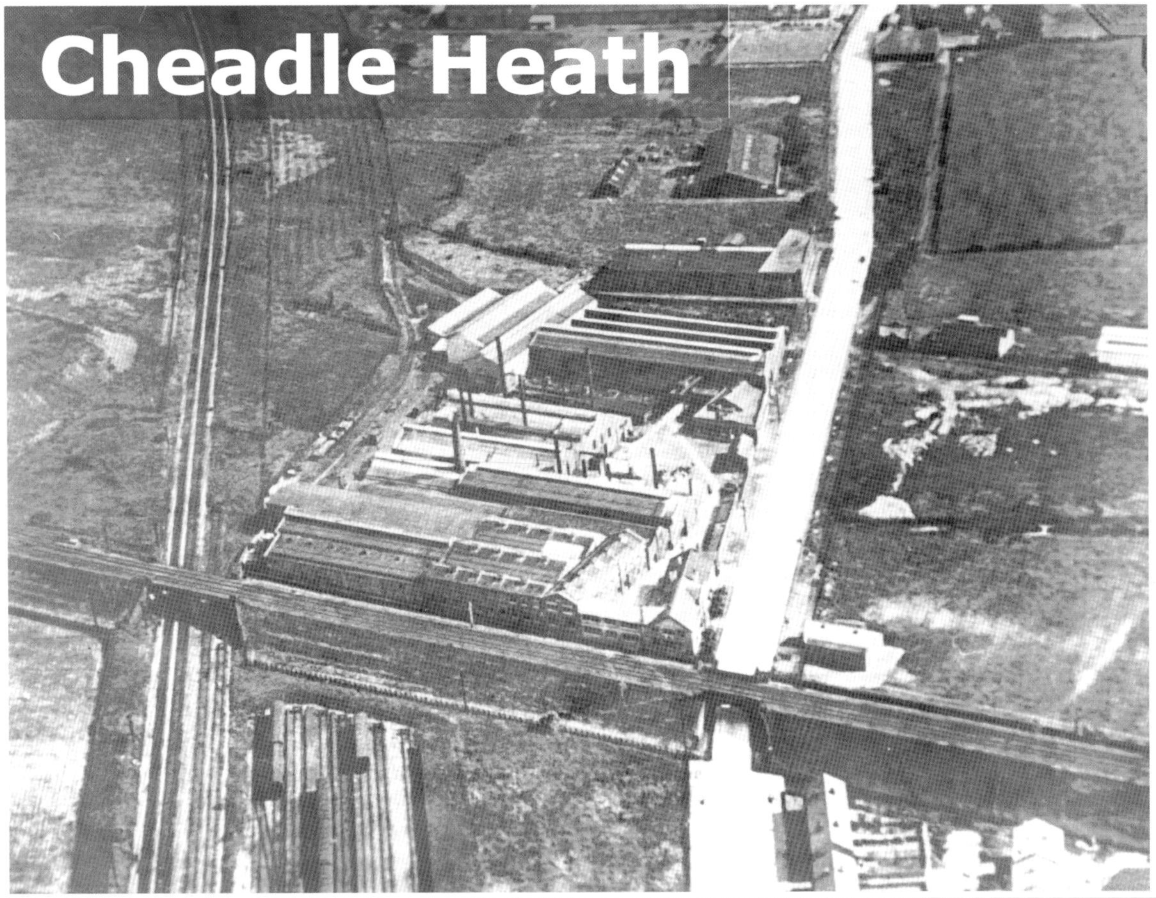

Cheadle Heath c1930

Cheadle Heath is a mostly residential area but the centre of the village is now dominated by large retail units, including two supermarkets, a DIY store and a large outdoor pursuits shop. Nearly all were built on the site of the old rail goods yard that was next to Cheadle Heath Train Station. The station, which was opened in 1902, closed on 2nd January 1967 - the same day as Tiviot Dale

Although big, these units are small in comparison with some of the factories that have existed in Cheadle Heath at the Birdhall Lane Industrial Estate. These pictures from the 1930s show Birdhall Lane just as it had started to develop. This land had previously been farmland but it was soon swallowed up by the new industrial buildings along the length of the road. Note the railway sidings in the top picture in the bottom left. This was just down the line from the train station and the goods yard.

Simon Carves Ltd were one of the first companies to build a factory here in 1926, and we can see their first building at the site below. A landmark 6-storey brick tower would be built to the left of the factory a few years later as part of a new building. The tower housed a working flour mill and was used for research to test flour milling machinery that the company produced. The tower was demolished in 2004. Note the cricket pitch at the top right of the image, to the rear of warehouse. This has now been built over. The new image is looking towards the railway bridge (above) from the opposite direction. Birdhall Lane is now the second largest industrial estate in Stockport after the estate at Bredbury, and continues to expand.

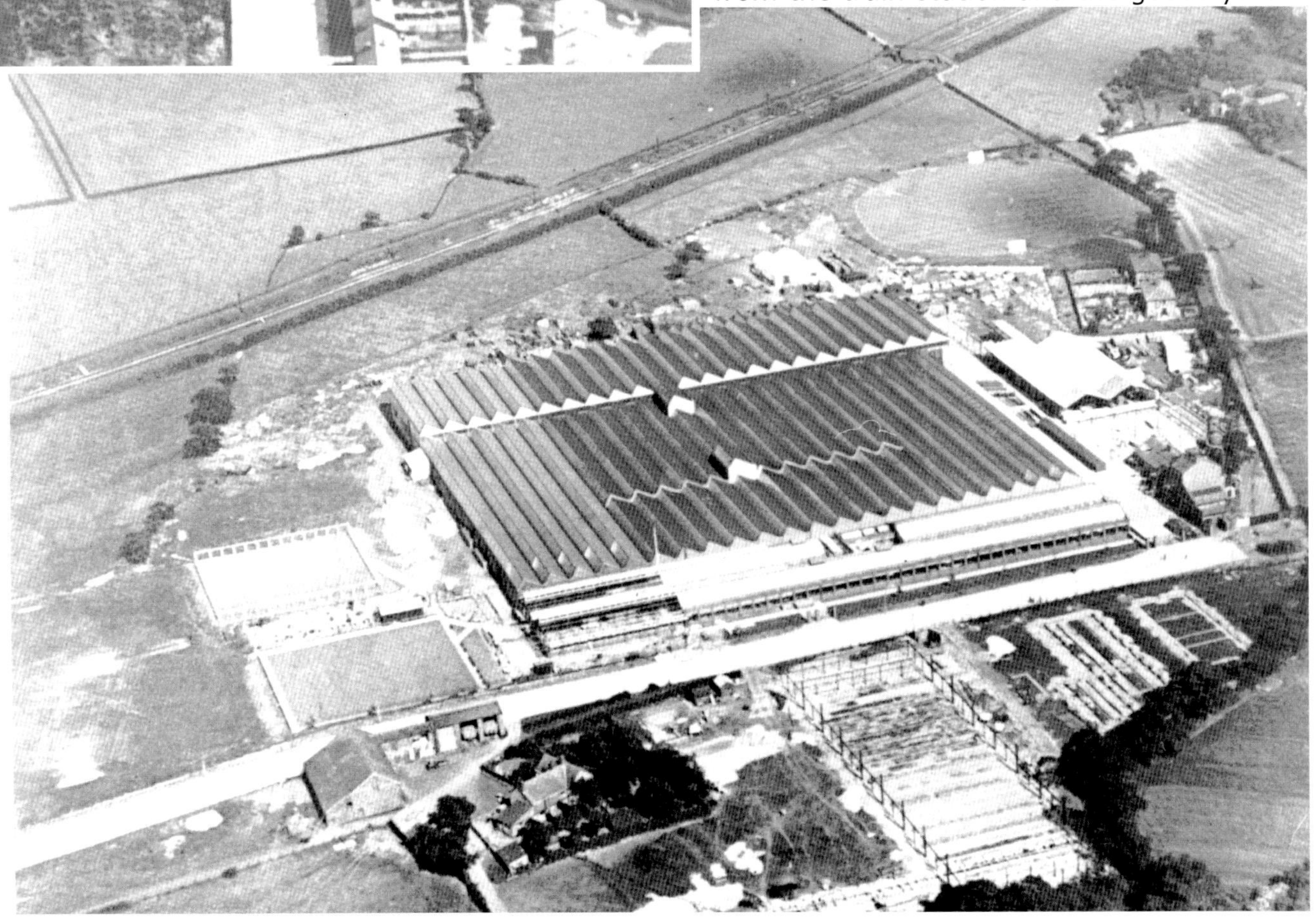

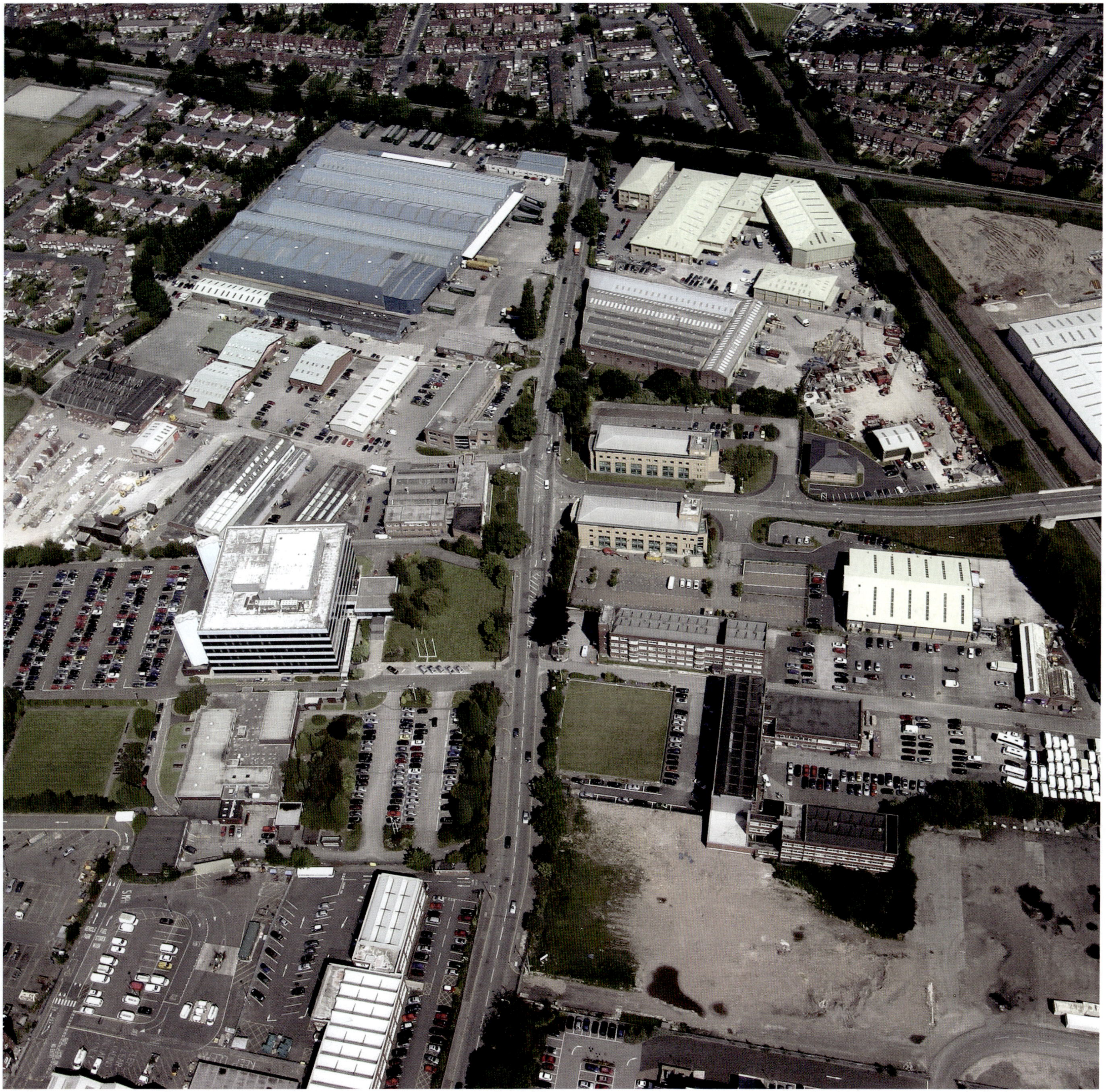

Cheadle

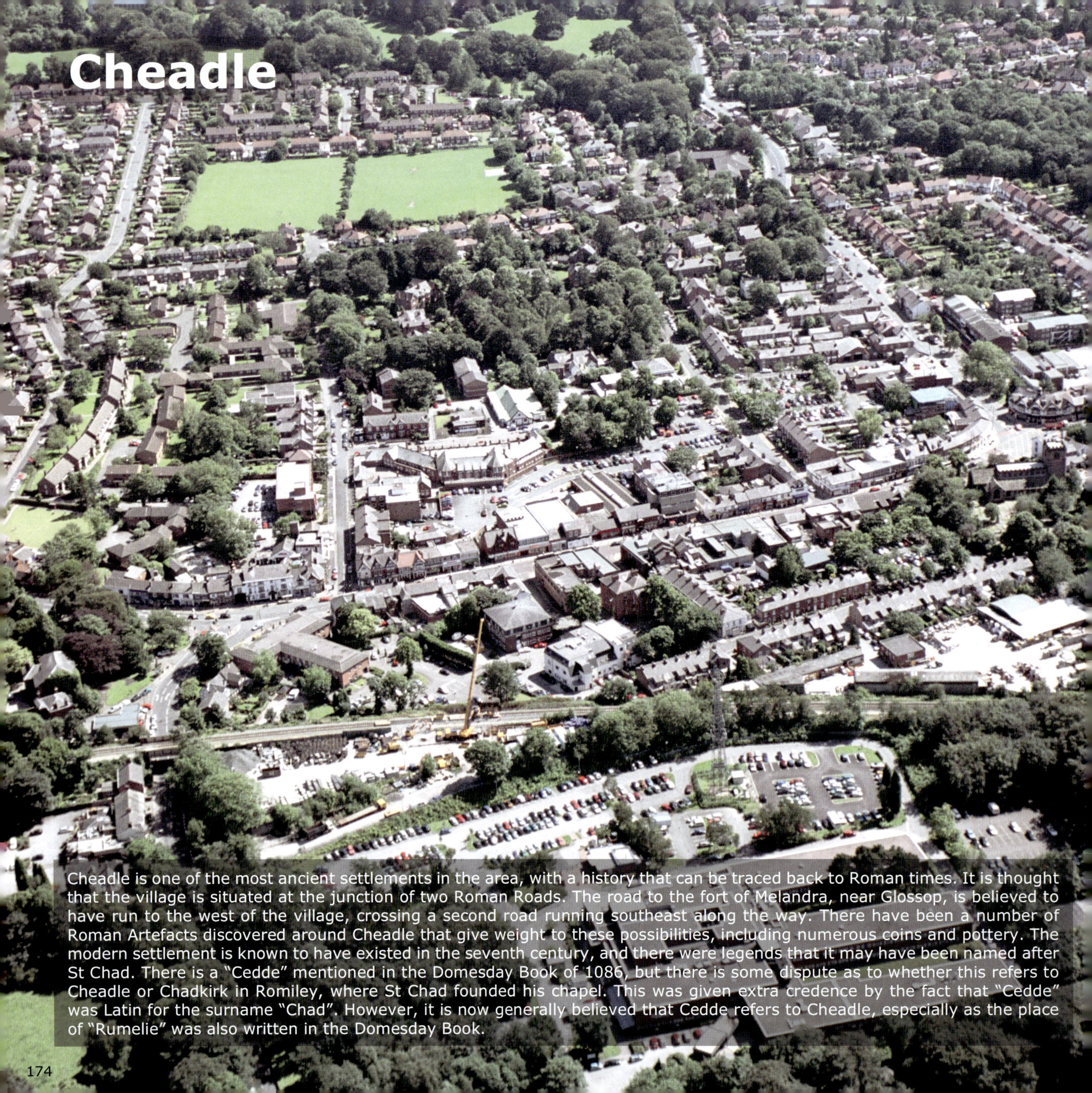

Cheadle is one of the most ancient settlements in the area, with a history that can be traced back to Roman times. It is thought that the village is situated at the junction of two Roman Roads. The road to the fort of Melandra, near Glossop, is believed to have run to the west of the village, crossing a second road running southeast along the way. There have been a number of Roman Artefacts discovered around Cheadle that give weight to these possibilities, including numerous coins and pottery. The modern settlement is known to have existed in the seventh century, and there were legends that it may have been named after St Chad. There is a "Cedde" mentioned in the Domesday Book of 1086, but there is some dispute as to whether this refers to Cheadle or Chadkirk in Romiley, where St Chad founded his chapel. This was given extra credence by the fact that "Cedde" was Latin for the surname "Chad". However, it is now generally believed that Cedde refers to Cheadle, especially as the place of "Rumelie" was also written in the Domesday Book.

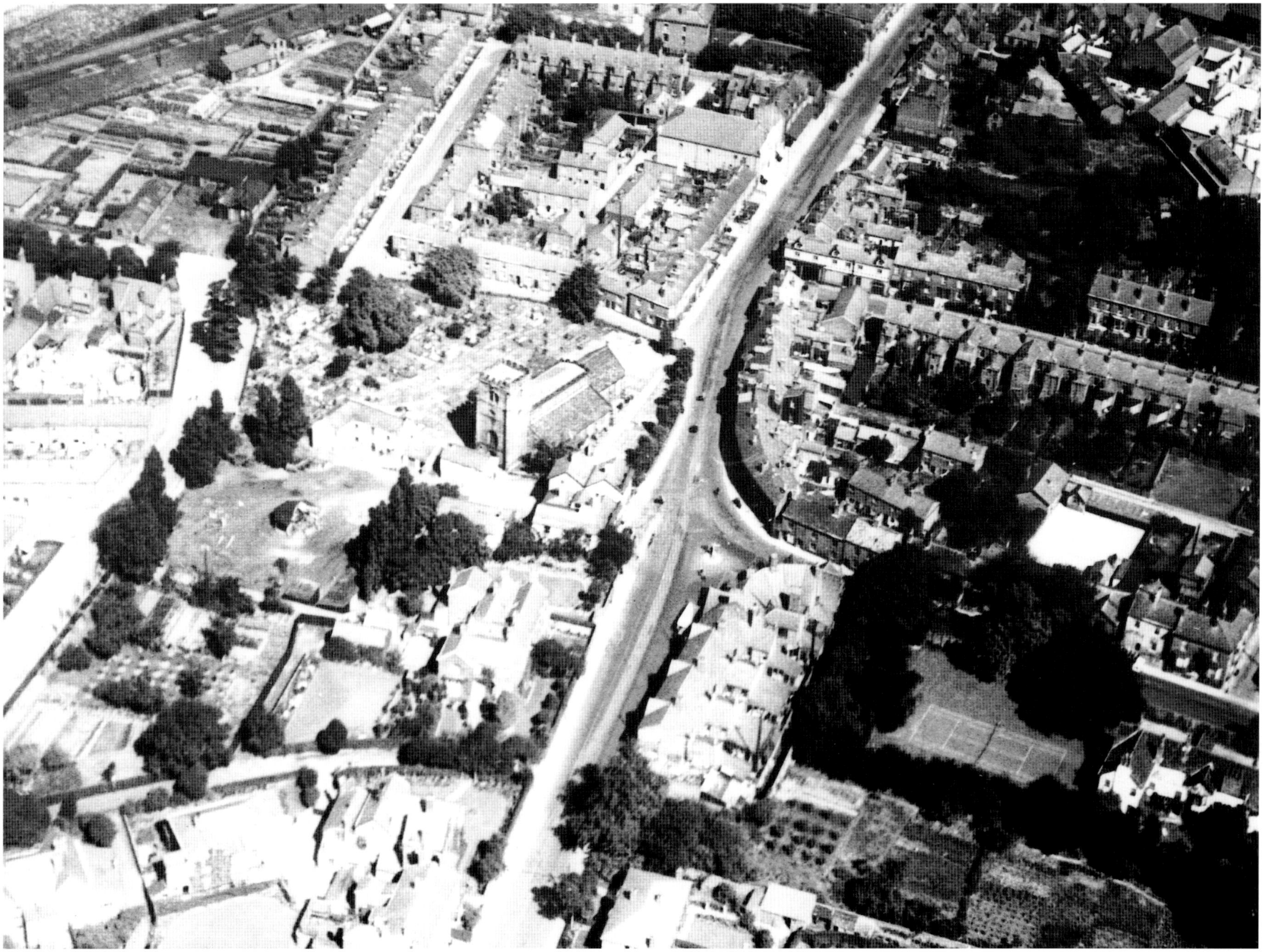

Cheadle Village 1927

By the 12th Century the village was known as "Chedle". "Ced" was an old Celtic word meaning "wood", and could also be the Cedde referred to in the Domesday Book. The old English "Legh", meaning "wood" or "clearing in a wood" (like at Edgeley, Heaviley, Romiley and Woodley) was added after the Domesday Book was written. This does means that the literal meaning of Cheadle could be "Wood, Wood", so the "Legh" may have been added at a time when the original place meaning had been forgotten. The industrial boom of the 18th and 19th centuries seen in other local districts such as Reddish and Edgeley largely passed Cheadle by. There was a bleachworks situated near to the site of Barnes Hospital and a couple of small printworks, but generally there were no large factories built around the village core. This has undoubtedly shaped the nature of the village as we see it today. There are no great swathes of terraced housing, save for a few close to the High Street, shown above in 1927, and there are still many areas of attractive villas from Victorian and Edwardian times. Cheadle is now a very pleasant, much sought after residential area that has managed to retain its history and heritage, although it's fair to say it could do with a lot less traffic on the high street.

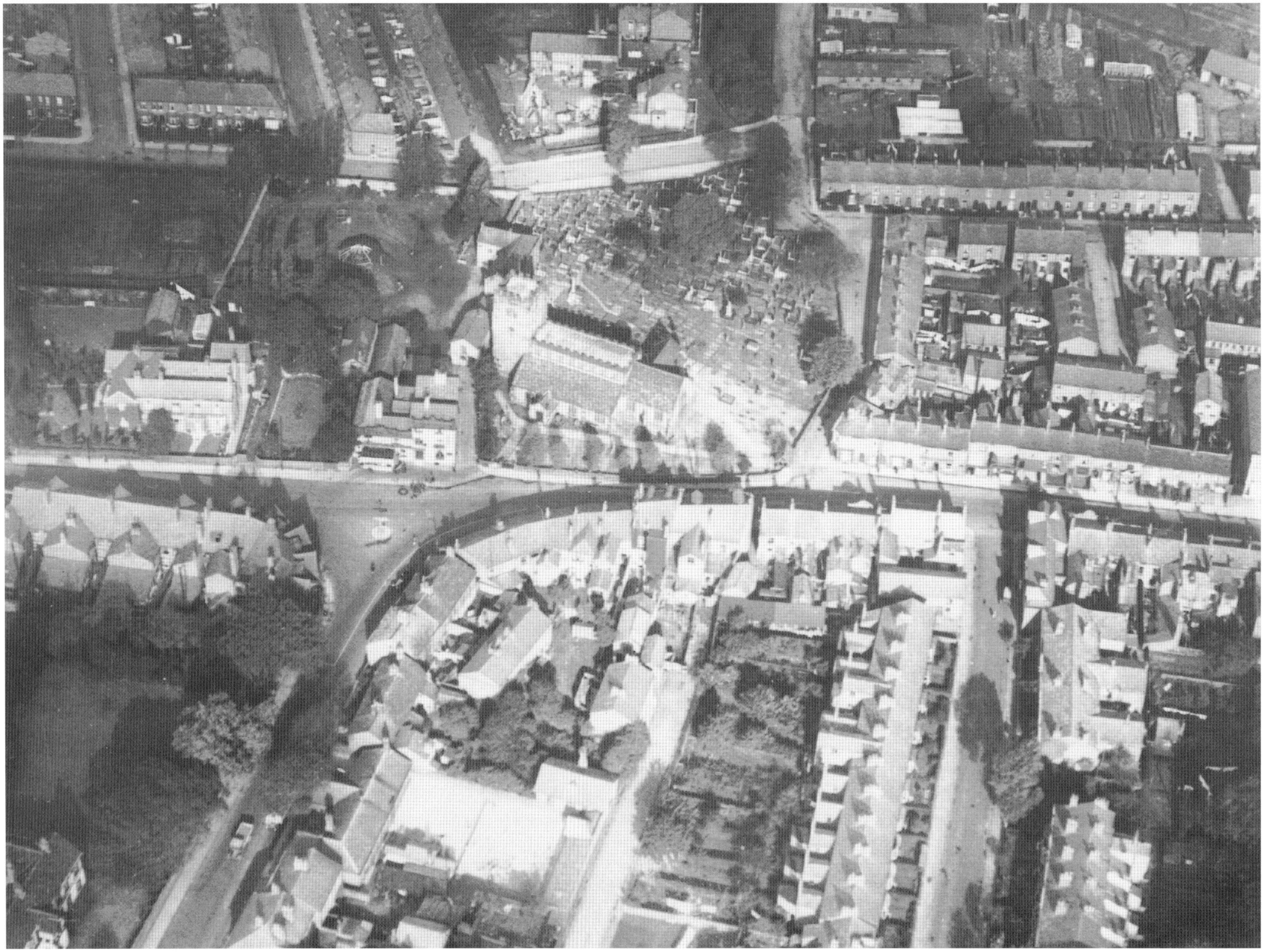

St Mary's Church 1927

St Mary's Church originally dates back to the 12th Century, but the present building was not begun until around 1520, being completed in about 1550. The church is home to the "Cheadle Cross" – an 11th century Anglo-Saxon stone cross that was found to the north of the church by the Micker Brook in 1874 during construction of Barnes Hospital. The cross is evidence that there may have been a parish located here at that time. Despite extensive renovations between 1875 and 1892, the church is now Grade 1 Listed and the chimes of the clock continue to ring out over the village every quarter hour. Next to the church is the old coaching house of the White Hart. This was one of two coaching houses built at either end of the High Street following the creation of a turnpike road in 1753. The other was the George & Dragon, at the eastern end of the village. The turnpike, following the Wilmslow to Didsbury road, was set up to provide funds to maintain the road and encourage an increase in horse-drawn traffic. Before the turnpike, Cheadle was an extremely quiet place with few people using the route. Two new stone bridges were built to help improve the journey. One was over the River Mersey to the north of the village, and the other was over the Micker Brook to the south.

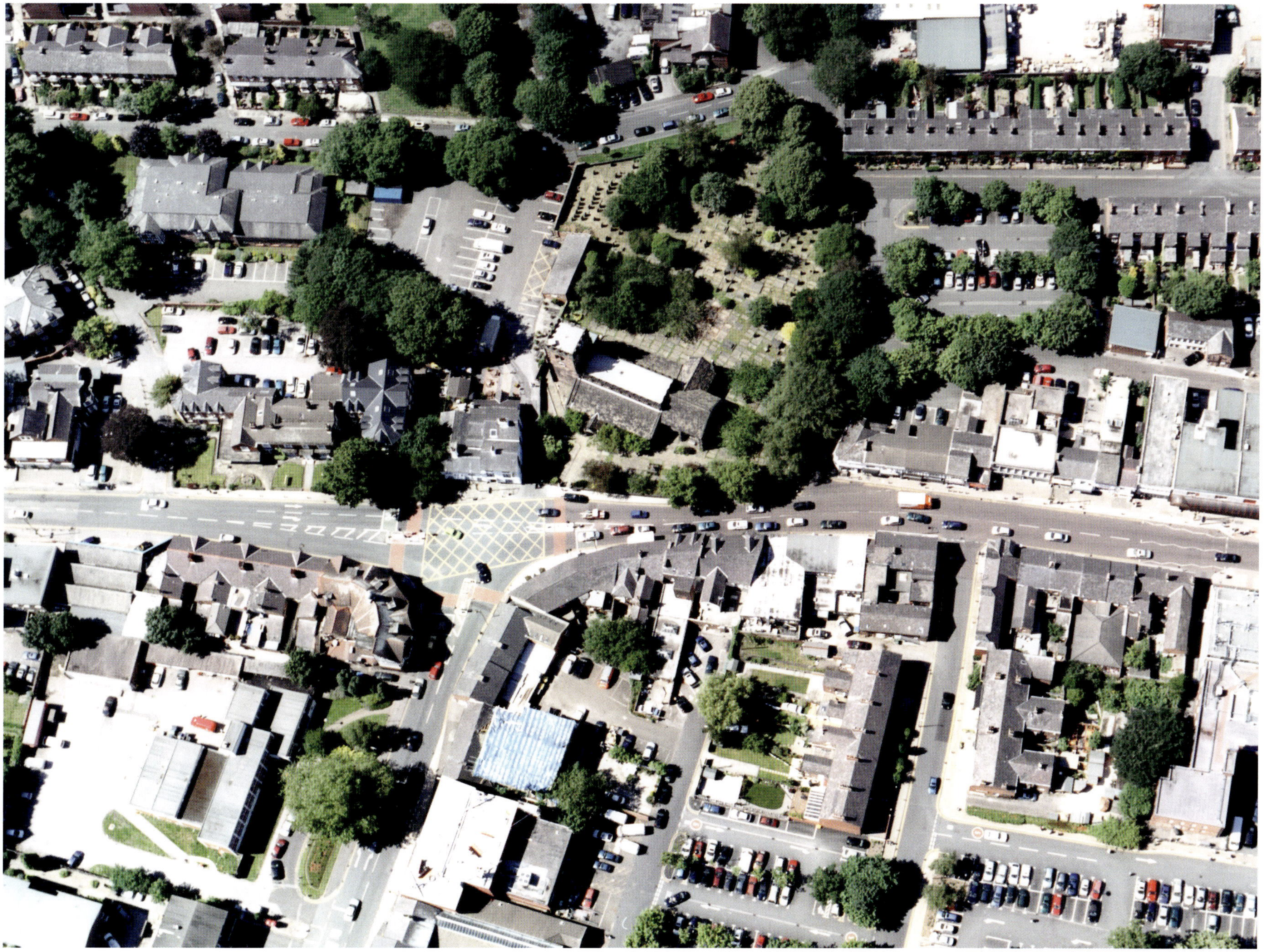

The new inns were built in anticipation of an increase in traffic - and therefore trade - when the turnpike opened. A later turnpike was opened in 1820 alongside the White Hart as part of the Stockport - Liverpool route, increasing the importance of the village. On the lower left is the site of the old Cheadle Rectory. This was a medieval, black-and-white timber-framed house built from materials left over from the building of St Mary's. The house is believed to have been the Manor House for the ancient township of Cheadle Bulkeley. Sadly, the house was demolished in 1939 and the rather bland box shape of the village post office is now on the site. The house is remembered in the name of Rectory Gardens, which lie at the front of the new building. These two remarkable images shows that very little has changed in nearly 80 years between the photographs, with all of the main buildings clearly recognisable. We can still make out the original circular shape of the churchyard, although some of the land has been lost. This shape is an indication that the site is an ancient place of worship, possibly dating to prehistoric - and therefore Pagan - times. There is also an ancient circular churchyard at St Mary's in the Market Place. Some of the housing to the right of the church around Lyme Grove, and on the bottom right of the image near Massie Street, was demolished in the 1960s to make way for car parks.

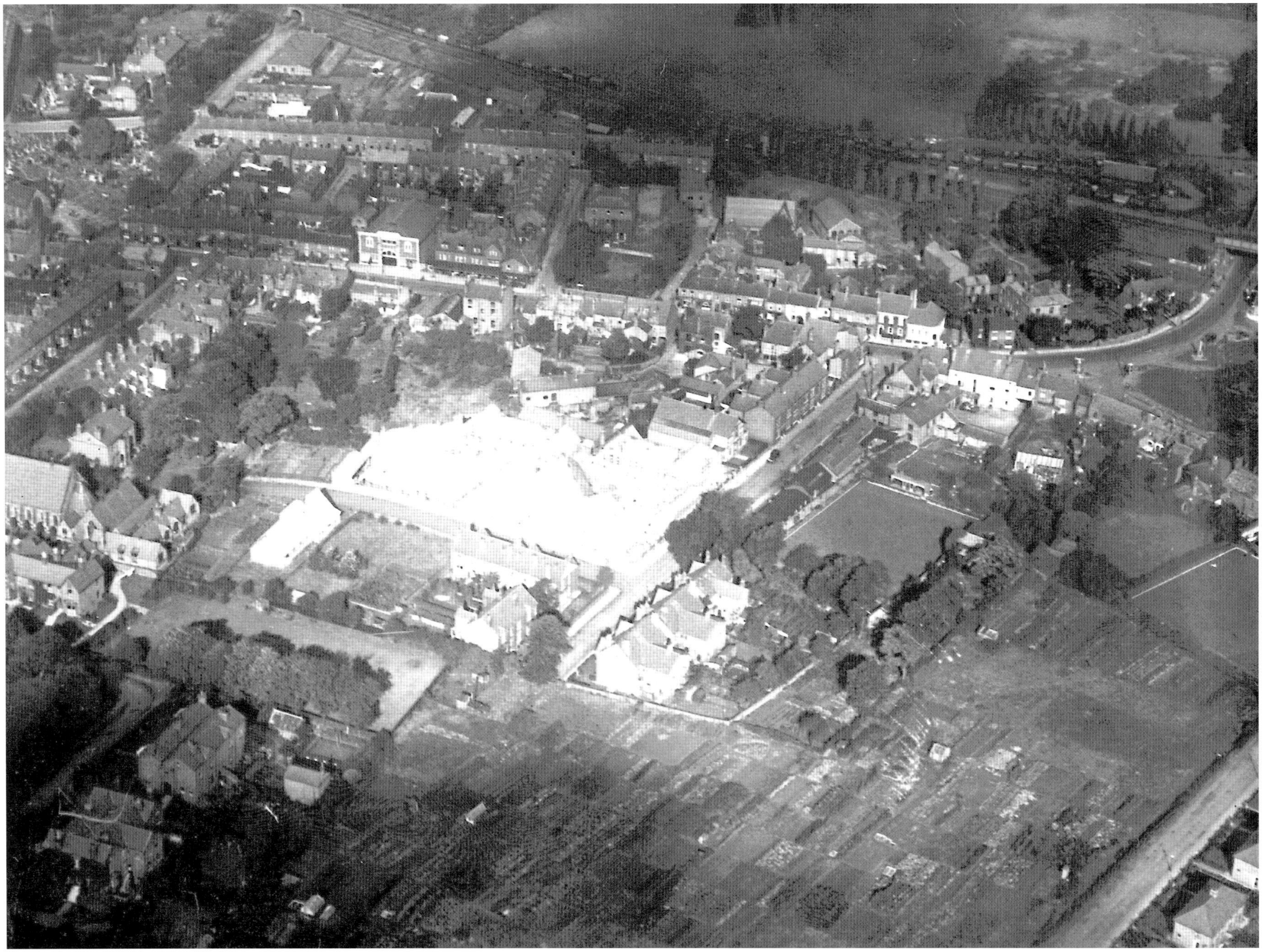

Cheadle High Street 1927

The majority of the buildings on the High Street date from the mid-to-late 19th century, with a few 20th century additions. They are generally two-storey houses with the ground floor as business or retail premises. Cheadle has managed to maintain its traditional look whilst still allowing new developments to take place. There are very few modern eyesores competing for space, with the possible exception of the telephone exchange building. That building is opposite the site of the old Electra Cinema, which is the large, double fronted building in the top left of this picture. A supermarket was later built on the site, but it was redeveloped again in the late 1980s into smaller retail units. Cheadle Green, on the extreme right, was protected from 1810 as part of the Cheadle Enclosure Act. The terms of the act stated that the land here "shall at all times remain unenclosed for the public accommodation and convenience of the said village of Cheadle". It was later renamed as Cheadle Village Green and is now protected as part of the village conservation area. The Ockleston drinking fountain, which also had a trough for horses and a basin for dogs, was erected in 1889 in front of the George & Dragon. It is visible in the middle of the road before the Green.

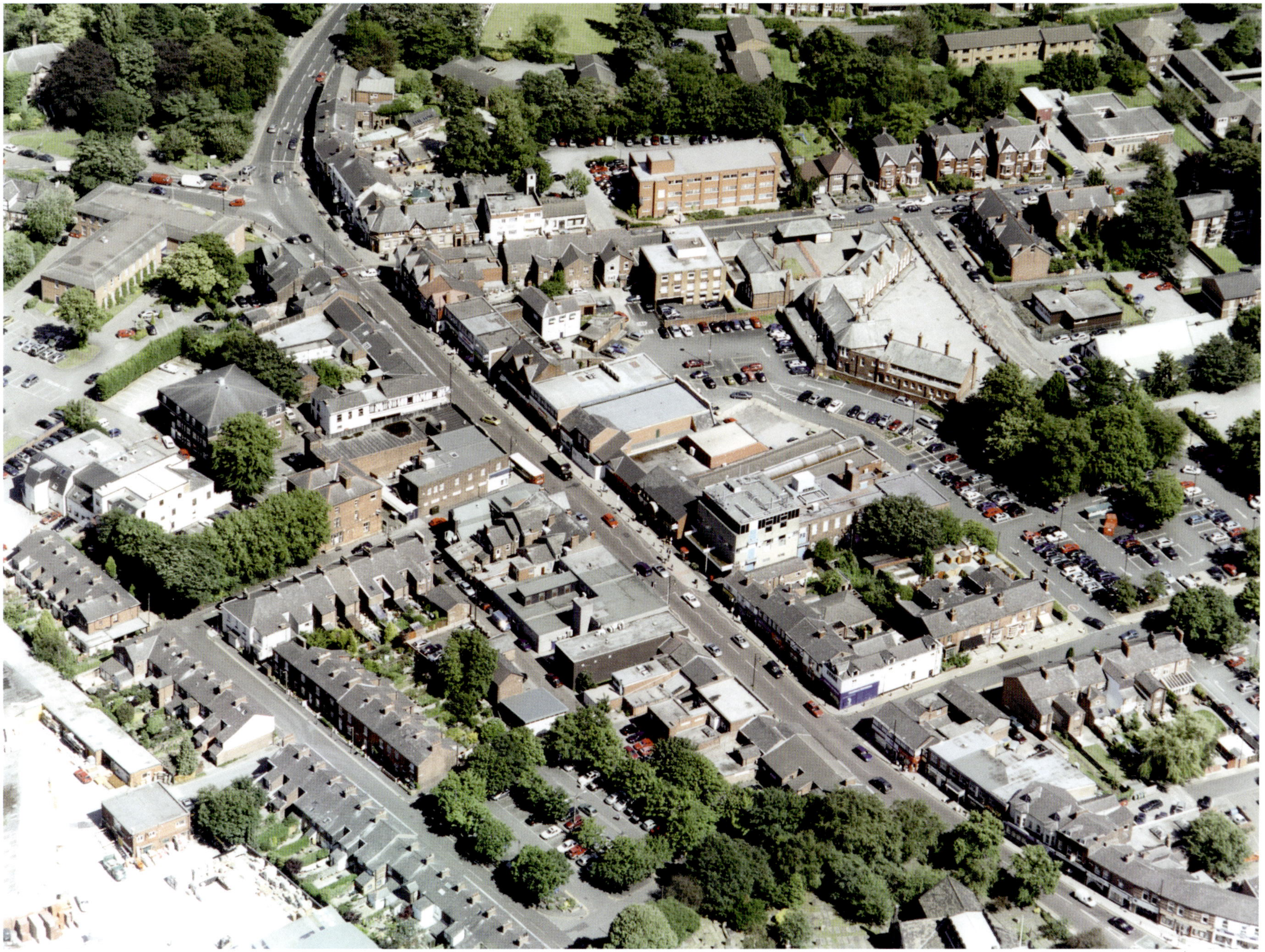

Today the village green is full of mature trees. The Literary Institute building next to the green (in the very top left of the new image) was erected in 1887. It was used as a library and reading room until 1966 before becoming council offices. The building closed in 2001 but has recently been refurbished as new offices. The Ockleston Fountain was moved to Queen's Gardens in 1967. A train station was opened to the north of the village in 1866 off Manchester Road close to the River Mersey, and this was followed later in the year by a second station within the village itself off Brook Road, just behind the High Street. The track can be seen at the top of the old photo, with the railway bridge passing over Manchester Road on the right. The Cheadle village station closed in 1917 after it was unable to compete with the Gatley to Mersey Square tram service that ran down the High Street. The Cheadle North station closed in 1964. The station building is now a restaurant within the grounds of the Golden Days Garden Centre. Cheadle primary School with its eye-catching angled wings (centre of old image), was built in 1908, but was known as Ashfield Road School. It opened the following year on April 1st and has been providing education for the youngsters of the village ever since.

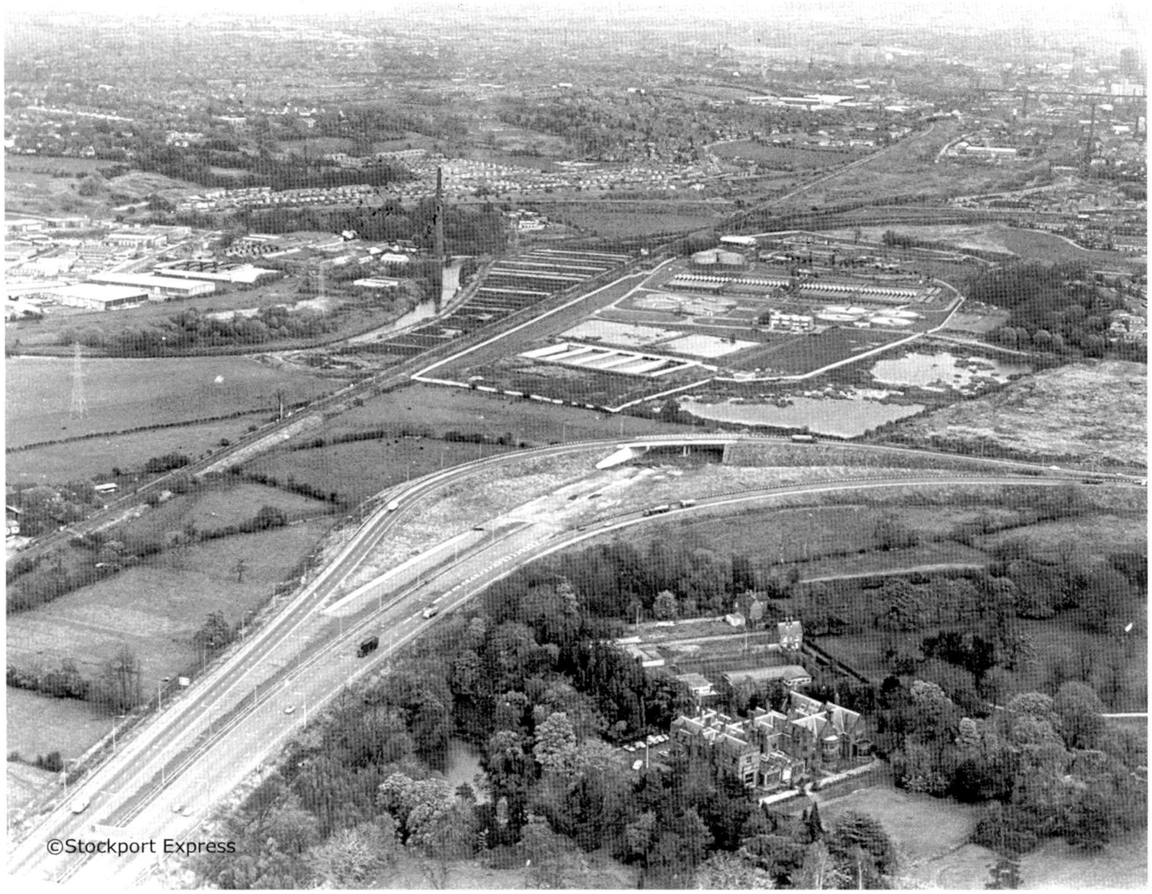

Abney Hall 1977

This fine mansion was built in 1847 for Alfred Orrell, Mayor of Stockport in 1842. He was a cotton mill owner and named the house "The Grove", as it was built on the site of the former Cheadle Grove printworks (opened 1760) which had burnt down earlier that year. Orrell would not get to live in the house though, as he died 14 months after construction started in January 1849 at just 33, before the house was finished. It was then bought by James Watts.

Watts was a member of the family who owned the largest drapery business in Manchester, S & J Watts. He would later go on to become Mayor of Manchester. Watts renamed the building Abney Hall and extended it to its current size. His family lived in the house for over one hundred years until the house and its grounds were sold in 1959.

Barnes Hospital 1927

Barnes Hospital was built in 1875 with funds donated by Robert Barnes, a former cotton merchant. The building took four years to build and was intended to be a convalescent home associated with the Manchester Royal Infirmary. Barnes donated £26,000 to develop and maintain the 46-acre site, although the total cost was around £52,800. The foundation stone was laid on 29th July 1871, but Barnes died on Christmas day of that year, so did not see the building completed. The gothic structure, with its impressive clock tower, was for many years completely rural. The initial plan was for the hospital to be a place of recuperation where patients could regain their strength in quiet surroundings. But as the years wore on the hospital's purpose changed. It was later used for geriatric care and also for the care of stroke patients. Running along the bottom left is the main line to Edgeley Station. This is visible in the new picture (opposite page), but is surrounded by trees.

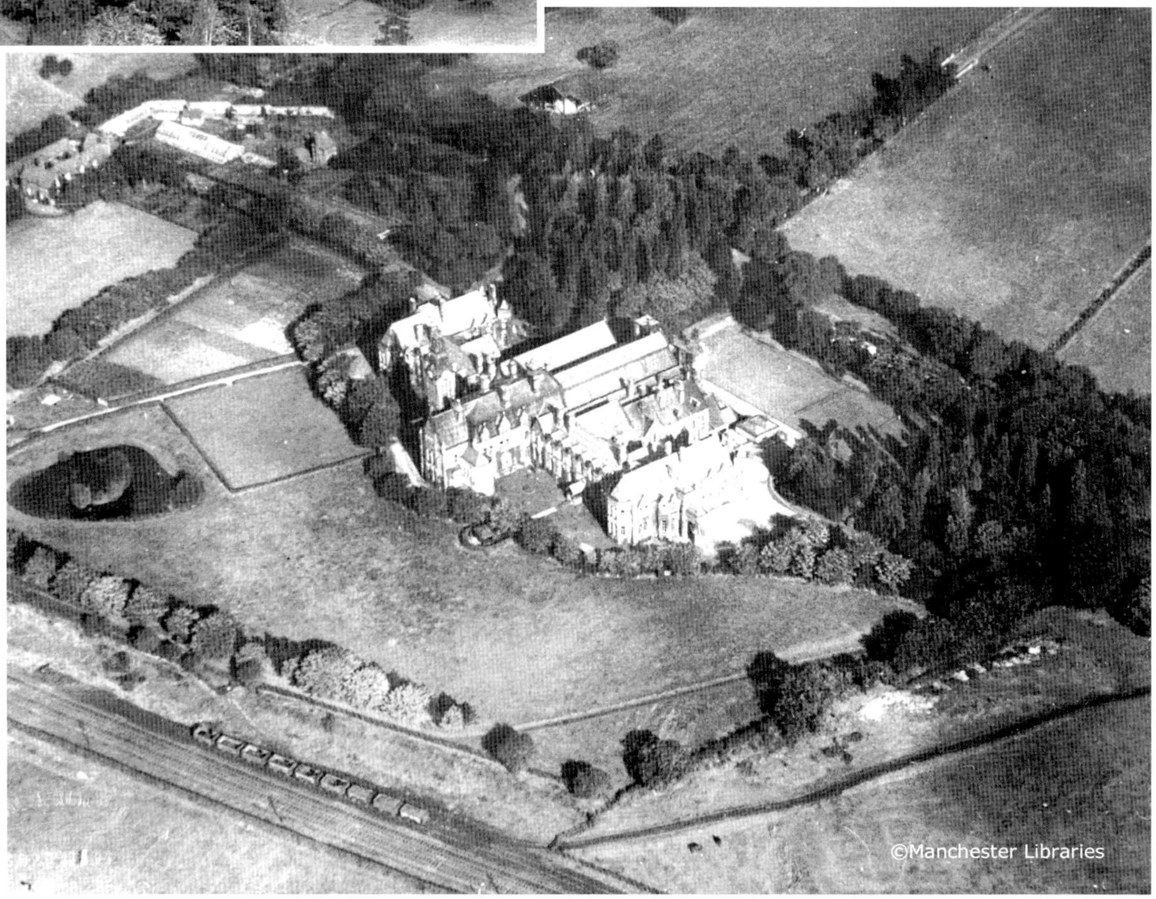

Abney Hall (continued)

The hall was bought by Cheadle & Gatley UDC for £14,000 and it became the new base for the council offices, replacing Bruntwood Hall. The hall remained in use as a civic centre until 1978, when it was leased out as offices. Now, the hall is under private ownership and has been fully converted to office use. It has also been joined by an almost equally large new building to the rear, built in a style to try and match that of the original house.

Abney Hall Park is open to the public, although the grounds are only one tenth of the original size. Much of this land was lost when the M63 motorway was constructed up to Cheadle Heath, as shown in the image from 1977. The park today is a tranquil haven, despite the noise from the nearby motorway, and contains some of the last remaining wetlands in Stockport.

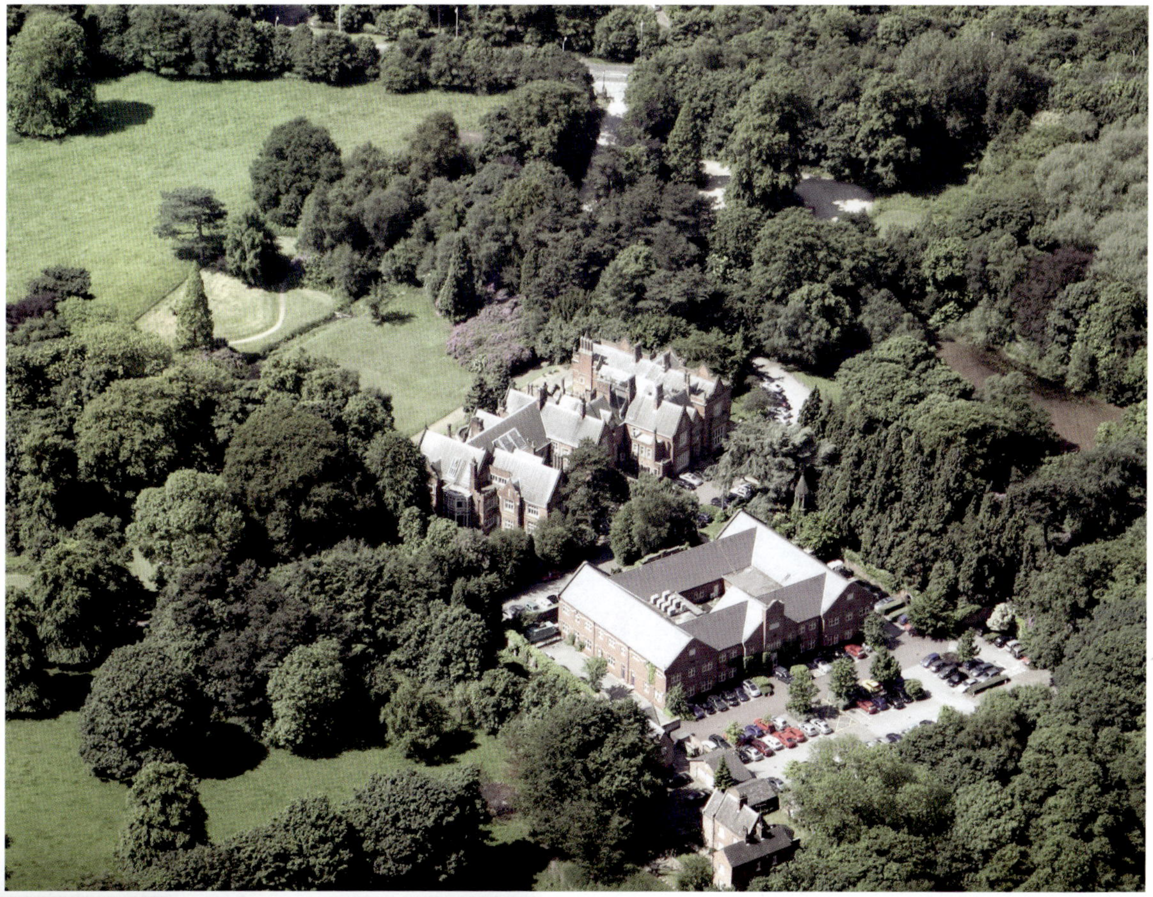

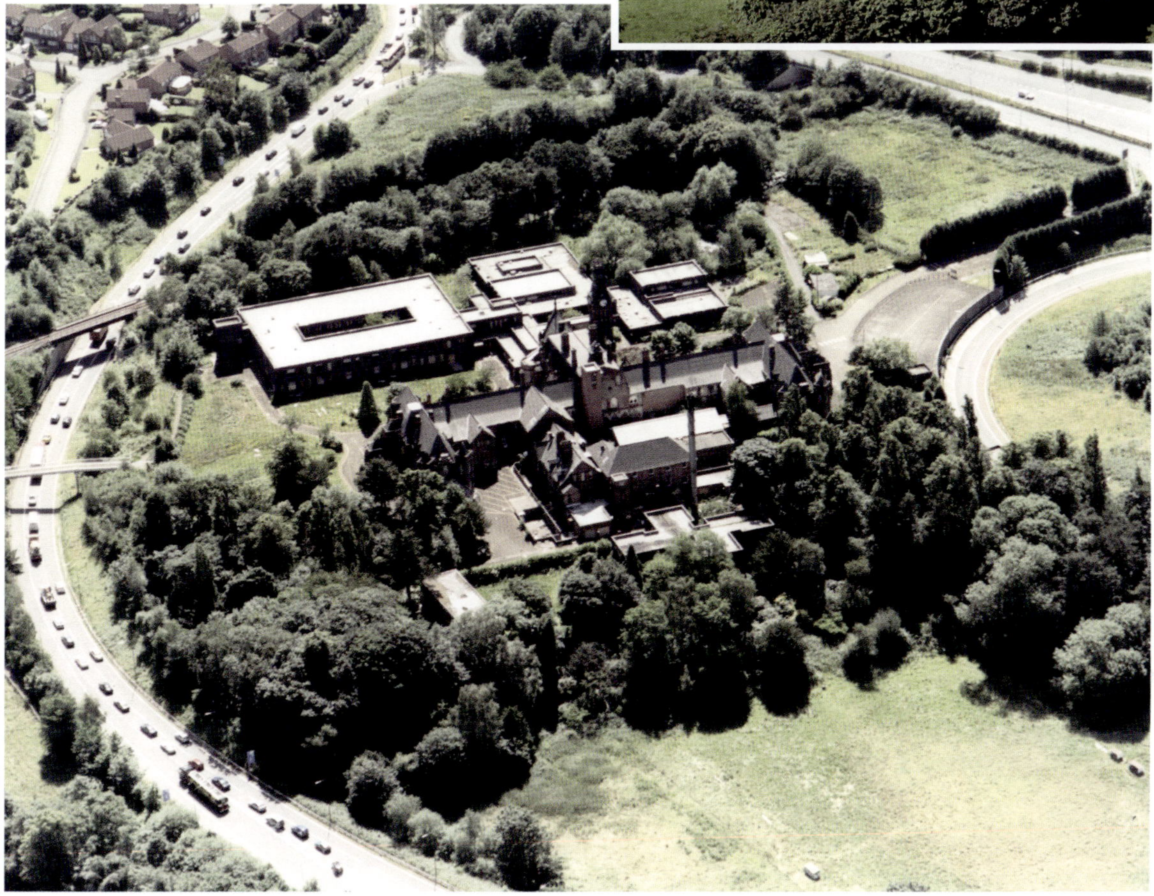

Barnes Hospital (continued)

Peace and quite is something that is now unattainable at Barnes Hospital, as the building has been completely surrounded by its own mini ring road, which is part of junction 3 of the M60 motorway. The building closed as a hospital in September 1999, but was made a Grade 2 Listed building the following November. It has since fallen into disrepair and is awaiting redevelopment as flats, but the modern extensions will be demolished. Note that there is an old football pitch on the bottom right, with the dug outs visible on either side of the pitch. This ground was briefly used by a team called Manchester Royal FC in the 1990s and early 2000s who played in the Manchester League. It is not a suitable place for a football ground, as the goal at the end just off the picture backs onto the motorway, and the rather small fence that was in place would not have been much help in stopping wayward shots landing amongst the traffic. The club folded in 2002.

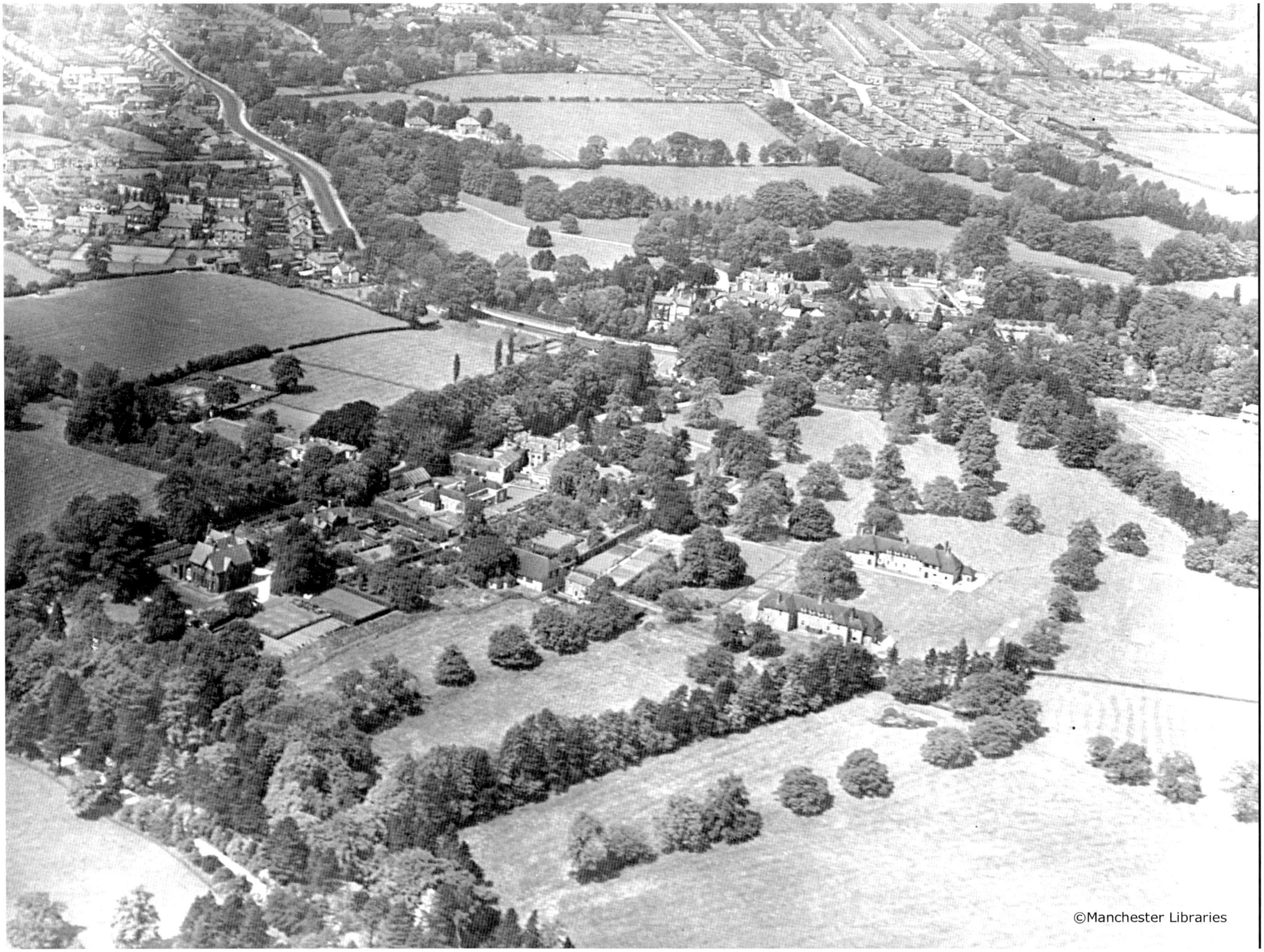

Schools Hill 1933

In 1933 Schools hill was still a quite, semi-rural backwater. The road was situated a fair way from the village of Cheadle and saw little development until the mid 19th century. It was at this time that the building boom following the expansion of the railways took off, and Cheadle was no different. The area quickly became a place for wealthy merchants to settle, and Schools Hill developed as one of the more exclusive areas. Many large villas were built in the vicinity, and today it remains an area of large, exclusive homes. In this picture we can see some of the elegant Victorian Mansions that were built along the hill, with the road itself shrouded in trees. Schools Hill is now a busy connecting route from the junction of the new A34 and the newly developed business and retail parks at Cheadle Royal. The two identical buildings on the right are the school buildings of the Children's Garden Village of the Boys and Girls Welfare Society, situated within the Belmont estate. The society bought the estate in 1920 and the two buildings were built in 1923 and 1925 for orphaned and destitute children. The society is now known as The Together Trust.

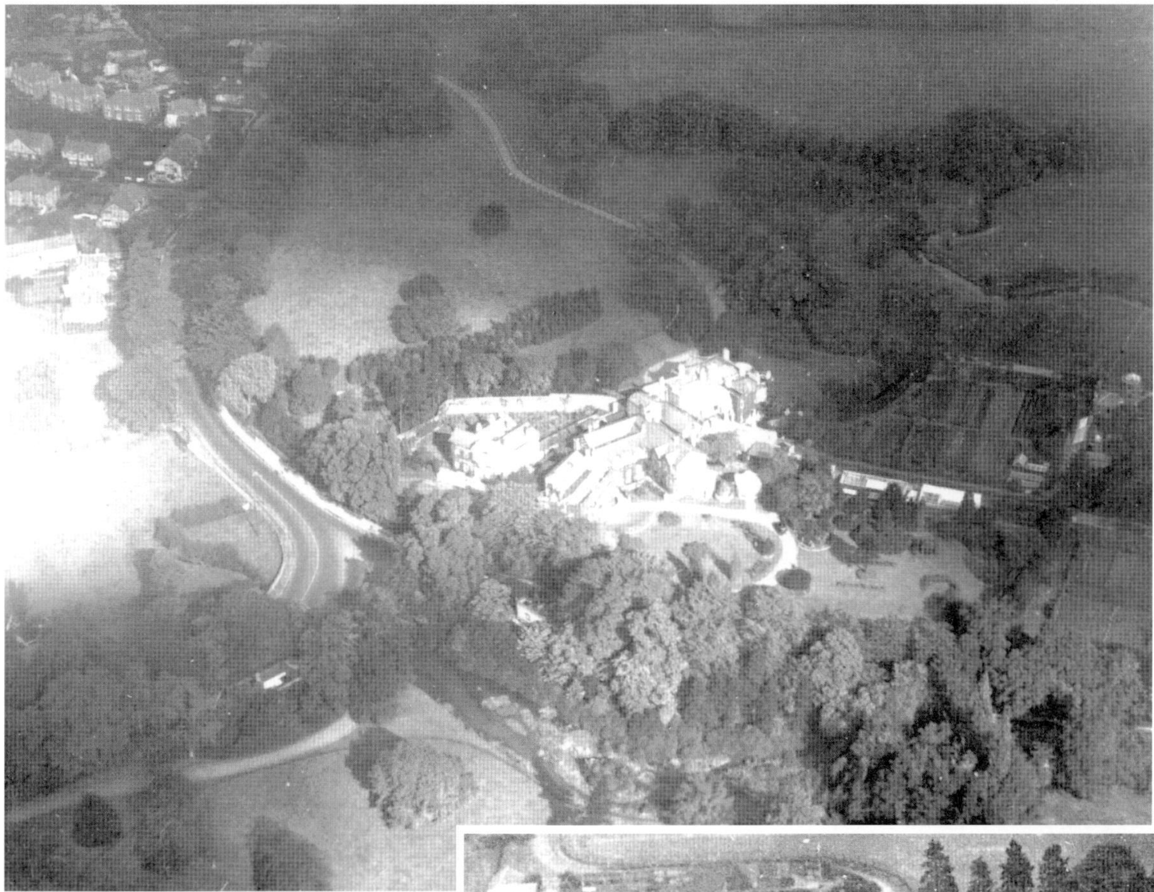

Moseley Hall & Brookfield Hall 1928

Moseley and Brookfield Halls at the foot of Schools Hill was the location for the first state Grammar School of the Education Act of 1944 in the UK – Moseley Hall Grammar School. It was initially a mixed school until the girls moved to a new site further south on Cheadle Road in 1956. The new school was called the Cheadle County Grammar School for Girls, but the site would undergo a series of changes in the following years. The Boys school moved to the new site in 1970 and built a new building next door. It was later renamed the Manor, which then merged with the girl's school to become Margaret Danyers College. In 1995 it was renamed Ridge Danyers College after merging with Marple College. In 2004 the college was renamed again to Cheadle & Marple Sixth Form College. The site of the two old halls was built over in the 1990s and is now home to the Village Hotel.

Bruntwood Hall 1928

Bruntwood Hall opened in 1861 and was originally a private residence. It was owned by John Douglas who named the estate and the house after Bruntwood, a village in Ayrshire. The estate became a public park during the 1940s, and at around 128 acres is one of the largest urban parks in Stockport. The hall was bought by Cheadle and Gatley UDC in 1944 and was used as their main offices until 1959, when they moved into Abney Hall. The building has been converted into offices and is now not open to the public, but the Victorian conservatory (shown here to the left of the main building) has been converted into a restaurant, and is open year-round.

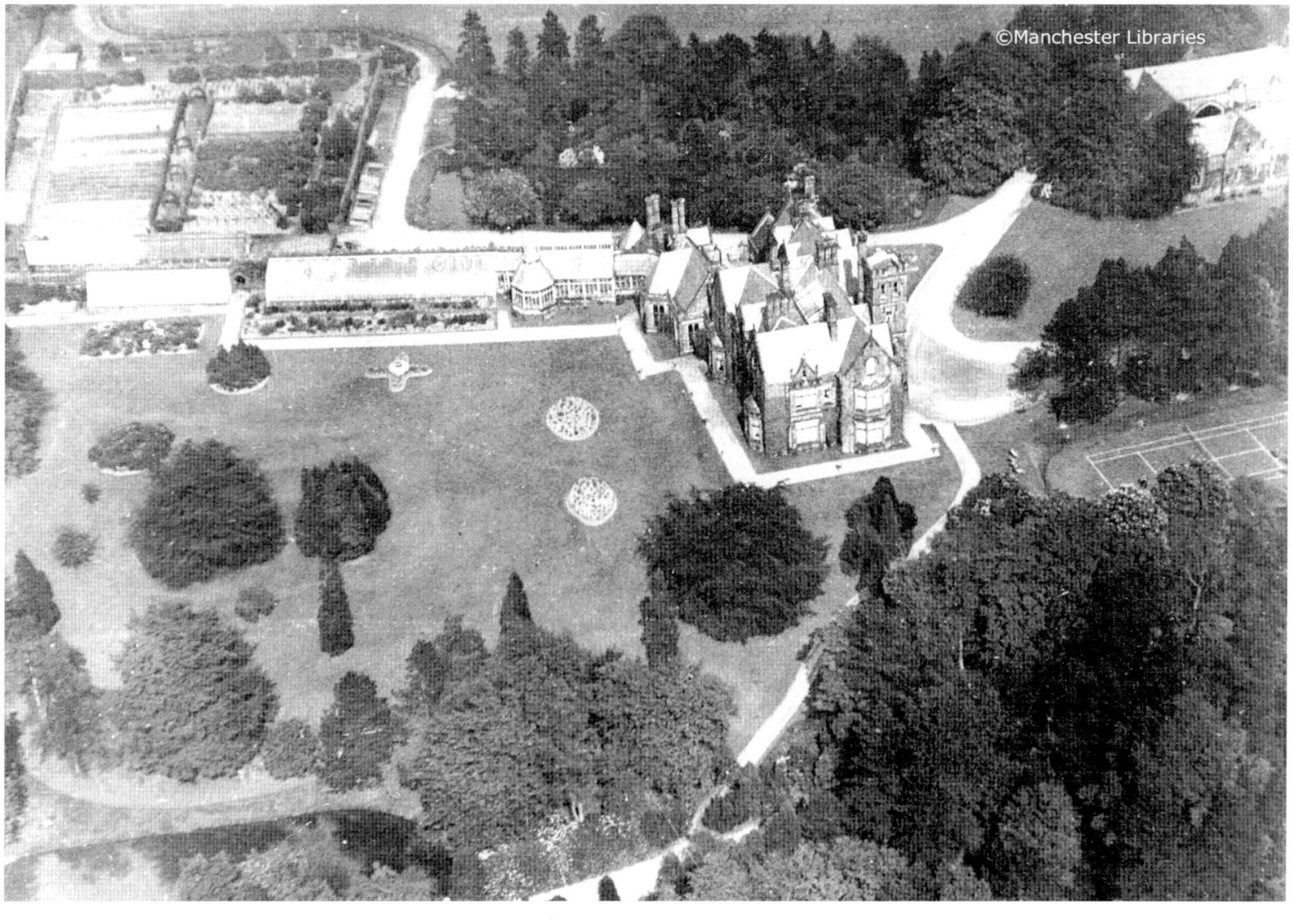

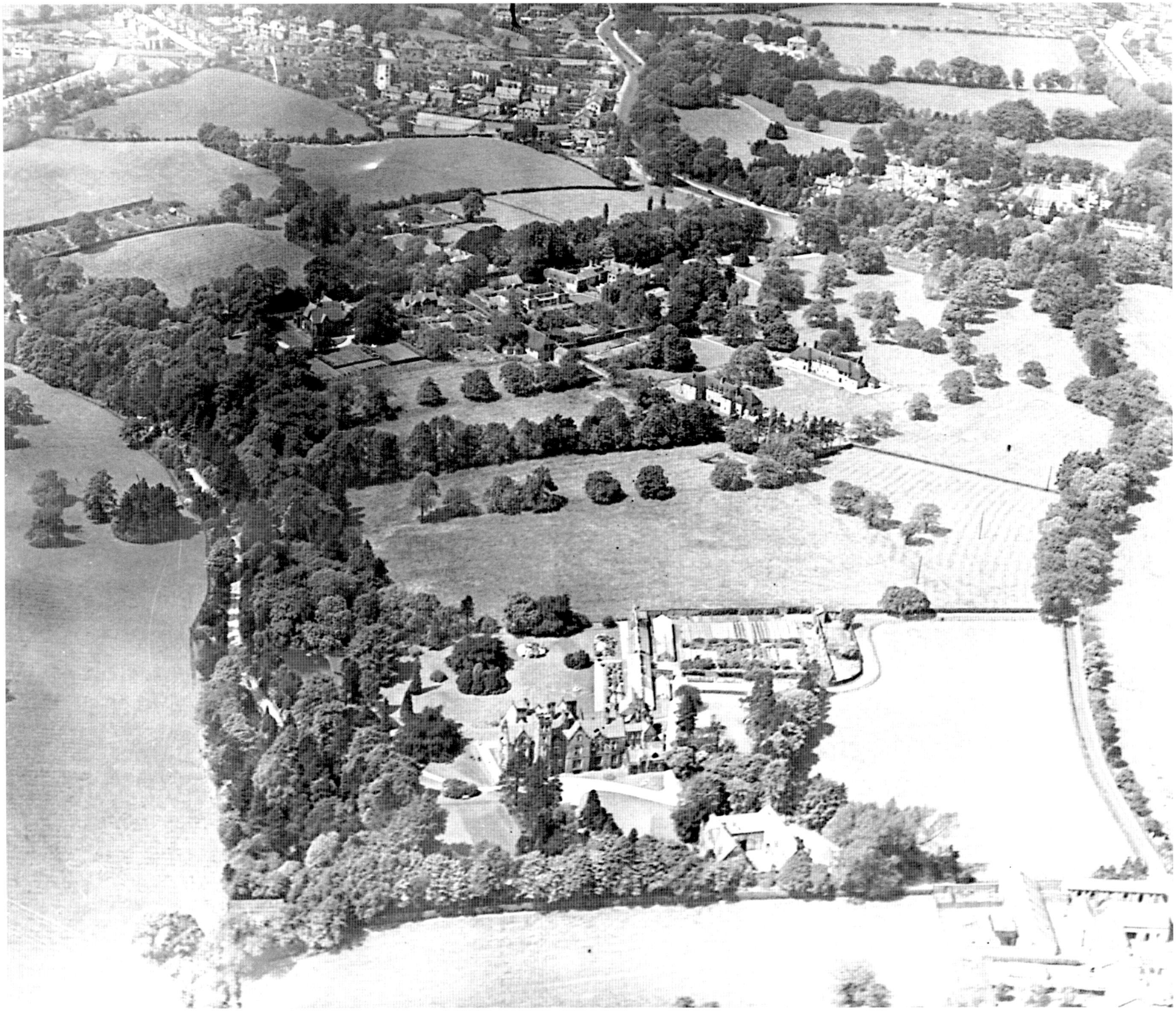

Bruntwood Park 1933

Here we can see the greater extent of the park as we look back towards School Hill and Cheadle Village in the distance. The park has many facilities for activities, including a pitch-and-putt golf course, children's play area and a BMX track, and also contains attractive gardens and many secluded woodland walks. A large chunk of the park was lost to the development of the new A34 road in the 1990s, just to the left of the picture.

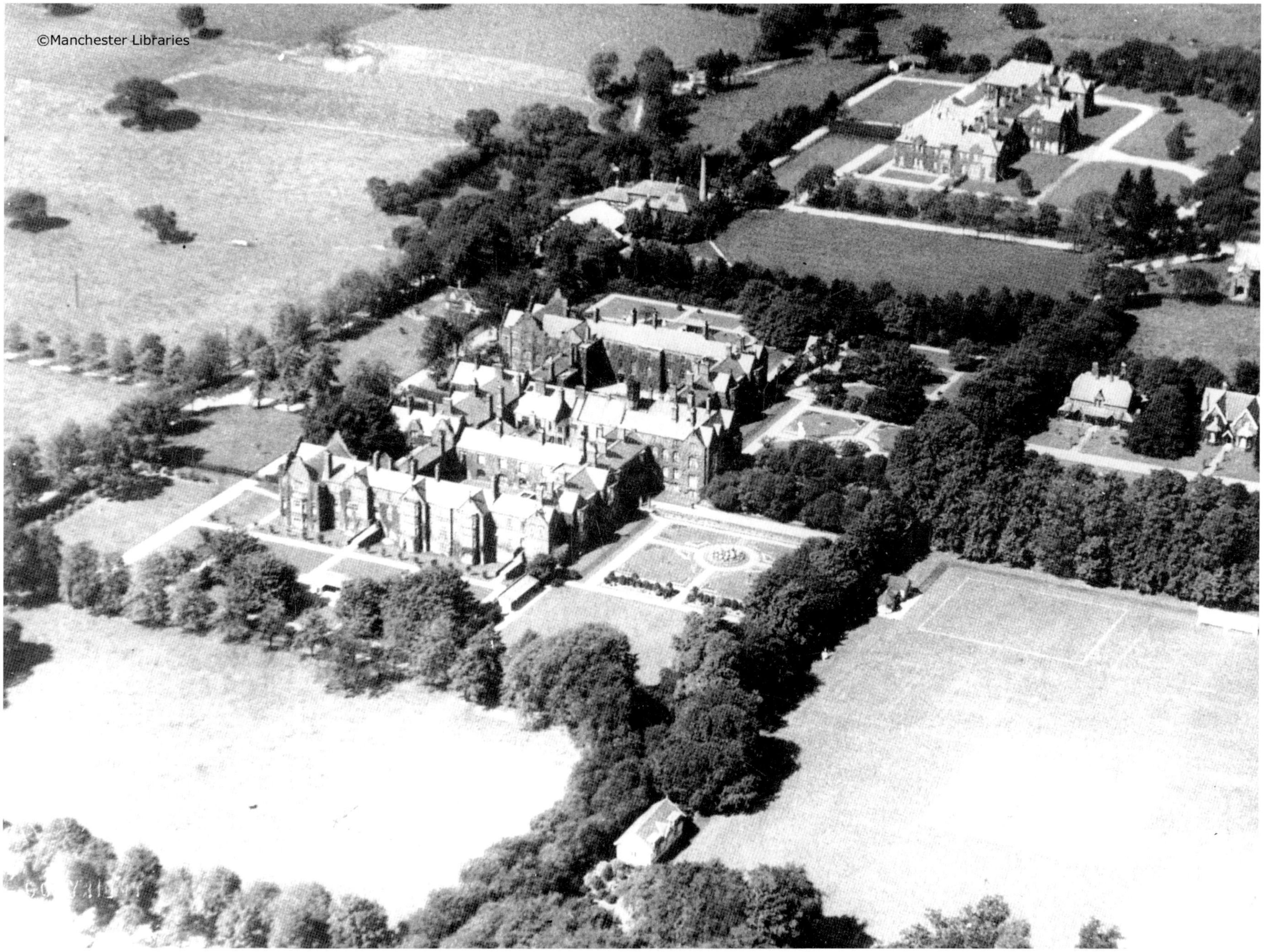

Cheadle Royal Hospital 1933

Cheadle Royal Hospital was founded in 1763 as the Manchester Royal Lunatic Hospital. It was first based in Manchester city centre and was associated with Manchester Royal Infirmary before it moved to the present site in 1848 where this fine Gothic-style building was erected. It was built on 37 acres of land that was previously part of Finney Farm in Stockport Etchells, and opened a year later in 1849. The architect of the building, John Lane, was also responsible for designing the Infirmary opposite the Town Hall. The hospital was extended three times, in 1861, 1877 and 1892, and by 1949 it had become known as the Cheadle Royal Lunatic Asylum. The equally impressive looking building standing next to the hospital is St Anne's Hospital, which was a private hospital for epileptic children. St Anne’s was bought by Cheadle Royal Hospital in 1887. Up until the 1990s the area here was still relatively peaceful despite a fair amount of traffic, but that was all to change when in 1994 permission was granted to construct a large business park and retail units as part of the development of the new A34 road. In total, the new business park covers 67 acres of land, and development is still ongoing. This was accompanied by the arrival of the combined John Lewis & Sainsbury’s stores on Wilmslow Road in 2000, opposite where the hospital stands.

Cheadle Hulme

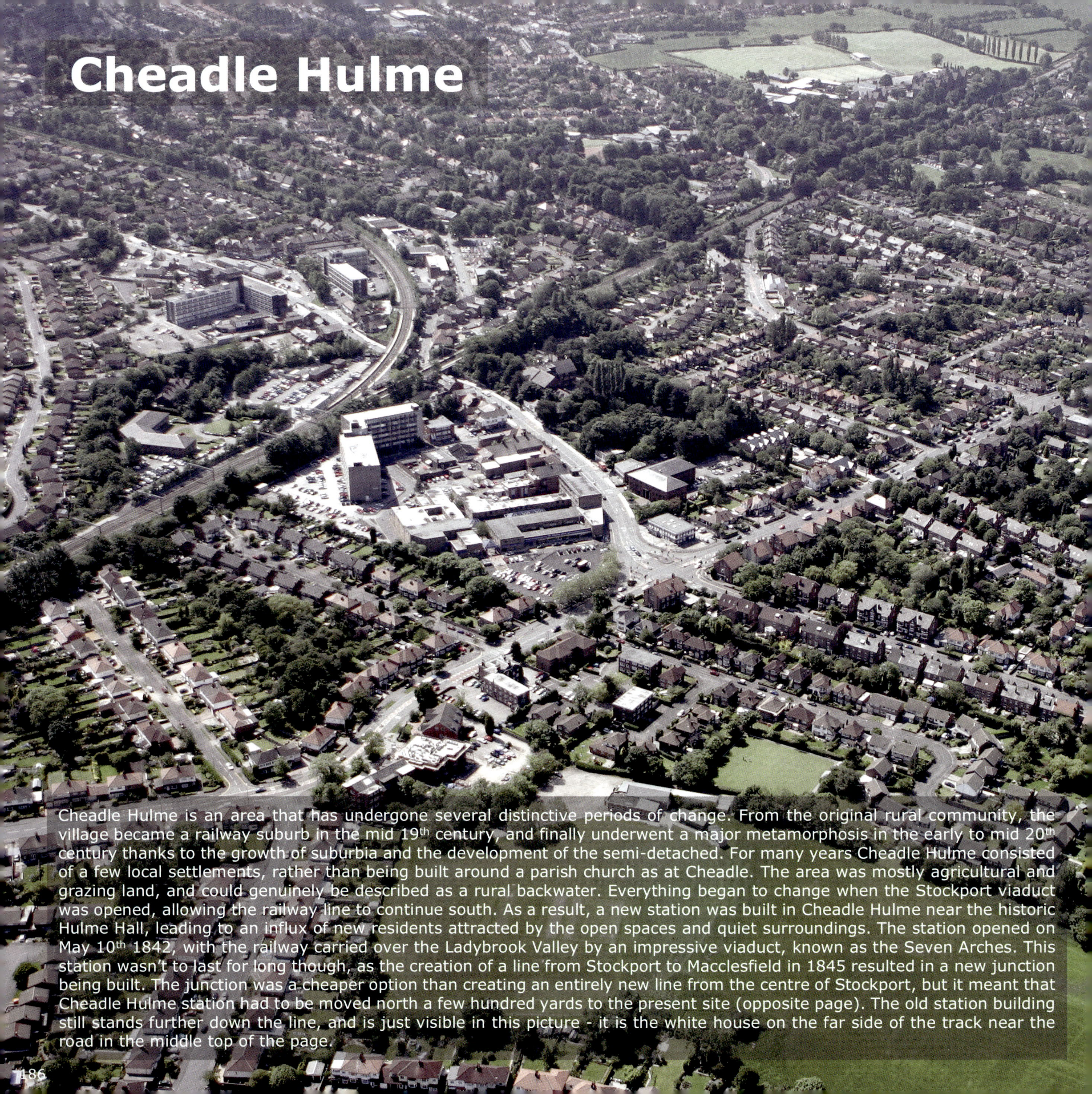

Cheadle Hulme is an area that has undergone several distinctive periods of change. From the original rural community, the village became a railway suburb in the mid 19th century, and finally underwent a major metamorphosis in the early to mid 20th century thanks to the growth of suburbia and the development of the semi-detached. For many years Cheadle Hulme consisted of a few local settlements, rather than being built around a parish church as at Cheadle. The area was mostly agricultural and grazing land, and could genuinely be described as a rural backwater. Everything began to change when the Stockport viaduct was opened, allowing the railway line to continue south. As a result, a new station was built in Cheadle Hulme near the historic Hulme Hall, leading to an influx of new residents attracted by the open spaces and quiet surroundings. The station opened on May 10th 1842, with the railway carried over the Ladybrook Valley by an impressive viaduct, known as the Seven Arches. This station wasn't to last for long though, as the creation of a line from Stockport to Macclesfield in 1845 resulted in a new junction being built. The junction was a cheaper option than creating an entirely new line from the centre of Stockport, but it meant that Cheadle Hulme station had to be moved north a few hundred yards to the present site (opposite page). The old station building still stands further down the line, and is just visible in this picture - it is the white house on the far side of the track near the road in the middle top of the page.

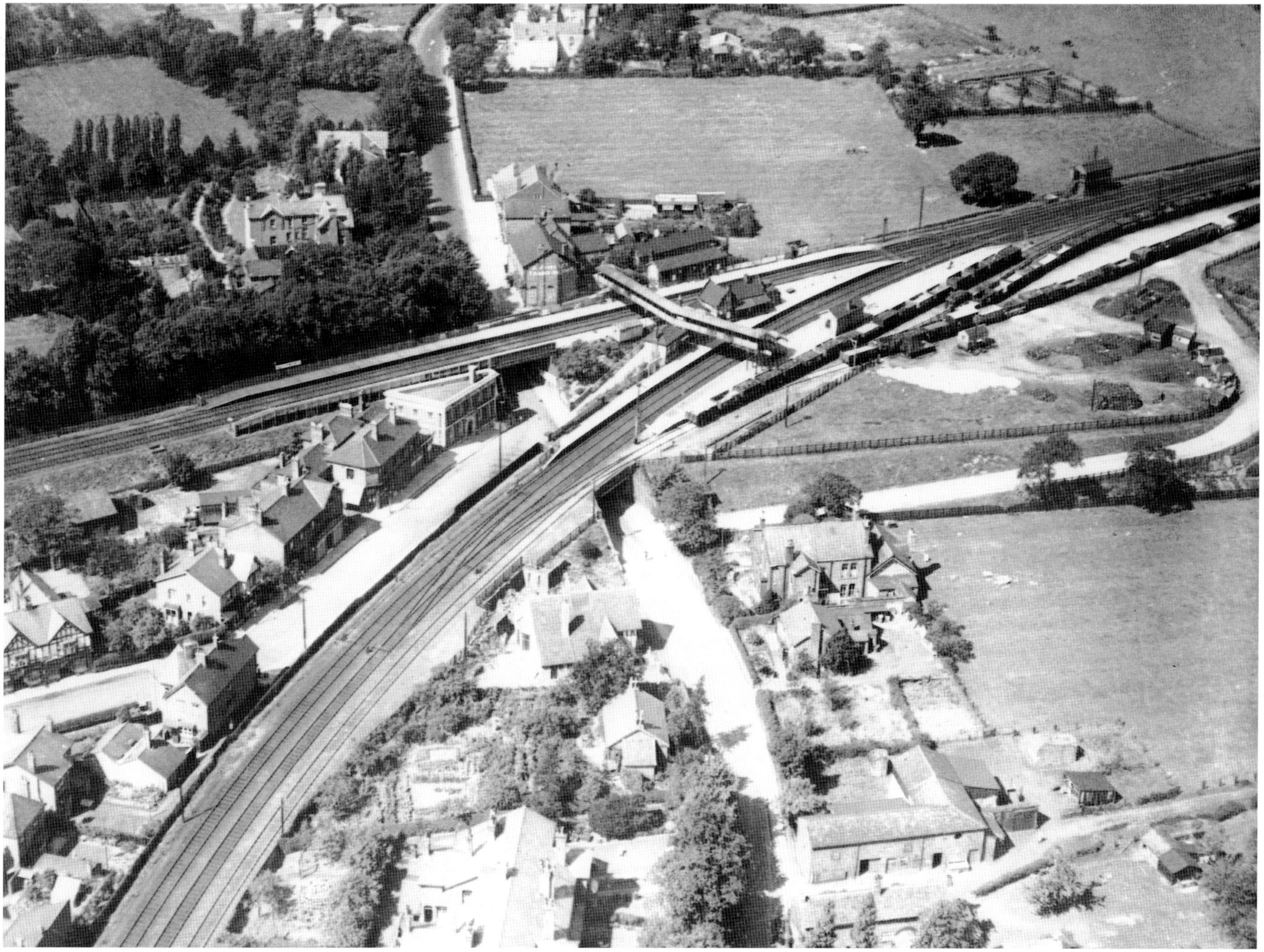

Station Road 1927

This view has changed dramatically since 1927, yet is still instantly recognisable as the centre of the village. The picture shows the rail junction that was created by the addition of the line to Macclesfield in 1845 (the track heading to the bottom of the picture). The area around the train station was still somewhat surprisingly undeveloped at the time, with many fields still prominent. Most of the local villages had seen more development along their high streets by this time. One of the most noticeable differences is the presence of a covered walkway over the station platforms and the traditional looking station waiting rooms on either side. The station even had its own mini goods yard, mostly used for coal, on the bottom right. The walkway collapsed following a crash at the station in May 1964, when a train took the bend too quickly and derailed. Three people were killed in the accident. Today, there are concrete boxes where the platform buildings were, and the goods yard is the station car park. The first building beyond the station is Pimlott's Butchers, which is still there and trading to this day. Beyond that there were fields and houses right up to the junction with Ladybridge Road. The road leading off to the left is Mellor Road.

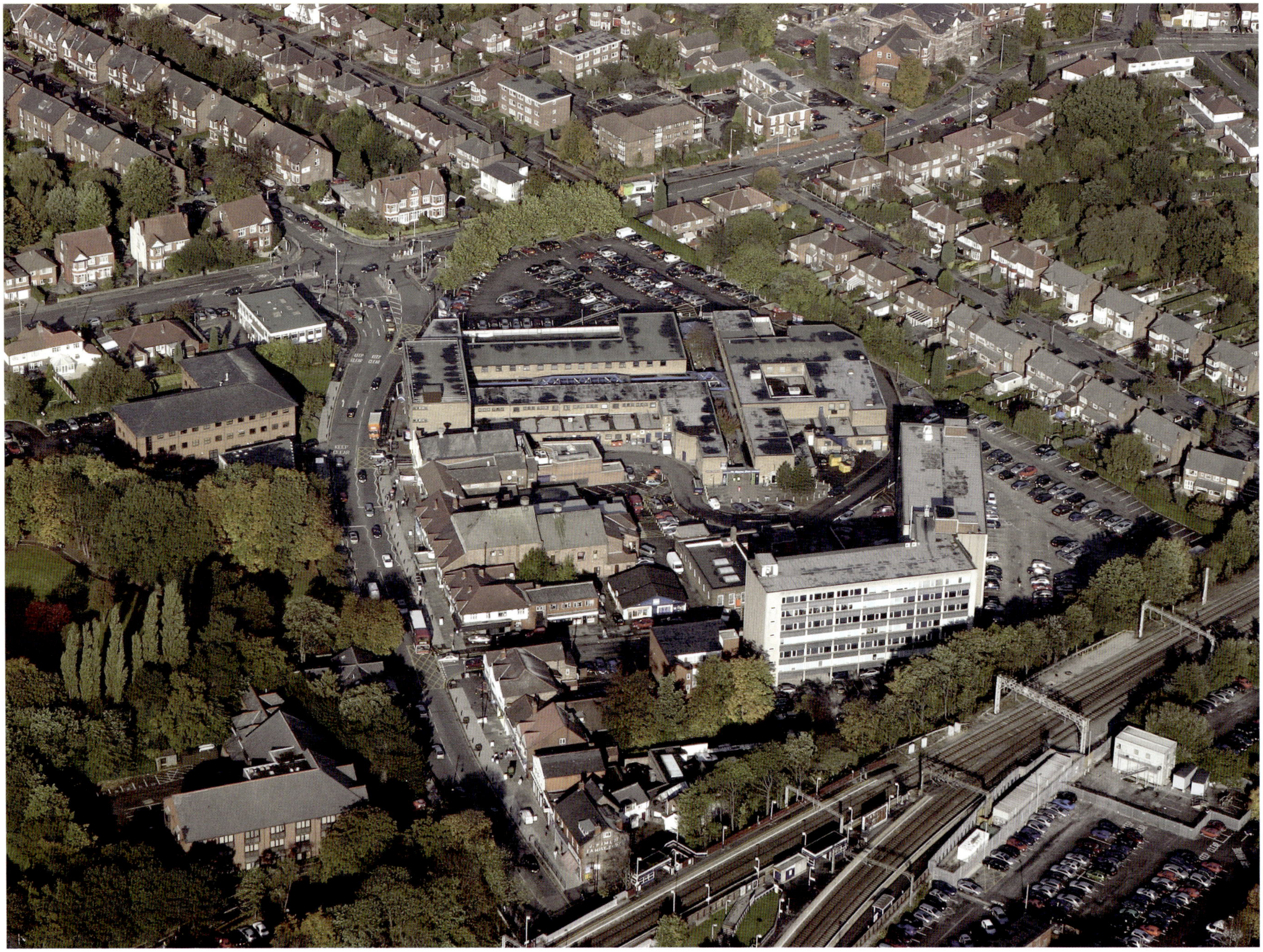

Station Road

The area around Station Road today is dominated by the modern shopping precinct and the grey office building of Simon Carves Ltd. It would be fair to say that the presence of such overly large offices mean that the centre of the village has lost some of its original charms. There are more offices in the opposite direction, parallel to Mellor Road (opposite page). Despite this, there are still many attractive buildings in the village, including the shops on the north side of Station Road opposite the peaceful haven of Oak Meadow (on the left). These include the old Elysian Cinema (now Bryants furniture shop) and the old Kings Hall (opened 1937). From the air the big offices look out of place in such a small local high street, and probably should not have been built, especially as many of them are currently lying empty. If permission were sought to build similar buildings today it would almost certainly be refused. However, one major new building was recently given permission for construction: A large new Waitrose supermarket opened in 2007 on the site of the former Cobden House office building (ironically, probably the most attractive of the offices buildings in the village) in the bottom left. Only time will tell if this is to become another mistake.

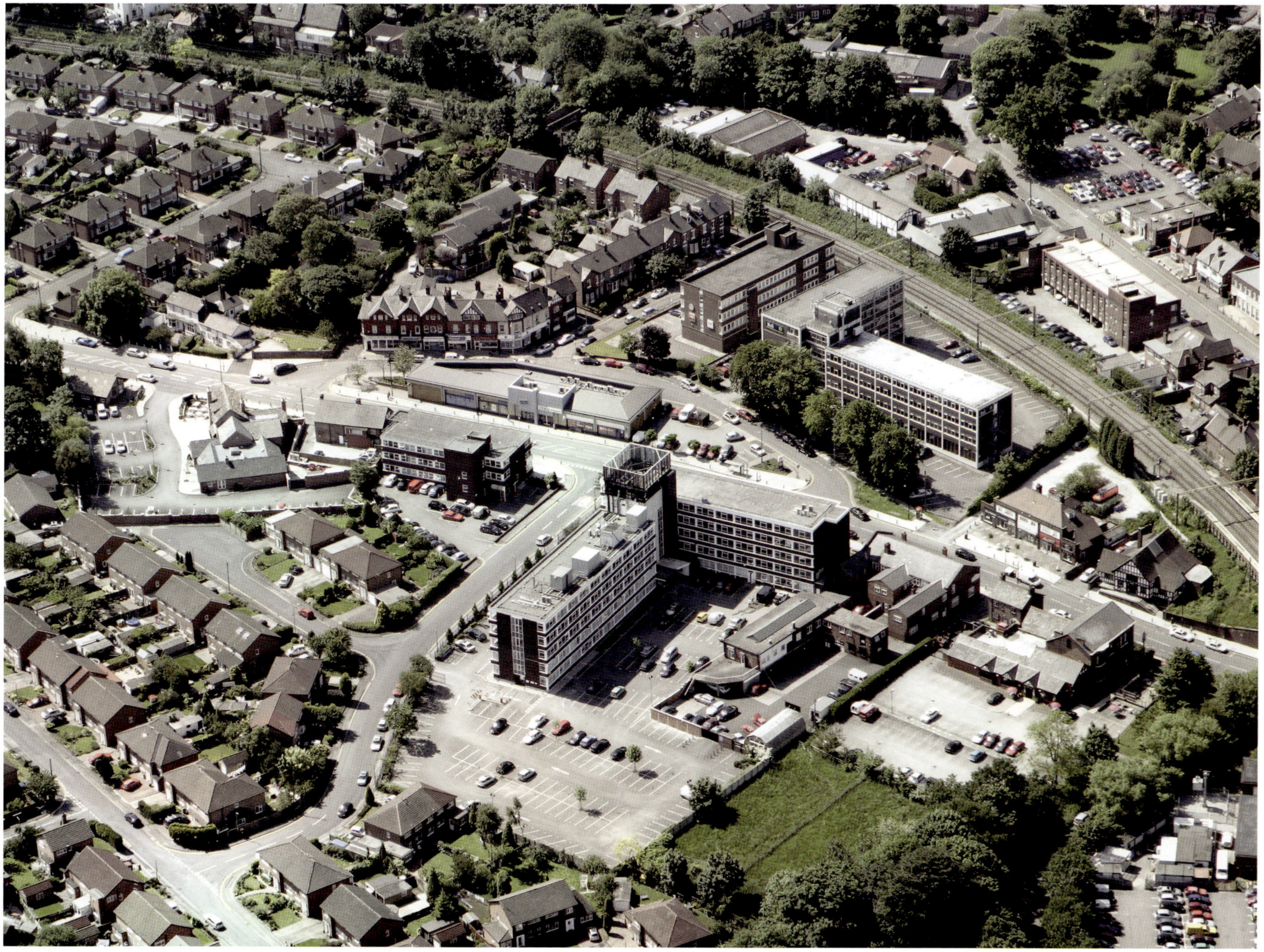

Station Road & Mellor Road

This view further down Station Road shows us the conflict between the old and the new. The traditional local shops on the far side of the road are literally dwarfed by the size of the neighbouring office blocks, where as the L-shaped block on the near side is gargantuan in comparison to the neighbouring houses. However, some historic buildings do remain. On the middle left of the image is Millington Hall (on the right hand side of the car park entrance). The hall dates from 1683 and was built as the residence of John Millington, a local Alderman who died in 1694. The building was later used as a place for silk weaving before becoming a restaurant in the 20th century. It has recently been converted again into a public house. On the top right is Mellor Road. At the very end of the road is Chads Theatre, partly hidden by the surrounding trees. The Cheadle Hulme Amateur Dramatics Society (or C.H.A.D.S. for short) was founded in about 1921. The society was originally based at the parish hall on Church Road before moving to temporary premises near the present site in 1928. The current theatre dates from around 1959, and is one of the few amateur theatres remaining in the area, including the Garrick Theatre next to the Hatworks and the Forum Theatre in Romiley.

Cheadle Hulme School 1928

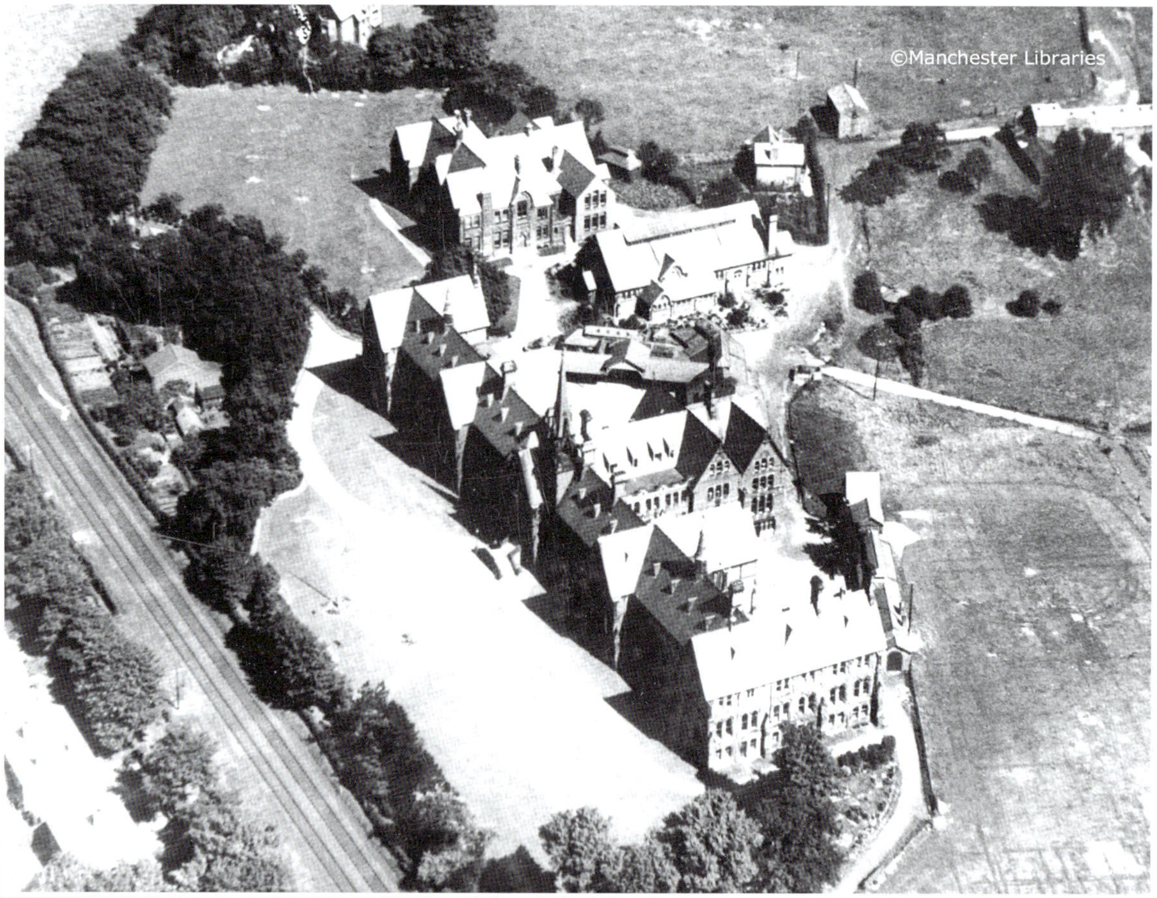

Cheadle Hulme School off Claremont Road is without doubt the most impressive building in Cheadle Hulme and a rival to any other in Stockport. It originally opened as The Manchester Warehousemen and Clerks' Orphan Schools in 1855 and was based in that City in the Ardwick region, having previously moved from Flixton. The purpose of the school was to provide education for "orphans and necessitous children", but it quickly outgrew its early premises and sought to move to a new site.

Five acres of land were bought in Cheadle Hulme and the magnificent Gothic style building, with a particularly impressive central spire, was built between 1867 and 1869. At first it consisted of the central area of the main building, but wings were added in 1878 and 1899.

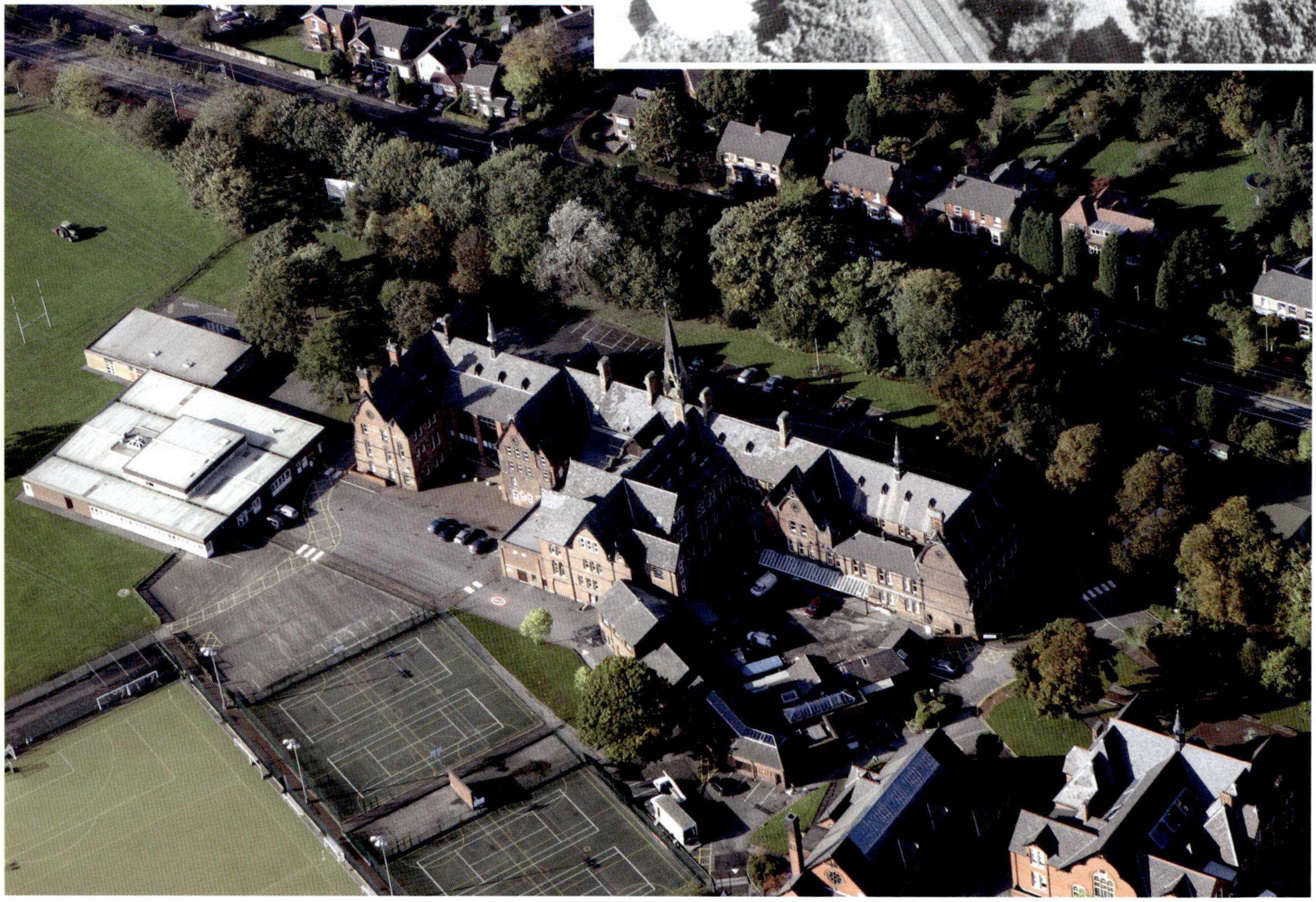

The separate swimming pool building (the building with the pitched roof with the transparent section in the middle) was opened in 1912, and the grounds were extended in 1913 when a further 30 acres were bought to the rear of the school. This land is now mainly utilised as sports pitches.

The name of the school was changed to Cheadle Hulme School in 1931. It is now a private boarding school with over 1400 students, and is one of the top performing establishments in the country. The original name is preserved in the name given to its former students - Old Waconians.

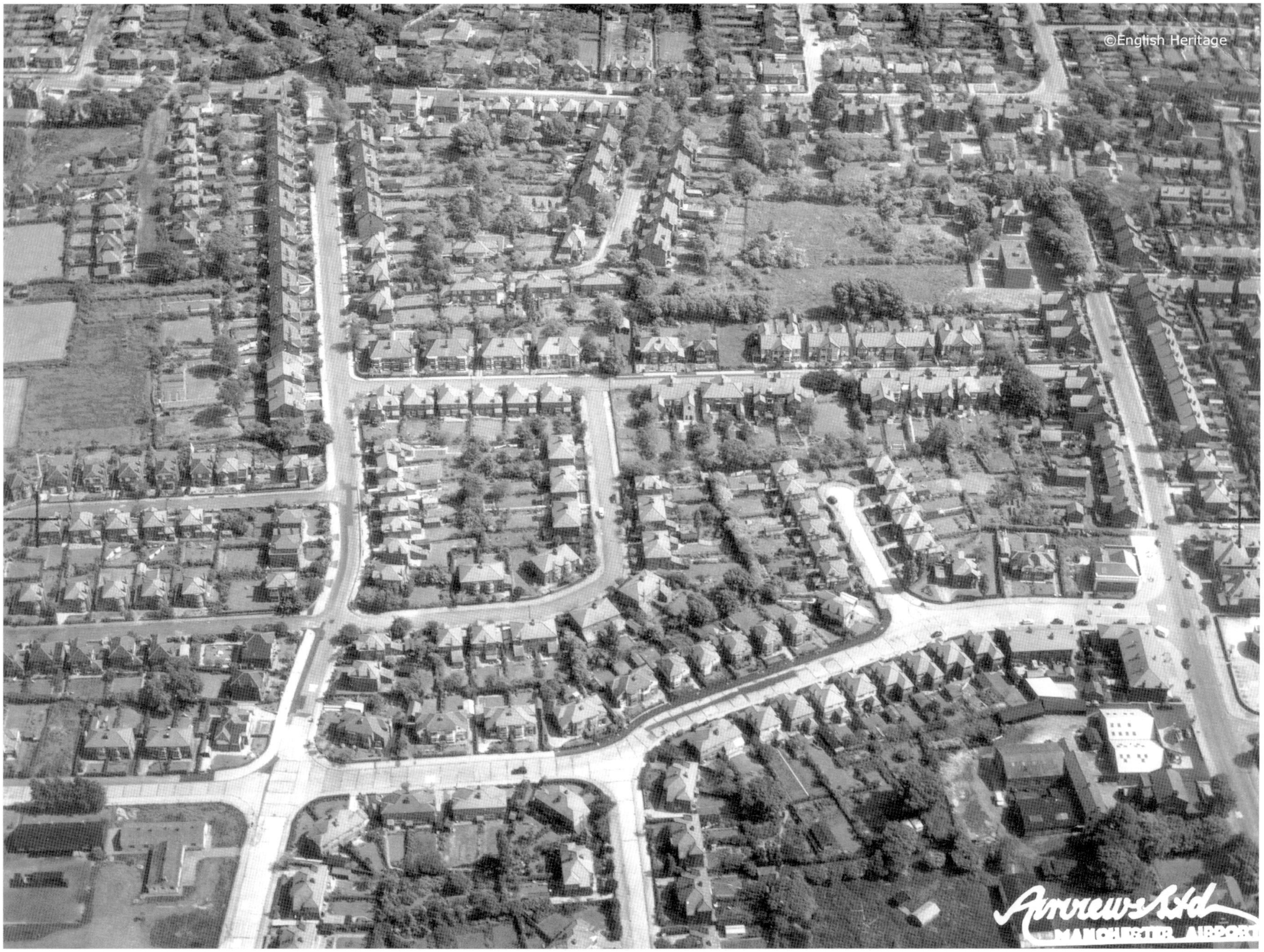

Queen's Road 1959 (looking east)

Cheadle Hulme experienced massive growth between the 1920s and 1950s. Increasing wealth and conditions after the war led to a boom in both property and the quality of life. The old living conditions of the big towns and cities became unacceptable, and so enormous house-building programmes were undertaken throughout the land, giving people the chance to move into leafy suburbia. Cheadle Hulme was one area that saw unprecedented development. The major new house of the 1930s was the semi-detached, and the area around the eastern end of Queen's Road (the long road on the left running from the top to the bottom of the picture) shows us a fine example of the "semi" at its best. The houses here would no doubt have been far removed from those that the new residents had previously been used to. These houses in particular were of an excellent size and had very spacious gardens. Curving away at the top of Queen's Road road is Station Road at the junction with Ladybridge Road. Note that the land on the far side is still covered by houses and gardens. Today it is the large car park for the shopping precinct, and shows that the main route through the village would still have preserved its traditional feel seen in the image from 1927.

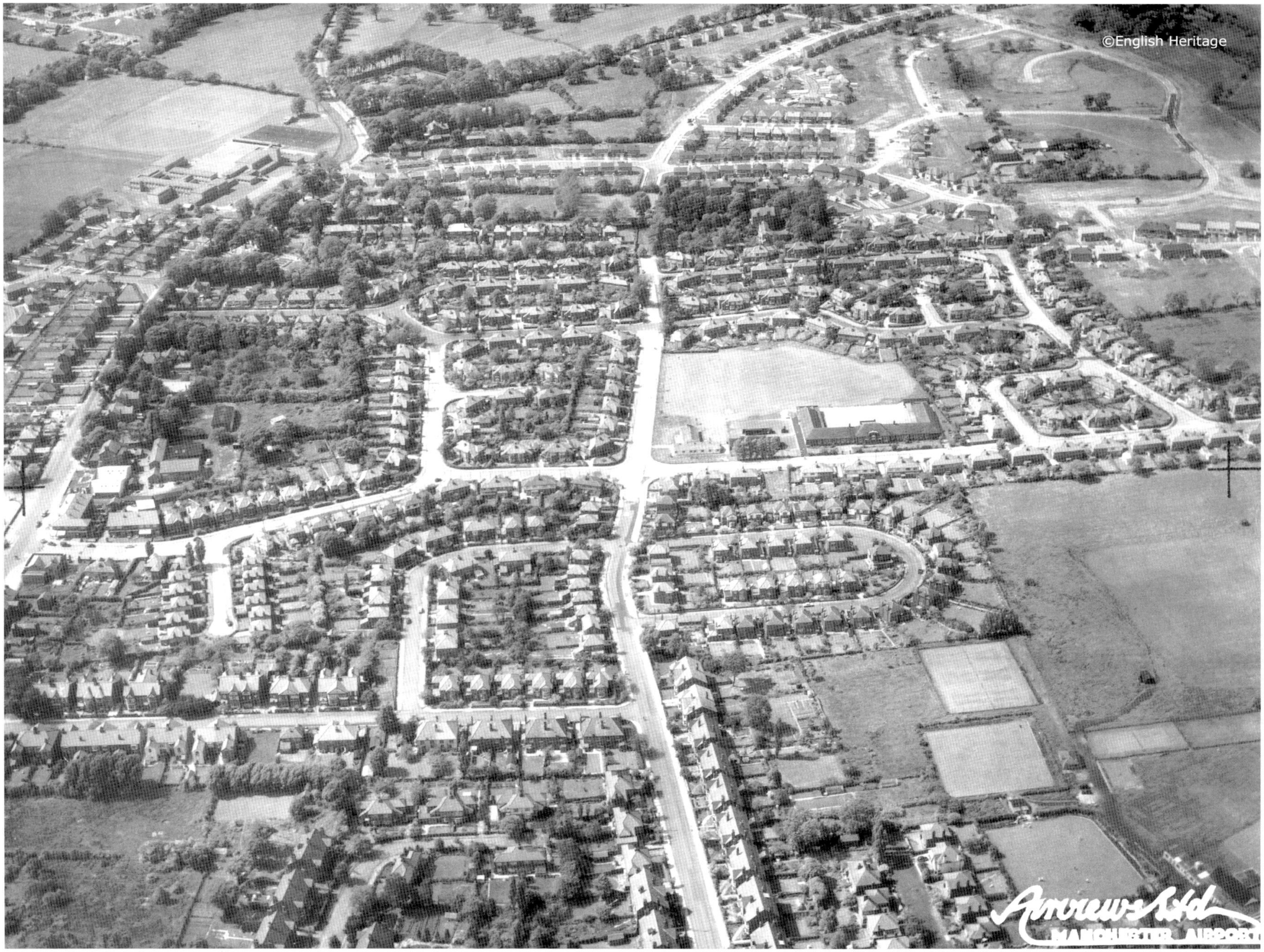

Queen’s Road 1959 (looking west)

The explosion of house building continued well into the 1950s. This image is looking in the opposite direction down Queen’s Road towards Cheadle. It shows us the greater extent of the 1930s estate, as well as new developments further along the road. In the top right streets have been laid out in readiness for more new houses to be constructed around Radnormere Drive. There are clearly foundations in place, as well as houses part-way through construction that have yet to have their gardens divided. This second new estate was made up of larger detached houses. In the top left along Cheadle Road is the site of the then newly built Cheadle County Grammar School for Girls that is now Cheadle & Marple College. The school in the centre is Queen’s Road Primary, and on the right are the grounds of the Ladybridge Sports Club. Today, the two areas either side of Queen’s Road have blossomed. The streets and houses remain much as they were when first put up, and the abundance of greenery makes the area a very attractive one for families and commuters. On the opposite page we can see the area around Cheadle Road (top) and the area around the u-shaped Radnormere Drive (bottom) with the same street pattern discernable from 1959. At the top of this picture is Cheadle & Marple College, next to Cheadle Golf Course.

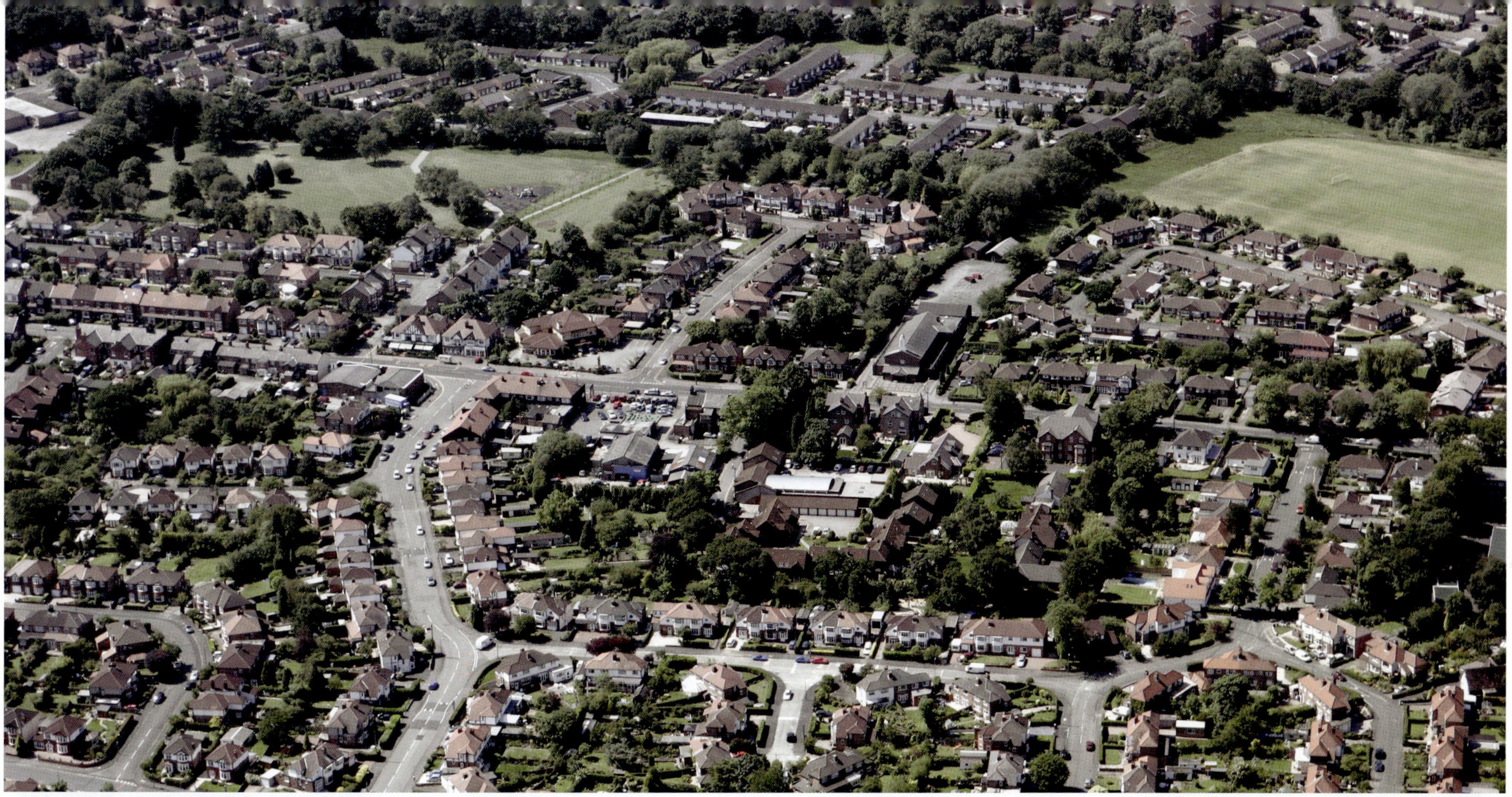

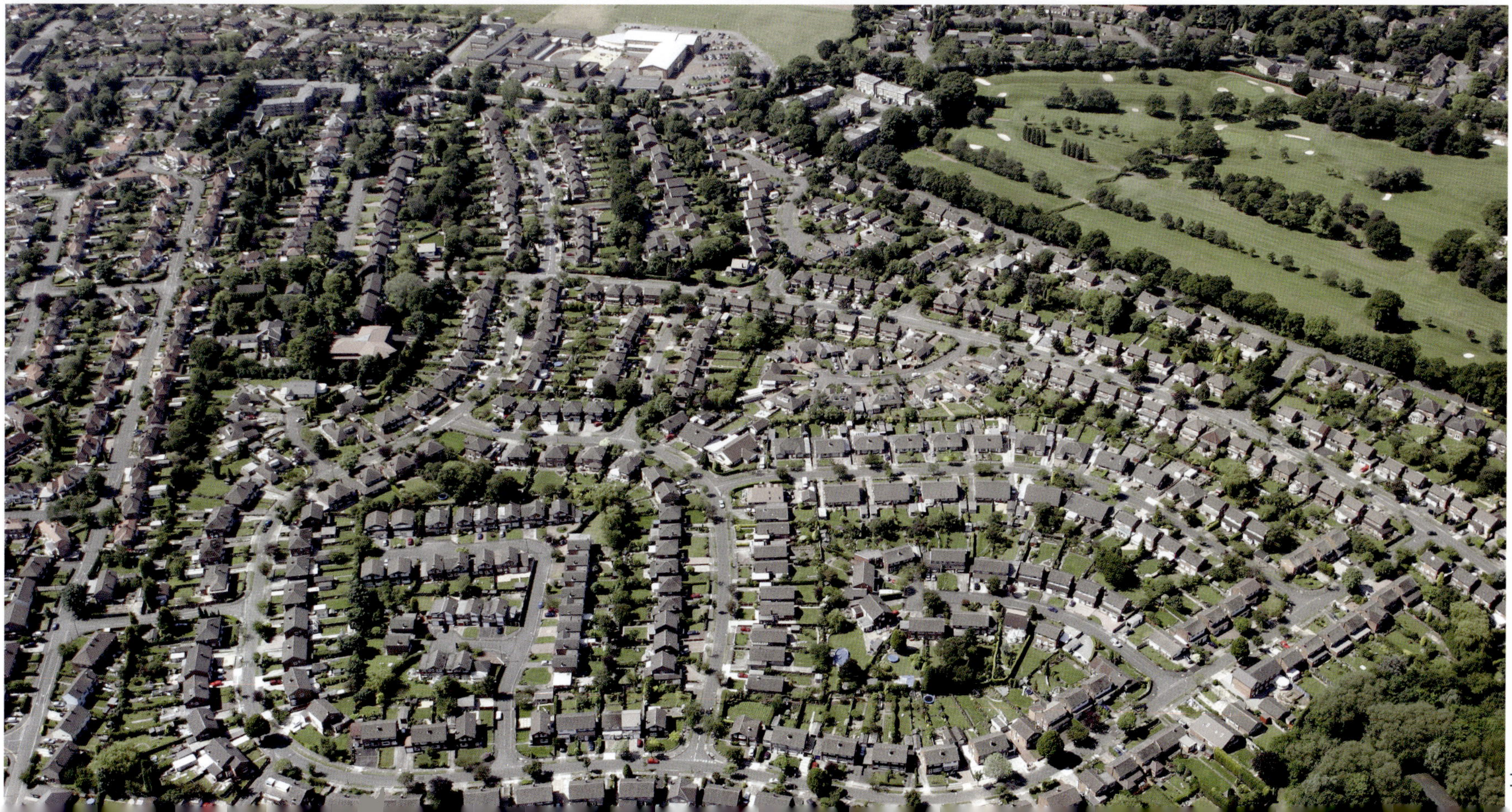

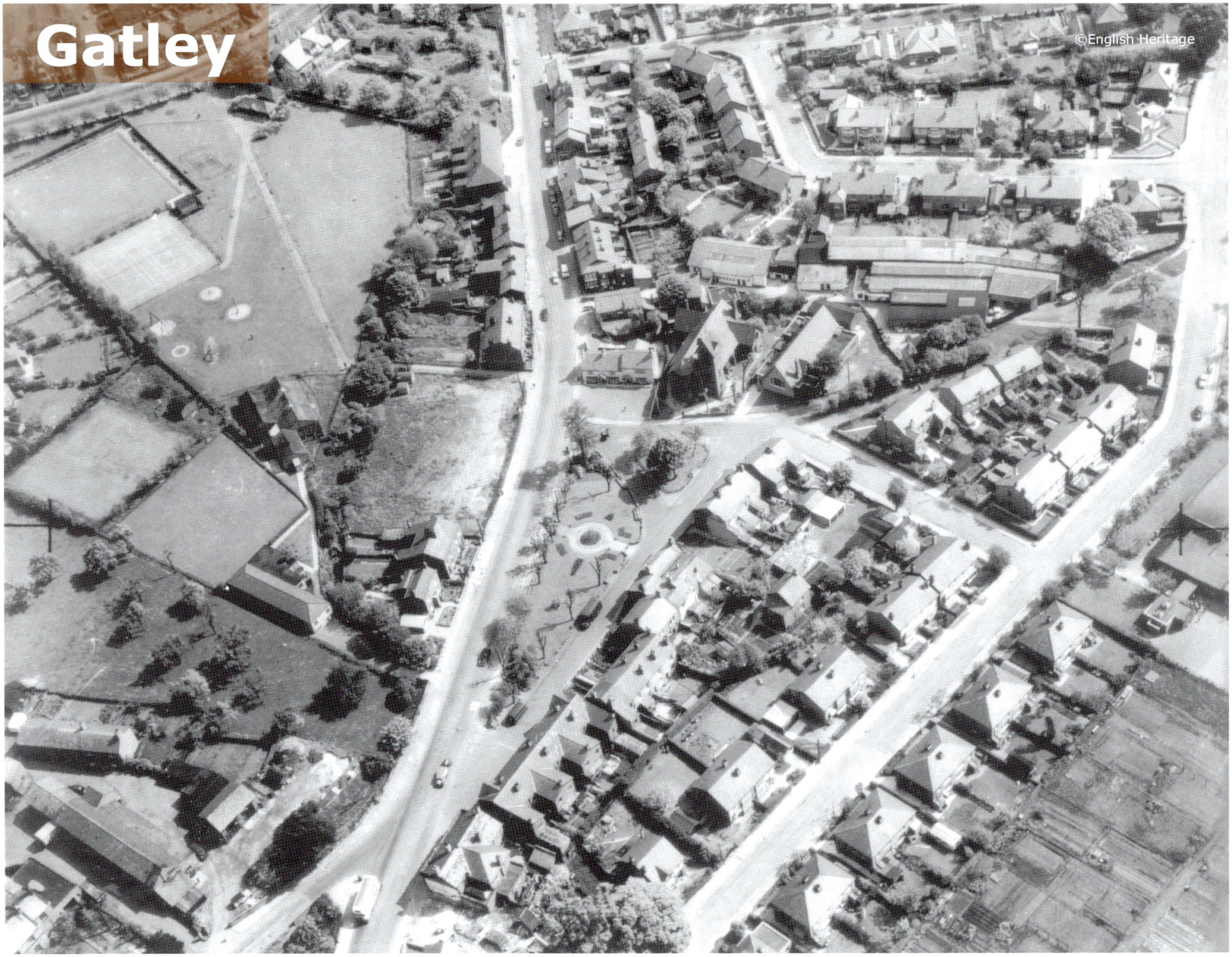

Gatley Green c1956

Gatley & Heald Green were known collectively as Stockport Etchells as far back as the 13th century when it was part of the Stockport Barony. The Township, along with the neighbouring township of Northern Etchells (the modern day Northenden in Manchester) was often simply referred to as Etchells, and in 1894 it was absorbed into the newly created Cheadle and Gatley Urban District. The name of Stockport Etchells was eventually abolished in 1930. At the time of the barony, Gatley would have been known as Gateclyve or Gaticlyve, which in Old English meant "a bank or cliffs where goats were kept" Gatley station opened on 1st May 1909, and it was also the last stop for trams travelling from Mersey Square. The terminus was outside the Horse & Farrier pub, at the junction with Church Road, where the trams used to turn around and head back. This image is of Gatley Green further down Church Road away from the village centre. The layout of the Green is still the same, although the trees are now much larger. The Green is now protected as part of the local conservation area.

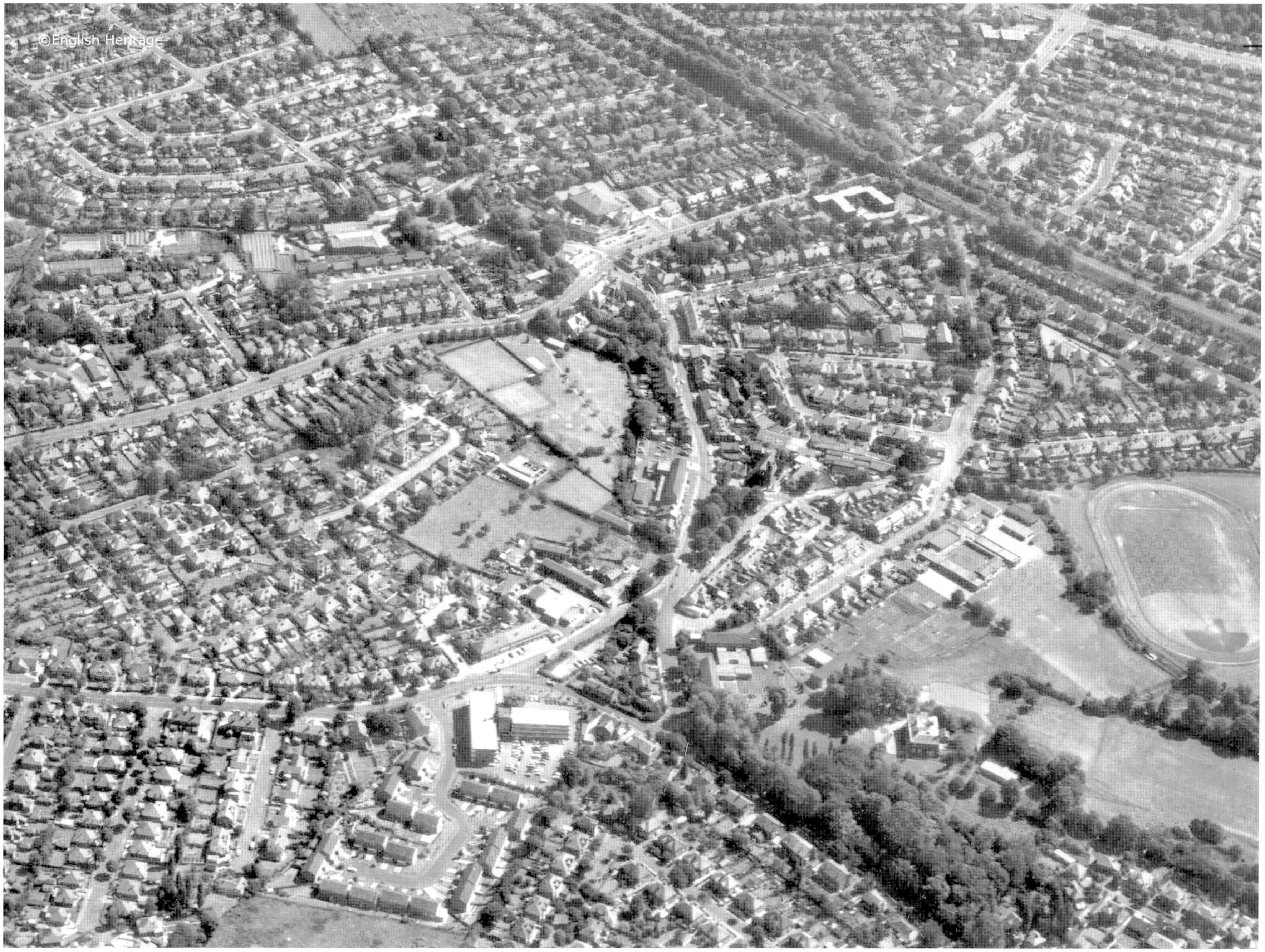

Gatley Village 1975

This image shows the village more or less as it appears today. Gatley Green is now shrouded in mature trees and there is a new row of shops opposite, whilst on the right are the William Scholes playing fields and the athletics track. The centrepiece of the village was the Tatton Cinema, seen here at the top of Church Lane next to the Horse & Farrier. It opened on October 14th 1937 and featured three screens of differing sizes – the "Major", the "Mini" and the "Minor". At first the cinema had just one screen, but the "Minor" was added in 1971 where the former restaurant had been, seating only 111. In 1975 the original auditorium was split in two to create the third screen. The main stalls area became the "Major", with 647 seats, whilst the former circle became the "Mini", seating 247. It was an extremely popular venue, and people would visit from miles around to take in a show. Sadly, the cinema could not last. Pressure from new multiplex developments nearby and decreases in customer numbers led to the picture house being closed in January 2001. A campaign to reopen the cinema was to prove unsuccessful, and the rear of the building was eventually demolished. The superb art deco facade at the front remains, with plans to incorporate it into the future redevelopment, but at the time of writing the site is still derelict.

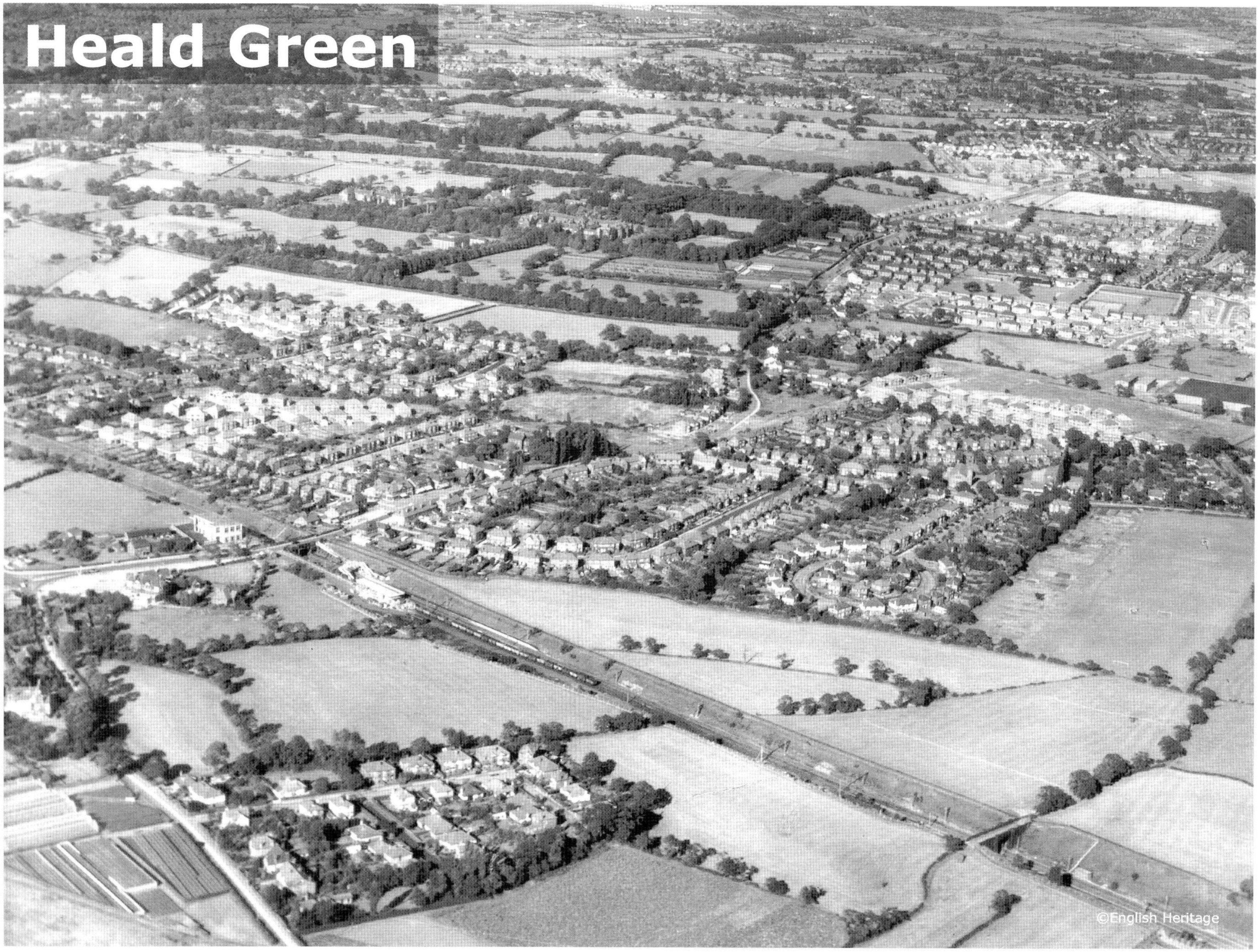

Heald Green c1959

Heald Green is in the very south west of Stockport, situated extremely close to Manchester Airport. Life in the village is accompanied by the near constant roar of aircraft coming in to land at Ringway, although twenty percent of the time they will take off in the opposite direction. To give some comparison, the aircraft pass over the town hall at 1600 feet, but by the time they reach Heald Green they are just over 400 feet above the ground. It was around the time that these pictures were taken that the building boom experienced in neighbouring areas like Cheadle Hulme was in full swing. There are new estates under construction here on either side of the main road, as well as a new platform at the train station. Heald Green was still an extremely rural area at the time, separated from the increasing urban sprawl by rolling fields between Cheadle and Cheadle Hulme, which can clearly be seen in the distance in the area close to Bruntwood Park and Cheadle Royal. Most of these fields would be swallowed up in next to no time. Despite this, the village has managed to maintain a great sense of space, with plenty of generous gardens compensating for the loss of the open land.

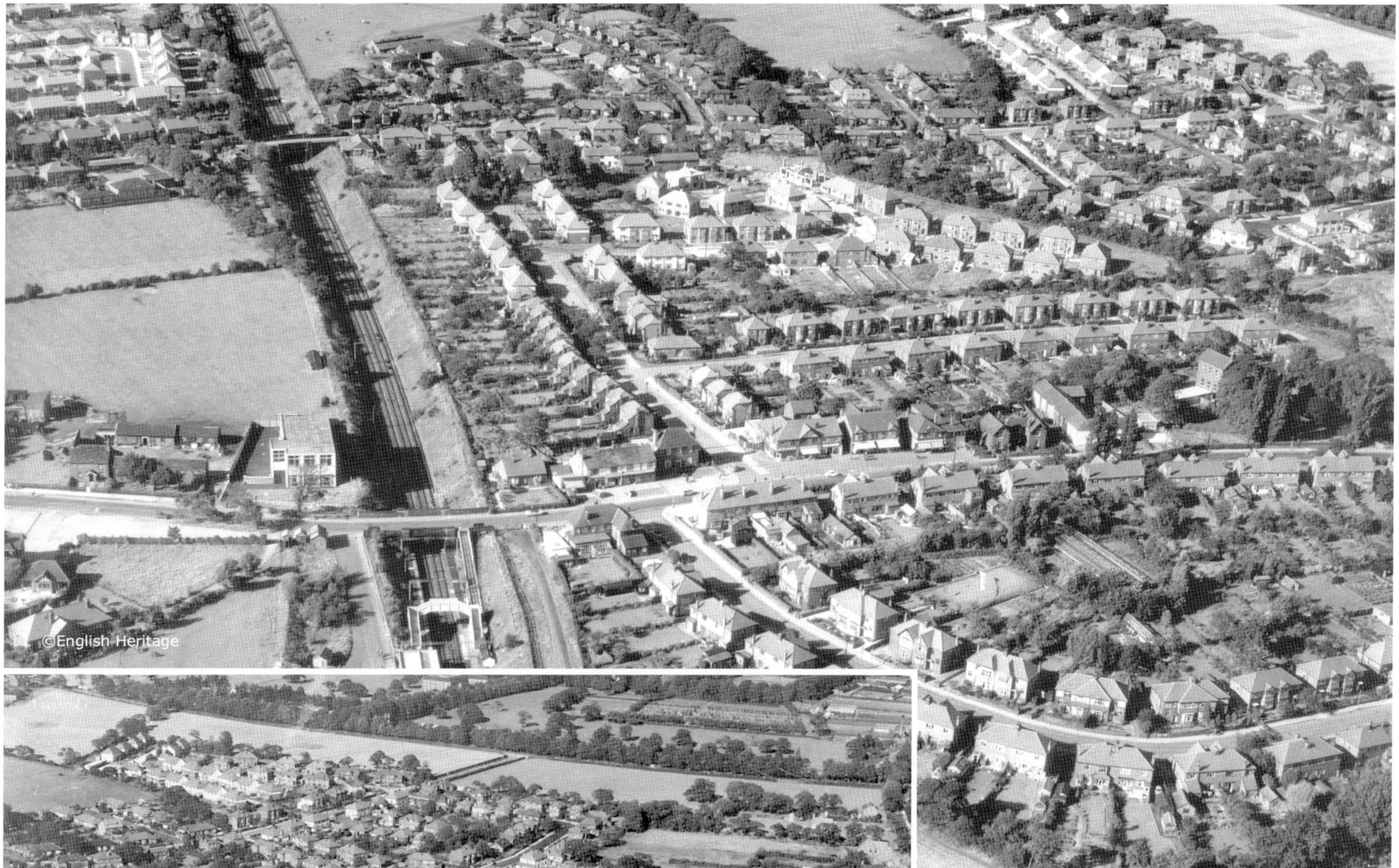

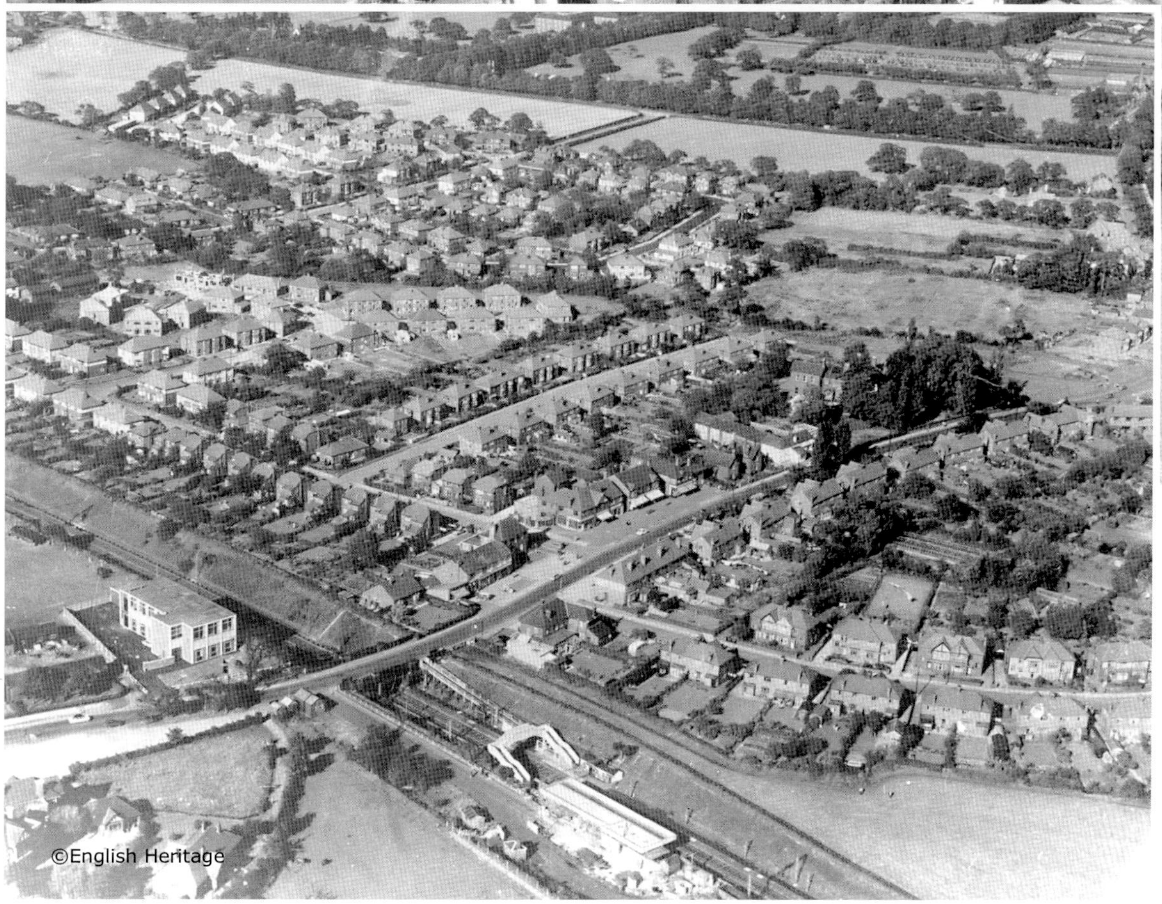

Finney Lane c1959

The village centre is based on Finney Lane, which contains a long row of local shows. Back in the 1950s, this row was less than half the length it is now, and contained only a handful of premises. The new shops were built on the land to the right, which was still undeveloped at this time. We can also see a close-up of the new platform at the station. The station opened in 1909 as part of the Styal Line from Crewe to Manchester.

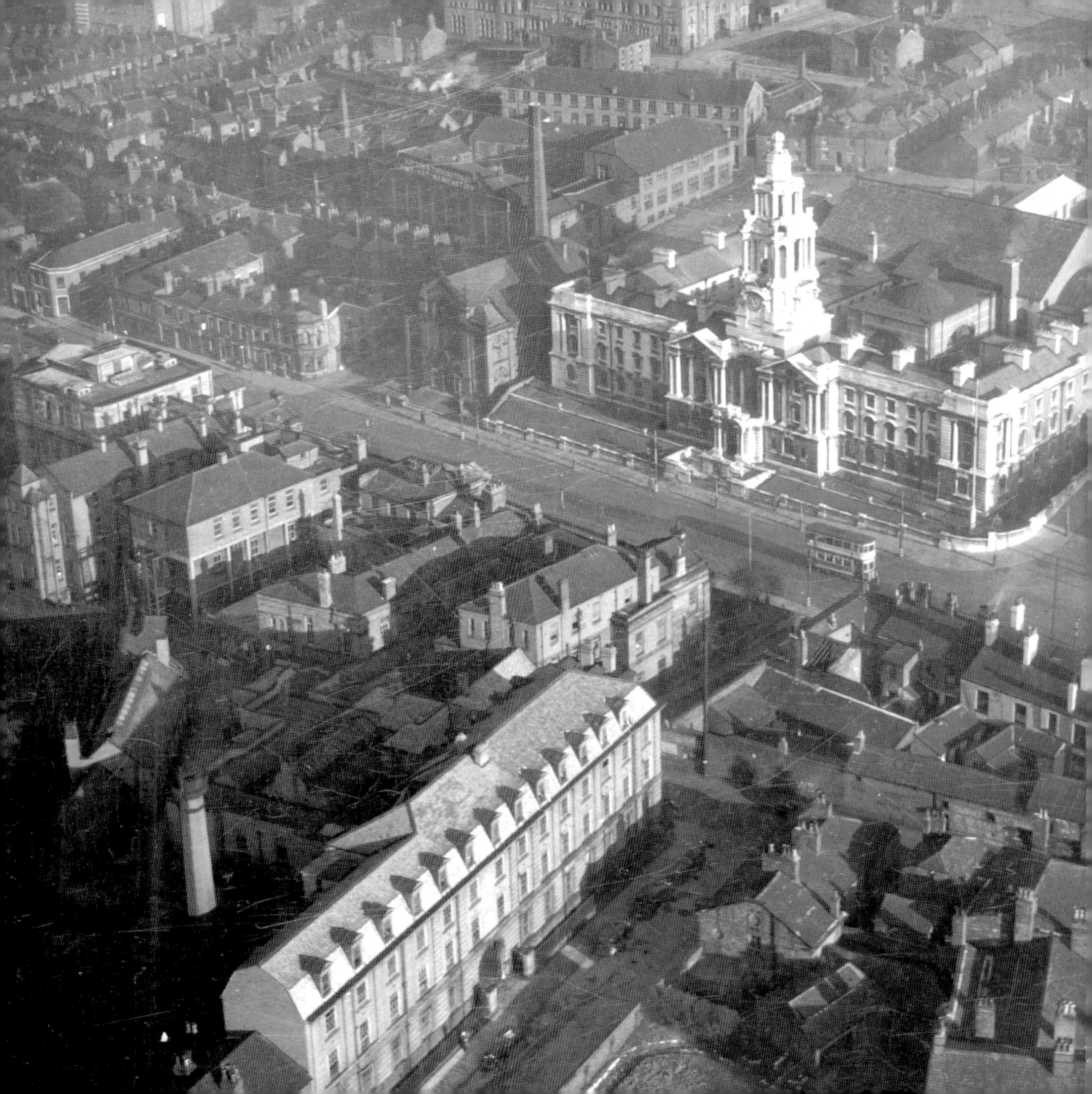

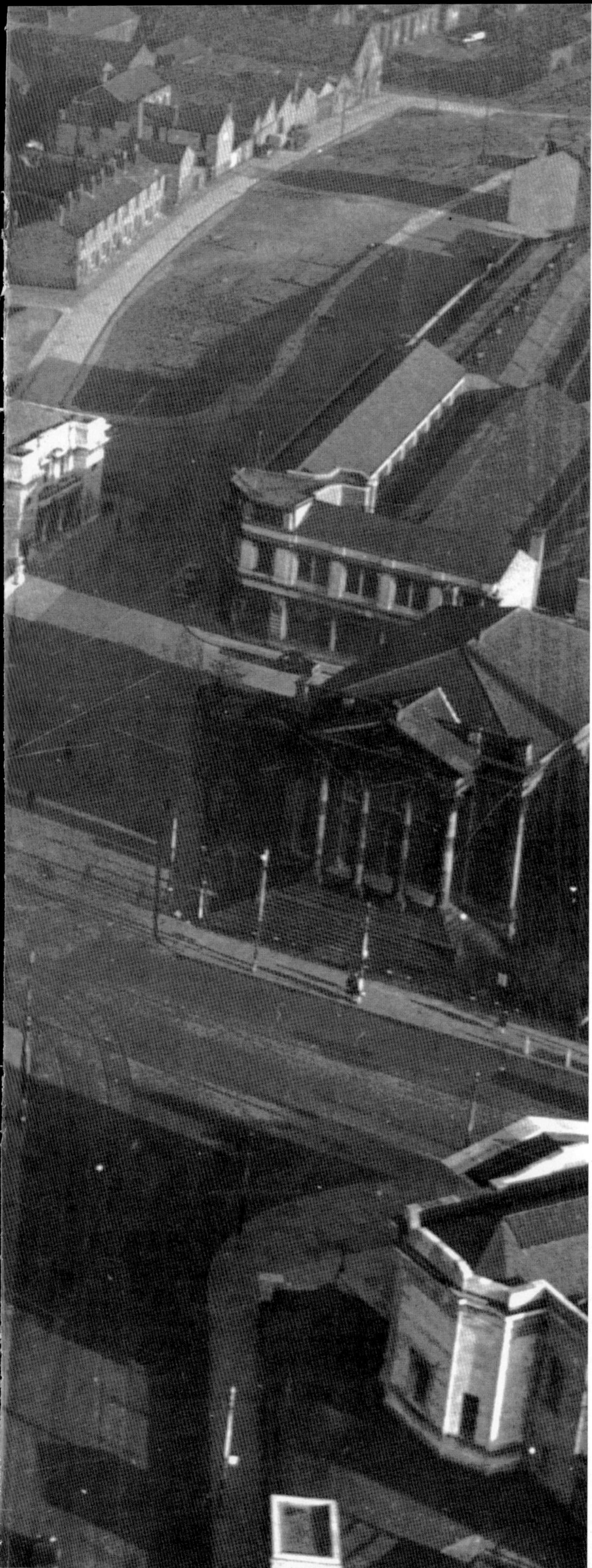

Subscribers

Muriel & Ron Addison	–	Mile End
Christine Bailey	–	Poynton
Doris K. Bridge	–	Lower Brinnington
Vanessa Brown	–	Bredbury
Tracy & Ian Coburn	–	Mile End
David Collatine	–	Bredbury
Eileen & Arthur Collister	–	Brinnington
Shiela Crossley	–	Cheadle
Alice Daniels	–	Brinnington
Dave & Deb	–	Offerton Green
P Davies	–	Offerton
William Drabble	–	Romsey, Hampshire
Amanda Dranfield	–	Heaviley
Mary & Laurence Eyre	–	Bredbury
Alan Forshaw	–	Rojales, Spain
Eric Forshaw & Robert Kearsley	–	Brinnington
Colin Fretwell	–	California, USA
Ken Gee	–	Larne, County Antrim
Martin Green	–	Bramhall
Tim Gwilt	–	Heald Green
B.D. Hall	–	Cale Green
Chris Hallworth	–	Offerton
Ian Hammond	–	Reading, Berkshire
Peter John Hill	–	Brinnington
Derek Houghton	–	Offerton
Alan Houldcroft	–	Edgeley
Ralph Hurst	–	High Lane
Richard Jones	–	Heaton Moor
Jim Leigh	–	Cheadle Hulme
Lynne Land	–	Heaton Chapel
L Maddocks	–	South Reddish
Matt & Margaret	–	South Reddish
Janet McMurray	–	Cheadle Hulme
Ken Millward	–	Offerton
George Harry Moore	–	Offerton
Frederick Moseley	–	Offerton
David Mumford	–	Cheadle
Helen Nance	–	Heaton Chapel
George Martin Nelstrop	–	Bramhall
Majorie Noble	–	Oban, Argyll
Ray Preston	–	Offerton
C.A. Sheeran	–	Hazel Grove
Jim Stewart	–	Offerton
Trevor Stokes	–	Hazel Grove
Logan Sykes	–	Great Moor
Brian Thurling	–	Edgeley
Bernard Timms	–	Bridge Hall
Jonathan Webb	–	Bramhall
Treasa Wilde	–	Openshaw, Manchester
Brian Winfield	–	Heaton Chapel
Elaine Wright	–	New Mills
Joanna Yates	–	Bramhall
Conservation & Heritage Department	–	Stockport MBC
Legal Services	–	Stockport MBC
Stockport Heritage Library	–	Wellington Road South
Wilde Consulting Engineers	–	Adcroft Street

First published in the United Kingdom in 2007
by SBP Publishing

All Images from this book can be purchased, along with the hundreds of other images of Stockport that we hold that we did not have room for in this book. Please contact the publisher for further information.

Front Cover: The Pyramid
Back Cover: Bramall Hall
Page 198-199: Stockport Town Hall 1949

ISBN: 978-09557265-0-7

Printed and bound in China